A HISTORY OF WORLD CIVILIZATION

Volume 1

A HISTORY OF

WORLD CIVILIZATION

MAX SAVELLE, *General Editor*

IRWIN ABRAMS, *Antioch College*
WILLIAM C. BARK, *Stanford University*
CHARLES BARKER, *Johns Hopkins University*
GIOVANNI COSTIGAN, *University of Washington*
CYCLONE COVEY, *Amherst College*
MARY E. HARDWICKE
ELEANOR HUZAR, *Southeast Missouri State College*
MARIUS JANSEN, *University of Washington*
GEORGE H. KNOLES, *Stanford University*
ALBERT J. LYND
FRANZ MICHAEL, *University of Washington*
DAVID ROBERTS, *University of Washington*
C. EASTON ROTHWELL, *Hoover Library, Stanford, California*
MAX SAVELLE, *University of Washington*
MERRILL T. B. SPAULDING, *Hoover Library, Stanford, California*
HELLMUT WILHELM, *University of Washington*
HERBERT J. WOOD, *State College of Washington*
GORDON WRIGHT, *University of Oregon*

Henry Holt and Company · New York

PREFACE

The march of time in the twentieth century has brought about a situation in the community of the world that makes it imperative for every educated citizen to have at least an elementary understanding of the major civilizations in the world other than his own. It is no longer sufficient for a citizen to know the history of his own country, important as that is; nor is it any longer sufficient for the citizen to be acquainted with the history of western civilization. The world today is, in fact, a close community of peoples, and the citizens of every country are being called upon with increasing frequency to think about events and people in areas of the world that, until the second quarter of the twentieth century, were relatively unknown to them.

This book is an effort to provide a broad and scholarly basis for such an understanding.

To achieve its purpose, any such book must attempt to present the *whole* of human civilization. While it is true that there have been—and are—many separate civilizations in the world, it must be recognized that each one is but a distinct variant within the total picture of the cultural achievements of humanity. Thus the first objective of this book is to present the entire picture.

At the same time, any such study must be a true history of civilization. It is not enough to list kings, analyze political institutions, or describe wars. On the contrary, to arrive at an understanding of any given civilization the student must know how the people lived, what their literature was, and what their art and their music were. Most of all, no study of any civilization can be even superficially complete without some reading of the speculative, religious, and philosophical formulations of the given civilization's understanding of the meaning of the drama of human existence.

While the over-all objective of the book thus must be to give the student a vision of the whole tapestry of human history, it also should be possible, in such a book, to find a complete, though necessarily brief, history of each separate civilization from its beginnings to the present. Thus it should be possible to grasp, in substantial outline, at least, the history of the Mediterranean area, of China, of India, of Russia, or of the Atlantic civilization, each one throughout its course.

Such are the objectives of this book. We have attempted to write in a fashion worthy of the intellectual maturity of college students, without in any way "writing down," and, at the same time, to provide a genuinely scholarly and authoritative history without losing the interest that is inherent in the human drama.

And because we believe that a dependable history of any civilization can be written only by an expert, the various chapters of this book, dealing, as they do, with widely different histories, have been written by specialists in those fields. At the same time, we have striven to coordinate all the separate histories in such a way as to present to the student an integral picture of the completed tapestry of the whole.

This is a vast and complex story, this history of the rise of civilizations and of civilization built upon the aspirations, the struggles, the triumphs—aye, and the failures—of men. It is not an easy story to relate. Yet he who can seize upon it, both in its details and in its broad, sweeping perspective, should find it enjoyable; above all, he should better understand his fellow men thereby, and be, for that, a better and a wiser man himself.

We are indebted to many individuals and many institutions for aid in the preparation of this book: to the libraries of our respective colleges and universities, and to the many museums that have aided us in the collection of pertinent illustrations. Of particular assistance have been Mr. George J. Lee, Curator of Oriental Art, the Brooklyn Museum, and the staff of the Metropolitan Museum of Art. A special debt of gratitude is due to Mlle. Sylvie Rimbert, of Paris, who made many of the maps, and to Professor Raymond Muse, of State College of Washington, who read the manuscript in its entirety and made many helpful criticisms and suggestions. Professor Donald Treadgold, of the University of Washington, read parts of the manuscript, as did, also, Professors Scott Lytle and Harry Woolf, of the same university.

It must be recognized, of course, that errors of various sorts will inevitably creep into a book of this kind and scope. We have made every effort to find and eliminate such errors; where they still remain, the responsibility for them is claimed by the individual authors alone.

THE AUTHORS

January 15, 1957

The figures on the cover are the Parthenon (p. 120), elevation of a portion of the exterior of Reims Cathedral (p. 543), and a gateway to the Great Stupa at Sanchi (p. 314); those on the halftitle, a Bull Seal (p. 304), a Greek (p. 104) and a medieval coin (p. 482); those on the title page, a Greek amphora (p. 124), *Madonna and Child* by Andrea del Verrocchio (Courtesy of the Metropolitan Museum of Art), and *Kneeling Bodhisattva* (p. 385).

CONTENTS

Maps

Chronologies

INTRODUCTION

TO HISTORY

History, by apprizing [the people] of the past, will enable them to judge the future; it will avail them of the experience of other times and other nations; it will qualify them as judges of the actions and designs of men; it will enable them to know ambition under every guise it may assume; and knowing it, to defeat its views.

Thomas Jefferson

Students beginning the study of the history of civilization may well ask, "What is history?" Not only will they wish to know what history is about, but probably they will also wish to form some idea of why they undertake the study and what they may expect to get out of it.

History has been variously defined. A famous definition sets forth that "history is past politics." But this view is out of date, because we now recognize that it leaves out any consideration of economic forces or religion or science, and man's past cannot be understood without these elements. Another famous definition makes history a record of the past, *"wie es eigentlich gewesen ist"*—as it actually happened. This makes plain the need of getting at the truth of man's past, but it does not make place for the historian's interpretation of events. And without such interpretation, the record has little interest or usefulness. In a more recent definition, history deals with "all that we know about everything man has ever done, or thought, or hoped, or felt." This is a more satisfactory view, because it is more inclusive. Still another idea is included in a definition that many historians now accept. In their understanding of it, history is "a genetic social science, which is concerned with reconstructing, as far as may be possible, the best thoughts and activities of humanity."

Because of the limitations of space, a history of civilization must leave much unsaid. But, as far as space permits, it must seek to present in a continuous narrative the most important incidents and movements, ideas and institutions, in the complex human past. It must keep a proper balance, not stressing any one aspect of history, such as politics, at the expense of the others, and it must come down to the present time. The past forms a whole, and the beginning student of history must learn to see it as a whole.

THE CONSTANT THEMES IN HISTORY

Though history forms a complex whole, like a tapestry embroidered with many colors and depicting numerous scenes, in it may be discerned certain constant and universal themes. The great problems of mankind remain fundamentally the same, whether they present themselves to the pastoral peoples of the Middle East, the peasants in farming settlements in Egypt, India, or China, the trading and often wandering Greeks, the barons and serfs of the Feudal Era in the history of the west, or the industrial workers of today.

1

The Economic Theme

For a society, a nation, a tribe, or an individual, the first and most fundamental problem is how to make a livelihood—that is, how to get food and shelter. Where the climate and soil are good, a group of men set down in a new place might find agriculture to be the easiest way of procuring a living. But where the soil will grow nothing but grass, the same men might take to raising cattle and sheep. Where both soil and climate are unfavorable but near-by seas are teeming with fish, these men might find fishing a more satisfactory way. Or they might turn to commerce or to an industry that makes use of rich minerals beneath the soil. Thus geographical location sometimes suggests the answer to the economic problem that all men must face.

But too much emphasis must not be placed on geography. Other factors also help to determine the way in which men make a living. One of these factors is the size of population. Herds of livestock, grazing upon open grasslands, can support a sparse population, but a dense population usually must till the land or develop commerce and manufactures. The presence of hostile neighbors is another factor that sometimes affects economic development, for the danger of war gives stimulus to warlike industries. Thus one or another factor may influence a certain people to gain their living by a specific economic pursuit, but the basic problem of earning a livelihood is one that all peoples must solve in some fashion. This story of the methods, practices, institutions, and laws that have developed out of their struggle merely to live is what constitutes the economic phase of history.

The Social Theme

Social organization is the second constant theme in history. Man is a social animal; because of his heterosexuality, he cannot live alone. And for other reasons besides the need of reproduction, he finds it convenient to live in groups. He finds strength in groups. As a general rule, he does everything better—from hunting or building a pyramid to amusing himself—by joining other men.

As men form groups, certain social habits or customs develop for regulating the conduct of the members of the group, and often these habits or customs become so strong that they have the force of law. The story of the institutions, methods, and customs of social life that have arisen in response to men's need for social organization constitutes the social aspect of history.

The Political Theme

From the political problem arises the third constant theme of history. Throughout the ages, in every place, men have recognized the need of some sort of authority for the government of individuals composing a social group. A great variety of forms of government have been tried in various areas and epochs. Many of these have been successful— even some that are diametrically opposed to each other. But all political institutions, events, and ideas are answers to the same basic problems, common to all peoples and as old as civilization itself. The form of government has varied according to time and place, but the need for government does not change.

The Religious Theme

Men have almost always and almost everywhere had some kind of religion. For our purposes, we may define religion as "the complex of emotions and ideas that have made men seek to keep in harmony with the unseen powers governing the universe." The forms of religious expression are various, from primitive animism to the esthetic naturalism of the modern age. But these are all expressions of similar religious impulses. For, like the other basic needs of men, the need to feel "at home" in the universe remains a constant. Over the course of the ages men have found as many answers to this need for spiritual security as they have found to the need for economic and political security.

The Philosophic and Scientific Themes

Closely akin to religion is philosophy— the ideas that have arisen out of men's attempts to explain and understand the nature of the universe about them. Many philosophies have been based upon religion, attributing the creation and the governance of the universe to a god or gods. But other philosophies, such as those to which certain Greco-Roman and Chinese thinkers sub-

scribed, have given only a minor role to the gods. And with the advent of modern science, many of the older, more primitive religious interpretations of the universe have been discarded or revised. Some modern philosophies, such as pragmatism or naturalism, are not based upon religion at all but, rather, on the findings and implications of modern science.

The problem of understanding the universe remains the same, however the problem is answered, and the impulse to seek an answer to it has never been stronger than in our own time. For modern science is the newest of the intellectual instruments that men have devised for finding an answer to the riddle of the universe. We of this age make use of science for answering many questions that men in former times sought to answer by means of religion or philosophy. But there still seem to be areas of human outlook with which science cannot successfully deal.

The Flying Machine of Leonardo da Vinci. Man has always dreamed of flying, and in 1495 the great Renaissance artist (see p. 587) designed this flying machine. Leonardo also developed a practical helicopter and designed a tank and an armored car. The wheel was, perhaps, man's most important invention, but long before A.D. 1 the Egyptians had experimented with pistons that worked by compressed air, and Hero of Alexandria shortly afterward invented many contrivances that worked by steam. (Courtesy International Business Machine Corp.)

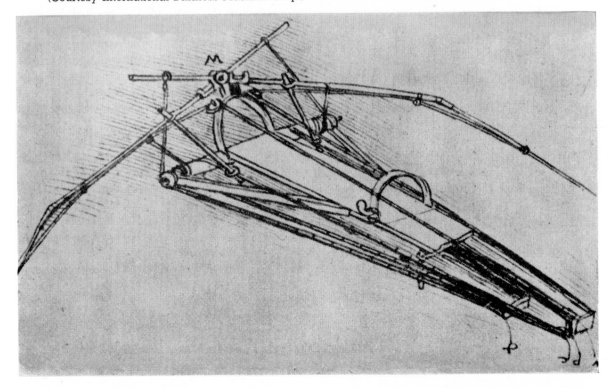

Literature and Music as Constant Themes

Literature is another thread running through the whole fabric of the history of civilized men. Allied with both the religious and the philosophical impulses, the literary impulse has progressed with them—from the childlike tales of the fireside storyteller to the modern psychological problem novel, from crude tribal songs to the refined, delicate, abstract, often abstruse, philosophical or fanciful lyrics of a Shelley, a Rupert Brooke, or a T. S. Eliot.

Nor can literature be considered without attention to music. Much of primitive literature is song, and much of modern music may be described as the expression in sound of thought and emotions for which mere words are inadequate.

We find it difficult to measure the importance of literature and music in the progress of history. Who can weigh the influence of such a piece of literature as the Bible? Or the works of Shakespeare? Or Plato? Or of such music as *"La Marseillaise"*? In literature and music we have another of the constant themes of history, and the impulse to expression in these forms has played an incalculably significant role in the march of civilization.

The Esthetic Theme

Man has shown a constant impulse to see beauty in—or to beautify—his surroundings. Evidences of this appear among some of the oldest human cultures—among the Cro-Magnon men, in the beginnings of the Chinese and East Indian cultures, and among the earliest settlers in the Valley of the Nile. Certainly one cannot form an adequate idea of the great civilizations of Egypt, Greece, India, China, or western Europe without giving serious consideration to the history of architecture and the other arts. Some say that the architecture and arts of any civilization are the most accurate representation of the "mind" of that civilization. However that may be, it is clear that art and architecture are integral parts of history, no less significant, perhaps, than religion or literature.

Great Personalities in History

At certain times in the course of history, individual men of outstanding importance have had a powerful influence on the stream of events. Some historians, notably Thomas Carlyle, have believed that these great men are the decisive factor in history. In this view, history is "the essence of innumerable biographies."

Some men have, indeed, had a role of exceptional significance in the affairs of their time. Individuals, such as Caesar or Genghis Khan or Napoleon or Adolf Hitler, have altered the course of history simply by the sheer force of their own character.

But too much importance should not be given to the role of great men in history. Large as was the importance of Hitler in his time, he probably would never have been heard of had he been born in Austria in the age of Caesar. Nor would Napoleon have become the ruler of Europe had he been born in Corsica 1000 years instead of two centuries ago. For all their strength of mind and character, the individuals whom we know as great men of history could not have attained prominence unless they had been born into situations that gave them opportunities to play leading roles. Yet the situation into which each was born was itself the product of previous history, over which these men had no control. Thus, while it must be recognized that the character of individual men counts for much in the course of history, it is also true that the lives of individuals are in large degree influenced—if not actually determined—by deep social and economic forces over which they have little or no control.

CULTURE AND CIVILIZATION

Everything that human beings have ever done, even in the most remote times, is of interest to the student of history. Customarily, however, we speak of history as beginning at that point in time when a primitive "culture" passes through the metamorphosis that transforms it into a "civilization."

As we use these terms in the study of the past, *culture* comes before *civilization*. We speak of culture as beginning whenever and wherever human beings began to use and invent mechanisms other than the human body as means of aiding them in their struggle for survival. Thus culture took its start when men began to use sticks and stones as weapons instead of their bare hands; or when they began to build their own shelters instead of sharing natural caves with the bears; or when they began to organize themselves into groups for purposes of the hunt, of defense, of social intercourse, or of economic enterprise. To be sure, other creatures besides men form groups for common endeavors—ants live in colonies, for example, and beavers work together to build dams. But human culture alone shows *conscious* invention and planning, and human culture alone is handed down from one generation to the next. (The social behavior of certain animals and insects is generally thought to be merely instinctive, not the product of thought and memory.)

So far as we know, all true men—as distinguished from anthropoid apes—have had cultures, however primitive and rudimentary. The study of the cultures of primitive men is the concern of the anthropologist. Ordinarily the historian is interested in them only when they become civilizations.

We cannot draw a clear and sharp line, however, between a culture and a civilization. Every civilization grew out of a culture, though not every culture has developed into a civilization. The North American Indians had a culture but hardly a civilization; the barbarians who overran the Roman Empire had a culture; Rome possessed a civilization that ultimately civilized the barbarians.

Stonehenge, Wiltshire, England, is so oriented that the axis through the Slaughter Stone (upper right) and the Friar's Heel (top right) points directly to the rising of the sun at the summer solstice. It was also a temple that dates to possibly 2000 B.C. (British Information Services)

The Erechtheum, Athens, Greece. The last (c.421–409 B.C.) of the temples to be built on the Acropolis in the great Athenian Age, the Erechtheum was probably designed by Mnesicles. Although irregular in shape, because of the site and because of the sacred places and altars it housed, it is considered the high point of architecture in the Ionic order (see p. 121). It was also supposed to be the burial place of Erechtheus, early hero and legendary warrior king of Athens. (Trans World Airlines photo)

As a rough rule in this book the following are taken as the marks of a civilization:

(1) Every civilization occupies a fairly definite territorial area, has a characteristic, though often diversified, economic life, and characteristic political forms, although it may not be politically united under one government.

(2) Every civilization has an organized intellectual life, usually centering in common ideas or religious beliefs that are accepted by most members of the society.

(3) Every civilization has a system of writing that permits a more effective communication of ideas and assures their preservation from one generation to the next.

(4) Every historical civilization has centered in towns or cities, with their dependent food-producing areas, in which the economic, political, and religious functions in the life of society tended to be specialized: the farmer produced food and the ironworker, weapons and tools; the priests administered the affairs of religion; and the kings and their officers performed the functions of government.

Many primitive cultures have had some of the marks of civilization: a fixed abode, an adequate supply of food, social and political organization, religion, art, and oral literature. Such cultures are nearly at the stage of civilization. The one clear line that separates them from civilization is that they have not devised or acquired a system of writing. When they make this decisive step, they become civilizations. At this point their history begins.

The Great World Civilizations

The earliest civilizations, in the sense in which the word is used here, arose in six separate areas on the earth's surface—in the river valleys of Egypt, Mesopotamia, India, and China and in the high mountain valleys of Mexico and Peru in America. Possibly some of these civilizations, such as those of the valleys of the Indus and the Euphrates, shared a common beginning in a remote time in the past, though probably they arose independently of one another. At a later time, other civilizations were to develop around the Mediterranean and along the shores of the Atlantic Ocean.

Two of these earliest civilizations have practically disappeared: those that arose among the Incas of Peru and the Mayas and Aztecs in Mexico were submerged when the Europeans began their conquest of the New World. In other areas, however, civilization has survived from its first appearance down to our own time. Yet civilizations do not show the same vigor in all periods. Rather, each one seems to rise from its beginnings to a Golden Age, then to pass into stagnation or decline. Sometimes, after a long period of stagnation, a civilization enjoys a new burst of creativity or a "renaissance."

Historians have long sought to find an explanation of why this happens. Some have seen it as simply the unfolding of God's plan with men. Others have believed that history moves always in cycles. Many nineteenth-century historians believed that history is a record of steady human progress. The English historian Arnold Toynbee believes that cultures and civilizations have grown as a "response" to the "challenge" presented by the problems of satisfying the basic wants of men in the differing environments in which men have found themselves. Whatever the explanation, it does appear that civilizations do vary in the degree of their vigor, and though no great civilization has ever entirely disappeared, some have become stagnant, while others have continued to advance.

The Pyramidal Temple at Chichén Itzá, capital of the flourishing Second Mayan Empire (A.D. c.1000–2000) in Yucatan. The early history of the Maya is still completely obscure. (Burton Holmes from Ewing Galloway)

Interior of Reims Cathedral—looking from the choir toward the main doorway, above which is the famous rose window. Built between 1212 and 1241, Reims is one of the finest Gothic cathedrals—the soaring expression of a deeply religious age. The vaulting in the nave is 124 feet high—a height made possible because Gothic builders, although still working in stone, had advanced far beyond the Greeks who built the Erechtheum, having developed the pointed arch, vaulting, and the flying buttress. (University Prints)

WHY STUDY HISTORY?

So far we have been endeavoring to describe what is involved in the study of history. But most students will also wish to know what is its purpose. "Why study history?"

History as Heritage

One good answer is that history is a sort of jewel box containing the cultural heritage of every individual born into the civilization of the modern world. A moment's reflection will show that if all the knowledge, ideals, institutions, and material wealth accumulated in the past should suddenly be taken from us, we should instantly revert to the condition of wild beasts. What would our civilization be like without the art of the ancient Greeks, the East Indians, or the Chinese? What would it be like without the Bible or the religion of Christ or the great religious teachings of Buddha and Mohammed? What would it be like without the Gothic cathedrals that we have inherited from the Feudal Era in Europe or the art that we owe to the men of the Renaissance? Or what would it be like without the steam engine, invented some 200 years ago, or the radio, invented two generations ago? Or without the writings of Shakespeare or Confucius or Plato or George Santayana? The cultural heritage of the modern student is the richest in the history of the race.

The Practical Uses of History

Nor can we avoid the practical uses of history. Civilization as we know it is what it is because of what it has been. The past not only still lives among us, it gives us the golden key for understanding things as they are.

This practical aspect of history is what makes the study of the past so valuable to the citizen of a democracy. In history he will learn to see as a whole the problems that arise in the social life of mankind, and he will learn, too, the many different ways by which men have sought to solve them. Thus he will gain a better understanding of these problems, and he may become more tolerant of ideas and institutions other than those he encounters only in his own experience. History, as a record of constant change in the past, should show him that constant change must be expected in the future. And a knowledge of history should

Buddha—an eighth-century stone relief. Today millions of peoples in Asia are followers of the great religious teacher who was born in India c.563 B.C. (Courtesy of the Metropolitan Museum of Art)

make it easier for him to meet the basic problem of intelligent living, which is only —in its last analysis—the problem of choosing and supporting those changes—since change is inevitable—that will be most conducive to the deepening and enrichment of his life and the life of his society.

Suggestions for Further Reading

The following books are suggested as valuable to the beginning student in the history of civilization. While most of them refer to the history of civilization in the west, all are of a sufficiently general nature to be useful in the study from beginning to end.

Suggested books dealing with narrower or more specialized parts of the story will be found listed at the end of each chapter.

Readings on the Study of History

Article "History," in the *Encyclopedia of the Social Sciences*.

An excellent discussion of what history is, its materials, its methods, and its objectives, with special sections on the historiography of the most important areas of civilization, written by distinguished specialists.

Article "History," in the *Encyclopedia Britannica*.

A good brief explanation.

Harry Elmer Barnes, *A History of Historical Writing* (Norman, Okla., 1937).

This is a rapid survey of the work of the most important historians in the west. It is careful and interesting.

Marc L. B. Bloch, *The Historian's Craft* (New York, 1953).

A brief and thoughtful essay on the nature of historical study, by one of France's greatest modern historians.

R. G. Collingwood, *The Idea of History* (Oxford, 1946).

This is a brilliant philosophical essay on the nature of history and the growth of the idea of history in western civilization. A classic.

Louis Gottschalk, *Understanding History* (New York, 1950).

This is a brief and highly interesting introduction to the chief problems of method in the study of history.

Edward M. Hulme, *History and Its Neighbors* (New York, 1942).

An interesting attempt to explain what history is, and history's relationship to the other social studies.

Allan Nevins, *The Gateway to History* (New York, 1938).

An introduction to the problems and critical methods of historical study. One of the best.

James H. Robinson, *The New History* (New York, 1912).

An essay upon the modern concept of history that includes in that study sociological and intellectual phenomena as well as politics.

James T. Shotwell, *Introduction to the History of History* (New York, 1922).

A brief history of history-writing.

James W. Thompson, *A History of Historical Writing* (2 vols., New York, 1942).

A scholarly, somewhat advanced history of historical writing.

General Histories of Civilization or of Continuing Aspects of History

H. E. Barnes, *An Intellectual and Cultural History of the Western World* (rev. ed., New York, 1941).

This is an encyclopedic survey of the cultural history of civilization in the west, from the ancient Mediterranean civilization to the twentieth century. Most useful as a reference book.

C. Crane Brinton, *Ideas and Men; the Story of Western Thought* (New York, 1950).

A very readable and interesting history of ideas and the men who held them.

Lewis Browne, *This Believing World* (New York, 1930).

A popular history of religion.

Sheldon Cheney, *The Theatre: Three Thousand Years of Drama, Acting, and Stagecraft* (New York, 1952).

A good, readable survey.

Sheldon Cheney, *A World History of Art* (New York, 1937).

A useful survey.

Herrlee G. Creel, *Chinese Thought, From Confucius to Mao Tse Tung* (Chicago, 1953).

A useful survey.

W. C. D. Dampier, *A History of Science and its Relations with Philosophy and Religion* (3d ed., Cambridge, England, 1942).

A very interesting, brief survey.

Clive Day, *A History of Commerce* (4th ed., New York, 1938).

A near-classic.

Will Durant, *The Story of Philosophy* (New York, 1950).

A popular history of philosophy in the western world.

Will Durant, *The Story of Civilization* (5 vols., through the Renaissance, New York, 1935–53).

A fine popular, but lengthy, history. Chiefly cultural.

Alfred Einstein, *A Short History of Music* (New York, 1938).

A good, dependable survey.

Sir James G. Frazer, *The Golden Bough* (abridged ed., New York, 1952).

A classic history of magic and superstition.

R. J. Harvey-Gibson, *Two Thousand Years of Science* (New York, 1929).

A good survey.

Talbot F. Hamlin, *Architecture Through the Ages* (rev. ed., New York, 1953).

A useful survey.

John H. Hammerton, ed., *Universal World History* (10 vols., New York, 1937).

Actually a history of civilization in the west. Useful as a reference work.

P. H. Lang, *Music in Western Civilization* (New York, 1941).

A useful, but dull, survey.

William L. Langer, ed., *An Encyclopaedia of World History* (rev. ed., Boston, 1948).

A highly useful reference work on historical events.

Kenneth S. Latourette, *A Short History of the Far East* (rev. ed., New York, 1951).
This is a useful survey of the history of the Far East; it contains usable bibliographies for further study.

H. Leichtentritt, *Music, History and Ideas* (Cambridge, Mass., 1938).
A provocative essay relating the development of music to the other parts of history, particularly intellectual history.

John A. Macy, *The Story of the World's Literature* (New York, 1925).
A good survey.

F. S. Marvin, *The Living Past, A Sketch of Western Progress* (5th ed., Oxford, 1931).
A brilliant set of essays showing how much of an influence the past still exerts upon the present.

The Oxford History of Music (2d ed., 7 vols., London, 1929–1938).
This is a standard history. Very scholarly and technical; chiefly for relatively advanced students.

John H. Randall, Jr., *The Making of the Modern Mind* (rev. ed., New York, 1940).
This is a very useful survey of the intellectual development in the civilization of the western world from the Feudal Era to the twentieth century.

D. M. Robb and J. J. Garrison, *Art in the Western World* (New York, 1935).
A good survey.

James H. Robinson, *The Mind in the Making* (New York, 1921).
A brilliant essay upon the growth of the "mind" of western civilization, and the relation of intellectual life to social forms.

Bertrand Russell, *A History of Western Philosophy* (New York, 1945).
A generally sound, sometimes biased, often irreverent, and always entertaining history of philosophy in the western world. Nontechnical, easy to understand.

George H. Sabine, *A History of Political Theory* (rev. ed., New York, 1950).
A fine modern survey of history of political thought.

George Sarton, *Introduction to the History of Science* (3 vols. in 5, Washington, 1927–1948).
A scholarly work by the greatest historian of science.

Homer W. Smith, *Man and His Gods* (Boston, 1952).
A rationalist's history of religion in the western world.

George N. Steiger, *A History of the Far East* (Boston, 1936).
A good survey.

Anthologies of Original Writings from the Literature and the Thinkers of the Great World Civilizations

Columbia College, *Introduction to Contemporary Civilization in the West* (2 vols., New York, 1946).
An excellent and extensive anthology of selections from the most important thinkers of the western world, from the Feudal Era to the present. Chiefly economic, social, and political writings.

George H. Knoles and Rixford K. Snyder, eds., *Readings in Western Civilization* (rev. ed., New York, 1954).
A very useful selection of readings from the most important writers in the civilization of the western world from the ancient Egyptians and Babylonians to the twentieth century.

Lin Yutang, ed., *The Wisdom of China and India* (New York, 1942).
An excellent set of selections from the most celebrated writings of India and China.

Stith Thompson and John Gassner, eds., *Our Heritage of World Literature* (rev. ed., New York, 1942).
A good collection of selections from the great literature of the world down to about 1900. Weakest on the Far East.

Robert Warnock and George K. Anderson, eds., *The World in Literature* (2 vols., Chicago, 1950–1951).
Probably the best anthology of selections from the literature of the great civilizations.

Atlases

Encyclopedia Britannica Atlas
An excellent atlas, constantly being revised.

William R. Shepherd, *Historical Atlas* (8th rev. ed., New York, 1956).
A superb reference work, recently brought up to date.

1

The Earliest Human
Cultures

The Lanyon Quoit or Dolmen, Cornwall, England. Remains of a long barrow (see pp. 34–35), from which the earth has been removed. (British Information Services)

The characteristic feature of human culture that most clearly distinguishes it from the behavior of other animals is the inheritance by each human generation of much of the pattern of behavior of its ancestors. In each generation men invent or discover new techniques for survival or the good life, or they improve their institutions or add to their store of knowledge. These gains are handed down to the succeeding generation of men, which, in turn, makes new additions to the human cultural inheritance.

This is what we mean when we speak of *progress*, when we say that the present is the heir of the past. We may not go so far as to say that there is an inevitable law of progress, but we do have warrant to say that human culture involves a process of accumulation and inheritance, both of knowledge and of skills.

This cumulative process began long before the period of recorded history, which takes its start only with the invention of writing some 5000 years ago. Though this was of enormous importance, writing came about only at a relatively late date in the long, continuous process of human progress, and many other advances of equal importance—such as the use of fire—occurred much earlier. At the time when recorded history began, therefore, man was already the heir to a cultural patrimony accumulated by many previous generations. Hence, before setting out upon the study of the historic period, we must take note of what had been accomplished in the preceding epochs of human existence.

THE UNIVERSE, THE EARTH, AND TIME

The Universe

Man is a latecomer among the creatures that inhabit the earth, and the earth itself has only a relatively short and recent history as part of the universe. Scientists tell us that the universe is made up of luminous gases in the form of nebulae, which eventually condense into incandescent stars and solid bodies. We cannot even hazard a guess as to how long this process has been going on. We can only say that stars have been forming and disappearing for millions of millions of years, and that the oldest of the stars that now exist are millions of millions of years older than the newest. And we know that the process of the formation and extinction of heavenly bodies is still going on today.

Our sun condensed into its present mixture of gas and other matter about 7 trillion years ago. It is not the newest of the stars—Sirius is only 2 trillion years old, and Capella is a mere trillion years old. Both of these are much larger than our sun, and other stars are still larger. Betelgeuse, for example, has a mass about 50 times that of our sun, and a volume about 27 million times greater.

Our whole solar system, of which the earth is only a tiny part, is of infinitesimal size when compared, for instance, with the solar system of the Andromeda nebula. We gain a vague impression of the size of this nebula when we learn that light, which travels at about 186,300 miles a second, takes about 30,000 years to cross Andromeda. Light crosses the whole of our solar system in only eight hours.

We gain some further realization of the vastness of space and time when we note that light, which covers almost 16 billion miles in a day, takes about 900,000 years to come from Andromeda to the earth, a distance that is simply too great for imagination to grasp. We see Andromeda today by light waves that left there at a time when the earliest human beings were stumbling about the earth in their endless search for food. During the whole span of human existence, these light waves have been hurtling through space, to reach earth only in our own time. In order to find out what is happening in Andromeda at this minute, we would have to wait almost another million years.

The Earth: Man's Home

After such astronomical figures concerning space and time in the universe, it is a relief to come down to earth. We have noted that stars apparently come into being by the condensation of nebulae. But this does not complete the process, for sometimes the stars break down into solar systems of planets rotating about the parent star. And sometimes the planets themselves give birth to satellites, as have some of the planets that revolve about our own sun.

The birth of the earth took place somewhere in the neighborhood of 2 billion years ago—a time much more recent than the formation of the sun. But not until hundreds of millions of years later did life appear upon the earth. For a time—which is probably more than half the earth's age—before the first appearance of living creatures, the earth underwent vast geological changes. The outer crust buckled and folded, and eruptions and earthquakes took place, making over the whole surface. Wide oceans rolled where now the greatest continents have raised themselves above the waters. Huge areas of land existed for epochs, only to sink again beneath the spreading seas. Eventually, the primary rocks of the earth's surface were worn down by wind and weather, so that dust, rubble, mud, and sand were deposited in the lowlands. Thus was created an environment that could support the simplest forms of life. But not for many millions of years after that, not until the most recent geological epoch, was the earth hospitable to so highly developed and complex a form of life as the human species.

The Origin of Life

What life is and whence it came is a question that no one has answered in terms that all men can understand and will accept. Many religions, both ancient and modern, have offered explanations that attribute the creation of life to a supernatural power. Some of these explanations, and other theories that were also put forth in both ancient and modern times, have been abandoned with the increase of scientific knowledge of the earth and man. But scientists themselves have not yet discovered a wholly satisfactory answer.

Scientists have discovered, however, that the simplest forms of living matter are not very different from nonliving matter. Certain processes that go on in the simplest organisms are not unlike the changes undergone by some of the more complex crystals. Some scientists suggest, therefore, that the essence of life is a matter of chemical reactions. These reactions could take place anywhere, at any time, if conditions were favorable. And conditions on the earth became favorable for such a transition from nonliving matter to living organisms at a time some millions of years ago.

Geological Time

The first forms of life appeared on the earth over 500 million years ago, though no creature resembling man appeared until about one million years ago. The span of time since the first appearance of life is divided into three principal eras which themselves are subdivided. These are: (1) the Paleozoic Era, or Era of Ancient Life, (2) the Mesozoic Era, or Era of Middle Life, and (3) the Cenozoic Era, or Era of Recent Life.

The Paleozoic Era is much the longest of the geological eras, being more than twice as long as the Mesozoic. These first two eras together cover nearly 430 million years, while the Cenozoic Era has lasted only about 70 million years.

The Cenozoic Era comprises two subdivisions: the Tertiary Period, or Age of Mammals, and the Quaternary Period, or Age of Man. The longer Tertiary Period includes about 69 million years, while the short Quaternary includes only the last million years. Some scholars prefer to include the Quaternary Period in the Tertiary because the Quaternary is so much shorter. But here we shall speak of the Tertiary and Quaternary as separate periods because the Quaternary is the age in which man appeared, and it is therefore the period with which this book primarily deals.

The Tertiary Period is usually subdivided into five epochs: (1) the Paleocene, (2) the Eocene, (3) the Oligocene, (4) the Miocene, and (5) the Pliocene. The Quaternary Period is subdivided into two epochs: (1) the Pleistocene and (2) the Holocene. The Pleistocene is often spoken of as the Ice Age and continued for slightly less than one million years. The Holocene is often referred to as the Recent Period and includes only the last 10,000 years. This is the epoch during which the races of modern man first appeared and in which human civilization arose.

Man

Early man, as distinguished from all other animals including the anthropoid apes, probably appeared during the early part of the Pleistocene Epoch of the Quaternary Period, roughly about one million years ago.

This was near the beginning of the Ice Age, when the Earth's climate underwent a series of changes. This Ice Age included four successive glacial ages, each of which was followed by a warm period. We live today in the last of these warm periods. Why these great climatic changes should have come about at the beginning of the Quaternary Epoch, we do not know. We can, however, see the effect they had on the history of man. We know that in the periods of glaciation, much of the land was submerged by water, and during the warm or interglacial periods, the land rose up again and the weather became dry. At times in these warm interglacial periods, Europe and Africa

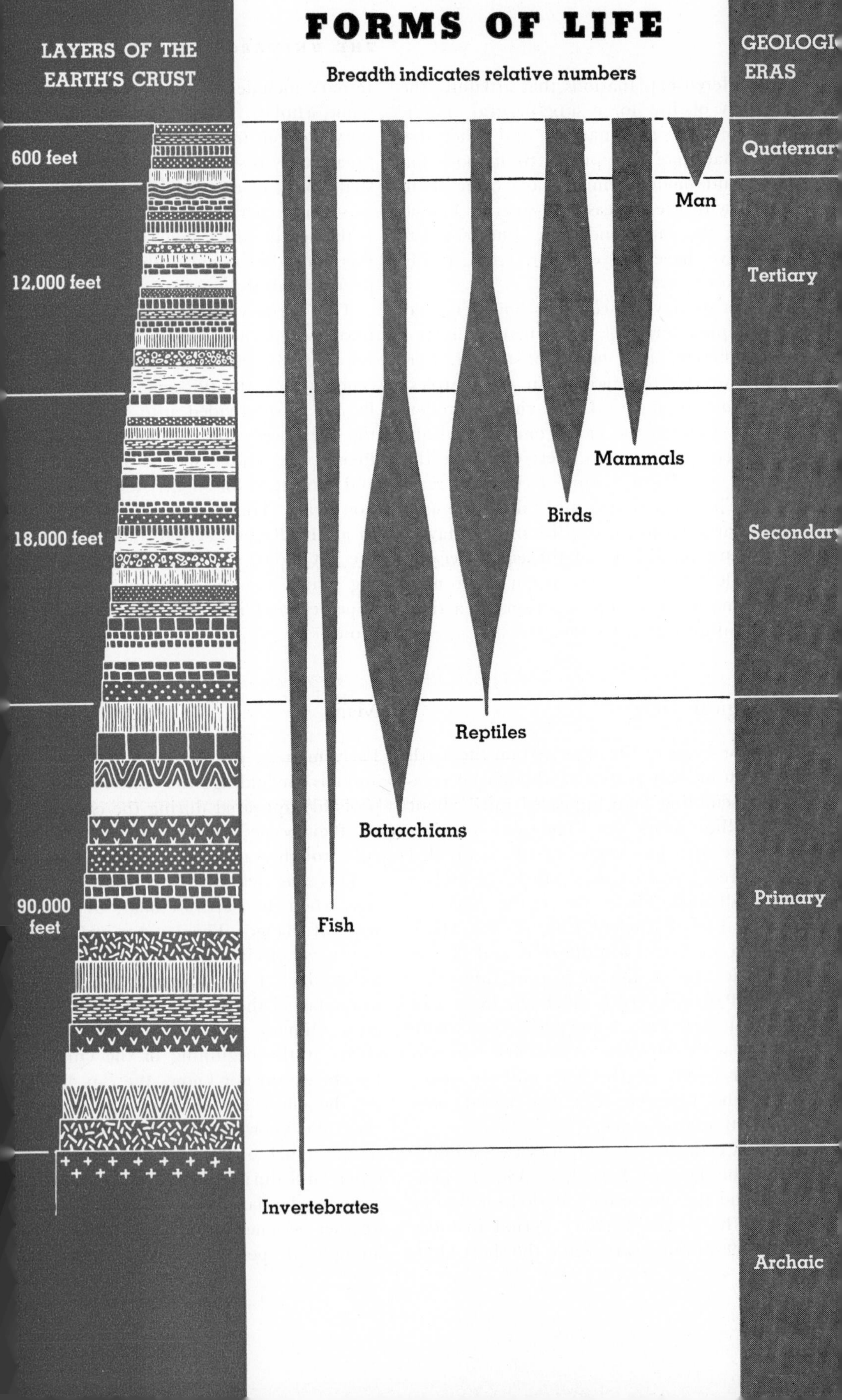

FORMS OF LIFE

Breadth indicates relative numbers

LAYERS OF THE EARTH'S CRUST

600 feet

12,000 feet

18,000 feet

90,000 feet

GEOLOGIC ERAS

Quaternary

Tertiary

Secondary

Primary

Archaic

Man

Mammals

Birds

Reptiles

Batrachians

Fish

Invertebrates

GEOLOGIC PERIOD		GLACIAL EPOCHS	Ages of MAN	CULTURAL AGE	INDUSTRIES
	Holocene (Recent)	Postglacial		Iron Bronze Neolithic	
	Pleistocene	Fourth Glacial	Homo Sapiens		Azilian and Tardenoisian Magdalenian Solutrean Aurignacian
		Third Interglacial	Homo Neanderthalensis		Mousterian
QUATERNARY		Third Glacial			Acheulian
		Second Interglacial	Homo Heidelbergensis		Abbevillian Chellean
		Second Glacial			Pre-Chellean
		First Interglacial		Paleolithic	
		First Glacial			
TERTIARY	Pliocene		Pithecanthropus Erectus(?)	Eolithic	

formed only one continent, joined at Gibraltar and Sicily, and the British Isles were part of this huge continent. The climate of southern Europe and northern Africa was not the same then as now. Southern Europe must have been much warmer, and northern Africa humid, rather than arid, for evidently the elephant, rhinoceros, and hippopotamus used to migrate from Africa into Europe, withdrawing again to the south when the cold glacial period returned.

The Age of Man

The human race, which made its appearance at some time about the beginning of the Ice Age, seems to have originated somewhere in southern and eastern Asia, where mammalian life abounded.

One of the oldest specimens of man known is the Java ape-man, or *Pithecanthropus erectus,* whose remains were discovered in Java in 1891. This remote relative of Homo sapiens, the present species of man, lived in the early Pleistocene Age, between about half a million and a million years ago. We know nothing of the predecessors of *Pithecanthropus erectus,* although remains recently discovered in a mine in northern Italy appear to be those of a human being who lived long before *Pithecanthropus.*

Scientists are not agreed that this specimen is human. At first some regarded him as not human at all but rather a giant gibbon. Others have conceded only that he represents a transitional, prehuman stage. Unfortunately we do not have enough remains to know quite what he looked like. Because the jawbone is missing, we do not know whether his face projected, like an ape's, or was vertical, as with modern man. But the skull is long, in relation to its breadth, and this differentiates *Pithecanthropus erectus* from the anthropoid apes. Though we may be sure he was not what we should call a handsome man, we know that he was rather tall, that he could hold himself erect and walk about like a man, and that he lived on the ground rather than in trees. He probably deserves the name of ape-man, for he was neither wholly an ape nor wholly human.

From two skulls found near Peking (Peiping) in 1921 and 1930, we gain more knowledge of early man. These remains seem to date from the early Pleistocene period, but they give evidence of creatures closer to modern man than to the Java ape-man, *Pithecanthropus erectus.* The species represented by these two skulls is known as *Sinanthropus pekinensis,* or Peking man. It is believed to be near to the type of human being from which evolved the extinct Neanderthal men and also the modern races of man.

Evidence of another early species of man is provided by remains found in 1907 in a sandpile near Heidelberg, Germany. Only the lower jaw was found. This is chinless and massive, as in the anthropoid ape, but the spread of the dental arch is like that in a human being. And the teeth, sixteen of which were present in the jawbone when it was found, are unmistakably human. This species has been named Heidelberg man, and he lived either in the warm period preceding the onset of the Ice Age or in the first or second interglacial period. He was clearly much nearer to modern man than to the ape.

We have much more knowledge of still another species, known as Neanderthal man. The name comes from the valley in Germany where the first remains of this species were found in 1856. But other remains of the same species have been found in many places in Europe and Asia Minor, and we have specimens of some twenty Neanderthal men, women, and children.

Neanderthal man was not a prepossessing individual. He was short of stature, with a massive head and bulky body. He had a huge face, like an anthropoid ape, and a low, sloping forehead. But his brain was much larger than an ape's, and he had a receding chin, which gave him a more human appearance than Heidelberg man, who had no chin at all.

This species survived over a period of perhaps several hundred thousand years and did not die out until as little as 20,000 or 80,000 years ago. It may have been living in Europe when more advanced types of men appeared. Some anthropologists think that modern man may have descended from Heidelberg man, though others believe that both this species and *Homo sapiens*, which is the species we belong to, split off from a common parent stock.

With Rhodesian man, we complete the roster of the most important predecessors of modern man. His remains comprise a skull, lacking the lower jaw, and some few bones that were found in a cave in Rhodesia, Africa, in 1921. Like the other species that we have noted, Rhodesian man combined simian and human characteristics, and he shows a considerable resemblance to the Neanderthal man. We cannot establish the time at which he lived.

How modern man is related to these and other possible predecessors of whom we learn more from time to time, we cannot say with assurance. All we know as certain is that these early species have many similarities to Homo sapiens, as well as to the anthropoid apes, and that Homo sapiens himself made his appearance about 10,000 to 20,000 years ago.

Homo sapiens, it must be noted, is the product of a lengthy development. Long isolation of groups of men, combined with other factors, produced a number of "stocks," but these are not races. Since his appearance, Homo sapiens has existed as a *single* species, although in various "stocks," or types. Thus although the terms linger in our vocabularies, the division of humanity into Caucasian, Mongoloid, and Negro *races* was a classification that is now obsolete.

Similarly peoples who spoke certain languages were formerly assigned definite physical characteristics. Language is a distinctive and exclusive mark of the human species, but the origins of languages are so remote that we know nothing of them—except that they came long before writing. Languages also change and develop, so while it is customary to divide languages into "families"—Indo-European, Semitic, etc.—it is quite probable that these developed from earlier languages which are unknown to us.

Restorations made by Dr. J. H. McGregor of the heads of prehistoric men: *Pithecanthropus*, Neanderthal man, and Cro-Magnon man (p. 23). (Courtesy of the American Museum of Natural History)

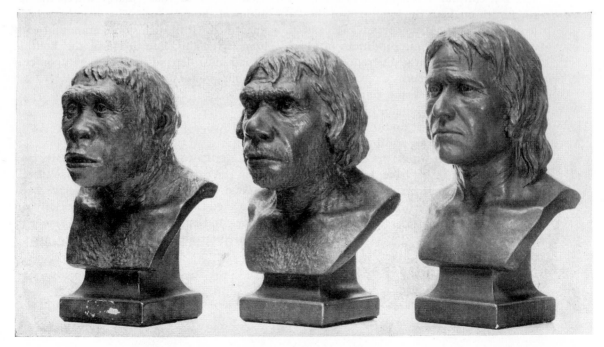

THE BEGINNINGS OF HUMAN CULTURE:
THE PALEOLITHIC AGE

Now that we have surveyed the ancestry of our hero, man, we are ready to witness the opening of the human drama. Our beginning is with the earliest development of human cultures.

The Prehistoric Cultural Ages

In the study of prehistoric human cultural development, it is customary to speak of four great epochs—the Paleolithic or Old Stone Age, the Neolithic or New Stone Age, the Bronze Age, and the Iron Age. Sometimes we also speak of other periods besides these four. For example, the period just before the Paleolithic or Old Stone Age is sometimes called the Eolithic or Dawn Stone Age. Sometimes a Mesolithic or Middle Stone Age is designated between the Old Stone Age and the New Stone Age, and a Chalcolithic Age, between the New Stone Age and the Bronze Age.

The Paleolithic Age lasted much longer than those that came after it; it lasted, roughly, from the beginnings of the earliest human cultures down to the Neolithic Age, which began about 5,000 or 6,000 years ago. But cultural development was not continuous throughout the long span of the Paleolithic Age. The rate of advance varied, rather, according to the conditions of physical environment and the different abilities of successive types of men.

Many of the bones and implements that give us evidences of human life in the Paleolithic Age have been found in the terraces that were formed long ago by rivers as they widened and narrowed or changed their courses. Other relics have been found in caves. Some of the richest of these finds have been made in France, which for that reason has always been a center of archaeological studies.

From the debris of tools, weapons, and burned bones, from the paintings on the walls and ceilings of the caves that they inhabited, and from their burial places, we have been able to learn much about how primitive men lived. Sometimes the dirt and debris in the caves are as much as thirty feet deep. These deposits were not necessarily made by peoples who dwelt continuously in the same cave. Sometimes a cave was inhabited for a long period, became vacant when the original dwellers moved to another place, and then, at a later date, became the dwelling of some other people.

The Dawn Stone Age

Some archaeologists believe they can identify certain stones as eoliths—that is, stone implements used in the Eolithic or Dawn Stone Age. But it is often difficult to distinguish between stones that owe their shape to natural causes and those shaped by men. Some stones have been found that give such clear indication of having been intentionally chipped that they must be recognized as man-made. However, no such stones have been found in those places where the remains of the most primitive men have been unearthed. Until such stones are found with human remains, knowledge of the Eolithic period must depend in large part upon reasonable guesses.

The Lower Paleolithic Age

With the Paleolithic Age, we reach a period when the existence of human culture is well attested. Remains of this period have been discovered all over Europe, especially in France and Spain, on some of the islands of the Mediterranean, in parts of Africa, and in

India and China. Implements made of bone and horn, works of art, and burial places contribute much to knowledge of this period. But a special significance is attached to the vast number of stone implements that have been discovered, for they tell a continuous story of human progress throughout the Old Stone Age.

Pre-Chellean Culture. The Pre-Chellean is the earliest of the several cultural epochs into which the Old Stone Age is divided. In this period appear not only tools but also weapons of flint, chipped in various ways to perform different services. Unlike eoliths, these are unquestionably artifacts—that is, products of human handiwork. Suitably shaped stones were selected, then rough flakes were knocked off with a hammer stone, and finally the implement was retouched—that is, small flakes were chipped off to give a point or a sharp edge and to shape the tool so it could be firmly grasped. Such implements could be used for making wooden tools, of which none has survived, or for cutting flesh and dressing hides, or for boring and planing.

The Chellean Epoch. The artifacts of the Chellean epoch—so-called because of the deposit found at Chelles-sur-Marne in northern France—indicate a considerable step forward in primitive human culture. They give evidence of a hardy people, who had achieved much more control over their environment than had men of the preceding period. Apparently the men of the Chellean epoch made great strides, especially in hunting, as their enlarged armory of weapons suggests. Wild life was abundant in their time, though some of the tropical animals were no longer to be found in Europe.

The most typical instrument of the Chellean epoch was the *coup-de-poing*, or hand ax. This ax was made of a piece of flint or quartzite, flaked to a rough almond shape and, as Chellean skill increased, to other shapes as well. The point and its edges were usually sharpened, while the other end was shaped so as to be held in the hand. These hand axes were from four to eight inches long and weighed as much as a pound. In its various shapes—almond, oval, disk, and spear—the instrument was used for a variety of purposes, such as hacking, sawing, chopping, cutting, scraping, stabbing, and, perhaps, for throwing. Small pointed flints were also developed, perhaps principally for boring, but these were not essentially different from the coup-de-poing, which was the instrument-of-all-work of Chellean man.

Recently the historical anthropologists have come to combine the Pre-Chellean and the Chellean cultures under one name, Abberillian, which is derived from the region of Abbeville, in France.

Acheulian *Coups-de-poing* (p. 22). Some of the Acheulian hand axes are masterpieces of craftsmanship, far beyond mere technical necessity. Although it has been suggested that the hand-ax people were still communicating by gabble and gesture, the men who made these tools must have formed in their minds an image of what they were working to achieve. The standard hand ax was not a product of one mind, but of men in successive generations, copying and improving the products of their predecessors. The development of speech greatly aided these processes. (Collection *Musée de l'Homme*, Paris. Photograph by Tendron)

Acheulian Culture. The artifacts of the Acheulian epoch—named for the deposit of remains discovered at St. Acheul in France—show considerable improvement in workmanship, though little that is new. The Acheulian *coup-de-poing* is smaller than the Abberillian, better made, and shaped more symmetrically. Careful flaking and retouching by pressure-chipping gave the flintworker more control over his product. And not only was the core of the piece of flint used, as before, but also the flakes struck from the core, which were used as knives, planes, scrapers, drills, and pointed instruments. Toward the end of this long period, still further improvements were made in the *coup-de-poing*, which became the masterpiece of Acheulian workmanship. The technique of chipping had so far improved that sharp, thin dagger and knife blades could be fashioned from flint flakes.

The Mousterian Culture. The Mousterian epoch gets its name from the remains discovered at Le Moustier, again in France. This period began at the close of the temperate third interglaciation, but it continued into the fourth glacial age (see chart, p. 17). At that time the climate of Europe was cold and damp as far south as northern Spain and Italy. Even the birds and mammals that lived in the arctic regions now migrated southward. Except during the summer months and in the temporary warm periods of the glaciation, the climate was too cold for the warmth-loving Asiatic beasts. In their place the mammoth, the reindeer, the woolly rhinoceros, and the cave bear roamed the forests and plains of Europe, along with those still-surviving beasts that preferred a temperate climate.

The Mousterian epoch of the Paleolithic Age is much better documented than those before it. For the first time the fossil finds include many remains of human beings as well as their artifacts, so we can form a much better idea of the men of this time. We can identify the creator of the Mousterian culture as the heavy-set, apelike Neanderthal man.

As the climate became more severe, Mousterian man gradually left the river banks, along which earlier men had lived, and took to the caves. In this period a good example of the influence of climate on human institutions is found, for it was at this time that man first developed the family and a simple form of communal life. Apparently a whole tribe would take to a cave in cold weather, first driving out the bears, then defending their home from the ferocious beasts without. These must have been difficult tasks—in one cave the skeletal remains of more than 800 bears have been discovered. The force of adverse circumstances compelled men to cooperate with one another. And the conditions of cave life also created a favorable environment for social development. We have evidence that some attention was given to burials, and this may indicate the beginnings of religious consciousness.

We must not overemphasize the social development in this epoch, however, for Neanderthal man lived most of the time outside the cave. At best, his home could not have been comfortable. Only the mouths of the caves were habitable as a rule, and the protective fires at the cave entrance could hardly have done much to temper the winter cold. The caves must have been smoky, and many of them were damp, as is shown by the diseased bones of both men and animals.

Hunting occupied a large share of Neanderthal man's time, for he needed the fur, fat, and flesh of his bestial contemporaries. Though his weapons were none too helpful, he was surprisingly successful. This is known from the numerous bones of large animals that have been found in the ashes of man-made fires. Since the bones were split—obviously for the purpose of extracting the marrow—we are sure that men must have caught the animals and brought them to the site of the fire. Since the bones of the mammoth, the woolly rhinoceros, and the cave bear have been found in the debris of cave fires, Neanderthal man must have captured these huge animals, even though his weapons were not powerful enough to overcome them. Presumably the hunters must have dug pits in which to trap them, or come upon them when they were wounded by accident or in fighting with other animals.

At one Mousterian site small quartzite balls were found, indicating a new use of stone. How they were used is not clear, but it has been suggested that they were fastened together by long thongs and used as bolas— weapons to hurl at and entangle an animal.

The first known industry in bone also appeared in the Mousterian epoch. Large bones were used as chopping blocks and, perhaps, for retouching flints. Bones were also broken and used for skinning and preparing hides.

Toward the end of the fourth glacial stage, the Mousterian culture came to its end. At the same time the Neanderthal man, who created this culture, disappeared. This disappearance was amazingly sudden, for Neanderthal man was at once replaced by the *parent* of Homo sapiens, and no trace of Neanderthal man has been found in the later Paleolithic Age. It may be that the older race was deteriorating, and when it was confronted by a species superior both mentally and physically and, perhaps, equipped with better weapons, it was either driven away or annihilated.

As the lower—or middle—Paleolithic Age ended, the climate of Europe again became temperate, though not so warm as before. This was the time when a new species of man, Homo sapiens, made its appearance. We can date this event with more confidence than any before: this transition from a lower to a higher species of man took place between 25,000 and 50,000 years ago.

The Upper Paleolithic Age

The dominant race of Homo sapiens in Europe during the Upper (later) Paleolithic Age, which now began, was the Cro-Magnon, so called from the name of the small cave in southwestern France where the first skeletal remains were found. Cro-Magnon man was not related to the Neanderthaloid races that he supplanted, and probably he originated somewhere outside of Europe, into which he seems to have migrated. It is believed that his original home was in Asia, from which he first moved into Africa, before passing on into Europe. Before reaching Europe, Cro-Magnon man had already developed his culture. But it is possible that he took over a part or the whole of the culture of the peoples whom he displaced.

For the most part, the Cro-Magnons were straight-limbed, large-chested, and tall—their average height, at a favorable early period, was perhaps more than six feet. They were long-headed, having skulls with an unusually large brain capacity, and broad of face, with prominent cheekbones and aquiline noses. From their brilliant cultural achievements, we may presume they were notably intelligent.

Cultural remains of the Upper Paleolithic Age are much more varied and much richer than those of the Lower Paleolithic. They indicate a more aggressive attitude on the part of the relatively modern men—the Cro-Magnons and others—who now inhabited Europe and most of the Mediterranean Basin. No longer is the work of man confined almost entirely to stone and bone. For although Homo sapiens continued to manufacture instruments of war and peace, his work now began to show evidence of thought and imagination, expressed in religious and artistic creations, which become profuse and impressive.

The Aurignacian Culture. No one knows whether the Aurignacian flint industry, which next appears, was derived from the earlier Mousterian culture or was imported by the invaders coming into Europe at this time. At any event, it shows an improved skill and wider scope. In the course of this cultural stage, larger flakes came into use, and an improved art of retouching. Of the

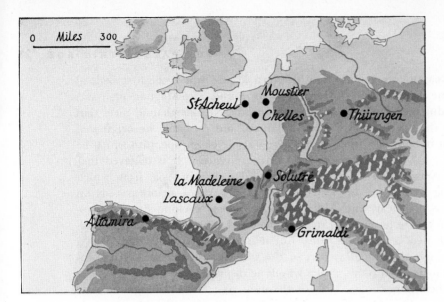

Location of Prehistoric Caves in Western Europe. Recently similar caves, containing hundreds of paintings, have been discovered in a remote region of Africa.

greatest significance in the development of the stone industry were the new implements used for engraving and carving. Many new instruments were also devised by Aurignacian man for hunting and fishing. These implements range in size from tiny, sharply pointed "microliths" to large spearheads. Bone was used more than ever before, and now ivory and horn were carved, a process which required unusually sharp tools.

The Solutrean Epoch. The chief advance in technique in the Solutrean epoch, which followed the Aurignacian, was the new mastery of pressure chipping. By this means of flaking the flint, the artisan could make a much thinner instrument than before. The new process made possible the manufacture of the pointed flint implements of the laurel-leaf and willow-leaf shapes, for which the Solutrean epoch is famous. The willow-leaf shapes were fitted with a shouldered point, a new invention that increased the effectiveness of the weapon. These shouldered points were long, very narrow flints, with part of the base chipped away so as to leave a notch and stem. The stem made it possible to attach the flint to a shaft, so that the weapon could be thrust or thrown, and the notch made sure that, once the weapon struck home, the point would remain fixed in the victim's flesh.

Other kinds of flint points, also finely shaped, were made for drilling and boring shell, bone, and ivory. Bone and ivory needles, pierced at one end, are found more often than before, as are drilled horn batons or ceremonial wands.

The Magdalenian Culture. The products of the flint industry of the next cultural epoch, the Magdalenian, reveal much less skillful workmanship than those of the previous epoch. The art of chipping declined. No more are found the beautifully flaked leaf blades of the Solutrean culture.

Despite these signs of decadence, stonework was not wholly given up. Many small implements were still made, especially for boring and drilling and performing other services in connection with the bone industry. And one important new discovery was made in flintwork—the chipping of long, thin flakes from a flint core by a single sharp blow. This was much easier than the tedious process of chipping and retouching and gave a remarkably keen edge.

What skill and inventiveness the men of the Magdalenian epoch lost in their flintwork, they made up by their rapid progress in the use of bone and horn. The new developments in this field prove that Magdalenian man had lost nothing of imagination or initiative but had merely turned his attention to a new problem.

The javelin point, first appearing in the Aurignacian epoch, and the harpoon, both made of bone and reindeer horn, were the most notable products of Magdalenian workmen. A regular process of improvement, too, may be observed in the making of harpoons. At first, the barbs were small and numerous, but eventually they became fewer and longer and less sharply curved. Later it became customary to equip the harpoon with a double rather than single row of barbs.

Very fine bone needles were made in this epoch, polished and sharpened on carefully selected stones. The baton—the purpose of which remains a mystery to us—is found in almost all the regions of Magdalenian culture, as in some regions of the earlier cultures. Dart throwers, made of horn (as were the needles and batons), became much more numerous in this period. Javelins, harpoons, batons, and dart throwers were decorated, bearing further testimony to the lively and imaginative minds of their makers.

All the new artifacts of bone and horn show that the men of the Magdalenian age were rapidly changing their world. In our own age, when invention is a commonplace occurrence, we find it hard to realize how important were the inventions of the Magdalenian—or even to realize that something as simple as a javelin point once had to be invented. But an invention like this or like the discovery of the principle of the harpoon was a milestone on man's road to dominance over his environment—as significant as the work of the genius of the earlier ages who first began to select naturally shaped stones, and as significant in their effects upon human life as some of the greatest inventions of the modern age.

The harpoon made it much easier for Magdalenian man to catch fish, and this made his supply of food more secure. The javelin, straight and barbed, gave him a better weapon for hunting animals. The dart thrower was another valuable extension of man's reach and power. The excellent needles of this period proclaim that clothing was becoming more important, and this is an indication of a more complicated society. Buttons may have been used, too, since bone and ivory were fashioned in such a form as might have served this purpose.

From the foregoing discussion of Upper Paleolithic culture, you can see that the cave-dwelling people of Europe in this age were highly inventive and technically skillful. They were clearly the superiors of their Lower Paleolithic predecessors, who had lived along the same river banks and in the same caves that the later Aurignacian, Solutrean, and Magdalenian men took over.

Cave Drawing at Lascaux. Such pictures often have been found in the deep recesses of caves where no families ever lived and where no daylight penetrates. We can marvel even more at the results when we realize the artist had to work by the dim light of a stone lamp, crouched on a narrow ledge or standing on a companion's shoulders. (French Government Tourist Office)

Where it took earlier men scores and hundreds of thousands of years to win some little control over the forces of nature, these later men in a few thousand years improved their flints, worked in horn and bone, produced needles and clothes, dart throwers, javelins, and harpoons.

The Birth of Religion. The life of later Paleolithic man was one of hunting and fishing, with much wandering from place to place, but it was more comfortable and secure than that of Mousterian man. And those remains that reveal their spiritual and esthetic life speak more vividly than anything yet encountered of the kind of man who, for the first time, tried to express his love and appreciation of the beauty of life and his misty hopes for the future.

Even before the appearance of modern man, Neanderthal man had expressed his awe of death by placing certain flints and ornaments with the bodies of his dead. Now, the new races devoted more attention to their burials. The skeleton of a man of the Aurignacian epoch, found in Wales, was painted red. Somewhat similar treatment was given a skeleton and the accompanying ornaments that were discovered at Brünn in Czechoslovakia. Other skeletons that have been discovered show that the bodies were carefully stretched out, with the arms folded. Ornaments, weapons, and sometimes even food were placed with the body. From the care given to the bodies of the dead, we know beyond question that these early men had some definite beliefs about death and future life. The remains are too scanty, however, and their meaning too mysterious, for us to gain a precise knowledge of these beliefs.

The Birth of Art. But there is a further source of information about early man's thoughts and feelings—the highly illuminating pictures that were engraved and painted on cave walls, incised on weapons and ornaments, molded in clay, and carved in the round. The personal ornaments, which have been found in abundance, are in the form of necklaces, pendants, and chaplets of bone, ivory, shell, or teeth. Such decorations give us an indication that the cave men and cave women were not unaware of their appearance or reluctant to improve it. And because necklaces made of seashells have been found far inland, it is presumed that the men of this time must have engaged in trade. Other examples of movable art works are engraved pebbles, decorated implements, and figurines.

For the most part, the subjects of primitive art were the animals among whom the artists lived. Those animals used for food were represented more often than those that were fierce enemies of man, and the more important they were as a source of food, the more often those animals were pictured. The horse, deer, mammoth, and bison appear far more frequently than the lion and hyena. Pictures or figures of birds and fish are found much less frequently than those of animals, and representations of plant life hardly at all. Human figures sometimes are found, but these are not so well done as the representations of animals. Decorative figures, based either on geometrical designs or forms of life, also appear.

Gradually the engraver and painter attained greater skill. The finest examples of their work are the superb animal figures found on the ceiling of the caves at Altamira in Spain and in the caverns of Font-de-Gaume in France. These are not simply in profile but show the figures in a variety of positions and with much detail. Beasts were represented in motion, lying down, chewing the cud, bellowing, or grouped in herds. Their eyes, hair, horns, and hooves are portrayed with remarkable accuracy. A feast might be depicted or animals crossing a stream, with fish swimming about them. Sometimes the shaft of a hunter's dart or spear protrudes from the flesh of an animal —probably the painter was working a primitive magic charm to assure success in hunting. The skill of the early sculptor is also shown by the impressive figures of animals that are carved in relief—that is, partly raised above the rock—on the walls of these caves, and in figurines carved in the round from bone, horn, and ivory, and in dart throwers that were fashioned in the shape of animals.

Perhaps human beings were depicted less frequently than animals because the human figure is more difficult to represent, or perhaps the artists were more concerned with using their skill to work magic for their success in hunting. Whenever the human form does appear in primitive painting and sculpture, it is presented nude. The female is shown more often than the male, perhaps because the female represented fertility and increase. Magic significance sometimes attaches to the human figure in primitive art, as is known from the representation of sorcerers in disguise, notably in the paintings of the cavern of Trois Frères in France. From the emphasis placed on the sexual characteristics of the men and women represented, we know that the prehistoric artist was deeply interested in the mysteries of sex, which, as one of the unknown forces of nature, he must have considered a suitable subject for the magical powers of the artist.

The Azilian and Tardenoisian Epochs. The Magdalenian, last and greatest of the Upper Paleolithic artistic periods, was followed by the Azilian and Tardenoisian epochs, which brought to a close the Paleolithic Age. We do not know why the change took place, but we do know that these new epochs marked an abrupt break with the past. We know, too, that they were accompanied by racial changes in the European population. The Cro-Magnons and other European Paleolithic races largely disappeared, though some traces of them remain in western Europe and the near-by islands. After the Magdalenian epoch the races of Europe and the Mediterranean Basin begin to show the three main types that are dominant in that region today.

The Azilian-Tardenoisian period, which dates back some 8000 to 10,000 years from our time, was the last stage of the Old Stone Age. Unquestionably it was a period of cultural decline. This deterioration may have come about because the craftsmen gradually lost their skill, or because the older peoples of Europe were submerged by an invasion of peoples in an inferior stage of culture, or because of poorer materials. Whatever the reason, the signs of decline are unmistakable in the flints of this transitional age, which show a deterioration of workmanship from those of Magdalenian times, and in the bone implements, which are neither so varied nor so well shaped as before. At about this time the reindeer, whose antlers give a hard horn suitable for making implements, disappeared from Europe.

The Azilian-Tardenoisian period produced no such art as that of the earlier stages of the Upper Paleolithic. Painted pebbles were the sole work of decorative art from the Azilian culture. Smooth, flat pebbles were selected, and the paint, made of red ochre, was applied by the fingertip or a brush on just one side of the pebble. The designs were varied—bands, points, crosses, and many others. Some of the patterns bear a close resemblance to characters later used in one or another alphabet, but this does not necessarily mean that they were used in a system of writing and calculation. Interesting as are these decorated pebbles, they do not represent nearly so high a form of art as that of the epochs immediately preceding.

Despite these signs of faltering, one must not lose sight of enormous advances made in the whole of the Paleolithic Age. Starting as a species hardly differentiated from the great anthropoids, man had begun to learn about his environment and how to cope with it. He had proved that, unlike other animals, he was not simply the creature of his environment but also capable of mastering it. He had taken stone and bone and fashioned hunting weapons from them; he had learned to fish; he had begun to use animal hides for clothing. He knew, too, how to use fire—to keep warm, to keep beasts from entering his cave, to give him light, and to cook his food, at least to soften the marrow of bones. His creations in art, such as the paintings of the French and Spanish caves, are an amazing revelation of his sense of beauty and his mastery of technique. Family and tribal life as well as religion and magic were doubtless well established by the end of the Paleolithic Age. Man had risen above the utter bestiality in which he had started. His culture was still feeble and insecure, but he had made the beginning of a series of advances that would achieve, in our own time, an almost complete conquest of the physical environment.

The rate of human advance, moreover, was accelerating. It took hundreds of thousands of years for man to arrive at the stage of culture marked by the beautifully chipped flints of the Solutrean epoch and the admirable art of the Upper Paleolithic, but only tens of thousands of years from the improved implements of Aurignacian man to the polished stone and settled life of Neolithic man. The age of bronze and iron, which came next, was to last only a few thousand years, and the age of steel, our own age, began, as it were, only yesterday.

THE NEOLITHIC AGE

The Neolithic or New Stone Age, as the name indicates, was an age of a new kind of work in stone. But this is not all that marks the passage from the Old Stone Age to the New. The Neolithic Age brought a whole new cultural complex, extending beyond the achievements of the Paleolithic Age in many more respects than merely the method of preparing stone implements. Because of these advances, the Neolithic is much closer to our own age than to the Paleolithic— a man of the Neolithic Age would find himself more at home among us, if he could be transported into our times, than he would if he were somehow set down among men of the earlier Aurignacian epoch.

Certain other advances made by Neolithic men were of revolutionary importance. For it was Neolithic men who first began to domesticate animals and to plant and grow hitherto wild plants for food. The result of these two achievements was the so-called "Neolithic revolution," in the course of which food-gathering tended to become less important and food production more so. It was this revolutionary economic change that, in turn, tended to make men settle down and remain in one place rather than constantly wander in search of food.

Social Progress

One of the most significant advances of Neolithic man was his discovery that he was a social being, who got along much better in communities than singly or in only the small family group. This sharply differentiated his life from that of the nomadic, food-gathering family groups or small tribes that were characteristic of the Paleolithic Age. It permitted and encouraged cooperative ventures, which tended to make man a settled rather than nomadic creature and gave him much more control over his environment. This development of community life deserves to be considered one of the most important revolutionary movements in human history, for it was at once a social, economic, and political revolution, and it had a most important influence on the industrial, artistic, and religious life of man.

Neolithic Industries

The men of the Neolithic Age continued to use flint for a variety of instruments, which generally were better made than formerly and sometimes show beautiful workmanship.

Excellent saws, daggers, and spearheads were produced, as well as well-barbed arrowheads (the bow had already come into use before the close of the Paleolithic Age).

The crowning achievement of the Neolithic stoneworkers was the polished ax head, or *celt*. The stone for the head was first flaked, then ground and polished until the desired sharpness and a smooth, bright surface were attained. Afterward a haft was attached. Such tools, which were made in a variety of shapes and sizes, were much superior to the heavy, wedgelike axes of the preceding age. At the same time, however, Neolithic men discovered how to make pottery, and pottery-making began to be one of the important Neolithic industries among the peoples of the Middle East.

The development of communal life was closely related to the improvement of the flint industry in Neolithic times as well as the development of other, newer crafts. The growing population, gathered in settlements of increasing size, had need of more tools and weapons than ever before. Hence Neo-

lithic artisans had need of more flint in order to meet this demand. Moreover, a better grade of flint was required, and this meant freshly mined flint, instead of old, thoroughly dried stone. Consequently mining, which had begun in the Old Stone Age, now became an industry of impressive proportions. And villages and workshops multiplied about the pits and shafts that were dug into the best deposits.

Neolithic Dwellings

The dwellings of the Neolithic and immediately succeeding ages were built both on land and over water. The simplest type of land village was composed of round huts, made of poles and branches, covered on the outside with clay and built over shallow pits. Later in the period more elaborate and substantial houses were constructed. Commonly, a village would be established near a river or lake or near a flint deposit, and usually a site was chosen with a thought to defense

Neolithic Lake Dwellings—a model of Swiss lake houses, constructed in Switzerland. (Courtesy of the American Museum of Natural History)

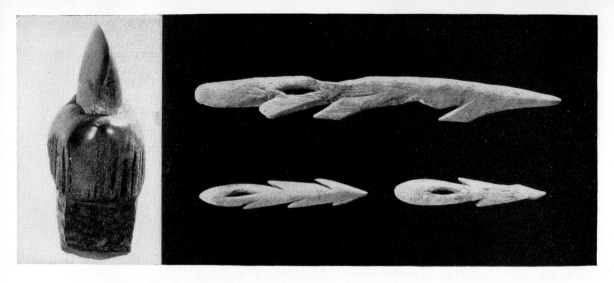

Neolithic Tools. A polished stone chisel set in a bone handle, found in Switzerland, and stone harpoons, found in France. (Collection *Musée de l'Homme*, Paris)

against attack. The existence of fortified walls shows that prehistoric man already resorted to violence, and that other men, as well as beasts, were among his enemies. Evidence of this is found in gruesome remains, such as human skeletons with death-dealing weapons still fixed in the solid bone, and human skulls well scarred by the blows of stone axes wielded by Neolithic warriors.

Remains of Neolithic lake dwellings were first discovered in Switzerland in 1853–1854, when an unusual drought lowered the water level. Since then lake villages of the same type have been found in many other places throughout Europe. Some of these belong to the Neolithic, others to the succeeding age. The building of a lake village was a difficult and complicated operation, requiring the placement of thousands of piles, then the construction of floors, and finally the building of the houses. Dwellings built on lakes had the advantage of being comparatively safe from attack. Besides, the villagers could fish from their own doorsteps, dispose of their refuse simply by dumping it in the lake, and make use of boats for communication and transportation. As a safeguard against attack, these dwellings were sometimes left unprovided with bridges to the shore, which the villagers reached only by boat.

Boatbuilding

Though Paleolithic man seems to have known something of the art of navigation, the oldest known boats are of Neolithic manufacture. It is clear that the art of boatbuilding was first extensively developed by men of the more recent period. The boats were made of tree trunks, which were shaped and hollowed out by the use of stone implements and fire. Some of them were surprisingly well made, considering the inadequate tools with which the prehistoric shipbuilders had to work. One boat dating from the Neolithic Age is forty-nine feet long and almost five feet wide.

Neolithic Commerce

Like navigation, trade also had its beginnings in the Old Stone Age but did not flourish until the New. We have indications that the trade in flint must have reached a considerable volume, for the mining operations, in places where there were deposits of the best flint, were on a larger scale than would have been required to meet the needs of only the settlements nearby. We have further evidence of this commerce in the discovery, over a wide area, of objects made of types of flint, obsidian, and jade that could have come only from certain, limited deposits. Other objects, too, can be identified as having been transported some distance for purposes of trade. These include shell, amber, gold, stone used for ornaments, salt, and pottery.

In this early period, quite as much as today, commerce played an important part in the building of civilization. Not only were material things carried from place to place and exchanged in trade, but—even more important—ideas were also exchanged. New ways of making tools, of shaping and ornamenting pottery, of cutting amber, of building boats—all these techniques were passed from one region to another. And as they passed, older and less efficient techniques were replaced by new and better ones.

Pottery Manufacture

Paleolithic man knew fire and made timid use of it—for protection from animals, for preparation of food, and for illumination of the dark caves—but it remained a dangerous though beautiful mystery to him. Neolithic man made much more constructive use of fire, both in the building of boats, as has been mentioned, and in the making of pottery. To us nowadays the art of the potter seems so simple that we find it hard to real-

ize that this is one of the greatest achievements of Neolithic man. Yet the humblest little vase made in our time, as well as the most beautiful examples of the potter's craft in all the period of historic time, are the outcome of a long, slow, painstaking development in the prehistoric ages. Once the idea had been conceived, there had to be a gradual improvement in the process of shaping the clay, then the discovery of the potter's wheel—first used, apparently, in Mesopotamia in the early part of the fourth millennium B.C.— and, finally, the discovery of baking, which gives durability to vessels made of clay. Not only were the containers that the potters made extremely useful—indeed, you can hardly imagine how men got along without them—but they offered great scope to the esthetic talents of their makers. Their shaping, coloring, and decorating afforded large new opportunities for artistic expression.

The making of pottery is one of the activities of Neolithic man that indicates he lived a sedentary life. Nomads hardly ever have the time to develop the ceramic art, nor can they conveniently carry pottery with them in their wanderings. Other achievements of Neolithic man also bear witness to a settled existence. These include the discovery and development of agriculture, the domestication of animals, and the making of textiles, all of which are perhaps the most significant accomplishments of the New Stone Age. Man had by now progressed so far that he

Prehistoric Trade Routes. As Neolithic groups began to produce surpluses, they traded over a wide area, and what at first were luxuries began to be necessities. With food surpluses, it became worth while to keep prisoners as slaves instead of killing them —because a slave can produce more than his keep.

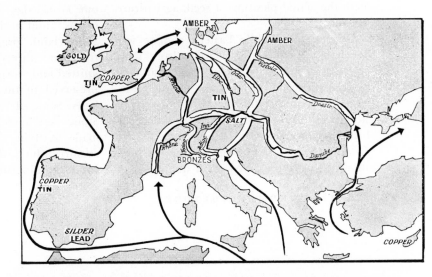

Neolithic Pottery, Denmark. *Musée de l'Homme.*

could provide his own supply of food, instead of always moving from place to place in search of it. He was changing from a hunter to a peasant—a landsman who settled in a fertile spot and made the land support him.

Agriculture

We cannot say precisely how and where men first stumbled upon the art of making plants grow. But it is obvious that this was one of the most valuable of the discoveries of our Neolithic predecessors. At first, Neolithic men and women—and probably the people of the Old Stone Age before them—must have gathered the edible roots, plants, and seeds that they found as they moved from one temporary home to another. Eventually they noticed that these valuable foods grew more abundantly in some places than in others. Then, when some person of imagination and understanding proceeded to experiment with the actual planting of seed, agriculture began.

Because the Middle Eastern climate was much more suitable to plant culture than was that of Europe, it seems likely that agriculture started there, perhaps in the Mesopotamian region, later spreading outward in all directions. Our knowledge of the early history of agriculture in Europe comes mostly from the Swiss lake villages, among the piles of which were preserved great quantities of

Neolithic grains and plants. Wheat and barley were the grains most commonly cultivated. Peas, lentils, poppies, flax, apples, carrots, grapes, and many other fruits, nuts, and vegetables were also grown or gathered from wild supplies. A digging stick was used in the cultivation of crops. Gradually this was improved to become the hoe. Still later, perhaps not until the Bronze Age, the plow was developed.

The Domestication of Animals

Equally important was the domestication of animals. In the dog, whom he first domesticated, man found a valuable helper in the hunt and a faithful guard and friend at home. The ox, hog, sheep, and goat, which were domesticated soon afterward, assured a constant supply of meat and milk and also gave service as beasts of burden and a source of fibers for making textiles. The horse, which Paleolithic man had used for food, may have been domesticated by Neolithic man, and certainly in the Bronze Age the horse was used for riding. The domestication of these animals must have occurred after the discovery of agriculture, since at least some of the animals would have to be fed during the winter on the products of the cultivated fields.

The Manufacture of Textiles

Another important advance, coming close upon the domestication of plants and animals, was the making of textiles. Here again our knowledge comes principally from remains found in the Neolithic lake villages of Switzerland. Fragments of spinning apparatus, looms, threads, ropes, raw flax, nets, and knitted and woven fabrics have been found, preserved in the peat under the Swiss villages. Some of the cloth produced by these Stone Age men is almost incredibly well made, testifying still further to their skill and resourcefulness and the rapidly increasing comfort and security of their life.

Neolithic Art

In Neolithic artistic expression, there is a marked deterioration from the strikingly naturalistic cave paintings and engravings of the Paleolithic Age. Men of the new age no longer haunted the great natural caves, as their predecessors had done, and no longer were their interests so seriously concentrated upon their animal contemporaries, especially those they hunted for food. The more recent artists no longer tried to reproduce a perfect bison or horse but were content with a rough sketch only suggesting the form. This does not mean that Neolithic artists lacked the genius of their forerunners. Rather, it may be a sign that Neolithic men were developing their powers of generalization, which were later to lead them to the invention of a system of writing. Moreover, one must not judge their artistic talent solely on the basis of pictures and sculptures, for Neolithic men had many other opportunities for artistic expression, such as the decoration of their pottery.

Neolithic Music

Music seems to have been a form of artistic expression enjoyed by Neolithic men, for bone flutes that date back possibly 25,000 years have been dug up in western Europe. The beginnings of musical expression, however, must have been still farther back, for men must have sung—if only monotonous chants reiterating a single tone—long before they invented the first instruments.

We have little notion of the earliest music, for the oldest music of which we have knowledge, such as the simple dirges of primitive peoples and the oldest examples of plainsong, are already so complex that the tonal and rhythmic systems they exemplify must have taken ages to develop. "Primitive" music is almost always linear—that is, its appeal does not depend upon harmony but involves subtle distinctions between intervals of less than half a tone in the melodic line.

The Art of Healing

We know little of how Neolithic man treated illnesses and injuries, because the simpler kinds of medical treatment would leave no traces. But we do know that Neolithic man had some skill in the healing art, for in remains of this period have been found skulls showing the marks of a surgical operation known as trepanation. This operation may have been performed as part of a religious rite rather than as medical treatment, but, in any event, it bears witness to considerable skill on the part of the primitive surgeon. We presume that men who could perform such an operation must have been experienced in treating wounds and other injuries.

Neolithic Religion

It is difficult for us to interpret the meaning of prehistoric remains relating to religious beliefs and practices, because the religious consciousness of early man was itself evidently quite vague, and the meaning of his own religious symbols probably remained mysterious, even to himself. Undoubtedly early man was impressed by the great forces of nature—wind, rain, thunder, and lightning; fire, whose colorful flames both devour and give off warmth; the wild beasts who were both enemies and providers of food; and the mysteries of sex. He certainly did not understand these forces, but he learned to fear or respect them, and he tried to influence them in his favor. Consequently he drew pictures of animals on cave walls and drew or carved them on his dart throwers, knives, and shaft straighteners. He carved female statues emphasizing sexual characteristics, and he drew pictures apparently portraying fertility rites. Fear and ignorance doubtless led him to other and often cruel practices, for we know that some Neolithic peoples, such as the Aztecs and the Mayas, offered human sacrifices.

From the study of contemporary savages, we may infer that much of the life of early

The Alignments of Carnac, Brittany. Over a period of several millennia menhirs, crom-
lechs, and alignments were erected from Britain to China to serve as astronomical observatories—see also page 5. (French Government Tourist Office)

man was governed by taboos, and that he
composed rituals designed to placate the
powers of nature. Such surmises are confirmed, to some extent, by what we know of
the art and crafts of prehistoric man. We
may suppose, therefore, that in his mind religion—the reverential attitude toward the
mysterious forces of nature—was not differentiated from magic—the sly attempt to
bring those mysterious powers into man's
service by placation or by powerful charms.
Religious worship and magic rite were both,
apparently, believed necessary, if man was to
deal successfully with the good and evil
spirits that animated all nature. The earliest
clearly recognizable religious worship is that
of the "Mother-Goddess cult" of the early village communities of the Middle East.

We have stronger basis for our conjecture
as to early man's religious beliefs when we
draw upon evidence of his burial practices.
Remains from a time as early as that of
Mousterian man show that our predecessors
believed in some kind of life beyond the
grave. Reverence for the dead evidently became much stronger than before among the
men of the New Stone Age. Their burial

customs varied considerably. Some bodies
were burned; others were buried either in
simple graves or in natural or artificial caves
or beneath great boulders or in carefully
contrived burial chambers. Occasionally a
tumulus grave was used: an earth mound,
round or long in shape, sometimes covering
smaller stone chambers.

The most interesting and revealing of Neolithic burial practices were those connected
with the megaliths, or great stones, which
have been found in especially large numbers
in France. They are generally given the
names that were first used for the monuments found in Brittany. A *menhir* is a single, large stone, set on end. A *cromlech* is a
circular or rectangular enclosure, made of
several of these great stones. An *alignment*
is a formation of stones set in rows. A chamber made of several stones, topped with a
large, flat tablestone, is called a *dolmen*. Because the dolmen was the type of monument
best suited for making a burial chamber, it
was widely used. Megalithic monuments of
this kind have been found in parts of Asia
and Africa, as well as Europe and pre-Co-
lumbian America. Sometimes one or more

dolmens were covered with earth, to make a long or round tumulus. The larger dolmens were sometimes composed of several chambers, with passages that gave entrance and connected one chamber with another. Toward the end of the New Stone Age, such megalithic burial chambers were used less often, being supplanted by *cists* made of small stones, which were designed for one or more corpses, or by inconspicuous individual graves.

Not all megalithic monuments were built to provide burial chambers, but what the purpose of the others was we are not sure. Sometimes they are closely associated with dolmens, and this seems to imply that they had some religious significance conncected with burial. In other locations they have no apparent relationship to burial practices but seem rather to have been built for ritualistic purposes, like those of a temple. Notable monuments of this sort are to be seen at Avebury and Stonehenge in England and at Carnac in Brittany.

These great stones bear witness not only to Neolithic man's respect for the dead and fear of supernatural powers but also to his prowess as a builder. Some of the great menhirs weigh many tons and had to be transported over a long distance before they could be erected in the desired form. How men of the Stone Age contrived to move such immense stones remains one of the many mysteries of human prehistory. We are tempted to presume that the architects and engineers who put up the megaliths must have discovered the usefulness of rolling pins in moving heavy objects. Perhaps they were led still further: to the discovery of the wheel, one of the most powerful and useful technical aids that men have ever invented.

TRANSITION: THE AGE OF METALS AND THE BEGINNING OF RECORDED HISTORY

Transitions from one great historical period to the next are always gradual, and such was the transition from the Stone Age to the Age of Metals. Copper was in use in the Middle East as early as the fifth millennium before Christ, and perhaps in Egypt, too. Bronze appeared in the East in the fourth millennium, a little later in the Aegean, but not in the western Mediterranean until the third millennium B.C.

The Use of Metals

Probably copper was discovered by accident, when some campfire was built upon stones containing copper ore. Presumably, some keen-eyed Neolithic observer noticed the metal that was thus smelted by the heat of the fire and later reproduced the process by design. For a time—the interval is sometimes called the Chalcolithic or Copper Stone Age —copper was used in the pure form in which it was thus obtained. But pure copper is too soft to make useful tools and weapons. The next step was the discovery that the addition to copper of only a small proportion of tin makes bronze, an alloy that is much harder and much more useful than pure copper. Probably men first made bronze by accident, also, when the ore they smelted happened to contain both copper and tin. Thereafter, presumably, they must have experimented until they could make the alloy at will. The discovery of bronze made it possible for men to fashion a host of new and better utensils—vases, saws, swords, shields, axes, trumpets, bells, and others. At about the same time men also learned how to smelt gold, silver, and lead.

One brilliant discovery leads to another, sometimes soon after. Thus, only about

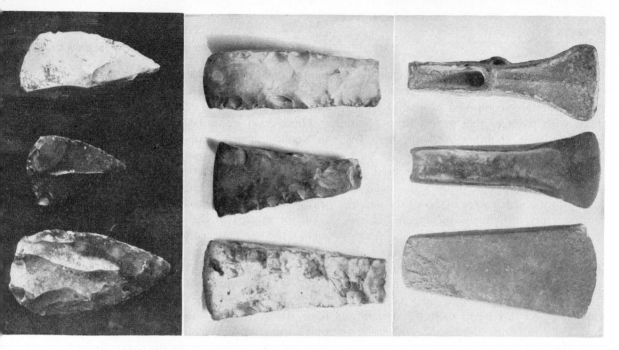

A Comparison of Tools. Paleolithic tools from Le Moustier, France; Neolithic shaped hatchets from Denmark; and Bronze Age axes—from the end of the third interglacial period, about 50,000 years ago, to about 4000 B.C. (Collection *Musée de l'Homme*, Paris)

2000 years after the discovery of copper and bronze, iron also came into use. This new metal was known as early as the second millennium before Christ, but for a long time iron was rare and expensive and its use was not widely established in Europe until about 500 B.C. As men proceeded to experiment with the use of iron, discovering the process of tempering, they gradually came to realize its immense superiority.

But with mention of the discovery of iron, we pass beyond the limits of prehistoric times and invade the era of written history.

We may therefore close the chapter at this point, having traced the progress of prehistoric man from a state devoid of culture to the cultural riches of the Bronze and Iron Ages. As this new era dawned, culture was in several places ripening into civilization. With the appearance of the settled, complex, and brilliant cultures that arose in Egypt, Mesopotamia, India, China, Mexico, and Peru, after hundreds of thousands of years of slow and tedious prehistorical preparation, comes the beginning of the history of civilization.

Suggestions for Further Reading

On the Antiquity of the Earth and Its Inhabitants

Sir A. Keith, *The Antiquity of Man* (2 vols., Philadelphia, 1925).

A standard survey of the various anthropological types and their antiquity. (The chapters on Piltdown Man should be disregarded, in the light of more recent scientific investigations.)

H. H. Newman, ed., *The Nature of the World and of Man* (Chicago, 1927).

This is an excellent collection of essays by astronomers, physicists, chemists, and biologists on the scientific nature of the universe, matter, life and mass.

On the Culture of Prehistoric Men

F. Boas, *The Mind of Primitive Man* (New York, 1938).

Studies stress basic question of hereditary differences and likenesses of races and environmental influences. Readable interpretation of cultural developments, showing close intellectual ties of primitive and modern man, fallacy of racial mental characteristics.

C. W. Ceram (pseudonym for K. W. Marek), *Gods, Graves, and Scholars* (New York, 1951).

A very interesting description of the work and some of the achievements of the archaeologists in revealing the earliest origins of civilization.

V. G. Childe, *The Bronze Age* (Cambridge, England, 1930).

This is a well-organized account of man's development culturally during the early age of metals. An account of the great progress of modern scholarship on primitive man.

V. G. Childe, *The Dawn of European Civilization* (New York, 1925).

One of the first good general characterizations and summaries of the period. Tells of prehistoric archaeology, concentrating on the Neolithic and Copper ages. Sketch of contributions of these periods.

V. G. Childe, *New Light on the Most Ancient East* (New York, 1934).

Prehistoric archaeology of the Nile, Tigris-Euphrates, and Indus river valleys. The relative age, independence, and interrelation of these cultures. Sound scholarship.

H. Frankfort, *The Birth of Civilization in the Near East* (Bloomigton, 1951).

A consideration of the question of the growth of civilization in Egypt and Mesopotamia. Treats growth not as gradual, and birth not as slow, but as the results of sudden and intense change and creativity. City life considered the key to the growth and decline in both civilizations.

A. A. Goldenweiser, *Early Civilization* (New York, 1922).

Standard text in anthropology, treating of all primitive peoples, especially American Indians, and the growth of their cultures from early origins. A relatively old work.

E. A. Hooton, *Up from the Ape* (New York, 1946).

This book is concerned with the evolution of physical types of man. It is a study of individual ancient specimens; attempts to relate physical development to mode of life, disease, etc.

W. W. Howells, *Mankind So Far* (New York, 1944).

Physical anthropology. Concerned with the development of man by evolution from early man to Homo sapiens, then development of Homo sapiens in terms of physical changes.

A. L. Kroeber, *Anthropology* (New York, 1948).

A regular, well-organized, sound, survey textbook. Concentrates on race and origins of culture, beginnings of civilization.

R. Linton, *The Study of Man* (New York, 1936).

A layman's presentation of the developments within anthropology. Tries to work out patterns, within the new science of anthropology, for human origins, race, family, tribe, state, cultural developments.

R. H. Lowie, *An Introduction to Cultural Anthropology* (New York, 1940).

Presents questions: What is culture? Why and how does it develop? Why is it different in various societies? In answering questions, the author describes various illustrative societies, chiefly primitive ones.

G. G. MacCurdy, *Human Origins* (New York, 1924).

Convenient, well-proportioned study of European archaeology, stressing the cultural evolution, but with regard to the organic and geological factors. Early man through the Iron Age. Sound and free from bias.

J. L. Myres, *The Dawn of History* (New York, 1911).

A simple, brief book, tracing the gradual change of primitive peoples into civilization and individuality. Study for Egypt, Babylonia, and the Mediterranean peoples.

H. F. Osborn, *Men of the Old Stone Age* (3rd ed., New York 1924).

A relatively old work, but presenting a thorough review of the evidence and conclusions to that point. Deals with Paleolithic archaeology and excavations. Written for laymen.

H. Peake and H. J. Fleure, *The Corridors of Time* (10 vols., New Haven, 1927–1936).

All ten volumes in this series are brief and readable. They trace early developments from primitive men to law, religion, trade, travel, and war. Easily used, well written.

PART I

The Ancient Civilizations
of the Mediterranean Area

The earliest true civilizations had their beginnings in the valleys of the Nile River in Egypt, of the Euphrates and Tigris rivers in Mesopotamia, of the Indus River in India, and of the Wei and Hwang Ho rivers in China. A little time later, and quite independently, two comparable civilizations arose in the American hemisphere, in the mountain valleys and plains of Mexico and Guatemala and in the mountain valleys of Peru. (These civilizations will be discussed in Chapter 27 of this book.) Then, while the Egyptian and Mesopotamian civilizations were at their height, another civilization arose around the shores of the Aegean Sea. This took its start on the islands of Crete and Cyprus and spread to the Greek peninsula of the mainland, where centers developed at Mycenae and Tiryns. Trade and other relations soon developed between this civilization and those of Egypt and Mesopotamia. In the second millennium B.C., the Hellenes, who were barbarians from the north, overran the Aegean civilization and eventually remade it into the more sophisticated civilization we know as Greek.

At about the same time, too, while the Hellenes were invading Greece, certain cousins of theirs, known as the Latin tribes, were moving into the Italian Peninsula, and a Semitic people—the Phoenicians—were establishing a far-flung empire, with its center at Carthage, around the southern and western shores of the Mediterranean. This Carthaginian Empire and the Roman Empire, which the Latins created, were destined to wage a mortal struggle for domination of the Mediterranean world—a struggle that would eventuate in the death of Carthage and the triumph of Rome.

But Rome, too, would eventually die. And a new Rome—Constantinople, rebuilt upon the Bosporus at Byzantium—would carry on the Greco-Roman tradition in the new "Byzantine" civilization. Meanwhile, out of the Semitic lands at the eastern end of the Mediterranean would come Christianity, to add a new religious ingredient to the Mediterranean civilization. And after that, again out of the Semitic east, would arise yet another religious empire, that of the Moslems, stretching around the southern border of the Inland Sea, westward as far as Spain and eastward into India, China, and the remotest Orient.

Though each of these civilizations would flourish only to decline into minor significance, much of the achievement of these peoples around the Mediterranean—Egyptians, Mesopotamians, Greeks, Phoenicians, Romans, Jews, and Arabs—was to endure. Without the art, literature, philosophy, law, and science that all of them contributed, the later great civilizations of the western world could not have developed so rapidly and richly as they did.

The story of these civilizations is the first great chapter in the history of civilization.

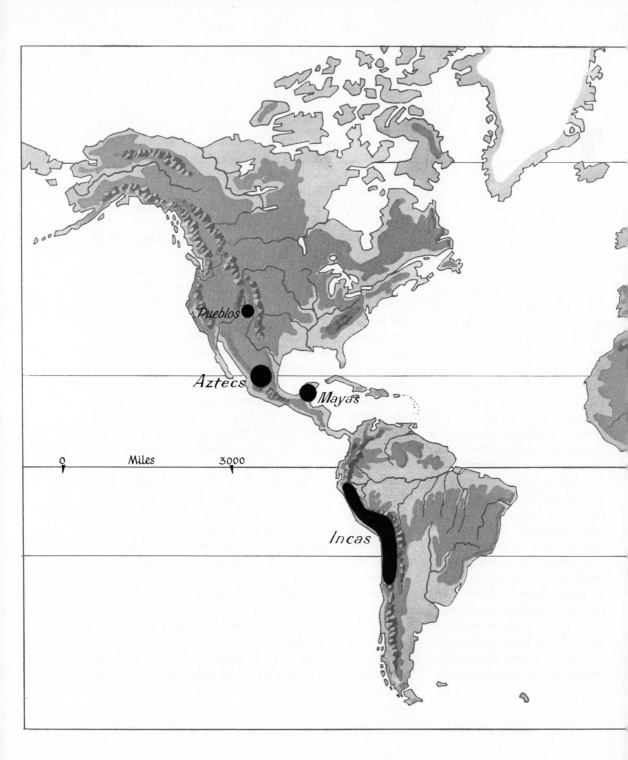

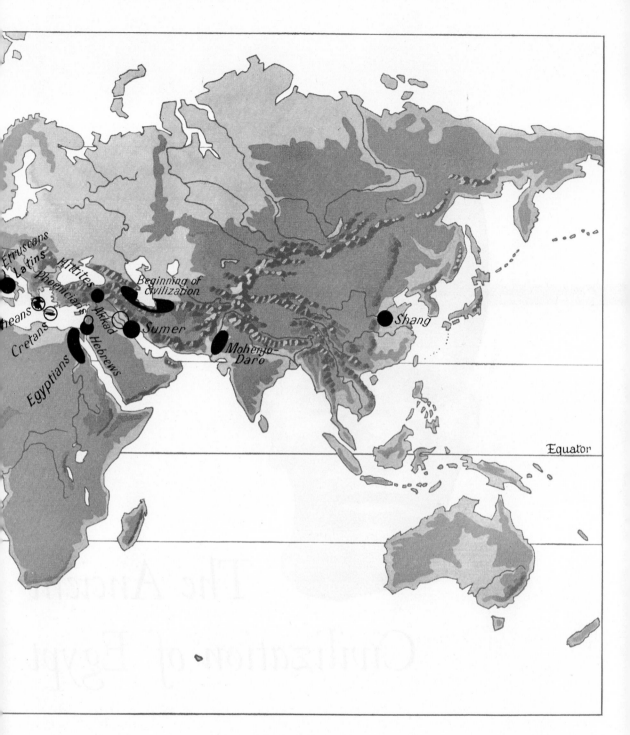

Early Foci of Civilization

2

The Ancient
Civilization of Egypt

Amenemhet III (?), 1842–1797 B.C. Sculptured head, 19″ high, black-green slate. See page 55. (NY-Carlsberg Glyptothek, Copenhagen)

Egypt has always seemed a land of mystery. In ancient times the Greek traveler and historian Herodotus found it a realm of incredible wonders, where people seemed to do everything in strange and unfamiliar ways. The old Greek's superstitious awe is not surprising, for, although twenty-four centuries have elapsed since Herodotus visited Egypt, belief has never entirely died out that the Egyptians built their pyramids according to a special and prophetic kind of mathematics and that they put a curse on anyone who disturbed the tombs of their dead. But today, Egypt works its spell on us for more tangible reasons—the great Sphinx, the pyramids themselves, the colossal statues that the Egyptians carved in the living rock, their temples and obelisks, the colorful paintings in which animal-headed gods appear, and the mummies that have been preserved for tens of centuries.

Much of the mystery that clings to the name of Egypt is due simply to ignorance. The sometimes oversubtle Greeks felt sure that the Egyptians, like their Sphinx, knew something they were not telling. Other peoples have had much the same feeling—perhaps because so much of the record of the Egyptian past remained unintelligible until recently.

Much of the mystery of Egypt fades away, like fog on a summer morning, as modern research penetrates the darkness. Yet not all our awe of Egypt disappears, for we have good reason to marvel at the Egyptian contribution to man's conquest of his environment. We need not attribute magical powers to the Egyptians in order to admire the people who invented or helped to invent our calendar, worked marvels of engineering, and created an architecture of monumental grandeur. Far from being magical, their achievements were pre-eminently material and practical. And the more we know of them, the better we appreciate the greatness of the Egyptians.

THE UNIQUENESS OF EGYPT

Egyptian civilization is distinguished from others of ancient times by several characteristics. Although the Sumerian civilization of Mesopotamia perhaps has as good a claim to being the oldest of civilizations, the Egyptian was unquestionably the longest lived:

over 3400 years elapsed between the beginning of the First Dynasty in 3110 B.C. and the triumph of Christianity, near the end of the Roman period (30 B.C.–A.D. 324). when the old Egyptian civilization may be said to have died.

A second remarkable characteristic is the cultural integrity of Egypt. Although there were periods of brilliance and periods of decline—and some of these extended over a longer stretch of time than the whole four and a half centuries of American history—Egyptian civilization was basically the same throughout its long span. And even some of the racial stock has remained the same. In the course of time the Egyptians absorbed many invaders, but there are today individuals who have the same physical appearance as their ancestors who figure in the art of ancient Egypt—short and slight of build, dark of hair and complexion. Not always was this trait of stubborn persistence an advantage, because Egyptian civilization withstood many changes that might have been for the better.

A third characteristic is the importance of religion. All ancient peoples, to be sure, were to some degree under the influence of religion, but in the Land of the Nile this influence was at first very strong. Although a certain amount of secularization soon developed in the historic period, much Egyptian activity—in government, economics, art, and every other field—continued to have religious meaning.

The River and the Sun

Ancient Egypt is appropriately called the Land of the Nile, for civilization developed only where the river made it possible. And this was not along the entire course of the Nile, which is 4000 miles long, but only along the last 500 miles below the First Cataract, which is near Aswan. Upper Egypt is the name given to the narrow valley of the Nile, only ten or twelve miles across, between Aswan and Memphis. At Memphis the river divides, forming a delta, called Lower Egypt. This delta region was much more humid than Upper Egypt, and in ancient times much of the land was marsh. The coast, where the delta touches the Mediterranean, takes in only about 150 miles. Ancient Egypt thus was a small country.

Although to some degree isolated (see map, pp. 40–41), Egypt was not too remote to maintain trade and cultural intercourse with other lands. To the south lay Nubia, the land of the cataracts of the Nile, with which Egypt kept contact throughout most of its history. To the west lay the Libyan Desert, out of which invaders sometimes came to raid the delta region. To the east lay the Arabian Desert, across which caravans proceeded on their way to the shore of the Red Sea. The Mediterranean coast on the north also afforded opportunity for contact with foreign peoples, both friendly and hostile. The most traveled route, of course, was the narrow passage from Africa to Asia across the Isthmus of Suez and Arabia Petraea. By this route came and went most of the trade between the Valley of the Nile and the Fertile Crescent (see next chapter), and across this land bridge marched the armies of Egypt, Assyria, and Persia.

Though its natural frontiers were not formidable, Egypt was not often invaded. The reason for this is that Egypt lies at a considerable distance from the steppes of Central Asia, from where, in ancient times, came the great waves of semibarbaric peoples. Most of these inundations broke their force upon the Fertile Crescent and Asia Minor. Some of them, however, did sweep as far as Egypt.

The land was well favored in several respects. Stone and valuable metals were available in the neighboring cliffs and deserts—in Nubia and the Sinai Peninsula. This made it possible for the Egyptians to develop metalwork and construct the great stone buildings that are the most impressive and almost indestructible records of their long past.

Then there was the climate. Although less dry than at present, when the climate is exceedingly dry, in prehistoric times the region above the humid delta was always hospitable and healthful to man as well as to animals and birds. Even in the winter, when for four months the weather is comparatively cool, there is little rain in Upper Egypt. And over the centuries the increasing dryness of the air has preserved many of the written records of the Egyptian civilization —a boon to historians.

But the fortunes of Egypt depended principally on the river and the sun, for Egypt's comparative isolation, mineral wealth, and dry climate would have meant little had not the Nile provided its rich silt and fructifying floods and the sun its life-giving light and warmth. Yet the river had to be carefully watched. The annual inundation that fertilized the valley began early in July and continued late in October; the waters had to be controlled, so far as possible, so they would not ruin the land; reservoirs and irrigation canals had to be built, because too large or too little an inundation meant disaster. It was this necessity to control the Nile that led the early Egyptians to combine with one another and coordinate their efforts—a union that was almost forced upon them.

Once the inundation was over and the difficult feat of supplying the stored-up water to the fields was accomplished, the Egyptians had one of the most fertile agricultural lands on earth. Enormous crops of wheat, barley, millet, grapes, flax, and vegetables were grown, while the pastures were filled with cattle, sheep, and goats. So richly productive was the valley that the Egyptians had little need for foreign trade or colonization.

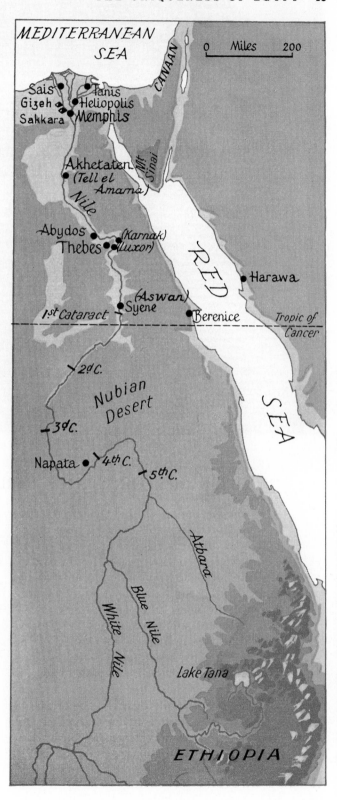

Ancient Egypt

The Rosetta Stone. Found in 1799 near Rosetta, Egypt, by troops of Napoleon's army, this basalt slab was inscribed by the priests of Ptolemy V (p. 150) in hieroglyphs, demotic script, and Greek (top to bottom). It was the key by which the great French Egyptologist, Jean François Champollion was able to decipher the Egyptian hieroglyphic writing. (Courtesy of the British Museum)

THE PREHISTORIC AND EARLY DYNASTIC PERIODS

At the beginning of the Quaternary Era, while Europe was still suffering from the effects of the great glaciers, the region in Africa west of the Nile was a fertile plateau where men and animals found an easy living. With declining rainfall and the progressive desiccation of the plateau—now the Sahara Desert—animals and men were forced to retreat eastward into the Valley of the Nile for water and forage. Here, in a hospitable new homeland, men still in the Paleolithic stage made the transition to Neolithic culture, while their contemporaries in Europe continued a roving existence. Out of their settlements emerged Egypt's earliest magnificent civilization.

Sometime in the dim ages of the Prehistoric Period—today the Prehistoric Period is roughly dated as about 4500 to about 3110 B.C.—the old clan organization was supplanted by a territorial political organization. The country was divided into districts, later called *nomes*, which comprised a number of villages and, eventually, cities. When Menes, a king in Upper Egypt, conquered the delta region and united Egypt, the prehistoric period came to a close.

Possibly there was a union of Egypt before this time, but it cannot be proven and remains speculative. With Menes begins Egyptian dynastic history—that is, history divided into periods according to the dynasties of the kings who reigned—and Menes is generally considered to be the founder of the First Dynasty. To distinguish it from the Old Kingdom, the period of the first two dynasties is now called the Protodynastic Period.

At about the time of the Protodynastic Period came the development of writing. Although there are traces of writing earlier, nothing is readable. Egyptian writing made use of conventionalized pictures—*hieroglyphs*. This was probably a Mesopotamian invention that the Egyptians took over and developed to suit their own ideas. From the start, an integral part of the system was an alphabet, which consisted of uniconsonantal (alphabetic) signs, and biconsonantal and triconsonantal signs, all used as both ideograms (idea signs) or phonograms (sound signs). It was a cumbersome method of writing, making use of more than 600 signs, but as time passed the writing of the signs was simplified, although the spelling of individual words remained the same. *Hieratic* and later *demotic* scripts developed as cursive renderings of the signs, and in demotic script the pictorial origin of the signs is almost completely lost. When not supplanted by Greek, this was the business and literary script of the Egyptians from about 600 B.C. to A.D. 300.

For years it was believed that the Egyptians had developed a calendar during the Prehistoric Period, and that July 19, 4241 B.C. was the first known date in history. Now we know this is not so, for the invention came somewhat later. The first Egyptian calendar of which we have any real information was a *lunar* calendar. Because twelve lunar months average 354 days, every two or three years it was necessary for the Egyptians to add a thirteenth month. This lunar year was regulated by having the heliacal rising of Sirius fall in the twelfth month. The calendar of 365 days—twelve months of thirty days and five epagomenal days, which were supplementary feast days—was developed about the twenty-ninth century B.C. as an *artificial lunar* calendar for business and administrative purposes. But the lunar calendar was not abandoned and continued to provide the dates for important festivals—just like our Easter, which is lunar controlled. The use of the 365-day calendar through the years led to the knowledge that the addition of one day every four years would keep it in place in the seasons, but the Egyptians themselves never took this step. It was Julius Caesar who applied this knowledge to reform the Roman calendar that eventually led to ours through the Gregorian reform.

THE OLD KINGDOM

Writing and the calendar were not the only developments of the Protodynastic Period. Over the years there was a slow but steady progress that led to one of the greatest epochs in Egyptian history—the Old Kingdom, coinciding with the Third to Sixth dynasties (2664–2181 B.C.).

During the time of the Old Kingdom the capital was at Memphis. Never before or after did Egyptian kings have such absolute power as the pharaohs who ruled in Memphis. Their monuments, impressive records of their grandeur, were never equaled.

The earlier dynastic rulers of Egypt had begun to establish contact with other lands, but the more powerful pharaohs of the Old Kingdom did much more to widen the sphere of foreign relations. They continued to take copper from the mines of Sinai, which Menes had seized. They also waged war against Nubia and sent expeditions into the Sudan and other regions of Central Africa. Trade or diplomatic relations were established with the islands of the Aegean and with near-by Asia. With the tribes of Libya to the west the pharaohs waged inter-

Egyptian Dynasties, 4500–2052 B.C.

Prehistoric Period   4500–3110 B.C.*

Protodynastic Period, First
    and Second dynasties   3100–2665

THE OLD KINGDOM

Third Dynasty   2664–2615
    Sozer   2664–2646

Fourth Dynasty   2614–2502
    Sneferu   2614–2591
    Khufu (Cheops)   2590–
      2568
    Khafre (Chephren)   2556–
      2562
    Menkaure (Mycerinus)
      2525–2508

Fifth Dynasty   2501–2342

Sixth Dynasty   2341–2181
    Neferkare Pepi II   2272–
      2182

FIRST INTERMEDIATE PERIOD

Seventh-Tenth dynasties   2180–2052

* The only reigns whose dates are exact to the year are the Twelfth Dynasty, the Twenty-sixth and Twenty-seventh dynasties, and the Greek and Roman periods. The other dates, in this and the following Egyptian chronologies, are not fixed, but the range of uncertainty is fairly small.

mittent warfare until the time of the Fifth Dynasty when the Libyans were completely defeated. Thereafter the Libyans provided mercenaries for the pharaoh's army. By water from distant Punt, on the southern coast of the Red Sea, came incense, aromatic wood, and other luxuries. But the most important foreign relations of the Old Kingdom were with Southwest Asia, where the Egyptians met with a civilization, originating in Mesopotamia (p. 67), that was as advanced as their own. Articles of Mesopotamian and of East Indian origin have been found in Egypt, and it is certain that ideas and customs came to Egypt from Asia along with the products of commerce.

Foreign affairs and all other activities of the state were under the control of the pharaoh. The Old Kingdom was a theocracy, and its king was deemed a god, so far above the people that they referred to him only indirectly, by the name of *Pharaoh*, which meant Great House. He was the owner of all the land in the kingdom, and he was a political and religious despot.

Strong kings, such as Khufu and Khafre of the Fourth Dynasty, personally discharged their most important duties, but weaker kings delegated their powers to lesser officials—even the ablest rulers had to make much use of subordinates. The official next in power to the king was the vizier, who directed the administrative organization and acted as chief justice. Other members of the complicated bureaucracy were the powerful priests of the god-king and other gods, the judges, the directors of the treasury, palace and the king's storehouses, the military commanders, and the *nomarchs,* who governed the nomes as agents of the king.

The royal family filled many of these offices—as, later, was the custom in Assyria and Persia. Sometimes the son or grandson of the pharaoh served as vizier, or chief minister. The other members of the bureaucracy were drawn mostly from the upper class, but men of the people sometimes gained high office, indicating at least a little elasticity in the social class structure.

Egyptian Society

At the top of the social register in the Old Kingdom were the relatives and favorites of the king, numbering a few hundred persons. Until the close of the Fourth Dynasty the nobles lived in the capital or near by. Gradually, through the Fifth and Sixth dynasties —especially the latter—when the central power was less strong, the office of nomarch became hereditary instead of appointive, and the nomarchs tended to live in their nomes instead of at Memphis and to exercise a rule all but independent of the king. At this time there was no separate priesthood, because priests were also officials and officials were also priests, one man holding many offices, both religious and administrative.

We know little about the middle class of professional men and artisans. Some of these —scribes, artists, and other educated men— were members of the priesthood. Others were craftsmen, such as the artisans who worked with the precious woods, metals, and gums brought from the south. There were few merchants, because trade did not attain to so much importance as in modern times.

The vast majority of the population belonged to the lowest class, comprising agricultural workers and herdsmen. Some of these were free men and reasonably well off. But most of them, though not slaves, were probably bound to the soil as serfs. They were miserably housed and poorly fed, despised and exploited by the middle and upper classes, and doomed to eke out a drab life under stern discipline.

Women, however, held an unusually high place in Egyptian society. This may have been because in the earliest times social organization was matriarchal. Consanguine marriage—that is, marriage between close relatives—was not at all unusual, and even the marriage of brother and sister was not uncommon. Often descent was reckoned through the female line.

The Economy

We have already mentioned that agriculture was the main source of wealth in the Old Kingdom, and that commerce, which was managed by the state rather than by independent merchants, was not large. Industry was also of minor proportions, concerned mostly with the production of luxury goods for the privileged classes. But one aspect of economic life in the Old Kingdom must be noted: the close supervision of economic affairs by the state. Egypt was a land where cooperation was essential to the production of the necessities of life. Hence it is not surprising that the state undertook to supervise this economic cooperation. The state saw to it, at first, that the peasants kept up the dikes, canals, and reservoirs upon which the welfare of the land depended. Then, as they became conscious of their strength, the pharaohs widened the area of their control, requiring their subjects to perform other services, such as work in quarries and brickyards and on the construction of pyramids and temples. Ultimately the state came to control nearly the whole economy.

Early Religion

By the time of the Old Kingdom, Egypt already had a long and complicated religious history. Religion was made up of many elements—the totemism of the early clans, the ancient myths connected with early conquests, local sects devoted to the divinities of specific cities and nomes, the developing religious ideas of the priests, and influences from foreign lands, especially Asia. Confusion inevitably ensued as to the traditions of the gods and the relationships among them, and the priests could not always have been clear on all points.

Belief in the forces of nature remained a dominant element in ancient Egyptian religion. From most ancient times dated a belief in the sky-god Horus, associated with the falcon that is often represented in statues of the early pharaohs. This ancient Horus fought against a god of darkness and desolation, named Set, who was a god of great and evil power. Though he was unpopular and worship of him was at times proscribed, the belief in his existence never died out.

Another myth presents the god Osiris, who came to be associated with vegetation and the fertilizing power of the Nile. According to myth, Osiris had once ruled on earth. In a battle with his brother Set, Osiris was slain.

Other gods were associated with special functions and abstract qualities. Thus Thoth, who was identified with the ibis, was the god of letters, law, and wisdom. The dog-headed Anubis came to be one of the allies of Osiris in the lower world of the dead. Ptah was the patron of the arts and artists. A throng of other divinities, both local and universal, also formed part of the vast, confused Egyptian pantheon.

One of the most significant of Egyptian religious beliefs concerned death and a future life. No other people has ever placed so much importance on the physical preparation for the future life. At first, however, these preparations were made in behalf of only the king and a few others of the privileged classes. Yet the king was supposed to be the protector of his people not only here but also in the future world, and the land of the dead was presumed to be well populated. Consequently, by the time of the Middle Kingdom the Egyptians seem to have revised their notion of a future life, so that the common people were also presumed to pass into the world of the dead.

The belief in an afterlife is responsible for some of the most impressive and informative records of life in the Old Kingdom. Since the king's death was not final, his body had to be mummified, so as to preserve it, and a suitable palace provided for it. This led to the building of the pyramids, which have always remained one of the wonders of the world. Not only was the mummified body of the king kept in the tomb but also food and other necessities and a statue that would show how the king looked in his prime.

Gradually this belief led to a more spiritual conception of religion. By the time of the last two dynasties of the Old Kingdom, it was no longer presumed that the pharaoh would have a future life merely because this was his due as a god. Rather, he would have to subject himself to a judgment of his deeds before going on to his eternal abode. Thus religion began to be a means of enforcing a moral code.

Khafre. Part of a seated statue that was found in the temple in front of the Second Pyramid of Gizeh, built by Khafre. Behind the head is the god Horus (p. 49), protecting the king with his wings. (National Egyptian Museum, Cairo)

But his sister-wife Isis found him and restored him to life, and his son, a second Horus, born to Isis after Osiris' resurrection, fought and killed Set. Thereupon Horus succeeded Osiris on earth, and Osiris dwelled in a lower world, where, as judge of all who would enter his realm, he became a force for moral betterment.

In the period of the Fifth Dynasty the ancient pre-eminence of the first Horus was usurped by the sun-god Ra. The priests of Ra at Heliopolis became immensely powerful, and the pharaohs included the name of Ra (or Re) in their own official names.

Architecture and the Arts

The huge edifices of the Old Kingdom are among the greatest ever built anywhere. The building of tombs made of stone, rather than of sun-dried brick, began in the time of the Pharaoh Zoser (2664–2646 B.C.) of the Third Dynasty. The Fourth Dynasty became the pyramid age par excellence. During that period were erected the splendid structures of Khufu, Khafre and Menkaure at Gizeh, the most impressive of which is the Great Pyramid of Khufu (Cheops). This monumental mass of limestone and granite blocks required an astonishing amount of materials and labor. Ten years were spent by thousands of men in the preparation of the causeway, then twenty years more were spent in the actual building of the Pyramid. That such projects could be conceived and carried out gives some indication of the grandeur of the pharaoh in the eyes of his subjects, the capacity of the Egyptians for organization, and the efficiency and wealth of the Egyptian state.

Each pyramid had a chapel or temple against its east face, from which a causeway led down to a valley temple, with its quay and canal leading to the Nile. Just to the north of the valley temple of Khafre's pyramid is the Sphinx, now regarded as a portrait head of Khafre, with the usual lion body. Probably it served as a sort of guardian image for the temple.

The power of the kings of the Fifth and Sixth dynasties was not so absolute and their pyramids not so imposing as those of Khufu. But their temples are somewhat lighter and more graceful, and some of them have reliefs and inscriptions that mean more to the historian than the mere size of the larger pyramids.

The Old Kingdom has left little painting that is separate from sculpture, for usually the painter was employed in coloring the carved reliefs in tombs and temples. These skillfully executed carvings present scenes

The Great Pyramid of Khufu and the Sphinx. Built almost 2700 years ago, the largest of the Egyptian pyramids covers 13 acres, measures 755 feet on each side, was originally 480 feet high, and is made of colossal blocks of limestone, some weighing 30 tons, that were quarried with metal tools across the Nile, ferried on rafts, and hauled up ramps to their final positions. Except for three small chambers, deep inside, and the narrow passages leading to them, the Great Pyramid is a solid mass of 2,500,000 cubic yards of stone. The Sphinx is 187 feet long and the head, 60 feet high. (Trans World Airlines Photo)

from the life of the times, providing us with much of our knowledge of the Old Kingdom. The figures are stiff, and, in some respects, unnatural to us, as in the combination of profile and front view. Sculpture in the round was also stiff and conventional, but it, too, was skillfully done, sometimes in the hardest stone. The majestic statue of Khafre on his throne has never been surpassed in its vitality and power.

The work of stonecutters, metalworkers, jewelers, and woodworkers shows the same excellence and the same long tradition as that of the craftsmen in the more important fields of art. These artists were close observers of the natural life and outdoor scenes that they loved to copy in all their products, whether temple walls or eating utensils, whether in diorite, in ebony, or in gold. Chairs, chests, and even beds show that the upper-class Egyptians were accustomed to many of the comforts of life and wanted these objects beautifully made and decorated.

Early Egyptian Literature

The Old Kingdom left many written records but little that can be called literature. Reading and writing were skills acquired by few, and those few were mostly the priest-admin-istrators. Yet the age had its proverbs, myths, and stories as well as the records of important events that were carved on stelai (stone columns) and in tombs.

The best examples of writing in this early period are the *Pyramid Texts,* which come from the pyramids at Sakkara, dating from the Fifth and Sixth dynasties. They speak of the future life in the realms of the sun-god Ra and Osiris and discuss ways to attain it. Though at the time the afterlife was only for the king and a few of the great, these writings show something of the intellectual and moral growth of the priests of the period.

The Birth of Science

Like all other intellectual and cultural pursuits of the Old Kingdom, science was practical. The Egyptians early developed the science of land measurement, necessitated by the annual inundation of the Nile that tended to move landmarks and make resurveys necessary. Some progress was made in astronomy, and the knowledge of medicine was remarkable, despite its strong admixture of magic. In all their technical processes—agriculture, stonecutting, irrigation, building, the fine arts—Egyptians of the Old Kingdom demonstrated a remarkable intelligence.

THE MIDDLE KINGDOM

Long before the end of the Old Kingdom there were signs that the tremendous power of the kings of the Fourth Dynasty was ebbing. For one thing, the pyramids were less impressive. Power was passing to the priests, especially those of Heliopolis, and the lords of the nomes. Even before the end of the Sixth Dynasty the old centralized power of the pharaoh practically ceased to exist.

An age of disorder followed. Upstart kings vied with one another for the support of the nobles, and invaders swept in from Libya and Asia. Finally the Eleventh Dynasty of Theban kings (2134–1999 B.C.) restored order and re-established the central power under Nebhepetre Mentuhotep in 2052 B.C. Their work made possible the glories of the Twelfth Dynasty, beginning in 1991 B.C., during which the civilization of ancient Egypt again attained a high development.

Political Change

In the Middle Kingdom the pharaoh never regained such unquestioned and absolute power as Khufu had wielded. No longer did he own the whole Land of the Nile and everything, including the people, in it. Now he had to share power with the priests and the nobles. Hence the Middle Kingdom is sometimes known as the Feudal Age of Egypt.

Yet the position of the pharaoh was far from weak. The kings of the Twelfth Dynasty developed a strong bureaucracy, practically a civil service, which kept the nobles in check, and they opened up more extensive foreign commerce, which provided another source of wealth besides the diminished taxes.

Social Change

The social organization of the Middle Kingdom was, in general, similar to that of the earlier period. The middle class grew larger than before, however, and the mass of people was probably better off. But the life of the peasants was still hard and insecure, and at the bottom of the social structure, slaves— mostly Nubians taken as prisoners of war— became more numerous.

A Static Economy

Economic conditions remained about the same as in the Old Kingdom. Agriculture was still, as always, the primary source of Egypt's wealth. Foreign trade, including private exchanges, increased a little, and commerce within the country became more lively during the prosperous period of the Twelfth Dynasty. The artisan crafts also flourished. Yet

Egyptian Dynasties, 2134–1570 B.C.

THE MIDDLE KINGDOM

Eleventh Dynasty 2134–1999 B.C.
Nebhepetre Mentuhotep II
2061–2011
Interregnum 1998–1992
Twelfth Dynasty * 1991–1786
Amenemhet I 1991–1962
Senusret I 1971–1928
Amenemhet II 1929–1895
Senusret II 1897–1879
Senusret III 1878–1843
Amenemhet III 1842–1797

SECOND INTERMEDIATE PERIOD

Thirteenth Dynasty (Thebes) 1785–1647
Fourteenth Dynasty (Xois) 1785–c.1603
Fifteenth Dynasty (Hyksos) 1678–1570
Khian 1647–1607
Auserre Apopi 1603–1570
Seventeenth Dynasty
  (Thebes) c.1600–1570
Kamose

* Because of coregencies, the dates overlap.

A Nile Boat. Such models were placed in Eleventh-dynasty tombs to secure for the dead man everything he had possessed in this life and might need in his life in the nether world. Each portrayed a feature of the economic life. This probably represents a fleet of river boats that had been owned by a prince or noble. (National Egyptian Museum, Cairo. *Archives Photographiques*)

there was no radical departure from earlier methods and conditions. The economic system remained patriarchal, under the management of either the king's officials or the powerful nomarchs.

Religious Change

The religion of the Middle Kingdom reveals several new developments. The supremacy of the sun-god Ra continued, but now Ra was forced to share the place of honor with a new Theban deity named Amon. After the beginning of the Twelfth Dynasty the two were spoken of together as Amon-Ra. The merger solarized Amon and gave him precedence over the gods of all other cities, at the same time that it stressed the power of the new dynasty that had come from Thebes. Another divinity that arose to prominence was the crocodile-god Sobek, who also became associated with Ra.

Most important were the changes in the worship of Osiris. Ra, though deemed supreme among the gods, was now elevated to a lofty, and therefore remote, position, whereas Osiris became the god whom the Egyptians took to their hearts. It was he who

bestowed immortal life, and this was a blessing that the practical-minded Egyptians could understand. Pilgrims from all over the land visited his shrine in the city of Abydos in Upper Egypt, and those who could do so arranged for their burial in the necropolis there. Abydos became the scene of lavish public ceremonies re-enacting the story of Osiris' life. This drama of death and resurrection, which perhaps symbolized the drying up of the land and its subsequent fertilization by the Nile, had a natural appeal to the people, who now for the first time were permitted to take part in the celebration of the rites connected with the winning of future happiness.

The popular worship of Osiris constituted a religious development much more far-reaching than that which the priests of Ra had accomplished long before. Immortal life was now a blessing available to all—not just the king and those whom he wished to have it—but it was given only to those who earned it by their good conduct. All men became equal in death, when all had to submit to the judgment of Osiris, who would weigh the heart of the individual against a feather representing truth and would open the gates of his realm only to those who had been true and good—although the fully developed form of the judgment before Osiris as revealed in Chapter 125 of the *Book of the Dead* is not attested until the beginning of the New Kingdom. Thus the Egyptians attained an exalted ethical concept nearly 2000 years before the time of Christ. They did not arrive at monotheism, however, because Osiris was never the sole god, only one of many and tolerant of other gods.

The new religion introduced still other changes. Now that everyone had a chance to enter the realm of Osiris, bodies of the dead of all classes were mummified, the mummies buried as safely as possible, and the tombs provisioned with food and other necessities. Magical charms were also supplied to ward off evil.

This reformation in religion had its counterpart in social changes. Not only did the nobles extend their power, but greater opportunities were open to others to rise to high positions in the civil service. Men of lowly origin now served their government in responsible posts.

The Art of the Middle Kingdom

In the Eleventh and Twelfth Dynasties came a notable revival of art. Unfortunately most of the architectural works of this period have perished, so we know them only by repute. Pyramids were still used as tombs, but they were not so grand as formerly. More wealth and labor were expended on temples, which, from what we know of them, seem to have shown good taste and careful planning. One of the most famous buildings of the time was the huge Labyrinth at Hawara, a great structure of gleaming white stone, with large halls and long passageways. In this age, too, obelisks were first used.

Reliefs and paintings decorated the monuments of this period, especially the tombs that the nobles had cut into the sides of cliffs. These tombs can still be seen. The scope of painting was somewhat broadened, since it was no longer so largely subordinated to the carving of reliefs, and the style of painting shows some attempt to break away from the conventionalization that was the rule in earlier works.

Notable examples of the sculpture of the Twelfth Dynasty still survive. The best works were statues of the kings, in which are shown a naturalistic tendency rarely encountered in Egyptian art. Carved portraits of Amenemhet III and his equally remarkable father, Senusret III, are among the most striking. They do not give the same impression of calm and unquestioned majesty as do the statues of rulers of the Old Kingdom, but this is not the fault of the sculptor—times had changed, and the kings no longer displayed such supreme majesty as before. (Compare the sculptured head of Amenemhet III on page 42 with that of Khafre on page 50.)

The Literature of the Middle Kingdom

Much literature has come down to us from this period, and it shows greater advances than were made in any other field except religion. Some of the writing that survives is on rolls of papyrus, which were found in the cliff tombs of the nobles. Other texts were inscribed on coffins, as charms giving protection to the dead, or carved on the walls of tombs and on stelai set up in various parts of the kingdom. These writings are much more varied, as well as more plentiful, than those surviving from earlier times.

The religious writings include songs and poems devoted to such subjects as the nature of life and death, directions for conducting the mysteries of Osiris, and the passage of the dead from this life to the next. Other writings are words of wisdom that often express sad reflections upon the uncertainties of life. Among treatises of instruction are the counsels written down by Amenemhet I, advising his son on how to act as a king. The nobles also recorded their wisdom and records of their just deeds, so as to win the approbation of their successors.

Sometimes the sentiment expressed in these writings is vague and pompous; often it is pathetically self-contradictory. But there is no need to deprecate these writings; instead we should recognize them as remarkable evidence that men, so very long ago, were striving to find and follow the right course of action. We should hail them as evidence that the human conscience was beginning to stir.

Quite a different kind of literature is the popular tale. One of these recounts the story of a shipwrecked sailor, who made a marvelous visit to a magic island ruled by a huge serpent. Another was the "Story of the Eloquent Peasant" and his attempts to obtain justice.

The Progress of Science

The Egyptians of the Middle Kingdom continued to show their greatest mastery of science in the field of practical works and techniques. Notable among their achievements were dikes, canals, tombs cut out of solid rock, the practical application of simple mathematics, and observation of the heavens.

Medicine was not far advanced beyond the stage of development it had reached in the time of the Old Kingdom. Though something was known of human anatomy and disease, doctors commonly prescribed substances having unpleasant tastes but no curative value—and they had a special fondness for prescribing castor oil. Surgery, however, seems to have made considerable use of scientific observation.

Arithmetic remained simple, and fractions were used only in an awkward manner, but some progress was made in both plane and solid geometry. That no greater advance was made, from practical to speculative mathematics, was another indication of the limitation of Egyptian thinking at that time. In solving the problems of life the Egyptians went only as far as they could see with their own eyes. Beyond that point, if they ventured at all, they were apt to turn to magic.

THE HYKSOS

After the death of Amenemhet III in 1797 B.C., the Twelfth Dynasty gradually lost its power. The kings of the Thirteenth Dynasty were so weak that for part of the time the country was again divided into a northern and a southern kingdom, and the people of the north suffered their first great foreign invasion since the beginning of the dynastic era.

The invasion of Egypt was not solely the result of weakness and dissension in the Land of the Nile. It was owing also to events in the east that now began to have important repercussions upon the affairs of Egypt.

In Southwest Asia the first centuries of the second millennium B.C. were a time of unusual disorder. The northern peoples called Indo-Europeans were then pouring out of Central Asia, to found kingdoms in Mitta and in Anatolia (Hatti) and to seize the Babylonian Empire in Mesopotamia. Their violent movements naturally caused upheavals in all the lands near their new settlements. The disturbance in Syria was especially significant for Egypt, because from and through Syria came the invaders who overran the delta of the Nile.

This horde probably included some of the older Semitic settlers and some of the newcomers from the east. Later the Egyptians spoke contemptuously of the leaders of this invasion as *Hyksos*, which has been translated *Shepherd Kings* and also *Rulers of Countries*. Actually, however, the warriors who swept into Egypt were not mere nomads of the desert, for in their conquest they made use of the latest discoveries of the civilized east. For example, they had chariots of war, drawn by horses, which were probably as devastating in their time as modern armored divisions are today. From these conquerors, too, the Egyptians learned much of the art of war, which later they were to put to use for their own account.

The Hyksos secured a firm hold upon the northern part of Egypt, but they also dominated the south, although there the Egyptians put up a stronger resistance. Eventually the Hyksos kings were Egyptianized and took on the outward appearance of native rulers. Nevertheless the southerners were not appeased, and a Theban dynasty—the Seventeenth—kept up the fight with success under Kamose, the last king of the dynasty. Ultimately the conquerors were driven from the region of the delta and pursued into Palestine by Ahmose I, who founded the Eighteenth Dynasty about 1570 B.C.

THE NEW KINGDOM OR EMPIRE

Under the able rule of Ahmose I began the age of the Empire. In the next four centuries —under the Eighteenth, Nineteenth, and the early rulers of the Twentieth dynasties— Egypt enjoyed extraordinary wealth and grandeur, abandoning her former isolation and building up a great foreign empire.

The first period of Egyptian imperial expansion is contemporaneous with the Eighteenth Dynasty (1570–1304 B.C.). After the Hyksos invasion the Egyptians realized that they could not avoid contact with the east. Nor could they make themselves secure simply by occasional punitive raids upon Asiatic cities. They must undertake, instead, to gain mastery over their Semitic neighbors.

The attempt began in the reign of Thutmose III (Thothmes), who throughout most of his reign waged one campaign after another in Asia, from 1469 to 1436 B.C. When this greatest of Egyptian conquerors was done, he held control of all Palestine, Syria, and Phoenicia, and his power reached to the boundaries of Cilicia and the Euphrates. Subsequently, however, the Egyptians were driven back to their homeland, when the rising Hittite Empire rallied the native princes of Syria and led them in a revolt against Egyptian rule.

Not for some time did the Egyptians try to regain their empire. But the pharaohs of the Nineteenth Dynasty were vigorous, and one of them—Seti I (1303–1290 B.C.)—recovered part of the Egyptian holdings in Palestine and some cities in Phoenicia. His successor, Ramses II (1290–1223 B.C.), a great warrior, waged several campaigns in a vain attempt to add new territories to those that Seti I had regained. His successors fared no better, and though one of them—Ramses III of the Twentieth Dynasty—was a king of unusual vision and leadership, the Egyptian Empire was never restored to its earlier bounds.

Black Granite Bust of Thutmose III. His reign was concurrent with that of his sister Hatshepsut (p. 61). (National Egyptian Museum, Cairo. *Archives Photographiques*)

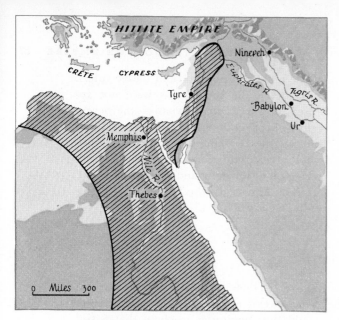

The Empire of Thutmose III about 1450 B.C.

Imperial Government

Under the stress of new conditions the government underwent changes. These were more subtle than dramatic but nonetheless important. The increase of responsibilities bearing on the bureaucratic system led to the appointment of two viziers, one of whom was stationed at Thebes and the other at Heliopolis. But there was little lessening in the power and majesty of the kingship, for the pharaoh was always a god and to some extent always unapproachable.

Imperial Commerce

The Egypt of the Empire underwent no radical social or economic change, except that trade with foreign lands increased, reaching to Nubia, Punt, Syria, Palestine, Phoenicia, Cyprus, the Aegean region, and even distant Anatolia (Hatti) and Mesopotamia. The riches that flowed in from trade and tribute produced a greater magnificence and luxury than ever before. There were, however, unfavorable consequences of the new wealth, and eventually softness in its possessors and corruption affected the political and economic stability of the country. Especially ominous was the unhealthy increase in wealth of the priests of Amon.

Imperial Society

One of the changes noticeable in the social order was the increase in the number of slaves, a consequence of the capture of prisoners in the wars. This introduced a sizable foreign element into the population, as did also the practice of hiring mercenary soldiers, to which the kings again began to resort.

The position of women, which never was so low in Egypt as in some of the Asiatic countries, perhaps improved further in this period. The Empire witnessed a period of unparalleled feminine influence in high politics. The great Hatshepsut, the first great queen of Egypt (1484–1469 B.C.), was a woman of powerful personality, and somewhat later the fascinating queens Tiy and Nefertiti also played roles of importance. The young, childless widow of Tutenkhamon, Queen Anches-en-Amon, sought to preserve her own power and establish the

Egyptian Dynasties, 1570–1075 B.C.

THE NEW KINGDOM OR EMPIRE

Eighteenth Dynasty	1570–1304 B.C.
Ahmose I 1570–1545	
Thutmose III 1490–1436	
Hatshepsut (queen) 1484–1469	
Amenhotep III 1397–1360	
Amenhotep IV (Akhnaton) 1370–1353	
Tutenkhamon 1352–1343	
Horemheb 1339–1304	
Nineteenth Dynasty	1304–1181
Seti I 1303–1290	
Ramses II 1290–1223	
Twentieth Dynasty	1181–1075
Ramses III 1179–1147	

succession, by requesting the Hittite king Suppiluliumas to send her as husband one of his sons. Although her request was granted, the young prince unfortunately was murdered en route to Egypt by nobles who probably had other plans for the Egyptian succession.

Though we do not have extensive remains of Egyptian law codes, we have reason to believe that the Egyptians did not lag behind the Babylonians and Hittites, who in this age were promulgating legal systems. The more conscientious of the kings left sufficient evidence to show that they were concerned with the cultivation of justice. Generally social and legal restrictions were loosened as the horizon widened in the imperial age. Yet we must not assume that Egypt underwent a fundamental social revolution. The vast majority of the people remained lowly agricultural workers, and society gave virtually no scope to what we regard as individualism and personal independence.

Imperial Religion

The Osirian revolution in religion continued its course during the Empire, assuring a future life to all who endeared themselves to the god of the dead by virtuous living—or who could afford to buy magical charms from the priests.

The growing power and wealth of the priests was one of the outstanding religious developments of the age. The priesthood now became a separate vocation, which it had not been before, and its members thus gained a privileged position. Thutmose III began the custom, which later kings continued, of making enormous gifts of land and booty to the god Amon upon the successful conclusion of a foreign campaign. This god of Thebes, who had been associated with Ra, had never lost his identity. As the divinity of the leading city of a great empire, he now became more imposing than ever before, and his priests gained prestige in proportion.

For a time, however, the priests of Amon were checked by the amazing religious revolution of Amenhotep IV (1370–1353 B.C.), who raised to a supreme position the sun-disk deity Aton, whose worship had begun earlier. Declaring Aton to be the *only* god, Amenhotep IV changed his own name to Akhnaton—"Pleasing to Aton"—and built the city of Akhetaton—"Horizon of Aton"—to which he moved the capital. So devout was Akhnaton that he attempted to obliterate all reference to the other gods, especially Amon, whose priests he banished and whose wealth was given to the priests of Aton.

The Offerings of Seti I and Ramses II—bas relief from the mortuary temple of Ramses II at Abydos, dedicated to Osiris, before whom Seti is making an offering, while the goddess Isis receives offerings from Ramses. (Courtesy of the Metropolitan Museum of Art)

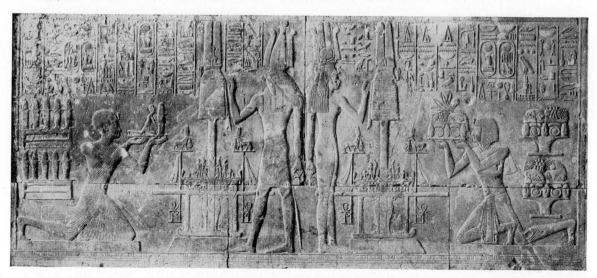

Akhnaton. Despite the conventionalized head-dress, the sculpture is naturalistic (p. 62). (Cairo Museum. *Archives Photographiques*.)

Akhnaton is, without doubt, one of the most interesting figures in the history of the Ancient Orient. In modern times he has been extolled as the first "individual" to appear in history, and his religious reform has been much praised. Perhaps, as some scholars believe, his religious revolution was an attempt to smash the *political* power of the priesthood of Amon and so restore the legitimate power to the kingship. Perhaps, as others hold, he was a poor ruler, thoughtless of the welfare of his people, tactless and violent in his attempts to force a new religion upon them. Whatever the judgment, Akhnaton remains a colorful personality.

Thus an abrupt change was made. Monotheism replaced the old polytheism. This seemed to mean that not only would all Egyptians worship one god, but all the peoples under Egyptian rule would worship the same god, for the worship of Aton spread beyond Egypt. This would have meant the achievement of a universal, monotheistic religion several centuries before the Hebrews and the Persians. It was a religion, moreover, that taught reverence for truth and for the world of nature, for this was the world that Aton created. It also had the power to inspire deep religious sentiments, as we know from the hymns that Akhnaton himself composed in honor of Aton. Even now, after 3300 years, these hymns evoke an emotional response in readers.

But the religion of Aton did not endure. Its dominance was wholly due to the strong-willed Akhnaton, who reigned for seventeen years. After his death, under his weak successor Tutenkhamon, the priests of Amon returned, and no trace remained of Aton. The ignorant and superstitious masses had never been captured by Akhnaton's lofty conception, and they hailed the return of Amon as the restoration of the "good old religion."

The Golden Age of Egyptian Literature

The literature of the Empire was extensive, lively, and varied. In addition to the usual religious poems and the *Book of the Dead,* which consisted mainly of written spells for the protection of the deceased, the hymns of Akhnaton were especially notable. Other poems commemorated the wars and victories of Thutmose III and Ramses II. Wondrous stories and wise proverbs were also written, as in the period of the Middle Kingdom, but perhaps more interesting are the biographies of nobles who accompanied their kings on campaigns and had such accounts recorded on the walls of their tombs.

This age left the most important documents of a historical character that have yet been found in Egypt. Among these are the annals of the campaigns of Thutmose III, written on the walls of the Great Temple of Amon at present-day Karnak (part of ancient Thebes), and documents found at Tell el Amarna, the site of ancient Akhetaton. These latter, written in the cuneiform script, in the Akkadian (Babylonian) language used for diplomatic correspondence, deal with international affairs involving Egypt in the reign of Akhnaton. More of these letters were later found in the ruins of the Hittite capital Hattusas (present-day Boghazköy) in Asia Minor. Another document of extraordinary historical interest is the great treaty concluded between Ramses II and the Hittite king Hattusilis (or Hattushilish) in 1270 B.C. Originally engraved upon silver plaques, a copy of the Egyptian version, in hieroglyphs, was found on the walls of the temple of Karnak, and a cuneiform text has recently come to light. This is the earliest known example of a political treaty and is surprisingly modern in some of its clauses.

Even in a brief glimpse of Egyptian literature, note must be taken of the love songs that disclose a side of the Egyptians rarely revealed in their monuments. We can more easily think of them as real men and women, with all the usual emotions, when we read the strangely pathetic song of the youth who thus tells us that when his mistress comes to him and kisses him, he is "happy without beer."

The Golden Age of Egyptian Art

The great wealth of the Empire was lavishly spent on buildings that surpassed in grandeur all earlier architectural achievements except the pyramids. In a valley west of Thebes—renowned as the Valley of the Tombs of the Kings—the pharaohs of the Empire built magnificent cliff tombs. Along the desert edge below the western cliffs were the temples in which were conducted the services for the dead king. The finest of these is a mortuary temple built by the formidable Queen Hatshepsut, which is approached by three colonnaded terraces. At present-day Luxor and Karnak, other elaborate temples were erected in honor of Amon. Like almost all the buildings of the Egyptians, they were heavy and adorned with massive columns. Some, like the Great Temple of Amon at Karnak, had huge hypostyle halls, in which rows of heavy columns support the roof. There the central rows are higher than those at the sides, leaving a clerestory to provide light for the dark interior. Such temples had pylons, which were huge towerlike walls, before the courts, and they were made even more impressive by tall obelisks.

Ramses II, like other kings of this period, made numerous additions to buildings that his predecessors had erected. Unfortunately, however, he saw nothing wrong in stripping the works of his predecessors in order to finish his own. But some of his structures—a great cliff temple at Abu Simbel and the Ramesseum, his mortuary temple—are among the most impressive in Egypt for

The Temple of Hatshepsut. Built on the slope of the western cliffs in the Valley of the Kings, where most of the Theban kings were buried, this temple was decorated with bas reliefs recording important events in Hatshepsut's life. (Courtesy of the Metropolitan Museum of Art)

Nefertiti, Akhnaton's queen. Cast of the original found at Tell el Amarna. The crown is painted blue with a gold band, inset with precious stones. (Courtesy, Metropolitan Museum of Art)

Especially notable are the statues done at the behest of Akhnaton, which reveal the new naturalism he favored. He commanded his sculptors to present their subjects as they saw them, and consequently their work departs radically from the tradition of conventionalized representation. The king is portrayed as a human being, not a god, and the head of Nefertiti, Akhnaton's queen, is justly famous for its natural grace. (See page 60.)

Relief sculpture—in which the gods, battle scenes, the hunt, and lesser subjects were depicted—also showed an increasing degree of naturalism. Again this was especially true of the work done in the time of Akhnaton. In view of the long tradition of unnatural conventionalism, it is hard to believe that Egyptian artists could have carved the lifelike reliefs that appear in the tombs at Akhetaton. The king must have commanded his artists not to spare him, for his appearance in portrait reliefs is quite unprepossessing. Though the weak points of the king's face and figure are shown almost as though in caricature, the artists certainly were masters of their art. Posture, facial expression, or the hang of draperies presented no difficulties that they could not overcome. Tremendous progress might have been made had this naturalistic art continued. Instead conservatism triumphed, and Egyptian sculpture turned back to the tradition of stiff carvings, conventionalized portraits, and colossal statues, more remarkable for size than any other quality.

Painting was another art that flourished under the Empire. But much of the work in this medium was done for the decoration of the palaces, and these structures were not built for permanence, so their decorations have perished with the buildings. Most of what remains is made up of paintings that were to illustrate the *Book of the Dead* or to ornament the walls of tombs and the floors of palaces. Pleasant scenes of daily life were the favorite subjects of imperial painters— representations of animals, ceremonies of various kinds, mourners, banqueters, hunting expeditions, water scenes with birds, fish and

sheer vastness, difficulty of work, and colossal size of statues and obelisks.

Thebes, where most of the building was done, must have been a magnificent city, with its brightly colored buildings, luxuriant temple gardens, vast pylons, towering obelisks, and the gorgeous palaces of kings and nobles. Since gates and obelisks were overlaid with gleaming gold and other metals, it is no wonder that visitors were overawed and that even the greatest kings of Asia thought that in Egypt gold was as dust.

Though sculpture in the round was not so distinguished in this period as in earlier times, some admirable work was produced.

aquatic plants. These are happy reminders of the good life that the wealthy men and women of the Empire enjoyed, and they gave ample opportunity for the use of gay colors that all Egyptians loved.

This age also left evidence of its wealth and elegance in the form of minor artistic works. Glassware, metal and wooden objects of many kinds, musical instruments, necklaces and other forms of adornment—all these also attest a civilization that knew refinement. Unquestionably the ancient Egyptians had a keen and lively artistic sense, and those who could do so provided themselves with comfortable houses, pleasant gardens, and finely wrought furnishings.

Egyptian Music

The Egyptians, especially in the time before the Hyksos invasion, were fond of the serene music of the harp and other soft-voiced instruments. A painting, found in a tomb at Sakkara dating from about the time the Great Pyramid was built, shows instrumentalists playing a vertical flute, a double clarinet, and a four-stringed harp. Four singers, who are shown seated, appear to be indicating the melody by movement of the hand and fingers. Evidently musical instruments were used only to accompany singers. Judging from their attitude and gestures and the lines that appear in their faces, one guesses that the singers must have sung in the same

nasal, tight-throated, high-pitched style that is characteristic of singing in the Orient in our own time. The literature of love songs, dating from the Twelfth Dynasty, indicates a secular musical tradition of refinement, perhaps comparable to the age-old religious music.

The Hyksos era brought a noisier popular music, though the quiet, classical music of the Old Kingdom hung on in school and temple under the supervision of the conservative upper class.

Unlike the music of Mesopotamia, which was based on a sensuous chromaticism, the native Egyptian music was diatonic—that is, two steps and a half step. The fifty or so ancient Egyptian instruments that have been discovered—especially woodwind instruments resembling the flute, clarinet, and oboe—are so constructed that they could not have played intervals smaller than a whole tone. Probably, therefore, Egyptian harps were tuned for diatonic melodies. However, the Mesopotamian influence undoubtedly colored popular music with a diversity of chromatic scales. For some reason the lute did not

Ancient Pillars in the Hypostyle Hall of the Temple of Karnak. (Trans World Airlines Photo) Many beautiful buildings have been built on

the post-and-lintel system. Stone posts can be high, but stone lintels cannot be long. Stone is weak in tension; hence the posts must be relatively close together.

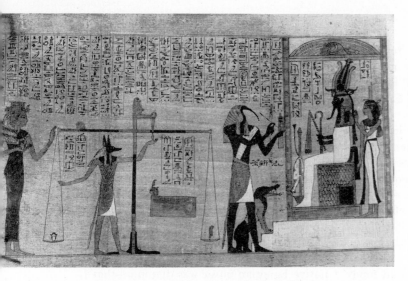

The Judgment of Queen Makeri. Twenty-first dynasty papyrus, showing Osiris sitting in judgment while the dog-head god Anubis weighs the queen's heart against a feather. (National Egyptian Museum, Cairo. *Archives Photographiques*)

appear in Egypt until the fifteenth century B.C., although it was known in Mesopotamia much earlier.

Other influences besides the louder and more chromatic idiom of Mesopotamia may have brought changes in the soft-sounding, upper-class art-music. Akhnaton's religious revolution, which brought forth psalmlike hymns to the sun and a "modern," realistic movement in sculpture, must surely have stimulated a vital new style of musical composition and rendition. But in the reaction following Akhnaton's death, presumably the conservative priests of Amon regained their former influence over Egyptian art-music, as they did over religious forms and ideas.

THE PERIOD OF DECLINE AND AFTERWARD

After Ramses III the pharaohs never again had an effective rule outside Egypt, and with the end of the Twentieth Dynasty about 1075 B.C. the Empire came to an end.

The remainder of the story of Egypt is quickly told. The years from 1075–656 B.C. are known to historians as the Period of Decline. For a while Egypt suffered another Semitic invasion, when the Assyrians overran the land in 671 B.C. But Assyrian rule did not last long, and under the Twenty-sixth Dynasty (663–525 B.C.), which had its capital at Sais, the ancient Egyptians enjoyed another period of independence. Persian domination, which began in 525 B.C., was interrupted in 404, but resumed in 341, to come to an end with the conquest of Alexander the Great in 332 B.C. and the subsequent establishment of the Ptolemaic Dynasty (see Chapter 6).

||||||||||||||||||||||||||||||||||||||||||||||||||||||||||||||||||||||||||||||||||||||

Egyptian Dynasties, 1075–332 B.C.

PERIOD OF DECLINE

Twenty-first–Twenty-fifth dynasties   1075–656 B.C.

SAITE PERIOD

Twenty-sixth Dynasty   663–525

FIRST PERSIAN DOMINATION

Twenty-seventh Dynasty   525–404

LAST INDEPENDENT KINGDOM

Twenty-eighth–Thirtieth dynasties   404–341

SECOND PERSIAN PERIOD

Thirty-first Dynasty   341–332

Suggestions for Further Reading

Source Materials

Anthologies and Collected Documents

E. A. Wallis Budge, ed., *From Fetish to God in Ancient Egypt* (London, 1934).
A highly interesting collection of texts from ancient Egypt.

G. H. Knoles and R. K. Snyder, eds., *Readings in Western Civilization* (rev. ed., New York, 1954), pp. 26–27.
A selection of texts from the "Book of the Dead."

J. B. Pritchard, ed., *Ancient Near Eastern Texts Relating to the Old Testament* (Princeton, 1950).
An excellent collection of ancient texts. Contains many documents emanating from Egyptian and other ancient civilizations as well as from the Hebrews.

Secondary Works

J. Baikie, *A Century of Excavation in the Land of the Pharaohs* (New York, 1924).
A lively, nontechnical account of the history of various excavations and of the archaeologists involved.

J. H. Breasted, *A History of Egypt* (New York, 1909).
One of the excellent early accounts of Egypt in the light of modern excavations. Very influential on later histories and, for the most part, still valid.

H. Frankfort, *Ancient Egyptian Religion* (New York, 1948).
Scholarly lectures.

S. R. K. Glanville, ed., *The Legacy of Egypt* (Toronto, 1943).
A group of essays written by specialists. Covers cultural, technical, religious, legal, political influences which have continued to our own time. The book is one in a series covering the heritage from antiquity.

A. Moret, *The Nile and Egyptian Civilization*, translated from the French (New York, 1928).
A comprehensive and readable synthesis from prehistoric time through the late foreign conquests. Covers political, cultural, and intellectual aspects. Good volume for the non-Egyptologist.

M. A. Murray, *The Splendour That Was Egypt* (London, 1949).
A general survey, giving a brief historical account and a full report on cultural aspects. Readable for laymen.

W. M. F. Petrie, *Social Life in Ancient Egypt* (New York, 1923).
Petrie, whose work has influenced all his successors, was one of the earliest and greatest Egyptologists. This is a short, simple account of the life of the people, justice, religion, trade, learning—still quite valid.

G. Steindorff and K. C. Seele, *When Egypt Ruled the East* (Chicago, 1942).
Concerned chiefly with the period of the Egyptian Empire, and fits Egypt into west Asia. Especially good for religion and art. Fairly brief, authoritative, and up to date, supplementing Breasted by new materials.

3

The Civilizations of the Fertile Crescent

The Goddess Ishtar on a Lion. Assyrian bas relief (see p. 85). (*Archives Photographiques*)

In the same millennia during which the Egyptian civilization was being formed, a similar development was taking place along the banks of the Tigris and Euphrates rivers only a few hundred miles away. There, as in Egypt, technical progress was occurring much more rapidly than in Europe. Before all the European peoples had taken up the use of metal, eastern peoples had passed through the Copper Age and the Bronze Age and gone into the Iron Age.

From its earliest centers in Egypt and the land between the Tigris and the Euphrates, civilization soon spread to the whole of the Fertile Crescent—the area of productive lands, shaped like a horseshoe, that stretches northward from Babylonia to the highlands of the Euphrates, then curves southward again through Syria and Palestine (see map, p. 68). Gradually civilization spread still wider—eastward to the land of the Medes and the Persians, northward and westward through Asia Minor, out to the islands and the peninsulas of Greece and Italy, and on to the distant shores of the Mediterranean as far as Spain.

SUMERO-BABYLONIAN CIVILIZATION

The scene of the earliest civilization in the Fertile Crescent was Lower Mesopotamia— the fertile plain lying between the head of the Persian Gulf and the point where the Tigris and Euphrates begin most closely to approach each other. In ancient times this region was known as the land of Sumer and Akkad or the Plain of Shinar and, later, as Babylonia. In ancient times, also, the region was smaller than now, for over the course of centuries the shore has pushed about 200 miles out into the Persian Gulf, and the two rivers are now farther apart than formerly.

Though the land is not now regarded as attractive, in the early days it had a number of advantages for human settlers. In flood season the two rivers overflowed their banks —as they still do—and, as the waters receded, a rich deposit of silt was laid down. With irrigation, for which the rivers provided water, the soil could be made to produce a wealth of fruits, vegetables, nuts, and grains.

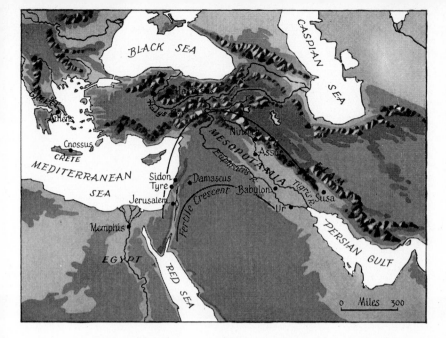

Ancient Mesopotamia— "Land between Two Rivers." The region that arcs westward from the valleys of the Tigris and Euphrates rivers through Syria and Palestine to Egypt was christened the "Fertile Crescent" by Professor James Henry Breasted— and the name has been used ever since by most historians.

And the hot winds of autumn ripened the dates, which were then—as now—a source of much wealth. The rivers afforded a good supply of fish, and the land abounded with animals and fowl. Yet these advantages would have been of no use except to a people of keen intelligence—such as were the Sumerians—because the products of orchard, field, and pasture depended upon constant irrigation, and this required engineering ability, continual maintenance, and cooperation both in planning and upkeep.

Though rich in sources of food, the Plain of Shinar was not otherwise well endowed. There were no trees to provide lumber and stone was rare. Consequently bricks had to be made to build temples, palaces, great houses, and city walls, while reeds were used for the houses of the common people. Because fuel was scarce, the bricks were sun-baked. As a result, even the greatest buildings have not endured so well as those of other ancient peoples who built in stone.

Sumer and Akkad

The lower valley of the two rivers was already settled when the Sumerians moved into it some time between 5000 and 4000 B.C.,

migrating probably from Central Asia. The northern part of the plain was then inhabited by a people of Semitic language, who had come there from northern Syria and were just emerging from the Neolithic stage of culture. Other Semitic-speaking peoples had migrated out of Arabia into the southern part of the delta.

Entering the land as invaders, after these Semitic peoples were already established, the dark-haired Sumerians set about conquering the Semites and imposing their culture upon them. The Sumerians, probably, were an Indo-European people, for their language was unlike the Semitic tongue, and they had apparently reached a high stage of civilization before their migration into Mesopotamia.

For centuries a struggle—both political and cultural—went on between the Sumerians and the Semites, with Sumerian institutions coming in time to dominate throughout the region. Later the Semitic element gained a political ascendance in this early civilization.

We know very little about the earliest history of the Sumerians. Evidently before coming into Mesopotamia they had passed beyond a simple tribal organization and had developed a society of stable settlements in towns. They owned flocks and herds and carried on agriculture, for which they had devised a plow and seed drill drawn by oxen. In their new homeland they soon learned to increase the natural productiveness of the river valley by building irrigation canals and using watering machines. They also learned to build their villages on natural or man-made mounds, so as to be safe from the flood waters as well as more secure from attack. By about 3500 B.C., as we know from excavations made at Ur, the Sumerians had attained a brilliant civilization. Probably their culture continued to dominate Lower Mesopotamia for more than 1500 years, through the reign of the dynasty of Hammurabi at Babylon.

The whole of Sumerian history was studded with invasions, wars, and the creation of empires. One reason for these wars—paradoxical though it seems—is that the land required peace, because the riches of the delta depended upon cooperation in the work of irrigation, and warfare disrupted this cooperation. Hence the rulers of small kingdoms often sought to increase their realms so as to make them more secure; but to do so, they apparently felt they must make war on neighboring kingdoms.

Another cause of war was the wealth of the delta, which tempted other peoples to invade the land. Especially troublesome were the tough, warlike peoples living in Elam, to the east, who swept down into the delta whenever the native rulers there relaxed their vigilance.

Still another factor in all the wars and invasions, down to the time of Hammurabi, was the rivalry between Sumerian and Semite for domination of the civilization that the Sumerians had created. Although the Semites were hardier, they were less advanced than the Sumerians, who knew more about the technique of warfare. While the Semites were learning how to wage war with better success, the Sumerians eased their grip on the sword. The result was that the once ignorant pupils finally became the masters.

The struggle of Sumerians, Semites, and outsiders for control of the Land of the Two Rivers took place against a background of urban rivalry. Each of the various cities of Sumer and Akkad had its own *patesi*, who was the hereditary civil ruler and chief priest, its own divine protector, and its own claims to the surrounding territory. The first of these urban dynasties arose in Kish in Akkad, and in Erech and Ur in Sumer. For centuries these and other cities waged war upon one another as well as on foreigners, until the intercity rivalry was brought to an end shortly before 2600 B.C. by Sargon of Agade, who created the first great empire in the Fertile Crescent.

Sargon and the First Empire

Sargon was a remarkable man, who rose from the humble rank of cupbearer to become the first of the Semitic empire-builders. He extended his dominion over the Assyrians, invaded the Zagros Mountains to the east, and even reached into Asia Minor and Syria as well as conquering the land of Sumer and making Semitic influence stronger there than ever before. By his conquests, Sargon won control over regions of great mineral and commercial wealth, which he

Crouching Dog Stone Urn. About 3000 B.C. (Louvre Museum. *Archives Photographiques*)

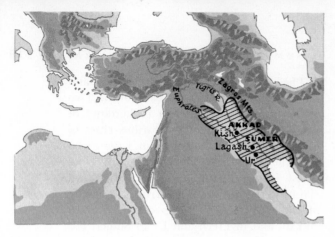

Mesopotamia about 1500 B.C.

2000 B.C., however, a strong new dynasty of Amorites or western Semites, which had arisen in the city of Babylon in the north, drove the Elamites out of the lower delta and once more united Sumer and Akkad under a large empire. The leader of these Amorite conquerors and founder of the new empire was Hammurabi.* Under his direction, canals and temples were built, fortifications and monuments were raised, and the laws of the empire were codified and inscribed in lasting stone.

In spite of Hammurabi's constructive work, the Babylonian empire proved no more permanent than the earlier creations of Sargon and Dungi. From without, tough and envious neighbors battered at the borders, while within the empire revolts wore down its strength. The outcome was the disruption and conquest of Babylonia. About 1600 B.C. the capital fell to the Hittites, while the Kassites, a fierce mountain people from the east who first used horses in war, took over the remainder of the empire.

intended to organize as part of his empire. But revolts interfered with his plan, and his successors could not hold the empire together.

Dungi

A period of foreign domination followed the decline of Sargon's empire, until eventually a Sumerian empire arose under the leadership first of Erech and then of Ur. In this empire the Semites were given as much political power as the Sumerians, and peace and order were restored. The great organizer in this last period of Sumerian prominence was Dungi, who through a long reign of fifty-eight years wisely guided the work of restoring civilized life to Sumer and Akkad. Unfortunately, however, he became involved in foreign wars, in which the strength of the empire was wasted. Ultimately the empire was overrun by the northern Amorites and the Elamites from the east, and a wholesale destruction was visited upon Ur, the capital.

Babylonia: Hammurabi

Civil war and disorder ensued, and the Elamites gained domination over the southern portion of Mesopotamia. Some time after

The Kassites

The Kassites—as well as the Hittites and a third Indo-European people, the Mitanni—had emerged from Central Asia by the first half of the second millennium B.C. if not before. Like some earlier invaders of Lower Mesopotamia, the Kassites had first come as traders to the cities of Babylonia. Soon the Kassite awe of the grandeur of the Babylonians changed to envy of their wealth and contempt for their smugness. The Kassites had not been made soft by civilization, and

* The dates of Hammurabi have never been accurately established. He was for years thought to have flourished about 2100 B.C. Then another system of dating placed him as 1955–1913 or 1948–1905 B.C. During the past twenty years, as scholars studied new evidence, the dates 1868–1826 and 1801–1759 B.C. were suggested. The recent discovery of documents pertaining to his contemporaries elsewhere suggests 1728–1686 B.C., but these dates are also questioned. Consequently no one yet can be sure just when Hammurabi lived.

when they saw something they wanted, they did not hesitate to fight for it. Thus it was that the virile mountaineers became the new masters of Babylonia.

Their rule lasted for almost six centuries, but their dominion was never so grand as the earlier empires of Sargon and Hammurabi; the period of their rule will be discussed only briefly.

Cultural Achievements

Thus far we have only sketched the background of migrations and invasions and noted the rise and fall of empires in Lower Mesopotamia in the period from about the end of the fifth millennium B.C. to the early part of the second millennium. We have said nothing of the accomplishments of the Sumerians and others during this period in those activities that make life worth living—the creation of government and law, the pursuit of prosperity and comfort, the cultivation of beauty, and the increase of knowledge. We must now turn back to take note of these cultural achievements.

The Sumerians were the pioneers in the political development of Lower Mesopotamia; the Semitic peoples who were established there before the Sumerians had been, indeed, much slower to develop a system of government. Under Sumerian influence, Sumer and Akkad gradually became a land of city-states, unified in language, religion, laws, customs, and economic activities. But these city-states remained proud of their independence and jealous of one another. They bitterly resisted political unification under a single government embracing the whole of Mesopotamia.

As is usual in simple societies, political and religious authorities were closely bound together. Like their predecessors in the Neolithic Age, the Sumerians pictured the unknown powers of the universe as grim and horrible beings, who were to be feared, worshiped, and placated. All these mysterious powers animating the universe were represented in the Sumerian pantheon, and each city had a patron god of its own. This god was thought of as the supreme ruler of the city, acting through a human agent—the *patesi*—who was both the civil governor and the chief priest.

Sometimes one of these *patesi* would make himself master of others, and thus kingdoms and empires would come into being. But the cities would still keep their pride of local patriotism, and an empire would last only as long as its ruler could maintain a forcible domination over the cities that formed his realm. At one time or another various cities—Kish, Erech, Ur, Lagash, Agade, Babylon—would hold mastery over some of or all the neighboring cities, but eventually its rule would break down.

Though no empire ever established strong and enduring political ties among the numerous cities of Sumer and Akkad, trade linked them with one another—and with foreign lands. Commerce exchanged the wealth of the delta for that of Asia Minor, Syria, Egypt, the Persian Gulf, Elam, India, and the Caucasus. And with trade, Sumerian culture spread abroad.

Economic Life

The basic economy of the rich delta of the Tigris and Euphrates was always agricultural. The irrigated fields brought forth rich harvests of grain, vegetables, and dates. Some of the land was privately held; some was owned by the ruler or controlled by the priests in the name of the gods they served; but much of the land was worked communally.

Commerce and industry added to the wealth of Sumer. The chief industry was cloth-making, though artisans were also employed in making tools, weapons, pottery, and other articles. But commerce was a larger source of wealth than manufacture. Trade reached out in all directions and in-

Ur-Nammu, Emperor of Ur. Found at Lagash and dating from about 3100 B.C., this stone bas relief was probably a votive offering. It shows Ur-Nammu (top left) with a mason's basket on his head, celebrating with members of his family the foundation of a temple, and (at the bottom) pouring a libation before his prime minister and his three sons. The names of the various persons have been inscribed on their figures in archaic cuneiform characters and in the Sumerian language. The background inscription at the bottom relates that Ur-Nammu brought in wood to build a temple. (Louvre Museum. *Archives Photographiques*)

volved all kinds of goods. Imports included stone, wood, and metals—none of which was available in abundance from local sources. Business operations were on a large scale, requiring business agents, letters of credit, and commercial loans, although no money was coined and all transactions were therefore on the basis of barter.

Babylonian Society

The people were divided into three social classes. At the top was a privileged group of officials, priests, and fighting men. Next was a class of free men, including business, professional, and laboring men. At the bottom were the slaves. Because of the constant menace of war, social prestige was in proportion to military service. Hence the aristocracy, which provided the military caste, lorded it over the lower class of free men, who were called upon to render military service only occasionally and in humble positions. Some of the free men lived a miserable existence, little better than that of slaves.

Slaves had some legal rights, and their owners took reasonable care of them, since they represented valuable property. Many slaves were taken in battle, but others were purchased or born into servitude because their parents were slaves. Since most of them were Sumerians or Semites, they were not looked down upon as an inferior race. Though not intolerable, their lot was unenviable, for in most respects they were at the mercy of their masters, who could beat them, sell them, or humiliate them at will.

Women were accorded a measure of respect and considerable freedom. They could engage in business, control property, and govern their children, and they had the advantage of monogamous marriage. However, a wife could be divorced more easily than a husband, and she had to bear children or her husband could lawfully take a second wife or a concubine. Women were also regularly required to serve as religious prostitutes in connection with those parts of religion that centered about the cult of fertility.

Babylonian Science

In the practical sciences the Sumerians and their Semitic pupils demonstrated a considerable degree of inventiveness. In response to the needs of agriculture, they invented, as we have mentioned, a plow and a seed drill, and they developed irrigation works. For the needs of war they made excellent weapons—axes, maces, spears, daggers, and bows. They also developed protective clothing and chariots of war, which at first were drawn by asses, then by horses. Standing armies were maintained, and the military phalanx was devised.

The scientific interest of the Sumerians was not confined, however, to such practical exploits. Though their astronomy was diluted with astrology, they began to map the heavens and worked out a lunar calendar. For business purposes the month was divided into thirty days, and the lunar system was adjusted from time to time to agree with the solar year. Studies in arithmetic and geometry led to helpful discoveries. An interesting feature of the Sumerian system of units is the frequent appearance of the number 60 and its multiples or divisors. Thus the year had twelve months and 360 days, which were divided into hours, minutes, and seconds according to the same system, and the circle was divided on a similar basis into 360 degrees. Geography was studied and maps were made, for the Sumerians seem to have been eager to measure anything they could see. In medicine, as in astronomy, science was mingled with superstition, but something was known about the treatment of diseases, and surgical operations were performed.

Babylonian Art

The brilliance of the Sumerians was revealed in their art as well as their science. Their architecture, though restricted to the use of sun-dried bricks, was impressive.

Large palaces with many rooms, decorated walls, and courts attest to the imagination and skill of the architects. The arch, vault, and dome were all used in the construction of the tombs of kings, and the weapons, tools, and ornaments that were placed in the tombs give evidence of the skill and of the refinement of Sumerian artisans. As early as 3500 B.C. the art of the Sumerians attained a peak that it was never thereafter to exceed.

We have more extensive knowledge of the buildings of a later period. In the time when the city of Ur was in its ascendancy, the dominant building was the ziggurat, a huge mound of bricks, provided with terraces and stairways and surmounted by a small shrine. Larger temples were built near by, housing sanctuaries and other chambers for which there was no room in the ziggurat. The king had an elaborate palace, while members of the aristocracy made their homes in two-story houses of many rooms, built around courtyards and supplied with chapels, bal-

Gudea of Lagash. Portrait sculpture c.2200 B.C. (Courtesy of the Metropolitan Museum of Art)

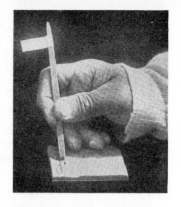

Sumerian Clay Tablet and Bone Stylus. Found in the palace at Kish, this is the earliest example of Sumerian script where cuneiform signs are used along with pictographic signs and probably dates about 3500 B.C. The stylus, in the hand of the discoverer, Professor S. Langdon of Oxford, has two ends: the larger (as shown being used) for making wedges and heads in ordinary size, and the smaller for inserting signs. By changing the position of the stylus in the hand, the user can make every variety of cuneiform sign. The bone stylus was an improvement over the earlier reed stylus. (Courtesy of the Ashmolean Museum, Oxford)

conies, lavatories, and drains. The dead were buried under the floor of the house—a practice that sometimes forced families to build new quarters, leaving the old house to its former inhabitants.

Though the shortage of stone was a hindrance, Sumerian sculptors were skilled artists, and their work is vivid and strong. Unfortunately some of the best pieces, done in bronze, were destroyed when the statues were melted down to recover the metal. Fine examples of their carving of seals and stelai have survived, however, and some of their stone carvings in the round.

Writing

The Sumerians were among the first peoples to develop systems of writing. Their earliest written language made use of pictures to represent things; then a simpler system was evolved, which used symbols to stand for syllables or whole words. But the Sumerians never made the next step: that of a phonetic alphabet, in which each sign stands for a sound.

Sumerian writing was inscribed on tablets of soft clay by means of a reed that made wedge-shaped (cuneiform) marks, and then the tablets were hard baked to preserve them. Even though the syllabic system was cumbersome and the clay tablets were by no means a convenient writing material, the Sumerians made effective use of their writing, and vast numbers of their records have come down to us.

Babylonian Literature

The uses to which Sumerian writing was put were varied, including works of a religious nature, such as texts of omens, charms, and hymns, as well as documents of commerce and codes of law. Beyond these practical uses, the Sumerians also ventured into literature, though this was closely connected with religion. The great *Gilgamesh Epic* tells the story of the Creation and the Flood, much as does the Book of Genesis in the Bible. Other writings recounted the adventures of heroes who went through harrowing and incredible experiences, involving gods, men, and abundant imagination.

A more sophisticated form of literature is seen in the lamentations, composed on occasions of great calamity, such as the fall of a city or the humiliation of its patron god. Some of these laments have the power to move the reader of today, as, for example, the one inspired by the tragic overthrow of Ibi-Sin, which tells how Ur was taken, the land devastated, and the king carried off into captivity in Elam.

Religion

The religious achievements of the Sumerians were rich and varied, but theirs was not an elevating religion of love and trust, inspiring peace and understanding. Rather it was a cult of fear and horror, in which the endeavor to exalt virtue was less important than the desperate attempt to placate capricious deities.

The Sumerian religion, which was taken over by the Semites, was polytheistic. Its numerous gods represented the important and impressive aspects and forces of nature. Among them were gods and goddesses of the sun, moon, earth, sky, the rivers, wind, rain, plague, love, and war. The relationships among these gods were confused, since, as we mentioned earlier, each city had a patron deity to whom it gave first place, and when one city won supremacy over another, it forced the vanquished city to recognize the supremacy of its patron god, who had assured the victory.

The gods were conceived of as anthropomorphic—of human form and personality—living in their temples in the cities, which their priests and devotees attended. Food and worship were provided for the gods, and even wives—the temple prostitutes—by whom they were believed to have children.

Life after death was not a matter of large importance, since the religion did not teach a belief in Heaven or Hell. But the dead were presumed to enter into a world of shades, and the living had to make offerings to insure the passage of the deceased to the netherworld. Otherwise their ghosts would take vengeance upon the living.

For these rites in behalf of the dead, as well as to provide magic charms for the cure

of illness, the services of priests were required. The soothsayers, too, performed the important function of reading the omens of the future and warning of impending disaster. One method of forecasting was by reading the omens in the liver of the sacrificial sheep. Another was by astrology.

From their role in rites such as these, as well as in the regular services of worship designed to propitiate the gods, the priests gained enormous power and wealth. The whole of society was at their mercy, and the poor were especially hard pressed to meet their exactions. At times the kings intervened to curb the priests, but so great was their prestige that a king who undertook such reform courted trouble and sometimes lost his throne in the outcome.

All education was in the hands of the priests, and thus their influence was paramount in the whole intellectual life of the land. In the temple schools, students were taught the intricate system of writing, so that they might become scribes, some of them in the service of the temples. Mathematics was also taught, and the Semitic as well as the Sumerian language. Students who so desired could pursue more specialized studies, leading to such professions as medicine, the priesthood, and architecture.

Hammurabi and the Great Code

The Code of the Laws of Hammurabi evidences the debt that the Semites owed to the Sumerians. The differences between the two peoples in their social, moral, and religious ideas can be seen by comparing the earlier Sumerian codes with that of Hammurabi, which dates from a time when the Semites were masters. Generally the Semitic laws are harsher, setting much more severe penalties for such crimes as adultery, helping slaves to escape, and offenses of slaves against their masters.

An interesting point about these laws is that they prescribe various penalties for the

Code of the Laws of Hammurabi. This is a front view of the 8-foot stele found at Susa, where it had been taken as war booty by an Elamite king. The Code, 3600 lines long, extends around the entire shaft. The bas relief at the top shows Hammurabi before the god Marduk, who is handing to the king the code of laws—the divine origin of the laws. The rays behind his shoulders show that Marduk is the sun-god. (Louvre Museum. *Archives Photographiques*)

same offense, according to the social class of the person who committed the offense. The aristocracy was favored in certain cases involving personal injuries, but in other breaches of the law the penalty for members of the upper class was harder than for the common man. The laws concerning property were complex, as would be expected in a thriving commercial civilization. Much attention was also given to moral offenses and those arising from a failure to respect obligations to the state.

THE HITTITES

During the nineteenth century a series of apparently unrelated archaeological discoveries were made in Asia Minor and the Near East, but not until the 1880's did scholars identify these as Hittite ruins and broach the idea of a Hittite empire. Despite mention in the Bible, the Hittites had been lost to history. During the last fifty years further archaeological studies and a vast amount of scholarship have done much to rid the Hittites of the mystery that surrounded them.

Although we do not know exactly where they originated, we do know that some time around 2000 B.C. the Hittites migrated from the northeast or the northwest into Asia Minor, subjugating the native peoples and establishing city-states, one of which was their capital, Hattusas, in the great bend of the Halys River, near present-day Boghaz-köy. The language that they brought with them is now known to be of the Aryan group, parent tongue of all Indo-European peoples.

Apparently the Hittites achieved great military power early in the second millennium B.C. They had already made conquests in northern Syria before they destroyed Babylonia about 1600 B.C. and had left the wreckage to the Kassites because control was impossible over such a distance. But not until the fifteenth century did Hatti become a great imperial nation. By that time the Hittite kings had begun to establish themselves strongly in northern Syria and Mesopotamia, and were receiving tribute even from Thutmose III of Egypt (see map, p. 78).

The great ruler Suppiluliumas (1375–1335 B.C.) began a new and more daring venture at expansion, pitting his strength against that of two powerful neighbors: the kingdom of the Mitanni, which at this time dominated Assyria, and Egypt, which held control of Syria. Against great odds, the Hittite king won complete success. Mitanni was forced to become a subject ally of Hatti, while northern Syria was wrested from Egypt. Mursilis II (1334–1306) consolidated his father's holdings, while waging further wars, and under his son Muwatallis (1306–1282) Ramses II was defeated at Kadesh on the Orontes (1296), barely escaping with his life. Since neither party wished to press the struggle to a conclusion, for further warfare would have taxed Egypt severely and Hatti was feeling the menace of the Assyrians, the treaty that we have already mentioned was eventually signed by Ramses II and King Hattusilis III (1275–1250), whereby northern Syria remained in the hands of the Hittites.

Gradually thereafter the empire fell apart. The alliances that the Hittites had made with the peoples to the east and to the west did not endure, and new migrations of unknown peoples poured across the borders. About 1200 B.C. Hattusas was burned, although Hittite culture was preserved for another 500 years in the city-states of northern Syria and Cilicia.

Hittite Culture

Though the Hittite civilization was not so original or so polished as the Sumerian, it made a number of notable advances. One of these was the use of the horse, which the Hittites learned from the Kassites. Another was the use of iron, which was smelted in the rocky Anatolian highlands of Hatti.

Iron provided a new and better material for the manufacture of tools and weapons, but the horse conferred a boon of no less importance. Although the ass and the camel continued to be used for common work, the horse was much more adaptable to the needs of men in western Asia. With a swift horse a man could traverse meadowland, desert, and mountain much faster than ever before. This made possible much closer relations between states. Hundreds of letters were carried back and forth between Assyria and Babylon and Egypt and Hatti and the cities of Syria and Phoenicia. Great treaties were made between states so far distant from one another that in earlier times they had had virtually no contact. New trade routes were

Bas Relief of a Hittite Deer Hunt. Chariots of most ancient people were clumsy carts with four solid wheels. It was the Hittites who perfected the light battle chariot, which, by the time of the great battle with the Egyptians, carried two fighting men besides the driver. (Louvre Museum. *Archives Photographiques*)

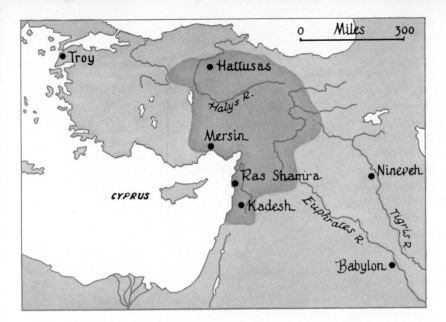

The Hittite Empire about 1350 B.C. The extent of the Hittite domain can only be guessed at from remains that have been unearthed over a wide area.

established, and with commerce, knowledge was carried far and wide. For example, the cuneiform writing of the Sumerians now spread throughout the Ancient Orient and was adopted for use in diplomatic relations by both the Hittites and the Egyptians. Such were the advances in civilization that the horse helped bring about.

As the empire began to emerge, the Hittite kings established a form of constitutional monarchy—probably the first in history—in which the king was to some extent responsible to a council of nobles, the *pankus,* and in which succession by the male heir was established by law. Since the Hittite rulers were never god-kings, their legal status was derived from the pankus. At the same time (*c.*1500 B.C.) a code of laws was written down. Although the Hittites borrowed much from the Babylonians and Assyrians, the code was surprisingly humane, not being based on the "tooth for a tooth" principle.

One of the best sources of information about the Hittites is their extensive monumental art. Some of their carvings were done on the living rock, some on separate blocks of stone. Many scenes are presented—gods and goddesses, religious processions (including priests and male and female worshipers), soldiers, hunting expeditions, lions,

sphinxes, double-headed eagles, libations, and feasts. These sculptures give evidence of how much the Hittites borrowed from neighboring peoples and show a fair mastery of the technique of carving on stone.

The sculptures also show how the Hittites looked and dressed. In appearance they were a not-unattractive people of the Armenoid type, with high-crowned heads and aquiline noses, a good deal sturdier in build than the Egyptians. Because their climate was cold and snowy in winter, they were well clothed, with shirts, mantles, hats, and upturned shoes. Their warriors wore high, conical hats and sometimes carried swords with curved blades. Women wore mantles and full skirts and high, round, brimless hats. In some carvings the men have pigtails; usually they are beardless.

The palaces, temples, forts, city walls, and gates of their cities indicate that the Hittites were builders of no little ability. The great palace of Hattusas, constructed of bricks and wood on a stone foundation, was a large edifice of many rooms, residential apartments, and halls, provided with courts. The forts were strongly built of stone, and they were strategically placed on heights.

Like their predecessors, the Hittites attached much importance to religion. Their ruler was a priest-king, and the priests had much influence. The chief god was Teshub, the storm-god, who is sometimes represented with a trident or bolt of lightning in his hand and sometimes astride a bull. Another leading divinity was the mother-goddess, with whom was associated a young male god. Her emblem was the lion, on which she is sometimes shown standing. There was a host of other divinities, representing favored regions and forces of nature, and one of the

few known pieces of Hittite literature is the *Prayers in Time of Plague,* addressed by Mursilis II to the weather-god.

By diverse means the Hittites stamped their impression on the records of history— by pioneering work in the use of iron, by their great empire that so strongly influenced the course of history in the second millennium B.C., by their adaption and transmission of the achievements of other Asiatic peoples, and by original contributions in art.

THE ERA OF THE SMALLER STATES

The centuries after the fall of Hatti were a period when no great power existed in the Ancient East. In Assyria, Babylonia, and Egypt no rulers of vigor or prominence held the throne. In the absence of great empires a number of small kingdoms were able to flourish. The peoples who had the most significant roles in the development of civilization in this period were the Phoenicians, inhabitants of the northern coast of Syria, who now stood forth as an independent nation of seafarers; the Philistines, the Aramaeans, and the Hebrews, all of whom were newcomers; and the Cretans, whose Minoan civilization will be discussed in the next chapter.

The Phoenicians

The Phoenicians were early settlers in the western part of the Fertile Crescent. Though one of the Semitic peoples, they were of mixed ancestry, as were the Canaanites. And like the Canaanites, the Hebrews, and the Philistines, the Phoenicians were never strongly organized as a nation. The cities that they founded shared a common culture, but they had no political links with one another, nor did they band together in trading ventures. They were able to maintain their independence as long as no great empire threatened them. But in the ninth century B.C. the Assyrians subjugated them.

Phoenician Settlements about 500 B.C.

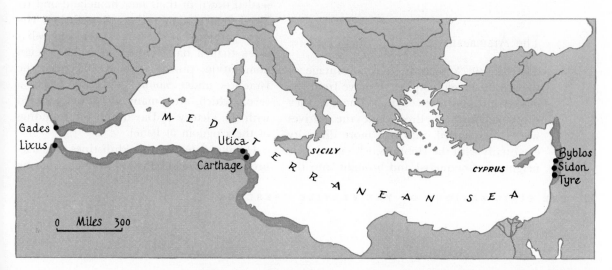

Gades
Lixus
Utica
Carthage
M E D I T E R R A N E A N   S E A
SICILY
CYPRUS
Byblos
Sidon
Tyre
0   Miles   300

In the period of their independence, however, the Phoenicians developed an extensive and lucrative commerce, especially by sea across the Mediterranean, taking goods —and ideas—from the civilized lands of the east to the backward peoples of Europe and the west. Among their oldest trading stations and colonies were Lixus on the Atlantic coast of North Africa and Gades (Cadiz) on the Atlantic coast of Spain, Utica on the Mediterranean shore of Africa and near-by Carthage which became their greatest colony.

The religion of the Phoenicians was far from admirable. It involved cruel superstitions, licentious rites in honor of the goddess Astarte, and the sacrifice of children, who were burned alive. Some of these customs penetrated to the Jews of Israel. For example, Ahab built a temple to the Baal of Tyre for Jezebel, one of his wives, who was a Phoenician.

Fortunately the Phoenicians had something better to contribute to civilization than their religion. Their greatest accomplishment was the alphabet they began to use about 1500 B.C., probably by a refinement of the Egyptian symbols. Among the peoples to whom the Phoenicians taught their alphabet were the Greeks of the Aegean, who improved it by adding vowels—the Phoenicians themselves used only consonants. Along with the new writing went the use of papyrus and ink, which they had learned from the Egyptians, which made a much less cumbersome process than inscription on stones or clay tablets.

The Aramaeans

The Semitic Aramaeans took advantage of the fall of the old empires to move from the desert into northern Syria. Though they easily subdued or drove out the natives where they settled, they had more difficulty eventually with the Hebrews, who were their neighbors. Conquered and brought into the Hebrew empire by King David, they later regained their independence. In the eighth century B.C. they were conquered by the Assyrians and thereafter did not recover their freedom. The Aramaean civilization did not disappear, however, but continued under alien rule.

The cultural career of the Aramaeans in the centuries after their defeat paralleled that of the Phoenicians, except that, instead of turning westward to the sea, they developed an overland trade toward the east. They adopted the Phoenician alphabet and transmitted it to the peoples to the east— Assyrians, Persians, Indians—as well as to the neighboring Hebrews. Their simplified writing and their extensive and valuable trade made them and their language known everywhere in the Near East.

The Hebrews and the Philistines

The Hebrews, like all their close neighbors except the Philistines, Egyptians, and Hittites, were a Semitic people. After a long period of nomadic wandering, they settled sometime before the end of the thirteenth century B.C. in the land of Canaan. Their invasion of Palestine was slow, involving much warfare and the gradual assimilation of the Canaanites, much of whose culture the ruder Hebrews adopted.

About 1200 B.C., in the midst of an upheaval of peoples that affected the whole of the Near East, the non-Semitic Philistines invaded Palestine and subjugated the Hebrews. In time, however, as the Philistines settled down in their new homeland and relaxed their vigilance, they allowed their Hebrew subjects to rearm. After somewhat more than a half century of harsh foreign domination, probably about 1025 B.C., the Israelites under Samuel and Saul began a revolt which, after many vicissitudes, ended with the victory of David and the founding of the kingdom of Israel.

Having defeated the Philistines, the Hebrew conqueror subdued all the neighboring peoples. Solomon (*c*.973–*c*.933 B.C.), the son and heir of David, ruled over a great and wealthy kingdom, far exceeding the meager holdings of his ancestors before the Philistine invasion. Yet even before Solomon's death, the Hebrew empire had begun to shrink, and soon it broke apart, giving rise to the two separate kingdoms of Israel (or Ephraim) in the north and Judah in the south.

Thereafter the glory of the Hebrew empire was gone for good. In the ninth century B.C. the Hebrews passed under the domination of the Assyrians, who, in the next century, destroyed the northern kingdom of Israel. Early in the sixth century B.C. the Chaldaeans laid waste the surviving kingdom of Judah, dispersing the population and carrying off part of it into captivity. Later on, when the Persians became masters of the Near East, the Hebrews gained a measure of freedom from persecution, but they did not recover their independence.

The Economic Life of the Hebrews. In their early days the tribes of Israel were shepherd people, and some of them always remained so, especially those living in the south. But after the conquest of Canaan, they also took up agriculture and the simple crafts, which they learned from the more advanced Canaanites. By the time of Solomon they had also built up an extensive commerce, the profits of which helped support the expensive grandeur of Solomon's court with its great temple and palace. Especially in the northern region of Israel did town life thrive, which meant that commerce and industry were flourishing.

Hebrew Society. In the time of Moses (*c.* 1200 B.C.), the social organization of the Hebrews was that of a simple pastoral people. With the beginning of town life, however, and later with the creation of the kingdom of David, conditions changed. The elders of the tribes, who previously had wielded authority, were replaced by a new aristocracy comprising the relatives and henchmen of the king. Another new element was the middle class, composed of the wealthy merchants of the towns, whose social rank was between that of the nobles and the poorer herdsmen. As in most ancient societies, slaves made up the lowest class.

The laws of the Hebrews reveal considerable concern for justice and an earnest attempt to maintain a high standard of morality. Women, though not the equals of men in Jewish society, were accorded a position of respect. However, the Jews of David's time were about as cruel and bloodthirsty as their neighbors, although their laws were superior to those of the Code of Hammurabi, which dates from perhaps 1000 years earlier.

Neither in science nor in art did the Jews distinguish themselves. Though they learned to carry on simple crafts and industries, they were so lacking in skill that Solomon had to import Phoenician artisans to plan and decorate his great temple and palace in Jerusalem.

Hebrew Literature. Literature was another matter. In this field, the ancient Hebrews knew how to express themselves admirably. In their legends, traditions, history, and poetry as recorded in the Old Testament, they created one of the greatest literary monuments of all time. The story of their wanderings, their wars, their crimes, their tragedies, and their successes was inspired and embellished by the magnificent motif, running through all their literature, of the development of their mighty religion, which was truly their most significant contribution to civilization.

Hebrew Religion. One reason why their religion is regarded as so remarkable is that it was the first and greatest of all the eastern religions to attain to a permanent monotheism. At its best, it taught the highest ideals of moral and ethical excellence, and it strongly influenced the later religions of Christianity and Mohammedanism.

Reverse of a Coin from Judah —showing a bearded man sitting on a winged wheel, supporting an eagle in his hand. The obverse shows a helmeted head. The bearded man is assumed to be Jahweh in the guise of the Greek god Zeus. Until the time of King Josiah, at the end of the seventh century, B.C., God was commonly pictured. Then the discovery of an old copy of what was probably Deuteronomy renewed and strengthened the injunction forbidding such representation. But the habit of picturing God died hard. Ezekiel was still preaching against it, and this coin was made in either the fifth or fourth century B.C. (Courtesy of Union of American Hebrew Congregations)

The superiority of the Hebrew religion was not gained all at once or easily. Rather it was the product of change and development over a long period of many trials and bitter misadventures. At the beginning of their history, in fact, when they settled in the land of the Canaanites and for long thereafter, the religion of the Hebrews was no better and no worse than other religions of the day.

From their earliest time, before they moved into Canaan and settled there, the Jews worshiped a god whom they called Jahweh. The worship of Jahweh was what held the Jews together as a people in the time when they were beset by Canaanites, Philistines, and other enemies. But their religion did not elevate their moral standards. The law of "a tooth for a tooth" was accepted; human sacrifice was tolerated; and the command not to kill did not prevent wholesale murders.

The age of Solomon, which marks the peak of the Hebrews' political power, was not an age of religious wisdom and advance. Solomon, like other despots of the time, paid tribute to foreign gods as well as his own, and he did much to bring the priesthood to a new and regrettable prominence. It was to the interest of the priests to magnify the importance of liturgy, sanctuaries, and other externals, and to insist upon a strict adherence to the exact letter of the law in all matters touching religion. After the breakdown of the Hebrew kingdoms, the power of the priests over their people was unrestricted.

Yet in this inauspicious period of political decline and priestly dominance, the religion of the Hebrews was made over into a more spiritual and exalted faith than any the world had known before. This revolution was the work of a succession of great religious teachers, or prophets, whose message is preserved in some of the most important books of the Old Testament. Foremost among them in this era were Amos, Isaiah, Micah, and Hosea.

The idea that these prophets set forth was that Jahweh was a god who valued justice, honesty, and kindness, who could not be propitiated by mere rituals of worship and sacrifices that meant nothing to the givers, who loved his people but nevertheless punished wrongdoing. The woes that were coming upon the Hebrews, the prophets proclaimed, were the punishment that Jahweh visited upon them for their pride, their love of wealth, their indifference to the sufferings of the weak.

The kingdom of Israel fell to the Assyrians in 721 B.C. To no avail later prophets repeated the warnings given before, and in 586 B.C., the Chaldean Nebuchadrezzar II destroyed Jerusalem. Soon after this disaster the prophet Isaiah took the final step toward the new religion when he proclaimed Jehovah [Jahweh] the one and only God, creator of all, thus expressly stating the Hebrew doctrine of monotheism.

ASSYRIAN CIVILIZATION

The Assyrian Empire

The creation of the Assyrian Empire in the ninth century B.C. brought to an end the era of the small states of Syria and Palestine. Thereafter the Assyrians held the center of the stage in western Asia until their fall at the end of the seventh century B.C.

Assyria lay in Upper Mesopotamia and the region to the east. The western part of the country was a high rolling plain, while the area east of the Tigris River, extending to the Zagros Mountains, was a land of hills, woods, and great streams. Here the Semitic Assyrians had settled before the middle of the third millennium B.C. (doubtless after much wandering) and had pushed still farther, until eventually their rule extended from Elam to the borders of Egypt.

The Assyrian Empire reached its peak under Sargon II (722–705 B.C.). He defeated the Israelites and all his other enemies, including the Egyptians, but when revolts broke out in Elam and Babylonia, the Egyptians seized the opportunity to regain their independence. Eventually a new power—the Medes—arose on the plateau to the east of Assyria. Allied with the king of Chaldea and the Scythians, another new invading people, the Medes, took and destroyed Nineveh, the Assyrian capital, in 612 B.C. Soon the remnants of the Assyrian armies were crushed, and the greatest empire yet created ceased to exist.

Assyrian Culture

The unprecedented conquests of the Assyrians were owed to their army, which was the most highly organized in the history of the Ancient Orient. In early times the army was based upon the conscription of the peasants, but later it became a standing army, made up of soldiers who took long-term service. Eventually foreigners had to be enlisted as well as Assyrians.

The army comprised several branches—engineers, whose services were used in siege

Assyrian Empire, 750–625 B.C.

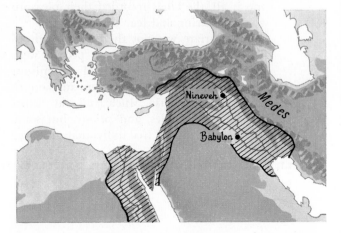

operation as well as on the march; cavalry; corps of chariots; and infantry, in which were included pikemen, slingers, and archers. The soldiers were provided with protective coats of mail, helmets, and metal or wicker shields. Much use was made of spies, and the topography of the region to be invaded was carefully studied before the start of a campaign.

In their conquests the Assyrians deliberately resorted to a policy of frightfulness. They not only killed or enslaved their enemies and laid waste the land, but they boasted in the most cold-blooded way of their atrocities. Towns were leveled to the ground or destroyed by fire and flood. The heads of corpses were cut off and heaped into pyramids or stuck upon the battlements. Victims were flayed alive, blinded, impaled, or entombed alive. Others were mutilated and left in the sun to die slowly. Holocausts were made of youths and maidens. And to top it all, the kings recorded their pleasure at the suffering and fear they caused.

But warfare was not the only pursuit of the Assyrians. Most of their people were peasants, tilling the land, and agriculture was the most important element in the economic life of Assyria. Much land was owned by the king, nobles, and priests, but some was in the hands of free individuals of lower rank. However, most of the peasants were serfs. The crops included grain, dates, grapes, vegetables, and spices, while sheep and goats were also raised by the great estate owners. Oxen were used for plowing, and horses in war and the hunt.

Commerce and industry, which the aristocracy scorned, were never so important in the Assyrian economy as in the Sumerian and Babylonian. These sources of wealth were left to slaves or foreigners, like the Aramaeans, who made much profit from trading. But mining was a source of wealth that interested the kings, and so was war, which was almost a business in Assyria.

The most privileged group in Assyrian society comprised the royal family, nobles, and priests. Next came the wealthy merchants, landowners, and artisans; at the bottom were the serfs and slaves, whose lot was hard.

The integrity of the family was highly respected by the Assyrians. For this reason, slaves were seldom separated from their close relatives. Women, however, were completely under the control of their husbands, who were regarded as the legal owners of their wives. The world of the Assyrians, like that of most other ancient peoples, was a man's world.

Like almost all religions thus far noted, except the Hebrew, the Assyrian religion

III

Assyrian Kings

Tiglath-Pileser I	c.1115–c.1102 B.C.
Ashurnasirpal III	c.884–c.860
Shalmaneser III	d.825
Tiglath-Pileser III	745–728
Shalmaneser V	728–722
Sargon II	722–705
Sennacherib	705–687
Esar-Haddon	681–668
Ashur-Bani-Pal	c.669–c.626

IIIIIIIIIIIIIIIIIIIIIIIIIIIIIIIIIIIIIIIIIIIIIIIIIIIIIIIIIIIIIIIIIIIIIIIIIIIIIIIIIIIIIIIIIIIIIII

was a somber belief, resting on ignorance and fear of the forces of nature, buttressed with magic and soothsaying, and offering almost nothing in the way of ethical inspiration and hope for the future. The chief god was Ashur, originally a sun-god, who was deemed the king of gods and the lord of all creation. He was eventually exalted to so high a position that the Assyrian religion verged on monotheism, but it never quite achieved this. Ishtar (p.66) was also worshiped, both as a mother-goddess of fertility and as a stern and chaste mistress of the hunt. Other divinities were Marduk and Nabu, who were of Babylonian origin, and Shamash, who became the sun-god as Ashur rose to the superior rank of king of gods. But the worship of these gods gave the Assyrians little more than a focal point for their fears and a stimulus to conquests. The future life was conceived of as a dull and ghostly existence, as it was by other Semites.

A large group of priests existed for the performance of the rituals of worship in the temples. Other priests served as interpreters of the divine will, foretellers of the future, and masters of magic charms that would hold off evil forces.

The great constructive work of the Assyrians was not so much a matter of what they invented as, rather, the organization and preservation of what they themselves inherited. This service is clearly exemplified in Assyrian science. Though the Assyrians

added practically nothing of their own, they were quick to take over Babylonian medicine, astronomy, and mathematics, and they performed a splendid work of organizing, rearranging, and clearing up details in this fund of knowledge. The huge library of Ashur-Bani-Pal at Nineveh is an indication of this ability and interest of the Assyrians. In it the royal scholars stored up all they could find of the Babylonian cultural heritage, much of which would otherwise have perished.

Besides preserving the earlier literature of the Mesopotamian world, the Assyrian scribes produced a new Assyrian literature. Much of this is in the form of letters, reports, omens, and historical records of the deeds of the kings and the events of their reign.

More impressive was the Assyrian accomplishment in art. Architecture was grand and ornate. Huge palaces were built of brick and wood on stone foundations and were decorated with reliefs, metal statues, paintings on the walls, and colored enamel work. Intricate arrangements of courts, rooms, stairways, passages, and gardens gave an im-

Assyrian Winged Bull. One of the bas reliefs from Sargon II's palace at Khorsabad. (Louvre Museum. *Archives Photographiques*)

pressive quality of grandeur, appropriate to the buildings of great conquerors. Vaults, domes, and arched doorways appear, and even the column. The ancient ziggurat was taken over.

Some notable work was done in the minor arts, particularly in metal work. The colossal lions and winged bulls placed at the gates of palaces are famous, but the best artistic creations of the Assyrians were in the relief sculpture that adorned the lower section of the walls. In them, the human figures are not nearly so well done as the scenes from nature. The representation of animal life, especially scenes from the hunt, seemed to release Assyrian sculptors from cramping conventions. Lions, wild asses, deer, gazelles, horses, hunting dogs, and birds are magnificently portrayed. These unsurpassed animal carvings are alone enough to establish the Assyrians firmly among the great artists of the world.

THE CHALDEAN OR NEW BABYLONIAN EMPIRE

Before the fall of the Assyrian Empire, Babylonia had risen to prominence as a subsidiary state, and Babylon had been sacked again, about 689 B.C., as the hotbed of attempted uprisings against Sennacherib. With the death of Ashur-Bani-Pal, Nabopolassar, the ruler of Babylonia, established Babylonian independence and, allying himself with the Medes and the Persians, helped to bring about the capture of Nineveh and the downfall of the Assyrians.

Although the mighty power of Babylonia was to last less than 100 years, its influence was immediately felt, and the empire that Nabopolassar created is known both as the Chaldean Empire and as the New Babylonian Empire. With the area of the Fertile Crescent securely his, Nabopolassar set out to curb Egyptian designs to re-establish their empire in the Near East, and after a series of engagements, his son Nebuchadrezzar roundly defeated the Egyptians in the battle of Carchemish in 605 B.C. Thereafter Syria passed under Chaldean rule, and when the Kingdom of Judah rebelled in 597, Nebuchadrezzar captured Jerusalem. Eleven years later, after a new rebellion, he sacked Jerusalem and left it in ruins, imprisoning the king and many nobles in Babylon—this was the so-called "Babylonian captivity" of the Jews.

Under Nebuchadrezzar the Chaldean Empire reached its height, and Babylon became briefly the city that the Greek historian Herodotus described. The great walls were rebuilt; temples and immense palaces were erected; and the famous terraced gardens—the Hanging Gardens that were one of the Seven Wonders of the Ancient World—were restored.

Whether the Chaldeans, whose name appears in history only shortly before the rise of the Empire, were exiles returned to Babylonia or a related Semitic people is unimportant. Their rulers, in any case, were antiquarians *par excellence* and sought to restore many aspects of the old civilization of Hammurabi—in government, law, literature, and industry.

When they met with poor success in attempts to revive the old Babylonian religion, the Chaldeans removed all human qualities from the gods and identified them with the planets. Later this "celestial" religion was to influence the Romans, and under them Marduk became Jupiter, Nabu, Mercury, and Ishtar, Venus. With the gods elevated

Chaldean Kings

Nabopolassar	*c.*625–*c.*605 B.C.
Nebuchadrezzar	*c.*605–562
Nabonidus	d.538

to such heights, in order to learn the future that the gods had prepared for them, the Chaldeans began an intensive study of the stars, which was a mixture of astronomy and astrology.

Until long after the fall of the empire the Chaldeans remained the most capable scientists in the Ancient Middle East. It was the Chaldeans who divided the week into seven days and the day into two twelve-hour periods, and one of their astronomers calculated the length of the year with an error of only twenty-six minutes. They mapped the entire heavens, and for centuries they observed and recorded all celestial happenings.

But temple-building, religion, and science were not enough. Nabonidus, the last king—in the Bible the last king is called Belshazzar—was so at odds with the priests and so detested by the people, that Babylon fell easily to Cyrus in 538 B.C., and Babylonia became an insignificant part of the Persian Empire.

THE RISE OF THE PERSIAN EMPIRE

The Persian Empire

For centuries before the creation of the vast Persian empire of the sixth century B.C. a succession of peoples from beyond the Caspian Sea had been moving westward. Some passed into southeastern Europe, while others spread over Asia Minor, destroying the Hittite Empire, ravaging Syria and Palestine, and even attacking Egypt. The most powerful of these invaders were the last to appear—the Medes of present-day northwestern Iran, who swept over Assyria and moved into Asia Minor.

But the Medes were not to be conquerors of all the ancient civilizations, for in 550 B.C. their king was overthrown by Cyrus, the ruler of the Persians, who were closely related to the Medes. These heirs of the ages, who were to build the last and greatest of the empires of the Ancient Middle East, had lived for an unknown length of time in the southernmost part of what is now Iran. Before starting on their wider conquests, their great king Cyrus defeated the king of the Medes and began to move westward. Within a short time Cyrus conquered the Lydian kingdom of Croesus in Asia Minor and the Greek cities on the coast. Subsequently he overran the Chaldean Empire. By 538 B.C., when Babylon fell, the Persian domain reached to the borders of Egypt, including all the other lands we have thus far studied.

Thus within eleven years Cyrus well earned the right to be known as "the Great," for he had made himself one of the foremost military leaders of all history. Unfortunately little is known about him, other than the bare outline of his victories. Deserving of special mention, however, is Cyrus' liberation of the Jews. Vague though he remains as a personality, Cyrus the Great is famous as the founder of an empire that lasted more than two centuries—until another genius, Alexander the Great, brought it to an end.

Cambyses, the cruel son of Cyrus, rounded out his father's victories by the seizure of Egypt in 525 B.C. Only three years later the

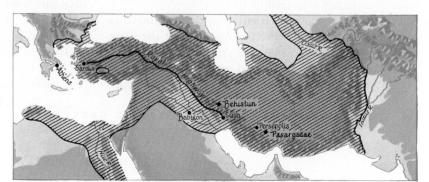

Persian Empire
about 500 B.C.

||||||||||||||||||||||||||||||||||||||||||||||||||||||||||||||||||||||||||||||||||||||||

Persian Kings

Cyrus the Great	550–529 B.C.
Cambyses	529–521
Darius I	521–485
Xerxes I	485–465
Artaxerxes I	465–425
Xerxes II	424
Darius II	423–404
Artaxerxes II	404–358
Artaxerxes III	358–338
Darius III	336–330

||||||||||||||||||||||||||||||||||||||||||||||||||||||||||||||||||||||||||||||||||||||||

king, who suffered from epilepsy, lost his mind and committed suicide. Revolution had already broken out in the empire, but this was soon ended by the nobles, who, in 521 B.C., made Darius king.

Darius, who was related to Cyrus and Cambyses, put down the revolts that confronted him, then undertook the conquest of Scythia, the region north of the lower Danube. The campaign accomplished little of importance, but it was counterbalanced by the conquest of the Punjab, the lower part of the Valley of the Indus in India. This Indian province enriched the Persian king more than any other province in the empire. Darius' next venture was to open the epoch-making series of clashes with the Greeks, to be discussed in the next chapter.

Persian Culture

Darius proved himself as constructive a genius as Cyrus, because he organized the empire that his predecessor had founded. His imperial system, which lasted for centuries, was one of the greatest political accomplishments ever recorded.

Like other Oriental monarchs and their gods, the Great King was deemed the favorite of the Persian god Ahura-Mazda. But the nature of the Persian religion was such as to permit tolerance of the gods of the other

peoples under Persian rule. Thus in Mesopotamia Cyrus associated himself with the Babylonian god Marduk, and in Egypt Cambyses and Darius associated themselves with Ra. Likewise the Jews were allowed to keep their religion, and respect was shown for the Greek shrine at Delos.

A similar policy of enlightened toleration was followed respecting local customs and traditions, and in the smaller kingdoms, where feasible, the native rulers were kept on as vassal kings. Thus the peoples under Persian rule suffered relatively little disturbance, though the Persians themselves remained a privileged people in their empire, and their homeland was relieved of regular taxation.

To earn the good will of the subject peoples, which was an obvious purpose of Darius' political system, the king contributed to rebuilding of religious monuments and carried out numerous public works. Such, for example, were the completion of a canal joining the Nile with the Red Sea and the construction of roads connecting the various parts of the Empire with Susa, its capital. These roads, such as the one which traverses the 1500 miles from Sardis to Susa, were provided with posting stations, so that royal messengers might continue night and day at the greatest speed. The roads were used by private persons—traders and travelers—as well as the officials of the government and the armies of the king.

For administrative purposes the Persian Empire was divided into twenty *satrapies*, or provinces, each supervised by a *satrap*, or governor, who had tremendous powers. To check the satrap, however, a secretary was appointed, who reported directly to the king; a military commander, likewise responsible only to the king, had charge of the garrison, over which the satrap had no power. A secret police—the "Eyes and Ears of the King"—afforded a further check.

By the standards of the times the Persian rule was humane, enlightened, and efficient. The governmental system was well in advance of any other that existed in the first millennium B.C. or before. By our standards the Persian king was cruel and despotic. He had no conception whatever of individualism but regarded his subjects as slaves, fit only to grovel at his feet. Though more humane than the Assyrians, the Persians of Darius' time did not hesitate to flay their enemies alive or mutilate them or inflict other barbaric punishments.

Socially and economically, the organization of the Persians at the time of their conquests was comparatively undeveloped. The population was made up principally of strong, rather uncouth, peasants, who lived a simple, agricultural or nomadic life on the plains and hills of the Iranian plateau. They were ruled over by a highly privileged caste of nobles, who owned vast estates and had great influence in the conduct of public affairs. Towns were few, and trade and industry were of little importance.

After winning their empire, the Persians had the good judgment not to interfere with the more productive economy of the lands under their rule. Instead they encouraged trade and industry and grew rich from it. A respectable coinage was issued, and the work of skilled artisans flourished.

The art of the Persians was borrowed largely from the Assyrians, Hittites, Babylonians, Egyptians, and even the Greeks, for the Persians themselves had no ancient esthetic tradition. Their art was called into being suddenly, to give splendor to the court of the king, and it had little influence after the Persian Empire disappeared.

The principal artistic work was in architecture and decorative sculpture, devoted to the building and ornamentation of palaces —the Persians never erected temples. Though Susa was the capital of the Empire, the grandest buildings were at Pasargadae and Persepolis in the remote land of Persia. Stone was easily obtainable and much used for foundations, stairways, and columns. The use of the column gave Persian palaces quite a different appearance from those of Mesopotamia, and the columns themselves were much lighter than those which the Egyptians used. Colossal statues of winged bulls recall those of Assyria. The walls of the great stairways at Persepolis are covered with relief carvings that show processions bringing tribute and performing other services. At Persepolis are also to be seen friezes done in brightly colored enamel. These, like the relief carvings, are well done but rather stiff and conventional. The tombs of the Persian kings that were cut in the living rock near Persepolis are also interesting and suggest an Egyptian influence.

The Persians derived their learning, like their art, largely from their more civilized neighbors. They took over the cuneiform writing of Mesopotamia, adapting it to their own language and devising a cuneiform alphabet. They also made use of Aramaic, which was already widely known through the western lands under their rule. The old

Winged "Genii." Part of a frieze of colored (not enameled) bricks on the palace at Susa. The two winged sphinx (or genii) with human heads have lions' bodies. Above them is the holy winged symbol of Ahura-Mazda (see p. 90). (Louvre Museum. *Archives Photographiques*)

Darius and His Prisoners. High above the great road from Babylon to Ecbatana is the Rock of Behistun, on which Darius told how he quelled a rebellion. The satraps shown here typify dress and ethnological peculiarities of the various peoples of the empire. (Courtesy of British Museum)

Persian language survives in inscriptions, such as the one carved on the cliff wall at Behistun. This gives an account of Darius' victories over the rebels at the time of his accession to the throne. It is inscribed in cuneiform in three languages—Old Persian, Babylonian, and Elamite, thereby providing a key for the reading of all three.

Zoroastrianism

Though otherwise much in debt to their more civilized neighbors, the Persians had no need to borrow in the field of religion. Their own religion, Zoroastrianism, was one of the greatest of all the religions of the Ancient Orient, rivaled only by that of the Hebrews at its best and by the Hindu religion of the Punjab that Darius conquered.

The great religious teacher of Persia was a man known as Zoroaster or Zarathustra, who lived, probably, in the last half of the seventh and early part of the sixth centuries B.C. Prior to his time the Persians had a primitive religion based on the worship of numerous gods representing the forces of nature. The rituals of worship were conducted by priests called *Magi*. Like the Hebrew prophets, Zoroaster sought to purge this religion of superstition and pettiness and raise it to a higher ethical plane. He succeeded in this, despite the opposition of the old priesthood, and his religious concepts were accepted by the court late in the sixth century B.C.

The religious reformation that Zoroaster inspired established the worship of one god, Ahura-Mazda, or Ormuzd. This was a god of righteousness and truth, who had revealed his precepts to his prophet Zoroaster. He was opposed by an evil spirit, Angra-Mainyu, or Ahriman, who represented the lie— that is, the negation of truth. The world of man was conceived of as a gigantic battleground, on which the forces of good and evil contended. Every man must elect to serve on the side of one or the other of these warring gods. He might, if he desired, serve Ahriman, and this god of evil would, of course, tempt him to do so. But if instead he chose to serve the god of goodness, he must take an active role as a warrior in the cause of goodness, showing no kindness or pity for those on the other side.

Zoroaster himself intended his religion to be monotheistic. He thought of Ahura-Mazda as a supreme power, who permitted men to choose between good and evil but punished those who made the latter choice. Some of his disciples, however, modified this monotheism when they taught that evil was the work of a second god, Ahriman. In later times still other divinities were recognized. Thus Mithra, one of the old Persian gods, reappeared as a helper of Ormuzd, and Anahita, a Semitic goddess of fertility, was taken over. Eventually the old priests, the Magi, regained power, and ritualism once more became important.

Zoroaster believed in immortality, and his teaching on this point is of crucial importance. For the god of evil was doomed to ultimate defeat, though he and his cohorts did not know it. This final defeat of evil would come on the day of the last great judgment, when the dead would be restored to life. In the meantime the souls of the dead would survive in another world, where they would receive such treatment as they earned in their life on earth. Three days after death each soul was taken to a great bridge, leading across the depths of hell. If the good the man did on earth outweighed the evil, his soul would cross the bridge to a world of celestial happiness. But if the man's deeds revealed him as a servant of evil on earth, the bridge would become narrow, and his soul would fall into the realm of heavy darkness and terrible punishment. Still, even these souls would not remain in hell forever, for that would leave many of Ormuzd's creatures in the hands of his enemy. Eventually, on a day of final reckoning, the evil would be purified in molten metal, which to the good is as pleasant as warm milk. Thus hell itself would be purified, and everlasting victory would lie with truth and goodness.

THE MUSIC OF THE PEOPLES OF THE FERTILE CRESCENT

Music had a place of much prominence in Mesopotamian life, as we know from the writings that often were cast in poetic form and from the depiction of musicians and occasional references to them in the surviving documents.

Music was already well developed in earliest Sumerian times. Shepherds sang to their flocks, using the lute for accompaniment; and in their temples the Sumerians both sang and danced. Among their musical instruments were the sistrum, a kind of rattle made of cross pieces of metal; the vertical flute; the *auloi,* which was a double-reed wind instrument; the cithara, which the Sumerians probably took over from Semitic peoples; and the harp, which was their most characteristic instrument. The earliest known example of musical notation is a Sumerian hymn dating, in the extant tablet, from about 800 B.C.

The music of the Ancient East was brought to its highest point of development by the Hebrews, especially in their temple music, after 1000 B.C. This included solo, choral, and antiphonal singing and music for the dance. The range of instruments used was wide. The Book of Daniel mentions the ram's-horn trumpet (*shofar*), the vertical flute, the harp, the sackbut (which was a kind of trombone), the psaltery, and the dulcimer. The Book of Psalms and Genesis also mention organs, timbrels, small drums, and cymbals. The instrument that David used when he played before Saul was a *kinnor* or Hebrew form of lyre.

After the destruction of the second temple of Jerusalem in A.D. 70, the lavish orchestral music of the Hebrews, which in former times was said to involve as many as 4000 musicians, died out. But the ancient vocal tradition persisted, and from it is derived a part of present-day synagogue singing. Although the Hebrews had no system of notation other than signs to remind the singers of the vocal line, their musical tradition has shown remarkable constancy. In our own time Jews of widely separated lands—Yemen, south Arabia, Iran, Poland, and elsewhere—use practically the same musical formulas in their ritual as in ancient times. And in this music are preserved not only the musical heritage of the Jews themselves but also elements derived from the whole Ancient Orient.

Suggestions for Further Reading

Source Materials

Anthologies and Collected Documents

G. H. Knoles and R. K. Snyder, eds., *Readings in Western Civilization* (rev. ed., New York, 1954), pp. 3–25.
Selections from the Code of Hammurabi and from the Old Testament.

R. H. Pfeiffer, *State Letters of Assyria* (New Haven, 1935).
Official letters of the kings and other officials of Assyria. Gives a fascinating insight into Assyrian life, official and otherwise.

J. B. Pritchard, ed., *Ancient Near Eastern Texts Relating to the Old Testament* (Princeton, 1950).
An excellent selection of documents on Mesopotamian history as well as on the Hebrews. Especially valuable on showing the intellectual indebtedness of the Hebrews to Babylonia.

Contemporary Writings

E. S. Bates, ed., *The Bible Designed to Be Read as Living Literature* (New York, 1936).

A. Heidel, ed., *The Gilgamesh Epic and Old Testament Parallels* (Chicago, 1946).

C. H. W. Johns, ed., *Babylonian and Assyrian Laws, Contracts, and Letters* (New York, 1904).

Xenophon, *The Education of Cyrus;* translated by Henry G. Dakyns (Everyman's Library edition, New York, 1914).
Xenophon was a Greek historian of the fourth century, B.C.

Secondary Works

On Mesopotamia

W. H. Boulton, *Assyria* (London, 1933).
A standard account.

W. H. Boulton, *Babylonia* (London, 1933).
A standard account.

G. G. Cameron, *History of Early Iran* (Chicago, 1936).
An excellent survey from the earliest historical period to the beginning of the Achaemenian dynasty. One of the few books for the period.

C. W. Ceram (pseudonym for K. W. Marek), *The Secret of the Hittites* (New York, 1956).
An interesting account for the layman of old and new archaeological discoveries and how ancient scripts were deciphered to yield information about the old Hittite Empire.

G. Contenau, *Everyday Life in Babylon and Assyria* (New York, 1954).
A delightful description, beautifully illustrated.

L. Delaporte, *Mesopotamia* (New York, 1925).
Study of the interplay of the various peoples who inhabited Mesopotamia. Historical survey, but chiefly in terms of culture, society, and crafts.

M. N. Dhalla, *History of Zoroastrianism* (New York, 1938).
The best history of this great Persian religion.

W. Durant, *The Story of Civilization: Our Oriental Heritage* (New York, 1935).
A very interesting history of the ancient civilizations, including the Indian and the Chinese. Excellent reference book.

H. Frankfort and others, *The Intellectual Adventure of Ancient Man* (Chicago, 1946).
A series of lectures for laymen. Attempts to understand the meaning of life, the function of the state, the reality of God, the role of mythology. Deals with the east, Mesopotamia, the Hebrews, and Greeks.

J. Garstang, *The Hittite Empire* (New York, 1929).
One of the first books to deal with the Hittites as a separate and significant people. Consideration of both literary and, especially, the new archaeological evidence.

C. H. Gordon, *The Living Past* (New York, 1941).
A well-written cultural history of the Near East. Short, lively style.

P. K. Hitti, *History of Syria* (New York, 1951).
A history showing the evolutionary development of Syria, Lebanon, and Palestine from the preliterary age to the present. Emphasizes the constant meetings of Syria with the rest of the world, interacting, transmitting, and borrowing from nations it touched.

C. Huart, *Ancient Persian and Iranian Civilization* (New York, 1927).
A very extensive, though somewhat uneven coverage of the period from the prehistoric Medes and Persians to the eighth century A.D. Clear and logical in presentation.

M. Jastrow, *The Civilization of Babylonia and Assyria* (New York, 1915).
An early description of these civilizations when they were first being worked out. Some discussion of excavations and the deciphering of the language. Civilization is studied both from the excavations and the literature.

S. N. Kramer, *From the Tablets of Sumer: 25 Firsts of Man's Recorded History* (New York, 1956).
Essays on Sumerian life and thought, reflecting everyday life as well as political and religious customs and beliefs.

T. E. Olmstead, *History of Assyria* (New York, 1923).
Views the Assyrians primarily as imperialists, but also as effective administrators as well as individuals and artists.

R. W. Rogers, *History of Babylonia and Assyria* (London, 1915).
A standard book, because it was long the outstanding example of American Oriental scholarship as well as one of the first in ancient Near East history.

C. L. Woolley, *The Sumerians* (Oxford, 1928).
A study of the Sumerians down to the time of Hammurabi. Shows the Sumerian base from which came much of the later ancient Near East culture, including the Hebrew civilization. Claim presented that the Tigris-Euphrates civilization is older than Egypt and contributed much to Egypt. Done by one of the most famous Sumerian historians. Good pictures.

On Palestine

W. F. Albright, *The Archaeology of Palestine and the Bible* (New York, 1935).
Chiefly a study of the archaeological digs in Palestine. Its final chapter deals with the Bible in the light of archaeology. Lectures written for laymen.

G. A. Barton, *A History of the Hebrew People from the Earliest Times to the Year 70* A.D., *Largely in the Language of the Bible* (New York, 1930).
An attempt to tell the Jewish story largely in the language of the Old Testament itself, with connecting commentary and introduction. Especially good for Biblical history.

J. Finegan, *Light from the Ancient Past: the Archaeological Background of the Hebrew-Christian Religion* (Princeton, 1946).
Uses all kinds of archaeological materials to tie the Hebrew Near East history in with Hellenistic and Christian medieval history.

R. Kittel, *The Religion of the People of Israel* (New York, 1925).
A brief account of both the history and the theology of the Jewish people, and their theological adaptations to varying fortunes and influences.

A. Lods, *The Prophets and the Rise of Judaism* (New York, 1937).
History of the Jewish nation from the eighth-century prophets to the end of the Greek period. History plus general conclusions. Shows knowledge of literature and historical judgment. Especially good for the prophets.

G. F. Moore, *The Literature of the Old Testament* (New York, 1948.)
A book-by-book analysis of the Old Testament, giving internal evidence and manuscript traditions for validity. Considers the Bible as literature and history as well as revealed truth.

W. O. E. Oesterley and T. H. Robinson, *A History of Israel* (Oxford, 1932).
Deals with the period from the Exodus to A.D. 135. Attempts to keep religion at a minimum when viewing the tradition as history. Traces movements of the people from nomadic and pastoral existences to a settled trading community. Shows that our knowledge of the Jews must be based on the Bible but can be judged also from archaeology and other literature.

J. P. E. Pedersen, *Israel, Its Life and Culture* (New York, 1938).
Deals chiefly with the cultural aspects and developments among the Jews. Shows remarkable scholarship and knowledge of the literature.

Recordings of Ancient Near Eastern Music
Music of the Orient (Decca DX-107)

4

The Aegeans and the Greeks

Harvester Vase, found at Hagia Triada, near Phaestus. Late Minoan, c.1550 B.C., 4 inches high, it is of black steatite and originally was covered with gold leaf. (Courtesy Candia [Crete] Museum)

ometime between about 2000 and 1000 B.C. a series of waves of migrating Indo-European peoples streamed into the Greek and Italian peninsulas. In the land around the eastern Mediterranean, these incoming northern barbarians found a highly developed maritime civilization, which is known as Minoan (Cretan) and in its later periods as Mycenaean. In the process of conquering this region, the migrating barbarians learned much, and, with the aid of their own fresh genius, they created a new cultural synthesis—the classical Greek—that far surpassed all that had gone before.

THE CIVILIZATION OF THE BRONZE AGE IN THE EASTERN MEDITERRANEAN

During the same millennia that saw the rise and decline of the Egyptian and Mesopotamian civilizations, a quite different civilization arose on the islands and along the shore of the eastern Mediterranean—on the island of Crete, the Greek mainland, the coasts of Asia Minor, and on other islands as far distant as Cyprus.

Minoan Culture

In this region a Bronze Age civilization arose about 3400 B.C. The people who created it were, for the greatest part, of the short, dark Mediterranean type. Since there was no influx of other people until the Indo-European invasions of the second millennium B.C., for a period of about 2000 years the Aegean peoples were left undisturbed. Thus they gained an opportunity to make use of their talents. That they took advantage of the opportunity and that their abilities were admirable is proved by the high quality of their work.

In what is sometimes called the Early Minoan period—from *Minos*, which probably meant *ruler*, as did *pharaoh*—the transition was made from the Late Stone Age to the use of copper and then of bronze. Dur-

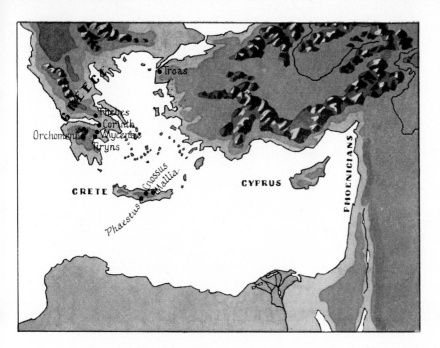

The Influence of Crete about 1550 B.C.

ing the Middle Minoan period great palaces were built in such growing urban centers as Cnossus, Phaestus, and Mallia, and trade was established with Asia Minor, Cyprus, and Egypt. In the first part of the Late Minoan period Cnossus became the dominant city of Crete and indeed of the Aegean world, and an age of unprecedented grandeur dawned. The rulers of Cnossus kept the seas free of pirates; trade flourished as never before; wealth poured into the island cities; and huge palaces arose. Gradually Cretan culture began to expand to the mainland Greece (see map, above), and the Cretans became dominant over Mycenae, Tiryns, and Corinth in southern Greece and Thebes and Orchomenus farther north. Eventually, however—about 1400 B.C.—the migrant Achaeans of the mainland threw off Cretan rule, invaded the island, and devastated it. For the next 200 years they dominated the Aegean world.

Archaeological discoveries tell us a great deal about Minoan civilization, but for many years archaeological evidence could not be supplemented by written material, because the several Bronze Age Cretan scripts remained undecipherable. Only very recently has the script known as "Linear B"

—a sort of proto-Greek—been deciphered, and some of the records and inscriptions at Cnossus and on the mainland have begun to clarify our knowledge of the later Minoan period. The earlier non-Greek Cretan scripts, however, remained unsolved.

The Minoan State

Political history in Crete followed the usual pattern. First there was clan rule; next a city-state organization. Then, at the end of the Middle or the beginning of the Late Minoan period, came the unification of Crete under the rulers of Cnossus, who eventually extended their authority to the Greek mainland.

The Minoan Economy

The great wealth of the Minoan world was produced by an unusually well-founded economy. Agriculture, vineyards, and olive and fruit orchards provided a large and diversified food supply. The Cretans kept their farms well stocked with goats, cattle, and fowl, while the sea was also a rich source of food. There was the small industry typical of great households in ancient times, and also the greater industry of palace and city.

By our standards Cretan society does not seem to have been sophisticated, but it would have seemed brilliant to our European forefathers only two or three centuries ago in comparison with their world. The Cretan cities were connected by good roads, and their well-built ships carried oil, pottery, wines, and metal to Asia, Egypt, Greece, Italy, Sicily, and beyond. From these lands they brought back other products and knowledge of other ways of doing things.

Minoan Society

Their economic diversification meant that the Cretans enjoyed a lively and varied social organization. As always in the ancient world, the large majority of the people worked for the advantage of the few—some as peasants, others as industrial or commercial laborers. But there were also skilled artisans, professional men, merchants, great landowners, and nobles.

Several features of the Minoan civilization indicate the gaiety and comparative freedom of its society. One of these is the beauty and delicacy of Minoan art. Another is the wide range of economic activity, which meant more freedom in the choice of livelihood. Still another is the exalted position of women, both in religion and in secular life. The women of Crete were not secluded creatures of the harem, as so often in the Ancient Orient. They were respected and admired, and they appeared in stylish gowns at games, dances, and in more serious pursuits.

The Cretans' love of dancing, music, and sport is itself an indication of their vivacity. The most popular of their sports was bull leaping, in which both men and women participated, and which probably had a religious meaning. In this sport a bull would be set loose to charge at a lithe youth or maiden, who would seize the animal's horns, be lifted up by the tossing head, and somersault onto the bull's back. Their love of play, such as this sport exemplifies, is one of the most valuable of the models that the early Aegeans bequeathed to their Greek successors.

Minoan Religion

In religion the Aegeans seem to have felt freer and more at peace in the world than their contemporaries, as their love of play attests.

For the most part the Aegean religion was an independent creation. The chief deity was a goddess—a Great Mother, symbol of fertility and of life and death. She is often represented partly clothed, with bare breasts, holding serpents in her hands. Sometimes she is symbolized by the dove. There was a god, too, but he was distinctly inferior in importance. Either the son or the lover of the great goddess, he represented the masculine force of reproduction. The bull came to be associated with this young male divinity, in whose honor bulls were often sacrificed.

Stones, pillars, trees, and animals had a place in Cretan religion in early times, and certain places, such as mountains, caverns, and groves, were regarded as holy. When cities were built, altars were set up in them, sometimes in little shrines, sometimes in the palace. But the great temples of Sumer and Egypt had no counterpart in the Aegean civilization, which favored a simple worship. Aegean rituals sometimes involved the sacrifice of animals or the offering to the goddess of gifts of fruit, grain, or wine. Priestesses, rather than priests, were in charge of the ceremonial sacrifices and libations, the singing, dancing, and offering of prayers. In this civilization the priesthood never became so powerful or so greedy as in other eastern lands, where men dominated the service of worship and gained strength from appeals to superstitious fear.

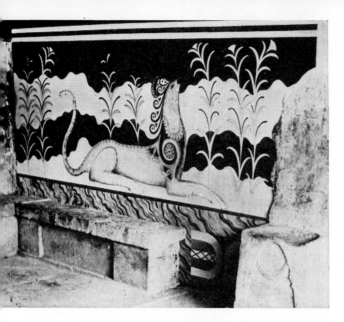

The So-called "Throne Room" in the Palace of Cnossus. Beside the monumental stone chair is a restored fresco of an eagle-griffin in a flowerbed. (British Information Services)

The Aegeans were not wholly free of religious fear, however, especially fear of what would happen to them after death. Accordingly they took pains—more than the Sumerians, though not so many as the Egyptians—with the proper disposal of the bodies of the dead. Tombs were provided for them, with supplies of food and drink, weapons, and little statues of their companions and servants.

Minoan Art

The esthetic creations of the peoples of the Aegean give the most impressive and revealing indication of their nature and their great abilities. Their work tells of a people delighting in beauty, imaginative, gay, and individualistic. Convention and ostentation are by no means absent from Aegean art; yet the artists were fascinated by nature and freer to experiment than were their contemporaries in Asia and Africa. Hence their art shows marvelous freedom and diversity.

The architecture of the Cretans and their neighbors was not, by conventional standards, their most admirable accomplishment.

To a modern observer it seems as though the architects of a building never quite made up their minds as to the plan. The palaces were expanded in a haphazard manner that would have sorely distressed the precise-minded planners of an Egyptian pyramid or hypostyle hall. Their floor plans and appearance therefore show a disconcerting indifference to symmetry. Columns were not placed uniformly, and doorways might be near a corner rather than in the center of a wall.

The greatest architectural works of the Ancient Orientals were temples dedicated to the gods; not so the Minoans. Their religious buildings were simple, and often sanctuaries were merely rooms within buildings of a nonreligious nature. The palaces were quite unimpressive when viewed from without; as a matter of fact, they were not built to be admired but to be lived in. The royal residents of the palaces made additions to them whenever and however they pleased, and the result was usually a vast but not majestic edifice. So far as possible, buildings were comfortable and convenient, arranged so as to receive ventilation, sunlight, and shade. One feature of the great palaces of Crete that shows the skill of the islanders was their superb plumbing system. Water for drinking and bathing was piped into the palaces, and a drainage system carried off the rain and waste water.

Aegean sculpture contrasts strikingly with that of Egypt. The Cretans confined their efforts to small works, made of faïence (earthenware), ivory, and steatite (soapstone), but these works were sensitively conceived and skillfully executed. The same high standard of craftsmanship was shown in work in metal and stone. Examples of this include gold trinkets, death masks, vases, rhytons of gold and silver, and bronze swords and daggers, which were wonderfully ornamented with delicate inlay and engraving. The Cretans also painted, with beauty, vigor, and color, in fresco and on vases, and their pictorial works also show that this playful, dancing people loved music.

THE RISE OF GREECE

We have already mentioned that the peoples of the Greek peninsula fell under the cultural influence of the Minoans of Crete, and that eventually they overcame the island cities. It is important to look a little more fully into the early story of these mainlanders, since they had a share in the formation of one of the most brilliant and constructive civilizations in history.

The Coming of the Achaeans

Some time about 2000 B.C., as we have said, there occurred in the regions east of the Caspian Sea one of those great movements of peoples that have so often and so deeply affected the historical developments in both the east and the west. It was in the course of this movement that related Indo-European languages were carried into India, Persia, and Mesopotamia. At the same time—possibly earlier—another group of Indo-European folk migrated westward into the Danube Valley, then southward into Greece. Their descendants became the Achaeans.

Gradually the warlike Achaeans pushed down through the peninsula as far as Attica and the Peloponnesus, becoming the new ruling people and introducing their language, which we call Greek. It is interesting to note that it is this Bronze Age script used by the Achaeans which was deciphered while the earlier Cretan scripts are still unreadable.

As the centuries passed, an old story was retold in the Aegean lands. Under the dominance of the Cretans, the Achaeans learned the superior ways of the more advanced civilization—the advantages of settled life, social organization, the business of piracy and trading, and the vastly important art of sailing. Meanwhile the Minoan kings of Crete, like their predecessors in Sumer and Babylonia, relaxed their vigilance—with disastrous results. About 1400 B.C. the Achaeans swept across the narrow sea separating the mainland from Crete, caught their masters napping, and crushed the power of Crete once and for all.

For the two or three centuries of the succeeding Mycenaean Age—so called because

Early Indo-European Migrations

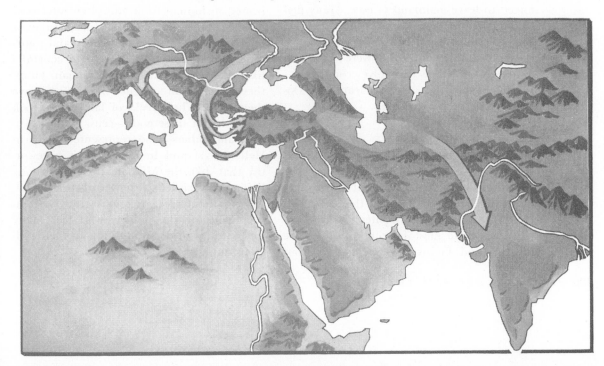

its center was Mycenae, on the Greek mainland—the Achaeans dominated the Aegean world. They superseded the Cretans in political hegemony, in trade with the islands and with Egypt, and in colonizing islands as far away as Cyprus. Though lacking in cultural creativity of their own, they contrived to extend Aegean civilization to its greatest limits in all directions.

The story of one of the sea raids of the Achaeans was given an embellished and lasting expression several centuries later in the *Iliad* of Homer. The thrilling tale of the warfare of the Achaean ships on the coasts of Troas (The Troad) in northwestern Asia Minor made so great an impression on the Aeolians, who lived to the south, that they passed it on for generations. Only long after the events it recounts was the story written down, probably about 850 B.C., in the form of the Homeric epic that we know.

The destruction of prosperous Ilium (Troy) seems to have been the last notable conquest of the bellicose Achaeans before they themselves succumbed to the superior power of the Dorians. These new invaders, related to the Achaeans, also spoke an Indo-European dialect. Their invasion began with a peaceable immigration that, about 1200 B.C., swelled to a torrent. Overwhelmed, the Achaeans were driven to more sheltered regions, such as Attica and Arcadia, or were forced to leave mainland Greece. Many fled to the coasts of Asia Minor, others to Syria and Palestine, while still others unsuccessfully attacked Egypt. Thus were the harsh conquerors of Crete themselves conquered. Warlike as had been the Achaeans, the Dorians were still less civilized.

Homeric Society

Something must be said about the society created by these new lords of the Aegean in their fortified cities. The sites of these fortress-towns, the most famous of which are Mycenae and Tiryns, have yielded generous archaeological remains. Another source of information is the poetry of Homer, which describes a society generally comparable with that of Mycenae, Tiryns, and the other great towns of the mainland. It is difficult to tell, from the poem itself, whether the society Homer describes was that in which he lived or a much earlier one.

By the time they conquered Crete, the Achaeans had passed from the backward pastoral stage of civilization to a stage involving a more advanced economy. The great families had made themselves as nearly self-sufficient as possible upon their estates; the care of the land and the raising of stock, especially horses, were occupations that a great prince could follow without shame. Other kinds of labor were less honorable, and for a time trade was considered unworthy of a well-born man. Piracy did not have the stigma of trade, however, since it involved warfare. Nobles could therefore engage in piracy, and ultimately some of them passed to the more honest forms of trade.

The religion of the Achaeans, like the rest of their civilization, was a composite: it took much from the Cretans and the earlier inhabitants of the mainland but also had some elements that the Achaeans themselves invented. Apparently the Achaeans first introduced the gods and goddesses who lived on Mount Olympus and who sometimes appeared in human form and often interfered in the affairs of men. As Homer presents them, these early gods were lusty and sometimes bloodthirsty, but they were generally likable, friendly, and almost human. Often they took pity on wretched mortals and gave them help. The Greeks of later times took over some of these gods—Zeus, Hera, Poseidon, and others—and represented them in Hellenic art and literature. It is noteworthy that, like the Minoan, the Achaean religion also lacked a powerful priesthood. Among the Greeks religious rites were in the hands of the nobles, who had many other things to do in addition to their religious duties.

The Greeks

Both physically and culturally, the Hellenes, or Greeks, were a people of mixed ancestry. The "well-greaved Achaeans" of whom Homer wrote had mingled with an earlier population that was of the Mediterranean type, as were the Cretans. Later the Dorians made their contribution to this stock of mixed blood. Hence the Greeks were the result of intermarriage between the short, dark, long-headed Mediterraneans, the round-headed Achaeans, and the Dorians, who were fair in complexion and big and strong of build.

The Land of Hellas

The term *Greece,* as used here, refers to all the settlements of the Greeks, not merely the mainland of Greece, because Greek civilization extended over a much wider area than the Greek peninsula of Europe. It included Greek settlements and colonies on the coasts of the Black Sea; along the shores of the northern Aegean as well as in the islands; in Asia Minor, southern Italy, and Sicily; and along the northwestern shores of the Mediterranean. Some of these outlying settlements were among the liveliest in the whole Greek world.

Yet the heart of the Greek world was in the communities of the Balkan Peninsula, where were located most of the great cities of classical Greece—Sparta, Corinth, Thebes, and Athens. This peninsula was not, like the Valley of the Nile and the Fertile Crescent, a rich and hospitable land. On the contrary, it presented a forbidding countryside, which only grudgingly gave up a meager yield of grain, olives, grapes, and vegetables. Because of the mountains, little of the land was arable, and most of this was rocky and poor. But sheep and goats could be raised on the hillsides, and these herds added to the income of the Greeks.

The land had some advantages to help compensate for its poverty. The mountains were of surpassing beauty, and the rivers, though turbulent and unsuited for navigation, added to the clear and vivid charm. The Greeks were far from indifferent to this majestic and inspiring natural beauty. The climate, moreover, was and is mild and healthful, more temperate than in the hot river valleys of lands farther south. And the sea around invited the Greeks to make use of their many bays and inlets, harbors, and protective islands. The Greeks exploited this resource, winning much of their wealth by fishing and maritime trade, and they used the sea as the highway to their distant colonies.

Throughout the rest of the Aegean, conditions were much the same as on the mainland. Most of the islands were rocky and poor, and mountain ranges separated the cities from one another. The more remote settlements, such as those on the Black Sea and in Sicily, found more favorable conditions for agriculture, but these were exceptions.

Geography and climate were thus important in the formation of Greek civilization. The Aegean region did not encourage slothfulness, but neither did it make the accumulation of great wealth easy or attractive. Because the sea gave them access to distant lands, the Greeks were open to the cultural influence of other peoples. But because the mountains divided their cities from one another, the Greeks could scarcely be expected to achieve political unification on a large scale.

The Dark Age: *c.*1200–800 B.C.

The Dorian invasions, which became irresistible after 1200 B.C., caused a widespread disruption of the old way of life. Some of the Achaeans from central Greece had gone across the sea to the northern coast of Asia Minor before the Dorian incursions became so powerful, and later others were forced to follow them. Other migrations took place

The Greek World

directly or indirectly, with them. As for the Dorians, they migrated to several new homes, principally in Laconia in the Peloponnesus, in Crete, and along the southern coast of Asia Minor.

When the invasions and migrations of this "dark age" had come to an end, the great centers of the old Aegean civilization had been destroyed, and, as we have said, civilization in European Greece had been set back centuries. Such of the earlier inhabitants as found it possible to remain in the peninsula had to find new homes and begin the slow process of rebuilding their civilization. Because the Dorians were the least prepared to appreciate what they had destroyed, their climb upward was slowest and most difficult. The coast of Asia Minor presented the strange and interesting phenomenon of three different groups of Greeks, all immigrants from Greece proper, speaking three different dialects of Greek: Aeolian in the north, Ionian in the center, and Dorian

within the Greek peninsula itself, generally from the northern to the central and southern regions. The Ionians, a group of especially uncertain origin, were forced to move from the Peloponnesus to Attica or across the sea to the islands or to the central section of the coast of Asia Minor, thereafter known as Ionia. Both in Attica and in Ionia they were in the forefront of Greek civilization, and most of the brilliant culture of the classical Greeks is closely connected, either

in the south. Yet the centuries of invasion and migration prepared the way for a great new civilization. And as the wanderers had finally settled down, after about 800 B.C., the patterns of a relatively stable culture began to emerge. This period of the first beginnings of settled culture, dated roughly from 800 to 500 B.C., is called the Archaic, or Formative, Age in Greek history.

The Archaic Age: *c.*800–500 B.C.

In this Archaic Age, which succeeded the Dark Age of confusion and groping, the institutions and attitudes characteristic of Hellenic society began to take shape. The society of this era is not easy to understand, for it was diverse, complicated, and changing. But it was the foundation on which later arose the classical Greek civilization, and to this period of beginnings can be traced those factors that were to give eternal luster to Greek culture, as well as those that were to limit and blight it.

Greek Colonization. One of the most important developments of this period was the spread of Greek settlements far and wide throughout the lands around the Mediterranean and the Black Sea, e.g., Byzantium was founded by Greeks from Megara in 658 B.C. The forces behind this expansion were simple, though numerous. The chief political cause was the old aristocratic family organization that prevailed among the Greeks. Under this regime, rights and privileges were in the hands of the members of the great families and, particularly, in the hands of the older men of these families. Ambitious and energetic younger men, impatient to make their names and fortunes, would thus be obliged to set out for new lands.

A more powerful force was economic discontent. As conditions became more orderly toward the end of the Dark Age, the population increased, and this produced land hunger. Since most of the land was already owned by the same great families that held political supremacy, and since they were disposed to hold on to it, many of the Greeks went abroad in search of fresh fields that they could call their own. Other economic motives were also involved. For example, some impoverished Greeks emigrated in order to take service as mercenaries at the invitations of the wealthy kings of the east. Others migrated to take advantage of opportunities abroad in trade or mining.

Colonies were planted from the western end of the Mediterranean to the eastern end of the Black Sea. The Propontis and the Euxine, as the Greeks called the Sea of Marmara and the Black Sea, attracted many settlements as did the shores of Asia Minor and the northern coasts of the Aegean and the islands scattered through the sea in this region.

Perhaps the most alluring of all the lands open to the Greeks was the west. Most of the colonies were in southern Italy, which was called Great Greece, and in Sicily. Among the more notable colonial cities were Syracuse, Naxos, Cumae, Neapolis, Tarentum, and Sybaris. But there were also numerous Greek colonies still farther west, even on the eastern coast of the Iberian Peninsula and the southern coast of Gaul. The most notable of these was Massilia, the modern Marseilles.

This protracted and far-flung colonizing effort had startling results. First, it gave the Greeks new sources of wealth to supplement the meager resources of their homeland. With wealth, the number of the Greeks increased, and their sallies across the seas were made in ever greater numbers. From their seafaring, they gained knowledge of other lands, and eventually they developed a trade that spread all around the Mediterranean. As commerce increased, fierce economic rivalries sprang up, which sometimes resulted in war among the rival Greek cities themselves.

The development of commerce led to the use of coinage. This made it possible for a

Greek Coins. (*Left*) Obverse and reverse of a silver tetradrachm of Athens, 480–470 B.C., shows the head of Athena and the owl, olive fruit, and abbreviated name of the city. (*Right*) Obverse and reverse of an electrum (pale-yellow alloy of gold and silver) one-third stater, probably struck in Lydia in first half of the sixth century, B.C. The series to which this coin belongs is one of the earliest Greek coinages. (The American Numismatic Society)

money economy to supplant the cumbersome system of barter. But the increase of commerce, making a greater demand for the products of agriculture and industry, also led to the greater use of slaves. Moreover it produced a new class of moneyed wealth. These developments brought with them ferment and change in the social order, which we shall discuss a little later in this chapter and the next.

THE RISE OF THE GREEK CITY-STATE

The Greek City-State

The economic, social, and political nuclei about which this prosperity and this expansion were developing were the Greek city-states. This form of political organization was not new, since it had existed in somewhat similar form among the Egyptians and the Mesopotamians. But the city-state had a special significance in the rise of the Greek civilization, since it was at once the visible political unit to which pertained the noblest ideals of social responsibility and the sociopolitical concept about which focused the Greek ideals of citizenship, individualism, and cultural creativity.

Like most political systems, the Greek city-state was the product of history and environment. Its origin goes back to the primitive Achaean society that Homer described. In this society the basic unit was the patriarchal clan, composed of those descended from the same divine ancestor. From time to time clans joined together to form a hereditary association known as a brotherhood. The next step was the union of several brotherhoods to form a tribe, which would still fur- ther increase their strength in time of war.

Since the tribesmen needed the protection of walls, they constructed fortified strongholds, in which they took refuge in time of need. As the fortunes of the tribe improved, the chief, or king, erected a more pretentious fortress, which was called the *polis*. Around this citadel grew up the dwellings of those who waited upon the king, and eventually this settlement became a city, as we use the term. Our word *political* comes from the Greek *polis*.

The society of these Achaean cities was dominated, it will be remembered, by the heads of the clans. Checking the power of their leader, who was king, was an advisory council of the lesser chiefs. There was also an assembly of the common men, but this had little authority.

Social Change

After the vicissitudes of the Dark Age, when the Dorians overran the Achaeans, changes came about in this social organization, especially in the cities founded by those Achaeans who fled to Asia Minor. In the upheaval the ties of the clans were loosened, and the kings lost power to the nobles. Eventually the society was wholly dominated by the aristocracy, and the king disappeared.

But no sooner did the nobility gain power than it met with threats to its pre-eminence. One of these came with the rise, in the seventh century B.C., of a new moneyed class, drawing its wealth from the trade and industry of the cities but lacking the prestige of the old landowning aristocracy. This menace the aristocracy met by allowing the *nouveaux riches* to marry into their families. Thus the aristocracy was transformed into an oligarchy—a rule by the few, but not necessarily by men "well born."

Another threat arose from the masses of poor peasants and artisans, whose economic and social position became miserable enough to raise the threat of revolution. From the protest of the popular classes came the impetus leading to democracy.

In some cities the first step toward democracy was "tyranny," an institution that has a peculiar meaning in Greek history. The Greek tyrant was usually a man of noble birth who became a champion of the people, stirred them to revolt, then seized personal power. The tyrant was not necessarily a harsh ruler. Usually he continued to favor the interests of the common people against the privileged classes, and often he hastened the coming of a genuine democracy.

Although most of the cities followed the same general pattern of political development, they sometimes differed widely in the form that their institutions finally took. We shall examine in detail the institutions of only two cities: Sparta and Athens. These were the most powerful cities of Hellas, and their institutions show a sharp contrast.

Sparta

No other Greek city ever acquired so much military power and prestige as did Sparta, and no other city made itself so often a force

for destruction and an obstacle to cultural advance. Thus the political system that Sparta devised has made the name *Spartan* signify rigorous military regimentation.

The reason why the Spartans developed their peculiar system was that they were a small minority living among conquered peoples. When the ancestors of the Spartans invaded Laconia, they subjugated those of the native pre-Dorians who were not killed or driven away. Some of these conquered peoples were reduced to the abject condition of serfs, called *helots,* while others, called *perioikoi,* were allowed to remain free but were excluded from citizenship. Later, in the eighth century B.C., the Spartans moved westward into Messenia, dispossessing the owners of the land and avoiding the need for overseas colonization. The Spartans themselves became a privileged, ruling caste. In itself, this was not remarkable, because in most Greek cities the upper class was outnumbered by the larger mass who did the work. What was distinctive about Sparta was that the Spartans comprised an extremely small minority, which was hated with exceptional bitterness by the subject masses.

The situation of the Spartans was therefore precarious, and it was not long before their security was menaced. Shortly after 650 B.C. a serious revolt broke out in Messenia, which the Spartans put down only after years of savage fighting. To protect themselves against another such outbreak, the Spartans reorganized their society, making it a military state. This they deemed unavoidable if they were to survive. But it meant that Sparta became an armed camp, and the Spartans had to bid farewell to any future development of the arts of peace that make up a rich culture.

In the reorganization of their society—a work that was attributed to the lawgiver Lycurgus—individualism was wiped out, and family life was ruthlessly forced into the mold prescribed by the state. Only healthy infants were allowed to live, the sickly ones being put to death. At the age of seven, boys

Picture on the Inside of a Spartan Kylix (Cup). Sixth century, B.C. Here, in black figures on a white background, King Arcesilas of Cyrene, a Spartan colony in Africa, is watching the weighing of goods—possibly "silphion," a plant widely used in Greek diet. The scene not only illustrates Greece's growing commerce but the growing realism in art. The pet animals of the king are remarkably—and humorously—well drawn. (*Cabinet des Médailles, Bibliothèque Nationale*, Paris)

were taken from their families, trained in a harsh curriculum of military exercise and subjected to hardships that would toughen them into redoubtable warriors. Only the elements of reading and writing were taught to them, since other subjects had little military use. At twenty, military service began. Until thirty, all men lived in barracks, and until the age of sixty, they remained under military discipline. Marriage was regarded only as the officially approved method of producing material for the army. Even married men continued during the period of their military service to take their frugal meals together in army fashion rather than at home. Girls were allowed to stay at home with their mothers, but they, too, were trained to be strong and active, so they would be fit mothers for Spartan soldiers. They were respected by their husbands—who also respected their fine horses and fierce hunting dogs. This inexorable regimentation inculcated in the Spartans personal austerity, abnegation of individuality, and selfless devotion to the state. And it achieved its end of developing an irresistible military power. But seldom in history has great power

been used to so little constructive purpose.

The political organization of this military state exemplified the conservatism of the Spartans, for Sparta never developed much beyond the stage of Homeric society. Sparta retained the ancient institution of kingship but in an unusual form—there were two hereditary kings. It also had a council, called the *gerousia,* made up of the two kings and twenty-eight men over sixty years of age, who were elected for life, and a college of five magistrates, called *ephors,* who were elected for one-year terms. Besides these, Sparta had a popular assembly, the *apella,* comprising all citizens over the age of thirty, but this assembly never gained much power. The *ephors* and the *gerousia* dominated the government, and both were strongholds of reaction. The average Spartan belonged to a privileged group, as compared to the *perioikoi* and the *helots,* but he was nevertheless subject to the rule of the influential nobles who controlled the *ephorate* and the *gerousia.*

The conquest of Messenia did not satisfy the hunger of the Spartans for land and power, so early in the sixth century B.C. attempts were made to conquer Arcadia. These failed, and thereafter Sparta pursued another method in its drive for power: it began the organization of the Peloponnesian League. Nominally this was an alliance among the cities of the Peloponnesus, in which all were equal; actually Sparta was the dominant power, and the League became an instrument for spreading Spartan influence in Greece.

Athens

The institutions and the culture of Athens contrasted sharply with those of Sparta. Spartan society was simple and devoted to a single purpose: building an army. Athenian society, on the other hand, was complex and constantly changing, and it had many goals. These may be summarized as the balanced cultivation of the life of the body, mind, and spirit.

How is this striking difference to be explained? For the answer you must look to the conditions in which the two cities evolved. In Sparta, as we have seen, social conditions required the Spartans to develop a military power to protect themselves against their subjects, and this power also gave them an effective instrument for waging war abroad. In Athens the social environment was such as to encourage the Athenians to cultivate their cultural abilities and allowed the citizen to think freely and to express himself individually.

The early history of Attica throws considerable light on later developments. During the period of the Achaean invasions, a people known as the Ionians had migrated into the sheltered little peninsula known as Attica. They came as peaceful settlers, not despoilers, and soon they merged with the native inhabitants. Thus there was no galling division between conquerors and conquered as in Laconia. Then, at the time of the Dorian invasions, Attica had the good fortune to be left undisturbed, and thus in this region the old Mycenaean civilization survived relatively intact.

Left in peace, Attica was able to develop independently. Good use was made of this happy opportunity, for by the end of the eighth century B.C. the various small communities of Attica were united under the leadership of the city of Athens. Athens itself had built up a flourishing maritime trade and a profitable industry, producing chiefly pottery.

With the unification of Attica under Athenian sovereignty, the political problem of rivalry among the cities of Attica was solved. But a serious social problem remained. Attica, like other Greek lands, inherited the tribal system of the Dark Age. This perpetuated the harsh domination by noble families, which always bred class strife. In Athens, as in most of the rest of Greece, the king's powers had been taken over by nine *archons,* selected from the nobility, and the legislative and judicial council, called the *Areopagus,* was also dominated by the nobility, since it was made up of the ex-archons. The poorer landowners and laborers were thus at the mercy of the noblemen who owned great estates. Many of the common people were reduced to slavery or a kind of serfdom.

The nobles might have continued to hold power over the mass of the people had it not been for two conditions to which we have already referred. First, Athens was not, like Sparta, a land of conquerors dwelling in the midst of a foreign population; the mass of the people was of the same stock as the ruling caste and had the rights of citizenship. Second, Athens had built up a prosperous trade and industry, and this development brought into being an industrial population. Men of this middle class were freer of control by the nobles than were the mass of peasants and artisans, and some of them were in a position to take the lead in curbing the nobles' power.

Solon. The reorganization of Athenian society was begun in 594 B.C. by Solon, who was given unusual powers as a mediator, charged with the task of removing the evils that threatened the peace of the state. So well did he measure up to his task that his name has since become a synonym for statesman.

Solon's economic reforms went far toward improving the wretched plight of the poorest members of society. He put a stop to the process by which free men were being reduced to servitude when they could not pay their debts. Then, as a step in preparation for political reform, he divided the population into four classes, according to income rather than birth. The upper classes continued to have a preponderance of political power, but the lowest class was made exempt from taxes and all but the lightest military duties.

The political reforms of Solon marked a first step toward democracy. These measures broke the hold of the old landed nobility over the government by giving to members of all the wealthy classes (not merely the nobility) the right to elect the executive officers of the government: the archons and other magistrates. The three upper classes also shared in electing a council (*boule*) of 400 members, which became a check upon the aristocratic council of the Areopagus. A popular assembly (*ecclesia*), composed of citizens of all four classes, also had a share in political decisions. Besides the right to participate in the *ecclesia,* the common people gained the right to serve on juries.

Solon's constitution solved some problems but left others unsolved and created new ones. Though enslavement was now illegal, it was still almost impossible for the free but landless poor to earn a living. Though the people gained a measure of power, the Areopagus could still block popular legislation. While the aristocracy suffered a setback, it was not willing to accept a diminution of its power and privilege. A step had been taken toward democracy, but many of the causes of social conflict remained.

Pisistratus. The next three decades were therefore filled with strife, which was abated only when Pisistratus established himself as tyrant about 560 B.C. A noble of great ability, Pisistratus is an excellent example of the mild and benevolent tyrant. To maintain his position, he had to keep popular support and hold the nobles in check. Hence he was driven to helping the friends and weakening the enemies of democracy.

Pisistratus caused the most hostile of the aristocrats to be slain or exiled; their estates were then distributed among the landless. He also made loans to the peasants and generally promoted their interests. The poor of the city were aided by elaborate public works, which not only improved their condition but also beautified Athens. So skillful and amiable an administrator was Pisistratus that he did not find it necessary to abrogate the constitution that Solon had devised. His rule of over thirty years—he was exiled twice before his death in 527 B.C.—was generally beneficial to the city. But his sons proved unable to carry on the tyranny, and soon after his death the way lay open for the further advance of democracy.

Cleisthenes. In the disturbed period following Pisistratus' death, some of the nobles tried to undo the reforms he had introduced and those of Solon before him. But the democratic faction now found a leader in Cleisthenes, who checked the reaction of the aristocrats without attempting to make himself tyrant. The result was that Athens became the first democracy in human history.

Cleisthenes saw that the greatest obstacle to social peace and freedom was the old system of tribes, comprising families, brotherhoods, and clans. He therefore abolished these old tribes, setting up new political entities which, though keeping the name of tribes, were actually based on territorial divisions and not on kinship. This daring innovation struck at the root of the aristocrats' political power.

Only a few other changes were made in the constitution. One of them, which was to prove important, created a board of generals (*strategoi*) alongside the archons. With the passing of time the generals gained power in civil as well as military affairs, and the chief general became the political leader of the faction in power. The generals were chosen from all classes, and, since they could be re-elected, they might hold office for long periods.

Another innovation that has been attributed to Cleisthenes was the curious practice of ostracism. According to law, the popular assembly could set a date once each year when the citizens might meet to vote the ex-pulsion of anyone they wished. Those who wished would write on a potsherd (*ostrakon*) the name of the person they would banish. Provided at least 6000 citizens took part in the voting, the citizen whose name appeared most frequently would then be ex-iled for ten years. Apparently Cleisthenes in-tended this law as a way of removing any aspiring tyrant, but it proved to have an un-fortunate effect. It became merely a way of getting rid of the leader of the minority party, and it caused the banishment of some able and devoted men.

THE CLASSICAL AGE, 500-323 B.C.

By about 500 B.C. Athens had thus emerged as a democracy, while Sparta, wedded to the system of a conservative oligarchy, had become the head of a great Peloponnesian League. Other cities, such as Corinth and Thebes, had also risen to prominence, but Athens and Sparta were to be the chief rivals for leadership in Greece. For the next century and a half Athens was to over-shadow Sparta and to hold rank as the cultural capital of the Greek world. This era is known as the Classical Age.

The Persian Wars

This was an age marked not only by cultural advance but also by constant warfare. Warfare arose, in part, out of a conflict between the Greek cities and the mighty Persian Empire that had gained control over Asia Minor as well as other lands of the Near East, where the Persians had subjugated a number of cities that had been founded by Greeks.

The proud and individualistic Greeks of Asia Minor did not submit readily to Persian power. Soon they revolted, under the leadership of Miletus, and called upon the other Hellenes to come to their aid. The Persian emperor Darius put down this revolt in 494 B.C., however, and proceeded to invade the Greek mainland by way of Thrace. When the Greek cities proved woefully disunited, it seemed as though Greece was doomed. Yet when the Persian host reached the plain of Marathon in 490 B.C. the Athenians rallied with surprising vigor and defeated the invaders. Athens was saved, but the danger was only deferred.

Fortunately for Greece, ten years elapsed before the Persians undertook another invasion. In the meantime the Athenians had built a navy, and when Darius' son Xerxes began the new attack, the Spartans agreed to send an army to hold the pass at Thermopylae while the Athenian fleet engaged the Persians at sea.

Although the Spartan soldiers at Thermopylae, under the command of Leonidas, fought with superhuman courage, they were betrayed by a renegade and finally overwhelmed. This disaster allowed the Persians to advance by land to Athens, which they sacked. At the naval battle of Salamis (480 B.C.), however, the Athenian fleet won a smashing victory, and this blow to Persian sea power helped the Greeks to keep up their struggle until the Persians were forced to withdraw from European Greece. By 479 B.C. the Greeks had beaten the greatest empire in the world, thereby making them-

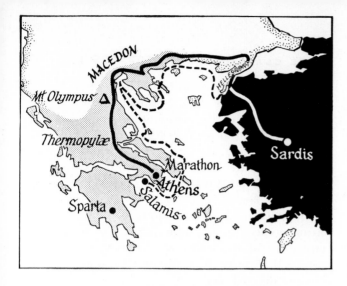

The Battle of Salamis, 480 B.C.

selves secure at home, freeing their brothers in Asia Minor, and winning dominion over the eastern Mediterranean. Their victory, which relieved them from fear of eastern despotism and made possible the free flowering of their genius, was one of the most important military victories in the history of western civilization.

The Athenian Empire

In the next fifty years Athens proceeded to build up its power over other cities of Greece, thus creating an empire of its own and becoming the leading state in Hellas. The first step in this process had been the formation of a maritime league, known as the Delian Confederation, for protection against the Persians. Athens presided over this league, which continued after the wars, and soon made it into an instrument of domination over Athenian allies.

Inevitably Sparta sought to block the rise of Athens. Recognizing this, the Athenian leader Themistocles, who had risen to prominence during the Persian wars and had taken the initiative in building up Athenian sea power, urged his fellow citizens to take measures against Sparta. Those of the upper classes in Athens who feared and hated de-

mocracy, however, chose to regard Sparta as an ally, for the Spartans were friends of oligarchy as against democracy. This faction caused the downfall and banishment of Themistocles, but the oligarchic reaction was short-lived. With Pericles, who rose to political leadership in Athens in 461 B.C., the democratic faction won a strong champion.

Pericles. Pericles was an intelligent and well-educated man, a compelling orator, a sincere patriot, and, though of aristocratic birth, an earnest democrat. His career coincides with the zenith of Athenian power, and his age is renowned for the glories of the cultural life of Athens.

Pericles induced the Athenians to take vigorous methods to offset Spartan opposition and strengthen their hold upon their own empire. Though he did not break the Spartan threat or establish a secure grip on the cities subject to Athens, he gained a considerable measure of success in his foreign policy. For the time being Athens kept peace in the Aegean.

At home, meantime, Pericles undertook further changes in the constitution, which distinguish Periclean democracy from the earlier form. Some of these changes worked to reduce the power of the Areopagus, which had remained a stronghold of the nobility, and of the archons, who until the time of Pericles were also representative of the upper classes rather than the common people. Another innovation, of large importance, was a system of payment for the performance of civic duties. Many citizens were, in practice, unable to take political office because they had to earn a living and therefore could not devote their time to public service. Pericles removed this barrier by providing pay for service in all public office except that of general or that of member of the assembly. He has been reproached for this measure on the ground that it encouraged the Athenians to be lazy, since poverty had not curbed their political power, and that it made them greedy to gain political office.

But Pericles judged it necessary in order that even the poorest citizens might gain practical education in democratic politics, and he thought it one of the best possible uses of public funds.

With these reforms, Athens became a genuine democracy—so far as involved the citizens. The rights of citizenship did not extend, of course, to all the inhabitants of the city. Not only were slaves excluded but also foreigners. And at the instigation of Pericles, Athens took a backward step: it limited citizenship to free men whose parents had been Athenians. In earlier times citizenship had been bestowed liberally on foreigners, because Athens needed to attract foreign craftsmen. But now that the city had become the rich and powerful head of an empire, that need had passed, and the Athenians judged that the fewer the citizens, the greater would be the advantage to those who held the rights of citizenship.

The Peloponnesian War, 431–404 B.C.

Although his domestic reforms proved lasting, Pericles was unable to achieve a comparable success in foreign affairs. Relations between Athens and Sparta remained uneasy, each city fearing the other and the city-states under Athenian hegemony resenting the loss of their freedom. Firm believer in democracy though he was, Pericles saw no solution to these problems but to maintain the supremacy of Athenian power. Perhaps there was no other solution open to him, for without its empire Athens would not have been rich enough to support the brilliant efflorescence of art and learning that proved to be its most splendid accomplishment. If Athens had not striven to maintain her empire, probably the other Greek cities would have lost their freedom, for when Athenian power was broken in 404 B.C. they simply passed under the dominance of Sparta until all Greece later fell under the rule first of Macedonia, then of Rome.

Since there was no better way out of the situation, Pericles probably did wisely when he determined to build up the Athenian maritime empire. Inevitably this meant war with Sparta, and war began in 431 B.C. Since Athens was a maritime power and Sparta a land power, warfare at first was confined to seasonal raids. Perhaps if Pericles had lived, Athens might have fared better, but he did not and disasters began to mount. First came the great plague of 429 B.C., which carried off almost half the population, including Pericles. Then in 415 B.C. an unwise decision was made to attack the Dorian city of Syracuse in Sicily in order to cut off Sparta's supply of grain. After this campaign ended two years later in complete defeat for the Athenian forces, the city had to face the revolts of its now subjugated allies as well as the increased arms of its enemies. The war dragged on until 404 B.C., when Athens was starved into capitulation. Thereupon the walls of the city were leveled, and Athens was deprived of its fleets, its empire, and even its democracy, for the victorious Spartans insisted on the establishment of an oligarchic government.

An Era of Confusion: 404–362 B.C.

The victory of Sparta only worsened the plight of the Greek world, now torn by fratricidal war. So crude and overbearing were the Lacedaemonians (Spartans) that they soon antagonized friend and foe alike. In reaction against Spartan clumsiness, the city of Thebes came to the support of the vanquished Athenians, permitting them to drive out the pro-Spartan oligarchy and restore their democracy. Meantime the Persians, after a brief alliance with Sparta, began to reassert their interest in Greek affairs and in 386 B.C. re-established Persian rule over the Greeks of Asia Minor.

Presently, in 377 B.C., Thebes and Athens formed a new league for their mutual protection against Spartan domination. But in this league Thebes took the leadership, and in 371 B.C., the Theban commander scored a smashing victory over the Lacedaemonians. Thereafter, for about ten years, Thebes was supreme in European Greece. Thebes, however, proved incapable of putting an end to the internecine rivalries among the Greek cities, and the quarreling Hellenes continued the tragic anarchy that eventually led to their subjection by foreign powers.

The Rise of Macedon

In 359 B.C. occurred an event of supreme importance for the future independence of Greece. In that year a redoubtable young man, known to history as Philip II, rose to power in Macedonia.

Macedonia is the land of fertile plains and hills that lies north of the Greek peninsula. Its people were related to the Greeks but had lagged behind them in cultural development. Cities were few, and signs of civilization were scarce until the fifth century B.C., when the kings began to Hellenize Macedonia. The population was composed of peasants and a powerful, warlike nobility, led by the king, whose rule was hereditary.

Philip II was determined to bring to completion the work of Hellenization that his predecessors had begun. As a youth he had spent three years in Thebes as a hostage, and during this time he learned to admire Greek culture generally and Theban military methods in particular. When he returned home,

as a start toward achieving his aim of making Macedonia the dominant state in the civilized world, he undertook a reformation of the Macedonian army, which he carried through with brilliant success. Shortly he was able to make rich conquests in Thrace and Chalcidice.

The new power of Macedonia represented a challenge to Athens, which the great Athenian statesman Demosthenes was quick to perceive. From 351 B.C. onward this fine orator delivered a series of scorching addresses, which are known in literature under the name of *Philippics*, exposing the schemes and subterfuges of Philip II. Though Demosthenes sternly warned the Athenians that they must meet the menace of Macedonia and must therefore build up their armed forces, for a long time he failed to shake his countrymen from their pinch-penny isolationism.

Eventually the Athenians began to heed Demosthenes and renewed their alliance with Thebes. But it was too late. In 338 B.C. Philip smashed the combined armies of Thebes and Athens and thus made certain the destruction of Greek freedom. On the heels of his victory he proceeded to form a new league of the Greek cities, in which he was master. At once he went on to summon his allies to prepare for war against the Persian Empire. The destruction of Persian power was the goal that he now set himself, and in 336 B.C. he made his first moves. But before he could go further with his plans, Philip was assassinated by one of his officers.

LIFE AND SOCIETY IN THE GREAT AGE OF GREECE

Economic Life in the Classical Age

Everywhere in Greece, as in most places in ancient times, agriculture was the basic economic activity. In Sparta most of the farming was done by the wretched helots. In Attica small citizen farmers, occasionally aided by a slave or two, wrested a meager

living from the fields. There were some large estates, too, on which slaves or tenant farmers worked under the supervision of overseers. But nowhere was the yield of the land abundant. Sheep were raised in some regions, principally for their wool, and also goats and pigs. Stock raising on a large scale was not feasible. In most places the land was given over to the raising of garden vegetables and fruit. In Attica barley and wheat were grown, but much more grain was imported than was produced at home. Olive oil and wine were important products of the larger estates. But the diet of the average Greek was frugal and lacking in variety. Meat and other luxuries seldom were part of it.

In the fifth and fourth centuries B.C. the development of maritime commerce made possible the growth of cities. Trading was mostly by sea, because of the difficulty of land transportation, but even seafaring was no easy matter. The ships that the Greeks used were small; wind and weather were unfavorable except in the spring and summer; and pirates were often a menace.

During the fifth century Athens dominated trade in all directions. Through her port passed the wares of the Ancient Orient, Etruria, and Great Greece and the natural products of the fields, forests, and mines of the Black Sea region, Thrace, Sicily, and Italy. But always the most important commodity was grain, which Attica could not produce in sufficient quantity for its own sustenance. Athens paid for its imports with olive oil, wine, manufactured goods, and silver from its mines. In addition, it had to make use of the wealth that it gained as tribute from the subjects of the

empire, for Athens spent more than it earned. Other cities, such as Corinth and Syracuse, also profited from trade, but many found their commerce restricted or destroyed by Athens.

Despite its growing importance, commerce never attained so much significance as in modern times, largely because commerce, like other kinds of labor, was held in low esteem. Only agriculture was deemed an honorable occupation. Trade was given over to the *metics,* or resident aliens, who were made welcome in the great cities and given certain rights, though not full citizenship. Their function was to attend to the management of trade and industry, so that the citizens might devote themselves to more respectable pursuits.

Industry also increased in productivity during the fifth and fourth centuries B.C., though it was not at all comparable to modern large-scale manufacture. Greek potters, masons, miners, smiths, and other artisans were workmen of admirable skill, but unfortunately they lacked machinery. Nor did they supply all the needed manufactures, because each household provided most of its own wants. In view of these circumstances, and the contemptuous attitude of the Greeks toward manual labor, it is not surprising that industry showed little signs of enterprise and inventiveness, for it did

Harvesting Olives—detail from an Athenian oil jar, c.525 B.C., 16 inches high. According to legend, when Athena and Poseidon contested for the land of Attica, Poseidon struck a rock with his trident and a horse, his gift to man, sprang out. Athena brought forth an olive tree, and the gods awarded her the victory. Later Erechtheus, legendary king and early hero of Athens, tamed the horse for man. (Courtesy of British Museum)

not attract the most talented of the Greek citizens. Industry was largely left in the hands of the *metics,* though some of the poorer citizens and some slaves were employed in the crafts. *Metics* predominated, also, in the professions.

This age witnessed some development of banking. Besides the simpler banking operations, such as changing money and arranging for the transfer of money between persons living in different cities, the bankers also accepted deposits which they invested. But because dealings of this kind involved the stigma that was always associated with trade, banking was not a vocation held in high repute. This is still another reason why the Greeks never made much progress in raising the standard of living. The growth of capitalism, which is the key to economic advance, requires the expanding use of credit, and this depends upon the development of banking.

Social Life in the Classical Age

Society in all Greek city-states was divided into (1) a citizen class, which held political power, (2) a free but unfranchised group, which carried on the business affairs of the city, and (3) an unfree class, which did all kinds of menial work. In Sparta the second class comprised the *perioikoi,* and the third class comprised the *helots,* both being natives. But in other great cities the *metics,* or resident aliens, made up most of the second class, and slaves composed the third.

Everywhere in Greece, the citizens were a privileged but far-from-homogeneous class. In Athens, which was typical of many other cities, the citizenry was divided between the oligarchic party, comprising the descendants of the nobles of earlier times, and the democratic party, composed of the mass of the poor peasants and such citizens as worked in the city as craftsmen and shopkeepers. Even though the poorer citizens ultimately gained a considerable voice in the government, rancor between the rich and poor citizens remained a curse of Greek society.

Slavery prevailed generally throughout Greece, even in democratic Athens, and even the best minds thought it a natural and proper institution. Indeed, slavery was general in the civilized world of that age. Moreover, the Greeks regarded as barbarians the peoples surrounding them, from whom most of the slaves were obtained. And the labor of slaves, the Greek philosophers pointed out, was necessary in order to assure the Greek citizens of the leisure required for their civic duties.

Most slaves in the Greek city-states of this period were taken as prisoners in war or were bought from slave traders, who obtained their human wares in such backward regions as Thrace and Scythia and from the interior of Asia Minor. In some regions, of course, such as Sparta, the slaves were part of a native population that had been conquered.

Slaves were used to perform all kinds of services. In Athens, where slaves numbered perhaps 80,000 (as compared with about 50,000 *metics* and 120,000 citizens, making a total population of some 250,000), many worked as domestic servants. But, probably, only the more prosperous citizens could afford to use slaves as household servants. Many more were employed as laborers in industry and commerce, as entertainers, or as workers in the silver mines.

Slaves were sometimes well treated, especially in Athens, and occasionally they were emancipated. Nevertheless, the slave was always at the mercy of his master, and if his master chanced to be a vain and selfish young aristocrat, his lot would be hard indeed. Outside Athens, slaves commonly found their treatment harsh and often revolted.

In the early pre-Greek society that Homer describes, women were loved and respected. By the fifth century B.C., however, their social position had declined, especially in

Athens. The Athenian girl in the Periclean Age was given only such training as would prepare her for managing a household and bringing up her daughters. Her marriage was arranged for her, and when she left her father's house, she passed from his supervision to her husband's. Her sons she watched over only until they were six years old, after which they passed most of their time outside the home. Her daughters she reared to pursue the same dull and narrow life that was her own lot. Though the men of Athens took part in the most brilliant intellectual life the world has ever known, the women had little share in it.

Education in Athens

Nothing tells us more about the ideals and achievements of a civilization than its educational theory and practice. On this score Athens made a glorious record. To be sure, the "liberal" education that was their finest distinction was not given to girls or to the sons of those citizens who had to work for a living. But apart from these restrictions, the Athenian conception of the nature and purpose of education has never been surpassed.

The education of the Athenian boy—and it was much the same everywhere else in Greece except in Sparta and Dorian Crete —was designed to make him a good citizen. Education was therefore well rounded, since the aim was to produce men who could think for themselves and provide them with high ideals. Such men, the Athenians believed, would be better prepared to live happily and honorably than those who acquired only specialized skills and practical knowledge but lacked the wisdom to distinguish between good and evil.

Primary education was given to nearly all Athenian boys, even the poor. This usually extended from the age of six to fourteen or fifteen. It consisted mainly of literature, music, and athletics. The sons of wealthier fathers then went through a period of secondary education, including mathematics and science, more literature, and some study of political science and philosophy. At the age of eighteen the boys were called up for two years of military service. Thereafter the citizen could go on to still more learning, if he chose. He might attend the lectures of wandering teachers, such as the Sophists, or the regular courses in the academy of Plato or at Aristotle's lyceum. Or he could devote himself to intelligent conversation in the market place, the enjoyment of the arts, physical activity in the gymnasium, and the exercise of his civic duties. The Athenian citizen's education did not cease abruptly; it was a never-ending pursuit of the good life, through cultivation of the body, mind, and spirit.

Formal education thus merged with everyday life. And it was a pleasant life that the Athenian citizen lived, although not what we should regard as exciting. The citizen of whom we are speaking did not work for a living, though he was not necessarily rich. He spent his time in talking with friends whom he would meet in the streets or the gymnasium and in attending to his political duties. Amusement was usually sought in private homes, at banquets and symposiums. The symposium was a drinking party, although its purpose was to enjoy witty conversation, not to get drunk. Plato's famous *Symposium* gives a lively description of such a party.

The Greek Outlook

The Greeks are distinctive as being one of the first peoples to develop the concept of individualism, and this was the feature of their civilization that most sharply marked off their society from that of the ancient Orient. In many of the cities, especially in Athens, it was possible, for the first time in history, for a man to stand out from the mass and to be honored for his own specific abilities.

Such recognition of the importance of the individual is a prerequisite of the idea of democracy. It is not surprising, therefore, that Athens became the first home of democracy. To be sure, the Athenian democracy did not grapple with the problem of the economic implications of democracy. What is important is not that Greek democracy fell short of perfection but that the idea of democracy should have evolved at a time when the rest of the civilized world was ruled by despots, and most of Europe was inhabited by peoples still not far above the Stone Age level of culture.

In the realm of social and political problems, then, in spite of all their shortcomings, the Greeks accomplished much. In the writings of great Greek thinkers in the social sciences are to be observed the qualities for which they are justly famous: idealism, originality in government—for example, the invention of democracy—and profound, constructive speculation on human problems. Their failures, on the other hand, are to be attributed mainly to the limitations of the city-state. It was the tragedy of the Hellenes that they could never advance from the city-state to a larger, more efficient social organization. The rivalry and dissension among their city-states, indeed, actually prepared the way for Philip II of Macedon, who put an end to Greek independence.

Suggestions for Further Reading

Source Materials

Anthologies

G. W. Botsford and E. G. Sihler, eds., *Hellenic Civilization* (New York, 1915).

A scholarly collection of documents illustrating many aspects of the social, religious, and political life of the Greeks. Highly valuable, especially as reference material.

G. H. Knoles and R. K. Snyder, eds., *Readings in Western Civilization* (rev. ed., New York, 1954), pp. 31–58.

Selections from the political writings of Thucydides, Plato, and Aristotle.

R. Warnock and G. K. Anderson, eds., *The World in Literature* (Chicago, 1950–51), Vol. I, pp. 85–171.

Selections from the *Iliad* and the *Odyssey*.

Contemporary Writings

The student is urged to read as many as possible of the works of the great Greek thinkers themselves. The following are among the greatest of the classics of ancient thought; they are all available in many editions, including "paperbacks."

Aristotle, *Politics*
Herodotus, *History of the Persian Wars*
Homer, *The Iliad; The Odyssey*
Plato, *Crito; The Republic*

Plutarch, *Lives:* The Life of Lycurgus
Thucydides, *History of the Peloponnesian War*
Xenophon, *Hellenica, or Grecian History; Oeconomicus*

Secondary Works

On Cretan Civilization

J. Baikie, *The Sea Kings of Crete* (London, 1926).

An account for laymen of archaeological excavations, attempting a lively account of the period. Analyzes old legends in the light of modern research. Notes especially Cretan and Mycenaean contacts with other countries.

A. R. Burn, *Minoans, Philistines, and Greeks* (New York, 1930).

Deals with the period 1400–900 B.C., the age of decline of the Aegean culture, the upsurge of the Greek. Traces the migrations of the Philistines, Etruscans, and Greeks, and their contacts with Egypt. Integrates legends with archaeology.

G. Glotz, *The Aegean Civilization* (New York, 1925).

A brief history of Aegean civilization as a whole, then an attempt to study the civilization as government, business, art, religion, funerary customs, architecture, etc. Done by one of the famous ancient historians.

H. R. H. Hall, *The Civilization of Greece in the Bronze Age* (London, 1928).

An attempt to make history from archaeology, dealing with the Cretan civilization to the Iron Age in Greece. Good simple presentation of the problems.

M. P. Nilsson, *Homer and Mycenae* (London, 1933).
A very able, moderate account of a wide variety of topics relating to literature and archaeology. Deals with the problem of the Homeric poems in relation to their ancient setting.

On the Development of Greece

W. R. Agard, *What Democracy Meant to the Greeks* (Chapel Hill, 1942).
A brief, selective history of the development of Greek culture from Homer to the later Stoics. Analyzes how and how well the Greeks, especially the Athenians, practiced democracy. Faces the problems as well as showing the virtues of democracy.

R. J. Bonner, *Aspects of Athenian Democracy* (Berkeley, 1933).
Traces the development of Greek democracy and stresses its various aspects. Clear, well-ordered presentation, though the book offers little that is new.

G. W. Botsford, *Hellenic History* (New York, 1948).
A good standard text, especially valuable for historical and economic problems of the period. Well illustrated, good maps.

J. B. Bury, *A History of Greece to the Death of Alexander* (New York, 1951).
A standard, high-caliber history of Greece, written in one volume but with considerable detail of information. Readable.

G. M. Calhoun, *The Business Life of Ancient Athens* (Chicago, 1926).
This book deals with an important but rarely stressed aspect of Greek history. A series of sketches on banking, capitalism, shipping, merchandising, mining gives the personality and practices of the man of business.

W. W. Fowler, *The City-State of the Greeks and Romans* (New York, 1893).
An old, but still valuable, book, tracing the city-state from its origins through the Roman oligarchy. Why and how the city-state declined.

G. Glotz, *Ancient Greece at Work* (New York, 1926).
Covers the period from Homeric to Hellenistic times. Discusses agriculture, industry, and trade.

G. Glotz, *The Greek City and Its Institutions* (New York, 1929).
Discusses the spirit of the Greek people as seen in their political institutions. Shows how the political machinery of the Greek city worked. Concentrates on Athens but includes the others.

T. R. Glover, *Democracy in the Ancient World* (New York, 1927).
Conversations with the ancients (in terms of their writings), about their concepts of democracy. Well done, simple and terse. The Greek section is much better than the Roman, since the Romans had little to say about democracy.

C. B. Gulick, *The Life of the Ancient Greeks* (New York, 1902).
A well-organized study of the domestic and personal life in ancient Greece, interestingly written. The archaeological and literary evidence are well balanced.

J. Hasebroek, *Trade and Politics in Ancient Greece* (London, 1933).
This careful, well-documented study surveys ancient Greek commerce and economics, with special stress on the relation of the state to the problems of trade and money.

M. L. W. Laistner, *A History of the Greek World from 479–323 B.C.* (London, 1936).
An expansion of the greatest age of Greek achievement, giving a detailed account, particularly of the political and military history. Sober, critical, and scholarly.

H. Michell, *The Economics of Ancient Greece* (New York, 1940).
A careful collection and synthesis of data for the economic structure of ancient Greek society from early times to the age of Alexander. A topical discussion, including mining, agriculture, labor, industry, commerce, banking, etc., it shows understanding of ancient techniques, and contrasts them successfully with present-day methods.

C. E. Robinson, *Every Day Life in Ancient Greece* (Oxford, 1933).
An elementary, well-written, pleasing, and worthwhile review of many aspects of Greek life in the Homeric and Classical periods. Discusses both city and personal life.

A. Zimmern, *The Greek Commonwealth* (Oxford, 1931).
Chiefly about Athens, this book deals with climate, geography, industry, and agriculture; attempts an analysis of attitudes of the citizens.

5

Greek Esthetic and
Intellectual Life

Athena—goddess of wisdom, of the arts and sciences, and of war. Marble relief, c.18 inches high, c.445 B.C. (Courtesy Acropolis Museum, Athens)

The individualism that was so important in the political and social life of the Greeks was no less vital in other phases of their culture. In the ancient Orient, art had been created at the command of the king, while intellectual life had been the province of the priests. In the city-states of Hellas, however, another situation prevailed. In their society, as it had developed by the fifth century B.C., individuals had emerged from the mass—men who were neither priests nor kings but nonetheless had a sense of their own particular being and worth, who took delight in expressing themselves, in exploring the world about them, and in interpreting and speculating about it. Art and learning were thus taken out of the hands of the few and made part of the lives of the many. This meant a revolution in the realm of artistic and intellectual activity.

Because so much of the Greek's life was taken up with service to the state and the effort to prepare himself for that demanding task, his outlook must of necessity seem "impractical" to many modern men. The explanation is found in the Greek's civic consciousness, based on his love of his city and his deep religious feeling. Material success was relatively unimportant, but to bring honor to his city by a victory at the games or the performance of a liturgy was highly admirable. An honorable Greek citizen always thought of something above him, worthy of all he could do for it, and that something was the state, the society that had brought him up and protected him and educated him. The moderation that created a well-balanced man, capable of serving the state as well as himself, was the prime virtue, and to as great an extent as possible life was guided in accordance with that virtue.

Another component of the Greek's view of life was his earnest desire to seek out the truth. The Greek was curious, and he wanted to know—simply for the sake of knowing. His attitude was the reverse of that of the Egyptian, who was restrained by superstitious fear from proceeding beyond the practical application of knowledge to scientific speculation. Indeed, the Greek was speculative almost to a fault, for he would much rather ponder the nature of the world than seek utilitarian knowledge.

Besides these basic attributes, there were other distinctive qualities of the Greek gen-

The Parthenon. Greek temple architecture was a refinement of the post-and-lintel system (see p. 63). Built during 447–432 B.C., by the Greek architects Ictinus and Callicrates, the Parthenon was being used as an ammunition dump by a Turkish garrison when, in 1687, the Venetians laid siege to Athens and a direct hit exploded the stored gunpowder, destroying the center section. The Parthenon is about 228 feet long and 104 feet wide, with columns 34 feet high. (Alinari photograph)

ius. One was a dauntless originality, which permitted the Greeks to break with tradition; another was an open-mindedness and love of freedom. But these qualities merged into a whole that served the great Greek ideal of the harmony of body, mind, and spirit.

THE ARTS OF GREECE

To the educated Greek, art was not something to be kept in museums and galleries but a part of everyday life. The Greeks did not "go to see" their art; they lived with it—in religion, in sports, even in the politics of the city-state.

Architecture

Students of Greek civilization are often struck by the fact that, while the public buildings of the Greeks were extremely beautiful, private buildings were dingy. The reason is simple. Architecture is an expensive form of art, and even the wealthiest Greek citizens were not rich enough to command this kind of art for themselves. But allegiance to their gods and to their city required them to erect handsome public edifices. Hence all Greek cities were adorned with fine temples, and when Athens became the rich and powerful mistress of the Aegean, her citizens spent the treasure of their city on the buildings that have helped make her name famous ever since.

The Hellenes won their notable success in architecture by adhering to principles of simplicity and grace. From the Achaeans they took over the basic form of their temples, which was a rectangular structure, first made of wood but later of stone. The *cella,* or main portion of the temple, was customarily provided with a porch; and a colonnade, or row of columns, surrounded both porch and cella. The pediment, or space below the angle of the sloping roof, was usually filled with brightly painted sculptures.

The style of the temple architecture is determined primarily by the shape and ornamentation of the columns. In the Archaic period, two styles were in use. The Doric style, which was popular on the mainland and in the west, made use of a plain, heavy column with sharp fluting. The Ionic, which appealed more to the Greeks of the islands and the Asiatic coast, used a more slender column, with flat fluting and a volute capital. The Corinthian style appeared later, about the end of the fifth century B.C. It closely resembled the Ionic except for a more ornate, bell-shaped capital, decorated with acanthus leaves. This style achieved its greatest popularity in the Hellenistic age and in Roman times.

The most famous of all Greek architectural works is the Parthenon, which Pericles directed to be built on the Acropolis in Athens. Though now in ruins, this temple of Athena, standing on the rugged hilltop above the city, still remains a triumph of calm beauty, grace, and symmetry. It has the usual rectangular cella, which is divided into two rooms. In the larger of these was placed Phidias' huge statue of the maiden goddess Athena. The Parthenon columns are especially remarkable for the clever way in which the builders created an optical illusion of straightness and symmetry—by making the columns curve in the middle, taper at the top, and lean inward.

Another outstanding example of Athenian architecture is the Erechtheum, which also stands on the Acropolis. Unlike the Parthenon, which is basically of the Doric style, the Erechtheum is typically Ionic. The plan is irregular, however, for religious reasons and because the unevenness of the ground required one of the three porches to be placed on a lower level than the others. One of these—the Porch of the Maidens—is also unusual in that six carved female figures take the place of columns.

Other notable pieces of Greek architecture that still survive are the Theseum, the Propylaea, and the temple of Athena Nike, all at Athens, and the temple of Apollo at Bassae, which has the oldest known columns of the Corinthian style.

One of the most interesting Hellenic constructions was the theater. Usually this was an open-air auditorium, semicircular in form, which was built on a hillside. From their seats on the sloping bank, the spectators had a good view of the circular orchestra below them. Behind the orchestra, which we would call the stage, was the *proscenium,* a row of columns, and behind that, a stage building used by the actors. An example of this kind of structure is the Theater of Dionysus (p. 128), which was built against the southern slope of the Acropolis (see p. 133).

The Three Architectural Orders. Although used to distinguish types of columns, more accurately *Doric* and *Ionic* refer to the rules that determine the proportions and relationships of the parts to the whole of a building. Corinthian is a variation of Ionic.

Doric Ionic Corinthian

Charioteer of Delphi—bronze, c.470 B.C. (Alinari photograph)

Sculpture

The first Greek sculptors doubtless learned much from their predecessors in the ancient Orient, particularly Egypt and Asia Minor. From the start, however, the Hellenes showed their independence, and before long they struck out on their own. By the early fifth century B.C., when the Archaic period passed into the Classical, Greek sculpture had become an original expression of naturalness and beauty.

Three figures appear in the earlier sculpture of the Archaic period—the standing nude male, the standing draped female, and the seated draped male or female. The statue is meant to be viewed from only one angle; the poses are stiff, and the style is conventional. The customary expression on the face, owed to a lack of skill in showing cheek and mouth muscles, is known as the "archaic smile"; the draperies of the standing female figures conceal the shape of the body, and the seated figures give an impression of heaviness. Nevertheless, these statues have vitality and strength. Later works of the period show considerable advance in technique—the stiffness has gone, the proportions are improved, and the meaningless smile has disappeared from the countenance.

Decorative sculpture was more varied. Often scenes from mythology, depicting many kinds of activity, were used in the relief sculpture that filled the triangular space offered by the pediment of a temple. Early sculpture of this kind was often done in limestone, as were some of the free-standing statues, and sculpture was commonly painted in bright colors. Marble was sometimes used.

Few pieces of free-standing sculpture of this period have survived. Many were in bronze and were later melted down for their metal. But we are fortunate in having two good examples that give an indication of this kind of work. One is the *Charioteer of Delphi,* serene and dignified of countenance, who is shown standing erect and holding the reins in his outstretched hand. The pose has a hint of naturalism, and the execution is skillful. The other is a nude figure of Zeus hurling a thunderbolt. The statue well conveys an impression of divine majesty.

Myron of Athens, whose work dates from about 475 to 450 B.C., was the best-known sculptor of this early time. His most famous statue is the *Discus Thrower*. The vigor and grace exhibited in this figure of a well-proportioned Greek youth show the artist's splendid success in capturing a moment of intense physical effort.

After Myron's time came the great age of classical sculpture. The two outstanding artists were Phidias (*c.490–c.432* B.C.) and Polyclitus (active *c.460–c.420* B.C.). Among the greatest works of Phidias were a colossal statue of Athena, which he designed for the Parthenon in Athens; another of Athena, which was placed on the Acropolis; and one of Zeus, which he designed for the temple at Olympia. None of these survives, but we presume that they must have been fine works, since the Greeks, whose taste we know to have been good, found them exceptionally impressive. It is from the remains of the Parthenon that we gain substantiation of Phidias' reputation, because the plan for this splendid temple was his.

Polyclitus of Argos did his work about the same time that Phidias was adding splendor to Periclean Athens. He chose to specialize in the figures of athletes. We know his work only from copies, but these attest his skill. In the *Doryphorus*, which shows a young athlete holding a spear, the sculptor exemplified his ideal of the human figure.

After the time of Phidias and Polyclitus, sculpture was restrained, dignified, and

Doryphorus (Spear Bearer), Roman copy in marble of Polyclitus' bronze, c.440 B.C., 7 feet high (Alinari photograph), and *Hermes and the Infant Dionysus* by Praxiteles, c.350 B.C., 7 feet 8 inches. (Courtesy of Royal Greek Embassy)

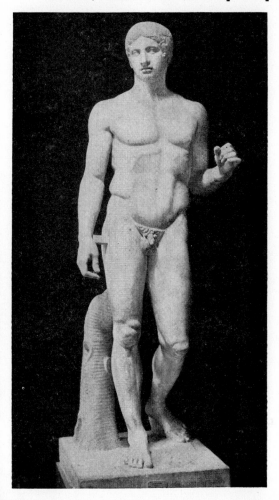

Attic Black-figured Amphora, signed by Exekias c.540 B.C. Although depicting one of the twelve labors of Hercules—the battle with the three-bodied giant Geryon—the armor was contemporary. (Louvre Museum, Paris)

advanced from the representation of simple geometric designs to well-drawn forms of plant and animal life and the human figure. The vase paintings are a valuable source of information about Greek life, since they illustrate types of dress, warfare, and athletics. They constitute one of the most attractive branches of Greek art.

From the first the ceramic art was highly regarded by the Greeks, and vase-making was an important industry in some cities. Much care was taken with vases of all kinds, from wine jugs and huge mixing bowls to small cups and containers for oil or perfume. All were embellished with scenes from mythology or everyday life.

The same good taste and love of beauty that are illustrated in the vase paintings are also shown in ivory and metal work, jewelry of many kinds, and the engraving of coins. Some painting of portraits and larger scenes was done in this period, but no examples have survived.

Music

Our word *music* comes from the Greeks. They applied it more broadly than we, however, using it to refer to all the arts presided over by the Muses. It thus signified all phases of intellectual culture, as opposed to physical culture. An ill-bred person would have been called "unmusical."

The Greeks themselves admitted that their musical tradition (using the word now in our sense of it) came from diverse parts of the Near East. Probably the Mycenaeans were largely responsible for transmitting it to them. Along with the Phrygian and Lydian scales, the Oriental *aulos* originally came from across the Aegean. The aulos came to be identified with the orgiastic cult of Dionysus, who was the patron god of the theater, and was prominently used in the theater, since the penetrating tone of the instrument was suited to use in the open air.

idealistic, though natural. The emotions were more openly expressed, and individualism was given freer rein. In the statue of *Hermes and the Infant Dionysus,* created by Praxiteles (active *c.*360–*c.*330 B.C.), the god leans gracefully, with curving body. The features are finer and the flesh more realistic than in the works of the earlier periods. Another notable work of Praxiteles is his *Aphrodite of Cnidus,* in which the goddess, represented as a nude young woman about to bathe, is portrayed voluptuously and with considerable sentiment.

Painting

Almost all we know of Greek painting comes from vase decorations. The artists of the late eighth and seventh centuries B.C.

Another instrument popular with the Greeks was the panpipe, which was played by blowing across the openings of the several tubes. It produced a flutelike sound. But the most important Greek instrument was the *cithara*, a large lyre of seven strings (often inaccurately called a harp). This instrument was identified with Apollo, the god of the Muses and symbol of moderation, and it was the instrument of the serious or professional musician and virtuoso. Its strains gave the accompaniment to the poetry of Sappho and Pindar, and vase paintings show Sappho herself plucking a cithara.

Singing, dancing, and playing upon musical instruments were accomplishments that were highly esteemed among the Greeks, who devoted a third of their educational curriculum to them. Contests in music were included in the Olympic and other pan-Hellenic games. The Greeks went so far as to ascribe ethical qualities to melodies,

according to the scale or "ethos" in which they were composed. And because they were convinced that the type of music that a citizen heard had influence on his character, Plato and other philosophers felt a need for some kind of musical censorship.

The Greeks concentrated upon developing possibilities of purely melodic music and never stumbled upon the concept of chords, which is fundamental to harmony. Nevertheless they made a notable advance in musical theory, and this became the most important Greek contribution to western music. The mathematician Pythagoras and some of his disciples discovered the basic principle of the mathematic ratios involved in the relationship of tones. They then proceeded to work out the ratio that defines mathematically the position of every musical note in relation to every other note in a given diatonic scale. Much later this discovery led to fruitful experiments in the development of harmony.

GREEK LITERATURE

In literature, as in art, the Greeks found a vital and satisfying form of self-expression. By means of the heroic epic, the noble elegy, the moving song, by the power of the drama, and in the forms of history, philosophy, and public declamation, they interpreted man and his world with sympathy and beauty. Their literature still lives as one of the most superb and inspiring achievements of the human spirit.

Poetry

The language of the Greeks was itself one of the outstanding products of their genius. Their alphabet originally came to them from the Phoenicians, but, as usual in their borrowing from the Ancient Orient, the Hellenes showed their originality by improving upon what they took over. This

they did with the alphabet by adding vowels, which the Phoenicians did not use. They proceeded to develop their language into one of great clarity and subtlety, which was at once flexible, powerful, diverse, and beautiful. Evidence of the power of the Greek language is our own dependence upon the Greek vocabulary in our writings on politics, philosophy, and science.

The first great figure in Greek literature known to us is Homer, author of the unsurpassed epics, the *Iliad* and the *Odyssey*. These remarkable poems, which are the only epics surviving from this early period, originated in Asia Minor in the ninth century B.C. It has been suggested that they are not the work of a single hand but composites, to which many poets contributed over a long period of time. Certainly other poets sang of great deeds, long before the *Iliad* and *Odyssey* were set down in writing.

Odysseus and the Sirens. This red-figured vase pictures Odysseus tied to the mast of his ship while the sirens sing on their rocks. It gives a good idea of Greek merchant ships in the early fifth century B.C. (Courtesy of British Museum)

But it makes little difference whether the poems are the work of one or more authors, when they succeed in their purpose of winning rapt listeners.

Homer wrote of the proud past of the Achaeans who had fled to Ionia. The age in which he told his stories was wild and turbulent, the society was aristocratic, and its virtues were heroic. But it was also a simple time, lacking the settled ways and complexity of the Athenian Age. This accounts in part for the universality of Homer's appeal. The qualities that he described with such fire have stirred men in all ages. Men of vigor and imagination will always continue to respond to the *Iliad's* valiant Achaeans and gallant Trojans and will forever be captivated by lovely Helen, mighty Achilles, noble Hector, and the pathetic Andromache. The *Odyssey,* with its tales of the wily Odysseus seeking to return from Troy to his home in distant Ithaca, tells us more about peacetime Achaean society than does the *Iliad.* The charm of Homer, shown in these two epics, may be described as youthful and exuberant. He is not abstruse, nor has he any trace of sententiousness or cynicism.

There were other poets in Homer's age, but their work has not survived. None of those who continued in the same tradition in later times is notable, until we come to Hesiod, who lived in Boeotia about the beginning of the seventh century B.C. His *Theogony* sets forth the origin of the gods. The *Works and Days,* a more personal composition, tells first of the Golden Age of men and subsequent ages, ending in the poet's own time with the Age of Iron. In the longer portion of the poem, Hesiod speaks bitterly of the evils of life and especially of the hardships of the Boeotian farmer. Unlike Homer, he projects himself into his story, expressing directly his ethical views and complaining of his own ill fortune. Hesiod has been called a teacher as compared with Homer, who amused, thrilled, and enchanted his auditors without attempting to instruct.

Only tantalizing fragments survive of the poetry of the seventh and sixth centuries B.C. The best known of the lyric poets of this time are Alcaeus and Sappho, both of whom lived in Lesbos in the sixth century B.C. Their songs are intensely personal and burning with passion. Alcaeus was a great admirer of wine, the virtues of which he found equal to any occasion, and he was also much interested in love. He had an arrogant disdain for the masses of men, which led him to favor oligarchy as against democracy. The celebrated Sappho conducted a school for girls, teaching them music and dancing, and she became deeply devoted to some of her students. Her verse gives expression to her love and the pain it caused her.

Pindar of Thebes, who flourished in the first half of the fifth century B.C., was the greatest of the poets who composed choral lyrics. Most of his famous odes were written in honor of victories won at the great pan-Hellenic games. His brilliant and vivid lyrics, written with extraordinary originality and power, brought him fame early in life. He became the friend of several of the greatest rulers of his day, especially the tyrants of Acragas and Syracuse in Sicily.

The Drama

In Athens in the fifth century B.C. the tragic drama, which was always in the form of poetry, became one of the most powerful and revealing vehicles of thought and emotion. Its origin perhaps was in a rude celebration in which a chorus of men danced and sang in honor of Dionysus, god of wine and fertility. The leader of the chorus gradually came to have an important part, addressing the chorus and receiving answers. Eventually, an actor, separate from the chorus and its leader, was added and, still later, the number of actors was increased.

Within a short time Greek tragedy outgrew its crude beginnings and became a noble and beautiful form of artistic expression. The singers, who originally wore goatskins and engaged in rough play, were made subordinate to the actors. The latter told the story, rather than acted it out, for the players wore masks and most of the action took place off stage. The stories were almost always taken from mythology, the characters being heroes and gods.

Performances of tragedies eventually became important occasions. Trilogies were commonly offered on a single day, the performance taking from early morning until dark. Contests were held, and prizes were given for the best tragedies. Public officials supervised the choice of the dramatists who were to compete and assigned to wealthy citizens the responsibility for preparing the chorus, which they had to do at their own expense. The actors were paid by the state. Thus the audience paid nothing, and even the poorest citizens could attend.

In the modern tragedy, the plot assumes much importance, and the dramatist feels free to present the misfortunes of individuals of all kinds, even the most degraded. The Greek writer was much less concerned with the plot, and he had much less freedom in choosing the characters. For he was not expected to probe the problems of specific men but to express something of the meaning of human life as a whole or the problems that are in some measure common to all men. Frequently the story told in the Greek tragedy centers in a character who is noble and admirable but who is confronted with forces beyond his control and inexorably led to awful deeds. He goes astray almost in spite of himself, as do even the best of men, and for this reason, his downfall and suffering are terrible to behold.

The Attic tragedy lives for us in the surviving works of three superb poets of the fifth century B.C.—Aeschylus, Sophocles, and Euripides. All three were intellectual giants, though each was unlike the others.

Aeschylus (526–456 B.C.), the son of a noble family, fought in the war against the Persian invaders of his homeland and saw them routed. He devoted the whole of his civilian life to his art, and he did more than any other man to give it form. He was responsible, in particular, for the introduc-

Theater of Dionysus, Athens. Greek theaters were always located in a precinct sacred to the god Dionysus, whose altar occupied the center of the orchestra around which the chorus performed.

tion of a second actor, for until his time only one actor had appeared.

Only seven of Aeschylus' many plays have come down to us. In the earliest of these, *The Suppliants,* the poet has not as yet developed his skill in dramatic dialogue, though the lyric poetry is charming. In *The Persians,* which is one of the few Greek tragedies based on history rather than mythology, he describes with sympathy and insight the emotions called forth in the Persian court by the Greeks' defeat of Xerxes. The play called *Seven against Thebes* is based in part on the story of Oedipus, and *Prometheus Bound* tells of the suffering that Zeus inflicted on Prometheus for aiding mankind by giving them fire.

The trilogy known as the *Oresteia* is considered the best of Aeschylus' work. The three plays, *Agamemnon, The Libation Bearers,* and *Eumenides,* set forth the fate of Agamemnon and his family. In the first, Agamemnon, the leader of the Achaean force at Troy, is slain by his wife and her lover. In the second, Orestes, Agamemnon's son, kills his father's murderers. In the third, the Furies pursue Orestes, but finally he is exonerated. The subject of the trilogy offered the dramatist an excellent opportunity to express a profound religious emotion, to build up towering dramatic crises, and to create some of the most impressive characterizations in all tragedy.

Sophocles (496–406 B.C.) is often regarded as the greatest of the Greek tragic poets. He must have enjoyed the self-confidence that dwells with those on whom good fortune attends; not only was he born to wealth and position, gifted with intelligence and charm, and honored with offices of trust, but in his plays he succeeded in capturing the public fancy. Only seven of his plays still exist. *Antigone* presents with tremendous force Antigone's religious devotion to her dead brother, in the face of the legalistic opposition of her uncle. *Electra* makes use of the familiar theme dealing with the house of Agamemnon. But the greatest of Sophocles' plays is *Oedipus the King,* the Greek tragedy best known to modern audiences. Here the courageous and intelligent Oedipus is led on by his inherent nature to inevitable conflict with the gods and to his own destruction.

Euripides (470–406 B.C.), a younger contemporary of Sophocles, was apparently a man of humble origin. In his own lifetime he was less popular than the other notable dramatists; in later ages, however, his fame has equalled or has surpassed theirs, and more of his plays have survived. He marked another step in the progression that we noted in comparing the mood of Aeschylus with that of Sophocles, because Euripides spurned the myth of the superiority of the gods to men and frankly exposed their weaknesses. This spirit of humanism and rationalism gained him favor with men of later times, and even now makes him seem closer to us in outlook than his predecessors.

Euripides made some notable innovations in the form of the drama, although he could not change its basic structure. Generally he sought to overcome the obstacles that hindered him from presenting the lives of ordinary human beings, rather than heroes, and he pushed the chorus further into the background in favor of the actors. He was unusual, too, in including realistic portrayals of women and according a great deal of importance to love.

The plays of Euripides are uneven in quality, but all are of interest. *Alcestis,* the earliest extant work, includes one of the most pathetic figures in tragedy. *Hippolytus* tells the story of that chaste youth's refusal of Phaedra's dishonorable love. *The Trojan Women* portrays the boundless grief and abject helplessness of the women and children of Troy just after the fall of the city. *Iphigenia in Tauris* is a tightly constructed play dealing with the reunion of Iphigenia and her brother Orestes in Tauris and their eventual escape from that land. *Electra* deals with a theme that Aeschylus and Sophocles had also used.

Greek comedy, like tragedy, had its beginnings in celebrations devoted to Dionysus. At first, it consisted of crude, coarse chants and revels, amounting to little more than rustic buffoonery in honor of fertility. Gradually actors were introduced, as in tragedy, and the form was refined. Its earliest development was in Sicily, but its highest peak was reached in Attica, where comedy became a surpassing art. Unfortunately our knowledge of it is limited, since the only writer of comedy whose works have survived is Aristophanes (*c.*444–380 B.C.), who lived in Athens and wrote during and after the Peloponnesian War.

As we might expect, comedy was freer from convention than the more serious drama and always retained considerable license. The players spoke with amazing frankness, often voicing open criticism of leading political figures. Aristophanes did not hesitate to treat love with ribald candor (as in *Lysistrata*) or to poke fun at Socrates (as in *The Clouds*) or to treat Zeus himself lightly. Sometimes his humor became what might be regarded as gross obscenity. But it must be remembered in some respects Greek society was more robust and less hypocritical than ours. And it was still close to the earth—hence the open and healthy enjoyment of everything considered amusing about bodily functions. The freedom with which Aristophanes was allowed to criticize public leaders even during time of war is an impressive testimonial of the Athenians' devotion to free speech. Aristophanes was unquestionably a poet of genius and a keen observer of society, but we must not put unquestioning trust in his comments, for at times he was narrow and prejudiced.

The Greek Historians

Prose literature developed later among the Greeks than did poetry, but it was no less estimable when it reached maturity. His-

Herodotus. Found at Benha, Lower Egypt, this bust is not a portrait of the great historian, because it was made probably in the fourth century B.C. (Courtesy of the Metropolitan Museum of Art)

tory, especially, provided the material for some of the greatest works in Greek literature. Later historians owed much to their predecessors, but we have knowledge of none of these before Herodotus (484–425 B.C.). A native of Halicarnassus, who traveled widely and spent much time in Athens, Herodotus has kept the name that Cicero gave to him—the "Father of History"—because, with him, literary history came into being.

The *History* of Herodotus is a work of vast scope, the first half of which surveys the civilization of the lands conquered by the Persians, while the second half tells of the wars between the Persians and the Greeks. For his material the historian drew upon the works of earlier writers and such documents as were available, but mainly he re-

lied upon the information he gathered from talking with people in the lands he visited. This method resulted in the recording of many myths and anecdotes that have great charm though little historical value. Herodotus had his faults—he was sometimes credulous, especially of religious superstitions; he could be careless; and he had his share of prejudice. Nevertheless the work of this astute and friendly observer has tremendous historical value.

Thucydides (*c.*471–*c.*400 B.C.), who shares fame with Herodotus as a pioneer in the writing of history, was the son of a wealthy Athenian family. Little is known of his life except that he held an important naval command in the Peloponnesian War, and, because of what was judged an avoidable failure, that he was exiled in 424 B.C. His enforced banishment of twenty years gave him the leisure to write his famous History of the Peloponnesian War.

Though Thucydides and Herodotus are both historians of the first rank, their method of research and manner of writing are quite different. Whereas Herodotus chose a vast theme, exploring earlier times as well as more recent, Thucydides wrote on a narrow topic, confining himself to the Peloponnesian War. In keeping with the spirit of philosophical thinking in his time, Thucydides adopted a cold and rational approach to his subject, and his method is considered much more scientific than Herodotus'. Because he wrote only from his own knowledge or information that he carefully checked, he earned a pre-eminent reputation for accuracy and objectivity. He is generally recognized as the greatest historian of antiquity and one of the most admirable of all time.

The principal successor to Thucydides in the fourth century B.C. was Xenophon (*c.*434–*c.*355 B.C.). His *Anabasis* and *Hellenic History* have both charm and historical value. Yet he cannot be ranked with Thucydides on the score of insight, objectivity, or ability to draw a clear picture.

GREEK RELIGION

Religion was one of the most influential factors in the growth of the splendid and original Greek civilization. Indeed, the enormous cultural achievement of the Greeks cannot be accounted for without careful consideration of their religious outlook. Whereas religion often played a destructive or obstructive role in the cultural development of the ancient Orient, for the Greeks it was often a constructive force and never a hindrance.

The Olympian Gods

The Greek religion took its start in the early period of the Indo-European invasions with a fusion of the religious ideas of the invaders and those of the Aegean peoples, who had borrowed from the peoples of Anatolia. Both Aegeans and invaders had believed in anthropomorphic gods, and their religions had been polytheistic. Moreover, the same gods were often known in different regions under different names, and the powers and respect accorded to certain of the gods also varied from place to place. Because of these variations, the Hellenes found it easy to accept foreign gods as manifestations of their own familiar divinities.

The poets Homer and Hesiod did much to bring order out of this confusion. In their writings they described the individual gods, defined their powers and functions, and gave them the aspects by which they were known in later times throughout Hellas. But the works of Homer and Hesiod never took on the nature of sacred religious writings, which could provide a basis for strict orthodoxy and the persecution of heretics. They contained neither an ecclesiastic nor a sacerdotal system to block the development of new thought in order to maintain old ideas and the privileges of a priesthood. Priests there were, to be sure, but in early times the heads of families commonly held the office of priest, and in the classical age, when the priesthood became a vocation, the priests never gained great power.

Thus the Greeks of the classical age had a religion that possessed little ethical content. Their outlook was not directed toward another world beyond the grave, for their religion did not stress a future life. Because their priests had little power, the Greeks were at liberty to inquire, to pursue freely knowledge of all kinds, with no fear of horrible deities, such as the Semitic Moloch or the monsters who peopled the afterworld of the Egyptians. Moreover their religion did not give them a gnawing sense of sin, which would make them think of the body as despicable and its functions—for example, the sexual—as shameful. Their anthropomorphic gods were genial and whimsical, sharing the same emotions as men, sometimes as ridiculous as men. Knowing gods of this sort, the Greeks could adopt a happy, secular outlook and develop their talents without anxiety.

At the head of the classical Greek pantheon was Zeus, the god of the sky, thunder, and rain. Zeus was regarded as the ruler of all other gods as well as of men. Majestic and terrible though he was, he was not beyond reach, for as the dispenser of justice and the protector of the helpless, he might be persuaded to intercede in behalf of other deities or mortals. His many peccadilloes were common knowledge, giving ample reason for the displeasure of Hera, his sister and wife, who was the protectress of marriage. Poseidon, one of Zeus's two brothers, was the god of the sea, while Pluto (sometimes called Hades), the other brother, was god of the underworld. The radiant Apollo was god of prophecy and patron of the arts. In his charge were laws, healing, the protection of youths, and the founding of cities. Athena, goddess of wisdom, who was born full grown from the forehead of

Seated Gods—probably Poseidon, Apollo, and Artemis. The complete cella frieze of the Parthenon represents in marble the annual Pan-Athenaic procession. This panel, c.40 inches high, from the east side, shows three of Athena's guests surveying the scene with Olympian calm. (Courtesy Royal Greek Embassy)

Zeus, was especially reverenced in Attica. Aphrodite, goddess of love, was the wife of Hephaestus, god of metal and handicrafts, and she was also the mistress of Ares, the god of war. Dionysus (Bacchus), who came into the Olympian pantheon later than the others, was associated mainly with fertility and the cycle of plant life. He was also known as a god of wine and a patron of the arts. Demeter was a divinity associated with the earth and its bounty. Hermes, the messenger of the gods, also symbolized fertility, but his worship never became a mystery, as did the cults of Dionysus and Demeter.

Oracles and Omens

The state religion of the Greeks was not free of superstition. The belief in omens and fortune-telling was particularly strong, and some of the gods were noted for their prophetic powers. The chief means of divining the future was through oracles, who were priests of a special kind, attending shrines where the gods were believed to make answer to questions addressed to them. The best known of these shrines was

that of Apollo at Delphi, where sometimes even foreign kings came to consult the oracles and seek revelations. By the answers that they gave in the name of the god, the priests sometimes exercised a large influence on affairs of great moment. On occasion they might take a bribe in return for a favorable prediction.

Mysteries

The Greek religion was generally sane and well balanced. But there was another current in Greek religion, revealed in the mystery cults, which was more emotional and other-worldly in outlook. These cults were called "mysteries" because they were built around secret rituals and initiations that assured members of salvation in a future life. Compared with the civic religion based on the Olympian pantheon, these mysteries were subjective—that is, the interest of the worshipers was solely in their own fate. Such cults arose because among the Greeks, as other peoples, there were always some who yearned passionately for an intimate, personal contact with some power stronger than themselves. This need for a strongly supernatural religion was filled by the Eleusinian Mysteries and by Orphism. These mysteries, however, while they were of considerable importance in the sum total of Greek religious life, were not typical of it in the classical age. They became much more important in the centuries that followed the collapse of Greek political freedom.

Festivals

There were several great festivals and games in which all the city-states participated, and these provided one of the most powerful forces working for cultural unification in Greece. Of all the great festivals, the games in honor of Zeus held at Olympia once every four years were the oldest and most renowned. Other celebrations were held at Delphi in honor of Apollo, and on the Isthmus of Corinth in honor of Poseidon. Festivals held at Athens attracted widespread interest, because of that city's prominent position. The Greater Panathenaea at Athens culminated in the grand procession that is depicted on the frieze of the Parthenon.

At these notable gatherings, which were state occasions of the greatest importance as well as religious celebrations, competitions of various kinds were held. The victors received only tokens, such as the wreath of olive leaves given to the winners in the Olympic games. But because success in competition was a matter of civic pride, the winners usually received other rewards of a more substantial nature when they returned to their own cities, to which their victories in the games had brought great honor and renown.

These festivals provide a striking illustration of the way in which Greek life was unified, for in them religion blended with other intellectual, artistic, and athletic activities. The physical sports—racing, wrestling, throwing the javelin and the discus— were only part of the whole. There were also contests in poetry and music, and the gatherings offered orators and writers a chance to make known their talents. The high ideals, both civic and religious, that were maintained in these contests and festivals helped to inculcate the spirit and tradition of good citizenship that distinguished Greek culture at its best. And when the games deteriorated in the fourth century B.C., this was a sign of the general decline of ethical standards in Greek civilization as a whole.

The Acropolis of Athens—center foreground, the Propylaea (gateway); front right, Temple of Athena Nike; rear left, the Erechtheum; rear right, the Parthenon. Many ancient cities developed around an acra, or hill. What once had been chosen for military advantages, later became the site for temples, palaces, and public buildings. After the Persians destroyed the old buildings and Pericles' program was completed, c.409 B.C., the Athenian acropolis was the dwelling place only of the gods and a sanctuary sacred to Athena. (From Martin L. D'Ooge, *The Acropolis of Athens*, 1909. The Macmillan Co.)

GREEK PHILOSOPHY

If it be considered that rational speculation hardly existed among the peoples of
the ancient Orient, the awakening of the
Greek mind in the sixth century B.C. appears to be an almost incredible miracle.
Seldom, if ever, has any more remarkable
pioneer work been done in the field of intellectual investigation and speculation than
among the Greeks in the great age of their
civilization.

The Ionic School

The first of the great figures to win fame
for their speculation on the nature of the
universe was Thales of Miletus (c.640–
c.546 B.C.), who is known as the "Father of
Philosophy." He attained prominence early
in the sixth century B.C., at about the time
when Solon was instituting his reforms in
Athens.

In attempting to explain the world,
Thales held that all things are made of water, which is the first and only element. The
differences among things arise only from
modifications of this prime element; ultimately, all things again become water. How
Thales explained the origin of water itself
and the process of its modification, we do
not know.

Another notable Ionic philosopher was
Anaximander of Miletus (c.611–c.547 B.C.).
He, too, was a materialist. But instead of fix-
ing upon one element as the substance of all
things, he took the "indefinite" or "boundless" as the first principle. Out of bound-
lessness, through a process of the separation
of opposites—such as heat and cold—arose
the world and the four elements that compose it—earth, fire, air, and water. Living
things came into being, he suggested, when
elements mingled, producing warmth and
moisture, and the simpler forms of life later
evolved into more advanced forms. Thus
Anaximander was the first to set forth a

theory of evolution, crude as it was. Finally,
he believed, all differentiated forms return
to the primary matter, undifferentiated and
formless, from which they had arisen.

A third great Milesian thinker of the
sixth century B.C. was Anaximenes, who
thought that the primary substance was air.
By a process of becoming thicker or thinner, air developed into the various forms of
matter. This process is induced by heat and
cold—heat rarefies air into fire, while cold
condenses air into water and solid matter.
Thus Anaximenes tried to answer the difficult and important question: how do changes
take place in the original stuff? All three
Milesians were speculative scientists, and in
their search for a reasonable solution to the
riddle of existence, all three hit upon matter as the source of all things.

The Pythagoreans

Quite a different philosophical bent is
shown by Pythagoras (c.582–c.507 B.C.),
who left his native Samos to settle in Croton
in southern Italy. Pythagoras was not a philosopher in the usual sense but a religious
teacher. Though he was interested in the
sciences, especially mathematics and musical theory, he did not, like the Ionian
thinkers, attempt a materialistic or physical
interpretation of the universe. His inclination was much more toward a metaphysical
explanation of things. Thus, he sought an
explanation not in, but beyond, the physical
world. His followers formed a religious order rather than a philosophical school, and
their aim was to set up a way of life that
would free the soul from its confinement in
the body. Unless the soul attained this freedom, they believed, it would be doomed to
a weary round of reincarnation.

The Pythagorean brotherhood believed
in the cultivation of the arts and sciences,
however, as well as religious speculation.
This led them to a philosophy based on

numbers. Number they regarded as the key to an understanding of the universe, and though their theory gave rise to a fanciful symbolism, they and their leader did much for the advancement of mathematics and astronomy, and they did even more to stir the mind and kindle the imagination of later thinkers.

The Eleatics

Xenophanes (active *c.*536 B.C.), like Pythagoras, came originally from the eastern Mediterranean. After a period of wandering he too settled at Elea, also in southern Italy. From the name of this town comes the designation *Eleatic* that is given to him and his successors. Xenophanes had no use for the mystic religion of Pythagoras and little more for the old anthropomorphic polytheism. In place of the old superstitions, he offered a pantheistic belief in the oneness of God.

Xenophanes' idea of the unity of the world was taken up by Parmenides and Zeno. Parmenides, born in Elea toward the end of the sixth century B.C., taught that eternal "being" is the only reality, whereas change and movement are mere illusion, known to us only by our unreliable senses. Above the senses, which mislead us, Parmenides put reason, which alone leads to truth. Zeno, who came a little later, supported his master's doctrine though he added nothing new to it, by attacking the opposing theory of plurality and change and by formulating intellectual puzzles that bring into question the findings of our senses and our usual conceptions of space and time.

Heraclitus

Heraclitus of Ephesus (active *c.*500 B.C.) resembled Parmenides, his contemporary, in developing an abstract philosophy and

giving high respect to reason. But in nothing else were the two alike. The Ephesian was a man of aristocratic birth and arrogant temperament, completely convinced of his own wisdom, scornful of those less generously gifted with intelligence, and contemptuous of the crowd. He despised both the customary religion and the philosophy of his predecessors.

Heraclitus believed that the only reality is the process of change or becoming. Reality cannot consist of sheer being, without change, for nothing ever remains unchanged. Rather, all things are constantly in a state of change. As an illustration of what he meant, he argued that a man cannot set foot twice in the same river, for the river has undergone change before he can put his foot in it for a second time.

The essence of the universe is fire, Heraclitus believed, because fire is the essence of change. The primal fire, he identified with reason, or wisdom. Involved in the process of change is the principle of strife, out of which comes the harmony of opposites. Life requires opposition, as appetite requires hunger, and rest requires fatigue. Thus Heraclitus accepted the endless process of change that nature revealed to him, and thus he accounted happily for the struggle of conflicting forces that is omnipresent in nature. The philosophy that he created was extraordinarily original and penetrating.

Empedocles, Anaxagoras and the Atomists

The leading philosophers of the mid-fifth century B.C. continued the work of the earlier thinkers. Empedocles of Agrigentum (*c.*500–*c.*430 B.C.) taught that there are four elements—fire, air, water, and earth— of which all things are composed. The varying proportions of the elements, when combined, account for the differences among things.

Anaxagoras of Clazomenae (c.500–c.428 B.C.) believed that all things are made of elements, which he called seeds, that abound in infinite number. The seeds themselves are everlasting, but they are always combining and dissociating. In this process of mingling and unmingling, like seeds seek to join together. Behind the process is a governing intelligence, giving order to the world, which Anaxagoras termed mind (*nous*). This conception of a universal directing mind or intelligence was a new notion in Greek philosophy that Plato was to develop. The emphasis Anaxagoras put on the idea of original seeds anticipated the view of the Atomists.

The atomic philosophy was founded by Leucippus, a little-known contemporary of Empedocles and Anaxagoras, and it was further elaborated by Democritus, a Thracian disciple of Anaxagoras who lived in the fourth century B.C. The Atomists recognized no all-powerful mind in the universe but insisted rather upon a stark materialism. For them, reality consists of atoms and the void or space in which the atoms move. These atoms are particles, so small as to be invisible, so many as to be numberless, all formed of the same matter but varying in size and shape. All things in the world, and the world itself, are made by the coming together of atoms falling through space. In this continuous falling, like atoms seek one another.

Leucippus did not attempt to explain motion, or the falling of the atoms in space, but said only that necessity required the union of like atoms. In his philosophy, however, there was no place for gods or a directing reason—the world was wholly material. His theory was more popular in later times than in his own, being adopted by the Epicureans and by more recent materialists.

The Sophists

All the philosophers so far mentioned were primarily concerned with the nature of the world as a whole. About the middle of the fifth century B.C., however, some thinkers began to concentrate upon the position of man, in particular, in the universe. The first of these new humanists, the Sophists, came to prominence at the time of the great surge of individualism that followed the Persian Wars and the spread of democracy throughout the Greek world. The Sophists found the search for a vague and elusive truth about the universe a waste of time. They thought it much better to study the more practical problem of man and his society. As teachers, their ideal purpose was to equip young men to assume their responsibilities as citizens. This aim was in harmony with the exalted conception of citizenship in the age of Athens, for the democracies of that time had need of the kind of man who would take good care of his public and private affairs, and to do so, the citizen must have a good education. Above all, he must know how to speak with eloquence in such public gatherings as law courts and the assembly.

Though most of them were teachers, the Sophists did not set up schools such as we know. Instead, each of them specialized in a subject of interest to him and traveled about from city to city, giving instruction to those who would have his services. Protagoras, the earliest and one of the greatest of the Sophists, was mainly interested in political science. Gorgias specialized in rhetoric, and Prodicus in grammar. Others had wider interests, and a few, such as Isocrates, offered a well-rounded course of education, including ethical as well as practical instruction.

The Sophists won a wide audience, especially in Athens, and their teaching had much influence. Generally they adopted a questioning attitude, examining in a critical spirit the old standards of morality and even bringing into doubt the existence of the gods. Teaching of this kind whetted the growing rationalism of the times, but unfortunately it did not have a constructive influence. The Sophists tore down old beliefs, but in their time no one arose to create a new system of thought to replace the ideas they attacked.

The spirit of the age, to which the Sophists appealed, was well expressed in the formula of Protagoras: "Man is the measure of all things." The author of this maxim understood it to mean that truth is what man experiences, and the world is what man makes of it. Others, however, put a more sophisticated interpretation on it: if man is the measure of all things, then each man decides for himself what is good and what is bad. This sense of the maxim suggests how it was that the teachings of the Sophists undermined the standards of morality.

Socrates

In Socrates (469–399 B.C.), the son of an Athenian stonemason, we meet one of the most interesting and attractive figures of all Greek philosophy. A man of indomitable personal courage and extraordinary endurance, he distinguished himself as a soldier in the ranks. And his good sense and balance marked his participation in the democratic government of Athens, when it fell to his lot, during the last years of the Peloponnesian War, to serve as a member of the Council of Five Hundred. Though in appearance he was decidedly ugly, the warm devotion of his friends and disciples attests to his charm.

Socrates was convinced that before men can begin to learn, they must recognize their own ignorance. Hence he tried first to clear the minds of his students of misconceptions. Only then could he lead them to a better understanding. To accomplish this, he made use of the dialectical method—that is, questioning the ideas of the student and making him think for himself—instead of lectures.

Socrates reached and inspired a number of brilliant young men in Athens—notably Plato, his greatest disciple—but the mass of men were left untouched. A number of the young men who attended his discussions belonged to the oligarchic party, and Socrates himself was therefore widely presumed to be in sympathy with this faction. Consequently, the philosopher was implicated when, with the restoration of democracy after the overthrow of Spartan rule, there was a reaction in Athens against the oligarchic party. In 399 B.C. Socrates was accused of teaching ideas hostile to the state religion and of corrupting the youth. Although he might have got off with a light sentence had he been willing to compromise his principles, he chose to stand his ground. He was therefore condemned to death and, in accordance with the set sentence, drank a poison brewed of hemlock. His death is movingly described in Plato's *Phaedo*.

We have no writings of Socrates' own hand, and consequently must depend largely on what Plato reports. Unfortunately, we cannot always tell how much of what Plato writes is Socratic and how much is Platonic. We do know, however, that Socrates did not formulate a systematic philosophy. Like the Sophists, he was concerned solely with men and their problems, and he sought to give men moral guidance.

Unlike the Sophists, Socrates emphasized that there are objective standards of morality. And the rules of virtue, which alone can give men happiness, are such that men can gain knowledge of these standards. For this reason, Socrates tried hard in his dialectical method to show his students the importance of straight, clear thinking. He was sure that if men could disabuse themselves of false conceptions and learn what is good, they would live virtuously and hence would win happiness.

Thus Socrates' teachings were in essence opposed to those of the Sophists. Where the latter were destructive, he was constructive. Where the Sophists left men wondering what good there was in anything, Socrates taught that virtue is within the reach of all men, if they will but use their reason, and the life of virtue will assure them happiness. Like the Sophists, he was a teacher, but he did not share their emphasis upon practical education. Instead he upheld the theory of a liberal education, which maintains that a man must learn how to live the good life before he seeks practical knowledge.

Plato

The greatest of Socrates' pupils was Plato (427–347 B.C.), a wealthy aristocrat who thought little of the democracy of his native Athens. After the death of Socrates, Plato traveled abroad for a time, visiting the west and probably also Egypt. Though he renounced politics at home, he hoped to see his theories of government adopted in Syracuse, which he visited three times. But his experiments in politics there ended in humiliation and failure. For most of his life, he was a student and teacher in Athens, where eventually he maintained a school known as the Academy.

Plato was much more interested than Socrates in formal philosophy. Unlike his master, he constructed a systematic body of thought that attemped to explain the meaning of the entire universe, and, again unlike Socrates, he left a large collection of writings. Most of these are cast in the form of dialogues, in which Socrates is one of the participants. The clarity and beauty of the dialogues are such as to establish Plato as one of the greatest masters of Greek prose. In his compositions, philosophy became literature par excellence.

Unquestionably Socrates was the teacher who exerted the deepest influence on the reserved and dignified Plato. The abiding respect and affection that the younger man felt for his master has made their relationship as student and teacher justly famous. There were several other sources of Platonic inspiration, however, that deserve mention, and we may be sure that Plato was aware of what had been done by earlier philosophers. Both Heraclitus and the Eleatics contributed to his thought, and he was also deeply impressed by the Pythagoreans. Like the latter, Plato was particularly devoted to mathematics. Another stimulus to his thinking was provided by the Sophists, the heretics of the age of Athens.

The core of Plato's teaching is his theory of forms or ideas. In his view, concepts or ideas are the only reality—immutable, universal, perfect. The material world, which we know through our senses, is merely transitory, an imperfect copy of the world of ideas. An individual dog, he would argue, is not real, for it is transitory and perishable, and it varies from other individual dogs. The reality is the idea of the dog, which is enduring and changeless and can be conceived only by the reason. Thus Plato believed that only ideas are real and that material things are actually unreal. The explanation is that he trusted reason and distrusted the senses as conveyors of truth. The world we know through the senses is like an image reflected in a mirror. The image reflects some properties, but others— such as odor or sound—it cannot report. The senses, like the mirror, give us some partial knowledge of the world of ideas, but only through reason, which is a far better instrument than the senses, can we wholly apprehend the realm of ideas.

The ethical position of Plato, like that of Socrates, was that man should use his reason to attain virtue. This is related to the conception that underlies his political theory, too, for in *The Republic,* Plato maintained that the love of virtue should be inculcated by the state. The cultivation of virtue is, indeed, the highest possible purpose of the state.

In the ideal state, as Plato conceived it, there were to be three classes: the lowest would do the work; the second would protect the state; the highest would govern. Admittance to the two upper classes would be based solely on fitness for the duties involved, and it would therefore require a rigorous education. Social life would be organized on a communistic basis. The amassing of wealth would be prohibited, and so would family ties. Women would share in education and also in military service.

In recent years Plato has often been bitterly criticized. Nevertheless, we are much in his debt, and Plato will find ardent champions as long as men read books of philosophy. Especially will he be appreciated for his liveliness, his exalted poetic imagination, his noble and humane ideals, the generosity and affection with which he always wrote of Socrates, and his gift for expressing lofty and stimulating thought in the clearest and most beautiful language.

Aristotle

Aristotle (384–322 B.C.) was born in the Greek city of Stagirus, in the northern Aegean. His father, who was the physician of the king of Macedon, may have given him his first introduction to scientific training. In 367 B.C. Aristotle went to Athens, where he attended the lectures of Plato at the Academy, and for twenty years he remained in close association with his master. Later he served for a time as tutor to the young Macedonian prince Alexander, before founding a school of his own in Athens.

Aristotle did a prodigious amount of writing, but the small portion that survives consists mostly of his lecture notes, which were not intended for publication. From them, we can see that Aristotle was a man of superlative brilliance and energy, but his notes lack the fire and imagination of Plato's prose.

Aristotle considered it essential for his students to know how to think clearly before beginning to think at all. To aid them in their thinking, he therefore worked out a complete system of formal logic. His further study led him to divide knowledge into

three parts. Speculative or theoretic knowledge has as its purpose knowing for the sake of knowing; it includes metaphysics, the natural sciences, and mathematics. Practical philosophy, which is directed toward the achievement of human happiness, includes ethics, politics, and economics. Under creative philosophy Aristotle put the theory of the arts.

Metaphysics, which is the study of being or reality, Aristotle considered the most important branch of knowledge. In this field, he took over Plato's teachings but greatly modified them. He reduced existence to matter and form, the latter meaning much the same as the idea in Plato's system of thought. Form is the universal, while matter is the particular; matter is what a thing is made of, while form is what it becomes. Where Aristotle sharply differs from Plato is in his insistence that in the realm of na-

Aristotle—a contemporary Greek Hellenistic statue. (Alinari photograph)

ture the two are inseparable—form, the universal reality, exists only *in,* and not apart from, matter, the particular.

In his physical system, Aristotle thought of all things as moving toward their end or purpose, according to nature's plan. At the bottom is unorganized matter, lacking form. Above is organized matter, which includes the whole range of beings having form and function. Highest of all is God, in whom perfect form is attained. This deity—the "Prime Mover," or source of all motion—is far above the world of men and has nothing to do with it. He is completely aloof, engaged solely in self-contemplation.

Although Aristotle's speculative philosophy is as abstract as Plato's, it is based on a careful study of the natural phenomena of the world we live in. Thus it allows a greater measure of respect for the material world.

Aristotle's practical philosophy is expressed mainly in his *Ethics* and *Politics.* His *Ethics* stresses moderation as the key to virtue and happiness. In his *Politics* he makes the happiness or welfare of the state the end to be sought. To attain this end, he does not favor such a far-reaching regimentation as Plato, but he does indorse the position that the state must control the individuals under its rule to secure the welfare of the whole. He was less critical of democracy than Plato, but he considered monarchy and aristocracy theoretically superior to democracy. In his study of politics he placed much reliance in the method of observation rather than the elaboration of political principles simply by logic, and he went to the trouble to investigate the constitutions of 158 states. Ultimately he seems to have concluded that no one type of government is the best in all circumstances.

GREEK SCIENCE

It will be clear from the foregoing survey of classical and preclassical philosophy that there were scientists among the Hellenes, but it will also be clear that the Greek science of this time was, in its own way, as one-sided as Egyptian science had been. For where Egyptian science was almost purely practical, the science of the early Greeks was chiefly speculative. Except for medicine, it was almost always allied with philosophy, which it served as a handmaiden. Many of the greatest philosophers of the sixth and fifth centuries B.C. were notable mathematicians or astronomers—Thales, Pythagoras, Anaxagoras, and Plato, for example; but their chief interest was the universe as a whole, not the parts of it, and their thoughts were prone to soar quickly and easily away from the concrete problems of the world. Yet these early scientists made a beginning, and their work is well worth consideration.

Very probably the first Greek mathematicians learned much from the easterners with whom they came into contact. Important additions were then made by the Greeks, especially by Pythagoras and his followers. Though they had mystical conceptions about the nature of numbers, they contributed a great deal to contemporary understanding of the subject, particularly in geometry. Several of the Sophists were good mathematicians and Plato, who was deeply influenced by the Pythagorean veneration for numbers, was always a staunch advocate of the study of geometry. Unfortunately the Greeks never devised a simple and flexible system of numerals, such as could have popularized the knowledge of mathematics, but this lack was no hindrance to speculation.

Some progress was made in astronomy, also, beginning with Thales, who is said to have predicted an eclipse. Again, however, the Pythagoreans were still more advanced. One of the brotherhood even rejected the geocentric theory of the universe; but this mistaken belief continued to be generally accepted. Considerable success in measuring time was achieved, and in the fourth century B.C. the solar year was reckoned at 365¼ days. As so often among the Greeks, speculation flourished, but the lack of instruments restricted the accurate study of the heavens, and the problem of creating such instruments evoked little interest.

Some attention was given to the biological sciences, but until the time of Aristotle little headway was made. That industrious student carried on research in a number of fields and collected an amazing amount of information, greatly surpassing anything that had been known up to his time. He made mistakes in his studies of animal life just as he did in his physics, but nevertheless he left behind him both a method and a mass of information of great value. It is unfortunate that this, perhaps his richest scientific bequest, was so long ignored. Aristotle's botanical studies were carried forward in the fourth century B.C. by his student Theophrastus; they were then allowed to lapse.

Medicine was practiced among the Greeks in very early times, but it was not until the sixth century B.C. that real progress began. As in the case of the other sciences, the first impetus came from the philosophers and, here, as elsewhere, a leading place was taken by the Pythagoreans, whose scientific work was as fruitful as their philosophy was fanciful. Although the names of a number of early medical men are known, the first great physician is Hippocrates of Cos, and even about him we know but little. In early Greek times the healing art was usually in the hands of guilds or families of priests devoted to the gods and heroes of medicine, and to one such group Hippocrates belonged. By this time—he was born about 460 B.C.—medicine was freeing itself of its earlier religious associations, and certainly there was nothing superstitious about Hippocrates' attitude. He sensibly regarded illness as a departure from the normal functioning of the body, not as the work of supernatural forces; and he treated it as such, regularly attempting to restore health by giving the body a chance to use its own recuperative powers. Drugs and surgery were employed sparingly, and the emphasis was put upon such things as diet and fresh air. He made errors, naturally—believing, for example, that there are four humors in the body which must be kept in the proper proportion to each other for the maintenance of health. Altogether his work was exceedingly valuable, and he even contributed some of the terms now customary in medical practice. The Oath of Hippocrates, which has made his name immortal, set the highest ethical and scientific standards for medical practitioners.

There was relatively little interest among the Greeks in the more practical sciences. Something was done in mechanics and, apparently, also in optics, but both these branches had to do with the building of temples and other public structures, the important point clearly being artistic rather than scientific achievement.

Why were the classical Greeks so much more interested in speculative than applied science? One reason is that the Greeks had a fondness for speculation that social conditions allowed them to indulge. Unlike the ancient Orientals, they were free to think and apparently they found it natural to think first; they did not frequently get to the stage of acting on their newly acquired knowledge. The chief apparent reason for this emphasis on speculative rather than applied science is that in Hellas the men who devoted themselves to science were not driven by the need for solving pressing practical problems, such as the storing of water against drought. They were usually men of the upper classes, such as Heraclitus and Plato, and they took rather a disdainful attitude toward utilitarian affairs. Their

Greek Terracotta. Not all Greek statues were heroic. Reproduced here, exact size, is a typical terracotta figure. These statuettes have been found in large quantities and in many places—houses, graves, sanctuaries. Their subjects range from gods and goddesses to children and nurses and humorous animals. Some may even be copies of large-scale cult statues. Evidently they were used for many purposes—as ornaments, as toys, as offerings to the dead, and as gifts to the gods. The artists who made them were humble craftsmen; probably many were slaves. Some of the figures were handmade; some were molded, and it is possible that the creators of the originals from which the molds were made were well-known sculptors. Although the terracottas date back as far as the late seventh century B.C., this is a fourth-century figure, showing a little girl carrying another on her shoulders—as part of a game or for a forfeit. (Courtesy of the Metropolitan Museum of Art)

whole philosophical and social tradition was responsible for this attitude. They were philosophers before they were scientists, and their chief interest was in searching for philosophical truth about the universe. As aristocrats, they considered the problems of agriculture, commerce, and industry to be the business of farmers, tradesmen, and slaves, except when the state as a whole was concerned. In the succeeding age this narrow outlook was to give way to a broader view, encouraged by Aristotle's productive work and made possible by changing social conditions.

CONCLUSION

Adjectives of many kinds could be used to describe Greek cultural life of the early and classical period. It was individualistic, secular, lively, original, relatively free, and certainly humanistic. It was also human, and therefore far from perfect. The Greeks were frequently conceited and arrogant. Their individualism and secularism sometimes led to materialism, as in the case of Athenian imperialism. There was a dark side to moral standards and social life, as indicated by the tolerance of slavery and, again, by the nature of Greek marriage, family life, and the status of women. The Hellenes were by no means free of superstition. Politically and socially they could be very lazy, refusing to adopt needed changes or even to rec-ognize the need for change when it was pointed out to them. Yet it was unquestionably true that the Greek city-states achieved some of the most significant cultural advances in the entire history of civilization, and that ever since, the Greek achievement has greatly enriched human experience.

Suggestions for Further Reading

Source Materials

Anthologies

G. H. Knoles and R. K. Snyder, eds., *Readings in Western Civilization* (rev. ed., New York, 1954), pp. 42–90.
Good selections from the *Ethics* of Aristotle, from Sophocles, and from Plato.

A. J. Toynbee, ed., *Greek Civilization and Character* (New York, 1954). (A Mentor paper-back.)
A collection of selections from the Greek classical authors.

A. J. Toynbee. ed., *Greek Historical Thought from Homer to the Age of Heraclitus* (New York, 1954). (A Mentor paper-back.)
A selection from the writings of the Greek historians.

R. Warnock and G. K. Anderson, eds., *The World in Literature* (Chicago, 1950–1951), Volume I, Chapter 2.
Selections from the Greek classics: Aeschylus, Sophocles, Euripides, Plato, Aristotle, Sappho, and others.

Contemporary Writings

Again, the student is urged to read as much as possible of what the Greeks themselves wrote, rather than secondary works about the Greeks. The following works are all classics; most of them can be found in any bookstore in cheap, popular editions.

Aeschylus, *Plays.*
Aristophanes, *The Eleven Comedies.*
Aristotle, *Ethics.*
Euripides, *Four Plays.*
Herodotus, *History of the Persian Wars.*
Plato, *Dialogues.*
Sophocles, *Tragedies.*
Thucydides, *History of the Peloponnesian War.*

Secondary Works

J. D. Beazley and B. Ashmole, *Greek Sculpture and Painting* (New York, 1932).
A good, short account of the chief works of Greek art, and of the changing artistic styles, techniques, and traditions. Well illustrated.

J. Burnet, *Early Greek Philosophy* (London, 1930).
A very satisfactory standard book on the early philosophers, from Thales to Leucippus. Fairly nontechnical both in history and philosophy.

L. Cooper, *The Greek Genius and Its Influence* (New Haven, 1917).
A famous book. Composed of a collection of statements, in individual chapters, from major modern scholars and writers, on the significance of the classics in the present day. Unusually well written.

F. M. Cornford, *From Religion to Philosophy* (New York, 1912).
Based on the thesis that philosophy stems from religion. Notes that in Greece this step was taken about the sixth century B.C., when the spirit of rational inquiry questioned the traditional beliefs, without breaking distinctly from the religious thought. A fairly technical book, both for philosophy and history.

H. N. Couch and R. M. Geer, *Classical Civilization: Greece* (New York, 1940).
A standard textbook. Stresses the cultural aspects of Greece, against a background of political-military history. An attractive, easily read book.

G. L. Dickinson, *The Greek View of Life* (London, 1932).
An excellent book, useful both for the novice and the expert in Greek history. A subjective

vital appraisal of the Greek attitude toward religion, the state, the individual, and artistic appreciation, based on ancient literary sources. Deceptively simple in presentation.

R. C. Flickinger, *The Greek Theater and Its Drama* (Chicago, 1936).
Discusses the development of drama, its origins, types, and how the traditions, religion, national ideas, and physical limitations of the stage influenced the developing drama.

E. A. Gardner, *A Handbook of Greek Sculpture* (New York, 1915).
A standard handbook, highly detailed in the description of individual pieces rather than presenting an over-all view. Fair illustrations.

A. E. Haigh, *The Attic Theater* (Oxford, 1907).
Treats of the technicalities of the stage, the public contests, the form of the theater, the scenes, costumes, etc. Little discussion of the individual dramas or dramatists.

E. Hamilton, *The Greek Way* (New York, 1930).
A sometimes able, often uneven, subjective study of the Greek attitude toward life and letters, contrasted with the modern point of view. Written for a wide public.

T. F. Higham and C. M. Bowra, eds., *Oxford Book of Greek Verse in Translation* (Oxford, 1938).
An authoritative and representative anthology.

G. Howe and G. A. Harrer, eds., *Greek Literature in Translation* (New York, 1924).
An excellent collection.

W. Jaeger, *Paideia: The Ideals of Greek Culture* (London, 1938).
A history of Greek culture and the ideals behind it as reflected by its writers. Stresses the educational training that made men think as they did. Assumes a knowledge of Greek history. A very important, stimulating book on an advanced level.

G. Murray, *Five Stages of Greek Religion* (Oxford, 1925).
A readable work, developed from public lectures. Deals with a highly controversial field, tracing a development from one kind of religion to another, and calling one higher than another. The book shows much religious insight and understanding.

M. P. Nilsson, *Greek Popular Religion* (New York, 1940).
Treats of religion according to popular beliefs and customs, superstition and folklore, that carried over in great part to the more formal religions. Shows even Classical Greek thought full of superstition. This changed with time and conditions up to Christianity.

G. Norwood, *Greek Comedy* (London, 1931).
A history of Greek comedy, tracing its origins, then working through the individual plays and playwrights, including some of the minor ones. Book written in terms of the individual works more than as an over-all summary.

G. Norwood, *Greek Tragedy* (Boston, 1920).
A tracing of the history of Greek tragedy in terms of the individual playwrights, with special emphasis on the three greatest dramatists and their individual works.

W. J. Oates and E. O'Neill, eds., *The Complete Greek Drama* (New York, 1938).
The body of Greek drama, in a variety of translation.

G. M. A. Richter, *The Sculpture and Sculptors of the Greeks* (New Haven, 1950).
A standard work, beautifully produced with a generous number of good pictures. Gives the historical background and later developments of art. An analysis of styles and techniques, and a discussion of individual sculptors.

H. J. Rose, *A Handbook of Greek Literature* (London, 1934).
A combination of encyclopedia, interpretation, and criticism of the major Greek literature. Useful as a reference work, listing authors, legends, types of literature, setting, etc.

H. J. Rose, *A Handbook of Greek Mythology* (New York, 1928).
A study in great detail of the history of the Greek myth; the early stories of the origins of things, the genealogies of the gods, and various Greek legends. Easy reference, sound.

G. Sarton, *A History of Science; Ancient Science through the Golden Age of Greece* (Cambridge, Mass., 1952).
The finest history of ancient science yet written —the first volume in a projected multi-volume history.

T. V. Smith, ed., *Philosophers Speak for Themselves* (Chicago, 1934).
Selections from the great Greek philosophical writings.

M. H. Swindler, *Ancient Painting* (New Haven, 1929).

Includes all ancient art; but quite naturally lays the heaviest stress upon the Greek. An able work, well illustrated. Thorough, but not too technical.

Recordings of Greek and Hellenistic Music
History of Music in Sound, I: Ancient and Oriental Music (Victor LM-6014)
Two Thousand Years of Music (Decca DX-106)

6

Alexander the Great
and the Hellenistic Age

The Deified Alexander—obverse of a silver tetradrachm of Lysimachus, king of Thrace (323–281 B.C.), struck at the mint of Lampsacus in Asia Minor; reverse, a seated Athena. (American Numismatic Society)

The conquest of the independent city-states of the Greek homeland (356–337 B.C.) by Philip II of Macedon set in motion one of the most important cultural transformations in the history of the Mediterranean. And the scope of the conquests that Philip began was enormously widened by his son Alexander. In Alexander's time no one appreciated the magnitude of the transformation that began with these Macedonian victories. Even the learned Aristotle, whose mind was engrossed with the political form of the already moribund city-state, failed to see the significance of the events taking place in his time. Yet this was the beginning of a new world drama.

The two centuries or so after Alexander are generally designated as the Hellenistic Age. This was a period of change not only in Greece but in all the lands we have studied thus far. In this age, Greece, as never before, felt the impact of the Ancient Orient, while the lands of the east were simultaneously undergoing a process of Hellenization. In this upheaval and fusion of cultures, the Greek creative genius found a much broader environment in which to operate. No longer was the city-state the center of the life of the Greeks. Their horizon now broadened to include the whole civilized world. Greek civilization, in fact, tended to lose its separate identity and to be fused with those of other lands in a sort of synthesis that included elements from cultures as far east as India and as far west as Rome.

Until recently it was the fashion to look down upon the Greco-Oriental civilization that arose after the conquests of Alexander, because it differed so much from the preceding Classical Age. It is true that the Greeks and Orientals of the Hellenistic Age failed, like their predecessors, to solve many of the political and social problems confronting them; but their efforts and experiments are not less worthy of consideration for that reason. In some respects they made notable advances and left useful models for later ages.

Scholars date the beginning of the Hellenistic Age in 323 B.C., when Macedonian power was established in Greece, but they do not agree as to what date to take as the end of the era, since it overlaps the beginning of the age of Roman grandeur. Here, we shall examine the Greco-Oriental world from the conquest of Greece to about 31 B.C., when the Emperor Augustus took over the administration of the Roman Empire.

ALEXANDER AND HIS CONQUESTS

Alexander, who was twenty years old when Philip was assassinated, was apparently a paragon in looks and charm. From childhood he was no less outstanding for the quickness of his mind, and his natural brilliance was enhanced by the best education obtainable, for his tutor was Aristotle. In temperament, even as a boy, Alexander was aggressive and ambitious, daring and uncontrollable. His energy and stamina were almost boundless. These traits, as well as others, were to be developed in the thirteen years of conquest that filled his life as king.

The Conquest of Greece

Upon his father's death, Alexander did not hesitate to assert himself at once. He took prompt action to deal with the revolts that broke out on his accession to power, and he effectively forestalled other outbreaks that were threatening. In 335 B.C. he invaded Greece to put down a rebellion at Thebes. The city stoutly resisted his attack, but in vain. Once it had capitulated, the young conqueror proceeded to take a frightful vengeance, so as to give a warning to any others who might contemplate opposition to him. The entire city was destroyed, except for religious buildings and the house of the poet Pindar, and all its inhabitants were sold into slavery. The policy of frightfulness proved successful, for Greek resistance disappeared overnight. Once his hold upon Greece was thus made secure, the youthful king was free to go ahead with his great plan for the invasion of Asia and the destruction of the Persian Empire.

The Eastern Campaigns

The story of Alexander's swift, daring sweep through the length and breadth of the Persian Empire is one of the most fascinating in the records of military history. In tracing his course we meet again the names of cities made famous by Nebuchadrezzar and Cyrus, by the Phoenicians of Syria and the pharaohs of Egypt; we encounter the strange wild peoples south of the Caucasus; and we range as far eastward as Afghanistan and India. So amazing was the speed with which Alexander made his progress through these lands that his conquests almost seem like a triumphal procession. And though we must recognize that circumstances gave Alexander a number of advantages, we must also acknowledge that his conquest bears witness to extraordinary military genius.

The expedition began in 334 B.C., when Alexander crossed the Hellespont with 30,-000 soldiers and 5000 horses—a force which we should call small. The Persians, determined to put a quick halt to the invasion, chose to make a stand at the River Granicus. But they were poorly prepared, and after a short, hard fight, in which Alexander narrowly escaped death, Macedonian arms won the field.

The following spring Alexander moved inland to Phrygia, then southward through Cilicia. There at Issus, in the autumn of 333 B.C., he was confronted by Darius III and the Persian army. Again Alexander proved his generalship, routing the Persians on the field and thus further weakening their prestige in the western parts of their empire. Next Syria succumbed, though Tyre put up strong resistance. A year after the battle of Issus the way into Egypt lay open before the conqueror, and Darius revealed his state of mind by offering to make peace on fabulous terms. He would give over to Alexander the whole of his empire west of the Euphrates, if the Macedonian would leave him the rest.

But Alexander was in no mood to accept a compromise. He proceeded into Egypt (332 B.C.), where he found a warm welcome, because the Egyptians thoroughly disliked the Persians. While in Egypt Alexander visited Memphis; founded the great city that still bears his name—Alexandria; consulted the oracle of Zeus-Amon in the desert west of Egypt; and was there hailed as the son of the god. Thus Alexander began to play a dual role, remaining a Macedonian among the Macedonians and Greeks, while becoming an Oriental god-king among the Orientals.

Before leaving Egypt the king sent an expedition into Upper Egypt to find out the cause of the annual floods of the Nile. The investigators discovered that these inundations were caused by heavy rains in the highlands of Ethiopia, which fed the headwaters of the Nile. The scientific interest that led Alexander to send out this expedition bears witness to the influence of his old teacher, Aristotle, who was delighted to have the information that the expedition brought back.

Early in 331 B.C. Alexander returned from Egypt to Syria and thence turned eastward, driving ahead steadily until he reached Gaugamela, beyond the Tigris, where Darius III awaited him. As before, the Persians had a much larger force, but their generalship was unequal to the genius of Alexander. Once more, as at Issus, the Persians were defeated, and Darius forced to flee. The victor marched south to Babylon and then moved on to Susa. In both these great cities he established Persian governors, leaving Macedonians to keep watch on them. Early in 330 B.C. he took Persepolis, where he captured the vast treasure that the Persian king had stored up.

The next year the conqueror advanced to the Hindu Kush and Bactria, where he spent the winter, and in the following year he crushed the remnants of Persian opposition in the region east and north of the Oxus River. Not yet willing to turn back, in the autumn of 327 B.C. he marched on into India, penetrating as far as the Punjab. The insatiable conqueror would have continued his campaigns in India, but his men, who had now traversed well over 10,000 miles of wild, inhospitable country, refused to accompany him. Neither by his charm nor by his sulking could Alexander persuade them to go on, so at last he had to return to the west.

Alexander spent the winter of 324–323 B.C. in Babylon, formulating new plans. He intended next to explore the coast of Arabia in search of a sea route from Babylon to Egypt and also to explore the Caspian. What still grander plans of exploration and conquest he may have had in mind we do not know, for in June of 323 B.C. Alexander fell victim to a malarial fever, and after an illness of eleven days, he died. He had not yet reached the age of thirty-three.

Alexander's Empire and the Route of Alexander's March

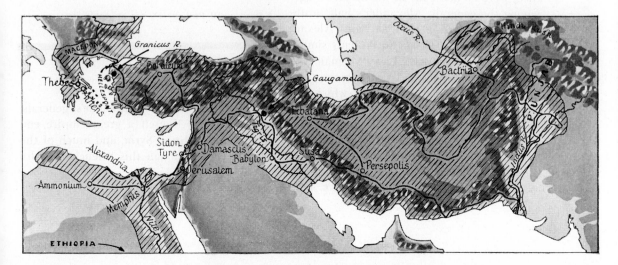

THE SUCCESSORS OF ALEXANDER

Alexander was always making plans for the future; but at his young age these naturally did not include provision for what would happen after his death. Hence his sudden fatal illness created a serious crisis. As soon as Alexander died, the army proclaimed his feeble-minded half brother, Philip Arridaeus, king. But when one of Alexander's wives, the Bactrian princess Roxane, bore a son two months after her husband's death, the boy became coruler with Arridaeus.

Arridaeus proved incapable of taking Alexander's place, and obviously the infant coruler could not. The real power therefore lay in the hands of Alexander's generals, among whom were several men of wide experience and ability. Yet no one of the generals could make himself sole ruler as successor to Alexander, nor could they agree among themselves on how to divide authority. Consequently the military men fell to fighting, and Alexander's empire fell apart.

The Ptolemies in Egypt

Out of the warfare among these generals—they were collectively called the *Diadochi*—which went on for half a century, several new dynasties arose. The first of these was established in Egypt, where Ptolemy set himself up as ruler. One of Alexander's generals, Ptolemy had been appointed to administer Egypt in behalf of Alexander's heirs. It soon came to pass, however, that there were no heirs, for in the fierce struggle among the generals, Alexander's half brother met his death in 317 B.C. and Alexander's son died in 310 B.C. So Ptolemy simply kept Egypt for himself. The Ptolemaic Dynasty that he established lasted more than three centuries, in the course of which the Greek rulers of Egypt engaged in various wars and schemes for aggrandizement at the expense of other Hellenistic kingdoms. The last ruler of the Ptolemaic house was the celebrated Cleopatra, whose charm proved insufficient to prevent Octavian (later the emperor Augustus) from taking over Egypt.

The Ptolemies of Egypt *

Ptolemy I	304–283 B.C.
Ptolemy II	283–246
Ptolemy III	246–222
Ptolemy IV	222–204
Ptolemy V	204–181
Ptolemy VI	181–145
Ptolemy VII (brother of Ptolemy VI)	145–117
Ptolemy VIII (driven from the throne by his brother Ptolemy Alexander, but later restored)	117–107, 89–81
Ptolemy IX (Ptolemy Alexander)	107–89
Ptolemy X	80
Ptolemy XI	80–58, 55–51
Ptolemy XII (younger brother and husband of Cleopatra)	51–47
Ptolemy XIII (also younger brother and husband of Cleopatra)	47–44
Cleopatra (lived 69–30 B.C., queen of Egypt and coruler with Ptolemy XII and Ptolemy XIII)	51–30
Ptolemy XIV (son of Cleopatra and almost certainly the son of Julius Caesar)	47–30

* Dates until Ptolemy IX are approximate.

The Seleucid Empire

Seleucus, another of Alexander's generals, staked out for himself a great empire embracing Asia Minor, Syria, and much of the Middle East. Though this Seleucid Empire later diminished as the more easterly regions fell away, it remained for a long time the largest of the succession states. A century after Alexander's death it still included Mesopotamia, southern Asia Minor, and even much of the old Persian realm between the Persian Gulf and the Caspian Sea.

Syria, which remained longest under Seleucid rule, was the administrative and cultural capital of this empire. But to pre-serve their hold upon Syria, the Seleucid rulers had to fight continuously—against the Parthians to the east, against the Gauls who invaded Asia Minor in the third century B.C., and against other Macedonian leaders. Finally, in the first century B.C., Rome terminated Seleucid rule.

The Seleucids of Syria

Seleucus I (conquered Susiana, Media and, later, much of Asia Minor and all Syria)	312–280 B.C.
Antiochus I (lost much of Syria to Ptolemy II)	280–261
Antiochus II	261–247
Seleucus II	d.226
Antiochus III (the Great. He regained much of the lost territories; invaded Thrace, 196 B.C., but was defeated in 191 and 190 by Romans when he interfered in Greece. Thereafter Seleucid Empire was reduced to an inland kingdom.)	223–187
Seleucus IV	187–175
Antiochus IV (brother of Seleucus IV, attempted to Hellenize Judea, with resultant uprising of the Maccabees; invaded Egypt successfully until Romans intervened in 168 B.C.)	175–163
Demetrius I	162–150
Demetrius II	146–141, 128

Macedonia and Greece

A ruling house was not established so quickly in Macedonia as in Egypt and Syria, for during the half-century following Alexander's death, Macedon was disturbed by repeated wars and invasions. Finally, in 276 B.C., Antigonus Gonatas, the grandson of one of Alexander's ablest generals, won control of the country and restored order. Meantime two great federations, the Achaean and Aetolian Leagues, arose among the cities of Greece, which fought intermittently against Macedonian rule but also—unfortunately for Greece—fought one another. Philip V sided with the Achaean League against the Aetolian League and Sparta in a war that ended in 217 B.C. His attempt to seize Roman holdings in Illyria began the

The Arch of Ctesiphon—the longest self-sustaining brick arch in the world. Under the Seleucids, Ctesiphon, or Seleucia, replaced Babylon as a great commercial city. This edifice, built there in the fourth century, B.C., remained intact until 1909 when a flood destroyed much of it. (Arab Information Center)

First Macedonian War (215–205 B.C.). The result was indecisive, so Philip resumed his aggressions in the Aegean area, until he was defeated in 197 B.C. by the Romans, whose help had been sought by both Rhodes and Pergamon (Second Macedonian War, 200–197 B.C.). Thereafter the Romans paid him generously to leave well enough alone. After his death his son Perseus again aroused the fears of Pergamon, and the Third Macedonian War (171–168 B.C.) meant the end of independence of both the Macedonians and the Greeks.

‖‖

Rulers of Macedon

Antigonus II (fought an alliance of Greek cities, headed by Athens, in Chemonidean war, c.266–c.262)	276–239 B.C.
Demetrius II	239–229
Antigonus III (regent 229–227)	227–221
Philip V	221–179
Perseus (died in captivity)	179–168

HELLENISTIC ECONOMIC AND SOCIAL LIFE

The Expansion of Agriculture and Trade

A number of developments in the Hellenistic Age encouraged economic expansion. First of all, the conquests of Alexander broke down barriers throughout most of the civilized world as it was known to the Greeks. As it became easier to move from place to place, many a Greek chose to emigrate from his old home in search of new economic opportunities. Migration was also made easier because a standardized Greek dialect, based on the Attic speech, gained wide acceptance throughout the lands that Alexander had conquered. Furthermore, the enormous treasure that had been amassed by the Persian kings and then seized as spoils of war provided a stimulus to industry, commerce, and agriculture. And since even the kings themselves were using their spoils to make a profit, aristocratic citizens were less apt now than before to have a contemptuous attitude toward the amassing of wealth through business.

Other factors that stimulated an economic boom were the more extensive use of coined money and the simpler systems of coinage that now came into use, the improvement of roads and harbors, and the spectacular increase in geographical knowledge.

Hellenistic Society

Society in the Hellenistic Age revealed a sharp contrast between extremes of wealth and of poverty. A few men, such as high officials, amassed enormous wealth, and the upper middle class prospered from the new trade with the east and with the rising republic of Rome. But the new wealth of the age brought little improvement in the condition of most of the Greek population, either at home or abroad, and scarcely any betterment of the position of the Oriental masses.

The gap between rich and poor became possibly wider than ever before, for as prices went up, to the advantage of the well-to-do classes, wages went down. The lower classes were forced into debt, and social unrest became widespread and especially pronounced toward the end of the period.

Some attempt was made to deal with the social problems. There were movements aiming at the cancellation of debts, the redistribution of land, and even the freeing of slaves. But these movements did not attain notable success, nor did they aim at reaching the source of hardship rather than its symptoms. Everywhere the wealthy men of Greek cities proved extremely generous in making voluntary gifts out of their own means. Their munificence took many forms, such as providing grain for the poor at a price below cost or even for nothing, furnishing amusements for the populace, contributing to popular education, and the like. Yet gestures of this kind did not solve the problem. The only men who attempted to get at the root of the trouble were revolutionary leaders and utopian philosophers.

In various other ways Hellenistic society demonstrated the same strange contrast between generous and humane impulses and an acceptance of suffering and hardship. For example, the institution of slavery continued, and slaves were often badly treated; yet the manumission of slaves became more common, and freedmen became an important element in society. Other signs of a more humane attitude were the greater tolerance now shown to foreigners, the friendlier relations between cities, the freer granting of citizenship, the growth of arbitration, and the attempts at lessening the cruelty of war. There was a general improvement in the social position of women, while at the same time infanticide was still permitted, and female babies were often put to death.

These contrasts—vast wealth beside sordid poverty, humane ideals beside brutality and cruelty—suggest that the Hellenistic society was a world in flux. And so it was. For while Alexander's dramatic attempt at building a world empire served to shatter old traditions and usages, and thus to set new developments in motion, his work was not brought to its completion. Before the time of Alexander, the Greek citizen thought first of his city, subordinating to it his own interests. After the time of Alexander, the city was no longer a universe in itself, to which the citizen gave supreme allegiance. But the citizen did not at once learn to identify himself with a larger political body. The consequence was that now he tended to think only of himself, and individualism, which had been a wholesome force under the discipline of citizenship in a city-state, became rampant and unbridled.

Allowed time enough, the people of the Hellenistic Age might perhaps have learned to measure up to Alexander's ideal, giving their allegiance to a new world in which all the peoples of the east and west would live in concord. Certainly they made some progress in this direction. Yet the Greeks did not, in point of fact, develop a political organization that would give substance to this internationalism, and the task of creating a universal state thus remained for the Romans to take up.

The Hellenistic World

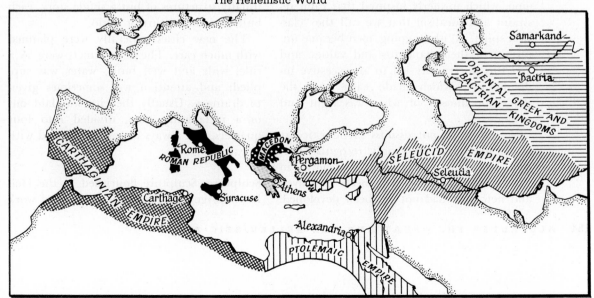

Dying Gaul—Roman copy in marble, 6 feet 3 inches long. The original bronze was cast about 225 B.C. to celebrate the victory of Attalus I (241–197 B.C.) of Pergamon over the wild tribes of Gaul who had crossed the Hellespont to invade Asia Minor. This sculpture shows the Hellenistic interest in individuals as such—in this case it immortalized an enemy—and in realism, not in idealism. Sometimes this statue is also considered to be an illustration of Stoicism (p. 160). (Anderson photograph)

HELLENISTIC CULTURAL LIFE

Hellenistic Art

In the art of the Hellenistic Age the genius of the Greeks is still to be seen, but notable changes are evident when this art is compared with that of the classical period of Greece. The mastery of technique remained superb, and the feeling for beauty continued. But there was a new tenor to Hellenistic life that was a departure from the simplicity and nobility of earlier days. Interest was in individuals, and one aim of the artist was to arouse the sympathies of his observers. This realism, though usually wholesome, was sometimes so extreme as to arouse revulsion.

Perhaps the reason for changes of this sort was the passing of the old civic religion, which formerly inspired that calm restraint and idealism that we call the "classical spirit." With its going, men became uncertain of their standards and values, and and this uncertainty led to an excessive individualism, which made each man the judge for himself of what was right and wrong.

Yet we must not dismiss Hellenistic art as decadent; we need only recognize that this art reflects a changing society, in which old traditions had been destroyed and new ones had not yet been developed.

Architecture. The two centuries after Alexander were a period when many new cities were built; and, since labor was cheap and the rulers rich and benevolent, the cities were well endowed with public works. These included not only temples but also such secular edifices as town halls, theaters and other places of amusement, palaces, gymnasiums, and more specialized buildings, such as libraries and lighthouses.

Cities grew larger than before, the greatest—Alexandria, Seleucia (p. 151), Antioch, Pergamon—having several hundred thousand inhabitants. Accordingly public buildings, such as temples and theaters, were on a larger scale. Private houses also became more comfortable, though still they were usually structures of but a single story, each built around a court or patio.

The new cities generally were planned with much care. The main streets were, as a rule, wide and well built; water was supplied; and attention was sometimes given to drainage. Usually the city was laid out on a rectangular plan, divided into four quarters, and always it was surrounded with a wall.

Sculpture. Sculpture flourished in the Hellenistic Age, and the rewards for good work in this medium were sometimes high. The Romans were especially eager to have works of art of this kind, and by the end of the second century B.C. the making of sculptures for the Roman market became a lucrative business for a number of Greek artists. Others supplied the demand in the rich cities of the east, and a large number of artists left the Greek homeland to settle in these cities, where patrons could more easily be found.

The student of Hellenistic sculpture is struck at once by the diversity of subjects, moods, and methods of treatment in it, and though the classical feeling for idealism and calm dignity was on the wane, traces of these qualities are still to be seen. One of the most famous pieces of Hellenistic sculpture is the *Winged Victory of Samothrace,* a work done in Rhodes about the middle of the third century B.C. This impressive statue shows Victory with her wings spread wide, her marvelously executed draperies blown by the rush of air, as she is about to alight on a warship. The statue has beauty, boundless energy and power, and irresistible dash —it is a superb memorial of victory. Even better known is the *Aphrodite of Melos,* popularly called the *Venus de Milo,* which is a product of the second century B.C.

The works just mentioned represent the Hellenistic sculptor at his calmest and best, when he combines nobility of conception with sure control and excellent technique. But these qualities are not to be found in a vast group of other Hellenistic works which reveal, rather, unrest, emotionalism, ornateness, and a vain striving for new effects. One work of this kind we know only by its great repute in ancient times, for it was destroyed by an earthquake. This was the Colossus of Rhodes, a gigantic bronze statue. Another work done on a grand scale was the frieze of the Great Altar of Zeus at Pergamon, dating from 180 B.C., which depicts the struggle of the gods and Titans. Though the technique is admirable, the scene is overcrowded with a riot of twisted figures, and the violence of the movement is excessive. Much the same may be said of the *"Laocoön"* group of the first century B.C. The spectator is more apt to be antagonized than moved by the anguish of father and sons, the writhing of arms, legs, and torsos, entwined in the serpents' coils, and the intense straining and violence of the whole scene.

Hellenistic sculpture gives evidence that the attitude toward the gods was not what it had been. They are now portrayed merely as men and women, with little or no trace of divinity. The *Apollo Belvedere,* for example, is a young man refined almost to the point of delicacy, while the Aphrodites of this period are little more than models of voluptuousness. In these pieces, as in the *Laocoön,* idealism has disappeared, and realism dominates the artists' moods. The same is true of the *Drunken Old Woman,* haggard and ugly, and the *Boxer,* a figure

Aphrodite of Melos—in her new setting. (Louvre Museum)

Hercules Finding His Infant Son Telephus. This is one of a series of large-scale murals found at Herculaneum, which was destroyed with Pompeii when Mount Vesuvius erupted in A.D. 79. Although it dates from the first century A.D., it is probably a copy of a second-century B.C. original in Pergamon. Telephus was the legendary founder of that city; Herculaneum was named for his father; and a cultural connection was known to exist. (Alinari Photo)

Painting. Our knowledge of Hellenistic painting is slight, for we must depend mainly on later copies, chiefly from Pompeii. From these works we can see, at least, that Greek painters in the postclassical period knew something about the restrained use of color, perspective, chiaroscuro, and the drawing of figures. Their subjects were mostly taken from mythology, and their main interest was in the depiction of human beings. Portraits, still life, religious and historical subjects were also painted. The great age of vase-painting was past, so we cannot add much to our meager knowledge from that source. Painted reliefs however do contribute some information about Hellenistic life.

Minor Arts. The Hellenistic period brought about a widespread demand for works of minor arts and crafts. Mosaics were greatly esteemed, and the intricate designs for mosaic floors developed in the east were widely copied in such cities as Pompeii and used as models by the Romans in the succeeding centuries. Craftsmen of this period were highly skilled in metalwork, producing embossed silver bowls and other metal pieces of intricate and beautiful design. The art of gem engraving—cameos and miniature portraits carved on precious stones—was also widespread, and brocaded cloth, interwoven with gold threads, was introduced.

with battered nose and cauliflower ears, both of which date from the second century B.C.

Sometimes, however, the realism is not unpleasing. The *Barberini Faun,* a lusty young satyr asleep on a rock, is a masterpiece of sensual realism, and the *Sleeping Hermaphrodite* reveals an interest in the grotesque. Portrait sculpture achieved a high excellence throughout this period, an indication of the continuing interest in outstanding individuals (p. 146).

Music

Even in the fifth and fourth centuries B.C., the musical taste of the Greeks was turning from the serene and simple music of earlier times to one that would give occasion for instrumental virtuosity. Various assortments of instruments were used in ensemble, and music became ever more embellished and colorful. To conservatives, this "ultramodern" music seemed confused and decadent. Thus both Euripides and Aristophanes voiced complaint at the new trend, while Plato and Aristotle denounced the new "romantic" melodies as immoral.

But music of this sort continued to develop, reaching full bloom in the Hellenistic period. The accents of the newer music were dynamic, following the beat of the melody rather than the rhythm of the poetry. In the *mime,* a new musico-dramatic genre that became more popular than the older tragedy, music and dance became more important than the text. Indicative of the interest in musical instruments, in contrast to the classical emphasis upon singing, was the invention of the hydraulic organ, reputedly by a Greek of Alexandria about 250 B.C., and the great processions, featuring hundreds of harpists, which the Ptolemies of Egypt often sponsored.

Yet the Hellenistic Age shows also a nostalgic harking back to archaic music. Evidences of this are found in the *Hymn to Nemesis* by Mesomedes of Crete (c.130 B.C.) and in one of the earliest Christian hymns, both of which seem to show a persistence of the classical Greek musical tradition. The Roman writer Seneca (c.4 B.C.-A.D. 65) gives us further reason to believe that vocal music had not died out by his time, for in one of his letters he writes: "I heard about midnight a furious clamor. I asked what it was. 'Vocal exercises' was the answer."

Literature

The Hellenistic Age saw a remarkable growth in the reading public. This was attributable to various factors, including the emancipation of women, who now took increasing interest in literature. Also the general progress of individualism meant that new and more diversified types of writing appeared and that more persons took an interest in their own edification and amusement. The advance of education, the larger number of books made from papyrus and parchment, and the endowment by wealthy rulers of libraries and institutions where scholars gathered encouraged this expansion too. An indication of the size of libraries is the 500,000 volumes that are said to have been amassed in the one at Alexandria and the 200,000 volumes at Pergamon.

Another occurrence of significance for literature was the widespread acceptance of a modified form of Attic Greek. This common language, known as *koine,* made intercourse easier among the diverse peoples of the Hellenistic world. It was used by traders everywhere; and in Rome a knowledge of Greek was valued by all educated men. A few Greeks still wrote in the old dialects, and easterners and Romans clung to their own languages for use among themselves, but the *koine* was unrivaled as the inter-

Contest of Apollo and Marsyas. This marble slab from Mantinea, Greece, c.350 B.C., is one version of a favorite Hellenistic subject. Marsyas, having found an aulos discarded by Athena, challenged Apollo to a contest. The god, playing on the lyre, won easily, and his challenger was flayed alive. Here the judge waits patiently, knife in hand, for Marsyas to finish. (Alinari photograph)

national language. The importance of this new tongue is shown by the fact that the Jews translated the Old Testament into Greek, and the New Testament was written in it.

Literature now had to satisfy many kinds of taste. No longer was there a single standard accepted by all who were interested in literature. What most people wanted in literature, as in sculpture, was verisimilitude, and the more lifelike a literary description, the better they enjoyed it. For them *lifelike* meant close to everyday experience; and a touch or more of obscenity whetted their appetite for what they regarded as literature. At the other extreme, scholars and learned men often showed a preference for an archaistic style of writing or the compilation of masterpieces of pedantry. Between the two extremes were a good many writers of merit. Unfortunately a large proportion of the literature of this period has perished, including the work of some authors very well thought of in their own day.

Poetry. Dramatic poetry was still written, but not as before. No tragedies have survived, and of comedy, only the work of a single writer, Menander (c.342–c.291 B.C.) of Athens. His work was polished, clever, and sometimes amusing; but he lacked the vigor and freshness and sincerity of Aristophanes. His characters were stereotyped, and so were his plots. Yet his comedies have the merit of telling us something about at least one side of life in Athens at the end of the fourth century B.C.

Most of the outstanding poets of the age were natives of Alexandria or established themselves there. For this reason the poetry of the Hellenistic Age is sometimes called "Alexandrian." One of the epics written in the third century B.C. is the *Argonautica* of Apollonius the Rhodian. Except for the understanding treatment of Medea, it is little admired. Apollonius was a native of Alexandria. But he left his native city, settling for a time in Rhodes, because he did

not get on well with Callimachus, who was one of the most learned men and poets of Alexandria as well as Apollonius' old teacher. Callimachus thought Apollonius wrote too much, and that the epic should be written in a briefer, more polished form.

Prose. The Hellenistic Age produced a vast amount of prose writing, though most of it, too, has disappeared. With the passing of democracy, political oratory lost much of its point, but there was no decline of interest in rhetoric or in the systematic study of persuasive speech, for the Greeks had an irrepressible passion for public speaking. In the popular rhetoric of the later Hellenistic Age, a florid and sometimes bombastic style known as the "Asiatic" gained favor at the expense of the more restrained and measured Attic style. Thus even oratory finally became a form of amusement, catering to the popular fancy for the sensational.

The great bulk of Hellenistic historical writing is now gone forever, but from what little survives we have further evidence of the interest in the individual that was characteristic of the age, and we can also find evidence of the absorption in events of contemporary importance. The greatest of Hellenistic historians is Polybius, whom modern critics rank second only to Thucydides. He was among a horde of hostages who were taken to Rome in 168 B.C., after the Romans inflicted a defeat upon the Macedonians and their Greek allies, and for twenty years thereafter he remained in Rome as an exile. During this long sojourn he made friends among persons of influence and gained respect for what the Romans were accomplishing.

The history that he wrote treats of the years 221–146 B.C., during which Rome emerged as the dominant power in the whole Mediterranean. His study shows his admiration for Rome, as well as his partiality toward the Achaean League, in which he had been a leader. His style is inferior to that of Thucydides, and he was not above suppressing evidence that ran counter to his own bias. Usually, however, he was careful and painstaking in collecting and using his evidence; he appreciated the magnitude of his subject; and he understood better than did many another historian of his time that the study of history can have significance for later ages.

We must also take note of the learned studies that occupied many earnest students at Alexandria, where the rulers of Egypt provided lavish facilities for collecting, copying, and interpreting the earlier works of Greek literature. The work of the librarians and philologists who preserved the original texts of archaic and classical manuscripts proved of immense value for later ages, as did their work in the scientific studies of language.

Hellenistic Religions

Nothing better reveals the decline of the *polis,* or city-state, in Classical Greek civilization than the changes that came about in religion during the Hellenistic Age. In the Classical Era, religion had centered in the city-state. Once the city-state was destroyed, the old religion was undermined.

Religion now became an individual matter, in which personal attitudes meant more than civic interests. Mysteries, such as the Eleusinian and the Orphic, gained many more adherents than ever before, and new cults developed for those who could not afford the expensive rites of initiation. Belief in magic and astrology grew, indicating a resigned acceptance of fate, and everywhere were signs of a yearning for personal salvation. Even philosophy took on a more religious cast.

These religious developments of the Hellenistic Age did much to prepare the soil for the later growth of Christianity, because in this period you can find evidence of a pronounced movement toward monotheism and a deep longing for something beyond this life, which the mystery cults did not fully satisfy. In due course the teachings of Christianity were to meet this need.

Hellenistic Philosophy

The older philosophical schools, drawing their inspiration from Plato or Aristotle, lost vigor in the Hellenistic Age. For a time Theophrastus continued the work of his master Aristotle; but times had changed, and men now wanted something new in

Silenus Holding in His Arms the Young Bacchus —third century B.C. Silenus, in Greek mythology, was a deity of forests and springs who taught Dionysus the culture of the vine. The names Bacchus and Dionysus were used by the Greeks in referring to this god, but the Romans knew him only as Bacchus. (Louvre Museum)

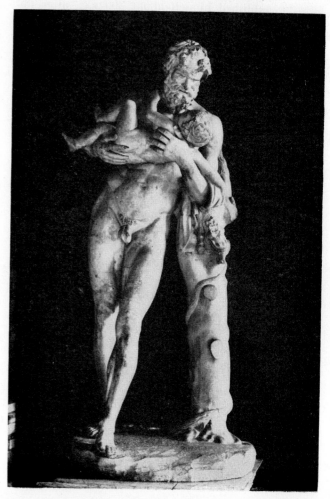

philosophy. The clear-headed, rational search for truth had become too difficult in an age of doubt and confusion. Men could no longer seek great truths about the universe and man—that was too big a task for them. Their aim, rather, was to find personal security in a world where their own position was uncertain and insecure. Thus once more we encounter the individualism of the Hellenistic Age, expressed in a concern for the individual rather than the world at large. No longer did the individual identify himself with the intimate, safe, and comfortable environment of a small city-state; instead, he felt himself tossed adrift alone on the vast sea of humanity.

Stoicism. One of the newer schools of philosophy that made answer to the need of the times was the Stoic, so named because its founder, Zeno (*c.*336–*c.*264 B.C.), began his teaching in the *stoa* or porch of one of the public buildings in Athens. Here he established himself about 300 B.C., after migrating from his native Cyprus. In the second century B.C. Stoicism spread to Rome, where it won a wide vogue.

Unlike the great teachers of the Classical Age, the Stoics had little interest in the question of origins. To solve this problem, they simply borrowed Heraclitus' doctrine that fire is the prime substance, in which all things have their source and their ending. Fire, in their teaching, is the same as God, and God is the same as reason. Since men, like all other beings, spring from fire and must return to it, fire is the essence of their nature. To be true to their nature, they must therefore live according to reason, which is identical with the divine fire.

The Stoics passed as quickly over the problem of knowledge, which they made simply a matter of sense perception. Thus they made truth completely subjective, for if we know only by our own senses, none of us can check whether the impressions we receive from our senses are the same as those that others receive from theirs.

The chief interest of the Stoics was not in such matters, however, but in ethics, and it was here that they made their important contributions. For in advising men to live according to nature, they meant according to reason or the divine intention. Hence men should not waste their time wanting what they do not have but should accept whatever place in life is allotted to them by the divine plan of the universe. Virtuous living thus means accepting one's own particular fate and doing the best one can within one's circumstances. In even simpler terms, virtue means doing one's duty.

This doctrine proved too austere for some of those who were drawn toward Stoicism, and accordingly they made modifications in it. These modifications were such as to make over the philosophy into something more like a religion. Some later Stoics even went so far as to accept divination and astrology.

Zeno believed in the brotherhood of all men, and he looked forward to a world state that included all. This noble ideal appeals to most modern students, but the Stoics sometimes get more credit for it than they deserve. The Stoic concept was too arid; there was in it nothing of the Christian ideal of brotherly love, for Zeno and his followers rejected love along with the other passions. Stoic "citizens of the world" would be automatons run by duty, ignoring the world as it is and vainly seeking to adjust themselves to "nature."

Epicureanism. The greatest rival of Stoicism was the school of Epicurus, an Athenian citizen, who, toward the end of the fourth century B.C. began teaching in his garden at Athens. Epicurus (*c.*342–270 B.C.), like Zeno, was a man of excellent character and he won many friends and universal respect. For his explanation of the universe, Epicurus had recourse to the atomic theory of Democritus. In this view, all things, including the soul, are held to be material, being formed by the temporary union of atoms.

When this union is dissolved, existence ceases. It follows that human beings exist only until such time as the atoms that compose their body and soul separate. This view rules out all possibility of a persistence of either the soul or the body after death. Thus Epicurus' teaching freed men's minds from the fear of death and encouraged men to make the most of the brief span of their existence by seeking such happiness as they might attain.

He also liberated his disciples from a superstitious fear of the gods. He did not go so far as to deny the existence of the gods, for that would have been too bold, but he taught that the gods dwell far away, caring nothing about the world of men.

Epicurus' ethical teaching was quite simple—the way to happiness is through pleasure. Some of his later disciples misinterpreted this to mean sensual indulgence. The Romans, especially, perverted Epicureanism into an excuse for the orgiastic indulgence of the appetites. Epicurus himself, however, counseled moderation in bodily pleasure. His ideal of bliss was to be achieved rather by the avoidance of pain of all kinds, including anxiety. What he meant by "pleasure" was not far from what we mean by "peace of mind." Those Epicureans who lived up to their master's ideals were often men of courage and honor. Indeed, they attached nearly the same importance to virtue as did the Stoics. The difference was that for the Stoic, virtue was a duty, while for the Epicurean, it was a path to happiness.

Cynicism and Skepticism. The minor schools of the Cynics and the Skeptics also show the temper of the times. The Cynics were followers of Diogenes (c.412–323 B.C.) a contemporary of Alexander, who once declared that if he were not Alexander, he would wish to be Diogenes. This was high praise, for the teachings of Diogenes were not meant for statesmen or others who accept social responsibilities. On the contrary, the Cynics spurned social conventions of all kinds, lived according to their own lights, and made no compromise with customs of which they did not approve. Some of them renounced wealth and position to live in poverty and utter simplicity, and the more extreme among them went about unkempt and in tatters. The more sincere did so in order to give other men an example of their philosophy of rugged defiance in the face of harsh fate.

The Spinario (Boy with Thorn)—bronze, probably first century B.C. The boy pulling a thorn from his foot is typical of the everyday subjects Hellenistic artists portrayed so successfully. This is probably a copy of a statue that Boethus made. (Alinari photograph)

The Skeptics were the ultimate product of the questioning attitude of mind that had developed in the Classical Age. As long as this outlook remained within bounds, its influence was wholesome. But in the unsettled atmosphere of the Hellenistic Age, the attitude of eternal doubting was carried to an extreme. The position of the Skeptics, the most notable of whom was Pyrrho, another contemporary of Alexander, was that nothing can be known for certain, and therefore there can be no rational purpose for human activity of any kind. Let us suspend judgment, they argued, and remain secure from emotionalism.

Hellenistic Science

The three centuries of the Hellenistic Age saw such a flowering of science as the world had never known before and was not to know again until the dawn of modern times, sixteen centuries after Christ. This accomplishment was the product of the marriage of Greek genius with Oriental knowledge, chiefly Chaldean and Egyptian.

Mathematics. Mathematics was the branch of science to which Hellenistic scholars made some of their greatest contributions. The first name to be mentioned in Hellenistic mathematics is that of Euclid. Early in the third century B.C. Euclid gathered together the existing knowledge in geometry and summarized it in a masterful treatise. His *Elements* remained the most widely used textbook of geometry from his own time nearly to our own, for it was still commonly used in the early years of this century. Euclid also did more advanced work in mathematics and in related subjects. Other mathematicians of note were Aristarchus of Samos (third century B.C.), Eratosthenes of Cyrene (*c.*276–*c.*195 B.C.), his contemporary, and Hipparchus (*c.*160–*c.* 125 B.C.), who is known as an astronomer as well as a pioneer in trigonometry.

Greatest of all Hellenistic mathematicians was Archimedes of Syracuse (*c.*287– 212 B.C.), who was also a great physicist. A number of anecdotes about Archimedes have come down to our time, making his name known to many who have little notion of the importance of his discoveries. One of these stories recounts that he noticed while in a bathhouse that the volume of water displaced by his body was equal to the volume of his body, and this immediately suggested to him a principle of large importance in physics. At once he dashed out of the bathhouse and ran home naked through the streets of Syracuse, shouting "Eureka!" (I have found!). Another anecdote relates how by means of pulleys he single-handedly launched a great ship for the ruler of Syracuse, remarking when he was done that if given a lever and a place to stand, he would move the earth itself.

Yet Archimedes himself regarded as trivial the practical application of scientific principles, which so often figured in the stories told about him. In his opinion, his important work was in pure mathematics, and in that field he made great contributions. For example, he worked out the value of *pi* and discovered the ratio between the volume and surface of a cylinder and an inscribed sphere. So great was his pride in the latter discovery that he had it commemorated on his tomb.

Astronomy. Astronomy was one of the scientific studies into which the Greeks branched out from mathematics. After examining the theories of his predecessors, Aristarchus advanced the bold hypothesis that the earth and the planets revolve around the sun. Had this suggestion been accepted, supplanting the geocentric theory that the earth is the center of the universe, the world would have been spared centuries of error and superstition. Unfortunately all the leading astronomers of the time rejected Aristarchus' hypothesis, and so did their successors for centuries. Much later, after astronomical knowledge had greatly expanded, Copernicus revived Aristarchus' hypothesis and made it the basis for his own brilliant achievement.

Hipparchus earned renown by working out the geocentric theory that was to prevail until the time of Copernicus. Though we now recognize this theory as erroneous, we must acknowledge that Hipparchus was a painstaking student, who made careful observations and took the trouble to learn from others, especially his famous Chaldean predecessor, Kidinnu. His calculations of the solar year and the lunar month were almost right, and his calculation of the sun's distance from the earth was much closer than Aristarchus'. His most important works included a catalogue of the fixed stars and his discovery of the precession of the equinoxes.

Geography. The study of geography was stimulated by the travels and explorations begun by Alexander. Notable in this field, as well as in many others, was Eratosthenes, who did much of his work in the museum at Alexandria. He made use of both the new advances in mathematics and the observations of such men as Pytheas, who in Alexander's time had traveled to northern Europe by way of the Atlantic. After a study of the extant knowledge of tides, Eratosthenes reached the conclusion that Asia, Africa, and Europe were all connected by land and that the surrounding oceans, too, were connected. Long before his time learned men had established that the earth is round, but he first boldly drew the conclusion that India, which Alexander had reached by going east, could also be found by traveling west. He also established the division of the earth's surface by lines of latitude and longitude, and he calculated with remarkable accuracy the circumference of the earth at the equator. Some of his work was improved upon by Hipparchus, and more was added to it in the first century B.C. by Posidonius.

Applied Sciences. The scholars of the Hellenistic Age were not quite so indifferent to the practical application of science as their Greek predecessors in the classical period. Archimedes invented a number of ingenious devices, such as gigantic burning glasses and huge catapults, for use when Syracuse was withstanding the Roman siege. He also devised the Archimedean screw, used for pumping water, and did much work with pulleys and levers. Some of his successors developed various kinds of pneumatic and hydraulic machines—even a kind of steam engine.

Medicine. Though little was accomplished after Aristotle's time in biology, some practical advances of importance were made in medicine and surgery. In the first half of the third century B.C. knowledge of anatomy was enlarged by the work of Herophilus and Erasistratus, both of whom came from their native Asia Minor to settle in Alexandria, then the center of scientific studies. Their most important discoveries concerned the brain and nervous system.

In appraising Hellenistic science as a whole, we must take due note of its shortcomings—the continuing though diminishing prejudice against all utilitarian study except medicine, the concomitant preference for speculation, and the lack of instruments for exact measurement and delicate observation. Yet, considering the circumstances of the times, we must conclude that the record was brilliant.

Moreover, the science of the Hellenistic Age did not die at the close of the period. On the contrary, it continued to stimulate later students. In the second century A.D. Galen recorded the accomplishments of the great Hellenistic pioneers in medicine, and by his efforts their work was preserved for later ages. Likewise, in the same century, Claudius Ptolemy (who, despite his name, was not related to the Egyptian dynasty) recorded much of Hellenistic astronomy and geography. Astronomy, especially, was preserved in the Middle Ages by the Arabs (see Chapter 11) and eventually it provided inspiration for Copernicus and others (see Chapter 23).

CONCLUSION

It is difficult to make a single, comprehensive evaluation of the Hellenistic Age. Unquestionably it made a large contribution to later civilization. And because it was in some respects more like our own time than was the Classical Age, it is easier for us to understand.

Yet in many ways it was less admirable than the Classical period. In politics the disappearance of the democratic spirit and the rise of a new absolutism mark a reversal of earlier trends. Nor was this a merely temporary setback, for the rising might of Roman power was already throwing a shadow over the age. With this ominous development in politics was associated the change in the spirit of individualism, which no longer meant the exaltation of man's glory as a human being, but, rather, a fearful and often emotional concern of each individual with his particular fortune. Even in the most brilliant Hellenistic expressions of individualism there was frequently a disturbing and almost frenetic quality. As the other lights grew dim, only science continued for a time to show a bright and reassuring flame.

Suggestions for Further Reading

Source Materials

Anthologies

G. H. Knoles and R. K. Snyder, eds., *Readings in Western Civilization* (rev. ed., New York, 1954), pp. 91–108.

Good selections from Lucretius, greatest of the Epicurean philosophers, Aristarchus, and Eratosthenes.

W. J. Oates, ed., *The Stoic and Epicurean Philosophers* (New York, 1940).

Selections from the great philosophical writers of the Hellenistic Age.

Contemporary Writings

The following are probably the greatest writings of the Hellenistic Age. They are easily available in many editions and in most libraries.

Lucretius, *On the Nature of Things.*

Plutarch, *Lives.*

Polybius, *Histories.*

Theocritus, *Idyls.*

Secondary Works

E. R. Bevan, *A History of Egypt under the Ptolemaic Dynasty* (London, 1927).

A lively, well-written account of the Ptolemies. Sound history, but written for the layman, with a fair share of personal anecdotes about the rulers and their ministers.

J. B. Bury, E. A. Barber, E. R. Bevan, and W. W. Tarn, *The Hellenistic Age* (Cambridge, 1923).

Four essays by experts in the period deal with physical science, literature, economics, and politics from the age of Alexander to the definite intervention of the Romans in the east. Shows the marked division between this age and the Hellenic.

M. Cary, *History of the Greek World from 323 to 146 B.C.* (rev. ed., New York, 1952).

A narrative history of Greece from the Macedonian to the Roman conquest. Thorough source on statecraft and culture. Illustrated.

P. Jouguet, *Macedonian Imperialism and the Hellenization of the East* (New York, 1928).

A good sequel to the ordinary histories of Greece which stop with Alexander. Especially good for Alexander's role as a political organizer. Discusses his autocratic successors. Contends that Greece and Macedonia should have turned west rather than east.

C. A. Robinson, *Alexander the Great* (New York, 1947).

One of several recent books on Alexander, this one better in dealing with the man than with his age. Careful scholarship, but written in popular fashion.

M. I. Rostovtsev, *Social and Economic History of the Hellenistic World* (Oxford, 1941).

This outstanding, original, well-written book shows unusual capacity to cut through detail to important information. Fuller on economic and social aspects than on political.

W. W. Tarn, *Alexander the Great* (New York, 1948).

An excellent two-volume reconsideration of the material about Alexander in an attempt to retrieve the personality of Alexander from legends. Stresses Alexander's brotherhood-of-man ambition. First volume narrative, second a source study and a breakdown of the problems such as the army, deification, world conquest.

W. W. Tarn, *Hellenistic Civilisation* (New York, 1952).

A fine comprehensive work, treating of the political, social, economic, and cultural aspects of the age. This edition is a revision of the 1930 book to bring it up to date with new evidence, but it is only partially successful in including all new material.

A. A. Trever, *History of Ancient Civilization* (2 vols., New York, 1936–1939).

An excellent source.

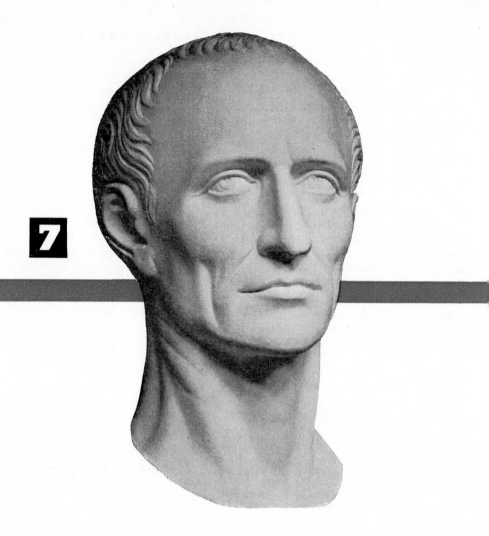

7

The Roman Republic

Julius Caesar. First-century B.C. portrait
bust. (Courtesy British Museum)

While the various waves of Hellenes were overrunning the Greek peninsula, other tribes were moving into the Italian peninsula, west of Greece, where the city-state of Rome was to arise. Rome was to flourish a little later than the cities of the Hellenes, but one day it would absorb them, as it would bring under its rule all the other lands around the shores of the Mediterranean. Eventually Rome would be the center of one of the greatest empires of all history, bringing peace and prosperity for a time to the entire Mediterranean world.

THE DAWN OF CIVILIZATION IN ITALY

The Land and the People

The Italian peninsula has two main divisions—the valley of the Po River, in the north, and the long, narrow peninsula proper, about equal in area to the Po Valley, stretching away to the southeast. The great mass of the Alps separates Italy from the rest of Europe, and the Apennines run the length of the peninsula. Italy is a larger and more varied land than Greece, and, though it has little mineral wealth, in ancient times it was covered with thick forests. Navigable rivers and good harbors are few, but the climate is mild. Because of these natural advantages, Italy early began to attract settlers from many other lands.

About 2000 B.C. the Stone Age inhabitants were overrun by Indo-European invaders akin to those who moved down into Greece from the region of the Danube River (see map, p. 99). Gradually the newcomers moved south from the Po and settled in the central and southern portions of the peninsula. The people known as the Latins were the most notable among these early immigrants. Another people, the Etruscans, who apparently orginated in the eastern Mediterranean, arrived in Italy about 800 B.C. A little later Greek colonists began to settle in southern Italy and Sicily. Both the Etruscans and the Greeks were to contribute much to the culture we know as Roman.

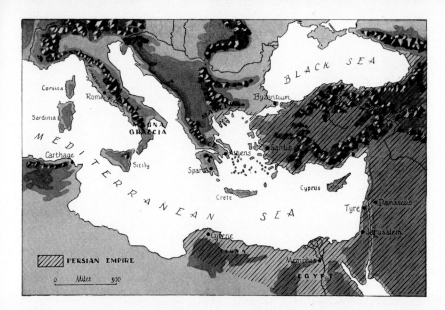

The Mediterranean World about 500 B.C.

But neither the Etruscans nor the Greeks were to rule over Italy. That was to be the mission of the Latins, who settled in the region known as Latium, south of the Tiber. Why the Latins, who were only one of the many peoples of mixed ancestry in Italy, should have won this role we cannot say. We do know, however, that they were predominant among those who made the earliest settlements on the hills beside the Tiber River at the site where Rome was to arise.

According to the legends that came down to later times, the settlement of Rome began in 753 B.C. Thereafter seven kings in succession ruled Rome, the later ones said to have been Etruscan conquerors. But the rule of the unpopular foreign kings came to an end in 509 B.C., when Tarquin the Proud was driven out.

No one knows how much truth lies behind these legends of earliest Rome, but there is good reason to believe they are not wholly imaginary. In any event, a kingship existed in Rome in remote times, and it resembled the kingship in early Greek society. The Roman king was a religious, military, and judicial leader. He held the *imperium,* or sovereign power, which was restrained only by established and revered custom. An advisory council of aristocrats and an assembly of the people could only approve or disapprove legislation, though later these bodies were to attain much importance.

Early Institutions

The general outline of developments in Rome toward the end of the sixth century B.C. resembles the pattern followed only a little earlier by the Greek city-states. The division between social classes was more rigid than in Athens, though not so sharp as between the social classes in Sparta. The patricians were a small upper class, composed chiefly of landowners, while the plebeians, who made up the mass of the people, were small farmers and artisans. The patricians were patrons or protectors of the plebeians, who had little wealth or political power. And, like the Greek nobles, the ruling class made use of religion to bolster its superior social position.

The first popular assembly, the *Comitia Curiata,* had only a passive role in legislation. Its organization was based upon the division of the Roman people, in earliest times, into three tribes, each comprising ten *curiae.* The *curia* was made up of several *gentes,* or clans, each of which included both patricians and plebeians. Each *curia* voted as a group, but since some *curiae* were smaller than others, this system of voting meant that a majority of the *curiae* might not represent a majority of the people as a whole. This long-continued practice of voting in groups obstructed the development of political individualism or democracy. Moreover, the patricians were more experienced in politics than the plebeians, so in practice they dominated the assembly.

Toward the end of the period of the kings a new assembly, called the *Comitia Centuriata,* began to take shape. Its organization was based upon military considerations. The Roman people were divided into five classes, according to their varying economic ability to purchase military equipment. The five classes were subdivided into groups called *centuries*—hence the term *centuriata.* Each of these groups had one vote, regardless of the number of its members. Thus the few rich in the upper classes had equal votes with the many poor in the lower classes and dominated the popular assembly, just as in earlier years

they had controlled the *Comitia Curiata.*

After the expulsion of the kings the patricians gained secure control of Roman society. The sovereign power that the kings formerly held was now delegated to two senior magistrates of equal power, known as the *consuls,* who were elected for a term of one year. The men elected to these two leading offices, as well as most other positions of importance, were always patricians. The Senate was the principal legislative body, even though, theoretically, it was for long supposed to be subordinate to the people's assembly. The Senate was so named because it was a council of elders. From the first it was an aristocratic body, and it remained so even after plebeians were admitted.

Though the Roman government was no longer a monarchy but a republic, it was not a democracy. It was an oligarchy—a system of rule by the few—in which the wealthy held the decisive political power. But this system had at least one virtue—those who gained privileges also accepted obligations, since they bore the brunt of military service.

THE ROMAN REPUBLIC

Expansion in Italy 509–265 B.C.

In the two-and-a-half centuries after the destruction of the monarchy, Rome won hegemony over the Italian peninsula. The rise was due, in part, to the character of its leaders, who were courageous, aggressive, and persevering. It was due, too, to the skill of the Romans in dividing their enemies and pitting one against another.

Rome was never a "good neighbor." Fearing its aggressive intentions, the other Latin cities made an alliance among themselves, from which Rome was excluded. But under the pressure of greater dangers from without, the Latin League was obliged to cooperate with Rome, and the Romans

were able to extend their power. With the help of the Latin League, Rome thus defeated two neighboring hill peoples, the Aequi and the Volsci, and by about 400 B.C. the Romans crushed their last important Etruscan enemy. Thereafter the Romans spread their influence southward into Campania and clashed with the warlike Samnites.

The southward advance of the Romans next brought them into conflict with Tarentum, which held leadership among the Greek cities in Italy. Violence broke out in 281 B.C. The next year the hard-pressed Tarentines hired the help of Pyrrhus, the brilliant king of Epirus, who crossed the Adriatic with a well-trained Hellenistic ar-

Via Appia—Today. The Appian Way (see map, page 180) from Rome to the port of Brundisium was only one of a network of roads. (Italian State Tourist Office)

my. Pyrrhus won a number of victories, but his losses were excessive—hence the name *Pyrrhic* for victories that cost too much—and he thought it wise to withdraw to Sicily. Eventually Pyrrhus retired to Greece, and shortly thereafter Magna Graecia became part of Rome.

Rome used several means to keep a firm grip upon the territories it conquered. First, it established Roman and Latin colonies among the vanquished peoples. The Romans who were settled as colonists retained the full rights of Roman citizenship, and the members of Latin colonies were given some of these rights. For example, they could marry and trade with Romans, though they could not vote. These partial rights of citizenship were granted also to the inhabitants of some of the old cities of Latium. As another means of bolstering their position, the Romans made use of alliances. But the Italian allies of Rome did not fare so well as the colonists. They might deal with Rome but they could not make alliances among themselves. Each of Rome's allies had to give up its independence in foreign affairs and make contributions to the Roman army or navy.

An excellent system of roads served to knit Italy together, under Roman leadership. The best known of these roads was the Appian Way, built late in the fourth century B.C. Originally it ran from Rome to Capua, but later it was extended to Brundisium. This ancient roadway still survives, and it was used by the British and American troops who landed in southern Italy in 1943.

Roman Democracy

The two-and-a-half centuries after the establishment of the Republic also saw a considerable movement toward democracy in Rome's government. This development occurred in the course of a long struggle between the patrician and plebeian orders. The patricians, as we have said, had gained the upper hand as soon as the kingship was abolished. But as Rome thereafter became embroiled in wars, the plebeians assumed a role of much importance, because the common people furnished such a large proportion of Rome's soldiers. Hence the patricians could not ignore the plebeians' demand for a share in the loot of war and a higher place in the state.

The popular class was goaded into raising such demands because the plight of the common people was serious. The peasants were in need of more land; but, in the fifth century B.C., although the government gained possession of much land in the course of the wars of conquest, little of this public land passed into the hands of the peasants. Generally it was monopolized by the patricians, who alone could afford to rent it from the government. Already impoverished, the peasants were forced into debt, sometimes even into slavery, whenever the harvest proved poor or when warfare prevented them from working the fields. Eventually the plebeians found an effective way to protest their plight—they simply withdrew from Rome. After several such secessions, the nobility found it wise to offer concessions.

One of the first gains won in this fashion by the plebeians was the right to choose officials to defend their interests. These officials were called the Tribunes. At first there were two Tribunes; eventually the number rose to ten.

The rise of the Tribunes was part of a larger development that at this time worked to the advantage of the mass of the people. This new development involved the formation of a new popular assembly, called the *Concilium Plebis,* or Plebeian Assembly, which was not to be dominated by the patricians as the older assemblies had been. Under this arrangement, the plebeians won the right to hold meetings of their own, not only for choosing the Tribunes but also for caring for other matters of concern to them as a class.

The power of the Tribunes was enormous. Their persons were inviolable, and they were available at all times to protect plebeians from mistreatment by any other magistrates. Eventually they won the right of veto over all official business and the right to initiate legislation.

The plebeians thereafter steadily continued to improve their position. About 450 B.C. they succeeded in having the laws written down, so that all might know their rights. Step by step they won eligibility to all the important magistracies, including the consulship and most of the priestly offices.

Nothing of importance, however, was done to relieve the economic hardships of the plebeians until 367 B.C. Then legislation was passed that aided debtors; provision was made for future allotments of land to the people; and the amount of land each person might hold was strictly regulated in the hope of avoiding the monopoly of land by the wealthy. In 287 B.C., with the passage of the Hortensian Law, the now-powerful plebeians won the final victory they needed for equality. Henceforth the acts of the Plebeian Assembly became law without the approval of the Senate. In appearance, at least, the government of the Roman Republic was now democratic.

While the plebeian class as a whole was gaining new rights, wealthier individuals within this class were beginning to form a superior caste, closer in spirit to the old patrician aristocracy than to the mass of the people. Few plebeians except the wealthy, indeed, ever passed through the prescribed course of honors—or successive political offices—that was a prerequisite for holding a consulship and then taking a seat in the Senate. The Senate, to which only rich men gained admittance, had much more importance than merely social prestige; and in the century and a half after passage of the Hortensian Law it again became the dominant force in the government of the Roman Republic, as we shall soon see.

The upshot of these various developments was that the old patriciate lost its former hold on the government, but a new aristocracy—the Senatorial class—made up of the wealthy inherited its power. The mass of the plebeians made little gain, and the government was no more democratic, in practice, than before.

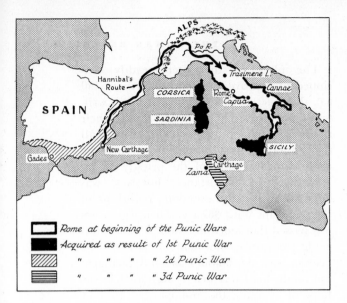

The Punic Wars

Conquest and Expansion Outside Italy

By 265 B.C. Rome had achieved an almost absolute rule throughout Italy and had gone far toward establishing a democratic government. The Romans might have stopped their expansion at that point and consolidated Rome's position, and Rome might eventually have become a democratic, national state. Actually, however, the Republic went on with its outward expansion, to create the largest empire in Mediterranean history. Sometimes, especially at first, war was forced on the Romans, but later they willingly took the initiative in waging war solely for aggrandizement. Rome grew rich on the spoils of imperialistic wars, but these conquests brought about a change in the character of its people and put a stop to its progress toward democracy.

The Punic Wars. Rome's first great overseas conflict was with Carthage, which controlled extensive territory in Spain, Sardinia, Sicily, and some of the smaller islands of the western Mediterranean as well as in Africa. Down to this time the oligarchy that governed Carthage had been friendly toward

Rome. The clash between the two great city-states came about when Rome deliberately interfered in the affairs of Sicily, where Carthaginian interests had long been strongly established. The Romans meddled in Sicily because they feared the growth of Punic— that is, Carthaginian—influence so near their own newly acquired dependencies. The First Punic War dragged on from 264 to 241 B.C. Although the Carthaginians had an able commander, Hamilcar Barca, the Romans eventually won. Carthage paid a large indemnity and gave up its holdings in Sicily. A few years later Rome seized Sardinia and Corsica.

In the succeeding years Hamilcar extended Punic influence in Spain, where eventually his son, the famous Hannibal, carried on his work. Though concerned, the Romans took no action, for they were engaged at the time in subjugating Cisalpine Gaul and were becoming involved in Greece.

Presently Hannibal was ready for war, which he brought on by attacking a Spanish city allied to Rome. He soon gave proof of his military genius. Setting out from Spain early in 218 B.C., he marched through Gaul and across the Alps with an army of about 60,000 men and a number of elephants. He remained in Italy throughout most of the Second Punic War, which lasted until 201 B.C., winning battle after battle and ranging about the countryside almost at will. Despite Hannibal's successes, however, his depleted armies were unable to end the war. And at last the Romans found a capable leader, P. Cornelius Scipio, who at the age of twenty-four was put in charge of Roman forces in Spain. Six years later, in 204 B.C., he went to Africa, where he did so well that Hannibal was recalled to defend Carthage. The issue was settled at Zama in 202 B.C., when Scipio emerged the victor. In the peace treaty Carthage lost its independence in foreign affairs, gave up almost all its fleet, and paid a huge indemnity.

The Second Punic War was one of the most important in history, for it effectively removed Rome's only dangerous rival. Now Rome, later to emerge as invincible ruler of the Mediterranean, could go on to conquer the Hellenistic east, draw off its wealth, and absorb much of its culture. To what did the Romans owe their victory? Less to the leadership of the Senate, which was far from brilliant, than to the courageous and steadfast citizens who made up the Roman armies and to Rome's loyal allies in Italy, upon whose desertion Hannibal had counted in vain. Rome's recently won control of the sea was also an important advantage. Finally, Rome owed much to Scipio, who had the good sense to learn from his enemy, Hannibal.

In the years following Zama, Carthage made a remarkable recovery. Rome watched with growing jealousy until Carthage became involved with Numidia, a neighboring state. This gave the Romans an excuse to renew the war and crush the enemy ruthlessly. In this Third Punic War (149–146 B.C.), Carthage itself was captured, the city utterly destroyed, and the people enslaved.

Rome and the Hellenistic Kingdoms. During the Second Punic War, Philip V of Macedon (see p. 151) had alienated the Romans by supporting Hannibal. Soon afterward, when Macedonia allied itself with the Seleucid kingdom, other states in the east appealed to Rome for protection, and the Senate seized this occasion to begin the Second Macedonian War (200–197 B.C.). In the outcome, Philip lost much territory and Macedonian sovereignty was impaired. Once embarked on this intervention in the east, Rome continued to extend its control. In

the Third Macedonian War (171–168 B.C.), Perseus, Philip's son, was defeated, Macedonia and Greece were plundered, and Macedonia was broken into four parts, which soon afterward were annexed by Rome. Gradually, thereafter, the cities of Greece were brought under Roman domination, although not until a century later was Greece made a Roman province.

In the period 200–150 B.C. the Romans experienced a marked change in their outlook. Gradually, in the course of years of victory and conquest, they became callous to the sufferings of others and contemptuous even of their allies. As their armies won victories, many a Roman gained fame as a military leader, and young men became ambitious to make their names famous in this fashion. Others amassed fortunes out of the pillage of conquered lands. As for the rank and file, they, too, became intoxicated with promises of boundless booty and glory. The conviction grew that Rome deserved to conquer and that any means to that end were justified.

An illustration of the new Roman attitude was given in the conquest of Spain, which was accomplished in 133 B.C. after twenty years of the most contemptible kind of warfare. In this campaign Roman treachery and brutality reached new depths, and the corrupting and weakening effect of the lust for money and power became evident even to some of the Romans themselves.

At about the same time Rome annexed the kingdom of Pergamon, which was willed to Rome by its last king and was renamed the province of Asia. Soon after, southern Gaul was conquered.

THE CONSEQUENCES OF IMPERIALISM

By the late second century B.C. Rome had thus won a great empire—but at a high price. As part of the price, the Romans had exchanged such democracy as they had for

a new oligarchical rule. And with the change in government came profound social, economic, and cultural changes that affected the whole Roman world.

The Decline of Democracy

By 287 B.C. the Roman government had become democratic so far as concerned its laws. In practice, however, the government remained an oligarchy, largely dominated by the Senate. Even in the best of circumstances, it would have been difficult to make democracy work in Rome; but after a century and a half of imperialistic war it became well nigh impossible. Imperialism demanded emergency powers for government, an increasing power in the hands of the military leaders, and secret and swift decisions. Enormous fortunes accumulated in the hands of the militarists, and the private power of the generals grew to the point of rivaling that of the state itself. Roman democracy was frustrated by Roman imperialism.

In the governing oligarchy were combined the remnants of the old patrician group and the more prosperous elements among the plebeians. This well-to-do, tightly organized, and experienced minority was able to control the elections to public office, including even the election of the Tribunes who were supposed to champion the interests of the common people. Its power was made more secure by virtue of the fact that a large proportion of the able and vigorous young men were away from Rome for years on end, serving in the armies.

Deterioration of the Economy

The wars of imperial expansion also brought social and economic changes of great moment. Agriculture was the foundation of the Republican economy in its best days, and the independent yeomen were the backbone of the citizenry. But wars brought ruin to the farmers who were chiefly responsible for Rome's victories. First, Hannibal had inflicted widespread devastation upon the country in his long occupation of southern Italy. The already impoverished peasants found it all but impossible to restore their buildings, equipment, and livestock; and the Senate gave them little or no help. Some of the men did not return from the continuous foreign campaigns, and their families were unable to carry on without them. Others who did return soon became hopelessly encumbered by the debts of their run-down farms.

A second factor that made it harder for the small man was the gradual growth of huge estates operated by cheap slave labor and owned or rented from the state by members of the well-to-do class that controlled the Senate. Still another factor was the importation of foreign grain that cost less than the grain grown at home. As the raising of grain became unprofitable, the land was put to use for vineyards, olive orchards, and cattle-raising. But these uses required extensive tracts of land and large capital investments, which were beyond the means of the small freeholder. Hence, though farming did not disappear from Italy, a large proportion of the former independent farmers were obliged to leave the land. Eventually this economic revolution proved disastrous. And its dire consequences were only slightly moderated by the increase in other business enterprises; Rome's industry and commerce were always on a small scale.

Social Change

These far-reaching economic changes worked comparable changes in Roman social organization. Rome had always been divided into classes, but now the division was sharpened, and the rivalry between classes became more acute. Thus, a problem arose as the peasants gave up their farms and moved to Rome or other cities. This migration produced an unwholesome growth in the urban population. Because there was not work enough in the cities to provide for the former peasants, the newcomers to the cities lived a wretched, hand-to-mouth existence, depending much of the time on private or public charity. A poor man having the rights of citizenship would attach himself as a "client" to some rich patron, attending him in public, voting for him, and doing menial service for him. In return the patron would contribute to the upkeep of the hanger-on. *Clientage*, as this relationship was called, became more widespread in this period than ever before, and it afforded a symbol of the degradation of the once-independent yeomen who were now reduced to a status that was hardly more than membership in the mob—ignorant, blindly cruel, envious, resentful, and a prey to demagogism.

The senatorial aristocracy, which took privileges and power for itself but refused to accept responsibility toward others, was partly to blame for this illness. In an earlier time, when Rome was fighting for its life, the entire Senate had discharged its duties and had done good work, but that time was now past. Some Senators seemed to think the world owed them a living, and many of them gave themselves over to lives of pleasure and frivolity. Stubbornly they refused to disgorge the public lands and other wealth they had seized both at home and in the provinces, or to make any reforms for the benefit of the common people.

There were others, too, who grew fat on the profits of war. These were the rising capitalists, the richest of whom became a new class, called the Equestrian Order. The name came from the old military order, under which only the richest men could afford to take service in the equestrian divisions, or cavalry. This new equestrian class became a disturbing element in Roman society, for many equestrians wished to exploit the provinces for their own enrichment, as did the members of the older senatorial aristocracy. Sometimes the two bands of self-seekers cooperated with one another; more often they competed in exploitation and plunder.

In the new circumstances the old Roman way of life underwent changes for the worse. The primitive Roman, though stolid and unimaginative, was at least sober, courageous, and honest. But the Roman was not strong enough to resist the temptations that now beset him, as Rome began to reap an ill-gained harvest of pillage from the conquered provinces and imported hordes of helpless slaves taken among the peoples whom it had vanquished. The rich gave themselves to ostentation, luxury, and dissipation. The gap between rich and poor grew wider, and the conspicuous display of the newly rich worsened a dangerous situation.

Street Musicians—a mosaic, c.100 B.C., by Dioskourides of Samos, which was found at Herculaneum. One way of earning a livelihood was as a wandering musician, playing and begging in the streets. Many musicians were Greeks or Greek-trained. Some found employment in military bands that were used to improve soldiers' morale, and others in the ensembles that played at games and contests. (Alinari photo)

CULTURAL LIFE PRIOR TO 100 B.C.

In the spheres of thought and art, the consequences of the Roman conquests were as significant as those affecting economic and social life. Previously Rome had lived in relative isolation; now it had become part of a much larger world. Along with material plunder, the Romans took what they could of the cultural riches of the Hellenistic lands Rome now held under its rule. The Romans became borrowers and imitators on a grand scale, and within a short time raised the level of their culture to a much higher plane than they could have attained solely by their own efforts in the course of centuries.

Education

The change was soon noticeable in the field of learning, especially as it affected education. In the older Roman society the education of boys was administered directly by their fathers, and it was largely practical in nature. The aim of education was to produce men with strong bodies and disciplined character, with only the slight book-learning considered necessary for future citizens. A serious attitude and a sense of duty toward the gods, the family, and the state were instilled by the reverential study of Roman legends and history. The respect for tradition that was thus taught them made the Romans slow to accept change in political, economic, social, or religious matters.

Nevertheless, intelligent Romans did not fail to appreciate the learning and literature of the Greeks they had conquered. They began to study Greek and to read such poets as Homer with sincere admiration. And they broadened their studies by the inclusion of Greek rhetoric and philosophy. Rhetoric they especially admired, because it had a practical use in public assemblies. Yet the Romans were not deeply affected by their acquaintance with the Greek mind, and some of them regarded the new learning with suspicion. While they borrowed from Greek culture, they despised the Greeks themselves as weaklings. Most of the Romans regarded liberal education—as opposed to vocational training—as a kind of frippery.

Literature

Latin literature took a belated start in the second half of the third century B.C. with the translation of some Greek poems into Latin and the copying of Greek models for Roman subjects. Thus early was the dominance of Greek over Latin established, in the character of the language, in literary forms, and, frequently, in spirit too; and this influence was to be lasting. Tragic drama had little attraction for the Romans, but two of their writers attained distinction in comedy. These were Plautus (c.254–184 B.C.) and Terence (c.190–c.159 B.C.), his younger contemporary. Both showed a dependence on Hellenistic models but also unmistakable signs of ability. Plautus was the more rugged and original, truer to the Roman spirit; Terence was the more refined and more imitative of his models.

In only one type of poetry—the satire—did the Romans achieve something original. Lucilius (c.180–c.102 B.C.), who established the satire in Roman literature, was a poet of vigor and independence. Latin prose made little progress in this period. The first considerable historical work in Latin, *The Origins* by Cato the Elder (234–149 B.C.), has perished, so Cato's treatise on agriculture is the oldest extant example of prose.

Art

In art, too, powerful foreign influences worked upon Rome. The Romans drew much inspiration from the Etruscans but even more from the Greeks, whose influence was so strong that in some fields Roman art seems merely a continuation of the Greek artistic tradition. The Romans had marked tendencies of their own, however, especially a preference for the specific and realistic, which was in contrast to the Greek propensity for idealism.

Architecture had much appeal for the Romans because it is an art with practical value and the Romans were a practical people. They showed a creative genius in the kinds of structure in which engineering is most important, such as bridges, aqueducts, and sewers. In their buildings the Romans were more versatile than the Greeks, whose best works were always temples. The Romans did well also in the building of baths, amphitheaters, triumphal arches, and basilicas, which were devoted to such public business as the sessions of law courts. In their architecture the Romans showed a bold willingness to experiment that was lacking in their other esthetic ventures. Much of their work is imposing and majestic—even such utilitarian works as aqueducts.

In sculpture Etruscan and Greek influences were still more pronounced. Etruscan sculpture was realistic, bold, and virile—qualities that the Romans prized. The Roman liking for Greek sculpture began during the conquest, when many Greek cities were looted. This new taste reinforced the old Roman habit of keeping life-sized images and masks of their ancestors and heightened a demand for portrait sculpture. In this field, as in the relief sculpture that they also fancied, the Romans insisted upon the utmost realism.

Religion

The primitive Roman religion was simple and unimaginative, and relations with the gods were upon a rather businesslike basis. Certain taboos were carefully observed; certain rites were meticulously performed; and, in return for this ritualistic show of respect, the gods were expected to smile upon their worshipers. Religion involved a belief in impersonal spirits called *numina,* which inhabited things and represented the forces of nature. Gradually more specialized powers were attributed to these *numina,* but spiritual and ethical ideas developed only slowly. As is common among agricultural peoples, the early Roman religion centered in the family, and gods of the household and fields were conscientiously propitiated. Among these were the spirits of the hearth fire (Vesta), of the doorway (Janus), and of the storeroom (the *penates*). The *lares*

Mourning Dancers—a detail from an Etruscan tomb fresco from Tarquinii, fifth century, B.C. Tarquinii, northwest of Rome, was head of the Etruscan League until it fell to Rome in the fourth century B.C. (Alinari photograph)

Roman Denarius—early second century B.C. On the obverse is the head of Bellona, Roman goddess of war, who, by the time this coin was struck, had long been identified as Roma, goddess of the city. (The American Numismatic Society)

were the spirits of the family fields, and the *lar familiaris* became the guardian of the whole household. The strong Roman feeling for ancestor worship accounts for the *genius,* originally a spirit of the household, which later represented the head of the family.

Alongside the cult of the family and the farm grew up a state religion that remained important throughout Roman history. At first, the king was the chief priest, but his place was later taken by the *Pontifex Maximus.* The state religion took over the old deities: Vesta—who was served by the Vestal Virgins—and Janus. Others among the old deities were Jupiter, originally a sky-god like Zeus, who became the chief god of the state religion; Mars, who changed from an agricultural divinity to a god of war; and Quirinus, who was at one time identified with Mars and later with Romulus, the mythical founder of Rome. These deities were served by special priests, called *flamines.*

As time went on the Romans borrowed freely from neighbors and subject peoples in religion as in other matters. The principal contribution of the Etruscans had been in superstitious practices, such as the reading of omens. The Greek religion gave much more: not only were some Greek gods borrowed whole, as it were, but others were equated with Roman divinities, whose character was thus changed. This identification of Greek and Roman gods—Hera became Juno; Athena, Minerva; Artemis, Diana— was advanced by the growing popularity of Homer and other sources of Greek mythology. A result of this invasion of Greek anthropomorphism, which was much more pronounced than the Roman, was a new attitude toward the gods, who were no longer universally regarded as awful beings, vague, mysterious, and remote. They now became beings not unlike men, with passions and impulses similar to those of humans; sometimes they got themselves into ridiculous and embarrassing predicaments. This new attitude led to a skepticism or cynicism that sharply contrasted with the older religious awe and veneration.

The later third century B.C. also saw the growth of emotionalism in religion. This came with the introduction of the cult of the Great Mother from Phrygia, the worship of Dionysus or Bacchus, and other mystery religions. These emotional forms of expression met a need unfilled by the state religion, which now became so cold and remote that it almost ceased to be a religion.

Philosophy

With other features of Greek culture came Greek speculative philosophy, which the better educated Romans were ready to receive and appreciate. The nature of the state religion was such that men of serious mind could attend its empty rites, which had mainly a political meaning, while devoting their main attention to philosophy. As Greek philosophical treatises were translated into Latin, Greek philosophers began to visit Rome to expound their ideas, and some remained there for years. At first the Epicureans were not well received, although the great Roman poet Lucretius (96–55 B.C.) was to become one of their foremost disciples. The Stoics fared much better. More than the other Greek philosophies, Stoicism proved adaptable to the Roman mind, for it could be interpreted with a practical meaning and it fitted well with Roman seriousness and sense of duty.

THE LAST CENTURY OF THE REPUBLIC

Eventually the Romans had to reap the harvest of their conquests and exploitations. Because of general conditions, the decline of republican government was inevitable. The last age of the Republic was a time when greed and corruption flourished, ambition ran wild, and long-standing hatreds burst out in bitter class warfare. Assassination, murder, and proscriptions stained the records of this age with blood. At times rioting was a commonplace occurrence, and conspiracy was the order of the day.

The Gracchi

By 133 B.C. Roman society was enmeshed in a tangle of grave problems. The wars had enriched the few but had reduced the many to beggary. The rural population, which should have been the backbone of Roman society, was being ruined. Those who moved to Rome and became clients of the rich ceased to have value as citizens in a republic. The Senate, representing a selfish clique of rich men, remained in full control of the state, and the upper classes continued to be heedless of the plight of the mass of the citizens.

The social problem was at last brought to a head by Tiberius Gracchus, who offered Rome a program of agrarian reform. He felt that Rome must do something to preserve the class of free farmers, and that to do so would mean an attack on the class of large landholders, who were making increasing use of slave labor. Consequently, when in 133 B.C. he was elected one of the ten Tribunes, Gracchus resolved to let nothing block the re-establishment of the peasantry. He submitted to the people an agrarian bill by which the land owned by the state was to be taken from those who illegally possessed it and distributed in small allotments among the needy. This seemed practicable and fair, because those in illegal possession of public lands were to receive a generous compensation when the land was redistributed.

Nevertheless, the Senate was hostile to this program—or any other kind of reform—and succeeded in blocking the proposal. Tiberius Gracchus had then to choose between giving up reform and taking extreme measures to push it through. He chose the latter course, determined to bend the law to suit his purposes. Thereupon a number of hotheaded members of the Senatorial party resorted to violence. Gracchus and his followers were attacked by a mob, led by some of the Senators, and the great Tribune and about 300 of his associates were slain. Thus the Senate won a victory, but only by establishing an ominous precedent of bloodshed.

Ten years later the work that Tiberius Gracchus had begun was taken up by his younger brother Caius, who won election as a Tribune in 123 B.C. The younger Gracchus was neither so idealistic nor so restrained as Tiberius, but in other respects he was the abler of the two brothers. He was as sincere in his wish to save the state but more conscious of the demands of practical politics. Accordingly he sought to make an alliance with the equestrians by offering them a larger share of control of the courts and of taxation, hoping to pit this group of capitalists against the landholding interest represented in the Senate. For a time this strategy promised success, but ultimately the younger Gracchus met much the same fate as his brother before him. An excuse to attempt to murder Caius was found when riots followed an attack by the Senate on part of his legislation. The Senate then proclaimed a crisis and ordered measures taken to put down the disorder. The "popular" party was defeated in the ensuing struggle, and Caius Gracchus committed suicide. With him died all hope of any immediate reform.

Italy about 50 B.C., as the Republic was nearing its close.

Marius and Sulla

It could not be expected, after the Senate set these precedents, that there would be no further appeals to the sword. In the decades after the death of Caius Gracchus, conditions in Rome grew worse. Out of the confusion there emerged a succession of military men—usually the successful generals of wars abroad. They championed now one cause, now another, but always they were moved principally by their own ambition for personal power.

The first of these new military dictators was Marius (c.155–86 B.C.), a man whom the aristocracy regarded as an upstart be-

cause of his equestrian background. An able commander, he first distinguished himself in Africa, where the Roman armies were engaged in a war against the king of Numidia. Aided by a brilliant young lieutenant named Sulla, Marius succeeded where several other commanders had failed. This triumph permitted him to launch upon a career in politics. Eventually, however, Sulla (138–78 B.C.), who had been his subordinate, emerged as his rival, forcing Marius to flee from Rome.

There followed many years of bloody rivalry between the "popular" party, which Marius had led, and the senatorial party, which Sulla now championed. In this era the Senate grew so strong and dictatorial that Rome was a republic only in name. Yet the success of the Senatorial oligarchy did not bring stability. Rather it produced a paralysis that could result only in ruin or a dictatorship.

Pompey and Caesar

One of the men then coming into prominence was Gnaeus Pompeius Magnus, or Pompey the Great, who was one of Sulla's supporters. Another was Crassus, the richest man in Rome. A third was Julius Caesar (100–44 B.C., see p. 166) who emerged as the leader of the popular party in Rome.

As the commander of the Roman armies in the east that conquered Armenia and the Seleucid Empire of Syria, Pompey (106–48 B.C.) established a great military reputation. On his return to Italy in 62 B.C. at the head of the soldiers he had led victoriously, he resumed a civilian status, expecting the Senate to approve what he had done in the east and give generous treatment to the troops who had served with him. But the Senate proved suspicious of him, and, in angered disappointment, Pompey made a political alliance with Crassus and Caesar. As long as this triumvirate held together, the Senate was helpless, and the three men had virtually a dictatorial rule.

But the alliance did not last long. In 53 B.C. Crassus met his death while in Mesopotamia, where he was in command of a military campaign against the Parthians.

Soon after, Pompey turned against Caesar, becoming a champion of the Senate. The two generals were to fight it out for supreme power in the state.

While allied with Pompey and Crassus, Caesar had gained a military command that enabled him to conquer Gaul and, in 54 B.C., to invade Britain. He used the conquest of Gaul for Rome's advantage and for his own. For Rome it meant that the northern frontier was moved back from the Alps to the Rhine and vast new territories could now be drawn upon for taxes and manpower. For Caesar it meant great personal wealth, a sphere of control in the west to set off against that of Pompey in the east, and a new vision of his power extending through a huge empire. By 49 B.C. he felt free to withdraw his legions from Gaul and embark upon civil war at home.

In Rome Caesar's conquest of Gaul had increased both his popularity among the people and the dread with which the Senate viewed him. Yet the Senate could find no better way to check Caesar's rise than to give more power to Pompey. So in 50 B.C., when gangs of political ruffians burned the Senate building and threatened all Rome, the Senate passed an "Emergency Decree" that made Pompey "sole Consul with full responsibility for restoring order." With the backing of the Senate, Pompey succeeded in keeping Rome tranquil—for the time being.

Caesar's proconsular command in Gaul was due to terminate in 49 B.C. (Proconsul was the title given to former consuls who after their term of office became provincial

Eastern Gate of the Old City of Damascus—built by the Romans about 60 B.C. When Seleucid power waned, Damascus was briefly an independent state. Conquered then by the Armenians, it fell to Pompey in 64 B.C. (Arab Information Center)

governors.) He hoped and planned to pass at once, when this command expired, to the consulship in Rome. He needed this office to make sure that his veterans were rewarded, so that they would remain loyal to him. He needed also to gain a new proconsular command for himself after his second term as Consul (he had been Consul in 59 B.C.), in order to maintain his position as a military leader. But the Senate, fearing Caesar's growing power, ordered him to resign his command in Gaul immediately, on pain of being declared a public enemy.

Instead of doing so, Caesar determined to lead his troops into Italy, and on the night of January 10, 49 B.C., he crossed the Rubicon River. This marked the boundary beyond which no general might lead his troops without breaking the law. By his march, therefore, Caesar committed treason and became an enemy of the state.

The law meant little at this time, however, because might determined right. And Caesar had the might he needed—five faithful legions behind him, and the Roman masses ready to hail him as their hero. Within two months he was master of all Italy. Pompey, driven from Rome, strove to rally his forces in Macedonia. But Caesar found the ships he needed to ferry his troops across the Adriatic and fight it out with Pompey. At Pharsalus in 48 B.C. Pompey was defeated and forced to flee to Egypt, where he hoped to take refuge. However, Ptolemy XII, recognizing that Caesar was to be the new ruler of the Mediterranean world, had Pompey slain as he stepped onto Egyptian soil. With the death of his rival, Caesar alone survived the Triumvirate, to become Rome's autocrat.

Caesar in Power

His task was clear. The Roman government had been mismanaged for more than 150 years. Both the Senate and the Assembly had used their powers selfishly, with little regard for Rome and none for the Empire.

So Caesar had to make his own precedents. Insofar as they did not hamper his own policies, he chose to preserve the traditional forms of government, although actually he controlled the military power. To give a cloak of legality to his position, he had himself made Dictator for life, Consul, Tribune, and *Pontifex Maximus,* though the offices were held in illegal numbers and with extralegal powers. The Senate, once all-powerful, now became a mere rubber stamp, and Caesar became personally responsible for his wide-reaching program of reform.

His measures for the empire were far-sighted. He viewed the empire as a commonwealth of peoples under the protection and guidance of Rome, not merely as lands to be exploited for the profit of the Romans. As a step toward realizing his conception of the empire, he increased the number of provincials who held the rights of Roman citizens, giving full or partial rights to the Transpadane Gauls, to many of his army veterans, and to great numbers of deserving individuals. Municipal governments were given a uniform administration, with the right to name their own tax collectors. The governors of the provinces were made responsible to the central government, no longer being permitted to rule as petty autocrats. Such measures of reform were among Caesar's greatest works, setting precedents that his successors could not ignore.

Within Rome itself, Caesar also undertook reforms. He made a start at reducing the number of citizens living on the public dole, encouraged a large number to migrate to overseas colonies, and distributed a considerable amount of land to small farmers. He also made plans for reconstructing buildings in Rome, where overcrowded living conditions were a factor in provoking disorder. Other public works included the draining of marshes, the planning of a harbor at Ostia to receive the shipments of grain bound for Rome, and the beginning of a road across Italy. He revised the calendar, as we noted when discussing the Egyptian calendar. Frequent public entertainments and banquets helped ensure the good will of the people. The scope of his vision and achievement is all the more impressive when we realize that Caesar was in power for less than four years after Pharsalus.

Despite his successes, the opposition rallied. Many of the Senators never reconciled themselves to the loss of power that the Senate suffered or to the passing of republican forms of government. Nor did Caesar do much to lessen their resentment. Like the Hellenistic kings, he had his image put on coins, his statue placed in temples, and a religious cult organized to give him worship. Then he assumed the purple robe and gilt throne of Rome's early kings—the final outrage to republicanism.

Though Caesar had the support of most of the people and the majority of Senators, many among the latter failed to realize how inevitable and complete was the collapse of the Republic. On March 15, 44 B.C., Marcus Brutus, Caius Cassius, and a number of other Senators drew swords on Caesar as he stood unguarded in the Senate building, and slew him in the name of liberty and the Republic. A majority of the Senators at once applauded. Like the conspirators, they assumed that only the death of the tyrant was needed to restore republican government. They did not see that the Roman people, the army, and the Italian populace had lost faith in the Senate, and that Caesar had been a bulwark against the rushing flood of civil war.

Rivals for Caesar's Power

The weakness of senatorial rule became apparent as soon as Caesar was dead. The conspirators had no idea what to do next and were uncertain of the temper of the people, who had idolized Caesar, so they let the initiative pass to Caesar's adherents.

Chief of these was Marcus Antonius, a bluff but good-humored and courageous patrician, popular with the soldiers and trusted by Caesar. Antony was quick to make donations from Caesar's wealth to woo the populace, turn public opinion against the murderers, and force the Senators to approve of whatever he did. Within a few days the "saviors of the Republic" were fleeing for their lives from the irate people of Rome. Brutus and Cassius went east, planning to gain control of the large armies and rich provinces in the east in preparation for civil war against the Caesarians. For a time Antony took a conciliatory attitude toward the Senate, which, in turn, was willing—however reluctantly—to cooperate with him to prevent further rioting and acquiesced in the necessity of allowing him to run the government in the same manner as Caesar.

Octavian

A new factor was soon introduced, however, in the person of Caesar's grandnephew, Caius Octavius. Intelligent, well-educated, of noble presence and unswerving will, this young man of eighteen had won Caesar's favor and had been named his heir, taking the name of Caius Julius Caesar Octavianus. Upon hearing of Caesar's death, Octavian came to Rome to assume Caesar's name and fortune. The fortune had been squandered by Antony, but the name of Caesar was enough to rally a number of the legions to Octavian's support. For a time Antony and Octavian maintained an alliance, but it was soon broken off, and Octavian found himself working with the aging Cicero (p. 187), who had come out of retirement to fight for liberty by a series of ringing denunciations of Antony. Yet when Octavian deserted him for a new rapprochement with Antony, and the Caesarians decided to eliminate their opponents by widespread executions and proscriptions, Cicero, as the denouncer of

Antony, was one of the first to die. In him died one of the last and greatest defenders of Roman liberty.

Meanwhile, Octavian and Antony allied with the strong Caesarian general Lepidus. Thus they followed the example of Caesar, Pompey, and Crassus by forming a second Triumvirate. Unlike the first, which had been a secret agreement, this second Triumvirate was legally recognized. Dictators in all but name, the three men now had complete charge of the army and the treasury, and they had the right to declare war.

Meantime Brutus and Cassius had been active in the east, assembling a substantial army, a large fleet, and adequate supplies and winning the allegiance of the provinces and dependent monarchs in that area. They took up a strong position at Philippi in Macedonia, but when Antony and Octavian led their forces there to do battle, the Caesarians emerged the victors, and both Brutus and Cassius committed suicide.

After the battle of Philippi, Antony prepared to make himself master of the east. However, he was soon bewitched by Cleopatra, the beautiful Egyptian queen, and deserted his wife and his duties in order to spend his time with her. News of these developments, reaching Rome, aroused public opinion against Antony, and in 31 B.C. Octavian secured a formal declaration of war against Cleopatra. Since Antony was practically her ally, this meant, in substance, war against him too. Once more Roman armies were pitted against Roman armies.

The advantage lay with Octavian, for Antony's soldiers were chiefly legionaries who shared the Roman antagonism toward Cleopatra. In the crucial land and naval battle at Actium, 31 B.C., these troops wavered, and when Cleopatra fled from the battle, with Antony following her, nearly the whole army and navy pledged allegiance to Octavian.

The war ended the following year soon after Cleopatra and Antony chose suicide in preference to captivity for her and disgrace for him. Egypt was made an imperial province of Rome, and its vast treasury was carried away to Italy to become Octavian's private wealth. Octavian spent some time settling affairs in the east before returning to Rome to celebrate the victory that had left him the supreme autocrat of the Roman world.

CULTURAL DEVELOPMENTS IN THE LAST CENTURY OF THE REPUBLIC

Religion

In the last century of the pre-Christian era, Greek and eastern influences on Roman culture became still more pronounced than in the age of the Gracchi. This was especially evident in religion. Doubts about their gods, which had begun to assail the Romans at their first contact with foreign religions, increased in this period, until all but the most resolute conservatives were turning to the eastern religions or philosophies.

To be sure, the worship of the old gods continued, but only as a ritual in which no one fervently believed. In the last stages of the decay of the Republic, a cult to Caesar was instituted, with the libertine Antony as high priest. This illustrates how the Ancient Oriental idea of deified men was gaining acceptance, how far gone was the old Roman awe of the unknown gods, and how religion was being used for political ends.

The patrician class, which formerly had provided the leadership for the public cults, now sought spiritual and ethical guidance in Greek and Hellenistic philosophies. Some were impressed by Plato, who extolled the conquest of the body by the soul, provided an incentive for morality, and made an adequate explanation of the world. Others responded to the Stoic conception of a god ordering the universe and encompassing the lesser gods. Still others, ignoring religion altogether, cultivated a morality based on personal integrity, social conscience, or mere expediency.

The poorer people, whose numbers were now swollen by foreigners, both slave and free, found little comfort in either the formal state religion or the abstract philosophies. Instead they turned to the mystery cults. These had been brought to Rome by soldiers fighting in the imperial wars, traders from the east, slaves sold in Rome, and other intermediaries. The masses of the inarticulate found a sense of personal worth in the Egyptian cult of Isis, for example, or in the religion of the Jewish Jahweh. There was a direct, personal element in the magic of the Chaldean astrologers who pretended to see through the uncertainties of the moment to the sure outline of the future. These gods and creeds offered a pageantry, a mystery, and a superstition that constituted a religious counterpart of the political and economic flight from reason manifested by the prevalence of civil wars and dictatorship. For a time the patricians held out against these influences that seemed to run against the Roman ideals of sobriety and dignity. But by the end of the Republic,

masters and mistresses were following their servants to the eastern rites, and foreign gods had official recognition in the Roman pantheon.

Unfortunately, few of the new religions did any more to foster morality than had the old state religion. Frequently they introduced practices long accepted in the east, which represented a break with the ancient Roman ideals. Even in the past, morality had stemmed not from religion but from pride in family ancestry and in the state. But pride both in family and in Rome had been lost during the period of aggressive and civil wars, which, though they might sometimes nurture courage and honor, were too often accompanied by inhumanity, lust, and disloyalty. The glory that the Romans had once sought for the Republic they now sought for themselves. And all too often the success of the dictators seemed to prove that the end justified the means.

Nevertheless, we should not conclude that religion was on the wane. Rather, from the growth of the mystery cults and the rise of Christianity in the next century, we should recognize that religious enthusiasm was merely disorganized, not extinguished. As the city-state grew into an empire, Rome was outgrowing its old gods, but soon it would be ready to accept a monotheism—appropriate to an all-encompassing empire.

The *Maison Carrée*. Many Roman temples were copies of Greek ones, some (as here) raised on a podium. Originally dedicated to two grandsons of Octavian, *Maison Carrée* was built at Nîmes in southern France about 16 B.C. It is 59 feet wide and 117 feet long, with Corinthian columns (p. 121). (French Government Tourist Office)

Philosophy

As the traditional religion waned, Greek philosophy gained a stronger hold on the Roman mind. In it, the vast majority of educated Romans found a broadened explanation of the physical world and a kind of answer to the social problems of the empire. They found as well an answer to their own demand for an acceptable code of personal morality. As they lost the old Roman sense of the abnegation of self in public duty, they gained a new vision of an intense personal inner life in disregard of chaotic outer events.

The philosophies remained, however, more eastern than Roman. For this reason few Romans made original contributions to them. Lucretius, the Epicurean who sought to present his philosophy in the compelling didactic poem *On the Nature of Things*, towers high above the other Roman philosophers. From him, it is a long step down to Cicero (106–43 B.C.), whose popular expositions of the eastern philosophies set forth no new philosophical concepts.

Stoicism continued to be the most popular of the philosophies, although its metaphysical complexities did not interest the practical Romans. Its rigid morality and its emphasis upon duty to the state, however, struck responsive chords, and equally appealing was its rationality, which gave to both gods and men roles that men could understand and that gave men self-respect. But the Romans paid little heed to the Stoic message of humanitarianism, even after the philosopher Epictetus (A.D. *c.*60-*c.*120), a Phrygian slave, began to expound his doctrine of the brotherhood of man.

Epicureanism, which had gained few followers in the second century B.C., won considerable popularity in the first. Its attraction lay in its materialistic approach to nature. Where Stoicism set forth unproved metaphysical explanations for the world, Epicureanism faced the problem in a spirit of skeptical investigation. And the answer it provided was one that made sense to the Romans—a view of the world as comprised of atomic particles of matter in a continuous process of change. The gods, in this view, remained removed from men and offered little or no ethical guidance. For want of such guidance, some of the Epicureans gave themselves over to gross self-indulgence. But the best of the Roman Epicureans, like the Greeks, found in this philosophy a retreat from the chaos of their times to an ethical and intellectual cultivation of their own garden.

Roman Law: *Jus Civile* and *Jus Gentium*

These philosophies, which the Hellenistic world had used for personal morality, the Romans applied to political life. Discerning men saw in the anarchy of the times an urgent need to reassess the traditional values of government and adapt the laws to the new needs. Foremost was the need for an international law, applicable throughout the empire, which law came into being through a gradual evolution. The old Roman laws, the *Jus Civile*, remained in force, but slowly and regularly the *praetors* and other jurists amended or supplemented them, often by adapting eastern usages to Roman needs. The provincial governors and the *Praetor Peregrinus*, who handled the lawsuits involving foreigners in Rome, were in an especially strategic position to effect these changes. Soon the concept of a "law of the peoples"—*Jus Gentium*—was developed as a supplement to the Roman law. By this was meant a law that applied throughout the empire, governing such universal problems as property, sales, and contracts.

Jus Naturalis

The final and most significant legal concept to be developed in the late Republic was that of *Jus Naturalis*. This "Natural

Law" stemmed not from judicial practice but from the Stoic idea of a rational god ruling the universe. It held that the law of nature surpassed all civil laws that men decree. Under it, all men are kindred and are endowed with certain inalienable rights, simply by virtue of being men. This Stoic concept contributed to the legists' idea that the peoples of the empire should be treated as fellow men to the Romans, rather than as mere animals to be herded or butchered for Rome's benefit. This basic principle has never been forgotten throughout the centuries that have passed since Roman times.

Cicero

Cicero deserves remembrance, not only for his achievements in other fields but as the originator and interpreter of some of the most progressive and humane ideas of political theory. In *The Laws* he restated the Stoic theory of natural law. In *The Republic,* imitating Plato, he set up his ideal state. Distrusting democracy, as did Plato, Cicero preferred a government based on a system of checks and balances. But to meet the needs of his own times, he favored a "first citizen" or "philosopher-king" with ultimate authority. He himself thought of Pompey in this role; later the theory was used as support for the principate (p. 192). Of more lasting significance was Cicero's emphasis on the duty of the citizen to devote himself to the welfare of the state. Thus, in his view, politics and ethics were linked together by social conscience.

Literature

The literature of the first century B.C. gave proof of the increasing sophistication of Rome. Books became common and inexpensive, even though they were inscribed by hand on scrolls—slave labor was cheap.

Circles of savants appeared, and politicians began to rely on their literary skill to secure or buttress their successes in public affairs. Roman writing was now more vigorous than the Greek, and more distinctively Roman than before. Latin as well as Greek was becoming the common tongue around the Mediterranean. In the process of expansion, Latin usage became more flexible and better suited to the purposes of literature.

Although poetry continued for the most part in servile imitation of Greek models, two Roman poets—Catullus and Lucretius—reached a level that was never excelled in Rome. Born in the provinces, Catullus (87–54 B.C.) came to Rome as a young man and immediately was swept into the lavish corruption of fashionable society. His passion for the profligate Roman matron Clodia inspired the most ardent of all Latin love lyrics. His spontaneous self-revelation, his emotional upheavals of love and hate, were not in the tradition of Roman austerity and discipline. But they well represented the new age of distraught egotism in Rome, and they showed the genius of a sincere indigenous art. In the best of his work, Catullus surpassed his Hellenistic masters, and he can be counted among the finest lyric poets of all time.

Of very different character was Lucretius, who combined the inspiration of a poet with the aims of a philosopher and religious teacher. His powerful epic poem, which sought by Epicurean arguments to free men from fears of death and the gods, was the most original monument of Roman philosophy. Lucretius taught a moral uprightness and loftiness of spirit more sublime than that of his Hellenistic teacher, and this nobility sustains the fire and intensity of the whole long poem.

In the whole view of Latin literature the work of this age in poetry was only a prelude to the Golden Age under the early emperors. Not so with prose, which reached its Golden Age in the century of Caesar and Cicero. Oratory became a powerful political

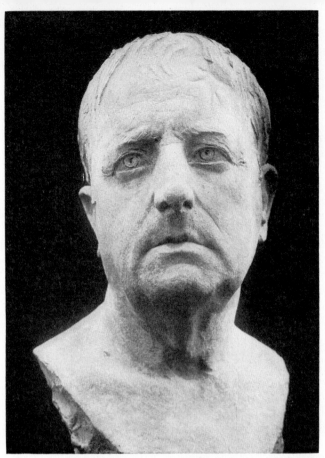

Unknown Roman—life-sized terracotta bust, first century B.C. In every Roman household a room was set aside for worship of living and dead ancestors. In contrast to the somewhat idealized statue of Augustus (p. 192), this portrait of an ordinary citizen is highly realistic. Yet both served the same purpose: veneration of the *pater familias*. (Courtesy of the Museum of Fine Arts, Boston)

History was also reaching new heights, both in style and accuracy. Sallust (86–34 B.C.) was one of the most successful of the new historians. He wrote on topics of which he had personal knowledge, such as the Jugurthine War and the Catilinarian conspiracy, and though he had a bias toward the "popular" party, he strove for accuracy. Using Thucydides as his model, he gave sketches of the leading figures to lend color to the narrative and put in their mouths appropriate, if fictitious, speeches. Even more effective was Julius Caesar, whose *Commentaries* on the Gallic and civil wars have remained guides for military historians. Their style is unmatched for lucid, concise prose. Lesser writers also contributed to the common literary fund. The most learned Roman of the century was Varro (116–*c*.27 B.C.), who wrote 490 books dealing with Roman religion, language, agriculture, antiquities, and other topics.

Art

Art proved slower than literature to break free of Greek domination. The conquest of the east brought shiploads of sculpture and other art objects from Greek and Hellenistic lands. Some eastern artists were brought as slaves to Rome, and others came voluntarily in search of work. The demand for works of art was thus well supplied, without need of the Romans themselves developing their indigenous art.

In subject matter the paintings of this period were often Roman, but the techniques were Greek. The sculpture, too, showed the roundness and refinement of Hellenistic work. In portrait sculpture, however, the Roman preference for literal realism persisted, despite Greek influences. This portrait realism was now carried over to the heads on Roman coins, as well; for the imperial coinage, like other forms of metal work in this century, also showed improvement in workmanship.

weapon, and the high stakes to be won in the forum brought the spoken and written command of the language to a new force. Supreme in this field was the versatile Cicero. His orations are masterpieces of persuasion and eloquence. His works on philosophy and political theory also rank among the classics of Latin prose. Of no less interest are his personal letters, which provide an intimate account of life in Rome in these critical years. Though not written for publication, these letters show the polished skill that was the natural expression of the most urbane of Roman writers.

Roman Architecture. The most distinctive Roman contribution in art in this period, as in the earlier Republic, was in the realm of architecture. Though world conquest introduced into Rome a medley of foreign architectural styles, generally the new public buildings followed the principle of the arch and the vault, enclosing great areas without intermediate support. Never before had the arch been used with such boldness. Largeness of scope and new engineering achievements were found also in such places of amusement as the circus and the amphitheater.

Eastern models now stimulated a demand for beauty as well as efficiency. Marble façades, lavish decorations, and bright colors replaced the plain stone solidity of the older Roman buildings. Men of wealth were able to add their own luxurious villas and palaces to the beauty of Rome, while monuments, arches, and columns commemorated the achievements of victorious generals. Nothing was done, however, at this time to improve the tenements in which the mass of the people lived. They had to wait another 200 years (p. 206).

Conclusion

The substantial progress in cultural life in Rome during the last century of the Republic stands in sharp contrast to the political chaos and disillusionment of the times. To explain this, we can only suggest that the challenge of the times stimulated men to greater efforts to solve problems—or to escape from them. Even those men most given to political ambition showed an interest in culture that was quite alien to their forefathers.

In some fields this century marked the peak of Roman achievements, while in others, it provided a solid foundation for the greater triumphs that came in the early years of the Roman Empire. In all, it achieved a synthesis of Roman culture with that of the east, and it saw the spread of this blended culture to the newly conquered barbarians of the west and north. This sharing of culture, which made possible a common understanding among the diverse peoples of the empire, was to prove more effective than the devices of politics in welding together the Mediterranean-wide empire.

The *Pont du Gard*. The Romans built for use, and many of their civil engineering projects resulted from their exploitation of the possibilities inherent in the arch as a building principle (see below). Their aqueducts functioned on the principle of gravity and brought water from mountain sources through systems of underground and open concrete channels, with ducts sloping in the desired direction. The *Pont du Gard* at Nîmes, c. A.D. 50, carried water 880 feet across a valley at a height of 155 feet. (*Archives Photographiques*)

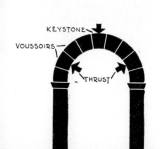

Suggestions for Further Reading

Source Materials

Anthologies

G. H. Knoles and R. K. Snyder, eds., *Readings in Western Civilization* (rev. ed., New York, 1954), pp. 111–123, 143–152.
Selections from Polybius, Caesar, and Cicero.

R. Warnock and G. K. Anderson, eds., *The World in Literature* (Chicago, 1950–1951), Volume I, pp. 317–367.
Selections from Cicero, Lucretius, and Plautus.

Contemporary Writings

Caesar, *Gallic War*

Catullus, *Works*

Cicero, *Essays on Friendship and Old Age*

Cicero, *Offices*

Cicero, *Selected Letters*

Livy, *The History of Rome*

Lucretius, *On the Nature of Things*

Polybius, *Histories*

Secondary Works

F. E. Adcock, *The Roman Art of War under the Republic* (Cambridge, Mass., 1940).
Good general observations on a very important aspect of Roman expansion and internal political changes.

F. Altheim, *A History of Roman Religion* (New York, 1938).
A study, chiefly of early religion, little on the Empire. Concerned with the origins from primitive Italian people, Etruscan, Greek, and eastern influences. Concerned not so much with cult and saga as with the place of religion in Roman life, especially political life.

F. Cumont, *Oriental Religions in Roman Paganism* (Chicago, 1911).
An original, exciting, well-written book. Takes each of the major Ancient Oriental cults that came to Rome and studies its impact on Roman thinking and religion.

R. A. L. Fell, *Etruria and Rome* (Cambridge, England, 1924).
Not so much an original book as a good summary of the relations of Etruria and Rome. Goes over questions of the origins of Etruria, its contact with and influence on Rome.

W. W. Fowler, *The Religious Experience of the Roman People* (London, 1911).
A standard work based on popular lectures. Treats religion as developed from primitive magic, which was lost in ritual, but reasserted itself later in various forms in spite of the austere and formal state religion.

T. Frank, *An Economic History of Rome* (Baltimore, 1927).
A readable and not-too-technical economic history. Deals chiefly with Republican times. Sections on slaves, freedmen, production, distribution, industry.

T. Frank, *Life and Literature in the Roman Republic* (Berkeley, 1930).
A book taken from lectures. Stresses the independence of Roman culture from Greek, as well as the dependence. Uses early and major writers to show literature of the Republic as centering about strictly Roman themes and experience.

T. Frank, *Roman Imperialism* (New York, 1914).
This book makes the expansion of Rome not aggressive, but the result of idealistic and democratic forces in Roman life. Well written and useful.

A. J. H. Greenidge, *Roman Public Life* (New York, 1901).
Traces the growth and working of the Roman constitution through the Principate in the central, municipal, and provincial governments. Theory and practice and estimate of how much continued into later times.

J. Hadley, *Introduction to Roman Law* (New Haven, 1931).
A simple account of Roman law, written for the student of ancient history and literature rather than of law. Sound.

T. R. Holmes, *The Roman Republic and the Founder of the Empire* (Oxford, 1923).
In spite of its title, this work deals with the last century of the Republic. Careful use of sources. Important for political and especially military history.

L. P. Homo, *Primitive Italy* (New York, 1927).
A lucid discussion of the difficult period of Italian prehistory. Well done, developing broad generalizations and interpretation soundly based on available evidence. Ties history in with geographic factors. Discusses mainly military and political history of Rome's external contacts.

L. P. Homo, *Roman Political Institutions from City to State* (New York, 1930).

Makes Roman constitutional history and development human, concrete, and readable. Background and personalities for the changes discussed. Better for the Republic than the Empire.

D. Randall-MacIver, *The Etruscans* (Oxford, 1927).

A brief but reliable and good popular account of the Etruscans. Good handling of a subject not too well known.

D. Randall-MacIver, *Italy Before the Romans* (Oxford, 1928).

A brief work, giving the archaeological evidence for the relationships of the various peoples of Italy and their influence on Rome. A good introductory account.

J. W. Mackail, *Latin Literature* (New York 1927).

Useful as a brief account of literature and appreciation of it, but difficult and disappointing to one looking for facts.

F. B. Marsh, *A History of the Roman World from 146–30 B.C.* (New York, 1939).

One of a series of books on the Romans. A straightforward, concise, clear presentation of this tangled period, with much material compressed into it.

T. Mommsen, *History of Rome* (New York, 1903–5).

An important book historically. One of the most influential and original books ever written about Rome; always used by later historians. Material old now, but much of it still valid. Stresses Rome's need for strong leaders, and especially favors Caesar.

H. H. Scullard, *A History of the Roman World from 753–146 B.C.* (New York, 1939).

One of a series of books on Roman history, sound and thorough, but traditional and conservative in interpretation.

G. Showerman, *Eternal Rome* (New Haven, 1925).

A good, readable book, sometimes subject to the author's biases. Good for fusing art with literature and history.

J. Whatmough, *The Foundations of Roman Italy* (London, 1937).

A discussion of the early inhabitants of Italy and their cultures, based on archaeology and literature. Especially good for the prehistoric period. Goes on through the Etruscans and the Roman unification of Italy.

8

The Roman Empire

Augustus as *Imperator*—marble statue, 6 feet 8¼ inches high, from Prima Porta. Augustus is shown addressing his troops, but the statue was made to be worshiped in a temple. Cupid signifies the divine origin of the Julian family. (Alinari photograph)

The years of bloody civil war that culminated in the battle of Actium saw the death of the Roman Republic, but the same bloodshed marked also the beginning of the peaceful era that was to follow. Octavian emerged from Actium with more personal authority and power than any man had ever held during the Republic. He had complete command of a well-trained army, and the prestige of victory made him sure of its loyalty to him. His vast wealth, which he had gained during the war years by inheritance, confiscation, and conquest, gave him the strength to carry through whatever reforms he chose and to give his veterans the generous rewards that would further assure their allegiance. But his most important asset was that he represented peace and order, and it was for this that the people, weary and sickened by the civil wars, longed. Although he received from the Senate the title of *imperator* (commander) in 29 B.C., two years later he assumed the title of *Augustus,* to indicate that his power was a sacred trust bestowed on him by the gods as well as men.

THE PRINCIPATE OF AUGUSTUS

In order to preserve the forms of Republican Rome and to give his rule an appearance better suited to an era of peace and order, Augustus had to abandon the role of unconstitutional dictator. In 28 B.C., accordingly, he announced that he would restore the control of the government to the Senate. But the Senate was as well aware as Augustus that it lacked the power to organize the government and prevent civil war without his help. So a compromise was established by which the Senate shared rule with Augustus, who was designated as *princeps* —first among equals—and hence his form of government is called a principate. Theoretically, the old Roman constitution was restored. Actually everyone knew this was but a screen for Augustus' military monarchy. The pretense was kept up merely for the sake of "peace with honor."

Political Change

In making political changes, Augustus could proceed with an almost free hand, for the Republic was dead, no matter what the pretense, and few of the former republican Senators were still alive.

Since he wanted to share the responsibilities of government with the Senators and Equestrians, Augustus early made a revision of the membership lists of these orders, to fill the ranks depleted by the civil wars and to make sure that the best men in the state were available for public office.

Only men of known virtue, who had held military rank or the political office of *quaestor,* could become Senators. Considerable wealth was also a prerequisite, but often the Emperor bestowed large gifts upon worthy men in order to make them eligible. Men of the Senatorial Order held the highest offices in the Empire, including the governorships of the senatorial provinces and top military posts. As a body, they were treated with much respect and deference, for Augustus frequently consulted the Senate and allowed it to act in legislative matters, although he always made the final decisions on questions of large importance.

The emperor was no less concerned with the caliber of the men admitted to the Equestrian Order. Prerequisites for membership in this, like the Senatorial Order, were ability, wealth, and moral character. Men of equestrian rank filled most of the civilian offices and the lesser military ranks, but some might aspire to positions of greater power, such as the governorship of the emperor's province of Egypt, the command of the emperor's personal Praetorian Guard, or appointment to the rank of senator.

Augustus' policy toward the plebeians was to try to keep them contented by honors and public amusements while lessening their actual political power. Thus he stressed the dignity of Roman citizenship, while he made it harder for freedmen or non-Italians to achieve citizenship, and he played up the glory of the Roman legions, in which the plebeians served as soldiers and lesser officers. Yet because of his fear that it might fall under the leadership of unscrupulous demagogues, Augustus made certain that the Plebeian Assembly had little voice in the government, and his successors reduced it to a role of no importance whatever.

With the increasing centralization of governmental power under a strong executive, Augustus had need of well-trained and reliable assistance. As a board of personal advisers, a sort of privy council, he formed the Council of the Princeps, which met regularly to discuss problems, establish the agenda for the Senate or Assembly, and expedite the top-level business of the Empire. Below this council was a vast bureaucracy that functioned far more efficiently than had the administration of the Republic, which had depended upon unpaid magistrates, elected for a term of only one year.

The army, which could either remain a support or become a threat to his rule, Augustus kept within careful bounds. He saw to it that the soldiers were well provided for and that they swore allegiance to him directly. But, recognizing the war-weariness of the people and seeking to rest his regime upon more peaceable bases of power, he reduced the size of the army to about one third of what it was in the period of the civil wars. It became primarily a force for guarding the frontiers. As a personal guard and a means of keeping a secure control over the capital, Augustus created the Praetorian Guard, a force of 9000 highly trained and well-paid soldiers, who were stationed just outside Rome. He also founded a permanent imperial navy, which put down the menace of pirates, protected the ships bringing grain to Rome, and transported troops to distant parts of the Empire.

By these measures, Augustus created a magnificent machine for the efficient operation of the government and the maintenance of order. Never before had there been such an efficiently organized and centralized government for an empire of comparable size and power.

Economic Prosperity

Augustus, who took prudent care of his own personal wealth, was also quick to protect and increase the wealth of the Empire. To assure a stable supply of food for Rome, he appointed a trained administrator to supervise the importation of grain from Africa, Numidia, and Egypt. And to prevent the widespread destruction that Rome suffered from frequent fires, he maintained a force of 3500 regular firemen. The roads linking Rome with the parts of the Empire were improved at his behest, and an imperial mail service was established.

Directly and indirectly, his reforms increased the prosperity of the Empire and served to provide a solid basis for economic prosperity, both in his own reign and in succeeding generations. From one end of the Roman realm to the other, trade could move freely along highways and waterways that were safe from brigands and free of the nuisance of boundaries. Thus the west could obtain the luxuries produced in the east, and from the west the east could obtain raw materials needed for building and manufacturing. Indeed, commerce spread even beyond the bounds of the Empire, because Augustus took measures to encourage trade with India and Arabia.

Agriculture flourished, too, with the return of peace. The breakup of the *latifundia,* the great landed estates, which had begun during the civil wars, now came to a stop, and some of the large estates grew even larger. But a decrease in the number of slaves, owing to the end of foreign wars, meant that more of the land was worked by free tenant-farmers, who were more productive workers than slaves. A trend toward specialization also contributed to the great-

er efficiency of agricultural production. Italian agriculture, for example, centered largely in the growing of grapes and olives, and eventually Italian wine and olive oil competed with the best products of the east.

Industry continued to center in small shops, except in such businesses as brickmaking, where natural monopolies of materials or techniques favored large-scale production. As in agriculture, free men or freedmen made up most of the labor force, though the use of slaves did not die out. As a mark of favor to the workmen and as a manifestation of the peace and political security of these times, Augustus now permitted the *collegia,* or fraternal organizations of workmen, which Caesar had suppressed in order to limit political rioting, to reorganize, although the state charters that limited them chiefly to social and charitable ends prohibited their again acting as an effective political force.

Territorial Expansion

During the civil wars that had marked the end of the Republic, Rome had ceased to extend the boundaries of its empire, and its hold upon the more distant lands had become less secure. Having been left without supervision, the western provinces were flaring into revolt, while the east was suffering from the requisitions that one dictator after another had levied.

The first task facing Augustus outside the Italian peninsula was therefore to re-establish a secure Roman power on the frontiers. Then he had to decide whether or not to enlarge the boundaries of the Empire by new conquests. The disadvantages of making new conquests were considerable, because this would require large armies in the field, under capable commanders, and these military leaders might be tempted to turn against Augustus and renew the civil wars. Moreover, the most desirable lands were already included in the Empire, so new con-

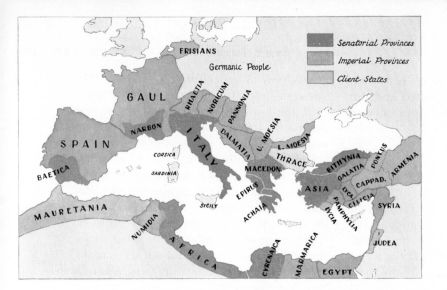

The Empire of
Augustus

Senatorial Provinces
Imperial Provinces
Client States

quests would probably cost more than the worth of the lands to be gained. Accordingly Augustus decided not to embark upon an ambitious program of expansion but to cope only with immediate problems of defense and trade. Yet even this cautious policy led him farther than he anticipated, and in his reign the boundaries of the Empire were considerably widened.

The relative peace in the east and south gave Augustus a welcome freedom to concentrate his troops in the unsettled northern and western provinces. The Gauls, whom Caesar had thoroughly subdued, would have showed little inclination to revolt if they had been left alone. But they were under constant pressure from the Germanic peoples to the east of them, and wars on the other side of the Rhine were inevitably accompanied by rumblings of discontent in Gaul.

For this reason, Augustus determined to advance the frontier as far as the Elbe River. This would make a shorter boundary that would be easier to defend. The Roman legions had no trouble in advancing to the Elbe and into Bohemia, but it proved impractical to maintain this new frontier, so Augustus ordered the troops to withdraw again to the Rhine frontier that Caesar had established.

More critical was the problem of establishing a frontier in the Balkans, where no imperial boundary had ever been permanently drawn. After a series of hard-fought campaigns, Augustus succeeded in establishing a defensible frontier along the Danube.

By the end of Augustus' reign the main outline of the Empire had been fixed. For the most part, it corresponded to natural features that gave strategic advantage— oceans, mountains, and deserts. Within the boundaries, well-organized frontier legions protected the vulnerable areas, and for generations the twenty-five provinces lived in secure peace—the *Pax Romana,* or the Peace of Rome.

Economic Organization

The economic reorganization of the Empire that confronted Augustus was even more critical than the political. The decades of unjust taxation, requisitions for the civil wars, and extravagant imports of luxuries from such countries as India and China had destroyed the prosperity of the provinces, especially those in the east, and had left them too unsure of the future to attempt a recovery. But now the years of peace under Augustus brought a revival of confidence and enterprise. Moreover Augustus took positive measures to foster economic recovery by making the Empire an economic unit, with protected trade routes and freedom of commerce, by encouraging local production, and by revising the tax system. An Empire-wide census was taken, to provide the basis for tax assessments, and the various taxes were revised so they would bear equitably upon wealth of all kinds and in such ways as to guarantee that the proceeds would reach the imperial treasury, instead of being drained off by the tax collectors for their own profit. And though the Italians continued to have special privileges, since they did not pay direct taxes, they were obliged to pay increased indirect taxes and thus bear a greater share than before of the economic burden.

The results of Augustus' fiscal policies were good. Throughout his reign the prosperity of the Empire increased, while the imperial treasury recovered from the ruinous drain of the last days of the Republic.

THE CULTURAL LIFE OF THE AUGUSTAN AGE

Cultural developments during the Augustan Age showed both good and bad trends. On the positive side, the peace and prosperity of the age provided leisure and an incentive for the growth of talent, and the emperor himself proved to be a generous patron of the arts. Moreover, a fresh perspective and new ideas came from the increase of contacts between east and west, among Greeks, Romans, and barbarians. However the monarchism of Augustus extinguished or dampened many creative fires that might have burned more brightly in the freer air of a republic. For the principal theme in education and the creative arts in this age was the expression of gratitude and praise for the blessings that the reign of Augustus was bringing.

Education

In education, the emphasis was increasingly upon the Roman rather than the Greek. The Latin language took on new economic and political importance as Rome rose to dominance in the Empire, and it was being used more satisfactorily and skillfully for literary expression than it had been before the time of Cicero. Many Romans now completed their education at home instead of going to Greece for the final stage of their schooling, as had formerly been the rule. Augustus favored this development, which gave sign of Rome's rise as a center of culture. To encourage it, he completed the building of a public library in Rome, which had been planned by Caesar, and he granted special privileges to teachers.

Philosophy

The all-pervading influence of Augustus reached far beyond the schoolrooms, constraining most men to shape their thoughts to the pattern of his own thinking. For the most part, his influence was a force favoring a conservative traditionalism. His own answers to the fundamental intellectual questions were mainly drawn from the Roman religion; consequently most philosophies adopted a more religious tone and gave less emphasis to rationalism than did the Classical Greek philosophies. An unsystematic eclecticism, corresponding to the spirit of shrewd compromise that animated Augustus, became more popular than those philosophies that were resolute and rigorous in following through their ideas to a logical conclusion. And the search for practical ethics, meeting the needs of everyday life, took precedence over that for answers to general problems, such as the origin of matter.

The Stoic and Epicurean philosophies continued to hold the widest favor. Epicureanism afforded a solace to many men who were denied an opportunity to gain pride and honor by service to the state. However, the Epicureans of the Augustan Age often debased the doctrines of Epicurus into a mere pretext for libertinism. And even the more refined among them, such as the poet Horace, understood these doctrines to mean only that men should submit to authority, while seeking simple pleasures that would fill out the brief and otherwise meaningless days before oblivion.

The Stoic teachings of fortitude and pride in self were well suited to the Augustan Age. Augustan Stoicism, however, put less emphasis than earlier teaching had done upon one's duty to serve the state, since the state was wholly under the care of the emperor. Instead Stoicism now emphasized, much more than in the age of the Republic, the importance of one's own moral improvement through discipline and mastery of the emotions. Its stress was upon the individual's duty to himself and his fellow men rather than his duty to the state. At the same time its orientation became more religious as the universal nature of the monotheistic Stoic God of Reason was made to justify the imperial rule and the individual man's existence in the universe.

Religion

Religion itself—wholly without stress on philosophy—held a place of central importance in Augustan Rome. The emperor himself launched a remarkable campaign to reinvigorate the traditional religious beliefs. Not only did Augustus rebuild temples that had suffered from neglect during the civil wars, rejuvenate the decadent priesthood, resume celebration of old religious festivals, and in 12 B.C. assume the office of *pontifex maximus,* but he also labored to infuse the rituals with real meaning.

It was by a revival of religion that Augustus hoped to overcome the despair and skepticism that had become widespread during the previous generation. He hoped to make the people believe in the gods as the protectors of Rome, and he wanted to use religion to make a wholesome family life and morality once more the backbone of Rome's strength. Accordingly, he himself in 17 B.C. led the *Ludi Saeculares,* a three-day ceremony of expiation to mark the end of the age of sin and despair and the beginning of a new era of peace and piety. Meanwhile he encouraged writers, such as the poet Vergil and the historian Livy, to tell of the role of the gods in establishing Roman power and to extoll the Roman virtue of dutiful devotion to the gods, the state, and the family.

Associated with this religous revival was the beginning of emperor worship, which was to continue in the Roman Empire for the next three centuries and which was to inspire the theory of the divine right of kings in more modern times. The practice was not new in Augustan Rome. Much earlier, Romulus, the traditional founder of Rome, had been deified, and so had various Greek heroes. In the east, rulers were commonly known as gods or the sons of gods. In recent times various successful Roman generals or governors had been hailed as divine by the people of the eastern provinces. And in Rome itself Caesar had been deified after his death, and a priesthood had been established for his worship.

Thus the deification of Augustus was a natural development from these precedents. It began in the east, where Augustus was proclaimed the divine successor to previous divine rulers. This homage in the east Augustus accepted, but he did not encourage worship of himself in Rome or elsewhere in Italy. Nevertheless, even in his lifetime, he was worshiped there by those eastern peoples who had settled in Italy and by the common people who were sincerely grateful to him for his work of restoring peace and order. Even more sophisticated persons, who did not think of Augustus as a god, were not averse to his worship, since he personified the state, and traditionally religion was always associated with the state. And those who hesitated to treat him as a god while he was alive had no reservation to worshiping him after his death. Only the Jews, who would accept no god besides Jehovah (and, later, the Christians), refused to take part in the worship of the emperor.

More spiritual religions were also gaining ground, for emperor worship did not exclude other gods and religious systems. The mystery cults continued to enroll new recruits, even though Augustus looked upon them with disfavor. These cults provided their members with a more colorful, more dramatic, and more emotionally exciting ritual than did the official religion, and they offered the worship of more spiritual and more moral gods who gave a reason for life here and a promise of joyous salvation hereafter.

Literature

In literature, as in religion, the impact of Augustus on the thinking and creative work of the time was so decisive and so personal that the period is rightly known as the Age of Augustus. His military and political suc-cesses made possible the peace, prosperity, and faith in the future on which literature throve; his masterful personality provided a new kind of hero to be celebrated; and his personal patronage gave financial support to many needy writers.

Unlike his successors, Augustus made no attempt to control the ideas that were expressed in literature. But most major writers came to recognize that the future greatness of Rome lay along the path that Augustus marked out, and even though some of them had been partisans of the Republic during the time of the civil wars, they now willingly expressed gratitude and heartfelt praise of the emperor.

The chief evidence of faith and pride in Rome's mission is the fact that the best literature of the Augustan Age was written as a glorification of the pageant of Roman history and the promise of Rome's future grandeur. The outstanding exposition of this theme was given by the poet Vergil (70–19 B.C.), who ranks among the best Roman poets of all periods. The well-educated son of a north Italian farmer whose land had been confiscated during the civil wars, Vergil first won imperial recognition when he appealed to Augustus to return the land to him. The emperor granted him this favor, as well as others, and soon Vergil became convinced that the Augustan settlement was the righteous conclusion of the

The Pantheon—built in Rome for the worship of all the gods. Reconstructed by Hadrian about A.D. 120 after fire had destroyed the earlier structure, it eventually became a Christian church. One of the world's most impressive domed buildings, its dome is 140 feet high and 142 feet in diameter. (Italian State Tourist Office)

The Attack of the Laestrygonians—one of the so-called "Odyssey Landscapes" depicting episodes from Books 10 and 11 of the Odyssey. Found in Rome about 1850 and dating probably from the first century A.D., this incomplete series of murals portrays space that attains grandeur. Hitherto classical artists had feared the infinite, but Roman artists opened men's eyes to the emotional possibilities of vast distances. (Alinari photograph)

civil wars. He became the most loyal of the court poets, singing the praises of the golden age that was dawning, when Rome would exercise a supreme, generous, and just rule under the guidance of the gods.

Two of Vergil's major works—the *Eclogues* and the *Georgics*—were poems of rural life. In them, he called the Romans back to the ways of their forefathers who had lived close to the land, because Vergil saw the strength and virtue of Rome as coming from ancient traditions, ancestral religion, and the simple piety of the country people.

On a much grander scale was Vergil's masterpiece, the epic poem known as the *Aeneid*. The outline of the story told in this poem was modeled on Homer's *Odyssey* and *Iliad;* the flight of the hero Aeneas from Troy, his trials and wanderings under the guidance and dictates of the gods, and the ultimate fulfillment of his divine mission, which was to found Rome and establish the Julian house from which Augustus was descended. But the differences between Homer's epics and Vergil's are profound. Homer recounted an adventurous tale of the struggles and conquests of the mighty and virtuous Odysseus. Vergil was not primarily concerned with Aeneas, as Homer was with Odysseus; for the hero of Vergil's epic is Rome, and the role of Aeneas is not that of a hero but an instrument of the gods, executing the divine plan for the founding of Rome. In the view of Vergil and the other Romans of his time, this did not diminish Aeneas's stature; rather Aeneas exemplified the subordination of self to the will of the gods and the mission of the state, which was the essence of *pietas,* the supreme Roman virtue. No greater tribute could have been made to Augustus as the traditional descendant of Aeneas than the homage that Vergil rendered in this epic, nor could a greater appeal have been made to the pride of the Romans in their sacred destiny.

Though lacking Vergil's profound depth of religious and patriotic feeling, the poet Ovid (43 B.C.–A.D. 17) also contributed to Roman civic and religious pride. Nowadays we know Ovid chiefly for his erotic and personal love elegies. But, like Vergil, he too helped glorify Rome's divine origins by recounting, in the *Fasti,* the legends of the gods and semidivine heroes who were commemorated in the calendar of Roman feast days. And in his *Metamorphoses*, which retells the stories of Greek mythology in a lively and graceful Latin style, he helped bring back to mind the religious myths that the Romans had taken over from the Greeks.

Historians as well as poets were finding in Rome's past the foreshadowing of the present glories of the Augustan Age. Foremost among these was Livy (59 B.C.–A.D. 17), who recounted the whole eight centuries of Roman history—from the founding of the city to the reign of Augustus—in a work of prodigious size. Livy remained a staunch republican, whose history gives an idealized picture of the Republic. Yet he served Augustus's ends, too. For believing that the real aims of history were edification and literary art, Livy strove to praise the simple virtues and religious devotion that had contributed to the achievements of the past and were to be the basis for Rome's future greatness.

Not all writers were concerned, like those we have just mentioned, with the glorification of the state and the emperor. Some were preoccupied with interests and problems of a more personal sort. Such was the poet Horace (65–8 B.C.). The son of a freedman, educated in Greece, Horace had fought for the Republic under Pompey against Caesar. But despite his having been on the opposite side in the civil wars, Augustus received him into the court circle, and the emperor's friend Maecenas became Horace's patron. For his part, Horace acknowledged the need and wisdom of the Augustan settlement. He did not, however, make praise of the Empire the principal theme of his poetry. Instead he devoted the bulk of his work to teaching men how to live contentedly in a world over which they had little control. An able satirist, he aimed good-humored laughter at the foibles of men and society and preached his own modified version of the Epicurean philosophy. The key to happiness, he taught, was to avoid excess, marvel at nothing, keep a wise indifference to the world, and make each moment full in a simple and contented life.

Art

The changes in art were less marked than those in literature, but such improvements as there were can again be attributed to the influence of Augustus, whose patronage attracted the most talented artists of both east and west to the imperial capital. Especially notable was the work done at his behest for the beautification of Rome. Of Rome, Augustus boasted that he found brick and left marble. There was exaggeration in this boast, of course, for he did nothing to replace the squalid wooden or brick tenements in which the poor lived, but it was true enough so far as it applied to temples and other public buildings. Large stretches of marshland were drained, and on a portion of this reclaimed land the emperor erected a new forum, providing space for buildings that could not be crowded into the older forums.

The Augustan construction was not limited to forums, however, but spread throughout the city, including baths, aqueducts, markets, docks, theaters, bridges, libraries, and granaries—all combining beauty with utility. Old temples were repaired, and new ones erected, and a massive mausoleum was built to provide a last resting place appropriate to the successor of the divine Julius.

Generally these buildings made use of the Roman style, which featured the arch and dome. But often they were ringed with Greek pillars or decorated with bright colored marble, showing the influence of the Hellenistic taste for rich ornamentation.

We have little of the painting of this period, because most of ancient art has been lost, but in what remains you can see evidence of considerable skill in depicting

Augustus—sardonyx cameo. (Courtesy Metropolitan Museum of Art)

nature, especially garden scenes. Portrait painting apparently died out, and portrait sculpture took its place. Such sculpture seems more natural and human than the work of earlier periods, and the portrait sculpture of children, especially, seems sensitive and alive. Fine work was also done in relief sculpture, which depicted historical events. Much of this appears on the sides of the triumphal arches that victorious generals erected to commemorate their successes, but some of the best is on the Altar of Peace, erected by Augustus in honor of the end of the civil wars. On this the emperor appears at the head of a ceremonial procession, followed by the imperial family, the Senators, and the people of Rome. The poses are nat-

ural, expressions on faces are realistic, and the work generally shows technical skill and a harmonious blending of the parts into the whole. It was still imperfect work, however, and the next century was to show greater skill and polish.

An Assessment of Augustus

It is only rarely that historians concede greatness to a statesman, for the historian often sees faults in his statesmanship that did not become evident until long after his death. Yet historians generally admit that Augustus deserves to be known as a great statesman, for his policies gave an enduring stability to the Roman state and Roman society. He succeeded in maintaining peace and order without resorting to an open military rule; he enlarged and made secure the boundaries of the Empire; and he stabilized the finances of the state. To be sure, his rule meant a loss of some of the freedom of the republican regime, but this was a small loss; only the aristocratic few, not the mass of the common people, had benefited from republican liberty. A more serious fault in his system was that it did not establish a secure balance of power between the *princeps* and the Senate. Yet nearly 200 years were to pass before the principate developed into an oppressive absolutism.

THE *PAX ROMANA*

The men who succeeded Augustus as *princeps* were personalities in their own right, each of whom put his personal stamp upon the developments of his time. The fundamental structure and progress of the Empire, however, had been established by Augustus, and his successors chose to adjust details rather than to overthrow the basic organization that had already proved its soundness and that was to continue to function effectively for centuries.

Tiberius

One major political problem that Augustus did not solve was the method of succession to his own position of *princeps*. Eventually this failure was to prove fateful; but in the short run it was not serious, because before his death in A.D. 14 Augustus arranged matters in such a fashion that his stepson Tiberius easily succeeded in taking over his position as *princeps*.

Tiberius (A.D. 14–37) was an able and experienced administrator and general, who worked hard at his job with a Roman sense of duty to the state. Yet he was never so popular as Augustus, and he lacked his stepfather's ability to assess men and get the best out of those he took into his service. Consequently he never felt sure of himself, and an atmosphere of uncertainty and suspicion hung over his court. Out of this, in turn, came intrigue, denunciations, and treason trials. Finally Tiberius withdrew from Rome, settling on the island of Capri, where he spent the last ten years of his life.

The "Five Good Emperors"

For a half-century after the reign of Tiberius, most of the men who succeeded to the office of *princeps* were incompetent or corrupt. This unhappy period came to an end only when the aged Nerva (A.D. 96–98) adopted the able general Trajan as his co-regent and heir to the principate. Trajan continued this practice of naming a capable heir and so did his immediate successors. The reign of Nerva thus marked the beginning of the period of the "five good emperors," which covered roughly the second century of the Empire's history.

Trajan. As *princeps,* Trajan (A.D. 98–117) continued to make use of the skill as a general that had led Nerva to select him for the succession. In the course of his reign Trajan waged almost continuous warfare and extended the boundaries of the Empire more than any other emperor since Augustus. He was not merely a general, however, but also a capable statesman. He showed a sympathetic understanding of the needs and problems of the provinces—Trajan was a native of Spain—and all parts of the Empire prospered under his rule. Not the least of his successes was his choice of a distant relative, Hadrian, as coregent and heir.

Hadrian. Hadrian (A.D. 117–138) proved to be one of the greatest emperors after Augustus. Able, energetic, and decisive, he instituted bold new policies that strengthened the Empire. Many of these aimed at improving the administrative system, and in the interest of efficiency he made a sharp distinction between civil and military administration. Thus he broke with the republican tradition of the soldier-statesman whose career would normally embrace both kinds of service. Moreover, he made larger use of men of the Equestrian Order, giving them more responsible posts in the public administration.

Unlike Trajan, he made no attempt to enlarge the Empire and even abandoned some outlying territories. But Hadrian's reign, like that of his predecessor, saw a continuation of the leveling process that was erasing the differences between Italy and the provinces and between east and west.

Antoninus Pius. Hadrian's successor, Antoninus (A.D. 138–161), earned little renown in history, for the happy reason that his reign saw no major crisis. The placid times were admirably suited to his temperate character. In recognition of his personal virtue, as well as a mark of gratitude for his

Bust of Trajan (Anderson photo)

fortunate reign, the Senate voted him the title of *Pius*.

Marcus Aurelius. In Marcus Aurelius (A.D. 161–180), the last of the "five good emperors," the Roman state produced one example of the philosopher-king of the type that Plato had regarded as the ideal kind of ruler. Marcus Aurelius was a disciple of Stoicism, and this austere philosophy, emphasizing duty to the state, was the inspiration of his reign. Not without much inner strain did he measure up to his task, for his was a retiring temperament and he was more inclined toward intellectual interests than a public career. This inner struggle between his native impulses and his sense of duty he describes in his *Meditations*, which is a moving human document as well as an epitome of the Stoic outlook on the world.

His reign saw much warfare, especially on the northern frontier of the Empire, and this put a severe drain upon the treasury. In the long run his decision to allow German tribesmen to settle in the frontier provinces as military colonists, personally free but bound to the land, was to have unfortunate consequences. So also did his choice of successor. Unlike the other "good emperors," Marcus Aurelius had a son, whom he made his political heir. And with the accession of Commodus, the best time of the Empire was over.

Political Stability

During the century that began with the reign of Nerva and closed with that of Marcus Aurelius, the Empire was a success. The provinces, now a federation of states under Rome, were well governed; peace prevailed everywhere within the Empire; and no disturbance occurred when one able ruler died and another took his place. Seldom since has the world known an era of peace and good will comparable to this epoch of the Roman Empire spanning most of the second century A.D.

Economic Prosperity

The political stability of the Empire was matched by economic prosperity. With better administration of the provinces and more equitable taxation, all the parts of the Empire could contribute to and draw upon a common store of wealth. Trade now bound the Empire together, while encouraging each region to develop its own economic specialization. Thus the areas of recent conquest began to obtain the luxuries produced in the older lands of the east, while these regions drew upon the virgin mines and forests of the barbarous lands. External trade developed, too, as caravans and ships brought in the wares of Scandinavia, India, and China. (See the map on pages 214–215.)

Notwithstanding the growth of trade, agriculture remained the basis of wealth and the occupation of most of the population. More use was made in this period of irrigation, crop rotation, and fertilization, and in some areas, agricultural production became more specialized—that is, crops were raised for market rather than to meet local needs for subsistence. But these changes were not radical, nor were they so significant as the decline of slave labor and the increasing concentration of landholding in large estates. Commonly the owners of these estates rented out the land in small tracts to free tenants, known as *coloni,* since the supply of slaves had dried up with the cessation of the warfare that formerly had provided large numbers of captives. The practice of tenant-farming worked more to the advantage of the landlord than the tenant, since the owner of the estate was assured of his rent, whether or not the harvest was good, whereas the tenant was forced into debt whenever the crop failed. Later the burden of debt was to reduce the tenants to a kind of serfdom. As yet, however, the benefits of tenant-farming outweighed its evils, for, as we have said before, the labor of free tenants was more productive than that of slaves, and, consequently, agriculture shared in the general economic prosperity of the time.

With the great new growth of trade, industry experienced a boom, and the middle class of merchants and artisans both swelled and prospered. Manufactures, however, were still produced primarily for the small minority of the population that commanded great wealth, since the mass of the people remained far too poor to buy anything but bare necessities. Industry therefore remained a matter of handicraft production in small shops, and factories did not develop.

Society during the *Pax Romana*

Social change in this era was in the direction of an equalizing and integrating of the various social classes. The old aristocracy of Roman and Italian stock virtually disappeared—many men of this class were killed in the foreign and civil wars, others were impoverished, while some simply became indifferent to their responsibility of rearing children and preserving the family fortune. Meanwhile ambitious men were rising up from the lower classes, forming a new plutocracy that took the place of the former aristocracy. This process of social advancement became relatively easy, for the army and the bureaucracy both provided means by which a man could rise to a higher station, and commerce afforded much opportunity to amass wealth. Indeed, it was no harder for a freedman to make a fortune than for a senator to hold on to what he inherited.

Class distinctions did not die out, however, and for reasons of social prestige, men still sought admittance to the rank of Equestrian or the higher rank of Senator. This social distinction the emperor frequently conferred upon men of wealth and ability from all over the Empire, as a reward for service in the public administration and as a means of assuring loyalty and subservience to him.

We know little about the common people who remained the bulk of the population and provided the strong backbone of the Empire. The satirists, biographers, and historians whose writings give most of what information we have were chiefly interested in depicting the virtues or foibles of the great. Seldom do they mention the small farmers, shopkeepers, artisans, and humble workingmen. Yet some knowledge of the common man can be had from the records of the fraternal associations called *collegia.* These were small social groups comprising workingmen engaged in the same trade. Their role, however, was not comparable to

"House of Diana," so-called —ruins and restoration (by Gismondi) of a five-story Roman apartment house at Ostia, second century A.D. Above the shops on the ground floor were small apartments for the shopkeepers and their families. A center courtyard provided light for the inner rooms. By the early fourth century, Rome was known to have had almost 50,000 similar apartment houses.

that of a modern labor union, because they confined their activities to performing religious rites in honor of the patron god of their trade or to collecting funds for payments to members who became ill and furnishing funerals for those who died. During this era, the *collegia* numbered some thousands, affording the average workman the sociability of an occasional feast day and the comfort of care in illness and death.

The lowest class in society, the slaves, shared in the general prosperity and good will of the period. The decrease in warfare resulted in the near elimination of the slave markets, because home-bred slaves were far harder to come by and far more expensive than the hundreds of thousands of battle captives. Prudent economics, therefore, dictated that slaves be treated more humanely in order to increase their working capacity. To an even greater degree, however, they profited from a new spirit of charity and brotherhood that spread from Stoic and Christian teachings. Not only the effective workers but also the young, the aged, and the sick were cared for as lesser members of the family of the owner. Indeed, the Stoics were questioning the whole basis of slavery, and manumissions were wholesale until the total economic structure of the Empire was shifted from slave to free labor.

Women of the upper classes were granted more privileges in this period than ever before. They were given an education; they had the right to hold wealth in their own name and to manage it themselves; and they were free to come and go as they pleased.

Some of them took part in politics, and others became sponsors of the new religious cults of the day. Many of them entered into marriage casually, knowing they could easily obtain a divorce and remarry, if they so chose, still keeping ownership of their wealth. Some of them earned the reproaches satirists directed against them on the score of license and extravagance. But the average woman did not give herself over to such excesses; she devoted her energies instead to the age-old struggle to survive and rear children.

The whole temper of life had changed. The intercommunication of the peoples of the Empire had made all areas cosmopolitan. And the vast increase in the number and size of cities, especially in the west, made for an urbanized culture that dominated even the much larger rural areas. Farmers' and traders' markets at convenient locations grew into towns, and merchants', veterans', and soldiers' families clustered in communities around the permanent frontier camps that later were to grow into such dominant cities as Vienna, Budapest, and Cologne. From the ever-growing and more numerous towns, the sophistication and styles of city life sifted down to rural areas. Country peasants craved town luxuries; former extravagances now seemed necessities; and the lure of excitement and ease drew sons and daughters of farmers to the cities. East and west, Africa, Asia, and Europe mingled, too, in these cities that drew men from throughout the Empire for business, education, and pleasure.

THE CULTURAL LIFE OF THE *PAX ROMANA*

The intellectual life of the period of the "five good emperors" reflected the political unity and cultural cosmopolitanism of the Empire. Men were free to move as they might wish from one end of the Mediterranean to the other, and the roads were traversed not only by traders but also by itinerant philosophers, who brought with them the intellectual wares of the far corners of the Empire. As a result, educated men everywhere in the Empire were exposed to numerous diverse philosophies, and instead of subscribing to any single system of thought, many now became eclectics, accepting some portion of one philosophy, a part of another, and perhaps bits of still others.

A concern with the practical problem of ethics was what ordinarily guided the choice, because the average Roman continued to be more interested in the propriety of his own actions than the pattern of the universe. More often than not, the counsel that seemed to him the best answer to the ethical problem was to accept fate, live in harmony with nature, and rule over his own life. This was the message common to the teachings of the Stoics, the Epicureans, and the Cynics, and it seemed sufficient to those who desired no more than ethical guidance. Those who felt need of something more— a sense of some divine power behind fate— generally turned to the mystery religions.

The Decline of Philosophy

Not all Romans of this time were eclectic; some upheld a specific philosophic system without borrowing ideas. Stoicism, for example, continued to have the strongest appeal. Now its teaching that all men were brothers, because all were creatures of the same fate that rules the entire universe, was in keeping with the leveling tendencies and the cosmopolitanism of the Empire. So was its teaching that all men should accept the duties that fate assigned to them. This message evoked a response among men in the highest as well as the humblest social ranks, and we have already noted that Marcus Aurelius was an outstanding exponent of Stoicism.

Another Stoic who deserves mention was Seneca (5 B.C.–A.D. *c.*65), who was one of the leading thinkers and writers of his day. He was less consistent than Epictetus (p. 186) or Marcus Aurelius, because he lived in great splendor while preaching the triviality of wealth, and he sometimes expressed aristocratic sentiments while upholding the democratic and humanitarian principles of Stoicism. Yet, despite such contradictions in his ideas, Seneca was honest, and as a political adviser to Nero, he sincerely tried to apply in government the Stoic teachings of toleration and charity. Indeed, so great was his generosity that in later days the Christians regarded him as one of their kind and believed that he must have been a pupil of St. Paul.

In contrast to Stoicism, which had an influence for good, Epicureanism in this period degenerated into an irresponsible sensualism, which often gave an excuse for the wildest debauchery. Its one attractive representative was Petronius, the "Arbiter of Elegance" at the court of Nero, who was a man of fundamental taste and intelligence despite his dilettantism and refined dissipation. His attitudes are well illustrated in his *Satyricon,* a novel of the extravagant adventures of scandalous rogues, whose license was occasionally relieved by sound and sober ideas.

There were others, too, who hearkened to the ragged itinerant teachers who expounded the message of Cynicism—disregard of convention and a limitation of one's wants to the barest of necessities. But those who sought freedom from earthly cares were less apt to take up Cynicism than one

Marcus Aurelius—gilded bronze, heroic size, about A.D. 175–180. This statue of the last of the Antonine emperors is known to be similar to a famous bronze statue of Trajan, which stood in the exact center of the Forum of Trajan that covered twenty-five acres in the heart of Rome. (Alinari photograph)

Religion

In religion, as in philosophy, the age of the Empire saw a mixing together of traditional systems. Previously religion had centered in the worship of deities associated with specific localities. Now that these local states had lost their political independence, having been absorbed into a single, cosmopolitan empire, the religious traditions associated with parochial deities were undermined. Yet a longing for some kind of religious association persisted, because the philosophers and the rich as well as the great mass of simple peasants living in small villages and the hordes of urban poor crowded into the slums of the cities had need of faith in a god or gods who would protect them.

The state religion did not meet this need. Augustus' success in revitalizing the official rites was not lasting and, after him, only the Emperor Claudius attempted any similar revival—with even less success. The other emperors treated the state religion simply as a formal and decorative symbol of political loyalty to Rome. The cult of emperor worship, which developed after the time of Augustus, proved no more effective than the older rites in winning the allegiance of the mass of the people.

Men seeking a more vital faith turned increasingly to the eastern mystery religions. What originally had been merely fertility rites practiced only in particular localities now developed into religions of universal appeal. In an age when men were despairing of reason, these mysteries offered a revealed theology and a ritual of purification. To persons who no longer hoped to control their own destiny, they offered ceremonies of initiation that would assure immortality. For those seeking intellectual justification, they explained their systems by a mixture of philosophy and theology. But to satisfy the larger number of men, those who craved superhuman guarantees of salvation, the mystery religions had recourse to astrol-

or another of the various other philosophies. Among these, Gnosticism gained prominence. This was a mystic philosophy, compounded of Greek and Hellenistic elements, teaching a revealed knowledge that equated sin with matter and purity with spirit. With the help of a destined savior, the Gnostics believed, men could win immortality by spurning the world and rising above matter to the pure realm of the spirit. In this kind of teaching the line between philosophy and religion was erased, for the believer in Gnosticism acknowledged that no philosophy was adequate and held that man had need of help from outside himself.

ogy, oracles, omens, and miracles. The drama of the ritual (which was performed by a consecrated priesthood), the color, and the pageanty—these enabled worshipers to lose themselves in religious ecstasy that gave relief from present woes.

In the first centuries of the Empire, as Roman rule extended into lands once held by the Persians, the cult of Mithra gradually became more popular than the worship of Isis, which previously had held first place among the mystery religions. Originally a Persian sun-god, Mithra came to represent the spirit of goodness that had overcome the spirit of evil and had created the world. Because this act of creation was symbolized by his having killed a mythological bull, the followers of Mithra were required to undergo a baptism in bull's blood, which would make them eligible for immortality, and to live a good and generous life in close brotherhood with other followers of Mithra.

Mithraism had a strong appeal, for it preached a positive doctrine at a time when men were prepared to live the good life strenuously. It was especially appealing to soldiers, who responded to the myths that portrayed Mithra as a victorious warrior for the good. For a long time Mithraism seemed destined to win a wider following than Christianity, which it resembled in many features: its teaching of the immortality of the soul and the resurrection of the body, its observance of rites of baptism and communion, and its emphasis on asceticism. It differed from Christianity, however, in one important respect, which seriously restricted its appeal; it did not take in women as members of the cult.

In the first centuries of the Empire, Christianity, which took its start in this period, seemed only another of the many eastern religions, comparable to Mithraism. Unlike the devotees of other sects, however, the Christians refused to acknowledge the emperor as a god. At first they were not molested on this score, because Christianity was considered to be a sect of Judaism, and the Jews had been given a special permission to worship only their own god. But when it became evident that the Christians were not Jews, the government began to look upon them with increasing suspicion. Their refusal to recognize the emperor as divine seemed to show a refusal of patriotic allegiance to the government, and, consequently, the government began to persecute the Christians, although it did not molest the members of other mystery religions. From the Roman point of view, Christianity was only one of a number of eastern cults, distinguished from the other mystery religions principally by the fact that its members were more troublesome. Only gradually did this new religion demonstrate the characteristics that were to set it apart from the other sects of the time as a superior answer to the universal demand for a strong new spiritual force.

Literature

The Augustan Age is widely known as the Golden Age of Latin Literature. The next century is rightly called the Silver Age. As silver is a precious metal, though not so valuable as gold, the literature of the later period has genuine merit, though inferior to that of the previous age. It gives evidence of virtuosity and even brilliance, but it does not give such rich expression to genuine emotions as do the writings of the Augustan Age, nor does it show such an optimistic purposefulness.

Many of the same themes were treated as in earlier days, but without the same spirit. Political writing was dangerous, unless it was chiefly a panegyric of the reigning emperor. Poetry became personal rather than patriotic, and frequently it was devoted to acid satire. Essays dealt with personal morality rather than the responsibility of the individual toward society. Yet this decline in quality did not mean a lessening of the quantity of writing. Imperial patronage was freely given to authors, and the number of libraries and recitation halls increased. Indeed, one author of this period, Pliny, complained that a Roman gentleman's time was endlessly occupied in listening to hopeful scribblers read their hopeless writings at public recitations.

Some of the best literary work was done in satire. Juvenal (A.D. 60–c.140), who permitted no levity to lighten his gloom, remains the classic example of the embittered satirist. With scathing pen, he laid bare the foibles of all kinds of men—emperors and politicians of former times, dispirited freemen and ambitious freedmen, dissolute women, sycophants, and the parasitic mobs, gathered from all parts of the Empire, that lived on the Roman dole. Other satirists, happily, found at least a mitigating humor in men's shortcomings. Among those who wrote in a lighter vein was Martial (A.D. c. 40–c.102), the author of keen, witty, and coarse epigrams dealing with contemporary life and love. His style combines Horace's zest and Juvenal's bleakness, with his own pithy wit enlivening the blend. Another major satirist was Petronius (d. c. A.D. 66), whose *Satyricon* has been called the first prose novel.

A natural expression of the Roman sense of imperial destiny was in the writing of history. The giant among the historians of this Silver Age was Tacitus (A.D. c.55–after 117), who is sometimes regarded as the last great Roman writer. His two major works—*Histories* and *Annals*—covered the period from the accession of Tiberius to the death of Domitian. His minor works include the *Germania*, an essay on the Germanic tribes, and the *Agricola*, a eulogy of his father-in-law, a general who did much to advance the Roman frontier in Britain. All these works are exciting reading, for Tacitus' style is swift and turbulent. He is supreme at sketching character with only a few bold lines. He has permanently blackened the names of the emperors he hated, while immortalizing the men he admired.

The other historians of the time seem pale beside Tacitus, but some of them deserve note. Plutarch (A.D. c.46–c.120) wrote in Greek—he was a Greek, not a Roman—the *Parallel Lives* of forty-six great men of Greece and Rome. His purpose was to celebrate virtue and fine deeds, but he took considerable pains with his research, and he shows understanding of the periods he treats. Suetonius (A.D. c.75–c.150) found scandal more exciting than virtue, for this is what spices his informative *Lives of the Caesars* and *Lives of Illustrious Men*. Apparently readers shared his taste, for his writings have survived, while the works of many other historians of more sober outlook have slipped into oblivion.

Also memorable was Josephus (A.D. c.37–c.95), a Hellenized Jew, whose *Jewish Antiquities* begins with the Creation and comes down to A.D. 66, thus relating the Roman Empire to Biblical tradition.

The age was sympathetic to didactic works and compilations of noncontroversial information. An example of this kind of writing is the *Natural History* of Pliny the Elder (A.D. 23–79), who attempted to systematize all knowledge in the natural sciences, geography, and art. Pliny suffered from a lack of critical faculty and an inability to integrate, and his readers suffer accordingly from intellectual indigestion, but his compilation includes much interesting fact as well as fiction. It was the works of Pliny and later second-century compilers of science, such as Galen the physician and Ptolemy the astronomer, rather than those of the earlier and more original Greek scientists, that were passed on by Rome to the new civilization that was yet to appear in western Europe.

The Art of Imperial Rome

The art of imperial Rome profited from the prosperity and technical proficiency of the time. There were no striking new developments, but the classical traditions were continued and even refreshed, for philhellenic emperors and other rich patrons spent large sums to revive the beauties of Greece.

The best of Roman art was portrait sculpture, which carried on a native Roman tradition. As in earlier times, the Romans honored their leading citizens with portraits, which showed them as they proudly were, never suggesting that they might have wished to be otherwise.

Also notable was the sculpture that appears as decoration on larger architectural or commemorative works, such as the triumphal Arch of Titus (p. 222) or the tall columns erected by Hadrian and Marcus Aurelius to celebrate their military successes. These were covered with sculpture in low relief, skillfully portraying scenes of military action. On the columns, for example, the spectator may view the preparation for war, the campaigns, the victories, and the booty taken by the victors, each stage being rep-resented in one of the series of panels that rise to the top of the column, each panel contributing to the grandeur of the whole.

On the larger public buildings the Roman talent for massive architecture was given full play. The vaulted and arched construction, which was suited to works of great size and imposing grandeur, was developed still further than in previous times, but Greek styles were not abandoned. One of the most famous of Roman structures is the Colosseum, a great circular amphitheater that was the scene of gladiatorial games, wild-beast fights, and other public spectacles. Spreading over six acres and rising four stories high, it seated 50,000 spectators. Like our own stadia, which are modeled on this style, the Colosseum had numerous entrances, stairways, and ramps to accommodate the crowds. But it was much more magnificent than any comparable modern arena, for it was provided with marble seats, plentiful statuary, and a great sunshade that could be drawn over the heads

The Arch of Trajan at Benevento. The arch was erected by the Roman Senate in A.D. 114 to celebrate the completion of the 200-mile *Via Traiana* from Rome to Brundisium. The sculptured reliefs on this side of the arch deal with Trajan's domestic achievements; those on the opposite side, with his foreign policy. To the left of the inscription, Jupiter, Juno, and Minerva welcome the emperor (at right), and Jupiter is about to hand Trajan his thunderbolt—a sign that emperor-worship was replacing the worship of gods. The inscription has served for centuries as a model for Roman lettering and many type faces. (Anderson photograph)

The Colosseum (Italian State Tourist Office)

of the spectators. Also notable was the Pantheon (p. 199) erected by Hadrian. This temple, dedicated to all the gods of the Empire, was the greatest ancient structure of concrete. Its tremendous circular dome, which is 142 feet in diameter, is so constructed as to require no supporting columns and gives an impression of clear line and dignified power. There were many other public buildings of great size in Rome and throughout the Empire. Most of them have fallen into ruins, however, except those few which, like the Pantheon and the Colosseum, were taken over as Christian shrines and thus preserved from total destruction.

Music in Imperial Rome

The yeoman culture of early Rome had not given much encouragement to music, but as the Romans had come into close contact with the Greeks, they had taken over Greek musical usage. The taste for bigness and loudness that developed among the Greeks in the Hellenistic Age was congenial to the imperial Romans, who made much use of Lydian trumpets and the Alexandrian hydraulic organ and often assembled huge choruses and great aggregations of instrumentalists. Nero's pretensions to skill on the cithara illustrate the prestige now given to the virtuoso, as well as the passing of the old feeling that a gentleman should have nothing to do with music. From sculptures, mosaics (p. 175), wall paintings, and literary references, it is clear that the Romans heard much music, although no actual examples of Roman music survive. Of more lasting importance, perhaps, was the development of the hymns and liturgical chants of the cults and the Christians, which were created in this period out of the plainsong heritage of the Ancient Orient and Greece.

THE DECLINE OF THE EMPIRE

Despite numerous signs of decadence after the reign of Augustus, the Empire continued for nearly two centuries to give the Mediterranean world the blessing of the *Pax Romana.* Taking good and bad alike into account, we may fairly say that these two centuries included some of the happiest years in man's troubled history. After the death of Marcus Aurelius in A.D. 180, however, nearly everywhere there were unmistakable signs of a critical decline.

Political Decline

This decline first became evident in political affairs, for the century following the death of Marcus Aurelius was marked by a recurrence of civil war and constant political insecurity. What precipitated this political breakdown was the failure of the Empire to solve the problem that seems always to arise in an absolute monarchy—how to assure that a strong and able man will gain rule in a time of crisis. With few exceptions, the men who succeeded Marcus Aurelius were unable to establish a firm rule, and most of them held power for only a short time. Usually they were men raised to the emperorship by one of the armies that were waging civil war upon each other in various parts of the Empire. Only occasionally did these emperors bother to obtain recognition by the Senate, which now declined in power and prestige until it amounted to little more than a town council.

With no strong ruler to organize the imperial defenses, the barbarian peoples living beyond the borders of the Empire found the frontiers almost unprotected against their invasions. Thus Dacia was given up to the Goths, various German tribes pressed into Gaul, the Saxons controlled the English Channel, while in the east the Persians took much of Asia and the Arabs broke off other fragments of the Empire.

Against such depredations the Romans took only sporadic action. Gradually they abandoned the former policy of maintaining a line of troops all along the border; instead they chose to keep a mobile militia some distance within the border, dispatching this force to any point where danger threatened at a given moment. But this meant that the barbarian peoples could cross the border whenever they chose, and only after an interval would the imperial legions arrive to drive them back. Hence the population near the border lived under the constant threat of raids.

In view of such widespread insecurity and uncertainty, it is not surprising that most of the population was pleased when a strong man made himself emperor, since only a strong ruler could stop the political collapse of the Empire. And it is not surprising that the people raised no protest as the emperors took on the role of Oriental despot. The trend toward despotism, which had begun earlier, reached its culmination in A.D. 284 when Diocletian, the commander of the imperial bodyguard, assassinated the reigning emperor and took the throne for himself. His reign marks the final breakdown of the principate. And with the passing of the principate, the spirit as well as the political forms of ancient Rome came to an end.

Later Roman Emperors

Commodus	A.D. 180–192
Pertinax	193
Septimius Severus	193–211
Caracalla	211–217
Decius	249–251
Valerian	253–260
Aurelian	270–275
Diocletian	284–305
Constantine	306–337
Romulus Augustulus	475–476

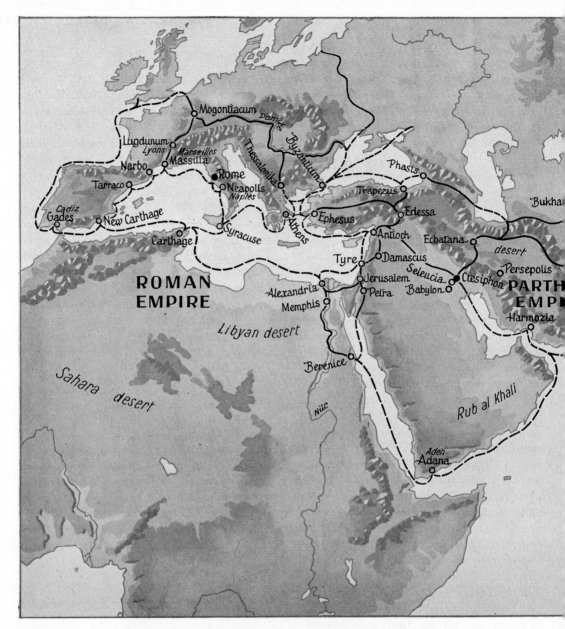

Trade Routes about A.D. 200

Economic Decline

The economic prosperity of the Empire had begun to wane before the end of the reign of Marcus Aurelius. With the civil and foreign wars after his death, there was almost total economic collapse. The bar-

barians raided; the soldiers plundered; the emperors spent recklessly; while always the swollen bureaucracy had to be paid and the public dole had to be kept up in order to quiet the restive people. Though the imperial treasury was being emptied, taxation could produce no more revenue, because

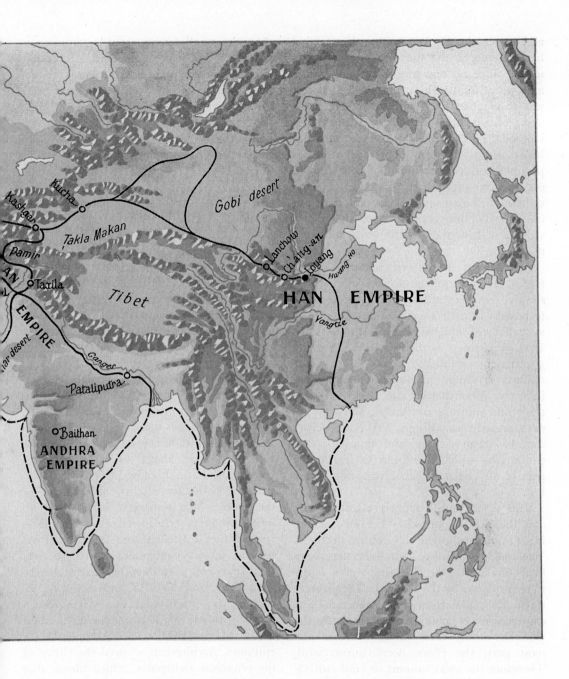

Kashgar
Kucha
Takla Makan
Pamir
Taxila
AN
EMPIRE
Gobi desert
Lanchow
Ch'ang-an
Loyang
Hwang Ho
HAN EMPIRE
Tibet
Yangtze
r desert
Ganges
Pataliputra
Baithan
ANDHRA
EMPIRE

little wealth remained upon which new taxes could be levied. Large areas of farmland along the frontiers were deserted, and trade was hampered by robbers and the deterioration of roads and bridges. The bureaucracy, now often staffed by uneducated army officers who had come up in the civil wars, was no longer an adequately efficient machine to handle the crises.

One device to which emperors resorted as a substitute for new taxes was debasement of the coinage. This had far-reaching effects. An immediate result was inflation, which completed the ruin of the middle and upper classes. Another result was that barter replaced the use of money in commerce, since no one would exchange valuable wares for worthless money. But barter was a cumbersome method of exchange, and consequently commerce dwindled in volume. This meant that each province had to supply as many of its own needs as possible, because it could no longer depend on trade to supply the commodities it required. It also meant that artisans were put out of work, since commerce no longer provided a wide market for the wares they produced.

As artisans began to abandon their trades, the government became alarmed. It simply required artisans and shopkeepers to remain in their vocations, and their sons were likewise obliged to take up the same work or business as their fathers. Thus the government established a new kind of hereditary servitude in both commerce and industry. Nevertheless, the decline in all trade and industry continued, and city life deteriorated accordingly. As the cities shrank, urban culture and municipal organization—which had been so intrinsic a part of all Greco-Roman civilization—were lost.

The agricultural pattern changed too, and the new organization became increasingly important as the city culture declined. The old, independent, small farmers were badly shaken by the changing times. Many were displaced by the barbarians, and great tracts along the frontiers lay barren. The emperors made some attempts to settle the Germans along these areas, but, for the most part, the efforts were unsuccessful. Therefore the total amount of land cultivation in the Empire decreased. For those farmers who had fled for safety or who had lost their farms through economic failure, the alternative was to settle as a *colonus,* a virtual serf, on one of the large estates that could offer military and economic protection. The government approved of the extension of the large estates, which, better than the small farmer, could guarantee to pay taxes, and it cooperated with the estate owners in attaching the *coloni* to the soil permanently as serfs. More and more administrative and judicial control fell into the hands of the estate owners as the municipalities resigned their duties. Thus, sometimes by contract and sometimes by unchallenged precedent, serfdom came to have the legal status of established usage that was its basis in medieval times.

Decline in Literature and Art

Inevitably intellectual interests, art, and literature suffered severely during the hard years of the third century A.D. To be sure, education was still widespread—there was an elementary school in nearly every village in the Empire. Nevertheless, the level of work had gradually been lowered as a reflection of the insecure and stultified spirit of the time. For example, as soon as the provinces became more self-sufficient and isolated, local dialects increased, with the result that, after about A.D. 200, standard Greek and Latin became mere formal languages for the learned, not the speech of the people. Men now were in no mood to seek enlightenment in Greek rationalism. Instead they turned in ever larger numbers to the mystery religions, which soothed their fears and gave them promise of respite from their troubles in a future life. In literature the intellectual decay was shown by the growing vogue for reducing the best works of earlier times to compendia or epitomes. Architecture showed the effects of the economic stringency, which meant that wealth was no longer to be had for ambitious building programs. Virtually the only branch of art that did not deteriorate was portrait sculpture. Here the Roman tradition of unflinching realism still brought forth fine works.

A notable exception to the general pattern of intellectual decline was the continued development of jurisprudence. Despite the troubled state of political life, a host of jurists continued the work of defining legal concepts and expounding legal principles. (For the chief divisions of Roman law, see page 250.) The jurists' work made Roman law one of the greatest legacies of the ancient world, a legacy perpetuated in our own time in the legal system of all European and American nations, especially the Latin countries.

The Spirit of the Empire

Deterioration of the Empire reached a critical point with the accession of Diocletian in A.D. 284. Not only did Diocletian complete the transformation of the Empire into an Oriental despotism, but he also began the partition of the Empire into two administrative units. The city of Byzantium—soon to be renamed Constantinople—became a second capital, in which Diocletian established his own residence, supervising the administration of the eastern portion of the Empire. At the same time an assistant emperor, named Maximinian, whom Diocletian appointed, took over the administra-

tion of the western portion, with Rome as its capital.

This division of the Empire became complete and permanent after the death of Constantine, who had acceded to sole power in A.D. 324. For a time the fiction was maintained that two "joint emperors" shared rule throughout the Empire, simply dividing the responsibilities as a matter of convenience. In practice, however, each of the two halves of the old Empire was now an empire in itself, quite independent of the other. Even the fiction of the unity of the two halves was abandoned after the death of Theodosius in A.D. 395. The East Roman Empire, with its capital at Constantinople, was to prosper, entering upon a new age of civilization, glory, and power. (For the history of this Empire, see Chapter 10.) But the West Roman Empire was to sink ever deeper into decay, until it became quite powerless to hold back the barbarian hordes pressing upon its borders. (The story of the barbarians is given in Chapter 17.) At last even the capital succumbed to attack—first in 410, again in 450, and again in 476. With these successive humblings of the imperial city, "the glory that was Rome" passed into history.

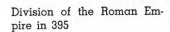

Division of the Roman Empire in 395

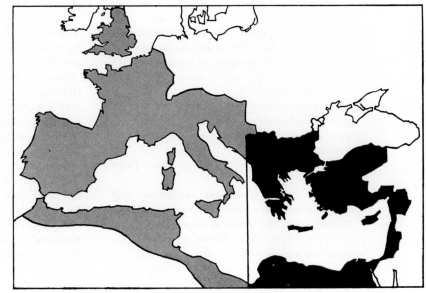

Suggestions for Further Reading

Source Materials

Anthologies

G. H. Knoles and R. K. Snyder, eds., *Readings in Western Civilization* (rev. ed., New York, 1954), pp. 123–143, 152–155.

Selections from Tacitus, Vergil, and Marcus Aurelius.

R. Warnock and G. K. Anderson, eds., *The World in Literature* (Chicago, 1950–1951), Volume I, pp. 367–440.

Good selections from Vergil, Horace, Catullus, Ovid, Juvenal, and Martial.

Contemporary Writings

THE GOLDEN AGE

Horace, *Odes.*

Livy, *History.*

Ovid, *Metamorphoses.*

Vergil, *Aeneid: Georgics.*

THE SILVER AGE

Josephus, *The Jewish Antiquities.*

Juvenal, *Satires.*

Marcus Aurelius, *Meditations.*

Petronius, *Satyricon.*

Pliny, *Natural History.*

Plutarch, *Parallel Lives.*

Seneca, *Moral Essays; Tragedies.*

Suetonius, *Lives of the Caesars.*

Tacitus, *Germania; Histories.*

Secondary Works

C. Bailey, *The Legacy of Rome* (Oxford, 1923).

Essays on various phases of Roman civilization and its contribution to subsequent ages, done by several competent scholars. Presupposes a considerable knowledge of Roman history and literature. One of the series of legacy books.

C. Bailey, *Phases in the Religion of Ancient Rome* (Berkeley, 1932).

A book constructed from popular lectures. A good introduction to the study of Roman religion and its development and importance in Roman thinking.

J. Carcopino, *Daily Life in Ancient Rome* (New Haven, 1940).

A book showing erudition, originality, and flashes of brilliance—but also some prejudices. Chapters on the physical aspect of Rome, society and family life, culture, education, religion, and amusements.

V. Chapot, *The Roman World* (New York, 1928).

A readable book. Treats the first four centuries not in terms of the city Rome but of the whole Roman empire. Gives the conquest and the description of individual provinces.

M. P. Charlesworth, *The Roman Empire* (Oxford, 1951).

A brief and vivid survey of the history of the empire, giving interpretation and a sense of development rather than a chronological account. Considerable social history included.

S. Dill, *Roman Society from Nero to Marcus Aurelius* (New York, 1905).

A general exposition and estimate of what was thought and felt in Rome during this time. Good for the influence on the Roman mind of the religion, superstition and philosophy coming to Rome from the Orient.

J. W. Duff, *Literary History of Rome from the Origins to the Close of the Golden Age* (New York, 1928).

This book, together with the following volume, forms by far the best account of Latin literature for the layman now available. Sets the literature into the historic background.

J. W. Duff, *A Literary History of Rome in the Silver Age from Tiberius to Hadrian* (New York, 1930).

An excellent, and quite sympathetic, account of the literature of the age of decline. Handles many of the lesser writers well.

G. Ferrero, *The Greatness and Decline of Rome* (New York, 1907–9).

A brilliant but uneven work, with many biases. Some of its conclusions should be treated cautiously.

T. Frank, *An Economic Survey of Ancient Rome* (Baltimore, 1933–40).

Five volumes by experts dealing with various provinces of the Roman Empire. Thorough, but quite technical, dealing with the various economic texts available, with suitable commentary.

L. Friedlander, *Roman Life and Manners under the Early Empire* (New York, 1908–13).

An interesting, full series, containing a number of comprehensive monographs on various manifestations of Roman life under the Empire. Carefully documented.

E. Gibbon, *History of the Decline and Fall of the Roman Empire,* edited by J. B. Bury (New York, 1896–1902).

A revolutionary book in its own time, still important for some brilliant sections such as the survey of the Roman Empire in the second century A.D., but too early for much consideration today. Viewed such things as the morality of the rulers as the cause of Rome's fall. Controversial estimate of Christianity.

M. Hammond, *City State and World State* (Cambridge, Mass., 1951).

An expansion of public lectures. Traces political theory from the early Greek monarchy through Athens, Plato and Aristotle, the Hellenistic world, Rome with Cicero and Polybius to Augustus. Shows the fate of the theory of the city-state vs. the practical necessity for greater political unity.

S. Katz, *The Decline of Rome and the Rise of Mediaeval Europe* (Ithaca, 1955).

A very interesting and scholarly little book. Chapters I and II discuss life in the Empire and the elements of decline in the period from the "Antonines" to Constantine.

F. B. Marsh, *The Founding of the Roman Empire* (Oxford, 1927).

Deals with the period of the end of the Republic and the change to the Principate. Argues that the forces of the time rather than the individuals caused the changes.

F. G. Moore, *The Roman's World* (New York, 1936).

A very good textbook for a course in Roman life and civilization. Readable, at the level of the layman, with a considerable amount of lively detail.

H. M. D. Parker, *A History of the Roman World from A.D. 138–337* (New York, 1939).

One of a series of books on Roman history, useful and sound. Some failure, not serious, to integrate political and military history with other aspects of life. But good for showing the effects of the extension of citizenship and reforms of Diocletian and Constantine.

M. I. Rostovtzeff, *Social and Economic History of the Roman Empire* (Oxford, 1926).

A very important book, original, profound, vital. Excellent illustrations well tied to text. Concentrates chiefly on economic history, attributing even the Fall to economic causes, thus filling a serious gap in the usual politically-centered histories.

G. Showerman, *Rome and the Romans* (New York, 1931).

A reliable book dealing with history and institutions, personal and public life. Especially good for showing the civilizing influences of Rome on the provinces. A work of popularization.

M. Yourcenar, *Hadrian's Memoirs* (New York, 1954).

Although modern fiction, this book will give the student a fairly accurate picture of the personality, problems, and power of this great emperor.

9

The Rise of
Christianity

The Archangel Michael—ivory carving, sixteen inches high, fourth century. As asceticism and contempt for the flesh spread among the early Christians, the Greek tradition of physical beauty—as here—was discarded. (British Museum)

In the reign of the Emperor Augustus, in 4 B.C., there was born in Palestine, in the little town of Bethlehem in the kingdom of Judea, a Jewish child named Jesus. This boy was to become the founder of one of the three or four greatest religions of the world.

Palestine in the Time of Christ

When Pompey organized the Roman province of Syria in 63 B.C., he left Judea, which was a part of Palestine, under the control of the Jewish high priest, subject to the Roman governor of Syria. In 40 B.C., Antony put Herod, a princeling sympathetic to Rome, on the throne as a client king. Thereafter Judea remained under the rule of client kings, under Roman supervision, until A.D. 70, when the Romans established their direct rule in the aftermath of a rebellion.

In the struggle for power between Augustus and Antony, the Jewish population had supported Augustus. Therefore, once established as *princeps,* Augustus showed special favor toward the Jews. Unlike other peoples under Roman rule, they were not required to take part in official religious ceremonies, since these rites would conflict with their own monotheistic religious beliefs. They were permitted to hold public office, and many of them were granted citizenship and the political privileges that went with it. In Palestine, as elsewhere, the Romans allowed the natives to run their municipal government for themselves.

What made Palestine unlike other Roman provinces was the use the Jews made of their privilege of local self-government. For the Jews were pre-eminently a religious people; indeed their government was based on their religion. Their religion taught them that there was but one supreme God, and that this God had made them His chosen people. Time and again the Jewish nation had suffered persecution because of its religious beliefs, and its faith was thus consecrated with blood. In the time of Christ this faith centered in the national sanctuary in Jerusalem and fed on the hope that soon a Messiah would come to lead the Jews in a struggle to regain their independence and establish their moral supremacy.

The Spoils of Jerusalem—from the Arch of Titus in Rome, A.D. 81. This panel on one side of the passageway of the arch shows servants carrying the seven-branched candelabrum and the sacred trumpets that Titus took from the temple of Jerusalem after his conquest of Palestine. Through this arch marched the victorious emperor and his soldiers followed by a train of captives and the trophies of war. (Anderson photograph)

Judaism at the Time of Christ

Naturally, in view of the importance of religion to the Jews, their high priests held the supreme social and political position among them. Generally the high priests were able both to serve Rome and to preserve the old Jewish customs. The next class under them, the aristocratic Sadducees, likewise cooperated with Rome, often adopting a tolerant and worldly Hellenistic culture that made for a broad interpretation of religion and set them apart from the rest of the people. On the other hand, the Scribes and Pharisees upheld a strict obedience to the Law—that is, the requirements of the Jewish religion. Yet sometimes they became preoccupied with a narrow-minded concern for ritual, rather than morality, which led Jesus to denounce them for hypocrisy. At their best, however, the Pharisees were worthy examples of upright living according to established law.

Still another group was the Essenes, or Zealots, about whom much has been learned with the discovery of the so-called "Dead Sea Scrolls" in 1947. These men and women gave themselves wholly to the observance of the religious Law, living together in small monastic communities and accepting severe discipline and sacrifice. John the Baptist may have been an Essene, and some of Jesus' followers came from this group. However, although Jesus Himself lived the life they advocated, His freedom with the Law alienated many Essenes, and they continued as an independent, often hostile, sect, until they helped to precipitate the insurrection of Jerusalem in A.D. 66, and immolated themselves in the destruction of the city.

The Jewish people also included a number of émigrés who did not live in Palestine but in other lands all around the Mediterranean. These Jews of the *Diaspora* (Dispersion) had been scattered when Alexander the Great was disrupting the Near East. Some of them had settled in Rome or other cities of the west, but most had established themselves in one or another of the commercial centers of the eastern Mediterranean. Though these Jews had no political allegiance to Palestine, their religious ties remained strong. They continued to place themselves under the authority of the high priest, sent money to Jerusalem, and were supposed to make a pilgrimage there before they died.

Jerusalem was thus a city in which religion dominated all aspects of life and in which several diverse religious and cultural influences came to a focus. For not only were the Jews divided among themselves in their attitude toward their Law, but they were also influenced by Greco-Roman ideas as a result of their inevitable dealings with their Greek neighbors and Roman conquerors.

THE LIFE OF JESUS OF NAZARETH

It was in this atmosphere of intense but diverse religious conviction that Jesus grew to manhood and began His mission as a religious teacher. Until the age of about thirty He earned a humble living as a carpenter in the little town of Nazareth, not far from His birthplace in Bethlehem. Then He gave up His livelihood to become a wandering preacher, living in utter poverty. By no means did all to whom He preached respond to his message, but gradually He gathered about Himself a small band of disciples, most of them poor people.

We know little of Jesus other than what is told of Him in the Gospels, which recount the events of not more than fifty days of His life. But this is sufficient to reveal a man of extraordinary virtue and magnetism. His whole being was a manifestation of the goodness that He taught, and it was His personal virtue that gave Him His hold upon His followers. Foremost of His qualities was His charity, for He showed a disinterested love and kindness toward all He met. But no less remarkable were His courage, honesty, and humility. To His followers, these qualities seemed to be sufficient proof that Jesus was God.

The Teachings of Jesus

The teachings of Jesus were based on the Jewish tradition of monotheism. In no respect did He contradict the religious beliefs sanctioned by the Old Testament. Like the prophets before Him, He did not change the Law but called upon men to honor its spirit and not merely the letter.

Yet His message was not the same as that of the earlier prophets, and the difference was enough to provide the basis for a new religion. What made Jesus' teaching unique was the supreme importance He attached to love. Never before had love been made the basis of a system of ethics and an essential feature of God's will for man, nor its meaning made so broad. For love as Jesus meant it—or charity or brotherhood or kindness, which were other names for the same virtue —was not a measured duty but a joyous and total gift of every act toward God and one's fellow men. Such love required that a man give up all thought of himself and submerge his own being in service to others.

It was this conception of love which was behind Jesus's teaching that all men are brothers, and that God's love goes out to the sinful as well as to the righteous. Thus Jesus raised up the poor and despised, dignifying them as the children of God and blessing them as the ones best able to enter Heaven.

Since love was the first and greatest of the Commandments, morality (or a way of life based upon love for others) was far more important than rituals of worship. An outward show of religion without an inner dedication to the principle of charity was merely hypocrisy, and this was one of the worst of sins.

To those who hearkened to Him, Jesus brought a message that the Kingdom of God was near and that He Himself was its herald. He taught that this world of sin and trouble would soon come to its end, and that God's children would enter into a new kingdom of righteousness and peace where they would be in the very presence of God. The death and resurrection of Jesus seemed to His followers to symbolize the salvation of men and the transition to the new age of blessedness.

Jesus's Trial and Death

Jesus Himself foretold His own death and resurrection as the necessary condition of man's atonement and salvation. Far from fearing His fate, he even hastened it; by denouncing the Pharisees as hypocrites, He forced them to meet His challenge. In their view, His teachings seemed a criticism of the sacred word of God, as well as an attack upon the established social and religious order. With good conscience, therefore, the orthodox leaders of Judaism sought to eliminate Him. Taken prisoner by Roman soldiers, Jesus was first brought to trial before the Jewish court known as the Sanhedrin, over which the high priest presided. But because this court lacked the power to impose the death sentence that the orthodox Jews demanded, He was then brought before Pontius Pilate, the Roman procurator of the province. Pilate was impressed by the dignity of Jesus' bearing and was willing to release Him. But this would have provoked disorder among those Jews who were outraged by Jesus's teachings. Consequently Pilate imposed the death sentence, and Jesus was executed.

THE GROWTH OF THE EARLY CHURCH

Christianity as a Jewish Sect

Like Jesus, all His earliest followers had been reared as Jews. After His death they continued to regard themselves as Jews, upholding the traditional Hebrew laws and ritual and setting themselves up as a separate synagogue. What was unorthodox, however, was their belief that Jesus had been the Messiah whom the Jews had long awaited and that as the Messiah He was the Son of God. Moreover, these early Christians believed that they themselves were inspired by the Holy Ghost, and that their visions and prophecies came from God.

The Jewish priests were as scandalized by these unorthodox beliefs of the early Christians as by the teachings of Jesus Himself. Within a few months after Jesus' death, therefore, the anti-Christian party condemned to death, for the crime of blasphemy, a Hellenized Jew named Stephen, who was one of the followers of Jesus. His death by stoning was soon followed by a general persecution of those Jews who were known as Christians. Many of them fled to other lands of the eastern Mediterranean, where they soon won new converts.

Christianity as a New

Hellenistic Religion

One of these converts, who was destined to become the greatest of all Christian missionaries, was a Hellenized Jew named Paul, a native of the city of Tarsus in Asia Minor. He was a member of a prominent family that had gained the privilege of Roman citizenship, and he had been reared in a Greco-Roman environment. Yet he remained staunch in his devotion to the Jewish faith, as did many others of the Hellenized Jews of the Diaspora. He was present in Jerusalem, pursuing religious studies, at the time when the first persecution of the Christians began. As a devout Jew, he took an active part in the campaign to suppress the new Christian sect. But in A.D. 35, as he was traveling to Damascus to organize persecutions there, he had a profound religious experience in the course of which he believed he saw a vision of Christ. Converted at once to the new religion, he became as zealous in preaching Christianity as he had formerly been in persecuting it.

After secluding himself for three years in Arabia, while preparing himself for his ministry, he began a missionary career that was to continue until his martyrdom a quarter of a century later. More than any other of the early Christian leaders, Paul caught the essential spirit of Jesus' teachings and conveyed it to the rest of the Church. Particularly he dwelt upon the great theme of Christian love, translating this conception into Hellenistic terms that the Greco-Roman world could understand and follow as a philosophy of life.

As a missionary, Paul had a large influence in the decision to admit Gentiles as well as Jews into the Christian Church. This was not an innovation, for Jesus had taught that His followers must love their Gentile neighbors as well as their Jewish kinsmen. Even before Paul's time, Gentiles had sometimes become Jews, and some had accepted the Jewish Law in becoming Christians. But Paul boldly declared that Christianity was a new church, not a sect of Judaism, and a convert might become a Christian without first becoming a Jew. This decision meant that Christianity could make a much broader appeal, seeking adherents not only among the small number of Jews but also among the tens of millions of Gentiles who made up most of the population of the Roman Empire.

By the dauntless labors of Paul and other missionaries, the Christian Church was firmly established by the end of the first century. But as time went on the Christians had to realize that the end of the world was not at hand, as at first they thought, and, therefore, that they must learn to live together as members of the Church. This meant that they must clarify the beliefs that made them Christians and agree upon the proper practice of their religion. The first century of the Church had been marked by zeal, vision, and ideals; in the second century, while these did not disappear, dogma and organization attained more prominence.

The Life of the Early Christians

The adoption of the Christian religion demanded a completely new morality as well as a new theology. Jesus had said that faith must be reflected in good works, and, for the Gentile convert especially, this meant a major wrench from the pagan life he had known. Theaters, games, holidays, even public service, were forbidden as idolatrous. All possessions were shared and little thought was given to practical affairs, since the second coming of Christ would soon end the material world. Voluntary celibacy was praised, but strong family ties also were directed toward the glory of God.

Christian Ritual: The Sacraments

Gradually certain ritual practices came to be regarded as a mark of the Christian religion. Thus, all Christians were baptized. At first, when most Christians were adults newly converted to the faith, this rite was administered after a course of training. But the newborn infants of Christian parents were also baptized, and soon this became the normal practice. Other rituals, such as those performed at marriage, were also standardized.

Some Christian religious customs were adaptations of Jewish rites, but others were innovations. Sunday, the day of Christ's resurrection, became a day of rest, replacing the Jewish Sabbath. Friday, the day of

Chapel of the Ascension on Mount Olivet. (Trans World Airlines photo)

Christ's death, was observed as a day of fasting and mortification. Certain other days were set aside as the occasion of feasts.

The observance of religious customs and participation in religious rituals did not take the place of righteous living. In the first century the early Christians did indeed attain an extraordinarily high level of morality, although always there were sinners as well as saints among them. In the second and third centuries, as it grew in size, the Church included more persons of only moderate zeal, and this inevitably meant a smaller proportion of the total whose behavior gave striking proof of their Christian virtue. Yet even pagans acknowledged that the Christians generally were distinguished by their sincere moral purpose, their cheerful trust in divine guidance, and their love for one another, as well as their special beliefs and practices.

The Origins of Christian Doctrine

As the starting point in defining its beliefs, the Christian Church took over the basic ideas of the Jewish religious tradition. Thus the Christians adopted the Jewish belief in a single God Who was the creator and supreme ruler of the world. Like the Jews, moreover, they believed that God had revealed His will to men in the Bible and had made a covenant with men that assured immortal life to those who worshiped Him. These prime articles of faith gave the Christians the same sense of origin, direction, and purpose that was characteristic of the Jews, in contrast to the Greco-Roman sense of living as a matter of this world and the present time.

The chief point of departure between Christian belief and Jewish orthodoxy was that the Christians accepted Jesus as the Messiah. This meant that Jesus was the redeemer promised to the Jews, Who had come among men in order to establish the Kingdom of God on earth and Who, after His death, had again joined God. Also identified with God was the Holy Spirit that was thought to have been present with Jesus' disciples on the Day of Pentecost. God was now conceived of as a Trinity comprising Father, Son, and Holy Ghost. Jesus of Nazareth was regarded as the incarnation of this divinity, Whose death was ordained as a voluntary sacrifice for the sins of the world, an act of redemption to establish the reign of righteousness. His resurrection was regarded as the decisive proof of His divinity.

Thus the Christian Church added new beliefs that the orthodox Jews did not accept. Moreover, without repudiating the traditions of the Jews, the Christians stressed the spirit of love rather than the letter of the Law. And as the Gentiles became dominant in the new church, the Jewish Law came to be regarded as a standard that, however valid it might have been for its own time, was now superseded by Christ's teachings. As the Jews themselves rejected Christianity as a sect, the Christian Church changed from a national religion to a religious brotherhood composed of all those believing in Christ, regardless of national affiliation.

The Influences of Paganism

While acknowledging their debt to Jewish tradition, the Christians never intentionally borrowed from the Greco-Roman religions. Yet the Christians could not shut themselves off from the pagan ideas that were part of everyday life all about them. Some of these ideas were not far removed from Christian teaching, and when men and women who had been reared in Greco-Roman culture were admitted into the Christian Church as converts, some of the beliefs they had held as pagans tended to merge with the new message they now accepted.

Indeed, Stoicism actually possessed a certain common ground with Christianity, because it had turned away from the ancient mythology in the direction of monotheism.

It also emphasized reasonable patterns of morality. Stoicism, in fact, had preached the brotherhood of man, as did Christianity, although without the emphasis upon the compassionate love of fellow man that became an essential part of the Christian idea of brotherhood.

The pagan belief that probably exerted the most substantial influence on Christian thought was Neoplatonism. This was a system of thought, combining portions of Plato's philosophy with other ideas closer to theology and mysticism, which was worked out in the third century A.D. by the Egyptian philosopher Plotinus (c.205–270) and his pupil Porphyry. The Neoplatonists believed in a divinity that controlled the universe and men, and they constructed a religious system upon the distinction that Plato had made between the tangible world and the world of ideas. Man's aspiration, they taught, must be to rise from the imperfect world—by sacrifice, prayer, discipline, and the observance of the proper rituals—to the perfect realm of the spirit, to a mystical fusion with the divinity. Thereby they would compensate for the struggles of this life in an eternity of happiness. The successive steps in this rise were: first, the achievement of social virtue; then personal asceticism; understanding by means of reason; and, finally, an ecstatic union with the absolute being above the material world. Neoplatonism thus verged on mysticism, yet it remained an intellectual belief, having little of the color and drama and promise that religion affords.

On the other hand, though lacking some attributes of religion, Neoplatonism contributed to the strong tradition of mysticism in the Church and to the division made between the world of sin here and the world of glory hereafter. Church fathers, such as Clement, Origen, and Augustine, found a reconciliation between these beliefs and Christianity; but the harmony, like that with other pagan philosophies, was reached by the development of an ever more complex and more "intellectual" theology for the Church.

The pagan mystery cults also had something in common with Christianity. Many of them, such as Mithraism, were dedicated to a being who was both god and man and who sacrificed himself in expiation for man's sins. Most of them assured the believer of personal salvation, and some spoke of this as a mystical unity between God and the believer. Some made use of a ritual of baptism and a rite of eating or drinking together. So striking are the parallels, indeed, that Christianity has been called the mystery religion of the Jews.

Yet the differences are more significant than the similarities. The central beliefs of Christianity came out of Jewish monotheism (which owed nothing to the mystery cults) and from the teachings of Jesus. Unlike the "saviors" to whom the mystery cults paid homage, Jesus had lived as a man among men, and numerous witnesses testified to His teaching. In the mystery cults the rite of initiation was sufficient in itself to assure the believer of salvation, while in the Christian Church, the rite of baptism only made it possible for the believer to gain salvation; after baptism, he must measure up to grave responsibilities if he were ultimately to enter the gates of Heaven. Especially he must demonstrate his love of his fellow man— even those outside the Church—whereas the initiate of the mystery cult was under no obligation to be "his brother's keeper."

There is no question but that the mystery cults had an influence upon Christianity, as did the Hellenistic philosophies. But it is also true that ultimately the Greco-Roman world became Christian, while Christianity remained the antithesis of paganism.

Organization of the Church: The Clergy

The institutional organization of the Church was the outcome of a gradual evolution. In the earliest time of the new religion, the

Christians met together in private homes, sharing the Eucharistic meal, repeating prayers, and recounting stories of Jesus' mission. As membership in the Church increased, a sharper distinction was made between the *catechumens*—those newcomers to the religion who were receiving instruction in the faith—and those who had been baptized and were permitted to take part in the Eucharist and other sacred rites. This separation of the catechumens from the faithful became especially important in times of persecution, when strangers sometimes sought admittance to the Church and profaned the holy rites in order to spy upon the Christians. The drawing of the line between those who were and those who were not members of the Church marked one step toward the organization of the Church as an institution.

Another step was the marking off of the clergy, who became the governing officers of the Church. The earliest authorities in the Church were the Apostles—those disciples to whom Jesus Himself entrusted the primary responsibility for continuing His work. But as the Church spread out, each congregation had need of a leadership of its own, to teach the increasingly complex creed, to administer the sacraments, to manage the property that the congregation owned in common, and to provide for the material needs of its members. The members who assumed these duties were known as deacons and presbyters. The latter, who were ordained by a special sacrament and were regarded as having the power to dispense God's grace, became the priests of the Church. Above them were the *episcopoi* (overseers), or bishops, in charge of one or more churches in an area, who were the successors to the Apostles. Both bishops and priests held office for life. Customarily they were unmarried, for celibacy was regarded as meritorious, but not until many centuries later (see Chapter 20) did this custom become obligatory upon all members of the clergy.

Church Councils

The clergy of each congregation kept in close touch with the clergy of other congregations. This association among the clergy did much to strengthen the Church, for it permitted one congregation to help another in time of need; it helped check the spread of heresies; and it made possible consultation among a number of congregations on how to cope with troublesome problems—for example, whether or not to put trust in an itinerant preacher. But this association also worked to strengthen the position of the clergy over the lay members of their congregation.

As time went on the Church tended to follow the pattern of organization used in the administration of the Roman Empire. Thus congregations were grouped according to the municipalities and provinces in which they were situated. The bishops of the leading cities came to be known as "metropolitan" bishops and gained pre-eminence over the bishops of lesser municipalities. By the third century these metropolitan bishops had begun the custom of convening provincial councils, to which were summoned the representatives of the clergy from all parts of the province. Occasionally "ecumenical" councils, or assemblies of all the bishops of the Christian world, were convened to deal with issues that involved the entire Church.

Some of these ecumenical councils, such as the one which met at Nicaea in 325, were very important in the history of the Church. Yet they did not meet so often or exercise so great an influence as might be expected. This was owing in part to the difficulties that arose in arranging for men to travel from all over the Empire to a common meeting place, and then inducing them to reach agreement on the issues presented for debate. But it was also owing to the increasing prestige of the papacy, which likewise claimed to represent the Church as a whole.

Some of the Early Popes

Silvester I	A.D.	314–335
Julius I		337–352
Innocent I		401–417
Leo I		460–461
Gelasius I		492–496
Gregory I		590–604

The Rise of the Papacy

The pope was the bishop of Rome. But his role involved much more than supervision of the diocese of Rome, for he claimed to be the spiritual head of the Church, blessed with the special guidance of the Holy Ghost, and all Roman Catholics acknowledged this claim. It rested upon the ground that Jesus designated the Apostle Peter as the head of the new Church, and Peter, who became the first Bishop of Rome, passed on his stewardship of the whole Church, not only the diocese of Rome, to those who succeeded him as Bishop of Rome.

Other circumstances helped the pope gain a position of leadership. At a time when the whole Empire was accustomed to looking toward Rome as the political center of the civilized world, it was natural for Christians all over the Empire to look toward Rome for spiritual guidance. Thus the pope became a counterpart of the emperor. Later, when the Empire was divided into two parts and the emperor established himself in Constantinople, the pope gained still more prestige, for he continued to represent the principle of Roman leadership. Moreover, a number of the earliest popes were men of remarkable stature, who made good use of their position in maintaining the power of the Church over the state. In the east the emperors generally controlled the churches. And, whereas the churches in the east (where the Greek tradition of philosophical speculation remained strong) were often embroiled in doctrinal controversies, such strife rarely stirred the churches in the west. So Rome came to be known as a bulwark of orthodox Christian doctrine.

Model of Old St. Peter's in Rome—torn down in the fifteenth century to make way for the present edifice (p. 585). Built by Constantine (p. 244) on Vatican Hill, Old St. Peter's was the prototype of many early Christian churches—called *basilicas*. Approach to these churches was through an open courtyard (*foreground*), called an *atrium*. Architecturally, atrium and basilica were derived from the old Roman private house. (Anderson photograph)

THE EARLY SPREAD OF CHRISTIANITY

It has been said that the greatest miracle of Christianity was its own spread and eventual triumph as the dominant religion of the western world. No one would have prophesied that the new religion would long endure when, at Jesus' death, it passed into the charge of the twelve Apostles—a little band of poor and illiterate men, members of an oppressed race dwelling in a remote province of the Empire, whom even the Jews themselves disavowed. Yet within a generation after Christ's death His teachings were known throughout the Mediterranean world.

To be sure, the Christian missionaries had certain advantages, for the common language and ease of communication within the vast Roman Empire helped speed the spread of ideas. Moreover, the government was disposed to tolerate all religions, provided only that they were not politically troublesome.

But other circumstances increased the handicap under which the Christian missionaries labored. Because their religion originated in the east, the Romans of the west often looked upon Christianity as only another of the many Oriental mystery cults. Because its message did not pretend to rest upon logic, those who were educated in the Greek philosophical schools looked down upon it as mere superstition. Because the Christians took pains to exclude nonbelievers from their sacred rites, outsiders often accused them of indulging in erotic orgies, or even cannibalism. Because their monotheism prevented them from worshiping the emperor and participating in civic ceremonies, the Christians seemed unpatriotic and antisocial. And eventually the government began to persecute them, which made it still harder for them to win recruits to their faith.

But these obstacles were mostly in the realm of practical considerations. The success of the early Christians was owed, rather, to the triumph of intangibles—faith, persistence, and heroism.

The First Converts

At first the missionaries of the new religion addressed themselves to Jews. Usually they appeared in a Jewish synagogue and proclaimed Christ as the Messiah. Sometimes they would win over the whole congregation at once; more often, they would be driven away. Ordinarily, however, at least some of the Jews would respond favorably and would follow the missionaries, who would help them set up a new synagogue dedicated to Christian teachings. Thus at the outset the new faith took the form of a reforming sect within Judaism.

The critical break came when the Christians, largely at the urging of Paul, decided to direct their appeal to Gentiles as well as Jews. From then on Christianity clearly stood forth as a new religion. By A.D. 100 it was one of the chief religions of the Roman Empire, and by 200 it had gained the allegiance of a large part of the population. By the fourth century the Church whose members once had been a persecuted minority had become the official religious institution, enrolling a majority of the population and persecuting the minority that remained pagan.

The Persecution of the Christians

The persecutions that afflicted the Christian Church in its first three centuries began in the time of its founder, for the first of the martyrs of the new religion was Jesus himself. The Jews who brought about his crucifixion kept up their attack upon his followers. So bitter did the strife become between Jews and Christians that the Romans often had to intervene to keep the peace.

But after A.D. 70 when the Jews suffered severely in an insurrection against Roman rule, they no longer constituted a serious menace to the Christians.

At first the Roman government took little or no part in the persecution of the Christians, and sometimes Roman officials even shielded Christians from the violence of Jewish or pagan mobs. It was the policy of the imperial government to permit the peoples of the Empire to belong to whatever religious sects they wished, provided only that they also took part in the official worship of the Roman gods and official rites of emperor worship. These official rites were not merely a religious service but the mark of political allegiance to the Empire. And since nearly all the pagans were polytheistic, they did not object to recognizing the Roman gods along with their own.

As we have already noted, the Jews were an exception, for their religion was monotheistic. The Romans, knowing that the Jews had a stubborn devotion to their own religion, gave them a special dispensation, so that they were not required to take part in the official religious ceremonies of the Empire. And at first the Romans were willing to grant the Christians the same dispensation, since the Christians seemed to be a Jewish sect.

It soon became apparent, however, that the Christians were not to be treated as Jews, for they did not consider themselves as Jews, and neither did the Jews so regard them. Yet the Christians refused to take part in the official religious ceremonies of the Empire, and they also refused to take public office or serve in the army, since this would require them to swear oaths in the name of the pagan gods. Thus Christianity became a matter not only of religious dissent but of political sedition. Moreover, the religious meetings that the Christians resolutely kept secret defied the Roman law against unauthorized associations. The government, accordingly, took steps to suppress this challenge to its authority.

In the first two centuries official persecution of the Christians was only sporadic. Some emperors—particularly Nero, Domitian, and Severus—took stern measures, but at other times the laws that made Christianity a crime were seldom enforced. Ordinarily, Christians were persecuted only when they refused to take part in the state religion, and the government took action against them only when a private citizen made a specific accusation against a particular Christian individual or group. Once a Christian was thus denounced, he was given a chance to renounce his religion and gain pardon. If he refused, he was put to death. The manner of execution was often cruel— the victim might be torn to pieces by wild animals or slain by gladiators—but this was not a fate reserved only for Christians; it was the common custom to make a spectacle of the execution of criminals who were not Roman citizens.

In the third century the periods of persecution became more infrequent but much more severe. Three emperors—Decius, Valerian, and Diocletian—made successive attempts to hunt out and destroy all Christians throughout the Empire. To force the Christians into the open, orders were given requiring all persons to offer public acts of worship to the gods of the state, and sentences ranging up to imprisonment and death were imposed upon all who refused. Under pressure, many Christians deserted their faith but many others stood firm. Ultimately the government was forced to abandon the persecutions, because the number of staunch Christians was so large and so influential that it proved impossible to exterminate them all. The last large-scale campaign against the Christians was terminated in A.D. 311.

The Conversion of the Empire

Soon afterward Christianity won legal toleration. In 313 the Emperor Constantine is-

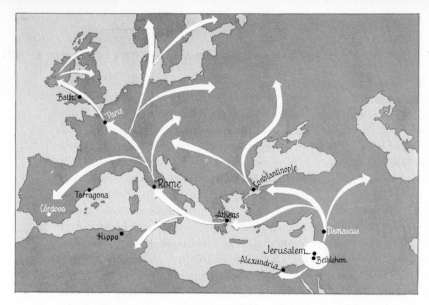

sued a decree, known as the Edict of Milan, which excused Christians from the obligation of making sacrifices to the pagan gods and taking part in emperor worship and gave their religion the same toleration accorded to all others. Though Christianity did not become the official religion of the Empire until some time later, Constantine showed much favor to Christians in the later years of his reign, and the Christian Church soon numbered a majority of the population of the Empire.

THE CRYSTALLIZATION OF THE CHRISTIAN THEOLOGY

Early Heresies

At the same time that the Church was suffering from the external pressure of persecution, it was passing through a series of inner crises that arose from uncertainties among the Christians themselves as to what was the exact definition of their beliefs. Jesus' own teachings were not worked into a complete system and were open to various interpretations. Nor had any of the Apostles undertaken to express the message of the new religion as a systematic body of ideas. Each missionary propounded his own version of Christianity, and each congregation determined its own beliefs. Some of those who had been brought up as Jews continued after their conversion to adhere to the Hebraic Law of the Old Testament, while others, who had been pagans, sought to integrate their new religion with the customs of pagan worship. Such differences in belief and practice gave rise to debate as to what was orthodox and what was heretical—that is, true and false in matters of Christian teaching.

Debate of this kind became more intense as Christianity came into contact with Greek philosophy, because the Greeks who inhabited the lands of the Hellenistic east attached as much importance to understanding as the Jews did to righteousness. As Christianity spread among them, they began to raise questions that the Church was obliged to answer, and the Church, which had been based almost entirely upon faith, was now forced to work out rational explanations for Christian belief.

The Problem of the Nature of Jesus

One of the most basic controversies concerned the nature of Christ. The position that the Church accepted as orthodox was that Jesus was both God and man, being identical with the Divine Father, while also sharing the attributes of a human being. Nevertheless a number of Christians continued to hold heretical beliefs, some denying that Jesus was a man, while others denied that He was identical with God. For example, the Docetists believed that the human body of Jesus was only a phantom, and the Nestorians taught that God merely dwelt in the body of Jesus, as in a temple. The Monophysites, from whom are descended the present-day Copts in Egypt, the Jacobites in Syria, and the Christians of Armenia and Abyssinia, insisted that the nature of Jesus was wholly divine. The strongest of the heresies was the one led by Arius (c.256–336), an ascetic and eloquent Egyptian priest. He taught that Jesus was not of the same essence as God, but neither was He a man quite like others; His nature, rather, was something like that of an angel—less than God but more than human.

The Council of Nicaea

Arius won so large a following within the Church that a bitter dispute over his teachings soon threatened the peace of the entire Empire. In the interest of public tranquility, the Emperor Constantine therefore took action to settle the question one way or the other. Accordingly he summoned the leaders of the Church to meet together at Nicaea, and more than 300 bishops thus assembled for the first ecumenical council of the Church. This council drew up a statement of Christian belief, known as the Nicene Creed, which defined the nature of the Holy Trinity and condemned Arianism as a heresy.

Despite this condemnation, however, Arianism continued to show much strength.

Constantine himself showed favor to the Arians, and if it is true—as tradition holds—that he was baptized as a Christian just before he died, it was probably an Arian priest who administered the baptism. For a time, indeed, the Arians seemed on the verge of triumphing. But in 380 the imperial government denied toleration to the Arians, and in 381 another ecumenical council, meeting in Constantinople, reaffirmed and expanded the orthodox trinitarian doctrines expressed in the Nicene Creed. Thereafter Arianism disappeared throughout the Empire, though it lingered on for generations among some German tribes beyond the bounds of the Empire.

The Problem of Good and Evil:

Gnosticism

Another great dispute arose over the problem of good and evil. The most challenging of the heresies growing out of this debate was Gnosticism (see p. 208), which arose about the middle of the second century. Like some of the Oriental religious cults, Gnosticism made a sharp separation between matter, which is evil, and spirit, which is good. In accordance with this view, the Gnostics regarded the divine spirit as above both the God of the Old Testament and Jesus, Who had concerned themselves with the physical world. And they taught that the path of man's redemption was through asceticism and mysticism, by means of which his spirit might be liberated from the evil of the material world and brought into union with the divine spirit.

The orthodox Church condemned these teachings, which placed the Christian God beneath another, still-higher spiritual being, which declared that man was not responsible for his actions since there could be no moral evil, and which made mysticism and asceticism more important than the behavior of men toward one another while on earth. Yet Gnosticism long continued to have adherents, especially in the east, and the heresy made a serious rift in the Church.

Basic Christian Doctrines

The heresies that arose in dissent from orthodox teachings of the Church bear witness to how difficult a task it was to define the doctrines of the new religion. Yet the gradual disappearance of the heresies also testifies to the success of the Church in formulating the beliefs that were to remain the core of orthodox Christian doctrine. Foremost among these were, first, the belief that Father, Son, and Holy Ghost are equal members of the Trinity that is God and that each is an expression of divine perfection; second, that Jesus was both God and a man, born of a virgin, Who died to redeem other men and then rose from the dead; third, that all Christians are members of one Church, which is under divine guidance; fourth, that the clergy are successors to the Apostles; and, fifth, that through the Church, men may be kept free from Hell and enter upon an everlasting life in Heaven. On these beliefs the Church was to stand firm throughout all the centuries of its existence.

THE LITERATURE OF THE EARLY CHURCH

In the course of defining and expounding its message, the early Church brought forth a copious literature. Though much of it was stylistically crude, it did possess the vital purpose and sincere message that most of the more polished pagan writing lacked; and the best of its writers used a skillful classical style to express Christian doctrine. Of the earliest Christian writings the most important, and the most impressive in simplicity and integrity, were the Gospels and the Epistles, which became the principal source of Christian doctrine. The other writings of the first two centuries A.D. include tales of Christ and His Apostles, the lives of Christian martyrs and saints, and accounts of the early Church. Many of these writings were later lost or suppressed as apocryphal, but some have come down to us in traditions of the Church that supplement the New Testament.

The Apostolic Fathers

There were also works of morality, which spoke little of theology but stressed a sane, ethical life of charity, virtue, and repentance. Most of these works were anonymous or were linked with names we know to be false. Some of the authors are known, however, and special honor is given to a few called the Apostolic Fathers, who were believed to have kept more closely than other writers to the apostolic traditions.

Such a Father was Ignatius, Bishop of Antioch, whose vigorous, warmly personal letters to his flock, written while he was awaiting martyrdom (c.107), exhort the faithful to virtue and purity. Because, too, of his special concern for preserving Christian doctrine from error—a concern that did not become widespread in the Church until after his time—Ignatius has been called the Father of Orthodoxy.

The Apologists

His successors in the struggle to establish orthodox doctrine were the writers known as the Apologists. Their works, which date from the second century and later, were no longer simple expressions of zealous faith, as most of the earlier writings had been. Their main endeavor was, rather, to standardize and systematize the Church's teachings, harmonize them with the rational spirit of Greek philosophies, and preserve them from heresies.

Origen. One may better understand how difficult was the task of distinguishing between true Christian doctrine and heresy when it is realized that two major Apologists of the Church were later condemned for having propagated heresy. One of these was Origen (c.185–254), famous as a teacher at Alexandria in the early third century. Aware of the basic importance of the Bible in Christian thought, he wrote a great deal in an attempt to solve some of the problems that arise in its interpretation. His most enduring contribution was a work in which he compared and commented upon six different texts of the Bible. In his time Origen was widely held in reverent esteem for his piety as well as his teaching. After his death, however, a number of his teachings were brought into question, and 300 years later, a Church council decreed that his writings contained a number of heretical doctrines, which Origen had innocently developed in his attempts to harmonize philosophy and theology.

Tertullian. A similar fault was found in the work of Tertullian (c.160–c.230), a zealous churchman living in Carthage at about the same time that Origen was winning renown as a teacher in Alexandria. A passionate defender of the Church, Tertullian made use of his training in law and the classics to refute the various charges of crime that were levied against the Christians and to demonstrate the religious and philosophic superiority of Christianity over pagan beliefs. His were the first important Christian writings in the Latin language, which he established as the language of the Church in western lands. Yet, despite the burning rhetoric and passionate conviction with which he sought to uphold orthodox doctrine, he was himself accused of heretical beliefs.

Chrysostom. One of the greatest of the Greek Fathers—those who lived in the east and wrote in Greek—was John Chrysostom (c.347–407). Reared in Antioch, his great gifts of grace and eloquence as a preacher caused him to be summoned to Constantinople, where he became patriarch, or archbishop. Like the other Apologists, he harmonized Christian teaching with Greek learning, giving new Christian meanings to ancient philosophic terms, such as charity. In his sermons he upheld a morality that would brook no compromise with conven-

A Roman Surgeon Teaching Anatomy. In 1956 Vatican archaeologists discovered an early fourth-century catacomb in Rome. Its frescoes, depicting a wide variety of subjects, included this lesson in dissection and anatomy. Previously, 1281—nearly 1000 years later—and Bologna, Italy, had been accepted as the date and place of the first known human dissection. The central figure is presumed to be quoting Galen (p. 163) from memory. (Wide World photo)

ience or passion, and a charity that would bring all Christians to an apostolic life of communal poverty and devotion. But this pious message made him unpopular with the imperial court and even with some members of the clergy of Constantinople, and eventually he was banished, to die in exile.

The career of John Chrysostom illustrates the unfortunate involvement of Church and state in the eastern lands of the Empire. It was in the east that the state came to dominate the Church, and, as almost always, the result was bad for the Church. Under the pressure of political supervision and interference, which destroyed initiative and silenced opposition, the Greek-speaking Church settled down into a rut of mediocrity. It never again produced a spokesman of the stature of Chrysostom or regained the fervor and faith of its early years.

Only in the west did the Church continue to show new vigor. The political collapse of the West Roman Empire after Constantine's death made it possible for the Roman Church to proclaim its independence of the state and even to assert that the Church was superior to the state. Moreover, the west became a citadel of religious orthodoxy, for while the eastern theologians were often tempted to make Christianity subordinate to Greek philosophy, the churchmen of the west never regarded learning as equal in importance to religion. In their view, learning must be the servant of religion.

As the split in the Empire widened, so did the division between the western and the eastern branches of the Church. The Latin fathers were studied almost exclusively in the west, and the Greek fathers were studied in the east, and it was from the Latin Fathers that the Christian heritage passed down to western Europe.

Ambrose, Jerome, and Augustine

The most influential of the Latin Fathers were Ambrose, Jerome, and Augustine. Of the three, the first to become famous was Ambrose (c.340–397). As Bishop of Milan, he proved himself an able and practical administrator, who gained influence by virtue of his commanding personality as well as his writings. Of great and lasting significance was his success in compelling the Emperor Theodosius to do penance for his sins and thus admit that he was subject to the same moral dictates as other Christians. This dramatic achievement of Ambrose did much to establish the western tradition that the clergy, as officers of the Church, had the power to discipline even the highest secular rulers.

Ambrose also helped to Christianize and Latinize the heritage of pagan learning. In particular he labored to adapt the moralistic writings of Cicero to the uses of Christianity and to assimilate some elements of Stoicism, such as its emphasis upon duty. Another of his endeavors was in music. He is said to have originated Latin church singing, and some of the most beautiful of the Roman Catholic hymns are attributed to him.

Like Ambrose, Jerome (c.340–420), was well educated in the Latin and Greek classics, but he was also a master of Hebrew. His linguistic accomplishments fitted him for his major work—the translation of the Bible into literary Latin from the various extant Greek and Hebrew texts. His translation, known as the Vulgate or People's Bible, was widely used in later centuries as a textbook for the study of the Latin language, as well as for the study of the Scriptures, and the Catholic Church still regards it in our own time as the authoritative version of the Bible.

Perhaps the greatest of all the Fathers of the Church was Augustine (354–430). Educated as a pagan, Augustine was drawn first to Manichaeanism and Neoplatonism before becoming a Christian. But once within the Church he wholly surrendered himself to it and became one of its foremost servants. So great were his talents that when he became Bishop of Hippo, he made this little town in North Africa one of the leading centers of Christendom.

A redoubtable controversialist, Augustine undertook the refutation of several heresies. But the most monumental of his writings was *The City of God,* which he wrote after Rome had been captured and pillaged by the barbarian Visigoths in 410. The pagans blamed the Christians for this catastrophe, arguing that Rome had known only triumphs under the pagan gods and had met defeat only after espousing Christianity.

Augustine's answer to this charge was that God was not the protector of Rome. The City of God, rather, comprises all those living on earth who are worthy Christians and all the blessed dwelling in Heaven. Alongside this City of God is the City of Earth, to which belong all those who live on earth according to man's needs and standards, which express the human impulse of selfishness rather than according to God's commandment to love one another. Men may not expect God to help them so long as they choose to dwell in the City of Earth, but only if they give their allegiance to the City of God.

This great work of Augustine is not only a moving expression of Christian faith but a fitting symbol of the age that marked the transition from the ancient Mediterranean civilization to the new civilization arising in western Europe. But, in the very work in which he says farewell to the Rome once known as the Eternal City, Augustine helped pass on to the new Christian civilization some portion of the cultural heritage that once had made Rome great.

ESTHETIC EXPRESSIONS OF CHRISTIANITY

Early Christian Art

The early Christian Church expressed itself less quickly in art than in literature. One reason for this was that, from the first, the Christians felt an urgent need to record the life of Christ and to set down in writing the basic truths of the Church in order to spread the Christian message and check the growth of heresies. They felt also a desire to express their religious ideals of faith, hope, and love in the medium of art, but the need of doing so was less pressing than the need that gave rise to Christian literature. Art, moreover, requires wealth, whereas literature does not. So Christian art could not develop until the Church acquired some measure of wealth.

Once the emperors became Christian, they provided the funds that were needed to support a Christian art. This art flourished first, therefore, in Constantinople and Rome, the two capitals of the Empire, and in Ravenna, which later supplanted Rome as the western headquarters of the imperial administration. The principal churches in these cities were provided with rich decorations, altar pieces, and sacred vessels, and elaborate tombs were provided for the relics of martyrs. For the most part the early Christian art followed in the Greco-Roman traditions; and in architecture, the Church adapted for its purposes the design of the Roman basilica, an enclosed building whose original function had been to house the law courts and places of business or public assembly.

What was new about early Christian art was mostly its use of symbolism, for the Christians at first were hesitant to attempt a representation of God. This reluctance was owed in part to the persistence among them of the Jewish tradition that forbids the portrayal of Jehovah, but it was also owed to their own repugnance for the heathen practice of worshiping idols. Thus the early Christian artists only rarely made statues in the round; no image of Christ on the cross is known to have been made before the fifth century. Instead of a human figure the fish was used as a symbol for Christ. Likewise the peacock was used as a symbol for immortality

The Good Shepherd Separating the Sheep from the Goats. The Church of Sant' Apollinare Nuovo in Ravenna is famous for its mosaics. Those made about A.D. 250 represent scenes from the life of Christ, who is shown here as youthful, unbearded, with blue eyes and brown hair. The later mosaics were commissioned by Theodoric (p. 247) and are in the Byzantine style. (Anderson photograph)

and the good shepherd as a symbol for Christ's salvation of sinners. Because these images were meant as symbols, there was no need to make them realistic—the fish that stood for Christ need not look like a real fish. Hence early Christian art did not keep up the Greco-Roman tradition of naturalism; instead it became conventionalized and abstract. Especially in the east, the media of mosaics and marble forced a flat, conventional art; and the lavish use of gold and high colors made for a rich and monumental, though not a humanistic, art. Still, the artists of both parts of the Empire, though building with many of the techniques and materials left from the decadent Greco-Roman art, infused into their work some sense of the forcefulness and intensity of the new faith.

Early Christian Music

During the Roman epoch the liturgical music of the Church took on the forms that were to remain standard during the later eras of western history and that still persist today in the services of the Roman Catholic Church. In part, this music was taken from Hebrew sources, but much of its inspiration was Greek. Its development was more rapid in the eastern countries than in the west, which was farther removed from the Greek and Hebrew sources.

Gregory I, who was pope from 590 to 604, did so much to standardize the music of the Mass and other services that the plainsong melodies used in the Catholic Church are still known as Gregorian chants. There is little doubt that the main body of Gregorian chants as we know them have come down to us in an unbroken tradition from the time of Gregory I, although it is not clear just how much Gregory himself had to do with giving them their form. It does seem probable that he edited out the more voluptuous melodies that were previously used in some churches, and that he founded or re-established in Rome the Schola Cantorum (School of Song, or choir) for the perpetuation of those melodies which he retained.

For a long time the Gregorian chants were sung without accompaniment and without harmony. Having little rhythm or sensual appeal, this music had a spiritual quality—ethereal, serene, timeless—that perfectly expressed and reflected the temper of Christianity. It thus had a close kinship with the other forms of Christian art, which also favored the abstract as against sensual realism. And it likewise harmonized with those elements in Christian theology—especially those showing the influence of Neoplatonism—which expressed a desire to subordinate an unsatisfactory world to a spiritual or mystical oneness with God.

ASCETICISM AND MONASTICISM

We cannot hope to understand the spirit of the early Christian Church without understanding its ideals of asceticism and monasticism. Behind the monastic movement was the eager desire of the zealous Christian to bring about the union of his soul with God even while he was alive on this earth, as well as to prepare for such a union after death. To achieve this union, he must make his soul master over his body. This meant asceticism, the complete renunciation of all the temptations of the material world, the voluntary acceptance of suffering and deprivation. To attain this detachment from the world, he must either live in solitude or band together with a small number of others of like mind and temperament. The movement that resulted in the establishment of communities of men pledged to asceticism and living in seclusion from the world is known as monasticism.

The impulse toward asceticism and monasticism is not peculiar to Christianity. It appears in other religions, both before and after the time of Christ, and among some individuals who profess no religion. But it was wholly in keeping with the spirit of Christianity, because, by words and deeds alike, Jesus preached that salvation could best be won by renunciation of worldliness and complete surrender to God.

In the third and fourth centuries other influences gave added force to the impulse toward asceticism and monasticism and brought these ideals to a practical realization. One of these was the influence of the dualistic philosophies of Gnosticism and Neoplatonism. Even though the Church condemned these philosophies as pagan or heretical, zealous Christians could not help but hearken to their teaching—which resembled that of the Church itself—that the universe is the arena of warfare between good and evil, that the material world is the realm of evil and the spiritual world is the realm of goodness, and that men should therefore strive to enter into the world of the spirit. Nor were Christians unaware of the Stoic hope of *apatheia*—peace of mind through detachment from the world. Yet another influence arose out of the new circumstances in which the Church found itself, once Christianity became an accepted and even official religion. No longer, as in former centuries, could the Christian demonstrate his zeal simply by accepting the risk of martyrdom or by devoting himself to propagating the faith as a missionary. Now those who wished to give heroic proof of their religious zeal must seek a greater hardship than would come to them simply by virtue of their being Christians and continuing to take part in the usual pursuits of the world or even taking up the vocation of priest. The Church as an institution did not establish monasticism. It was a movement of enthusiasm and self-sacrifice, imbued with a spirit of denial relating to the everyday world—a movement among laymen that the Church then blessed as in its own spirit.

Asceticism

Some of those who sought the rigors of asceticism chose to leave their homes and live alone as hermits. Such a life was regarded as a way to conquer one's human nature and gain God rather than as a mere retreat from temptation.

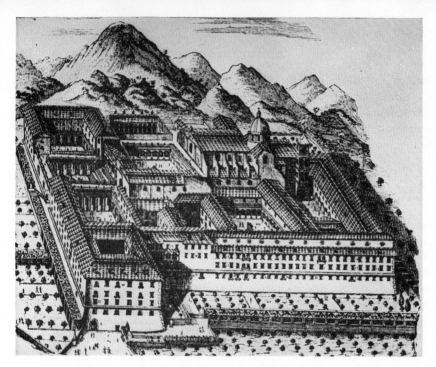

Monte Cassino—the abbey established by St. Benedict in 520. The buildings were destroyed during World War II but are being rebuilt. This general plan was made about 1751. (The Bettmann Archive)

Typical of these ascetics was Anthony of Egypt (251–c.356), who has been called the Father of Monasticism. Though born to wealth, he chose to give his riches to the poor and go off into the desert. Taking shelter in an ancient tomb, year after year he struggled against temptations that seemed to him to be directed by Satan in person. As word spread of his unflinching battles with the Devil, a crowd of disciples gathered around him, seeking inspiration and guidance from him, and many of them settled in nearby caves striving to follow his example.

Monasticism in Western Europe

About A.D. 340 reports reached Rome of the virtuous exploits of Anthony and his followers in Egypt. At once great numbers of Christians in the west began to imitate them, and Italy soon promised to match Egypt in the fervor of its hermits. Ireland, too, became the home of many "saintships," or communities of men and women living together under regimes of austerity and sacrifice.

In the west, those seeking a life of asceticism more often chose to band together in monastic communities than to live alone as hermits. One reason for this was that the climate in Europe is more severe than in eastern lands, and it is therefore less feasible for a man to live by himself. But it was also, perhaps, a reflection of the practical, Roman preference for organization, as opposed to anarchic individualism.

The man responsible for organizing the monastic movement in the west was Benedict of Nursia (480–543). He took the initiative in setting up twelve monasteries for men, while his sister became the sponsor of a number of convents for women. For the monasteries he founded, Benedict drew up a Rule, or body of regulations governing the behavior of the members. This Rule required the monks to take vows of poverty, chastity, and obedience to their superiors, to follow a routine of prayer and meditation, and to perform some kind of work. The routine he prescribed was rigorous, but it did not permit the monks to overdo their asceticism, for it made self-discipline rather than self-castigation the ideal.

Most other monasteries and convents adopted the Benedictine Rule, and the total number of them soon grew large. The fact that the fate of a monastery was dependent not upon one individual but upon the entire order gave the community strength and its plans continuity. Each individual, forgetful of self, was willing to contribute some small share to a great project, whether or not he would live to see its fruition. It was this very strength and stability that made the monasteries centers of civilization during the chaotic centuries following the barbarian invasions and the deterioration of the Roman Empire, and that made the monks who retreated from society, in part at least, the saviors of the culture of that society. Their schools, operated first for boys entering the clergy, then for anyone, were the only centers of education left. From the time of the historian monk Cassiodorus (*c*.480–575), a code was followed for monastic education that included pagan as well as Christian learning and that preserved much of the best of the ancient literature by the orderly copying and protecting of manuscripts in the monastery libraries. And the organized welfare work of the monks provided hospitals, orphanages, poor relief, and care for Christian and barbarian alike.

Within the Church the monasteries grew in favor and influence. Their membership continued to be made up chiefly of laymen, and so remained distinct from, and independent of, the clergy, supporting rather than conflicting with it. In matters of doctrine the monasteries could be counted on for orthodoxy and so won the further support of the Church. It is indicative both of their influence and good favor that in 590 a Benedictine was elected Pope Gregory I. With Gregory, we are already moving into the new civilization of the west.

THE TRIUMPH OF CHRISTIANITY

The reign of the Emperor Constantine marked the close of the age of the persecution of Christianity and the beginning of its triumph. By his Edict of Milan, in 311, the Church at last was given legal toleration. It seems probable that Constantine himself became a Christian, as tradition relates. It is clear, in any case, that his interest in Christianity was more political than religious, and in granting toleration to the Christian Church, his main desire was to put an end to a religious strife that was sapping the strength of the Empire.

The End of Roman Paganism

Constantine's successors went further than he. While continuing the toleration he had granted to Christianity, they began the persecution of paganism. This campaign against paganism, which began in 341, was halted temporarily by Julian—known in Christian literature as Julian the Apostate—who reigned as emperor from 361 to 363. While continuing to tolerate Christianity—he persecuted only a few Christians, who were especially troublesome—he made an attempt to revitalize the worship of the Greco-Roman gods by linking this worship with Neoplatonism. His endeavor proved vain, however, and with the death of Julian in 363, paganism was doomed. Shortly after, paganism became illegal and by the end of the century had virtually disappeared.

Why Christianity Triumphed

Any study of the beginnings of Christianity must take note of its eventual triumph, within only four centuries after the time of Jesus. And this inevitably gives rise to the question: Why did it gain this triumph?

Christianity itself makes an answer to the question—the Church considers itself a divine institution, founded by God and supported forever by the power of Divine Providence. But this answer satisfies only those who share the Christian faith in a supernatural power. Other answers, based on reason and history rather than religious faith, can also be given.

One such reason for the success of Christianity is to be found in the time of its appearance. In the age when Jesus preached His message, men everywhere in the Empire were feeling the need of a new religion. Confidence in the old religious beliefs had been lost. Nothing remained of them except a vague belief that God must be one and all-powerful, and that ethics must be based upon an absolute good. Pilate gave voice to the despairing mood of the age when he asked, "What is truth?" And Jesus gave the answer that men like Pilate sought. To know absolute truth and righteousness, to have implicit trust and faith in a Divine Father, to be wrapped in a mantle of divine and human love—this was the boon that Jesus offered those who hearkened to Him. Above all else, His was a message of love—and the principle of Christian love proved stronger than the authoritarianism of the ancient empires and more soul-stirring than the rigid, legalistic monotheism of the Hebrews.

Another explanation of the success of the new religion was the strength of the Church as an institution. The Church proved wise in choosing to open its brotherhood to all who sought admittance—women as well as men, rich and poor alike, slave or free, without distinction as to race. It was wise, too, in adapting itself to the customs of the times in all respects that did not compromise its fundamental beliefs. Thus it proved capable of becoming a universal church, understanding all men and dealing sympathetically with all their problems.

The Church's devotion to the principle of the brotherhood of men under God explains more than why Christianity displaced the other religions of the ancient Mediterranean world; for it suggests also to us why it was that Christianity gained a larger influence upon men's lives than any religion before it. Because of this principle, perhaps, more than any other, the Christian Church was to become one of the greatest guiding forces in the history of the western world.

Suggestions for Further Reading

Source Materials
Anthologies and Collected Documents
J. C. Ayer, ed., *A Source Book for Ancient Church History* (New York, 1913).
A good selection of early Christian documents and writings.
H. S. Bettenson, ed., *Documents of the Christian Church* (New York, 1947).
A very useful collection.
G. H. Knoles and R. K. Snyder, eds., *Readings in Western Civilization* (rev. ed., New York, 1954), pp. 167–209.
Selections from the New Testament and from St. Augustine's *Confessions* and *City of God*.
R. Warnock and G. K. Anderson, eds., *The World in Literature* (Chicago, 1950–1951), Volume II, pp. 47–66.
Selections from the New Testament and the Nicene Creed.

Contemporary Writings
Augustine, *The City of God; Confessions*.
The Bible.
Especially Isaiah, Matthew, Mark, Luke, John, The Acts, and Second Epistle to the Corinthians.

Secondary Works
A. Alfoldi, *The Conversion of Constantine and Pagan Rome* (Oxford, 1948).
A book dealing with a controversial question, which argues that Constantine did become a Christian. Traces the changes in Constantine's attitudes, and why he changed.
M. Burrows, *The Dead Sea Scrolls* (New York, 1955).
Clearly written, complete story, by an outstanding authority, of the ancient Dead Sea scrolls discovered in 1947. Includes extensive translations from the documents themselves.

C. N. Cochrane, *Christianity and Classical Culture* (Oxford, 1940).

Discusses the impact of Christianity on the Greco-Roman civilization. Has excellent characterizations and appraisals of the period and persons. Some distortion to biases.

C. T. Craig, *Beginning of Christianity* (London, 1943).

A standard text, using much modern material. Written about and for an understanding of the New Testament. Sympathetic to Christianity.

L. M. O. Duchesne, *The Early History of the Church* (New York, 1909–1924).

A good general account of Church history from post-Apostolic times to the end of the fifth century. Largely ignores the social background of the Church and its pagan rivals. An authoritative, objective account, vividly told. Shows interest in people of time.

S. Katz, *The Decline of Rome and the Rise of Mediaeval Europe* (Ithaca, 1955), Chapters 3–6. A fine and readable brief account of the rise of Christianity and the Greco-Roman legacy to the world.

M. L. W. Laistner, *Christianity and Pagan Culture in the Later Roman Empire* (Ithaca, 1951). Discusses the method and material of the early education of Christians. Shows the training within the Church and in the everyday world. Traces the influence of the pagan teaching material on the leading spokesmen of the Church. An able book.

K. S. Latourette, *A History of the Expansion of Christianity* (New York, 1937), Vols. I and II. The first two volumes of a large series, tracing the expansion of Christianity to the present day. An unbiased, competent history, making a rational study of Christianity as a major social phenomenon. Little discussion of dogma.

J. Lebreton and J. Zeiller, *A History of the Primitive Church* (London, 1949).

A sound, historical work, done by eminent Roman Catholic scholars. Sympathetic to the Church and religion. One of the best available histories.

J. Moffatt, *The First Five Centuries of the Church* (London, 1938).

Traces the split between the Greek East and Roman West, with the independent development of the Roman Church. Shows the relatively slow development of the Church, and its solidarity in response to the needs of the first four centuries of its existence.

A. T. E. Olmstead, *Jesus in the Light of History* (New York, 1942).

The story of Jesus himself. An attempt to disentangle him from prejudice and legend. Sympathetic to Jesus. A scholarly work.

D. W. Riddle and H. H. Hutson, *New Testament Life and Literature* (Chicago, 1946).

A good, convenient summary of the scholarly point of view and information. Well-organized criticism. Has the weakness of answering positively, rather than mooting, all the debatable questions.

J. Weiss, *A History of Primitive Christianity* (New York, 1937).

An advanced study, assuming knowledge of the ancient world and the Church. Follows the available evidence closely in telling the story of the Church's development. Works out a philosophy as well as fact. Places the Church in the Roman-Hellenistic world.

E. Wilson, *The Scrolls from the Dead Sea* (New York, 1955).

A readable account by a layman of the recent discovery and implications of the Dead Sea scrolls.

The Byzantine Achievement

Eleventh-century Ivory Madonna. Although Constantinople produced little large statuary after the Iconoclastic Controversy (p. 258), there was no prejudice against ivory carvings. This typical Byzantine Madonna furnished Europe with its visual imagery for Mary for nearly 700 years. (Archiepiscopal Museum, Utrecht)

When the Emperor Constantine built his new Rome on the shores of the Bosporus at the outlet of the Black Sea, he laid the foundation for a new civilization. This civilization was not new, of course, in the sense of being a wholly new creation; but it was really new in its synthesis of ancient Middle Eastern and Mediterranean cultural heritages. In one sense it was the direct heir of the Hellenistic Age; in another sense it was one of the great cradles of institutionalized Christianity; in a third sense it was the matrix of a new philosophy, a new literature, and a new art that were peculiarly its own.

FROM CONSTANTINE TO JUSTINIAN

In A.D. 330 the Emperor Constantine established his court in the city of Byzantium, which he had rebuilt and dedicated to the Virgin. At that time Constantine was the sole ruler of the Roman Empire, which still embraced all the lands bordering on the Mediterranean. But even before the time of Constantine, as we noted in Chapter 8, it had proved impossible to administer imperial territory solely from Rome. Hence it had become customary for two emperors to share the ruling power, one administering the western half of the Empire, while the other took charge of the eastern half. When Constantine himself had become emperor in 306, he participated in this dual system of control. It was only in 324 that he became undisputed master of all Roman territory.

When Constantine moved the seat of his government to Byzantium—later renamed Constantinople in his honor—his decision seemed merely a matter of convenience in administration, and in no sense did it imply the breakup of the Empire. Nevertheless the move was a portent. There was now little doubt that the old city of Rome had lost its primacy and that the political center of gravity had shifted to the new eastern capital.

Events were soon to show that the move had still larger significance, for when the Empire was again divided after Constantine's death, the western half continued to decline. The city of Rome never re-established an effective rule over territories nominally under its control, and in 476 the West Roman Empire ceased to exist.

On the other hand, imperial rule in the east proved durable, for it actually lasted for more than ten centuries. You may think of this government as a continuation of the Roman Empire, since both the name and many of the institutions of the old imperial state were retained. Actually, however, Constantinople was a new Rome, predominantly eastern in character. Hence the empire that the city headed is usually known as the Byzantine Empire. We shall use that term here, although you will frequently find "East Roman Empire" used elsewhere by other authors, especially for the period after 800.

In the course of time this empire became the home of a distinctive Byzantine civilization, rooted in Hellenistic and Roman traditions and decisively influenced by the new Christian faith. Such a mixture of Greek, Roman, and Christian elements eventually led to philosophical and artistic achievements that were peculiar to the lands under Byzantine control and that left their mark upon the cultural development of a much wider area.

Constantine and His Successors

The first three centuries of the Byzantine Empire were perhaps its greatest age. Constantine himself was a ruler of remarkable vigor. We have already noted that he reunited the whole of the Roman Empire, and we have also referred to his decisive action in granting legal toleration to Christianity in 313 and in summoning the first ecumenical council at Nicaea in 325 to establish the basic doctrines of orthodox Christian belief.

After Constantine's death the Romans were hard put to withstand the pressure of the Visigothic tribes that sought to breach the frontier. These invasions were temporarily checked during the reign of Theodosius the Great (379–395), who again—and for the last time—reunited all Roman lands under a single ruler. The reign of Theodosius is also memorable for the founding of the great University of Constantinople and for the compilation of the laws of the Empire in the *Codex Theodosianus*.

In the next century the Visigoths overwhelmed the defenses of the western half of the Empire and swarmed unchecked through Italy, Gaul, and Spain (see Chapter 17). Though this meant the utter destruction of Roman power in these areas, the westward movement of the Visigoths relieved the pressure on the Byzantine forces in the east. Such a development was fortunate, for otherwise the Byzantine Empire might not have had strength enough to cope with the menace of the Huns, the Ostrogoths, or, finally, the Persians, who were again expanding their power.

Meanwhile the Empire was confronted with grave internal problems. One of these grew out of the need for maintaining large armies to protect the borders, which led to a dangerous reliance upon mercenaries. Another was the result of an attempt by the government to organize the population of Constantinople into political bodies known as *demes*. This measure was meant as a way of granting the people a degree of self-government, but it misfired in an unexpected and alarming manner, for the demes became unruly political factions. Two of these, known as the Greens and the Blues, grew so powerful that at times they were able to defy the emperor and terrorize the entire city.

The Monophysite Controversy

Still more serious were the religious controversies that the Byzantine government found itself obliged to arbitrate. The Arian heresy, as we have seen, was effectively combated at the Council of Nicaea and the question of Christ's divinity was thereby officially settled. Discussion now centered upon the relationship between the divine and human natures of Jesus. Some Church members wished to emphasize the divinity of Christ, and when this position was pushed to its extreme—as was done by a group known as Monophysites—the humanity of Jesus was virtually ignored. Other Church members insisted that Christ's human nature was of crucial importance, for only by undergoing human suffering could he atone for the sins of men and thus make possible their salvation.

To the modern student, the point at issue may appear so abstract that the whole controversy seems absurd and devoid of real significance. But to the citizen of the Empire, the debate was of vital and overwhelming interest. You must remember that the men of those times attached supreme importance to their spiritual redemption. And no problem seemed to them more pressing than the question of whether or not they would be recompensed for their unhappiness on earth by eternal happiness in Heaven. A satisfactory answer to this question might well depend upon their right understanding of the nature of Christ.

Moreover, the debate had serious political implications. The government could not avoid taking some kind of stand on a problem that the citizens regarded as of burning importance. If it favored the position of the Monophysites, it would affront their adversaries, who were strong in Constantinople. If, on the other hand, it opposed the Monophysites, it might well lose its political hold on certain territories, particularly Syria and Egypt, where Monophysite doctrines had gained a wide following.

The issue was settled by an ecumenical council at Chalcedon in 451, which condemned the Monophysite doctrine as heretical and recognized the position of the Patriarch of Constantinople as superior to that of the other patriarchs and virtually on the same level with the papacy in Rome. By-

zantine authority in Church matters thus seemed strengthened; but the decision produced ominous dissatisfaction among the Monophysites in Syria and Egypt.

Imperial Problems

Shortly after the Monophysite controversy came to a head, the Byzantine Empire had to cope with the problem presented by the complete collapse of Roman authority in the west. After 476 no one even pretended to rule in Rome as emperor, and Byzantine authorities were forced to deal singlehanded with the Ostrogoths, who were now pressing upon imperial territory with the same vigor that their Germanic kinsmen, the Visigoths, had previously displayed (maps, pp. 256, 422).

The Emperor Zeno (474–491) endeavored to solve this problem by encouraging the Ostrogoths to occupy Italy in his name. The Ostrogoths promptly did so, though their leader, Theodoric, showed little readiness to take orders from his nominal overlord, the Byzantine emperor. However, Zeno's strata-

||||||||||||||||||||||||||||||||||||||||||||||||||||||||||||||||||||||||||||

Byzantine Emperors, 324–578

Constantine (the Great)	324–337
Constantius II	337–361
Julian (the Apostate)	361–363
Jovian	363–364
Valens	364–378
(Interregnum caused by Valens' death in battle)	
Theodosius I (the Great)	379–395
Arcadius	395–408
Theodosius II	408–450
Marcian	450–457
Leo I (the Great)	457–474
Leo II	474
Zeno	474–491
Anastasius I	491–518
Justin I	518–527
Justinian I (the Great)	527–565
Justin II	565–578

||||||||||||||||||||||||||||||||||||||||||||||||||||||||||||||||||||||||||||

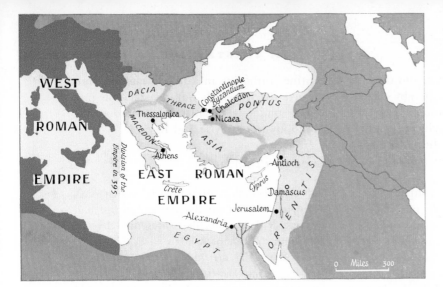

gem succeeded at least in removing the pressure of the Ostrogoths from his own eastern realm. And this respite permitted him to organize his defenses against the remnants of the Hunnish Empire and to withstand fresh attacks by the ever-dangerous Persians.

At the same time Zeno sought to conciliate the churchmen of Syria and Egypt by interpreting the decisions of the Council of Chalcedon in a manner favorable to the Monophysite point of view. His successor, Anastasius I (491–518), went still further in this direction—perhaps too far—for his concessions to the Monophysites provoked bitter opposition at home and led to serious difficulties with the pope in Rome.

Justinian the Great

Anastasius I was followed on the throne by a rough, almost illiterate soldier, Justin I (518–527). His reign is of importance chiefly because it brought into prominence the man who was to become the most famous of all Byzantine emperors. This was Justinian the Great (527–565), a nephew of Justin I.

Theodora. Justinian did not rule alone. Some time before his coronation, he had become acquainted with one of the most beautiful and notorious women in Constantinople: an actress and courtesan named Theodora, whose father apparently was keeper of the bears in the Hippodrome, the great public arena of the capital. Justinian had promptly fallen in love with her and, after obtaining the good-natured consent of his uncle, had married her. This created a veritable sensation in gossip-loving Constantinople. Theodora's reputation was in fact so bad that respectable people sought to avoid her, because it was considered the worst kind of luck to meet her on the streets.

As empress, however, Theodora played an honorable and often an effective role. She had a keen sense of political realities, and her advice on such matters as religious or foreign policy was usually sound—though not always followed. She also exhibited great courage in meeting a serious challenge to imperial authority on the part of the political factions of Constantinople. Refusing to flee from the city during a bloody riot that these factions had instigated, she induced the emperor to take a firm stand against revolutionary disorder. The wisdom of such a course was demonstrated by the speedy collapse of the insurrection and the eventual reduction of such factions as the Greens and the Blues to a state of political impotence.

Justinian's Conquests in the West. An Illyrian by birth and a westerner at heart,

Justinian was obsessed with the idea of recovering Roman territory in the central and western Mediterranean area and thereby restoring the old Roman Empire. This involved a grave danger, because it meant the neglect of the defenses of the eastern frontier, thus exposing the Byzantine Empire to the attacks of the formidable Persian monarchy and inviting still other incursions by the nomadic Avars, who now had taken the place of the Huns as the Empire's chief enemy from the steppes of Central Asia. Justinian, nonetheless, was determined to realize his dream of ruling the entire Mediterranean Basin. Accordingly, the Byzantine armies moved westward.

The Vandals, who had established themselves in northwestern Africa, were easily subdued, but the Ostrogoths in Italy put up a stubborn resistance. Years of fighting ensued, and the Italian peninsula was ravaged more completely than during any of the previous Germanic invasions. Ultimately Ostrogothic power in Italy was broken; the Visigoths were dislodged from the southern part of the Iberian Peninsula; and a Byzantine foothold was secured in northwest Africa.

The success that Justinian won in this venture was illusory, however. Looking at a map showing the territories brought under his rule, you are led to believe that he came close to restoring the old Empire. But if you examine the matter more closely, you see that the vital core of Spain was left in the hands of the Visigoths, that long stretches of the strategically important North African coastline remained unconquered, and that the key province of Gaul was still under the control of Frankish rulers. Thus Justinian's territorial gains were dangerously incomplete—and quite difficult to defend. Yet, in order to achieve such gains, he had spent the military strength needed to protect the Empire from its more dangerous northern and eastern enemies.

Campaigns in the East. So humiliating, indeed, was the situation along the northern and eastern frontiers that Justinian had little reason to take pride in his western conquests. The barbarians living along the Danube

The Empire of Justinian

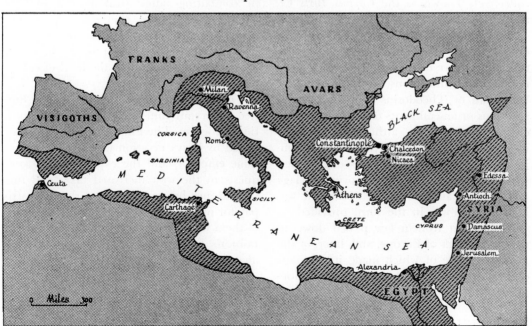

raided the Empire almost at will, and the Persians, now ruled by one of their greatest kings, Chosroes I, of the Sassanid dynasty, were able to break through the Byzantine defenses and capture Antioch. Only by repeated payments of tribute could Justinian prevent further Persian inroads into the Empire's eastern provinces.

The Justinian Code

In his internal policies Justinian achieved more genuine and lasting success than in the showy but unwise attempt to resurrect the old Roman Empire. Perhaps his greatest contribution was the codification of Roman law. This task occupied his attention until the end of his reign. The result was the publication of: (1) a *Code*, which brought up to date and systematized the laws of Rome since the reign of Hadrian; (2) a *Digest*, which compiled the principal legal opinions of the great Roman jurists; (3) an introductory textbook, called the *Institutes*, which discussed the principles of Roman law; and (4) a supplement to the *Code*, which included the laws promulgated after the *Code* had been completed. The four works are collectively known as the *Corpus Juris Civilis*.

Justinian's codification of Roman law was one of the most monumental contributions to jurisprudence ever made. It far surpassed the earlier codifications, such as those of Diocletian or Theodosius the Great. Later additions or amendments did not materially change its substance, although eventually, under the influence of Christianity, the punishments prescribed by law became milder, stricter control was established over marriage and divorce, and the status of women was improved. It was in the form provided by Justinian that Roman law passed down to the new nations of Europe, and, later, of the Americas, some of which made it the basis of both their political and legal development.

Justinian's System of Government

The political system that Justinian headed —and that expressed itself so forcefully in the *Corpus Juris Civilis*—was a regime of monarchical absolutism. Justinian did not create this system—he inherited it from Diocletian and Constantine—but it was one that suited his temperament, for he was a man of autocratic inclinations.

Nevertheless, he did his best to make his despotism enlightened and humane. While he required his subjects to pay heavy taxes and to render him strict obedience, he wished to give them, in return, an efficient and paternalistic government. His program, accordingly, aimed at reorganizing the cumbersome Byzantine bureaucracy, at making the law courts more efficient, at abolishing venality of offices, at checking the growing power of the great landed aristocrats, and at increasing happiness and prosperity in the entire Empire by a vast program of public works and a series of economic and social reforms.

There is no doubt that Justinian was sincere in his desire to carry out these ambitious plans. The earlier years of his reign saw much promising legislation, particularly in combating administrative and judicial abuses. He also took energetic steps to aid the commercial class, weaken the power of the large landowners, and prevent the entire peasantry from sinking to the level of *coloni* or serfs.

Unfortunately, his resources were too limited to permit him to carry out this ambitious program. The Empire was already burdened by heavy taxation when Justinian became emperor, and the expense of his conquests in the west increased taxes still further. Hence he could not find the means to pay for many of his projected reforms. Some of them were carried out in a very imperfect fashion, while others were ignominiously abandoned.

There was one administrative reform, however, that proved to be of lasting importance. This was the decision to give both military and civil authority to the governors of certain provinces that were especially liable to attack. The governors of these provinces were thereby enabled to raise and maintain larger forces for defense. To be sure, this reform weakened the control of the central government in favor of local authorities. Yet it provided a more effective means of repelling foreign enemies; and, by organizing the army primarily upon a territorial basis, it helped reduce the number—and the dangerous influence—of mercenary groups.

Justinian's Religious Policy

Justinian was none too successful in his handling of religious affairs. His wars to recover the western Roman provinces compelled him to seek the pope's friendship; consequently,

he was forced to take a sterner attitude toward the Monophysites, whom the pope as well as the leaders of the eastern Church regarded as heretical. This naturally antagonized the religious leaders of Syria and Egypt, who remained sympathetic to the Monophysite doctrine.

Prompted by Theodora's wise counsel, Justinian later attempted to reach a compromise with the Monophysites. At his behest, another ecumenical council, meeting in Constantinople in 553, reconsidered the decisions taken by the Council of Chalcedon, and the interpretation it placed on them was thought to be more acceptable to the Monophysites. Unfortunately, this new definition of doctrine failed to bring about lasting reconciliation. By the end of Justinian's reign bitter religious controversies had flared up once more, and it was therefore extremely difficult for the imperial regime to keep the loyalty of its Syrian and Egyptian subjects.

Emperor Justinian and His Courtiers—one of two mosaic panels, c.547, in the apse of the Church of San Vitale, Ravenna. Flanked by soldiers and courtiers and preceded by clergymen, Justinian is represented as a symbol of unity between the temporal power of the state and the spiritual force of the Church. (Anderson photograph)

Hagia Sophia—Byzantine masterpiece. Built in 532–537 by Justinian, it became a mosque in 1453 and the minarets were added separately later. The dome, rebuilt in 563 after earthquakes destroyed the original, is 184 feet high. (Marburg photograph)

BYZANTIUM'S GOLDEN AGE

In the realm of culture Justinian's contributions were more positive and enduring than in political affairs. Indeed, his reign is regarded as the Golden Age of Byzantine civilization. Out of Hellenistic naturalism, Roman engineering skill, Persian decorative design, and eastern Christian emotionalism, Byzantium was now able to bring about a new esthetic and cultural synthesis—one that has earned the Byzantine Empire a place of honor in the world's intellectual history.

Architecture

The most spectacular achievement of Justinian's reign was in architecture, particularly in the building in Constantinople of the great church of Hagia Sophia, or Holy Wisdom. A huge structure, the dome of which measures more than 100 feet in diameter, it is said to have required the labor of 10,000 men over a period of five years. It was to become a model for other churches in the Empire, and its methods of construction were to influence the architects of many distant lands.

The outstanding feature of Hagia Sophia (or Sancta Sophia) is the dome, in the construction of which the Byzantine architects solved a problem that neither the Greeks nor the Romans had ever mastered. The Greeks never learned to make a dome, and the Romans could do so only if the dome were placed on circular walls. The building of Hagia Sophia was thus a revolutionary step in the development of western art. It demonstrated that a dome could be erected over a square area, if it were placed upon the four arches spanning the sides of the square and likewise upon pendentives (triangular concave sections of masonry that extended between the keystones of the four arches and that, like the arches, rested upon pillars at the corners of the square).

The Minor Arts

Along with these architectural triumphs went a display of great skill in interior decoration. The walls and dome of Hagia Sophia —and of the churches patterned after it— were covered with gold mosaics that took the place of fresco painting. Effective use was also made of colored marble and of carved geometrical designs. On the other hand, the sculpture of figures, both in the round and in high relief, was neglected. Eastern Christianity strongly opposed "graven images" in places of worship, and this fear that art might lead to idolatry virtually reduced the sculpture of the Byzantine Empire to low reliefs and to miniature carvings, particularly in ivory. The latter were gilded or colored, and they could, therefore, be regarded as a kind of embossed painting. The fineness and technical perfection of such ivory carving —as well as similar proficiency in the manufacture of jewelry, enamelware, inlaid bronze, and embossed satins—produced a group of "minor arts" that played a major role in Byzantium's cultural legacy.

Literature

The artistic achievements of Justinian's reign were paralleled—but in no sense equalled—by developments in literature and scholarship. In history, Byzantine writers ably upheld the traditions of classical antiquity. The outstanding historian was Procopius (c.490–c.562), who listened perhaps too attentively to the scandalous gossip of his times but who displayed a great talent for vigorous prose and vivid historical narrative. His account of Justinian's wars is one of the great works of early historiography, and his gossip-laden and at times embittered history of the imperial court provides fascinating reading.

It was probably no accident that the most colorful and enduring works of Justinian's reign were those of historical writers. History counted very heavily in Byzantine culture, while the masterpieces of classical literature were so well known and so profoundly respected that the study and imitation of such works appeared more important to the Byzantine man of letters than any original and creative work of his own. There was, in effect, a "tyranny of the classics," which weighed as heavily upon Byzantine culture as it did, in subsequent centuries, upon certain intellectual movements in western Europe. This was particularly true of poetry, in which only the religious interests of an

The Nave of Hagia Sophia (Marburg)

expanding Christianity could find vigorous and sustained expression.

Yet this "tyranny of the classics" was not without some advantages. It bred a respect for good education, including training in grammar and rhetoric, and—later—in philosophy, arithmetic, geometry, astronomy, and music. It familiarized a surprisingly large number of Byzantine citizens with classical masterpieces, particularly the works of Homer, which were often learned by heart. It prevented overzealous churchmen from forcing literature into the narrow channels of theological dogmatism. And it led to the production, not only in Justinian's age but in the centuries that followed, of an impressive collection of scholarly works dedicated to the task of preserving and interpreting the great scientific and literary achievements of antiquity.

Music

Despite the persistence of Hellenistic musical traditions throughout the ancient east, Byzantine music came to bear little resemblance to that of the earlier Greeks. The change came about largely because a Christian culture required a new music to express its new values.

Although the aulos and cithara remained temporarily in use, the hydraulic organ became the real instrument of Byzantine musical expression. It was employed mainly for ceremonies of courtly pomp rather than as an accompaniment to religious singing. For instance, when the emperor entered the Hippodrome, the Greens and the Blues would hail him with conventional "acclamations," singing alternately to the accompaniment of two portable organs made of silver.

Aside from the use of organs in imperial pageantry, Constantinople displayed few characteristic Greco-Roman musical tendencies. This was especially true after the Church had put an end to the theater, pantomime, and virtuoso music. More and more, the musical tradition of the Near East overlaid the Greco-Roman musical heritage. The most distinctive development of Byzantine music was consequently a vast body of hymns, which followed Syrian models in melody and rhythm as well as in the text. Like other forms of Byzantine liturgical music, these hymns were usually chanted in unison by a chorus of boys, while sometimes bass voices provided a droning accompaniment. The melodies were written in a neumatic system—that is, a system of marks placed above the words to guide the singer. It was derived from Syrian antecedents and diverged markedly from the classical Greek musical notation.

This Byzantine ecclesiastical music—unaccompanied male choirs chanting Greek texts in an Oriental style—was introduced into Russia about A.D. 1000. From it the Russians developed the so-called "znammeny chant," which represents the most impressive achievement of the Byzantine musical tradition.

BYZANTINE CIVILIZATION ON THE DEFENSIVE

Justinian is a figure of such great importance that he casts a shadow over the emperors who followed him. Yet his successors in the late sixth and early seventh centuries were, for the most part, worthy of their heritage; and their reigns—up to 629—were a continuation of the first period of Byzantine power and political greatness.

A number of Justinian's conquests in the west were abandoned after his death, but not all. Sicily remained for some time under Byzantine control, and until the middle of the eighth century Ravenna was a Byzantine outpost on the mainland of Italy; years later it was still a gateway through which came powerful Byzantine cultural influences.

The Persian Threat

Meanwhile Byzantium emerged victorious in its struggle against Rome's hereditary foe in the east—the great Persian monarchy. After Justinian's death, Persia had resumed its attacks, and at the beginning of the seventh century the ambitious Sassanid king, Chosroes II, ravaged Syria and Palestine, finally taking possession of the city of Chalcedon across the Bosphorus from Constantinople. This Persian threat was brilliantly parried by one of the Empire's most heroic leaders, the Emperor Heraclius (610–641), who in 626 struck deep into Persian territory while Persian armies, allied with the northern Avars, were besieging Constantinople. When Heraclius reached Ctesiphon, the Persian capital, the Persians hastily made peace.

Heraclius was acclaimed as a conquering hero when he returned to Constantinople in 629. The patriotic ardor and religious enthusiasm of the Byzantine citizens was expressed in the same exuberant spirit in which the emperor himself announced his victory: "May the heavens rejoice and the earth tremble with joy . . . and may all Christians render thanks unto God. . . . For the haughty Chosroes, God's enemy, has fallen. . . . He has been hurled down into Hell, and his memory has been blotted out on earth."

There appeared to be ample reason for such enthusiastic rejoicing. For rather unexpectedly, and quite brilliantly, the Byzantine—the East Roman—Empire had succeeded where its western predecessor had failed: it had defeated the Iranian peoples of the east and held its own against the majority of its western enemies.

New Threats to the Empire

History, however, can play some very cruel tricks. It was the misfortune of the Byzantine Empire that its period of existence largely coincided with a great epoch of Asiatic expansion. As an outpost of European civilization, it bore the brunt of attacks from the east, and its people were compelled to wage frequent and at times disheartening warfare to protect themselves from their new enemies. The latter's strength was at first so great that the Empire was forced to take desperate defensive measures. Not until late in the ninth century was it able to re-establish the power and prestige that it had enjoyed under Justinian.

Among the Empire's new enemies the most formidable were the Arab-led Moslems. In the next chapter we shall discuss more fully their fierce onslaughts in Arabia, Persia, the Nile Valley, and, finally, their advance along the entire southern shore of the

|||||||||||||||||||||||||||||||||||||||||||||||||||||||||||||||||||||||||||||||||||

Byzantine Emperors, 578–867

Tiberius II	578–582
Maurice	582–602
Phocas	602–610
Heraclius	610–641
Constantine III and Heracleonas	641–642
Constans II	642–668
Constantine IV	668–685
Justinian II	685–695
Leontius	695–698
Tiberius III	698–705
Justinian II (restored to power)	705–711
Philippicus	711–713
Anastasius II	713–715
Theodosius III	715–717
Leo III (the Isaurian)	717–740
Constantine V	740–775
Leo IV (the Khazar)	775–780
Constantine VI	780–797
Irene	797–802
Nicephorus I	802–811
Stauracius	811
Michael I	811–813
Leo V (the Armenian)	813–820
Michael II	820–829
Theophilus	829–842
Michael III (the Drunkard)	842–867

|||||||||||||||||||||||||||||||||||||||||||||||||||||||||||||||||||||||||||||||||||

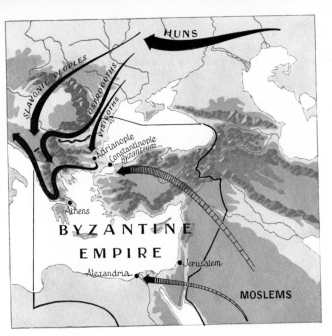

Barbarian Invasions of the Byzantine Empire from 378 to 717

tine resistance at this point, they could penetrate deep into Europe through the Balkan Peninsula and the plains of Hungary. The prospect was so inviting that on two separate occasions the Moslems massed their forces for all-out assaults on the Byzantine capital.

The first of these attacks began in 673 and continued until 677. While a Moslem fleet blockaded Constantinople, Moslem troops attempted to storm the city. But both the emperor (Constantine IV, 668–685) and the people of the city resisted heroically. Moreover, they had the advantage of a new and secret weapon known as "Greek fire." So well did they conceal the method of producing this fire that even today we are not sure of their formula. In all probability they made a mixture of quicklime and such other substances as sulfur and naphtha that would burst into flames as soon as water touched it. This weapon could be used in siege warfare, but it was especially formidable in naval engagements, when the mixture could be sprayed upon the sea near enemy ships or poured upon them with water-fed siphons.

Thanks to this weapon and to the splendid morale of the defenders, Constantinople withstood the attack. In 678 the Moslem ruler sued for peace, promising to pay an annual tribute.

The second Moslem onslaught occurred in 717. Once more, Moslem troops, led by an able general and supported by a strong fleet, besieged the capital, and this time the Empire, weakened by civil strife, seemed doomed. In all likelihood it was saved by the courage and resourcefulness of a heroic soldier, Leo III (717–740), known as "the Isaurian." Returning from the Asiatic front where he had served brilliantly as a general, Leo made himself emperor, ended the civil war, organized Constantinople's defenses, and in 718 forced the Moslems to abandon the siege. They reportedly lost 150,000 men, and only ten vessels are said to have remained of their fleet, most of the rest having been destroyed by a storm. For the Moslems it was a disaster without precedent.

Mediterranean. Here we need only note the ease with which the Moslems smashed the Byzantine defenses in disaffected areas and the slower and more costly progress they made when attacking more loyal Byzantine territories.

The Inroads of Islam

As we previously noted, it was in Syria and Egypt that the allegiance of the civilian populations had been most seriously undermined by the prolonged Monophysite controversy. So feeble, indeed, was the Egyptian defense that a Moslem force of less than 10,000 men was able to drive deep into the lower Nile Valley and capture the key city of Alexandria after scarcely a show of struggle. Farther west, however, Carthage put up stout resistance and withstood the Moslems until the close of the seventh century. Sicily and southern Italy held out even longer.

The most spectacular and decisive struggle between the Byzantine Empire and the Moslems occurred on the shores of the Bosporus. If the invaders could smash Byzan-

This repulse of the second Moslem attack on the capital did not mean the end of the Moslem threat. Syria, Palestine, Egypt, and North Africa remained under Moslem rule, and the Byzantine provinces in Asia Minor had to keep on the alert for new assaults. However, the Arab supporters of Islam made no further attempt to seize Constantinople, and as time wore on their threat to the Empire grew less serious. Not until the Arabs lost their leadership of the Moslem world in the eleventh century, giving way to the Seljuk and Ottoman Turks, did Islam resume its great offensive against Byzantium.

The Slavs

While the Moslems were pressing their attacks on the Empire, other adversaries—the Slavs—appeared in the Balkan Peninsula. The origins of the Slavs remain obscure. At the earliest time we know of them, they were established in the region of the upper Dnieper and Pripet rivers in what is now Russia. The swamps and forests of this region afforded them protection from attack—and also kept them relatively isolated from other peoples. Their language, however, belongs to the Aryan or Indo-European group, so we presume they were related to the Indo-European peoples who appeared as invaders in Greece and Italy in the early Classical period, and who, as Germans, overwhelmed the Roman Empire in the west.

The Slavs remained in their obscure isolation until the fourth century, when the Huns began to pour out of Central Asia into Europe. The Hunnish invasion set the German tribes in motion, and the German migrations, in turn, induced the Slavs to spread outward from their earlier homeland.

In this Slavic expansion three main streams appeared. One stream flowed westward into what we know as Poland; another moved eastward along the Dnieper, Don, and Dniester rivers; and a third spread southward, quietly but irresistibly, into the Balkan Peninsula. Those who took part in this migration into the Balkans are known as Yugoslavs, or South Slavs.

At first the Byzantine Empire was satisfied to establish merely a loose suzerainty over the South Slavs. They were usually permitted to maintain their tribal organization, and some of them, such as the Serbs, were allowed to form federations of tribes. As trade spread among them, bringing Greek culture with it, the South Slavs gradually became more civilized, and Byzantium could reasonably expect that eventually they would become steadfast supporters and ultimately loyal subjects of the Empire.

The Bulgarians

This hope of peaceable relations with the Slavs was doomed to disappointment. Serious trouble, however, did not start with the Slavs themselves so much as with the Bulgars. A people of eastern origin and obscure background, speaking a language that suggests kinship with both the Finns and the Turks, the Bulgars pressed westward into the Balkan Peninsula late in the seventh century, subduing a large proportion of the Slavs who had settled there before them.

At first the Byzantine rulers made use of the Bulgars as allies: for example, Leo the Isaurian called upon Bulgarian troops to assist him in repelling the Moslem besiegers of Constantinople. But during the eighth century the Bulgars became increasingly hostile. A formidable new Bulgar kingdom had developed north and south of the Balkan Mountains, in which a Bulgar aristocracy ruled over the Slavic-speaking masses. Ultimately this Bulgarian kingdom became strong enough to undertake a major offensive against the East Roman Empire.

In 811, under the leadership of a fierce Bulgarian warrior named Krum, the onslaught began. A large Byzantine army was trapped in rough Balkan country and completely overwhelmed, and its commander, the Byzantine emperor Nicephorus I (802–811), was killed in battle. To celebrate his triumph, Krum had the emperor's skull made into a goblet, lined with silver, which he used in drinking toasts with his nobles at great state banquets.

In 813 Krum laid siege to Constantinople. But the Byzantines under Leo V, aided by their superior military and scientific knowledge, proved more than a match for the barbaric invaders. After ravaging most of the surrounding countryside, Krum had to abandon the siege, and, with his death in 814, the danger to the Empire subsided. Dissensions within the Bulgarian kingdom now sapped its striking power, and gradually the cultural influence of Byzantium became so strong among the Slavicized Bulgarians that they adopted the Orthodox Eastern form of Christianity. Boris, the Bulgar leader who decreed their conversion, was the great-grandson of the terror-inspiring Krum.

Adoption of Christianity by the Bulgarians. The conversion of Boris and his Bulgarian subjects was important for two reasons. First, it lessened the likelihood of further Bulgarian attacks upon Constantinople, since this was the citadel of Orthodox Eastern Christianity. Second, it made easier the conversion to Orthodox Christianity of most of the other Slavic-speaking peoples of the Balkans.

A leading role in the conversion of the Slavs was played by two brothers, Cyril and Methodius. These famous missionaries helped prepare the way for the acceptance of Christianity by both the Bulgars and the Serbs, and they ventured even as far as Moravia, now a part of Czechoslovakia. Unlike the Roman Catholic Church, which insisted upon the use of Latin, the Orthodox Eastern (sometimes incorrectly called Greek Orthodox) branch of Christianity permitted the use of the language spoken by the members of the congregation. In their work among the Slavs, Cyril and Methodius therefore used the Slavic language spoken in the Bulgar kingdom. Known now as "Old Church Slavonic," this language is still used in the Orthodox Eastern churches of eastern Europe.

The Cyrillic Alphabet. Moreover, these two missionaries devised an alphabet for setting down the Slavic languages in writing. Since the Greek alphabet did not easily lend itself to the reproduction of the sounds used in Slavic speech, Cyril and Methodius had to invent a new alphabet. Eventually this "Cyrillic alphabet" became the basis for the written language of the Bulgarians, the Serbians, and the Russians; in somewhat modified form, it is used by millions of Slavs today.

The Iconoclastic Controversy

By the middle of the ninth century Byzantine foreign policy had achieved considerable success, for the offensives of both Moslems and Bulgarians had been checked. In its internal affairs, the Empire was not so fortunate. A bitter religious dispute, known as the "Iconoclastic Controversy," had arisen in 726 at the beginning of the reign of Leo the Isaurian and led to more than a century of serious political and religious disturbances.

The dispute grew out of the strong aversion that many Asiatics felt for the use in religious services of sculptured and even of painted images. It seemed to them that such images—or ikons—were idols. This view was held by the Moslems as well as by some Christians, and the Moslems did not hesitate to taunt the Christians as idolatrous in their worship. In their zeal to free themselves of this reproach, mobs of Christians would sometimes destroy the ikons used in the churches. The word *iconoclast* means a destroyer of ikons.

Not all Orthodox Eastern Church members shared this repugnance for ikons, however, and the quarrel became long and embittered. Finally the issue was compromised:

religious sculpture, already in disfavor, was barred, except for special work in low relief; paintings were allowed. To this day they remain an important feature of Orthodox Eastern religious life.

The "Iconoclastic Controversy" had political repercussions beyond the Empire's frontiers. The papacy in Rome, which looked with favor upon the use of both painting and sculpture, was not pleased with the ultimate decision to ban one of these forms of religious art, and its displeasure worsened the growing estrangement between Rome and Constantinople. Hitherto, the papacy

had recognized the right of the Byzantine emperor, beginning with Justinian, to confirm the choice of each successive Roman pontiff. In the course of the "Iconoclastic Controversy" this custom, marking a political link between the papacy and the eastern Empire, was terminated. Henceforth, the popes sought protectors among the Franks, whose political position in western Europe had already become dominant. The ultimate step in this evolution came in 800, when Pope Leo III crowned the Frankish king Charlemagne as Roman emperor (see p. 431).

THE MACEDONIAN DYNASTY AND ITS SUCCESSORS

In 867 a new dynasty, commonly called "Macedonian," gained the throne in Constantinople. This dynasty ruled for almost 200 years, giving the Empire as great a measure of political stability, economic well-being, and cultural distinction as it had enjoyed during the reign of Justinian the Great. It also launched a second expansionist movement that, though not regaining all the territories held in the time of Justinian, made the Byzantine Empire the greatest power of its age in the western world.

Basil I

The founder of this dynasty was a peasant named Basil, born to a family of Armenian origin that had migrated to Macedonia. Strong and handsome, but utterly unscrupulous, Basil went to Constantinople to seek his fortune, won the acclaim of the city's sporting public by defeating a famous Bulgarian wrestler, attracted the attention of the then-reigning emperor, Michael the Drunkard, by taming an unruly horse which Michael owned, and finally gained high imperial favor by marrying—and conferring respectability upon—one of Michael's mistresses. Once his position in the government

seemed secure, Basil organized a palace revolution that resulted in Michael's assassina-

Ikon of Vladimir. **This eleventh-century painting had immense reputation for almost miraculous power. (Historical Museum, Moscow)**

Basil I (founder of the Macedonian dynasty)	867–886
Leo VI (the Wise)	886–912
Alexander	912–913
Constantine VII (Porphyrogenitus)	913–919
Romanus I (usurper)	919–944
Constantine VII (restored to power)	944–959
Romanus II	959–963
Nicephoras II (Phocas) — (co-emperors, or usurpers, during the minority of Basil II)	963–969
John I (Tzimisces)	969–976
Basil II	976–1025
Constantine VIII	1025–1028
Zoë	1028–1050
Romanus (husband of Zoë)	1028–1034
Michael IV (husband of Zoë)	1034–1041
Michael V (joint ruler with Zoë)	1041–1042
Constantine IX (husband of Zoë and co-ruler with Zoë and her sister Theodora, the "aged virgin")	1042–1055
Theodora (sole ruler)	1055–1056
Michael VI	1056–1057

tion. Thereupon he ascended the throne and governed the Byzantine Empire in effective fashion during the rest of his life (867–886).

Not all Basil I's successors inherited his administrative talent and political ambition. Some of them—too indolent, too young, or too much absorbed in literary pursuits—allowed prominent military leaders to take over, as co-emperors, the major task of ruling the Byzantine state. The most famous of these soldier-statesmen were Nicephorus Phocas (963–969) and John Tzimisces (969–976). The former seemed almost grotesquely miscast for his imperial role. In the vivid narrative of a tenth-century chronicler, he is described as "a monstrosity of a man, a dwarf, piglike by reason of the close bristles on his head, with tiny mole eyes, a big belly, small legs, and neck scarcely an inch long." Nevertheless, this "dwarf" proved himself an outstanding military strategist, driving the Moslems from the islands of Cyprus and Crete, recapturing the cities of Aleppo and Antioch, and, shortly before his assassination, laying plans for the recovery of Jerusalem. His successor, John Tzimisces, actually launched such a crusade, which seemed to be on the verge of success when John succumbed to illness.

The Russians

John's offensive against the Moslems had been delayed by the intrusion of a new and quite formidable enemy—the Russians. The attempt of this eastern Slavic people to create their own state is discussed in Chapter 26. Here we need only note that by 969 the Russians were strong enough to push their way beyond the Danube and threaten the approaches to Constantinople. To meet this danger John Tzimisces made full use of his great military and diplomatic skill, forcing the Russians to withdraw to their own territory along the Dnieper River. The conversion of Russia to Christianity soon followed, and the ensuing growth of cultural as well as commercial relations transformed medieval Russia from a hostile neighbor of the Empire to a new outpost of Byzantine civilization.

Basil II

Nicephoras Phocas and John Tzimisces had governed the East Roman Empire during the minority of Basil II, a direct descendant of the founder of the Macedonian dynasty. When Basil II ascended the throne in 976, he proved himself an able statesman as well as a military organizer who could almost match the record of his brilliant predecessors. Civil warfare, which he effectively suppressed, prevented him from continuing John's crusade against the Moslems. Later he completely abandoned this attempt because of ominous threats from Bulgaria, a nation now returning to the aggressive policies of the long-remembered Krum. Basil II took speedy and quite ferocious measures to meet this new danger. In a series of campaigns he pushed the Bulgarian forces back to the Adriatic and finally trapped an army of 15,000 men. Dividing his prisoners into groups of one hundred, Basil ordered that ninety-nine men in each group be blinded, leaving the hundredth man to guide his sightless comrades back to the Bulgarian ruler. When the latter saw this pitiful array of what were formerly some of his best fighting men, he collapsed from shock and died shortly afterward. Within a few years the once-mighty Bulgarian state was annexed (1018) by the still mightier Byzantine Empire.

Basil II also succeeded in stabilizing the eastern frontiers of the Empire and consolidating the remnants of the Byzantine territories in southern Italy and Sicily. By a series of reprisals against North African pirates and by astute alliances with the rising Italian commercial cities, notably Venice, he was able to protect and foster a profitable commerce, bringing revived prosperity to the Christian lands bordering on the Mediterranean.

The prestige accruing from such success in war and diplomacy was enormous. The papacy, to be sure, remained independent within its own Italian territories. But the Germanic—or Holy—Roman Empire, which under Charlemagne had defied Byzantium, now entered into surprisingly close relationships with its eastern rival. One of its rulers married a Byzantine princess, who startled the none-too-fastidious Germans with her taste for luxuries and her habits of regular bathing. Her son, the future emperor Otto

III, became such an admirer of Byzantium that he "loved to speak Greek and surround himself with what he thought was the true Greek ceremonial."

Basil II died in 1025, leaving an enlarged empire, an unchallenged government, and a well-filled treasury. He had also increased the popularity of the Macedonian dynasty, so much, in fact, that two of its last members—the amorous Zoë (1028–1050), who overindulged her passion for new lovers and unusual cosmetics, and her younger sister Theodora (1055–1056), "the aged virgin" who left a convent to become joint empress in 1042—retained the loyalty and even the affection of their subjects.

Cultural Developments during the Macedonian Period

The period of Macedonian rule was one of outstanding cultural developments, which rivaled and sometimes even excelled the achievements of Justinian's reign. In applied science there were notable contributions in such fields as drainage, water supply, fortification, the use of drugs, and the organization of hospital services. In law and jurisprudence Basil I and his son, Leo the Wise (886–912), modernized and expanded the work of the great Justinian. In classical scholarship, Latin again became a frequently read language, while the writings of ancient Greece continued to be diligently studied, although they were all too frequently abridged. In historiography Leo the Deacon ably and vividly related the stirring events of the tenth century, and his eleventh-century successor, Michael Psellus, proved himself more scholarly and perhaps even more entertaining than the famous Procopius of Justinian's age. In philosophy Psellus achieved further distinction by championing a significant and fruitful revival of Platonism. And in literature, despite a discouraging fondness for preparing encyclopedias and commentaries on classical authors, there were contributions of marked originality—particularly in the writings of epigrams and in the composition of Byzantium's one great popular epic, the *Romance of Digenis Akritas,* which has been favorably compared with the *Song of Roland* as a brilliant account of frontier warfare against the Moslems.

Architecture. The most notable accomplishment of Byzantine architects in this period was the development of a new design for church buildings, based on the Greek cross, which has four arms of equal length. This was not a wholly new form, for buildings had previously been constructed on a cruciform plan. Hitherto, however, the entire building had formed a cross. During the Macedonian period a more intricate method of building was perfected, whereby the ground story of the building was square and only the upper stories took the shape of a cross. The arms of the cross were then surmounted by barrel vaults, while four subordinate domes occupied the angles between the arms. From the standpoint of engineering the design was admirable, for the thrusts of the subordinate domes and the barrel vaults neutralized each other, and all combined to meet the thrust of the great central dome, which was usually raised upon a drum.

Sculpture and the Minor Arts. The most noted contributions to sculpture during the Macedonian period were in some of the minor arts, such as the carving in low relief of ivory figures (p. 244). These small carvings, which were often colored, dealt primarily with Christian themes. Usually, they were made for ornamental bowl covers, caskets, or triptychs (carvings or paintings in three compartments) placed on church altars or in private chapels. They revealed exceptional skill in realizing a kind of ornamental symmetry as well as the artist's mastery of technical detail.

Painting. The same superior craftsmanship was shown in pictures painted on gilded wood or metal. Mural painting was still subordinated to the ever-popular mosaics, but fresco work was in progress. Out of this beginning was to develop the great fresco painting of the thirteenth and fourteenth centuries, which was to have a notable influence on the early art of the Italian Renaissance.

One of the most striking features of the pictorial arts of the Macedonian period was the attempt to revive the Hellenistic tradition of naturalism. Without abandoning their own traditions of formalism and emotional intensity, the Byzantine artists of this time achieved a more graceful representation of the human figure and a greater degree of realism than had been shown in the stiff and conventionalized portraiture of earlier centuries.

The Schism between East and West

In theology and religion the Macedonian period did not witness any such outburst of creative vigor as was demonstrated in the splendid artistic achievements of the time. There was no new sign of the intense religious zeal that had earlier given rise to bitter doctrinal controversies, such as those in which the Arians and the Monophysites had figured. Nor was there a drive for puritanical reform, such as had inspired the long-remembered Iconoclastic movement.

Of large importance, however, was the growing movement among Byzantine churchmen to challenge the fast-growing authority of the Roman papacy. The result was a schism of far-reaching significance between the eastern and western branches of the Christian Church.

The circumstances that brought about the schism were not new. One source of dispute grew out of certain differences in liturgy and ecclesiastical custom, such as the easterners' desire to conduct church services in the vernacular, and their dislike of "idolatrous" sculpture in the round. Another issue centered in theological differences concerning the "procession of the Holy Ghost." The Orthodox easterners maintained that the Holy Ghost proceeded from the Father alone, while the Roman Church added the famous *"filioque"* clause to the creed, which meant that the Holy Ghost was linked not only to God the Father but also to God the Son.

But the crucial issue was whether the patriarch of Constantinople (the eastern equivalent of the pope) and his clergy should continue to recognize the spiritual overlordship of the Roman bishop, who had already defied the emperor's temporal authority. This issue had been raised during the ninth century by an ambitious and energetic Byzantine churchman, the Patriarch Photius, and the ensuing quarrel had almost brought about a rupture. In 1054 an even more ambitious Byzantine patriarch, Michael Cerularius, pressed the dispute to the critical point, and the outcome was a decisive split between the two branches of the Church, with the partisans on each side denouncing their opponents in passionate terms. Except for a short period of truce early in the fifteenth century, the schism has persisted to this day.

A New Enemy: The Seljuk Turks

The break occurred at an unfortunate time. For just as the quarrel between Rome and Constantinople reached its climax, the Seljuk Turks were preparing to test the eastern defenses of the Empire.

Like the other Turkic-speaking peoples, such as the Avars and the Bulgarians, the Seljuks apparently came from Central Asia. By the early eleventh century they had made themselves masters of Persia, and in 1055 their leader entered Baghdad and was proclaimed sultan. Soon afterward Seljuk forces invaded Armenia. An energetic but unduly rash emperor hastened eastward to meet this Turkish threat, but forced marches and poor strategy weakened the striking power of the Byzantine army. The imperial troops therefore met with an overwhelming defeat at the battle of Manzikert in 1071.

Manzikert was not in itself an irretrievable disaster. Nevertheless, its effects were far-reaching. Long years of power and prosperity, together with the lessening threat of foreign invasion, had bred a certain indifference to military matters in the governing circles of Constantinople. Dangerous pacifist ideas began to be entertained by civilian officials, who not only disliked army leaders as unwelcome opponents but resisted the lat-

Religious Divisions in Europe and Western Asia after the Schism between East and West

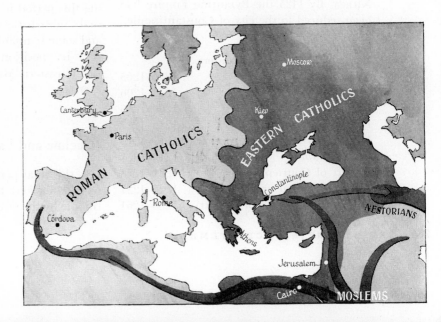

Byzantine Emperors, 1057–1453

Isaac I (resigned and appointed Constantine Ducas as his successor)	1057–1059
Constantine X	1059–1067
Romanus IV	1067–1071
Michael VII	1071–1078
Nicephorus III (overthrown by Alexius Comnenus)	1078–1081
Alexius I (founder of the Comnenus dynasty)	1081–1118
John II	1118–1143
Manuel I	1143–1180
Alexius II	1180–1183
Andronicus I	1183–1185
Isaac II (founder of the Angelus dynasty)	1185–1195
Alexius III	1195–1203
Isaac II ⎱ joint	1203–1204
Alexius IV ⎰ rulers	1203–1204
Alexius V	1204

[Isaac II was restored to power in 1203 after his son Alexius IV appealed for help to the leaders of the Fourth Crusade. The overthrow of these emperors in 1204 by Alexius V led to the storming of Constantinople by the Crusaders, who then set up a feudal empire in the Balkan Peninsula and the Greek archipelago. Almost immediately this empire began to crumble under Greek, Bulgarian, and Turkish attacks, and in 1261 Constantinople fell to Michael VIII, emperor of Nicaea. By 1425 the Byzantine Empire had been reduced to the city of Constantinople.]

Latin Emperors

Baldwin I (Count of Flanders, elected by Crusaders)	1204–1205
Interregnum	1205–1206
Henry of Flanders	1206–1216
Peter of Courtenay	1216–1217
Yolande (wife of Peter, regent)	1217–1219
Interregnum	1219–1221
Robert of Courtenay	1221–1228
John of Brienne (regent)	1228–1237
Baldwin II (brother of Robert)	1228–1261

Restored Greek Emperors (Palaeologus Dynasty)

Michael VIII	1261–1282
Andronicus II	1282–1328
Andronicus III	1328–1341
John V	1341–1376
John VI (usurper)	1341–1355
Andronicus IV	1376–1379
John V (restored to power)	1379–1391
Manuel II	1391–1425
John VIII	1425–1448
Constantine XI	1448–1453

ter's demands for an emergency mobilization of the Empire's resources to check and eventually throw back the Turkish invaders. The results of this policy were calamitous. The greater part of Asia Minor was lost to the Turks almost by default, thus depriving the Empire of one of its strongest defense areas, its best recruiting ground for the army, and a number of its most prosperous provinces. These were so ravaged by the Turks that they never recovered their old productivity.

In desperation, the Byzantine Empire now appealed to Europe for assistance against the infidel invaders. Europe's response was the movement known as the Crusades. But this was a dubious kind of assistance. Although the Crusades temporarily stemmed the Turkish invasion, the struggle used up most of the Empire's political and economic vitality. True, the Empire was to endure—in name, at least—for another four centuries, and during this period it was to preserve its intellectual and artistic life, its Orthodox religion, and some remnants of its imperial authority. But its position as the dominant state in the eastern Mediterranean was gone forever.

"Decline and Fall"

It is this final period of Byzantine history—from Manzikert to the capture of Constantinople by the Ottoman Turks in 1453—that alone deserves to be associated with Rome's "decline and fall." To be sure, these four centuries show flashes of the Empire's old military skill and political cleverness. Yet in any evaluation of Byzantium's historical role they form little more than a melancholy appendage to the centuries of Byzantine glory, which extended from the reign of Constantine the Great to that of Basil II, and which, despite grave military and political crises, never saw the Empire stripped of its latent power or relegated to the position of a second-rate state. The real Byzantine achievement occurred during these earlier centuries, with which this chapter has been almost entirely concerned. The remainder of Byzantine history should be viewed as a part—and often as a very minor part—of a confused, turbulent and dramatically transitional epoch in which crusading movements from the west and Turko-Tatar invasions from the east were to play the decisive roles.

Ruins of Rumeli Hisar—Ottoman fortifications on the European side of the Bosporus, 15 miles above Constantinople, where the straits are only 800 yards wide. (Three Lions)

THE BYZANTINE ACHIEVEMENT

Even when the effective period of Byzantine rule is so reduced in time, the Byzantine achievement must be acknowledged as truly impressive. For more than half a millennium the Empire was the most prosperous and most civilized state of Europe and western Asia. During most of this period it dominated the economic life of the areas around the eastern Mediterranean and the Black Sea, and it usually played a successful role in military and political affairs.

Few empires can match this record. The great eras of Assyrian, Babylonian, and Persian imperial rule were not long, and the empire of Alexander the Great broke up at his death. As for the Roman Empire, which is generally regarded as a model of imperial accomplishment, its era of greatness takes in less than five centuries. When you make such comparisons, you are forced to reject the verdict of Gibbon that the whole history of the Byzantine Empire was one of continuing decay. Rather, you must regard the Byzantine achievement as a striking example of imperial stability.

What outstanding services did the Byzantine—or East Roman—Empire render to the peoples of its time, and what were its major contributions to later ages?

The Bastion of the West

Perhaps the most obvious contemporary service was the Empire's resistance to successive attacks coming from eastern Europe or Asia. Certain of these onslaughts the Empire decisively defeated. Others, like the great Slavic and Bulgarian incursions, were slowed down until the invaders had begun to assimilate Christian civilization. Still other attacks Byzantium could not repel but could only turn aside. For example, the Magyars, another group of eastern invaders, were merely diverted from the lands of the Empire, later progressing along the Danube Valley into Central Europe; while the Moslems, unable to push through the main Byzantine defenses, proceeded across North Africa into Spain and southern France. We must not conclude, however, that Byzantium saved itself at the expense of the other lands of Europe to which these invaders turned. The Magyars had been sufficiently exposed to Byzantine influences to be able to set up a flourishing Christian state of their own: the kingdom of Hungary. And the Moslems, in their struggle with the Byzantine Empire had absorbed so much Greco-Roman culture that, by the time they reached Spain, they were themselves a civilizing force.

The Economic Achievement

A second major contribution of the Byzantine Empire is to be found in the stimulus it gave to contemporary European trade and the influence it exerted upon subsequent commercial development. As we have seen, Byzantium was the economic dynamo of the Mediterranean and the Near East. Its business interests reached as far as the interior of Africa and—until the rise of Moslem power in the seventh and eighth centuries—to the Indian Ocean. Byzantine maritime commerce declined after the Moslems seized Egypt and Syria, but trade continued on the overland routes to the east, especially those passing through Asia Minor and over the Black Sea to the great port of Trapezus (Trebizond), which tapped the resources of Central Asia. Meanwhile Slavic and even Scandinavian merchants from the north and Italian merchants from the west had begun to take full advantage of the water routes leading to Constantinople. These contacts did much to raise western Europe out of the rut of feudalized self-sufficiency and to launch the great movement of medieval commercial expansion that reached a climax in the thirteenth and fourteenth centuries.

The Transmission of Culture

A third major contribution of the Byzantine Empire lay in the salvaging of the intellectual and artistic treasures of antiquity and the transmitting of them, along with Byzantium's own cultural wealth, to the peoples of western Asia and Europe. Probably the chief agents in this process of transmission were the Empire's pedantic, unimaginative, but enormously conscientious scholars, who compiled, annotated, and eventually made available to other peoples the great masterpieces of Classical and Hellenistic times. The artists and architects of the Empire deserve almost equal credit, for their professional skill produced a wide variety of models—ranging from elaborate church buildings to delicately carved ivories—which western craftsmen could profitably imitate. Another magnificent legacy was provided by the Byzantine lawyers, whose opinions, codes, and textbooks have formed the basis of much of modern Europe's legal development. Without these three major bequests, it would have been far more difficult for western Europe to attain the cultural maturity and artistic brilliance that became so strikingly evident in the Renaissance of the fifteenth century.

Byzantine cultural influence was less spectacular in eastern Europe than it was in the west, but it proved more durable and far-reaching. All the eastern Slavs, as well as the Slavic-speaking Bulgarians, are indebted to the Empire for having put their languages

Interior of San Vitale, Ravenna—built between 526 and 547. Architects of this period had found a new solution to the problem of balancing domes, and that of San Vitale rests on an octagonal base by means of squinches—a series of small apsidal vaults inserted between the angles of the octagonal walls. Within the apse (right, lower center) may be seen the mosaic panel of Justinian (p. 251). (Anderson photograph)

into written form. Several Slavic peoples also owe their religion to the zealous work of Orthodox Eastern missionaries from Byzantium. And one Slavic nation, Muscovite Russia, showed the influence of Byzantium in almost the whole of its civilization. Moscow did not have the right to call itself "the Third Rome," for it never attained a cultural greatness rivaling that of Roman civilization; yet there was at least some basis for this boast of Ivan III and his Muscovite successors.

Byzantine Cosmopolitanism

A fourth major contribution of the East Roman Empire was its cosmopolitan outlook. Like its West Roman predecessor, Byzantium sought to create a multinational state embodying the principles of the *Pax Romana*. In the west, as we have seen, this ideal of a "Roman peace" had been largely realized by Augustus and his successors of the first and second centuries. During their reigns municipal self-government had flourished, national antagonisms had broken down, and a feeling of pride in the Empire and its historic mission had reinforced the great Roman tradition of law and order. Unfortunately the political autonomy that was so conspicuous in the western Empire could not be duplicated in the war-threatened Roman territories of the east. But another

feature of the *Pax Romana*—its broad spirit of internationalism—found ready acceptance in the east. The Byzantine Empire made the most of this heritage. Governing a wide variety of peoples, it showed little inclination toward chauvinism or race prejudice. It refused to indulge in systematic persecution of non-Christian faiths. It did not allow any ideology, social or religious, to interfere with the expansion of foreign trade. And while carrying on its official business in Greek, it was so reluctant to insist on linguistic uniformity that it aided its Slavic neighbors in creating their own alphabet and in conducting church services in their own language.

The response of the peoples subject to Byzantine influence and exposed to this tolerant system was most gratifying. During the period of Byzantine greatness the provinces —except monophysite Syria and Egypt—upheld the principle of imperial unity. After the fall of Constantinople in 1453, the victorious Ottoman Turks followed the old Byzantine tradition by attempting to set up a supranational state in which members of different races and religions were to share the tasks of imperial administration.

Despite all the Turkish, and even Muscovite efforts, there never has been a Third Rome. But the Second Rome on the Bosporus as well as the First Rome on the Tiber still exert their influence through the great ideal of international cooperation that they bequeathed to later centuries.

Suggestions for Further Reading

Source Materials

Contemporary writings

Procopius, *Secret History of Procopius* (Chicago, 1927).

The outstanding source for the reign of Justinian and the most famous Byzantine contribution to historical writing.

Liuprandus, *Works of Liuprand of Cremona* (London, 1930).

A vivid but unflattering description of Byzan-

tine civilization in the tenth century by a western observer.

Secondary Works

N. H. Baynes, *The Byzantine Empire* (New York, 1926).

A very good small book, written by an outstanding scholar, with separate chapters on Byzantine ecclesiastical, social, economic, and literary history.

N. H. Baynes and H. B. Moss, *Byzantium* (Oxford, 1948).

An introductory historical sketch, followed by a series of essays on various aspects of Byzantine cultural development, as well as a chapter on the Byzantine legacy to the modern world.

J. B. Bury, *A History of the Later Roman Empire* (New York, 1923).

A careful account, covering the collapse of Roman authority in the west and its development (through Justinian) in the east. Chiefly a study of political and military history, but with some social history and a fair amount of religious discussion. A well-organized survey of a difficult period.

Cambridge Medieval History, ed. by H. M. Gawtkin and others (9 vols., New York, 1911–1936).

A standard, though now relatively old, account of the Byzantine Empire and its contacts with the west. Volume IV is particularly useful.

C. Diehl, *Byzantine Portraits* (New York, 1927).

A collection of extremely interesting chapters on some of the more significant—and colorful—figures in Byzantine history.

C. Diehl, *History of the Byzantine Empire* (Princeton, 1925).

An outline of the story of Byzantium, divided by periods from A.D. 330 to 1453. An excellent condensation and appraisal.

E. Gibbon, *The History of the Decline and Fall of the Roman Empire,* edited by J. B. Bury (New York, 1896–1902).

A pioneer work in surveying Byzantine history and an acknowledged literary masterpiece. Unduly critical of Byzantine civilization.

F. Lot, *The End of the Ancient World* (New York, 1931).

A survey of the decline of the Roman Empire and its transformation into the early medieval kingdoms of western Europe and the Byzantine Empire. Deals with the period from Diocletian to the mid-eighth century.

D. T. Rice, *Byzantine Art* (New York, 1935).

A history and analysis of all the Byzantine arts, written with insight and understanding.

S. Runciman, *Byzantine Civilisation* (London, 1933).

A scholarly, well-written, and fairly detailed discussion of the various aspects of Byzantine culture. The chapters on political organization and economic policy will be found particularly helpful.

A. A. Vasiliev, *History of the Byzantine Empire* (Madison, 1952).

A straightforward account based on a course of lectures. Handles the Empire as an entity in itself, not as an unwilling annex to other civilizations. Discusses the historians of the time in some detail.

11

The Rise of Islam

Part of the Holy Mosque of the Prophet in Medina. (Arabian American Oil Co.)

About five years after the death in 565 of the great Byzantine Emperor Justinian the Great, there was born in the little desert town of Mecca, in Arabia, a man whose influence upon the history of civilization was to surpass by far that of the illustrious ruler of Constantinople. This man, known to us as Mohammed, was to found a new religion and set in motion a tide of expansion and conquest that was to sweep from one end to the other of the great Eurasian land mass, while the civilization based on this new religion was to produce a culture, known variously as Mohammedan, Moslem, or Islamic, which was to rival that of Byzantium in its Second Golden Age.

MOHAMMED AND HIS VISION

For centuries before the time of Mohammed, the Arabian Peninsula had been a place of little historical importance. From time to time Semitic peoples had migrated out of this region into the more hospitable lands of the Fertile Crescent, where they had become known to history as Babylonians, Assyrians, Phoenicians, or Hebrews. Those who remained in their Arabian homeland were never a threat to the great empires of the Near East.

Even today most of the inhabitants of the interior of Arabia remain nomads, ceaselessly wandering with their herds in search of pasture lands. In the seventh century the only bonds holding these nomads together were those of the tribe. Each tribe had its enemies, and warfare among them was almost constant. The warriors of these tribes, though skilled in cavalry operations, lacked the discipline that was needed to create a fighting force capable of sustained, large-scale campaigns. Along the coasts a number of towns developed, supporting themselves by trade. Like the nomads of the desert, the townspeople were governed only by the primitive tribal system, and tribal rivalries among them were compounded by their mutual competition in commerce. The townsmen were therefore no more united than were the dwellers in the desert.

Mecca was the chief city of the peninsula. Its importance was mainly religious, for most

The Kaaba—center of the Moslem world, the point toward which Moslems face when praying. Most sacred of Moslem buildings, the Kaaba is a small, nearly cubic structure within the mosque at Mecca. (Arabian American Oil Co.)

of the Arabs held to a primitive animism, and in Mecca there were many images and other objects that Arabs all over the peninsula regarded as having special religious significance. Most notable of these was a black meteorite, which was housed in a shrine known as the Kaaba.

Mohammed

Mecca was the town where Mohammed was born about 570. Orphaned at an early age, he was raised by a grandfather and an uncle and trained as a caravan agent. Presently he took employment as an agent for a wealthy widow named Kadijah, and soon he married her. This marriage gave him the ease and leisure to devote his time to religious contemplation.

In his trips along the caravan routes to the north, Mohammed had come into contact with Christians and Jews, and their monotheistic and spiritual religious beliefs had stirred his imagination, making him dissatisfied with the primitive animism of his own people. At about the age of forty Mohammed became convinced that God had chosen him to be a prophet, a successor to Abraham and Moses and Jesus. He believed himself to be the last and greatest in this series of prophets, and that to him alone had God given the whole of the divine revelation. Like the Jews and the Christians, Mohammed believed there was but one supreme God, and so uncompromising was his monotheism that he regarded the Christian doctrine of the Trinity as a sacrilegious concession to polytheism.

The Koran

The teachings of Mohammed were eventually written down—after the Prophet's death in 632—in a book known as the Koran. This became the sacred scripture of the new religion that is sometimes called Mohammedanism but is more properly called Islam—meaning, "submission to God's will." The Koran is composed of 114 chapters, or *suras,* which are arranged simply in the order of their decreasing length, for each is believed to be a separate divine revelation. The basic tenets are simple and few, summed up in five ordinances: the believer must acknowledge the "oneness" of God; say prayers five times a day, while kneeling with

THE SPREAD OF ISLAM

his face toward Mecca; give alms to the poor; fast from sunup to sundown each day during the sacred month of Ramadan; and, if possible, make at least one pilgrimage to Mecca.

The Koran also includes guidance for all phases of the life of the faithful. For example, it allows the Moslem to have four wives, but no more; forbids him to drink wine or eat pork; and encourages the custom of ceremonial ablutions. On the basis of such counsel, the religious leaders of Islam later developed elaborate rules governing social and political behavior as well as religious observances. The pious Moslem does not distinguish between religious law and political; he regards no rule of behavior as valid unless it has its source in the Koran.

Early Converts

Mohammed's first converts were members of his immediate family and his personal friends, who later gained great prestige among the Moslems as "Companions of the Prophet." Among them were his wife Kadijah, Abu Bakr and Omar ibn al Kattab, whose daughters were also married to the Prophet, and his nephew Ali, who married Mohammed's daughter Fatima.

As the little band of converts grew, some of the townsmen of Mecca became alarmed for fear that Mohammed's teachings would undermine the older religious beliefs that had made Mecca a place of holy pilgrimage. If pilgrims no longer came to worship at the shrine of the Black Stone, the merchants and traders of the city would suffer. Their distrust and antagonism was not lessened even when Mohammed agreed that Mecca was a holy city, which true believers should continue to visit.

Because of this growing opposition in Mecca, Mohammed was obliged to leave his birthplace and take haven in the neighboring city of Medina, which offered him a welcome. This hegira, or flight, took place on September 24, 622, which remains a memorable date in the annals of Islam.

In Medina, Mohammed persuaded the people to accept his new religion and organize a theocratic state, in which both public and private law as well as religious practices were based on the will of God as revealed to Mohammed. Inevitably Medina became involved in a bitter struggle with Mecca, in the outcome of which the Medinites, under the leadership of Mohammed, prevailed over their neighbors. By 632, when Mohammed returned to Mecca as a pilgrim shortly before he died, the Moslem faith was dominant in nearly all Arabia.

THE SPREAD OF ISLAM

Mohammed's Successors

When Mohammed died in 632, a problem arose as to who was to succeed him as leader of the new religion, for the Prophet had made no provision for the succession. Soon this problem was to give rise to grave dissensions and schism within Islam, but for the time being it was solved when the "Companions of the Prophet" elected one of their number to be their leader. This first caliph, or successor to the Prophet, was Abu Bakr

(632–634). During his reign Abu Bakr designated the man who was to succeed him—Omar, who became the second caliph in 634.

The First Caliphs

Abu Bakr	632–634
Omar	634–644
Othman ibn-Affan	644–656
Ali	656–661

Labels on image: Dauids thurn · Turris Dauid · Pi siner schloß · Jerusalem · Salomōs tēpel · Aurea porta · Gúldin port

Jerusalem the Holy—looking westward from Mount Olivet, with King David's tomb at upper left. This reproduction was made from a print from the original sixteenth-century woodcut by Sebastian Muenster. (Universitas-Booksellers, Jerusalem)

During the reigns of these first two caliphs, Islam made a remarkable expansion. Once the Arabs were united under the banners of the new religion, they became a formidable fighting force, which struck westward and eastward from Arabia, seizing territories under the rule of the Byzantine and Persian empires. The success of the Moslems was made easier by virtue of the fact that these two empires were exhausted from warfare with one another.

In 640 the conquest of Syria and Palestine was completed, whereupon the Caliph Omar made Jerusalem the third holy city of the Moslems, after Mecca and Medina, in the belief that the city had been visited by Mohammed. The reduction of Persia was accomplished in 652, in the reign of the Caliph Othman. Meanwhile the great and wealthy Byzantine province of Egypt had succumbed (639–642), because Constantinople had failed to take prompt and effective action to meet the Moslem threat. From

Egypt, the Moslems easily pushed on across north Africa to Tripoli and Tunis. These conquests were readily consolidated, for the Koran prescribed effective means for the treatment of the conquered peoples. Those whose religion was not monotheistic—the Persians, for example—were forced to become Moslems. But the Jews and Christians were permitted to retain their own religion, since these "peoples of the Book"—the Bible —believed, like the Moslems, in but one God. They were required only to pay a special tax, which was not levied on Moslems. In order to avoid this tax, large numbers of Christians, especially in Egypt, became converts to Islam, until the Moslems themselves, in order to be sure of having enough taxpayers, began to discourage them from accepting the True Faith. In lands where Moslem rule supplanted Byzantine, the new regime generally meant an improvement in the position of Jews, Christian heretics, and others who did not accept the Christian doctrine.

While this expansion was in progress, the question of the succession of the caliphate was again disputed. The second caliph, Omar, named an electoral college which was empowered to make the choice, and the election went to Othman ibn-Affan, another of the "Companions of the Prophet" and a member of the Omayyad tribe, which was prominent in the aristocracy of Mecca. This choice was protested by a faction led by Mohammed's nephew Ali, who argued that the caliphate should remain in the family of the Prophet. This dispute later gave rise to a division between the Sunna and the Shia branches of Islam.

After a caliphate of twelve years (644–656), Othman was assassinated during a rebellion led by Ali. Ali was then proclaimed caliph, whereupon he moved his capital from Medina to Kufah, on the eastern bank of the Euphrates River, not far from ancient Babylon. Not all the Moslems recognized Ali's election, however, and after five years of disorder, Ali, in his turn, met death by assassination in 661. Immediately Muawiya, one of Othman's generals and the leader of the Omayyad faction, seized the caliphate, moved the capital to Damascus, and securely established the ascendancy of the Omayyads.

The Omayyad Dynasty

To make sure of their hold on the caliphate, the Omayyads made the succession hereditary. This was a breach of the tradition of the election of the caliph, and its result was a great schism of Islam, beginning in 680. Those who recognized the Omayyad caliphate became the Sunna, or "orthodox" Moslems. Their adversaries, recognizing Ali and his son as their leaders, became the Shia. The schism still persists, but the majority of Moslems have always belonged to the Sunna. Since the seventh century the Shia have split into numerous small sects, dispersed throughout the Moslem world (see p. 281).

Under the leadership of the Omayyads, the Arabs continued their expansion eastward into Transoxiana and Samarkand, where they first came into conflict with the Mongoloid peoples; southward as far as the southern Punjab in India; and westward along the Mediterranean coast of Africa to Spain, which they invaded in 711. After defeating the Visigoths there, they pressed on into southern France, where their advance at last was checked, between Poitiers and Tours, in 732. Meanwhile, as we have seen in the previous chapter, they had begun

Mount Zion and King David's Tomb Today. Mount Zion is hallowed ground to Jews, Moslems, and Christians alike. (Israel Government Tourist Office)

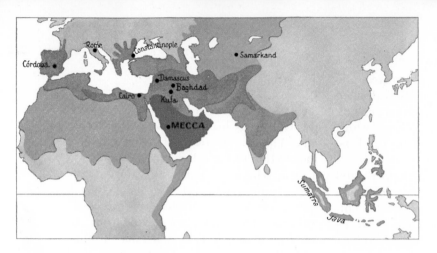

The Expansion of Islam

attacks on the Byzantine Empire. But Byzantium had successfully withstood these attacks, the first lasting from 673 to 677 and the second taking place in 717–718.

More important than the continuing expansion of Islam was the organization of a great Moslem state and society in the lands brought under Arab rule. If we recall that before the seventh century the Arabs had developed no social or political organization larger than a tribe or a town, we can only marvel at how rapidly they adapted themselves to the more advanced civilizations which they conquered. Their vast empire was divided into five great provinces—Iraq, Arabia, Egypt, Al Jezireh and Africa—while independent governors were appointed to administer Transoxiana and the Punjab. All seven governors had almost unlimited power to appoint their subordinates and levy taxes. These included a poll tax, which was imposed only on non-Moslems, and a tax on land. The governors were accountable to the caliph, since he was the head of all Islam, and an elaborate chancery and archives developed at Damascus, which remained the seat of the Omayyad caliphs. This administration was based on the Byzantine model; many of the clerks in it were Christians or Jews.

The social structure of the Empire revealed four main classes: Moslems of Arab origin; Moslems who were not Arabs; *dhimmis,* non-Moslems who were permitted to keep their own religion; and slaves. Although the law declared that no Moslem could be held as a slave, many of the slaves were Moslems, and some of them—especially eunuchs—rose to high position.

Because of the insistence that the Koran must be read and prayers recited only in Arabic, Arabic became the universal language of government and theology throughout the world of Islam. However, the Arabs soon began to assimilate Greek and Roman learning, which had been preserved in the lands now under their rule. As yet they were not quite ready to make contributions of their own to that heritage, although in architecture they developed a hybrid style, combining elements taken from Syria, Persia, India, and Spain.

The Omayyad Dynasty of Caliphs	
Muawiya	661–680
Yazid	680–683
Muawiya II	683
Marwan I	683–685
Abdu-l-Lalik	685–705
Walid I	705–715
Suleiman	715–717
Omar	717–720
Yazid II	720–724
Hisham	724–743
Walid II	743
Yazid III	743–744
Ibrahim	744
Marwan II	744–750

The Abbasid Dynasty

In 750 the chronic dissension over the succession to the caliphate once more broke out into an open struggle, in which the Omayyad dynasty was overthrown. The new dynasty that took over—the Abbasid—was descended from an uncle of Mohammed, and it was therefore more acceptable to the Shia than had been the Omayyad. A survivor of the Omayyads, however, fled to Spain where he established an independent emirate at Córdova (or Córdoba), which later became a full-fledged rival caliphate.

With the rise of the Abbasids, the Arabs lost their supremacy in the Moslem empire. As time went on the Abbasids came increasingly under Persian influence, and in 762 the capital was moved eastward to Baghdad. Soon Baghdad grew into a great and splendid city of Oriental magnificence, rivaling Byzantium in size and dwarfing the towns of western Europe in the ninth and tenth centuries.

THE GOLDEN AGE OF ISLAMIC CIVILIZATION

Baghdad

Under the Abbasid caliphs, Baghdad became much more than a religious center; it was also the economic, political, and cultural center of Islam. In the tradition of the ancient cities of Mesopotamia, it was the hub of a far-reaching commerce. In the bazaars of Baghdad were to be found not only the wares of Moslem lands but also porcelain and silks from China, spices and minerals from India and Malaya, textiles and slaves from Central Asia, honey, wax, furs, and slaves from what is now Russia and Scandinavia, and ivory, gold, and slaves from East Africa. The merchant was not a man of lowly station in Islam but the peer of the professional man, and both alike were accorded honor and patronage by the Abbasids.

Trade was one band that held Islam together. Another, more important, was its common language—the Arabic that was universally used in prayers, laws, and works of scholarship. Yet the insistence on the use of Arabic did not mean that the Moslems paid no heed to other cultures besides their own. On the contrary, the Arab was en-

The Caliphate about 750—about the time when the Omayyad dynasty was overthrown by the Abbasid dynasty.

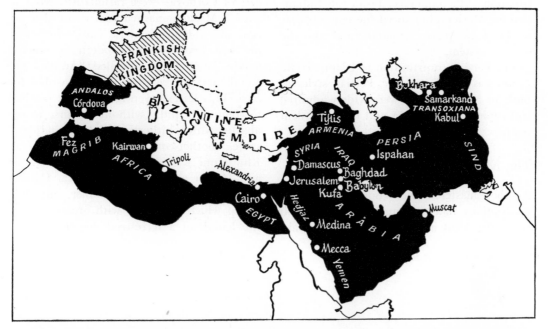

dowed with keen curiosity, and he soon demonstrated an appreciation for the learning and culture of the older peoples with whom he came into contact. Moreover, the non-Arabic peoples who became Moslems, either willingly or by conquest, carried over into Islam the traditions that had come down to them from earlier times. Hence, though unified by the factors of a common language and religion, Islamic culture became a blend of diverse elements—Hellenistic, Indian, Persian, and Syrian.

Much of the intellectual life of Islam centered in the "House of Wisdom" in Baghdad. This was an establishment comprising a school of translators, a library, and an academy. The scholars associated with it translated and studied the works of such Greek scientists as Galen, Euclid, and Ptolemy, the writings of Plato and Aristotle and the Neoplatonists, and also scientific treatises from Persia and India.

Indian sources contributed especially to the study of mathematics and astronomy. Knowledge of the stars was of much importance to the Moslems because of their concern to establish the direction of Mecca, toward which they must turn when they prayed, and because of the need of their merchant seamen and caravan drivers for some kind of reliable guidance on their long journeys. Mathematics was also of practical interest to them, because of their preoccupation with commerce. From the Indians also the Moslems borrowed the symbols that we know as Arabic numerals, and also the decimal system.

The Persian contribution to Islamic civilization was mainly esthetic. Persian styles in both art and literature were widely admired and copied by the Arabs and other Moslem peoples.

The Moslem Synthesis

As they mastered the wisdom that other civilizations had accumulated before their time, the Moslem scholars began to make new contributions of their own to this heritage. In medicine, Hunayn ibn Ishaq, a Nestorian Christian of the ninth century who worked with the Moslem scholars as a translator, drew upon his own experience in the practice of medicine to add to the knowledge of diseases. In particular, he made the most thorough study of the diseases of the eye that had been done up to his time. A generation later Al-Razi compiled a medical encyclopedia that subsequently came into wide use in western Europe. Among his duties as the chief resident physician and director of the great state hospital in Baghdad were those of setting up courses for the training of pharmacists and physicians, supervising the clinic for poor patients, and licensing medical practitioners. Another great physician of the Abbasid period was Ibn Sina (980–1037), known in Europe as Avicenna. Like many Moslem scholars, he was not only a physician but also a distinguished philosopher, philologist, and poet. His codification of Greco-Arabic medicine in the encyclopedic *Canon* was translated into Latin in the twelfth century and soon became the standard textbook for medical education throughout Europe. It remained in use until the seventeenth century.

Abbasid philosophy was derived mainly from Aristotle, though some Moslem philosophers were drawn to the mysticism of Neoplatonism, and a few—notably Averroës of Córdova—were rationalists. Notable among Moslem mathematicians of this period was al-Khwarizmi (fl. 820), who wrote the first textbook for modern arithmetic, making use of the so-called "Arabic" numerals and the recently devised symbol for zero. This latter invention made it possible to compute rapidly without recourse to the abacus, which hitherto had been indispensable. Another contribution attributed to al-Khwarizmi was the combination of Greek and Hindu elements into algebra. He was also a distinguished astronomer, one of a group which measured with great accuracy the length of a terrestrial degree and estimated the circumference of the earth at 20,400 miles. Al-Khwarizmi's astronomical tables, revised in Spain, were translated into Latin in 1126 and became the basis for the tables used in Europe. Other Moslems, making use of the work of Ptolemy, furthered the development of trigonometry.

Astronomy also owed much to Ptolemy, although the Arabs drew partly on Hindu knowledge and added much of their own. Especially significant were three astronomers of the tenth and eleventh centuries—al-Batani (c.850–929), al-Biruni (973–1048), and Omar Khayyam (fl. 1074–1123), noted for his mathematics as well as for his poetry. Al-Batani made important revisions in the work of Ptolemy; al-Biruni, Islam's most original and profound thinker in the physical and mathematical sciences, described the earth's rotation on its axis; while Omar Khayyam developed an improved calendar and a better system of algebra. Despite the great increase in astronomical knowledge, however, the widespread popular belief in astrology did not diminish.

The Moslem achievements in chemistry were worthy of note along with those in medicine, astronomy, and mathematics. As in other physical sciences, the Arabs went beyond Greek speculation to practical experimentation. Their chemists discovered many chemical compounds, accurately described the process of calcination and reduction, and improved laboratory methods. Many of their treatises continued to be widely used in Europe as well as Moslem lands until the eighteenth century.

So great were the advances in science during this Golden Age of the Abbasid reign that in later times Moslem scholars were content to revere and memorize the works of their predecessors rather than improve upon them. Except in Spain, which we shall consider shortly, the period following the decline of the Abbasids brought new developments only in literature and history, with merely a perpetuation of the scientific thought and accomplishment of earlier years.

Moslem Theology

Even more important in the eyes of the Moslems than scientific work was the vast labor spent on theology and jurisprudence. Most of those who wrote in these fields were of Arabian descent, and here we see most clearly the Arab contribution to Islamic culture.

The development of theology was hastened by the contact of the Moslems with Christians and Jews, for this forced the Moslems to define the distinctive tenets of their religion and make answer to the questions and criticism of the followers of the other two great monotheistic religions. The Koran remained the basis of Moslem doctrine, but other sources were also recognized. One of these was the Sunna, or traditions of the deeds and sayings of Mohammed. These traditions, giving precepts for all man's activities and duties, were set down in writing in the ninth century. A third source was *ijma*—the consensus, or opinions commonly held by the mass of true believers on points where neither the Koran nor the books recording ancient tradition give guidance. The Shiites do not accept *ijma* as a source of doctrine, but for the Sunnites, who, as we said, make up the largest number of Moslems, this provides a means of adapting Islamic institutions and beliefs to changing situations.

Moslem Law

In building up their science of jurisprudence, the Arabs relied as far as possible on the Koran and their religious traditions. But the teachings of the Koran, though including civil and legal prescriptions as well as commandments as to ritual and worship, were not adequate to cover all questions, especially those arising from the conquest of new territories. Nor was religious tradition enough of a supplement. Consequently jurists had to resort to the making of analogies, so as to treat a new case according to its resemblances to other cases for which the law was clear, and to the use of legal fictions. As Moslem law passed beyond the bounds of the Koran and other sacred writings, it made some use—as yet, we cannot determine just how much—of the principles and methods of Roman and Byzantine jurisprudence, especially in the laws governing commercial relations. The main basis of Islamic civil law, however, continued to be the Moslem religion.

The Moslem State

While the Abbasids vigorously sponsored and supported artistic and intellectual endeavors, their political system fell on evil days. From the deposed Omayyads, the Abbasid dynasty took over the principle that the caliphate should remain within the royal family. However, the succession did not necessarily pass to the eldest son of the caliph, for the latter designated as his successor whichever of his male relatives he liked best or regarded as most competent. This often led to bloody struggles between kinsmen, when the accession of the new ruler was challenged by those who had been passed over. This was especially apt to happen when one of several brothers was named as the successor.

After the middle of the ninth century the caliph's power diminished. Increasingly he busied himself with the delights of the harem and the other sensual indulgences that Baghdad provided in luxurious abundance, leaving to others the management of governmental affairs. Often the caliph became the helpless prisoner of his guards, who sometimes would remove him from Baghdad and shunt him about as they pleased from one city to another.

The pattern of governmental organization established by the time of the Abbasids continued to be followed for centuries. In many ways, especially in its complex bureaucracy, it resembled the Byzantine government. This is not surprising, since many of its officials in early times were Christians or Jews who had been trained in the service of the Byzantine Empire. Among the officers of the court were the chamberlain, who introduced foreign envoys to the caliph, the torturer, and the astrologer. The civil administration was under the charge of the grand vizier, an officer who—like the torturer and the astrologer—had a counterpart in the Persian court and government. As long as the grand vizier had the confidence of the caliph, his power was almost unlimited, but he could be dismissed as soon as the caliph withdrew his favor or came to regard the vizier as a rival. Under militaristic caliphs, the head of the armed forces—entitled the "Commander of the Commanders"—took the place of the grand vizier.

The most important department of the government was that of finance or taxation. This department was responsible for the collection of the *zakah,* a tax which was paid by Moslems on their wealth in the form of land, herds, or other property that could increase in value; tribute paid by defeated foreign powers; the poll tax imposed on non-Moslems; and the taxes levied on land and merchandise owned by non-Moslems. The *zakah* was used for the relief of the poor and the support of orphans, for payments to volunteers serving in holy wars against unbelievers, and for the ransom of captives. The other revenues were used to support the army, maintain mosques, keep up roads and bridges, and meet the large and varied expenses of the caliph.

Other departments were an auditing office; a chancery; a board of inspection, which resembled a court of appeals hearing complaints of miscarriages of justice; a police department; a department of justice; and a post office. The postal department was responsible for collecting data on geography and maintaining an intricate system of post roads throughout the Empire, and also for an intelligence service, which gathered information regarding the government of Moslem provinces as well as activities in enemy lands. The administration of justice was directly under the caliph or his deputies. Though generally the law was based on the Koran and Moslem religious tradition, civil suits between non-Moslems were settled according to the laws of the parties involved in the case.

In early times the organization of the army was haphazard, because mobile tactics, religious ardor, and hunger for pillage gave the Moslem warriors advantage enough to overwhelm their enemies. As time went on, however, the Moslems became astute practitioners of the military art, and more attention was given to the management of the army. The regular troops comprised a small number of élite regiments, which were supplemented in time of war by mercenaries, adventurers, conscripts, and bands of volunteers under their own commanders.

Within the regular army, special branches were organized: an infantry, equipped with spears, swords, and shields; a corps of archers; a cavalry, provided with lances and battle axes and fitted out with partial armor; naphtha-throwers, who wore fireproof clothing and threw incendiary material into the ranks of the enemy; and the engineers, who were in charge of siege machinery, such as catapults, battering rams, and mangonels. By the ninth century, the army also had

field hospitals and used camel litters as ambulances.

Until the middle of the ninth century the army was a centralized force, drawing its recruits from all over the Empire. But it proved difficult to maintain a centralized administration over so vast a territory, especially when weak men occupied the caliphate. Gradually the provincial governors, whose offices became hereditary, took a larger role in military affairs, raising troops of their own and paying them with land grants. This decentralization of military power was not peculiar to the Moslem Empire, however, for similar tendencies appeared at about the same time in feudal Europe.

The Malwiyah. Sacred to the Shiite sect of Islam, this unique spiral minaret is all that remains of the Great Friday Mosque, erected in 847 at Samarra about sixty miles north of Baghdad. From 836 to 876 Samarra was the residence of the Abbasid caliphs. (Arab Information Center)

Moslem Society

Society in the Abbasid period was diverse, and as Arabian supremacy receded, it took on a cosmopolitan character. At the pinnacle of society was the caliph, the religious leader and political master of all his people, who by a single word could—and sometimes did—make a man rich or take away the whole of his fortune. Next came an aristocracy with various grades, and an upper-middle class of scholars, writers, artists, merchants, and professional men. Because trade was an honorable vocation, many upper-class Moslems amassed tremendous fortunes by dealing in goods from all over the known world. Artisans and peasants made up the mass of the population.

Slaves became much more common in this period than before, especially in the households of members of the caliph's family and high officials in the government. Many of the slaves were well educated, either as scholars or musicians and actors. Women slaves were kept as concubines; indeed, few of the Abassid caliphs were born of mothers who were free women.

Industry and Agriculture

Industry and agriculture were no less important in the Moslem Empire than the wide-reaching commerce of which we have taken note. Western Asia produced rugs, tapestry, silk, cotton and woolen goods, furniture, and utensils. Persia was noted for its carpets and textiles, many of which were produced especially for the royal household. Kufah wove silks that were much in demand; Egypt revived many of its old manufactures; and Syria again produced large quantities of its superb glass. Damascus was pre-eminent in glazed tile and fine metalwork. After the capture of Samarkand in the eighth century, the paper industry spread from this center to most of the provinces of the Empire, reaching the Moslem outposts

in Spain and southern Italy in the twelfth and thirteenth centuries. Gems and metals were skillfully worked to satisfy the inordinate demand for jewelry.

After the establishment of the capital in Baghdad, much attention was given to building up the agriculture of the Tigris-Euphrates plain in order to feed the populace and increase the value of the land on which taxes were levied. Generally the Moslem government treated the natives of this region better than had their previous rulers; the natives, in turn, cooperated with the officials of the government who undertook works for reclaiming old agricultural areas, reopening silted-up canals, and in other ways restoring the productivity of the land.

Similar attempts were made to stimulate agricultural production in other parts of the Empire, until eventually many areas were bringing forth unprecedented harvests—to the great gain of the caliph's treasury. The staple crops included barley, wheat, rice, dates, sesame, cotton, and flax. Long before some of these fruits were known in Europe, the Moslem world was raising apples, apricots, peaches, plums, lemons, oranges, olives, pomegranates, and watermelon as well as such vegetables as eggplant, radishes, and cucumbers. Sugar cane was cultivated and refined, and many flowers were grown on a large scale for their commercial use in the making of perfumes, essences, oils, and unguents. The peasants who performed most of the labor were *dhimmis* —peoples permitted to worship in religions other than Islam—and many besides Jews and Christians were now included among them. The Moslem was content to live on the labor of the *dhimmi,* for though he had no disdain for trade, he regarded agricultural pursuits as beneath the dignity of the true believer.

The passing of time saw a gradual diminution in the number of persons in the Empire who did not accept the Moslem religion. Though the number of Christians and Jews remained large, most of the population chose to rid itself of the disabilities imposed on the *dhimmi* and gain the financial and political advantages that would come with their conversion to Islam.

The End of the Abbasids

As the Abbasid caliphate was passing into its decline, a new people—the Seljuk Turks—was rising to prominence. This was the first instance of a phenomenon that was to become familiar in later centuries—the rise of strong, uncivilized converts to Islam, coming out of Central Asia to overpower a luxurious Moslem regime and infuse new military vigor into the older, "softer," areas.

Under the leadership of Tughril Beg, the Seljuk Turks captured Baghdad in 1055. The caliph was treated with respect and allowed to keep his position as the religious head of Islam. He was obliged, however, to bestow upon Tughril Beg the new title of sultan—"the one who has authority." Henceforth the sultan exercised military and political power, while the caliph became a shadowy figure, brought out and exposed to public gaze on the occasion of special religious or ceremonial occasions. The Abbasids continued to hold the office until the last of the dynasty died in 1258 at the hands of the Mongols.

THE FLOWERING OF ISLAMIC CIVILIZATION IN SPAIN

Moslem Spain

Mention has been made of the capture of Spain by the Arabs early in the eighth century. This westernmost province was the first to break away from the rest of the Moslem Empire. The rupture occurred when Abd-al-Rahman, the sole suvivor of the Omayyad after they were deposed and massacred by the supporters of the Abbasids in 750, took refuge in Spain. There he quickly gained military support and defeated the Abbasid governor of Córdova; by 756 he had gained control of most of the peninsula. As he pressed northward some of the local rulers appealed to Charlemagne for help. In 778 this Frankish king crossed the Pyrenees to give them aid, but he suffered defeat at Saragossa, and as he withdrew again to France, the rearguard of his army was destroyed in the disastrous battle of Roncesvalles—later immortalized in the *Song of Roland*.

Thus Abd-al-Rahman emerged within a short time as emir—ruler—of all Spain. His descendants maintained a loose tie with the eastern capital of the Moslem world until 929, when the eighth ruler of the Omayyad dynasty in Spain asserted his complete independence by proclaiming himself caliph. For about a century thereafter the Omayyad caliphate of Córdova rivaled in material and intellectual splendor the Abbasid caliphate of Baghdad. Like most other Moslem governments, however, the caliphate of Córdova soon began to suffer from dissension in the court and tendencies toward decentralization, and eventually the caliph—as also in Baghdad—became the puppet of the palace guard. In the outcome of a palace revolution in 1031, in the course of which the caliph was deposed, the caliphate broke up into a number of independent states, with centers in Seville, Granada, Tóledo, Córdova, Badajoz, Valencia, Cadiz, Jaen, Elvira, and Saragossa. Thereupon the Christian states of Navarre, Leon, and Castile, which had risen in the north against the Moslem power, were encouraged to press more vigorously their endeavor to reconquer the whole of Spain for Christendom.

The policies set down by Abd-al-Rahman established the basic pattern of the Moslem regime in Spain as it persisted under his descendants and even after the breakup of the caliphate in 1031. As in other conquered

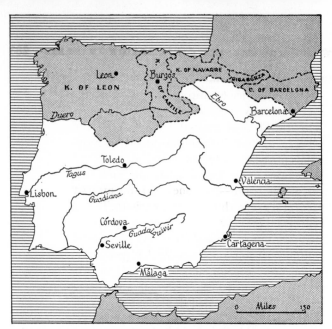

The Caliphate of Córdova

countries, a generous toleration was shown toward Jews and Christians, who were permitted to keep their own religion and— except in cases involving Moslems—even their own laws, although they were required to pay the poll tax that was imposed on nonbelievers. Land taxes were levied on much the same basis as in the other Moslem countries in the east, and generally the position of the peasants improved.

Many Christians chose to espouse Islam in order to gain the benefits accorded to Moslems. These converts swelled the ranks of the neo-Moslems, a class that attained considerable size in some cities and proved but a dubious support to the Moslem cause. On the other hand, many of the Christians who retained their own religion became admirers of the Arab civilization, which was much in advance of their own. They became masters of the Arabic tongue and students of Islamic culture, and it was largely owing to their labors that Arabic works were translated into Latin and thus made available to Christian scholars in other countries of western Europe.

In the tenth century Córdova was not only the capital of Moslem Spain but the most cultured city in western Europe. Its popu-

lace, spreading out into twenty-one suburbs, enjoyed such creature comforts as paved and illuminated streets and luxurious public baths, while its shops displayed merchandise gathered from all parts of the known world. Besides mosques and palaces, there were innumerable libraries and bookstores, twenty-seven free schools, and a university that attracted students from Europe, Asia, and Africa.

After the breakup of the caliphate into a number of petty states in the eleventh century, Córdova lost its pre-eminence, and Seville rose in importance. Presently Granada emerged as the leading Moslem state in Spain, under the rule of the Nasrids. In this beautiful mountain valley they built the exquisite and imposing palace known as the Alhambra, patronized learning and the arts, and gave refuge to Moslems fleeing from the Christian forces that were reconquering Spain. Córdova succumbed to this reconquest in 1236, Seville in 1248, but Granada held out, the last Moslem stronghold in Spain, until 1492.

The Culture of Moslem Spain

Intellectual progress in Moslem Spain was slower than in the Moslem lands in the east. The main reason for this was the lower level of civilization that the Arabs found among the natives of Spain (see Chapter 17). The Moslem conquerors of Spain did not have so much stimulus from the people under their rule as did their kinsmen who became masters of such lands as Egypt or Syria. Nevertheless, Moslem Spain produced a civilization that was unequalled in any other country of western Europe during the period from the eighth through the twelfth centuries. Moreover, the intellectual life of Islamic Spain was remarkably free, for the world of scholarship was open alike to Moslems, Jews, Christians, and converts to Islam.

Despite the political troubles of the period the eleventh and twelfth centuries were favorable to literature. Literacy was widespread in Moslem Spain, among women as well as men, at a time when elsewhere in Europe relatively few—not even all the clergy—knew how to read and write. The Arabic poetry of Spain—especially the lyric folk song originating in Andalusia—excited Christian admiration and emulation, while the wealth of imaginative and facile poems on platonic love became a model for some of the love poetry of the French and Provençal troubadours of the twelfth century. Many of the fables, tales, and fantasies of the feudal era in Europe bear a resemblance to Moslem writings that circulated in Spain.

Notable in the fields of history and geography was Ibn Khaldun (1332–1406), who traveled throughout the Moslem world and was everywhere received with honor. He developed a theory of history that considers the phenomenon of national progress and decline as the result of the physical factors of climate and geography as well as of moral and spiritual forces. As a historical philosopher, he had no peer in Islam—or in the entire western world of his time.

In the sciences, major advances were made in astronomical mathematics, botany, and medicine. As in the east, Spanish astronomers were led by an interest in astrology to make careful observations of the movements of the heavenly bodies and to make further progress in the study of trigonometry. Translations of their works circulated widely in Europe and proved valuable in connection with the explorations made during the late Middle Ages and the Renaissance. In the science of medicine, important contributions were made to surgery and clinical practice.

In the study of philosophy, the Spanish Moslems outdistanced even their Moslem colleagues in the east. Their problem was similar to one that the Christians had to face—to reconcile religious truth with the truth of reason as taught by the Greek philosophers. As philosophers, they insisted that truth is one and indivisible, and therefore they were obliged to reconcile the truth propounded by the Greek philosophers, in particular Aristotle and Plato, with the truth revealed in the Koran. They succeeded in harmonizing faith, reason, and science to their own satisfaction. Presently the work done on this problem by the Moslem philosophers of Spain was to have a great influence upon the Christian philosophers of Europe, whose similar endeavor to harmonize Greek philosophy with Christian theology is known as Scholasticism (Chapter 21).

Neoplatonism—which was better known in this period than the work of Plato—was the point of departure for one train of thought, which sought to adapt to the teachings of Mohammed the conception of man's spiritual union with a supreme being identified with pure intelligence. Eventually this contributed to a movement know as the *Sufi*, in which mysticism and pantheism were mingled with this Neoplatonic interpretation of Islam.

Portico of the Alhambra Palace, Granada—showing the intricate details of Moorish artwork. (Spanish State Tourist Office)

Averroës and Maimonides. But the greatest of the philosophers of Moorish Spain was Ibn Rushd, better known to the West as Averroës (1126–1198), who drew his inspiration from Aristotle. A scholar whose treatises on medicine, astronomy, and philosophy won him wide fame, Averroës was also active in the world of practical affairs, serving for a time as a jurist in Seville and Córdova and as a court physician for the rulers of Morocco. Orthodox theologians among the Moslems, Jews, and Christians frequently condemned Averroës' rationalism, for he insisted that all beliefs except revealed dogmas should be judged by reason. But his masterly commentaries on Aristotle were widely admired in Christian Europe, and his treatises, after having been censored to take out passages offensive to Christian faith, were made part of the course of study at the University of Paris and other universities of Europe.

Also notable was the Jewish scholar Ibn Maimum, or Maimonides (1135–1204), whose work resembles that of Averroës. His treatises sought to harmonize Jewish theology with Aristotle's philosophy and to vindicate scientific thought against narrow-minded religious fundamentalism. Like Averroës, Maimonides had an influence upon such Latin scholars as Thomas Aquinas, Albertus Magnus, and Duns Scotus.

Moslem Music

Mohammed had disapproved the use of music for religious purposes but not for secular diversion. The later Moslems showed much interest and aptitude for music of the latter kind, using scales based on notes that mark smaller gradations in tone than do the notes making up our scales.

Since stringed instruments are best adapted to producing minute intervals of tone, the Moslems developed a wide assortment of instruments of this kind. Among them were the *rebad,* the ancestor of the modern violin, and the *el'ud,* known in Europe as the lute.

The Moslems were also much interested in musical theory, and their aptitude for mathematics gave them help in this field. Especially notable among Islamic musicologists was Avicenna (p. 278). However, Moslem work in musical theory was of little assistance to Christian Europe, because the harmony toward which European music was groping had need of diatonic scales. Yet Spanish music, especially that of Andalusia, still shows a sensual and spirited character that is reminiscent of the Moorish tradition. And in the Feudal Era the troubadours of southern France were much indebted to the Spanish Moslems, whose costume and instruments they borrowed as well as their eastern conception of romance.

POLITICAL FRAGMENTATION AND RELIGIOUS CONQUEST

Spain was not the only province to secede from the Baghdad caliphate. The political organization of Islam was never tightly centralized, and an ambitious provincial governor might find it relatively easy to renounce allegiance to Baghdad and establish rule in his own name. The deep-rooted antagonism between the Shia and the Sunna sects was al-so a factor for disruption. By the tenth century various Islamic lands around the Mediterranean, as well as Asiatic provinces east of Baghdad, had broken with the caliphate. In their turn, these secession states gave fresh evidence of the weakness of the Islamic political system, for in most of them dynasties rose and fell in rapid order.

Expansion into India

East of Baghdad, decentralization proceeded apace. Early in the ninth century the governor appointed to administer this region established a dynasty independent of the caliph. This Tahirid dynasty gave way to the Saffarid dynasty in 867, and in 902, the Saffarids were dethroned by the Samanids. Under the Samanid dynasty, Bukhara and Samarkand became centers of learning and art, where Persian, Indian, and Arabic scholars found patronage. But in 998 the Samanids succumbed to the growing might of the Turanian Turkish tribes of Central Asia, who were becoming converted to Islam and would soon become its masters.

Before this came to pass, however, a Turkish slave named Ghaznawid, who had been exiled from the Samanid court, organized a force that conquered Afghanistan and the Punjab in 962. For a time the Ghaznawid dynasty that he founded continued to show vigor, but when strong rulers no longer occupied the throne, localist tendencies asserted themselves in this Moslem kingdom, as in most others.

Islamic Sicily

Sicily was another of the outposts of Islam. About the middle of the seventh century Moslem pirates began to make raids on Sicily, and in 832 they took Palermo and made it a base. From there, the Moslems launched attacks upon the mainland, striking at Rome in 846 and forcing the Romans for some years afterward to pay them tribute. By 902 the entire island of Sicily was under Moslem control. For a time they also held Bari, on the coast of the Adriatic. But they were never able to gain a secure hold on the mainland, and after two centuries of turmoil Sicily was conquered by Norman armies, aided by the Byzantines.

Under the Norman kings, who displaced the Moslems, Sicily developed an Islamic-Christian culture. In large part the pattern of government remained the same under the Normans as under the Moslems, and Jews, Christians, and Moslems were all admitted into the government without discrimination. Most of the population, which slowly turned to Christianity, was engaged in agriculture, but Moslem merchants continued to handle a flourishing trade, which made the kingdom one of the richest in western Christendom. The cultural influence of Islam also remained strong, especially in the reigns of Roger II (1130–1154) and Frederick II (1197–1250), who were suspected by their European contemporaries of being more sympathetic to Islam than to Christianity. Because of its mixture of the two cultures, Sicily became a bridge by way of which much Arabic knowledge was brought into western Europe. Spreading from Sicily to southern Italy and thence farther north, Moslem skill, art, and learning became one of the several factors producing the Italian Renaissance.

The Seljuk Turks

For a time the process of disintegration in Moslem lands seemed to be reversed when the Seljuk Turks, as we have noted, made themselves masters of Baghdad in 1055 and introduced a new vigor into the Islamic capital. Continuing the aggressive warfare that had brought them to prominence, they promptly began a series of military expeditions against the Byzantine Empire. The first major Byzantine defeat came in 1071 at Manzikert (p. 263); as a result, ten years later the Comnenus dynasty was returned to the Byzantine Empire and the new emperor appealed to the west for soldiers to fight Islam. This was the appeal that indirectly led to the launching of the First Crusade (1095–1099) against Islam by the new Christian society of western Europe.

Despite the comparatively recent emergence of the Seljuks from nomadism, they quickly acquired an interest in the cultural

Leaf from an Egypto-Arabic Manuscript, 1315. Much fine work was done in Egypt between 1250, when the Mamelukes, former slaves, seized power, and 1517, when the Ottoman Turks conquered the country. (Courtesy of the Metropolitan Museum of Art)

heritage of Islam. At the height of their power in the eleventh century they founded universities throughout their lands, especially in Baghdad, where such scholars as Omar Khayyam were to be found. By the end of the century, however, the Seljuk state had suffered the seemingly inevitable fate of all great Moslem states: it split into smaller states and principalities because of decentralization within and attack from without. It was because of the attack upon Baghdad by a Shiite shah of Khwarizm that the insignificant caliph appealed to the Mongols under Genghis Khan for protection, thus bringing upon the stage of the Middle and Near East one of the greatest conquerors of all time.

The Mongols

For centuries before this time the Mongols —who are also known as Tatars or Tartars— were nomadic tribesmen, wandering over the plains of eastern Asia. Late in the twelfth century these tribes were unified by the dynamic leadership of Genghis Khan (c.1162–1227) and made into a formidable fighting force. Their one aim was conquest, and their motive was not cloaked by any pretense of religious zeal, for their religious beliefs were merely a simple and primitive animism. Under Genghis' command, they proved themselves disciplined warriors, capable of moving with bewildering speed. They were utterly ruthless, for they had no regard for human life—they considered a good horse more valuable than a man. And they did not hesitate to wipe out a whole city, because they had no cities of their own but lived in movable encampments of tents. It is no wonder that the civilized peoples of Asia and Europe were stricken with terror when this savage horde descended upon them.

In the first stage of their expansion, in the thirteenth century, the Mongols pushed westward into Europe, overrunning Russia, Poland, and Hungary, and eastward into China, where their Great Khan made himself emperor (maps, pp. 367, 374). However, the Mongols did not at this time establish a secure hold on the westernmost lands into which they penetrated. One reason for this was that, when the Great Khan died, his male relatives were required by custom to return to their homeland for a meeting, known as the *kuriltai,* for the election of a successor. Several times it happened that the death of a Great Khan occurred at an opportune moment for the peoples of the west, who were thus granted a respite from the Mongol pressure.

Like other nomadic conquerors, the Mongols adopted the civilization of the countries they overran. After vacillating between Islam, Christianity, and other religions, most of their leaders—except those who became the masters of China—accepted the Moslem religion. But they remained tolerant of other religions and quick to take up new ideas and institutions. They were stern but just rulers, and their empire was a masterpiece of political organization. The government maintained roads, a postal service, hospitals, charitable institutions for the relief of the poor, and a system of price regulation. Under Kublai Khan (1257–1294), however, the empire broke up, and various provinces—such as Persia and northern India—became autonomous.

In the fourteenth century, a new Mongol invasion swept over the Moslem lands in the east. The leader of this invasion was Timur the Lame (*c.*1336–1405), or Tamerlane, whose adherence to Islam did not save Baghdad, Damascus, northern Syria, and India (see pp. 323–324) from cultural impoverishment. From these subjugated territories, he brought scholars, artisans, and workers to his capital at Samarkand, which entered into an age of new splendor. The greatness of his state disappeared soon after his death, but Tamerlane's career as a conqueror had lasting importance in two respects: first, by defeating the Ottoman Turks, he delayed for half a century their capture of Constantinople; and, second, by his pillage of the lands he invaded, he hastened the economic and cultural decline of the old Islamic civilization.

The Ottoman Turks

While the Mongols were making themselves the masters of much of East and Central Asia, the last great group of Turkish peoples were overrunning the Near East, most of North Africa, and sections of eastern Europe. The Ottoman—or Osman—Turks were originally not a tribe but an organization of

The Ottoman Empire
in the Sixteenth
Century

warriors, called *ghazis*, allied with economic guilds. The *ghazi* state of Osman eventually welded together the diverse units and began to subjugate Asia Minor and the Balkans. The Ottoman advance was halted for a time by Tamerlane, but after regrouping their forces, the Ottoman Turks went on to take Constantinople in 1453 and Syria and Egypt in 1517. In Europe their advance reached as far as Vienna, which they unsuccessfully besieged in 1527. By that time the Ottoman Turkish caliph-sultan, who had established his capital in Constantinople after its capture, ruled over the heart of the old Moslem world, as well as much of eastern Europe, and Tunis and Algeria acknowledged his suzerainty.

Thus the Ottoman Turks realized the long-standing ambition of the Moslems by bringing together under Moslem rule both the Byzantine Empire and the Islamic Empire of the Near East and North Africa.

Suggestions for Further Reading

Source Materials

Contemporary Writings

Arabian Nights.

Collection of stories, written from the tenth through the fourteenth centuries. Sources for the tales were found in the literature of the conquered lands, especially Persia.

The Koran.

An excellent translation is M. Pickthall, *The Meaning of the Glorious Koran* (New York, 1931).

Mohammed, *The Speeches and Table-Talk of the Prophet Mohammed,* edited by S. Lane-Poole (London, 1882).
Selections from the Koran.

Omar Khayyam, *The Rubaiyat.*
Best known is the Fitzgerald translation (London, 1859).

Secondary Works

T. Andrae, *Mohammed* (London, 1936).
A book written for the layman about Mohammed as a man, teacher, and ruler. Sympathetic to the man and his movement.

T. Arnold and A. Guillaume, eds., *The Legacy of Islam* (Oxford, 1931).
One of a series of books, a series of short essays, giving the results of the establishment of Islam, dealing with such subjects as the Crusades or Arabic medicine. Not concerned with Mohammed himself or with the religion, but with other ramifications.

C. Brockelmann, *History of the Islamic Peoples* (New York, 1947).
Although this book deals with the total history of Islam to the present, the first part includes a standard history of the establishment of the religion.

E. Dermenghem, *The Life of Mahomet* (New York, 1930).
A sound introduction to the study, well written. Shows all sides of the questions. Well based on the sources, though with little reference to them.

P. K. Hitti, *History of the Arabs* (New York, 1949).
A recent book by one of the outstanding scholars in the field. Deals with the whole history of the Arab peoples to the present, but good sections on the early period.

H. Lammens, *Islam* (London, 1929).
Deals chiefly with religious beliefs and social institutions of the Islamic peoples. Assumes considerable knowledge of the political history.

B. Lewis, *The Arabs in History* (New York, 1950).
A brief work more essay than history. Written at a popular level. Centers the total picture of the Arabs around the Islamic revolution.

C. C. Torrey, *The Jewish Foundation of Islam* (New York, 1933).
Traces the Jewish importance in Arabia and Mecca and its influence on Mohammed, who was an educated man and in contact with the Jews. Gives Mohammed much credit for ability and understanding.

G. E. von Grunebaum, *Medieval Islam; A Study in Cultural Orientation* (Chicago, 1946).
The best and most original presentation of Islam in some years. Discusses the originality of Islam and its share in the growth of world civilization. Greatest stress given to literature.

A. J. Wensinck, *The Muslim Creed* (New York, 1932).
A comprehensive study of the historical development of Muslim dogma, taken historically rather than systematically. Chiefly translations of the creeds and commentaries on them.

PART II

The Ancient Civilizations
of the Far East

The spread of Islam established a new link, stronger than ever before, between the western world and the Far East. While the new religion of Mohammed was spreading along the south shore of the Mediterranean and into the Iberian Peninsula of Europe, it was also penetrating eastward into Central Asia, China, India, and Southeast Asia, where the Moslems discovered civilizations that were already ancient, rich, and highly sophisticated.

The greatest of these civilizations were those that had arisen in India along the banks of the Indus River and in China in the valleys of the Wei and the Hwang Ho. These civilizations took their start at about the same time as those that developed in Egypt and Mesopotamia, and in much the same fashion—as men in various stages of Neolithic culture settled down to till the soil,

taking advantage of the rivers as sources of water for irrigation. From these centers in India and China, civilization gradually spread into the islands of the Japanese archipelago and into the islands off the southeast coast of Asia.

Little is known of the history of the civilizations of the Far East in the fourth and third millenniums B.C. Full knowledge of them does not, in fact, begin until some time during the second millennium, 2000–1000 B.C.—the same period when the Cretan-Mycenean civilization was at its zenith and the Hellenes were beginning to move southward into Greece and the islands of the Aegean Sea to make that older civilization over into their own. Archaeological study does show, however, that the beginnings of civilization in the Far East took place much earlier.

293

Eurasia in A. D. 200

12

The Beginnings of Civilization in India

Asoka's Lion Capital (p. 314). In the
Mauryan Empire, kings set up mono-
lithic stone pillars, the function of which
was to publicize moral rescripts. These
lions are today the symbol of the Republic of India. (Government of India Press
Bureau)

At about the same time when Neolithic cultures were developing into civilizations in the Valley of the Nile and the region of the Tigris and Euphrates rivers, a similar process was taking place in the broad valley of the Indus River in western India.

The Land of India

The great subcontinent of India, half the size of the United States, has the shape of a triangle, bordered by the sea on two sides and by mountains on the other. It comprises three principal geographical areas. The north is a region of mountains and hills; in the middle is a great semicircular plain, stretching from the Arabian Sea to the bay of Bengal; the south is a plateau area, known as Peninsular India because it juts out into the sea to form the southward tip of the great triangle. (See map, p. 300.)

Dominating the north are the lofty parallel ranges of mountains, known as The Himalaya, which extend for nearly 1500 miles. Scarcely any other country in the world has such a long, high frontier. More than a hundred peaks soar above 20,000 feet, and their beauty is as great as their towering height. These mountains provide India with an abundant source of timber and with water for the rivers that have always been avenues of trade and communication. In modern times the rivers are a potential supply of vast amounts of hydroelectric power.

Two of these important rivers of India rise in Tibet on the northern side of The Himalaya. One of them, the Brahmaputra, flows in an easterly direction along the length of the range, then turns south to join the Ganges near its mouth, forming a large, fertile delta in the region of Bengal, near the modern city of Calcutta. The other great river is the Indus. From its source, the Indus flows toward the western end of The Himalaya, then in a southwesterly direction for another 500 miles, to a point where it is joined by four other rivers. The region traversed by these five rivers before they merge is known as the Punjab—land of the five rivers. From the point where the other four rivers flow into it, the Indus continues in the same southwesterly direction for another 400 miles, passing through an arid region, known as Sind, before it empties into the Arabian Sea near Karachi.

On India's northwest frontier, stretching in a southwesterly direction from the point where, in our time, the borders of Siberia, China, and Pakistan meet, are other mountain ranges—the Hindu Kush, the Sulaiman, and the Kirthar. Like The Himalaya, these mountains have tended to isolate India from the rest of Asia, but they do not make so formidable a barrier as The Himalaya. Invaders by land have usually come through passes in these mountains, especially the Khyber Pass between the southern end of the Hindu Kush and the northern end of the Sulaiman.

The great semicircular plain that lies south of the mountainous frontier region is sometimes known as the Indo-Gangetic Plain, because it includes the region drained by the Indus and the Ganges rivers. Sometimes it is referred to as Hindustan, because it has been the traditional center of Hindu culture. Its geography as well as its early history may remind us of the Fertile Crescent in the Near East. Though its width is only 150 to 200 miles, the plain stretches 2000 miles in length. Its western end—the lower Indus Valley in Sind—is dry and worthless except when irrigated, but its eastern end is well favored with rainfall. Because of this, it has become one of the most productive and most heavily populated areas of the country. Just north of modern Delhi, where the mountains of the north and the hills of the south come close together, the plain shrinks to a narrow corridor, which forms a kind of gate between the western end of the plain and the productive eastern end, drained by the Ganges.

South of the Indo-Gangetic plain lies the great plateau area. In turn, this region is subdivided into two parts. The one nearer to the central plain is a region of mountains and rivers, extending from the Gulf of Cambay on the west all the way to the eastern end of the plain, near Calcutta. In this region, the Narbada River flows from east to west for a distance of about 600 miles, passing along a valley between mountains on the north and hills on the south. This valley provides the best route across central India, although the river is useless for navigation or irrigation. The area north of the valley is known as the Central Highlands or the Central Indian Plateau.

Below this division is the Deccan, including most of the region known as Peninsular India. The Central Highlands form the northern border of this region. Along the other two sides, which come to a point near Ceylon, are low ranges of hills known as the Western and Eastern Ghats. Those in the west are the higher, averaging 3000 feet in height and including one peak of 8700 feet. Hence all the rivers in the Deccan run from the west toward the east. Unlike the larger rivers of the north, which are fed by the perpetual snows of the great mountains, these rivers are supplied with water by seasonal storms, known as the monsoons. When the season of these rain storms is over, the rivers become quite shallow. Since the water supply is not constant, these rivers cannot be extensively used for irrigation.

Between the Ghats and the sea on each side of the peninsula is a plain extending in length for almost 1000 miles. The plain on the western side is narrower, but it is better provided with rainfall, for the winds that blow in from the sea during the season of the monsoons produce rain as they strike the higher lands of the Western Ghats. During the rainy season, which comes between July and September, short rivers are created, but they dry up again during the rest of the year. The southern part of this western plain is known as the Malabar Coast. Along this coast are several good harbors—Calicut, Mahé, Goa, Bombay, Daman or Damão, and Surat.

The plain on the eastern side of the peninsula is wider than that on the west, but it is drier, since it does not receive so much of the monsoon rain. There are few natural harbors, but some of the rivers provide roadsteads. The southern part of the plain, known as the Coromandel Coast, widens out as it approaches Cape Comorin, where the eastern and western plains meet at the southernmost tip of India. Off the southeastern end of the Coromandel Coast is a chain of islands known as Adam's Bridge, which provide an almost continuous connection by land with the island of Ceylon. Though not a part of the Indian mainland, Ceylon has always been closely associated with it. In the center of this island is a mountainous area, sloping to a coastal plain. The one good harbor is Colombo.

The climate of India is generally warm. In the south the temperature averages about 85 degrees over the course of a year, and in the north, about 75 degrees. The extremes of temperature spread over an enormous range, for bitter cold is characteristic of the high mountains of the north, and tropical heat of the extreme south. In some regions the range of temperature between day and night is also great, and from day to day. In the desert regions of the northwest, for example, the temperature sometimes rises and falls, within a period of twenty-four hours, through a range of 100 degrees.

Geography has had a relatively great influence upon the historical development of India. Especially important is the influence of the high mountains in the north, which have both protected India from invasion and rendered the land more habitable. The mountains not only provide a barrier against the dry winds that blow across Tibet and Central Asia, much of that vast area too arid to support a large population, but they also cause the monsoon winds to precipitate their moisture as either rain or snow. And it is this precipitation that provides the water for most of the rivers of India.

As a barrier to invasion, the mountains of the northeast have proved insuperable. Those in the northwest are not so formidable, and sometimes invaders have penetrated through the passes. There are three such passes, but two of them lead into dry, inhospitable desert areas, and for this reason invaders have seldom been tempted to use them. The Khyber Pass, however, leads into the rich region of the Punjab. It has therefore been the route most often taken by invaders, as well as the principal gateway by which India made friendly contact with the outside world. Hence Afghanistan and present-day Iran have had more prominence in India's history than other areas beyond her northern border.

Even after invaders have succeeded in making their way through the Khyber Pass, geography has continued to affect the course of their invasion. The Khyber Pass leads into the Indo-Gangetic Plain, which, as already noted, stretches from west to east across India. But near Delhi, where the plain shrinks in width to a narrow corridor, India's defenders have often made successful stands against invaders who have pressed through the Khyber Pass into the Punjab. And even when invaders have forced their way through this corridor into the eastern end of the Indo-Gangetic Plain, they have often found it difficult to penetrate the southern plateau region. Sometimes southern India has been able to maintain independence long after invaders have gained control of the northern plain area.

The mountains of the northern border have proved a barrier to the Indians themselves as well as to invaders. Because it is so difficult to cross them, the Indians have seldom attempted to extend their rule beyond the mountains. Yet in time of peace the passes have proved usable as routes for overland trade, which always provides a cultural as well as economic interchange among peoples. This intercourse has enriched India as well as the lands that have learned from it.

These factors of geography have given the Indians a sense of the unity of their land and civilization. When, as outsiders, we look at India, we cannot help being struck by the diversity of its geography, the enormous variety of its peoples and languages, and the prevalence of numerous small, rival states during most of India's history. The Indians themselves, however, have much more sense of their unity than we commonly realize.

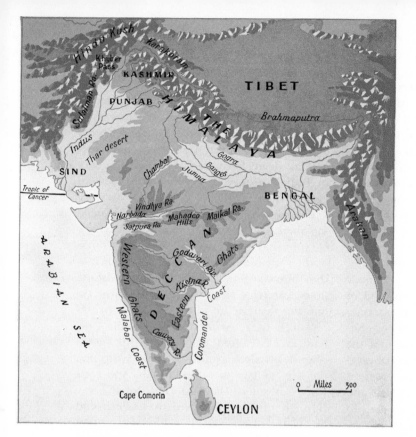

Physical Map
of India

The People and Their Languages

India has always been a great melting pot, in which numerous different peoples have merged with one another. Most writers distinguish four main groups among the peoples of India. First, there are those known as Aryans or, more precisely, Indo-Aryans. They are tall, fair-skinned people, often having long noses, who live mostly in the northern half of India. Most Hindus of high caste belong to this group. Their languages are derived from Sanskrit. Second, there are the Dravidians, who are darker of skin and shorter in stature. They live in the southern portion of the Deccan and speak a number of languages—Tamil, Telugu, and others—that have no kinship with Sanskrit. Third, there are the hill people, comprising scattered groups of primitive peoples living in the mountainous regions and jungles in isolated parts of the country. They are generally short, dark-skinned, and snub-nosed, speaking languages unrelated to the major linguistic families. Fourth, there are the Mongoloid peoples living in Burma, Assam, and along the southern fringes of The Himalaya. A snub nose, high cheek bones, and sallow skin are characteristic of them, and the men are beardless. These Mongoloid peoples and the hill people are probably remnants of the stock that populated India in Neolithic times. Presumably they were pushed back by succeeding waves of invaders into ever-more-remote places, and their numbers gradually reduced.

The languages of India are as diverse as its peoples. Hindustani is the most widely used of the fifteen languages of major importance. Two scripts are used in writing Hindustani—Hindi, which is based on Sanskrit script, and Urdu, which is based on a Persian script. The present government has made Hindi the national language of India, but the people of the south regard it as a foreign tongue.

THE DAWN OF INDIAN HISTORY

As yet, few written records have been found from which to reconstruct the story of the beginnings of Indian civilization, and we must depend primarily on the evidence of archaeological excavations. To supplement these findings, we do have a voluminous literature of hymns, rituals, philosophical treatises, and religious writings that all combine to give some further indication of early Indian history. There is also a collection of myths and legends, known as the *Puranas,* that include, besides stories of gods and saints, a long list of rulers and accounts of struggles among various tribes and kingdoms. Some of this material is obviously imaginative, but some of it is historical. From a later date we have the writings of foreigners, especially Megasthenes and other Greeks who visited India. These various sources enable the historian to reconstruct the record of ancient India—with many gaps —after the invasion by Alexander the Great during 327–324 B.C. But for the centuries before that time, our knowledge remains tenuous.

Stone Age Men in India

Remains of Paleolithic men have been found in many places in India. These men used tools made of quartzite and are therefore sometimes known as "quartzite men." They may have been Negritos, for apparently they had wavy hair, dark skin, and flat noses, and they were of short stature.

Remains of Neolithic men have also been discovered in almost all parts of India. These may have been descendants of the Paleolithic people, but we are not sure. We do know that they could make fire by friction, that they kept domesticated animals, and that they tilled the land. Ordinarily they lived in caves instead of building shelters, but they knew the art of making pottery by hand and also on the potter's wheel, and they

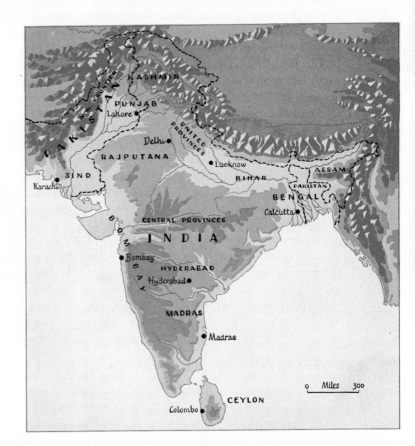

Modern India

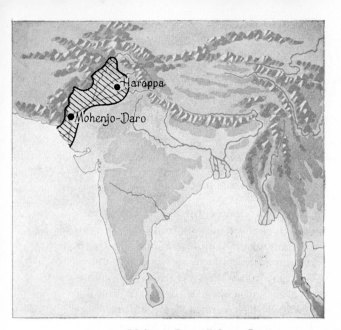

Mohenjo-Daro Culture Area

incised and painted decorations on their wares. They made simple boats, in which they sometimes traveled down the rivers to the sea. Their dead were usually buried in tombs made of three or more stones, propped together to make a circle, on which rested a heavy stone roof. Occasionally, however, the dead were buried in urns underground.

The shift from stone to metal implements was a slow and gradual process. In the north, copper was the first metal used, and iron appeared only several centuries later. In the south, however, no bronze artifacts have been found, so we presume that the transition was from stone to iron, without intervening stages of copper and bronze.

Toward the close of the Stone Age, the Dravidians emerged as one of the earliest civilized peoples of India. As yet we do not know whether they were a Stone Age people already established in India, who developed a higher civilization and then either conquered or drove off the other Stone Age peoples, or whether they were a people who originated elsewhere and entered India as invaders. Their agriculture must have been highly developed, because they built dams across the rivers to provide water for irrigation, and they were skilled in the making of

pottery and the use of metals. Their buildings included forts as well as dwellings.

Mohenjo-Daro and Harappa

Until the 1920's it was generally believed that civilization was introduced into India about 2000–1500 B.C. by invaders known as the Aryans. In the 1920's, however, a remarkable series of archaeological discoveries and excavations revealed the ancient remains of a flourishing civilization in the Indus Valley in the third millennium B.C.—well before the appearance of the Aryans in India. This civilization may have been founded by Dravidians, but no one is sure, for although seals bearing inscriptions have been found in these archaeological sites, the script has not been deciphered. Until scholars succeed in reading these inscriptions, we cannot establish just when these civilizations arose or who the inhabitants were or what became of them.

The two most important of the several sites that have been excavated are those at Mohenjo-Daro, on the Indus in Sind, and at Harappa, in the Punjab, 400 miles above Mohenjo-Daro. At the Mohenjo-Daro site the remains of seven cities have been discovered. Apparently a city was built on the site and later destroyed by flood, then a new city was built on the site of the old. This process was repeated until at least seven cities had been built, each on top of the ruins of the others before it. It is possible that the ruins of still other cities lie beneath those that have been dug up, but the seepage of water into the excavation has prevented archaeologists from digging deeper in order to find out. If it is true, as some believe, that the earliest of these cities dates from between 3000 and 2500 B.C., then the settlements in the Indus Valley arose at almost the same time as the civilization on the Nile and the Tigris-Euphrates rivers.

The excavations have brought to light the remains of numerous small and large houses, with doors, windows, paved floors, wells, drains, and bathrooms; and large public buildings, including a great bath with a pool surrounded by small rooms and galleries. The streets were wide and straight, with an elaborate drainage system. From this evidence, you can realize that the inhabitants had great skill in designing, building, and engineering.

The discoveries also reveal much about the life of the people. They had domesticated the elephant, camel, humped bull, buffalo, sheep, and possibly the horse. Their food included wheat of the same variety that is raised in the Punjab today, barley, palm dates, mutton, pork, fish, and eggs. Most of their utensils were of earthenware, some of which had been made on a potter's wheel, but other vessels were of copper, bronze, and silver. Iron was apparently unknown. Clothing was usually made of cotton, though wool was sometimes used. Both men and women adorned themselves with ornaments of gold, silver, copper, ivory, and precious and semiprecious stones, including jade, carnelian, agate, and lapis lazuli. Apparently the ladies knew the importance of make-up, for vanity cases have been found that contain tweezers, implements for piercing the ears to accommodate earrings, and such cosmetics as rouge and lipstick.

Beside the mass of the peasants who tilled the land and tended the herds, the population must have included a considerable number of artisans—blacksmiths, weavers, carpenters, masons, jewelers, goldsmiths, ivory-workers, stonecutters, and potters—and merchants who engaged in trade with other lands, as well as the shopkeepers who sold the wares of local origin. It is almost certain that tin, copper, and precious stones were obtained from outside, and it is possible that Mohenjo-Daro was a great inland port, carrying on commerce with Sumer, Elam, and perhaps Egypt.

Judging from the designs on the seals found at both Mohenjo-Daro and Harappa, which bear fine representations of real and mythi-cal animals, from the craftsmanship and design of ornaments, and from the stone images that compare favorably with some of the early Greek statues, we can be sure these people had a highly developed esthetic sense. But this artistic ability did not manifest itself in their buildings, which were commodious, strong, and utilitarian.

Few remains have been discovered that indicate the place of religion in this early culture. There seems to have existed a worship of a Mother Goddess, who perhaps symbolized the female principle of fertility. There is also evidence of the worship of a male god and the use of a phallic symbol that is almost identical with that used by Hindus at the present time in the worship of their god Siva. Some authorities hold that the religion of the Indus Valley people was the source of the Hindu religion found in India today.

Because we do not know how long this civilization lasted or how it happened to disappear, we do not know how much it contributed to the later civilization of India. It is possible that it came to an end before the Aryans invaded India, and that the later civi-

Clay Cart. This toy, nearly 5000 years old, was found in the Indus Valley. Like the Greeks (p. 142), the Indians did not confine their creative works to religious purposes. Throughout the world always, children have had their playthings. (Courtesy of the Museum of Fine Arts, Boston)

A "Bull Seal" from Mohenjo-Daro—about one and a half inches square. The reverse is engraved with a script that has not yet been deciphered. Apparently the seals were sawed out of steatite and then engraved with a burin, an engraver's tool. (Government of India Press Information Bureau)

lization of India arose—as was formerly believed—wholly by the efforts of the Aryans. But it is also possible that this civilization survived until the time of the Aryan invasion and that it had some influence upon that which the Aryans developed. As yet, no one can settle the point.

The Coming of the Aryans

In dealing with the story of the Aryans, the historian reaches firmer ground, though many points in this story are still obscure.

This fair-haired and light-skinned people probably entered India between 2000 and 1500 B.C., moving into the Punjab and the northwestern part of the Indo-Gangetic Plain. Their migration into India seems to have been part of the movement of Indo-European peoples (see map, p. 99) which, in this same period, also produced invasions of Greece and the Aegean and the Italian peninsula.

Some of the earlier inhabitants of India retreated to the south as the Aryans poured in, but others were captured and enslaved or reduced to the status of subject allies of one Aryan tribe that was fighting another. Eventually the Aryans spread southward into a portion of the Deccan. In time, a number of Aryan kingdoms arose, most of which had hereditary rulers.

The Aryan Kingdoms

By the beginning of the sixth century B.C. most of these petty kingdoms were merged into one or another of sixteen larger kingdoms. The rulers of these states commonly sought to make themselves absolute monarchs, but the actual power of the king varied from one state to another. Nearly every one of these kings had to consult a popular assembly and a council of elders, and sometimes the kingship was elective, though the choice was limited to members of the royal family. The Brahmans, or priests of the court (at that time membership in the priesthood was hereditary), also curbed the king's power, for often the Brahmans asserted that they were not under the king's orders but were equal to him. In the northeastern part of India there were even some republics, in which the affairs of government were managed by popular assemblies and councils of elders.

Of the sixteen kingdoms that had emerged by the beginning of the sixth century B.C., one called Magadha, in the southern part of present-day Bihar, had become more powerful than the others. Under a succession of capable rulers in the next two centuries, the authority of Magadha was constantly extended, sometimes by war or diplomacy, sometimes by dynastic marriages. Presently, under a ruler named Chandragupta and under another name (p. 318), this kingdom was to rise to exceptional prominence. In the northwest, no one kingdom grew to large size, and without a strong ruler to organize its defenses, the region of the Punjab became an easy prey to the rising Persian power on the west. Early in the fifth century B.C., the Persian ruler Darius I extended his control into this region, probably as far as the deserts of Rajputana, and made it into one of the provinces of the Persian Empire.

EARLY INDIAN CULTURE AND RELIGION

When Darius the Great invaded the Punjab shortly after 500 B.C. he found there a civilization that was probably equal and perhaps superior to that of his native Persia. In the preceding ten centuries the Aryans had been slowly building a stable and civilized society upon the cultural achievements of their predecessors, much as the Hellenes, their Indo-European kinsmen, had done in Greece. And the patterns of life that they evolved in the course of this process were to endure thereafter through all the centuries down to the present time.

To understand this civilization, you must turn to literature rather than to the records of changes in government and social organization—for change has never been so notable in Indian life as persistence of a traditional way of life, the origins of which are in the early Aryan period. And the Indians have never been so much interested in keeping records of political and social history as in developing a literature concerned with the nature and meaning of life itself.

We must therefore begin with a brief survey of that literature, before we can attempt to understand the ideals that shape and direct Indian life and set the Indian civilization apart from others.

Early Indian Literature

The literature of India in ancient times was created to be spoken or sung, and it was passed down from one generation to the next for centuries before it was written in Vedic, the parent language of Sanskrit. The earliest examples of this literature are poems or hymns that the Aryans sang after they came into northwest India. Later, as the migration spread eastward to new areas, the settlers added new songs, dealing with nature, their problems, their contact with the people whom they found in the area, and their hopes and aspirations. Still later these songs and poems were committed to writing, making up what is known collectively as the Vedic literature.

Vedic Literature. This literature includes the *Veda* (a Vedic word designating sacred lore and meaning, roughly, *knowledge*), the *Brahmanas,* the *Aranyakas,* and the *Upanishads.* The *Veda* is composed of four collections (or *Samhitas*), constituting the canonical books of the Indo-Aryan, and later the Hindu, religion. The first and oldest of these is the *Rig-Veda,* more than 1000 hymns written by the priestly class to accompany early sacrificial rites. The hymns are full of the joy of life, wonder at the beauties of the world, and praise of the gods of nature— Agni, the god of fire, Indra, the god of thunder and rain, Varuna, the god of the universe, Ushas, goddess of dawn, and others. Under the direction of the priests, ceremonies of thanksgiving were held, in which these praises of the gods were sung and animals were sacrificed according to a prescribed ritual. The *Sama-Veda* contains stanzas from the *Rig-Veda* arranged with reference to their place in the sacrificial ceremonies; they were intended to be sung. The *Yajur-Veda* is a collection of sacrificial prayers, some of which come also from the *Rig-Veda,* and its prose passages may be regarded as a manual for the officiating priests. The fourth *Veda, Atharva-Veda,* was written much later. A book of spells and incantations for appeasing and cursing the demon gods, it has been called the religion of the poor.

Each of the *Vedas* had its *Brahmana,* a prose text containing discussions by priests or instruction to their pupils concerning the various sacrificial ceremonies and the ritual to be used. Some of the discussions go into great detail, setting down certain rites that might last for days and nights and that were to be performed exactly as prescribed.

The third basic group in the Vedic literature consists of the *Aranyakas,* or "forest texts." At an early period in Indian history it seems to have been customary for some men to withdraw into the forests to meditate and speculate with kindred souls on the meaning of life and its problems as well as on the nature of the soul and the gods. These devotees did not have the facilities for the elaborate rites prescribed in the *Brahmanas,* but the ideas that came out of their meditation and speculation added new substance to the religious beliefs embodied in this literature.

In the *Upanishads* is to be found the further development of the religious speculation begun in the *Aranyakas.* In them this development becomes a transition from religion to philosophy. The *Upanishads* comprise nearly 200 treatises, dating from the eighth to the fourth centuries B.C., in which the Indian thinkers ponder basic problems: What is life? What is the ultimate self? What is the soul? What is the relationship between the soul of the individual and the soul of the universe? What is mind? What is matter? What is god? And the answers to these questions, which are suggested in the *Upanishads,* are both comprehensive and profound.

Supplementary to these four basic groups of Vedic texts, which Hindus regard as a set of religious "revelations," are other texts of a more technical nature. Written by priests, these give elaborate instructions on a variety of matters relating to the conduct of the rituals. Of special interest are the instructions for the laying out, measuring, and building of places for worship and sacrifice, because these include the earliest Indian writings on mathematics, especially geometry. They discuss, for example, the construction of squares and rectangles and the method of constructing a square equal to a circle or a circle equal to a square. Similarly the concern for the exact words to be used in religious rites gave rise to the study of phonetics, etymology, and grammar. A work written by Panini, who is reputed to have lived in Taxila, probably in the fourth cen-

tury B.C., is the first scientific treatise on grammar anywhere in the world, and it has remained the basis for the study of the grammar of the Sanskrit language.

The Panchatantra. Besides the sacred literature classified as Vedic, there is also a large amount of secular literature dating from this earliest period. Most famous are the tales to be found in the *Panchatantra,* a work translated into more languages than any other book except the Bible. From India, these stories were taken to Persia, thence to Syria and Arabia, and ultimately they passed to Europe. Some of them form the basis of the stories known to the western world as *Aesop's Fables.* Others appear in the tales of the *Arabian Nights,* in Gottfried von Strassburg's *Tristan und Isolde,* in Boccaccio's *Decameron,* and in the writings of Chaucer and Shakespeare. The stories of Jack and the Beanstalk, the Seven-league Boots, and the Magic Mirror have all been traced to Indian sources.

The Mahabharata and the Ramayana. The two pieces of secular literature that are most widely known among the Indian people are the great epics: the *Mahabharata* and the *Ramayana.* They occupy a place in Indian literature comparable to that of the *Iliad* and the *Odyssey* in Greek literature. The *Mahabharata* is much longer than the Greek epics. It was composed between 200 B.C. and A.D. 200 and is probably not the work of a single author but one to which many persons added in the long centuries before it was first written down. It is a tale of warriors in the great (*maha*) Indian war (*bharata*) —the struggle among the various Aryan tribes, which took place perhaps as early as the fourteenth century B.C. to decide the overlordship of northern India. But it is more than a saga of the heroism of warriors, for it includes tales of just kings, sages, dutiful wives, and beautiful ladies—indeed, the whole vast panorama of Indian life during the Vedic Age. It is still recited by professional storytellers who wander through the Indian countryside, by actors and poets, and by parents to their children. It has been translated into all the leading languages of India, and it has become part of the cultural heritage of all the Indian people.

The best-known and best-loved part of the epic is the *"Bhagavad-Gita"* (popularly known simply as the *Gita*), the "Song of the Lord," that Jawaharlal Nehru has called a "poem of crisis, of political and social crisis, and even more so of crisis in the spirit of man." The "Song of the Lord" has also been called the New Testament of India because it has been an ethical and spiritual consolation to generations of Hindus.

The poem is the story of a conversation between the warrior Arjuna and his charioteer, who is really the Lord in disguise. The great war was about to begin, but Arjuna hesitated to take up arms, even though it was his duty as a warrior, because he realized that on the other side were friends and relatives, some of whom would be killed and might even die by his hand. But through the charioteer Krishna, the Lord made answer to him, urging him to rise above these personal considerations and accept his duty—his *dharma.* In the course of their conversation there is revealed a code of ethics that stresses the importance of the spirit or motive behind action, teaches that right action must ultimately produce right results, though perhaps not immediately, and expounds the inevitable relationship between present action and the final purpose of the eternal universe. Near the end, Krishna proclaims "And even that man who shall hear this, full of faith and without malice, he too, being freed from evil, shall attain to the sacred region of those of righteous deeds." *

While the *Mahabharata* deals with men —men who are strong, vigorous, bold, and warlike—the *Ramayana* deals primarily with the love of a faithful wife, Sita, for her husband, Rama, and with the exploits of mythological and superhuman characters in forests inhabited by all sorts of animals and demons. Composed about the second century B.C., it is a shorter, more unified composition than the *Mahabharata,* but it is equally familiar to Indians, and its heroine Sita has been their ideal of womanhood.

The Hindu Religion

Each of these important literary masterpieces illuminates the "Indian way of life." It is from them that we gain what knowledge we have of the development of Indian religion and philosophy.

This religion is known now as Hinduism, but we may more correctly speak of it, in its early days, as a Vedic religion. It arose through a gradual merger of the religious beliefs of the Aryans with those of the people who were in possession of the land when the Aryans made their invasion. The religion that finally emerged was neither Aryan nor non-Aryan but a synthesis of both. Hence Hinduism has no one founder with a role comparable to that of Jesus or Mohammed, no specific beginning date, and no precise statement of its creed. Indeed, a variety of beliefs are embraced in Hinduism rather than a single doctrine, and this diversity is part of the strength of the religion. Hindus believe there is not any single way of attaining spiritual goals, but many ways. And because their religion expresses this conviction, it is not identified with any one race or linguistic group but has pervaded all India.

Nevertheless, there are certain essential ideas that all Hindus accept. First of these is the belief in the existence of *Brahman*— a single, eternal, unchanging essence or soul, which permeates the entire universe. Second is belief in the existence of the *Atman,* which is a part of this universal soul embodied in each individual. Like *Brahman,* of which it is part, *Atman* is eternal. This is a distinctive belief of Hinduism, unlike the belief of Christianity and some other religions that

* Edward J. Thomas, *The Song of the Lord* (London: John Murray, 1931), p. 122.

Brahma. Tenth- or eleventh-century stone statue of the Hindu god of creation and birth, one of the Hindu triad, more abstract and less popular than Vishnu the preserver or Siva the destroyer. (Courtesy of the Metropolitan Museum of Art)

the soul leaves the body at death to receive either an eternal reward or an eternal punishment. In the Hindu view, the soul is not created and cannot die; it can only rejoin the great soul of the universe, from which it has been sent forth like light from the sun.

A third Hindu tenet involves the conceptions of *maya* and *moksha*. Since the welfare of the eternal soul is the supreme consideration in life, it follows that material things are unimportant. If a man attaches importance to them, he is laboring under the illusion that they are important. This illusion is known as *maya*. To escape from this illusion, he must seek deliverance—*moksha*.

The process of gaining deliverance is long and complicated, and if, as often happens, a man dies before his soul has won release, the soul must be reincarnated in another body. Several such successive rebirths may occur before the soul is at last liberated from bondage to flesh and is reunited with the supreme soul of the universe. This is the basis of the Hindu theory of reincarnation, or the transmigration of the soul.

This conception leads to the Hindu belief in *karma*. The word has no exact equivalent in English, though it is sometimes translated as *fate* or *destiny*. Behind it is the belief that the good and bad actions of a man are added up to make a kind of score, which is charged against his soul. If an individual is born into a low status in life, this means that the score reckoned against his soul during its earlier incarnation in another body was unfavorable, and it is the *karma*—fate or destiny—of his soul to endure further suffering. If the man's good actions during this lifetime outweigh his bad actions, the good will accrue to the account of his soul in a future reincarnation. The man's life in the material world will not improve during his time—material improvement is an illusion, because material things are not of true importance—but his deeds will favorably affect his *karma* after his death.

We may note that this teaching makes it impossible for a Hindu to believe, in our sense of the words, that "all men are created equal." For at birth each man is subject to his *karma*, which represents the consequence of deeds in a former incarnation of his soul.

The conception of a single, eternal, universal essence was too profound for the average Hindu to grasp. Consequently, a number of divine beings were recognized, which outsiders sometimes regard as separate deities. The more educated Hindus insist, however, that Hinduism is monotheistic, and that these divine beings are not a group of gods but various manifestations of the one supreme being. Foremost among them are Brahma, the Creator, Vishnu, the Preserver, and Siva, the Destroyer (p. 326). All three are acknowledged by all Hindus, although worship is more often addressed to Vishnu and Siva than to Brahma, since the latter represents the principle of creation, and creation is an occurrence that took place only once, for all time. Numerous other divine manifestations, many of them resembling local or regional deities, are also recognized.

The Caste System

Closely related to Hindu religion and philosophy is the social and economic institution of caste, by which the population is divided among a number of classes.

Caste was unknown in the early days of the Aryans. There were warriors and rulers among them, of course, and hereditary priests who conducted what were then relatively simple ceremonies in praise of the gods, but these two classes were not sharply set apart from the rest of the population, which was composed mainly of peasants. But as the Aryans moved deeper into India and came into closer contact with the peoples who inhabited the land before them, the invaders may have developed social restrictions, to keep themselves separate from the darker skinned individuals who were not of their kind. These restrictions may have contributed to the development of the caste system.

Another circumstance contributing to the origin of castes may have been the development of more complex religious ceremonies, for as time went on, the conviction grew that the gods need not be praised so much as propitiated. Hence more power and responsibility was given to those who knew how to conduct the increasingly complex rituals dedicated to the gods. It was natural, then, for a priestly class to arise, composed of those who devoted their time to the proper study of the rituals and to the spiritual and intellectual training necessary for understanding, developing, and passing on the religious heritage. It was natural, too, for this class to assert its supremacy over all others—even kings and rulers—and to develop rules for keeping out all those who were not properly qualified for admittance to the priestly class.

As the tribes consolidated into small kingdoms and then large ones, it also followed that another small but distinct group would arise, composed of those who devoted their time to government and military affairs. In a religious age these rulers would require the blessing of the priests. In India, for a long time, the priests and the rulers struggled for supreme leadership, but eventually the priests won out.

Other social distinctions also arose as life in the growing kingdoms became more complex, and these distinctions also contributed to the development of castes. The great mass of the people tilled the soil and raised the food, while others distributed it and produced articles for trade. These occupations did not command so great prestige as the vocation of the priests or of rulers and warriors. Nevertheless, they were deemed reputable pursuits, and those who followed them were permitted to participate in the religious ceremonies of initiation, by which they were "born again." These three classes therefore came to be known later as the "twice-born."

But these classes did not take in the whole population. Below them were still those who were not permitted to take part in the initiation ceremonies that distinguished the "twice-born." Originally these were the dark-skinned people whom the Aryans conquered. As time passed, however, the distinction came to be a matter of religion.

Though the origin of castes and the date when they became rigid remain matters largely of surmise, the classes were distinguishable by the beginning of the Christian era. At the top were the *Brahmans*, the priests and teachers; next were the *Kshatriyas*, or rulers and warriors; after them came the *Vaisyas*, including farmers, merchants, and craftsmen; and finally, the *Sudras,* or serfs. At the bottom of the social order were those known as outcastes, untouchables, or —more recently—as members of the "scheduled" castes. They performed the menial, degrading, or unclean tasks.

Hindu religious teachings gave sanction to the social divisions of the caste system. One such sanction came from the teaching that the various castes all sprang from Brahma the Creator but from different portions of his body: the Brahmans from the mouth, the Kshatriyas from the arms, the Vaisyas from the thighs, and the Sudras from the feet. The social distinctions among the castes thus correspond to the relative importance of these parts of the body. The same idea is also expressed in another, subtler Hindu teaching. This holds that an individual combines in his nature three basic qualities: light, passion, and darkness. The proportion of these qualities varies as among individuals but generally corresponds to the distinctions of caste. The members of the higher castes have more of light in their nature, and this permits a fuller expression of the soul, while the members of the lower castes have more of darkness in them, which obscures the soul. Hence the caste system promotes the harmony and well-being of society by assigning to each individual the duties that correspond to the traits which predominate in his nature. Accordingly, each person must accept the responsibilities and perform the duties that are appropriate to his caste. This, we have seen, is the argument presented to Arjuna in the *Bhagavad-Gita.*

Gradually there developed regulations for the behavior of members of each caste, and these rules were often enforced by village councils, as well as by social and religious pressure. The rules became extensive and sometimes determined the most minute details. They defined the occupation that an individual must take up, the circle within which he might marry (ultimately only within his own caste), the group with which he

could associate, what he could and could not eat, where he could and could not go. When caste rules were broken—for instance, when a person of high caste was defiled by the touch of someone belonging to a low caste— certain ceremonies were prescribed for purification. These varied according to the degree of defilement.

Until recently, most Indians accepted the institution of caste as proper and natural. It put emphasis upon duty and obligation, rather than—as we do—upon rights, liberties, and privileges, and it imposed more onerous responsibilities upon the individuals in higher castes than those in the lower. It thus matched social prestige with obligations commensurate with the prestige. Moreover, it guaranteed that specialized skills would be preserved, since members of each caste had to continue the vocations appropriate to their caste, and it provided a constant reminder that each social group depended upon the others. The mouth may be more important than the feet, but a man has need of both; the Brahmans, who issued from the mouth of Brahma, may have a higher rank than the Sudras, who originate from the feet of Brahma, but society has need of both.

Religious Reform

While the Brahmans were organizing and systematizing Hindu religion and philosophy, they were challenged by skepticism. Near the end of the sixth century B.C. there occurred a period of intense questioning by members of the nobility, who were not satisfied with the priesthood, the rituals, and the authority of the *Vedas.* Out of this protest, which was largely transitory, came two reform movements—Jainism and Buddhism —that were to endure. Both originated at about the same time in eastern Hindustan; each had as a leader a member of the *Kshatriya* caste; both developed philosophical systems that retained much of the Hindu tradition—they accepted the idea of *karma* and reincarnation; both stressed the idea of *ahimsa*, nonviolence to any living thing; and both eventually developed into religions, Jainism becoming a separate sect within Hinduism and Buddhism becoming a separate faith.

Jainism. According to tradition, Jainism was originated by a succession of twenty-four saints. The last of these was Mahavira (the Great Hero), who was a wandering teacher for thirty years before his death in about 468 B.C. Mahavira taught that everything is eternal, including matter. To attain *Nirvana*, the release from the body and the restriction of matter, the lay member must pass through nine reincarnations; twelve years of self-denial and discipline suffices for the ascetic. To achieve salvation every person must follow the three-fold path of Right Faith, Right Knowledge, and Right Conduct. Mahavira's message was thus one of asceticism, which was the means of securing the release of the soul from transmigration. His followers, though never becoming a large force, played a significant role in India because of their rigid insistence on preserving life.

Buddhism. The founder of Buddhism was a man of the Gautama clan whose given name was Siddhartha (*c.*563–483 B.C.). In his youth, he lived a sheltered life at his father's home in what is now Nepal. As he reached manhood, he became distressed by the suffering he saw around him, and he began to deplore the inadequacies of the priestly religion. At the age of twenty-nine he left his beautiful wife and infant son to go in search of an answer to the question of how to relieve the sorrows of the world. This departure from home is known as the Great Renunciation.

During the next six years Gautama lived as a wandering ascetic, talking with others whom he met who were seeking spiritual guidance and practicing all kinds of austerities, including fasting. At last, as he was sitting one day under a pipal tree, the answer came to him. This revelation is called the Enlightenment, and thenceforth Gautama became the Buddha, the Enlightened One.

The answer given to Buddha comprises what have come to be known as the "four noble truths." First, suffering is widespread in the world; second, the cause of this suffering is the desire created in men by their craving for material things; third, the individual can free himself from self-seeking and desire; and fourth, the way to freedom from desire lies along the eight-fold path of right views, right resolves, right speech, right action, right living, right effort, right-mindfulness, and right concentration. As in Jainism, the goal is *Nirvana*.

In his teachings he emphasized almsgiving; knowledge; virtue; human charity; *ahimsa*, or nonkilling, even of animals ("let

Tower of Adinatha Temple—from the group of Jain temples at Khajuraho in Vindhya Pradesh, built between A.D. 600 and 1200. (Government of India Press Information Bureau)

them go free"); brotherhood ("the way of salvation is open to all"); and chastity. Although Buddha himself was opposed to monasticism, his disciples formed an order of monks, who wore yellow robes and took the vows of poverty, chastity, and obedience. Their monasteries, often located in the mountains, later appeared wherever Buddhism spread (see illustration, p. 320).

Buddhism remained a small sect, not unlike many others, until the great ruler Asoka (p. 313) was converted. Subsequently it spread widely and took on the form of an organized religion. Its doctrines were defined by a council of Buddhist leaders, and missionaries were sent into all parts of India and Ceylon and also to other countries in Asia.

Eventually Buddhism split into two schools: the *Hinayana* and the *Mahayana*. Those who adhered to the *Hinayana*—the Lesser Vehicle—were the orthodox minority, who held closely to the teachings of the Buddha himself. The larger number that adhered to the *Mahayana*—the Greater Vehicle —introduced a number of modifications into the teachings of Buddha, of the sort that would satisfy the desire of the common people for religious symbols and ritual. In this school Buddha was deified, saints were venerated, rituals were developed, and an elaborate theology and mythology was created. In both forms, Buddhism was a potent force in India in ancient times, originating as a reform movement within Hinduism rather than a rival religion.

THE RISE OF THE FIRST INDIAN EMPIRE

In the two centuries following Darius' conquest of western India, the hold of the Persians gradually weakened and then disappeared. As Persian power declined, a number of practically independent states arose in this region. One of the most important was Taxila, on the eastern side of the upper Indus. Its strategic location, on the main route from Central Asia to the interior of India, enabled its merchants to establish a famous market, while the numerous scholars who assembled in the capital made it renowned as a religious and intellectual center.

Alexander the Great

But before Taxila or any other of the new kingdoms grew strong enough to unite western India under a single rule, the Macedonian conqueror Alexander the Great (p. 149) began his career. After subduing Persia, Alexander determined to annex all the lands to which Persia formerly laid claim. Accordingly, he marched over the Hindu Kush in 327 B.C. and in the following year

crossed the Indus River. After receiving the obeisance of the ruler of Taxila, Alexander pressed on toward the east, intending to invade the Ganges Valley. But his army refused to go farther, and Alexander had to turn back, marching across what is now Baluchistan to Babylon, where he died in 323 B.C.

Alexander's conquest had little permanent influence on India, and no reference to it is found in contemporary Indian literature. For a time Persian or Macedonian governors tried to administer some of the lands in India over which Alexander had established rule, but part of the area was soon reconquered by Chandragupta, an Indian adventurer who emerged at this time as one of the most vigorous of Indian kings.

The Mauryan Dynasty

The kingdom over which Chandragupta (d. *c.*300 B.C.) eventually ruled was built on the ruins of the old kingdom of Magadha, the most important of the sixteen Aryan kingdoms that had arisen in northern India in the sixth century B.C. Like the others, Magadha had subsequently passed into decline, and about 320 B.C. Chandragupta marched eastward, deposed the ruling dynasty, and made himself king, establishing the new Mauryan dynasty which was to last about 150 years. After expelling Alexander's garrisons from northwestern India, he soundly defeated an invasion by Seleucus I in 303 B.C.

Asoka. Presently this dynasty brought forth a ruler who was to become one of the outstanding leaders in all Indian history. This was Asoka, who ruled from c.269 to c.232 B.C. The first half of his reign was not unlike that of other great conquerors. It saw the extension of Mauryan rule from its capital at Pataliputra (now Patna) over nearly the whole of the territory now comprising India and Pakistan, excluding the southern part of the Deccan but including Afghanistan.

However, Asoka's reputation does not rest solely upon his career as an empire-builder, for, while pressing his wars of conquest, he became appalled by the bloodshed and determined to proceed by a new method: "conquest by piety." Instead of dominating his people, he would instruct them in morality. Accordingly, he caused moral precepts to be carved on stone pillars in various parts of the country, ordered his officials to teach these principles to the people, and periodically toured the country to see what progress was being made. He himself became a deeply devout convert to Buddhism, aided in its propagation in India, and caused Buddhist missions to be sent to Ceylon and to southeastern Asia. Though he remained tolerant of Brahmanism, his patronage of Buddhism gave such aid to this religious movement that it became one of the principal faiths of the world.

The labor that Asoka spent in support of Buddhism proved of more lasting influence than his successes as a conqueror. The great empire that he built, uniting virtually all India for the first time under a single government, began to disintegrate soon after his death. Its breakup was hastened by attacks from the outside, especially those of the Kushans, an aggressive people from Central Asia, who poured into northwestern India about 100 B.C. and maintained an empire there from about A.D. 40 to 220. In the south the Andhra empire arose between the Godavari and Kistna rivers, gradually pushing northward and westward. It came to an end about A.D. 235 (maps, pp. 214–215, 294–295) . These two empires carried on a vigorous trade with the outside world. Roman and Indian records, as well as a large collection of Roman gold and silver coins found in north and south India, attest to the importance of Indian trade with settlements along the Persian Gulf, as far as the Red Sea, and even with Rome. At the same time Indian merchants were pushing north into Central Asia, eastward through Burma to China, and into areas of Southeast Asia that later were to develop into a number of Indian colonies (see pp. 325–328).

The Flowering of Indian Art

We know virtually nothing of art in India until the time when Buddhism made its appearance. The people of Mohenjo-Daro and

Asoka's Empire

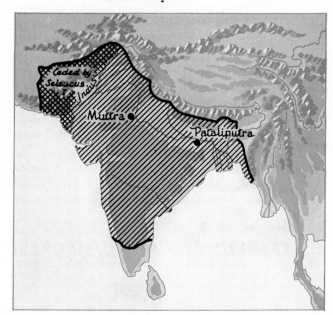

Harappa had a well-developed artistic sense and technical ability, as you can see from the photographs of some of the remains of their workmanship that have been brought to light. But nothing has been found to indicate that there was any art in India for 2000 years after the disappearance of the society represented by the ruins at Mohenjo-Daro and Harappa. We have reason to believe that work was done in art during this time, but none of it has survived.

At any event, we have numerous examples of art dating from the time of Asoka. Outstanding among them are the stone pillars on which Asoka caused his rescripts to be carved, and the buildings known as *stupas,* usually hemispherical, which the Buddhists used as shrines. The pillars, some of which are still standing, are impressive feats of engineering. The pillar itself, usually about 40 feet in height, was made of a single piece of stone, and much skill must have gone into the cutting and polishing of such huge columns. The capital, also made of one stone, displays ornamental carving, and commonly this includes the representation of an inverted lotus. This suggests a Persian or Greek influence, which may have been introduced by the Greeks and Persians who visited Asoka's court. One of these capitals depicted four lions (p. 296), which are outstanding for their detailed perfection and today are the symbol of the new Republic of India.

Asoka was an assiduous builder of *stupas* —he is supposed to have put up 84,000 of them. Most of these have disappeared, but other rulers after him continued the custom of building such shrines. In them were kept relics of Buddha or the Buddhist saints and pictures representing scenes in the life of Buddha. In these pictures, symbols were used, because Buddha was never shown as a person. The lotus flower stood for his birth, the pipal or bodhi tree for his conversion, the wheel of the law for his first sermon, while the stupa itself symbolized his death.

During the first three centuries of the Christian era, a notable center of art developed at Muttra (Mathura), a crossroads of trade southeast of modern Delhi. The sculpture that has survived from this center shows a more standardized use of religious symbols, and also a new method of depicting scenes in relief on a series of panels, rather than just one. These scenes reveal a sensual realism, very close to the spirit of the common man.

One of the most interesting schools of art in the post-Mauryan period was that known as the Gandharan, which arose in northwest India. This shows a considerable Greco-Roman influence and an unprecedented degree of realism. Even the figure of Buddha is represented, for in the north the Buddhists were mostly of the *Mahayana* school, which did not scruple at concessions to the literal-mindedness of the humble worshiper wishing to visualize Buddha and revere him as a god. From this school comes the conventionalized figure of Buddha seated in the posture of a Yogi (p. 9). The figure of the Buddhist Yogi is seen everywhere in Asia that Buddhism is found and is "as purely monumental art as that of the Egyptian Pyramids." It represents "the greatest ideal which Indian sculpture ever attempted to express."

Conclusion

By the end of the third century before the Christian era, then—about the time of Rome's second Carthaginian war—there had arisen a civilization of great brilliance in the subcontinent of India. In its economic, social, and political life, in its religion, in its art, and in its literature, this Indian civilization differed substantially from those that had appeared in the lands about the Mediterranean. Yet, in all these aspects, this civilization, at the time, say, of the great Asoka, was no less brilliant, no less significant in the broad history of human progress than they.

Suggestions for Further Reading

Source Materials

Anthologies and Collected Documents

C. H. Hamilton, ed., *Buddhism, A Religion of Infinite Compassion: Selections from Buddhist Literature* (New York, 1952).
Selections from Buddhist Scriptures, including commentaries by Hsüan-tsang and other Chinese writers. Contains, also, a condensed history of Buddhism and a bibliography of sources and secondary works.

Lin Yutang, *The Wisdom of China and India* (New York, 1942), pp. 3–564.
A fine collection of ancient Indian writings—from the *Rig-Veda*, the *Upanishads*, the *Ramayana, Panchatantra,* and the Buddhistic writings.

E. J. Thomas, *Early Buddhist Scriptures* (London, 1935).
Selections from important Buddhist documents.

R. Warnock and G. K. Anderson, eds., *The World in Literature* (Chicago, 1950–1951), Volume I, pp. 27–40.
Selections from the Vedic hymns (the *Rig-Veda*), the *Upanishads,* and the *Mahabharata.*

Contemporary Writings

The Bhagavad-Gita; translated by F. Edgerton (Cambridge, Mass., 1944).

The Ramayana and Mahabharata; translated by R. C. Dutt (London, 1910).
Versions of the two great epics of India.

The Song of God: Bhagavad-Gita, translated by S. Prabhavananda and C. Isherwood (New York, 1954).
An easily accessible translation. (A Mentor paper-back.)

Secondary Works

L. Barnett, ed., "Buddhism," *Life,* March 7, 1955; "Hinduism," *Life,* February 7, 1955.
Readable descriptions.

Cambridge History of India (New York, 1922), Volume I.
A standard reference work.

G. T. Garratt, ed., *The Legacy of India* (Oxford, 1937).
An excellent composite work on many aspects of Indian intellectual life.

G. S. Ghurye, *Caste and Race in India* (New York, 1932).
This volume with that by J. H. Hutton contains adequate descriptions of caste and its place in Indian society.

R. Grousset, *Civilizations of the East: India* (New York, 1931).
This book by the well-known French scholar deals primarily with works of art.

J. H. Hutton, *Caste in India: Its Nature, Function and Origins* (New York, 1947). See Ghurye above.

R. G. Majumdar, ed., *History and Culture of the Indian People* (London and Bombay, 1951).
Volume I of this new series on Indian history is *The Vedic Age;* Volume II is *The Age of Imperial Unity.*
Volume I of a new series on Indian history.

A. Mookerjee, *Art of India* (Calcutta, 1952).
An excellent collection, with some color illustrations, of outstanding works of Indian art.

K. W. Morgan, ed., *The Religion of the Hindus* (New York, 1953).
Written by six prominent Indians especially for non-Indian readers, this is the best single volume on the subject. Contains selections from basic sacred scriptures.

S. Piggott, *Prehistoric India* (Harmondsworth, England, 1950).
An easily available volume by a well-known British archaeologist. (A Penguin Book.)

S. Radhakrishnan, *The Hindu View of Life* (London, 1927); *The Philosophy of the Upanishads* (rev. ed., London, 1935).
These two authoritative works are by India's vice president.

Hugh G. Rawlinson, *India, A Short Cultural History* (New York, 1938).
A standard short history.

V. A. Smith, *Asoka, the Buddhist Emperor of India* (3d ed., Oxford, England, 1920).
The best biography of the great Mauryan ruler.

13

India's Golden Age

Standing Buddha—Gupta metal figure, c.500. With the increasing refinement of clear-cut shapes, the features of Buddha were established once and for all and had become stereotyped by the end of the sixth century. See page 9. (Courtesy of Museum of Fine Arts, Boston)

During the ancient period of its history, India had achieved a remarkable degree of cultural unity, but, except during the brief span of the Mauryan dynasty, it had not succeeded in welding the various kingdoms of the country into a political whole. India remained a collection of small states with ever-changing boundaries, some governed by their own rulers, others under the control of invading groups.

Although each of the invaders had added new racial strains to the population and new elements to the culture, the essential features of Indian life remained the same. Buddhism continued to be enriched by religious leaders, sculptors, and architects. At the same time, and despite the challenge of this newer religious movement, Hinduism continued to flourish and the class system became more rigid. Artists and artisans developed their native traditions, and merchants expanded their commerce.

In the second great period of Indian history, lasting from the second to the sixteenth century A.D., the historian is on firmer ground than previously in his attempts to reconstruct the story of the past. Not only are the sources more numerous, but they are more varied, and one account can be checked against another. The written records are of several kinds—religious literature, particularly new commentaries on the basic Hindu teachings; literary works produced by Buddhist monks; and dynastic histories and the accounts of the reigns of specific rulers. After the rise and spread of Islam, general Islamic histories included part of India and there also appeared a collection of Indian dramas that shed light on customs and ideas of the times. Finally, numerous inscriptions found on rocks, on gold, silver and copper plates, and in Indian temples provide descriptions of the government and of the life of villages and towns.

Accounts written by foreign visitors are extremely valuable for this period. Especially noteworthy are the writings of several Chinese Buddhist scholars, the most famous of whom were Fa-hsien, a careful observer who traveled extensively in India from A.D. 400 to 410, and Hsüan-tsang, who made a pilgrimage to scholarly centers in India between 629 and 645. In the eleventh century an Arab from Central Asia, Alberuni, who was a student of Greek philosophy, lived for some years in India, studying Sanskrit and

Indian philosophy, science, and the arts. These travelers wrote accounts of their visits that provide the only records for some events in Indian history. There were also a number of studies by Persians, Greeks, and Arabs of Indian astronomy and mathematics. Marco Polo described some of the cities of south India, which he visited late in the thirteenth century. Even before the great age of the explorers, some other Europeans, such as the Italian Niccolò dei Conti, visited parts of India and wrote accounts of their experiences.

Archaeological discoveries add further evidence. Among these are caves in several parts of the Deccan and the ruins of palaces, government buildings, temples, and universities that are to be found throughout India and in former Indian colonies elsewhere in Southeast Asia. Some of India's monuments from this period remain virtually intact, requiring little archaeological interpretation.

Yet there is a regrettable want of works by capable historians, written in this period. In China great scholars devoted their lives to the study and writing of history and the collection and editing of documents, for history was regarded as an intellectual pursuit of primary importance and necessary to the state. In India intellectuals concentrated their attention on the formulation, interpretation, and exposition of religious and philosophical ideas. Their efforts produced valuable works, expressing profound thoughts, but because of their lack of interest in history, little attention was given to keeping a chronicle of events in their time.

In terms of political development, the period from the second to the sixteenth century A.D. may be divided into two parts: the first lasting until the coming of the Moslems early in the twelfth century, and the second covering the period of Moslem rule until the country was overrun by new Islamic invaders —the Moguls. In the earlier of these two eras India was not united for any appreciable length of time except in the fourth and fifth centuries, under a dynasty known as the Gupta, and for a single reign—that of Harsha Siladitya—in the seventh century. For the most part, therefore, the political history of India in this era is a story of disunity, with one or another of the various states rising to prominence for a time, only to pass into decline while another state attained a short-lived vigor. From time to time new invaders added to the political disorder.

THE SECOND INDIAN EMPIRE

The Gupta Dynasty

The Gupta dynasty began its rise in one of the princely states that emerged in northern India after the breakup of Asoka's Empire. This dynasty was founded in A.D. 320 by a ruler who bore the same name—Chandragupta—as the ruler who was the founder of the earlier Mauryan Empire. The three most important rulers of the Gupta dynasty were this Chandragupta, who was its founder; his son Samudragupta (c.330–c.380); and his grandson Chandragupta II (c.380–c.412). By a three-fold policy of conquest, diplomacy, and skillfully arranged marriages, these three successive rulers accomplished the remarkable feat of uniting north India under native Indian rule.

Their empire extended over the Indo-Gangetic Plain as far south as the Narbada River, from the mouth of the Ganges to the tributaries of the Indus—though not including the valley of the Indus itself. South of the Narbada, the Gupta kings did not conquer, but by a shrewd policy of negotiation, they drew most of the rulers of the kingdoms in the Deccan and the ruler of Ceylon into a sort of vassal relationship. They may also have established a similar relationship with the Hindu kingdoms outside India in southern Sumatra, Java, Cambodia, and elsewhere in Southeast Asia (pp. 325–328).

The Indian State of the Guptas

Their empire was well governed. The succession to the throne was usually hereditary, though sometimes the king appointed his heir. The empire was divided into provinces and put under governors, usually princes, who were appointed by the king. These provinces were subdivided into districts, each ruled in part by subordinates of the governor and in part by representatives of the king. Each village had a headman, who worked closely with royal officials. In some villages there were assemblies comprising the whole adult population, while in others control of the village was in the hands of Brahmans and other local leaders. Committees in each village dealt with business relating to temples, holidays and festivals, and the administration of justice.

The main source of the government's revenue was the king's share—usually about one sixth—of all the produce of the kingdom. There were also other imposts levied on the rural population, regular charges on ports and ferries, and customs duties. In times of stress and danger, special taxes were levied. Most of these taxes were paid in kind.

To reinforce their power, the Gupta rulers made use of the theory of the divine right of kings. This theory was received with some skepticism, but generally the Guptas succeeded in gaining the good will of the populace, because the kings strove to give good government that would satisfy the needs of the whole community.

In seeking to establish their rule over the whole of India, the Guptas were not concerned merely to increase their own power. Their greater purpose was to free India from the almost constant fear of foreign invasions, which in the past had often threatened to overwhelm the entire country. They wished to make India strong within, so that it would be safe against enemies from without. Hence they encouraged what might today be called a cultural nationalism. As part of their design they gave their support to the traditional Hindu religion, which had begun to lose ground under the Mauryas, who had been patrons of Buddhism. Under the Guptas, consequently, Hinduism began a "rebirth."

But the Guptas were not religious bigots. On the contrary, toleration was their keyword. Though they showed a preference for Hinduism, they encouraged the free discussion of religion among all faiths, and they chose their officials without regard to religious qualifications. Likewise, scholars and artists of all religious persuasions were given royal favor, if they emphasized Indian themes in their work.

As a result of strong government, wise policy, and good administration, the Gupta period saw a marked economic prosperity. This prosperity, together with imperial patronage, helped make possible the flowering of what has been described as the Classical, or Golden, Age of Indian thought, literature, architecture, sculpture, and painting. The achievements of the Guptas in India were comparable to those of the Periclean Age in Greece.

After the death of Chandragupta II about 412, his successors proved unequal to the task of holding their possessions together. Dissension arose as conquered kingdoms began to reassert their independence. More-

The Gupta Empire

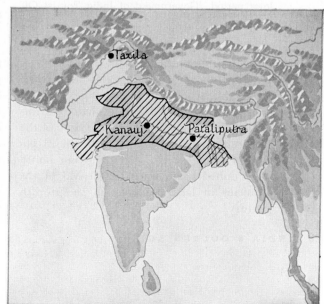

Harsha Siladitya—A Gupta Successor

Entrance to Cave I at Ajanta. The twenty-nine caves at Ajanta are Buddhist shrines and monasteries hewn in a rock cliff. Seven were built between the second century B.C. and the second century A.D., and the others were completed by the early seventh century. Cave I belongs to the later period. (Government of India Tourist Office)

over new invaders—the Huns—began to attack India from the northwest. Their repeated onslaughts, coming at a time when the authority of the Gupta rulers was already weakening, led to the virtual extinction of the Gupta Empire by the close of the fifth century. Subsequently, with the exception of a single reign, India was not politically united again until the arrival of the Moslems in large numbers in the twelfth century.

The one reign that was the exception was that of Harsha Siladitya. In 606 this ambitious ruler came to the throne of a small kingdom on the upper reaches of the Jumna River, north of Delhi. Within six years he forced most of the independent rulers in the lands of the former Gupta Empire to recognize him as their overlord. Thus he restored a unified rule in the area north of the Narbada River. But when he tried to push south of the Narbada into the Deccan, he met with a disastrous defeat and had to abandon the attempt.

More sympathetic to Buddhism than the Guptas had been, Harsha encouraged the building of Buddhist temples and helped support the Buddhist priesthood. He also patronized literature and the arts; and, perhaps in emulation of the great Asoka, he established charitable foundations for the relief of the poor and forbade the slaughtering of animals for food. His fame was widespread. He exchanged embassies with China, and he gave his daughter in marriage to a rising ruler of Tibet, who is believed to have introduced Buddhism to that land. Harsha is generally regarded as one of the great rulers of India, ranking with Asoka, Chandragupta II of the Gupta dynasty, and Akbar, whose reign came much later.

However, the government of Harsha was primarily an expression of the vigor of the ruler himself, not the work of an administrative system that could continue even under a weak king. When Harsha died in 647 and his forceful guidance was gone, the disruptive tendencies again prevailed. The empire that he had built disintegrated into its component parts, and once more we find the old pattern of numerous independent kingdoms, each struggling to maintain itself against its rivals, forming alliances and counteralliances, enlarging its boundaries for a time, only to give up its new territories as soon as another kingdom rose to an equally short-lived ascendancy.

THE NEW ERA OF INVASIONS

The Huns

During the centuries of political disunity India remained vulnerable to invasion, especially in the northwest. The first of several successive invading groups were the Huns, a people from Central Asia, apparently related to barbarians who were known to the Chinese as the Hsiung-nu and to the west, later, as the Mongols.

The Huns began to invade India in the fifth century, at about the same time that others of them were pouring into Europe to beset the declining Roman Empire. For a time the Guptas checked their advance into India, but when the Gupta dynasty disintegrated, the Huns were free to ravage northern India as they pleased. They destroyed many Buddhist and Hindu monuments and the great university city of Taxila, in what has been described as the greatest single blow that Indian civilization has ever suffered. Their depredations came to an end after the middle of the sixth century, when they settled down and eventually merged with the mass of the Indian population.

The Rajputs

The Rajputs, who have given their name to the area of India known as Rajputana, made their appearance near the end of the period of the Gupta dynasty. They may have been refugees fleeing before the Huns, but little is known of their origin. A sturdy and brave warrior people, they were soon absorbed into the Hindu caste of *Kshatriyas,* or warriors. They became intensely proud of their Hinduism and helped defend their new homeland against later invaders.

A clannish people, the Rajputs had no tradition of a great empire of their own, nor did they seek to resuscitate the Gupta Empire and make themselves masters of it. But their clans took over many of the small kingdoms that had arisen with the breakup of the Gupta Empire, and from the middle of the seventh to nearly the end of the twelfth century, much of northern and western India was under Rajput rule. These Rajput kingdoms provided a bulwark against the Moslems, whose empire soon spread eastward to the borders of India.

The Moslems

Moslem Arabs began in the seventh century to make raids on seacoast towns of western India, and in 712 an expedition of Arabs from present-day Iraq landed in Sind and established a base near the mouth of the Indus. From there they pushed northward and eastward until their advance was stopped by the natural barrier of the deserts and by the resistance of various Indian rulers. But what the Moslems gained, they held, and thus Sind became the seat of a new Moslem state in India under Arab rule.

In this state the Moslems at first sought to force the Hindus to adopt the new religion. But Hinduism proved too strong to be wiped out, and the Moslems soon had to modify their policy to one of toleration, allowing

Islamic Invasions of India

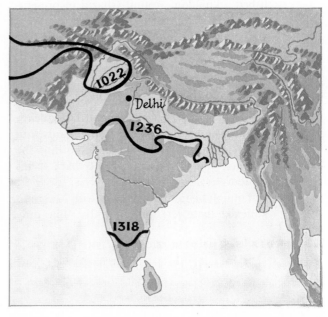

Hindu temples to stand and granting the Hindus the same right to maintain their own worship that was accorded in the west to Christians and Jews. In criminal cases the Arabs enforced Islamic law even upon non-Moslems, but in civil cases the Indians were permitted to settle disputes among themselves according to their own legal customs. Eventually, as the power of the caliph in the west declined and controversies arose between the rival Sunna and Shia, the Moslem state in Sind broke up into a number of petty kingdoms. After the ninth century it was cut off from the caliphate at Baghdad, and thereafter it remained an isolated Moslem outpost until the thirteenth century, when it was submerged in the course of a later Moslem invasion.

These early Arab settlements in Sind had virtually no influence on the rest of India. The Arabs were primarily interested in trade between India and the Moslem lands to the west. But from their contact with the Hindus in the course of their commercial dealings, the Arabs learned much in the fields of mathematics, medicine, and astronomy, and what they learned they passed on to the rest of the Moslem world. Thus the intellectual life of Baghdad was greatly enriched by the first Moslem penetration into India.

India's next experience with the Moslems came at the close of the tenth century. A short time before, a group of Turks had swept south from Central Asia and established a kingdom around Ghazni in present-day Afghanistan. In 998 the rule of this kingdom passed to Mahmud, who induced the caliph of Baghdad to recognize him as a sovereign. Two years later, angered at the behavior of some neighboring Indian rulers, Mahmud led a plundering expedition into northern India. Thereafter until his death in 1030, he made numerous other raids into India, devastating the land, despoiling the temples, and taking much booty back to his capital.

Though he raided almost at will, Mahmud annexed little territory in India. The only lands that he acquired were a Hindu kingdom in the extreme northwest and some small sections of the Punjab—areas that made secure his avenues of approach. His success was the result of his own vigor as a military leader. His successors never showed equal prowess, spending their strength in struggles among themselves and making no further encroachments upon India.

The next Moslem threat came from the state of Ghor, near the center of what is now Afghanistan. Under skillful and determined leadership, this state rose to prominence in the last quarter of the twelfth century. After 1190 the ruler of Ghor began a new attack upon India, which differed from the earlier raids in that this invasion involved a larger number of people, and that the invaders had the intention of settling in India, not simply making a raid and returning home with booty. Gaining strength from their avarice and religious zeal and benefiting from the rivalries among the Hindu states, which were unwilling to cooperate for their common defense, the newcomers had succeeded by 1200 in gaining control of most of northern India.

Once the conquest was assured, the ruler of Ghor, whose name was Muhammad, returned to his native kingdom, leaving one of his slaves behind as his lieutenant in India. In 1206 the successor to Muhammad recognized this lieutenant, once a slave, as Sultan of India. Subsequently, when Ghor was overrun by the Mongols, this sultanate, with its seat at Delhi, became independent. Thus was established what has come to be known as the Delhi sultanate, or the "slave" dynasty.

In time the Delhi sultanate established its rule over virtually all India. The original "slave" dynasty was eventually succeeded by a second, then a third Moslem dynasty. But in 1388 the Delhi sultanate at last collapsed, and a period of disorder ensued, lasting about sixty years, although local rulers continued at Delhi until the Mogul conquest in 1526 (see Chapter 36).

Tamerlane

The outstanding event in this period of chaos was the sack of Delhi in 1398 by the Turko-Mongol leader Tamerlane, who claimed to be a descendant of Genghis Khan. He is reported to have killed 100,000 captives in cold blood even before entering Delhi. He and his soldiers sacked the city, massacred a large number of its inhabitants, and took most of the artisans captive, transporting them to his capital, Samarkand, where their talents and labor were used to beautify the city. As he returned, he pillaged other Indian cities and ruthlessly destroyed all armies that tried to oppose him. He brought to India more suffering in a single invasion than any conqueror before him.

The Leading Kingdoms

A congeries of small kingdoms thus remained characteristic of Indian political life. In the early sixteenth century the foremost of these kingdoms in northern India were Bengal, Malwa, Gujarat, and Kashmir. Even when the Delhi sultanate was at the peak of its power, Bengal was able to maintain a considerable measure of political independence because of the distance that separated it from the capital. Malwa, in the area north of the central Vindhya Mountains, established its autonomy after 1401. Gujarat, in the area around the Gulf of Cambay, was well situated to develop trade. The Hindu state of Kashmir, in the north, came under the domination of a Moslem adventurer, though the state remained independent of Delhi. One of its fifteenth-century rulers is said to have forced Islam on his subjects.

South of the Kistna River, a Hindu kingdom, Vijayanagar, arose early in the fourteenth century. At its height it included all the territory south of the river to the tip of the peninsula, and its capital, which bore the same name as the kingdom, excited the wonder of foreign travelers. One of its kings, Krishnadeva Raya (1509–1530), ranks among the most brilliant rulers in all of Indian history. He was an able military leader, who treated his enemies with leniency and respect; he was interested in the economic prosperity of his state; and he encouraged art and literature. Gifted with an active and inquisitive mind, he was a scholar in his own right, and his personal life was pure and dignified. Krishnadeva Raya was praised alike by contemporary Indian writers and foreign visitors.

After the death of this great ruler, the kingdom of Vijayanagar entered into decline. In 1565 its capital was captured and sacked by a coalition of the Moslem kingdoms of the Deccan. The destruction, which went on for five months, was frightful, and every soldier in the invading army is said to have become rich.

What is most notable about Vijayanagar is that it was a *Hindu* kingdom during a period when almost all India was under Moslem control. Though other religions were tolerated, Hinduism was favored by the rulers, and for three centuries this state provided a refuge for the native Indian religion against the engulfing forces of Islam. But the kingdom never recovered from the invasion of 1565, and finally it, too, succumbed to the assaults of the Moguls.

Until the advent of the Moslems the Hindu civilization proved capable of absorbing those invaders who took advantage of the political weakness of India. The Moslems, however, resisted this assimilation. Though they eventually intermarried with the inhabitants, so that no separate racial stock of Moslem origin has endured in India, the Moslems clung fiercely to their own religion, which they have always regarded as superior to Hinduism. Consequently they have remained a separate religious community, with a culture of its own, distinct from that of the Hindus.

The influence of the Moslem invaders upon the Hindus was mainly destructive. Their invasions involved much bloodshed and hardship for the common man and led to the destruction of many of the great architectural monuments of the Hindus, which the Moslems detested as the shrines of idols and infidel gods. Nor were the Moslems able, even as conquerors, to provide the political unity that the Hindus had failed to achieve for themselves. As alien rulers, clinging to an alien religion and imposing heavy and discriminatory taxes upon the Hindus under their dominion, the Moslems could hardly have won the loyalty of the native population. And before long the Moslems themselves became victims of the ancient tradition of local political rivalries and a repugnance to government from a far-off capital.

Such was the political picture at the end of the fifteenth and the beginning of the sixteenth century, when two new sets of invaders were knocking at the doors of India—the Moguls, or Mongols, coming by land, the Portuguese coming by sea.

THE DIFFUSION OF INDIAN CIVILIZATION

The economic development of India in the first fifteen centuries of the Christian era was not largely affected by its political vicissitudes. Small farmers made up the mass of the population, and they were much more concerned with the problem of making a living than with questions of politics. No matter what government held power, they were obliged to pay taxes, but until the time of the Moslem invasions these taxes were not heavy. Under the Moslems the taxes were increased, especially in periods when punitive levies were imposed upon non-Moslems. Yet enough was left to the peasants to meet their simple wants, and despite the repeated pillage of the cities, the wealthier classes of Indians among the townsmen continued to prosper.

Industry and Commerce

Trade, both domestic and foreign, was extensive. Exports included foodstuffs, drugs and perfumes, ivory, jewelry, gold—though little silver—cutlery and armor, textiles (including silk, muslins, and brocades), and rugs.

Indian artisans were especially skilled in metallurgy. A striking evidence of this is a famous iron pillar, erected near Delhi in the fourth century A.D. This pillar, 24 feet tall and weighing about six tons, is made of a pure, rustless, malleable iron. It still stands, and after exposure to the weather for fifteen centuries, it still shows no sign of rust. A large statue of cast copper, seven feet high, is known to have been erected at the same time.

The principal imports were gold and silver, presumably sent in payment for the goods that India exported. As early as the first century A.D., the Roman writer Pliny the younger complained of the amount of precious metals sent to India in payment for luxury goods purchased in Italy. Most of the foreign trade centered at first in the seacoast towns of southern India. Later, however, in the period of the Moslem invasions, the northern kingdoms of Bengal and Gujarat gained prominence in the manufacture and export of textiles.

Indian traders not only exported their own manufactured goods, but also acted as middlemen in trade with southeastern Asia—Indochina, the Malay Peninsula, and nearby island kingdoms. From this region, Indian traders obtained spices, some of which they brought back to India to satisfy the demands of their own market, and some of which they shipped on to markets further west. This trade had much more than an economic importance, for it led to the spread of Hindu culture and the establishment of Indian colonies all through the regions of Southeast Asia.

Colonial Expansion in Indonesia

The migration of Indians into the islands of Indonesia may have started as early as A.D. 100, and it continued for the next seven centuries. The number of these settlers was never large in comparison with the population of the islands. But the newcomers were mostly merchants, who, intermarrying with the local population, came to form the nucleus of an upper class comprising Hindus and Hinduized Indonesians.

Srivijaya. Gradually a number of these Hindu colonies merged to become kingdoms. By the fourth century one of these Hindu kingdoms, Srivijaya, had gained ascendancy in southern Sumatra. Other Hindu kingdoms arose in central and west Java, and there were also several Hindu settlements in east Java.

In the eighth century a new dynasty—the Sailendra—assumed rule in Srivijaya. Probably this dynasty represented a new group of immigrants, coming from Bengal. The Sailendras were great builders, and one of their works—an impressive Buddhist monument known as Borobudur—still stands. It consists of a series of terraces, with floors and walls of stone. On the walls of the rectangular lower terraces are a series of elaborate sculptures, comprising about 1400 figures in relief, which depict the story of Buddha in his earlier lives, the Great Renunciation, the Enlightenment, and his teaching. Also carved in the stone are realistic conceptions of hell and the suffering in store for those who are not saved. On the circular upper terraces, there are only statues of the Buddha, some 400 in number, each in a pose of serene meditation, each protected by an open stupa. For grandeur of conception and skill of execution Borobudur is not matched anywhere in India.

Under the Sailendra rulers, the Srivijayan kingdom spread its influence northward from Sumatra to Malaya. In the ninth century a prince of this family gained the rule in Cambodia, in the southern part of what is now Indochina, and united several independent Hindu colonies into a single kingdom. Eventually the Sailendras extended their influence as far as southern India and Ceylon. Their kingdom reached its height in the twelfth century, when it controlled trade from the Strait of Malacca to Formosa and established colonies in Borneo, Celebes, the Moluccas, and the Philippines. But by the end of this century the task of administering its far-flung domains became too difficult, and a decline set in.

Majapahit. Meantime, the separate colonies in eastern Java were coalescing into a new Hindu kingdom—Majapahit—which by the fourteenth century spread over the entire island. Thereafter, bringing to an end the kingdom of Srivijaya, it gained control of Sumatra, southern Malaya, and most of the Philippines. Its capital, bearing the same name as the kingdom, became famous and prosper-

The Iron Pillar at Delhi. The shaft is about sixteen inches in diameter, and the purity of the iron (99.97 percent) accounts for the absence of rust. (Government of India, Press Information Bureau)

Dancing Siva—south India, bronze sculpture, tenth century. Siva is shown here in the dance of the universe through which he creates good and crushes evil, represented by the dwarf under his foot. (Government of India Information Services)

ous. The rulers took much profit from trade, for they levied taxes on produce, which were paid in kind, and the king thus gained a large supply of goods that could be sold to outsiders. Though Hinduism was the religion of the king and the upper class, it took deep root only on the island of Bali, and Buddhism, which was tolerated, became the predominant religion in Java.

The beginning of the end of Majapahit came when, at the death of a strong ruler, the kingdom was divided between his two sons. This gave the signal for other kingdoms to break away. The wars among them made the island easy prey for the Arabs, who were arriving in numbers all during the

fifteenth century. By the beginning of the sixteenth century, Majapahit had ceased to exist.

Thus the Indian period in Indonesia lasted from about the first or second century to the sixteenth. It had seen the introduction into the islands of Indian political organization, art and architecture, the two religions —Hinduism and Buddhism—and Indian language and literature. The caste system was also introduced, but it never became so rigid as in India, for there was much intermingling and intermarriage, and there were no outcastes. For official purposes, Sanskrit was important, but the local languages were never eliminated, and in the course of time a Javanese language known as Kawi spread through eastern Java and Bali. Much Indian literature was translated into Javanese, with additions that gave it a Javanese character. This is an instance of a tendency that gradually became pronounced—the adaptation of Indian culture to local influences, producing a culture best called Hindu-Indonesian.

Southeast Asia. At about the same time that the earliest Hindu colonies were established in Indonesia, others were appearing in the area that includes present-day Burma, Thailand, and Indochina. The Indian settlers did much to raise the cultural level of the primitive peoples who inhabited the region. Written language was introduced, and so was the Buddhist religion. In the eleventh century an Indian-influenced state, with its seat near where the city of Mandalay now stands, controlled much of southern Burma. Pagan, the capital, was a beautiful city, with many temples and buildings patterned after the architectural monuments of southern India. The Pagan kingdom remained strong until it was broken up as a result of attacks by the Mongols in the thirteenth century.

Farther to the east, in Thailand, the Indian commercial colonies coalesced into two weak kingdoms, one along the lower part of the Menam River, the other inland, up the river. To these colonies, too, the Indian settlers brought the cultural patterns of their homeland, which they passed on to the less-advanced population. In the eleventh century the lower kingdom was conquered by Cambodia, a kingdom lying to the east. In the thirteenth century the inland settlement was overrun by the Thais, who had been pushed out of southwestern China by the invading Mongols. Eventually the Thais were converted to *Hinayana* Buddhism, which still remains the prevailing religion of Thailand, as of Burma.

The third century B.C. saw the arrival of the first Indian traders in Cambodia, and by the second century A.D., several Indian colonies or small kingdoms had developed. In the ninth century these were organized into a single kingdom under the guidance of representatives of the Srivijayan kingdom of Sumatra. As elsewhere, the language, literature, and religion of India were introduced. Though the *Hinayana* form of Buddhism was tolerated, the predominant religion was Hinduism, with special emphasis on the worship of Siva (p. 326).

Early in the tenth century the rulers of Cambodia built a magnificent capital city— Angkor Thom, which remains an impressive sight, even though now in ruins. The city was five miles square and probably had a population of 1,000,000. A temple stood in the center, crowned with a four-faced statue of Siva, with one face looking toward each of the cardinal directions. The massive faces were formed of blocks of stone, fitted into place without mortar. There were also stone statues of Brahma and Vishnu. In the middle of each of the four walls that enclosed the city was a large entrance, the approaches flanked by huge seven-headed stone snakes over 100 feet long.

A few miles away was the great temple, Angkor Vat, which is still one of the most impressive monuments to be found anywhere in the world. The grounds are two thirds of a mile long and half a mile wide, and at the

Angkor Vat (Ewing Galloway)

top of a series of terraces stands a central shrine that towers more than 200 feet above the ground. Each of the terraces has covered corridors and hallways, the walls of which are filled with carvings in relief, depicting the life of the people and scenes from the *Ramayana* and the *Mahabharata.* After the kingdom of Cambodia was overwhelmed and destroyed by the Thais in the thirteenth century, the city was deserted and soon hidden by the jungle. The ruins were not discovered until the French began their penetration into the land in the nineteenth century.

To the Philippine Islands also, Hinduized Malayan traders and settlers carried Indian cultural patterns. So pronounced was this Indian influence that the people of the islands have been affected by it almost as much as they were by the later Spanish and American conquerors.

It is remarkable that the Indian homeland never established a direct political control over any of these lands in Southeast Asia into which Indian civilization was introduced. The conquest was owed simply to the superiority of Indian culture, spread by merchants and missionaries. With much reason, the modern Indians take pride in this example of an expansion that did not involve political conquest.

The spread of Indian culture in the other direction—from the homeland toward the west—was begun by Indian merchants who ventured into the lands around the Arabian and the Red Seas. After the rise of Islam, Arabs took over most of the trade in this region, but the westward diffusion of Indian culture did not stop, for the Arabs became students of Indian literature, philosophy, and science, especially medicine and mathematics, introducing this Hindu learning to Damascus and Baghdad. In turn, the Indians learned from Islam, for many of their artists and scholars visited Arab cities, and the Moslem religion was known and tolerated in India long before India was subjected to the raids of the Turkish Moslems.

Central Asia

Central Asia and Tibet also came to know Indian culture, brought to these lands by traders and missionaries. When *Mahayana* Buddhism was introduced into China, there developed a lively interchange between China and India along the overland route through Central Asia and by sea via Malaya and the East Indies. Hundreds of Buddhist monks and scholars traveled back and forth between the two countries. Chinese scholars collected thousands of Buddhist texts in India, studied Sanskrit and Pali, and translated the texts into Chinese. Since art was the handmaid of religion, it was only natural that Buddhist art, too, should penetrate China. (For a more detailed discussion of Indian Buddhist influence in China, see pages 375–377.)

The introduction of Buddhism into Tibet brought that land into a closer relationship with both India and China. Like the Chinese, Tibetan Buddhists traveled to India to study, and on their return they built monasteries on the Indian model. When Buddhism was attacked in India by the invading Moslems, thousands of Buddhist priests fled from India to Tibet. A tangible evidence of the scholarly contact among the three countries is a Chinese-Tibetan-Sanskrit dictionary, compiled in the ninth or tenth century, which still survives.

Thus, for most of the long period from the founding of the Gupta dynasty to the coming of the Moguls, India was a center of trade and cultural diffusion. And today the lands of Southeast Asia, and even China, still bear the unmistakable signs of their long and enriching association with India during these centuries—in art, architecture, religion, literature, the drama, and the dance. From these lands India learned less than it taught. Yet contact with the peoples of these lands must have been stimulating, and this stimulation may help account for the amazing creativity of India during this Golden Age of its history.

THE GOLDEN AGE OF INDIAN CULTURE

Sanskrit Literature

The Gupta period in Indian history has been called the Golden Age of Sanskrit literature. The Sanskrit language had originated much earlier and, as we have noted, a grammar had been compiled in the fourth century B.C. But the language continued to develop until the beginning of the fourth century A.D., and in the succeeding centuries it came to full fruition. This culmination of its creative use was owing in part to the consistent encouragement and patronage of the Gupta rulers. It was also stimulated by the increasing contact with other lands, for Sanskrit was the language used by traders in southeastern Asia as well as by scholars.

The production of literature in Sanskrit was enormous during the Gupta and post-Gupta periods. The great wealth of writings includes biographies, poems of all kinds, anthologies, works on astronomy, mathematics, and other branches of science, dictionaries, dramas, hymns, fables, philosophical and religious treatises, proverbs, and maxims. Especially notable were the anthologies, some limited to a single topic, others restricted to the work of a single author, and still others dealing with varied themes.

Poetry and Prose. The outstanding Sanskrit writers during the Gupta dynasty were poets, and foremost among them was Kalidasa, regarded in his lifetime and ever since as the greatest Sanskrit poet. Except that he was retained at the Gupta court, little of his life is known, but many scholars believe he flourished during the fifth century A.D. Kalidasa's poetry is of several types—philosophic and religious, romantic, epic—and includes poems descriptive of nature and everyday life. His *Meghaduta—Cloud Messenger*—is the most famous and original of a series called the "messenger" poems. In it, Kalidasa tells the enchanting story of a lover, separated by captivity from his beloved, who asks a cloud to take a message to her, telling of his longing. Half the poem is given over to the description of natural beauty, while the other half—with equally good effect—depicts the sorrow of the human heart.

The early part of the eighth century produced the Sanskrit poet who ranks next to Kalidasa. This was Bhavabhuti, who is known chiefly for the beauty of his language.

One of the great masters of Sanskrit prose was Bana. He was one of those rare scholars who write works of history that not only are valuable as records of events in the past but also attain literary distinction for their vivid description.

The Drama in India. Some excellent plays have come down to us from the period during and after the reign of the Guptas. Even in more ancient times drama had played a role in Indian life, but not much is known of it before this period. About the middle of the third century Bharata wrote a treatise, the *Natyasastra,* a compilation of ideas about the drama that had come down to his time. It listed and described the ten major types of plays, and this classification has been recognized for centuries since.

Generally regarded as the greatest Sanskrit play, however, is *Sakuntala,* or *Shakuntala,* by the poet Kalidasa. Translated into English in 1789, it was the first Indian play known to modern Europeans, and it made a deep impression on Goethe, who praised it highly. The prologue extols the beauties of nature; then the principal character, a king, makes his appearance in a chariot. In a woodland setting, he meets the beautiful maiden Sakuntala, the daughter of a hermit, makes love to her, and marries her. Suddenly the king is called back to his capital, whereupon an ascetic tells his wife not to mourn, for the king would be sure to remember her as long as she kept the ring he gave her.

One day, however, while traveling to show the king the ring, she loses it, and when she later appears at the palace, the king does not remember her and orders her away. As she leaves, dejected, she is whisked away to a distant forest, where their son is born. A fisherman finds the ring and gives it to the king, who at once remembers Sakuntala and sets out through the air to search for her. Miraculously he finds her and begs her forgiveness, whereupon they are happily reunited.

Another well-known play with a somewhat lighter touch is *Mrichchhakatika—The Little Clay Cart*—by Shudraka. Full of humor and melodrama, it contains some excellent descriptions, particularly one of a storm. It is the story of the love of the courtesan, Vasantasena, for an impoverished and virtuous Brahman, Charudatta. When Vasantasena goes to the house of Charudatta to leave some jewels for safe-keeping, she is caught by a storm and forced to spend the night there. The next morning, by mistake she chooses the wrong cart to take her home. The hero is suspected of having killed her and, after being haled into court, is sentenced to die. But a monk, whose life had earlier been saved by Vasantasena, comes to Charudatta's rescue, proving that Charudatta did not kill her and, indeed, that she was still alive. Charudatta and Vasantasena are reunited, and everyone is happy.

A comic interlude between the first and second acts introduces an entertaining character—a gambler who, after losing heavily, has taken refuge in a temple, where he poses as a stone statue. His pursuers, entering the temple, pinch the "statue," but the gambler does not move, whereupon they decide to play a game of dice at his feet. The "statue" resists the temptation as long as he can, then jumps down to join the game. His creditors recognize him and renew their pursuit, but he is saved by Vasantasena, who recognizes him as a former servant of Charudatta. In his relief and gratitude, he becomes a monk —the one who, later in the play, saves the hero and heroine.

Certain characteristics were common to most plays of the period. Usually they have a prologue and epilogue—the prologue of *Sakuntala* may have been the model that Goethe followed in writing a prologue for his *Faust*. The plays use both prose and verse. Characters of the upper classes speak Sanskrit, while the others use the vernacular. Almost always there are a hero, a heroine, a villain, and a jester. Tragedies are exceedingly rare—a respect in which Indian drama differs markedly from that of Greece. The plots often involve a number of remarkable coincidences, upon which the solution of the plot sometimes depends. The plays are generally quite long; Indians were apparently less heedful of time than westerners.

Linguistic Revolution

When the Moslems permanently settled in India after the thirteenth century, they introduced the Persian language and made it the official language of their courts. However, Persian did not find a permanent place. Instead there grew up a new language called Urdu, based on Sanskrit but infused with many words from Turkish, Arabic, and Persian. Urdu is still spoken in areas where Islam predominates, and it has become one of the official languages of the new Moslem state of Pakistan.

In reaction against the use of Persian, Hindu writers began to show a new interest in the vernacular languages of India. These had always been used by the common people, but hitherto scholars had preferred Sanskrit. Now scholars began to write in the local language of each area, and for this reason the period from the thirteenth to the fifteenth centuries has been called the "seed time" of the vernaculars. In the east the Bengalis still honor the poet Thakur, who translated the great epics into Bengali in the fourteenth century. In the same century a Turk named Amir Khusru began to use Hindi for literary purposes, writing in the vernacular a number of songs that are still sung in the villages of northern India. In some instances the growth of the vernacular literature was encouraged by Moslem rulers, who wished for political reasons to have a closer contact with the people. As the vernacular languages grew in importance, Sanskrit declined until eventually it became almost a dead language, studied only by the classical scholars, and still spoken by Brahman priests.

The Universities

Great universities, probably the first in the world, played a large part in Indian intellectual life during the Gupta period and thereafter until about 1200. These accepted only superior students—perhaps two or three out of every ten applicants—and many of those who were admitted were dismissed before finishing their courses. Students were given free tuition, board, and lodging, but they were not allowed to be frivolous.

Universities were located throughout the country, and some became famous for their specialization in specific subjects. Thus the university of Ujjain was distinguished for its study of astronomy, while the one at Ajanta attracted students who were interested in art. Benares became known for its orthodox Brahman teaching; it was, in addition, a center for philosophers who had new theories to develop. Foremost of all the universities was Nalanda, midway between modern Patna and Gaya. At one time it comprised several schools or colleges, offering instruction and research facilities in religion and philosophy—especially Buddhism—art, architecture, and agriculture. The school of agriculture even included a dairy farm. Its grounds included large libraries, observatories, numerous lecture rooms, and dormitories four stories high. Unfortunately the university was burned to the ground in 1197, and an immense number of invaluable Buddhist and Hindu manuscripts were destroyed.

Religion and Philosophy

Religion and philosophy continued as important parts of the lives of the Indian people. The main religions inherited from the past were Hinduism, Buddhism, and Jainism. The latter had remained relatively unimportant, but Buddhism had gained ground, aided by the patronage of Asoka and other rulers. Its split into two branches had hastened rather than hindered its spread, for while the *Hinayana* form of Buddhism remained rather austere, the *Mahayana,* making room for the use of images and ritual, made a more effective appeal to the people. Eventually *Mahayana* Buddhism lost much of its distinctive Buddhist character and took on a closer resemblance to Hinduism.

Hinduism and Buddhism interacted upon one another. While *Mahayana* Buddhism took over many practices of Hinduism as it became a popular worship, Hinduism also assimilated much of Buddhism, for Hinduism permitted the worship of many manifestations of the divine, and some of its believers accepted these manifestations and even images as minor deities. Ultimately Hinduism declared Buddha to be an incarnation of Vishnu. Not to be outdone, Buddhism identified Vishnu as one "destined to be a Buddha." By the eighth century, in India the two religions were scarcely to be distinguished from one another.

Hinduism, however, was so closely woven into the fabric of Indian life that its forms survived and remained closer than Buddhism to the Indian tradition. During the Gupta period in the fourth and fifth centuries, most of the monarchs were Hindus of the *Vaishnava* sect, which stressed the worship of Vishnu. Their desire to make India strong caused them to emphasize the distinctively Indian features of their society, and for this reason they encouraged the study of the *Vedas* and early religious practices. This brought about a new appreciation of Hinduism.

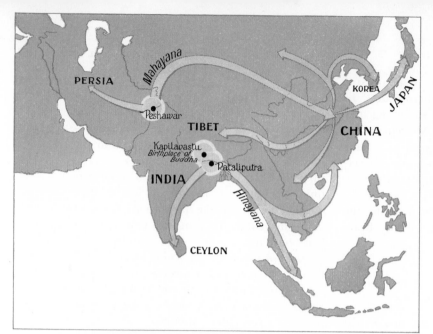

The Spread of Buddhism

Sankara. A significant stimulus to Hinduism and challenge to Buddhism came from the work of Sankara, a brilliant scholar who flourished about A.D. 800. A precocious child, who is said to have read all the *Vedas* by the age of eight, he accomplished his monumental work during a short span of time, for he died at the age of thirty-two. He was the author of the most famous of all the commentaries on the *Vedas,* and of other treatises dealing with the *Upanishads* and the *"Bhagavad-Gita."* In all these, he set forth the finest aspects of Hinduism, and in extolling its virtues, he attacked those—especially the Buddhists—who had deviated from the essential thought of the *Vedas.* He accepted the newer popular gods of Hinduism, and his acceptance helped make their position secure. But at the same time he attempted to purify popular Hinduism, since his purpose was not merely to encourage worship in the temples but to raise men's lives to a higher plane, to make them nobler and purer.

Though criticizing Buddhism, Sankara was favorably impressed by the devoted and disciplined Buddhist monks, and accordingly he founded ten religious orders to assist in the propagation of a reformed Hinduism. Four of these survived, and their monasteries became centers of pilgrimage. They helped—as did Sankara himself, by his travels throughout the land—to link the various parts of India closer together and thus compensate for its political division among numerous independent kingdoms. His career attests to the cultural unity of the Indian people.

The Decline of Buddhism in India. Sankara was not alone responsible for the disappearance of Buddhism from India, but he assisted in the process. Its gradual merger with Hinduism meant that it could no longer offer something new. Its patronage by some of the foreign invaders, such as the Kushans, had put a stigma upon it, and the emphasis that some Buddhist priests placed upon the *Tantras*—manuals explaining magic, witchcraft, divination, and mysticism—began to lessen its moral force after the seventh century. Moreover, the monastic orders, which had been a help in spreading Buddhism during the earlier centuries, lost their vigor after the Gupta period as monks spent more time in study than in propagating the faith.

Yet Buddhism left a mark upon Indian thought and life, even after its disappearance as an organized religion in India. Its teaching of a new respect for human life and its emphasis on *ahimsa,* or nonkilling, were never forgotten; it brought about a greater kindness toward animals and gave new impetus to vegetarianism; it influenced Indian art and architecture, and, through it, the arts of other Asiatic lands; it contributed the idea of the Great Renunciation. Even now the ascetic is honored in India as much as —more than—the leader in politics or business. Like Christianity, Buddhism flourished in other countries after its disappearance from the land of its origin. In some lands of Asia Buddhism became the dominant faith, and it was an important and influential religion in others.

The Moslem Impact. Both Hinduism and Buddhism originated in India and developed there without undergoing influences from outside. But Islam, which became the third religion of India and eventually displaced Buddhism as the leading rival of Hinduism, came to India from beyond its borders.

It was first brought into India, as we have noted, by the Moslem Arabs who established themselves in Sind at the beginning of the eighth century. Not for some centuries did the new religion provoke religious strife, for the Indians were neither narrow-minded nor intolerant of religious views they did not share.

But a bloody new chapter was begun when the Turks and others, who had become converted to Islam, entered India as conquerors, for these peoples sought not only to establish their rule over as much of India as possible but also to wipe out the "infidels" and establish the supremacy of their own true faith. These newer champions of Islam proved ruthless in their religious zeal, and under their pressure many Indians, especially in the north, became followers of the Prophet. Others, unwilling to abandon Hinduism for Islam but desiring to escape persecution, emigrated to central and southern India. Their migration strength-

ened Hinduism in those regions, but it meant that only a small minority of Hindus was left in certain sections of the north, which became predominantly Moslem.

Eventually the two religious communities learned to live together under an uneasy truce, because neither could wipe out the other. The Moslems remained so staunch in their monotheism and so sure of the superiority of their own religion that they could never be assimilated into Hinduism. Yet Hinduism was so deeply rooted in India's past and so self-assured that it would never yield to Islam.

Several attempts were made to reconcile the two religions. None of these succeeded, but one of them had a lasting consequence of minor importance. This was the endeavor by a man named Nanak, early in the sixteenth century, to found a new religion, with himself at its head, that would combine Hinduism and Islam. Nanak won a small number of followers and appointed a successor, who carried on his work. The sect, known as Sikhs, which stems from this movement has endured to the present time.

Indian Architecture

It is difficult to reconstruct the history of Indian architecture, for many buildings were wantonly destroyed by invaders. Although written records bear evidence that many cities of India were known for their splendid structures, few remain.

However, a number of temples have endured from the time of the Gupta dynasty and after. Among these are some famous cave temples (p. 320). The earliest of these were Buddhist and Jain but later there were also Hindu cave temples. The design of these temples and the sculpture in them reflect the gradual changes in religion that brought Buddhism and Hinduism closer together as time went on. Eventually, therefore, these came to represent an Indian rather than either a Buddhist or a Hindu art. But be-

The Mahabodhi Temple at Bodh Gaya. Bodh Gaya, or Buddha Gaya, is the site where the Buddha attained Supreme Wisdom under a pipal tree. The temple retains its early Gupta form, although it was restored at great expense in 1880–1881. (Government of India Information Services)

cause the art was created for religious purposes, not as an expression of the artist's personal inspiration, the artist himself was regarded as less important than his work. For this reason it is almost impossible to identify the work of individual architects, sculptors, or painters as can be done in Greece and elsewhere. Much of the work was undertaken by guilds, and it therefore represents the common effort of a number of artists.

The earliest Buddhist shrines and monasteries were built of wood, but later temples were carved in the rock of caves, and a new style, appropriate to stone rather than wood, was developed. In the cave temples there were large assembly halls, probably patterned after the halls used by guilds, with two rows of pillars supporting a roof. The main meeting room was in the middle, with aisles on the sides. At one end was the entrance, and there was a small stupa at the other.

One of the most interesting of these is the Kailasa Temple, devoted to the god Siva, which was built in the eighth century at Ellora. The temple takes its name from the sacred mountain in The Himalaya where the gods were believed to reside. The mountain thus had the same significance as Mount Olympus for the Greeks. The temple shows originality in its conception and marvelous workmanship in its execution. Using only the simplest tools—the mallet and narrow chisel—the builders hewed out a huge, solid block of stone, 60 feet high, 250 feet long, and 160 feet wide. This block was then hollowed out through openings that served as doors and windows, and the outside was ornamented with carvings in relief. Besides the temple, which stands as one of the finest achievements of Indian art, the builders also carved out a group of chapels and monasteries in the hills nearby.

Other parts of India, particularly the large cities, also had important shrines. Characteristic of them was the towerlike superstructure, known as the *sikhara*, which generally stood over the holy place. In northern India this was usually curvilinear, with a slight bulge in the center and a pointed top. In the south, the *sikharas* were usually in the form of a pyramid, comprising several stories, each set back from the one below. Many temples had smaller *sikharas* around the central one. Always the towers were decorated with sculptured figures in relief. In one area of southern India there was a distinctive development, which was the building of elaborately carved gateways or *gopurams*, in the walls surrounding the temple grounds. Sometimes these gates were so tall and so richly ornamented that they overshadowed the main shrine.

Although the Moslem invaders destroyed many Hindu and Buddhist temples when they first came into India, these invaders were lovers of art and architecture. Their destruction of temples was a matter of religious zeal, not a sign of indifference to beauty in building. They introduced into Indian architecture the true arch, the dome, and the minaret. In turn, they learned much from the Indians. So greatly were they influenced that the Moslem architecture in India is known as Indo-Saracenic. Most of the mosques, minarets, tombs, and palaces which the Moslems caused to be erected were built by Indian craftsmen. However, the Moslem religion did not permit so much use of decoration as the Indians admired; consequently, much of the beauty of the Moslem architecture in India is provided by the design. Calligraphy and inlaid floral arrangements provided most of what little ornamentation was permitted.

Many of the early buildings of the Moslem invaders have disappeared, as well as those that the invaders themselves destroyed. One spectacular Moslem monument that still stands is a tall tower, the Qutab Minar, outside Delhi, near the famous iron pillar mentioned earlier. It was erected near a huge mosque, now in ruins, and was begun by the founder of the "slave" dynasty early in the thirteenth century. It was perhaps meant as a minaret or as a memorial of victory. At the bottom of the tower is a tier of round columns alternating with angular ones; the next tier above consists entirely of rounded columns, and above that is a tier wholly of angular columns. Above these three tiers, which are made of red sandstone, are other tiers of columns of white marble. The whole tower, 238 feet high, is covered with exquisitely carved designs.

Moslem architecture was at its best in the early period. In succeeding centuries, the buildings became simpler and more formal, but had less distinction.

Indian Sculpture

In addition to the sculpture on the temple buildings, Indian artists made individual figures in stone, and statues cast in copper and bronze. In sculpture as well as other arts, the Gupta period was the Classical Age. So great were the achievements of the sculptors of this time that their work became "the ideal and the despair of Indian artists of subsequent ages." It was then that the forms of the divinities, both Buddhist and Hindu, were perfected (pp. 9, 308, 316, 326), to be copied in lands to which Indian culture spread.

The Qutab Minar at Delhi. (Indian government)

Indian Painting

Though Vedic, Epic, and early Buddhist literature makes reference to the painting of murals and individual portraits, virtually nothing survives of Indian painting before the beginning of the Christian era. But the earliest works which have endured give evidence that art must have had a long period of cultivation before these works were done.

At some time before the third century A.D. the six basic principles of Indian painting were formulated and recorded. The first of these principles deals with the knowledge of appearance and includes the study of nature and the figure, landscaping, and architecture. The second is the idea of correct perception—proportion, or perspective. The third principle involves "the effect of the mind on the body," to which Buddhist artists paid much attention. The fourth idea is the "infusion of grace," which is closely related to the fifth principle—truth. The sixth is concerned with technique, discussing the proper use of materials and tools.

After the seventh century no paintings of any significance are known until almost 1000 years later—after the Moguls had arrived in the land and put their impress upon Indian culture. But that is a time beyond the period we are considering here.

Indian Music

By Vedic times India had developed a musical tradition that, we have reason to believe, has endured with but little change down to the present day. The earliest Indian musical instruments were much the same as those used in ancient times in Egypt, Babylonia, and Palestine. But from the first, Indian music was distinguished from that of the Ancient Orient by its use of hand-beaten drums, on which complicated rhythms were produced.

In remote times the Indian scale was divided into twenty-two microtones. These intervals of tone are much smaller than on the scales we use—indeed, so minute that western peoples sometimes cannot detect the difference between the tones. For this reason Occidentals find it hard to appreciate Indian music, although it is not so far removed from the western tradition as the music of some other Oriental lands.

Another distinctive characteristic of Indian music that is of remote origin is its use of rigidly specified melodic and rhythmic patterns. The patterns of melody are called *ragas*. The word *raga* means *color* or *passion* and indicates that the various melodic formulas are invested with specific moods. These moods are taken as corresponding with nine sentiments: love, tenderness, humor, heroism, terror, anger, disgust, surprise, and tranquillity.

Ragas have their counterpart in the equally complicated rhythmic patterns known as *talas*. The drummer may beat two different *talas* at the same time, one with each hand, and thus produce overlapping patterns of miraculous complexity.

This system of combining prescribed patterns of rhythm and melody has worked to prevent any fundamental change in India's music for thousands of years. Yet "art is in limitation," and the limitations imposed on the Indian musician did not stifle his creativity. Paradoxical though it may seem, freedom was as characteristic of the Indian musical tradition as was confinement.

The Golden Age of Indian civilization came to its close at the end of the fourteenth century. By that time the Delhi sultanate had dwindled until it took in but a small area around the capital. There were other Moslem kingdoms in the north and center of India, and the Hindu state of Vijayanagar in the south, but none was capable of meeting the political problems of the day. Indian traders had lost control of the seas and trade routes; the Indian colonies in Southeast Asia had been taken over by others; and contact with China had almost ceased. Hinduism was producing few great thinkers, and

Buddhism had disappeared. India was weak and divided, ready to succumb should a determined new invader appear on her borders. And such an invader did, indeed, appear, when the Mogul (or Mongol) hordes began to sweep into India from the north.

Suggestions for Further Reading

Source Materials

Anthologies
R. Warnock and G. K. Anderson, eds., *The World in Literature* (Chicago, 1950–1951), Volume I, pp. 40–71.
Kalidasa's *Shakuntala.*

Contemporary Writings
al-Biruni, *Alberuni's India;* translated by E. C. Sachau (London, 1910).
Written by an early Moslem visitor to India.
Shudraka, *The Little Clay Cart,* translated by A. W. Ryder (Cambridge, Mass., 1905).
One of the outstanding Indian plays.
T. Watters, ed. and trans., *On Yuan Chwang's Travels in India, 629–645,* (London, 1904).
Account of Yuan Chwang's pilgrimage to the India of Harsha.
The Panchatantra; translated by A. W. Ryder (Chicago, 1925).
A collection of some of the stories.
A Record of Buddhistic Kingdoms (Travels of Fa-Hien); translated by J. Legge (Oxford, 1886).
Account by another prominent Chinese visitor to India.
The Travels of Fa-hsien; translated by H. A. Giles (Cambridge, England, 1923).
Same as above.

Secondary Works
P. Brown, *Indian Painting* (Calcutta, 1918).
An outstanding British authority discusses India's painting.
A. K. Coomaraswamy, *The Dance of Shiva* (Bombay, 1948).
Contains stimulating comments on many aspects of Indian life.
A. K. Coomaraswamy, *History of Indian and Indonesian Art* (New York, 1927).
The recognized authority on the subject.
T. G. Garratt, ed., *The Legacy of India* (Oxford, 1934).

A collection of articles on many phases of Indian life. A useful work.
R. Groussett, *In the Footsteps of the Buddha;* translated by M. Leon (London, 1932).
An engrossing account of Yuan Chwang's trip to India and his reception there by Harsha.
A. B. Keith, *A History of Sanskrit Literature* (Oxford, 1928).
The authoritative work.
A. B. Keith, *The Sanskrit Drama; in its Origin, Development, Theory and Practice* (Oxford, 1924).
A standard history of the Sanskrit drama.
R. G. Majumdar, ed., *History and Culture of the Indian People: The Classical Age* (Bombay, 1954); *The Age of Imperial Kanauj* (Bombay, 1955).
Volumes III and IV of a new history of India.
B. Rowland, *The Wall-Paintings of India, Central Asia and Ceylon* (Boston, 1938).
A good historical account with beautiful reproductions.
V. A. Smith, *A History of Fine Art in India and Ceylon* (2d ed., rev. by K. Codrington, Oxford, 1930).
A general history.
B. H. M. Vlekke, *Nusantara; a History of the East Indian Archipelago* (Cambridge, Mass., 1943).
The first three chapters discuss the Indian influence.
R. O. Winstedt, ed., *Indian Art* (London, 1947).
Three lectures on phases of Indian art.
H. R. Zimmer, *The Art of Indian Asia,* completed by J. Campbell (2 vols., New York, 1955).
Indian philosophy and mythology as reflected in Indian art. Magnificently produced and illustrated.

Recordings of Indian Music
Music of the Orient (Decca DX-107).

14

The Beginnings of Civilization in China

Black and Red Lacquer Box with Lid—Late Chou Period. The fantastic animals, intricate scroll work, and excellent workmanship of similar objects suggest an elegant society. (Nelson Gallery and Atkins Museum, Kansas City, Missouri)

The civilization of China had its most remote origin in the great Chinese plain along the banks of the Hwang Ho and the Wei. These rivers originate in the high plateau of western China, in what are now Tsinghai and Kansu provinces, whence they have for ages carried down the yellow earth, or loess, to the vast plain below.

But the Hwang Ho—*Hwang* means yellow, and *Ho,* river—is given to disastrous floods and frequent changes of course. From very early times, therefore, some device has been needed to control the river and bring its precious water to the parched lands beyond the river's banks. Without a system of water control, involving dams, canals, and terraces, agriculture could not be maintained, and a settled, urban culture could not be developed.

This system of water control involved a large degree of social cooperation and created a need for a bureaucracy to supervise the works that were necessary for the survival of the society. Since the earliest times, therefore, close social organization and a bureaucracy have been characteristic of the Chinese civilization. Both, as we have already seen, were also characteristic of the early civilizations that arose in Egypt, Mesopotamia, and the Indus Valley, and all these civilizations are sometimes grouped together as belonging to the "Oriental" type of society, which depends on the manipulation of the water supply.

THE DAWN OF CHINESE CIVILIZATION

Archaeologists and anthropologists believe that some of the culture sites in China are among the oldest known to have been inhabited by creatures resembling men. The earliest progenitor of the modern Chinese—Sinanthropus—belongs to the Quaternary Age (see p. 18).

Most of the remains dating from the Early Stone Age have been found on the margins of China, rather than in its heartland. These give evidence of emerging civilization in three separate regions—a northern civilization, covering much of what is now Inner Mongolia and extending into northern Man-

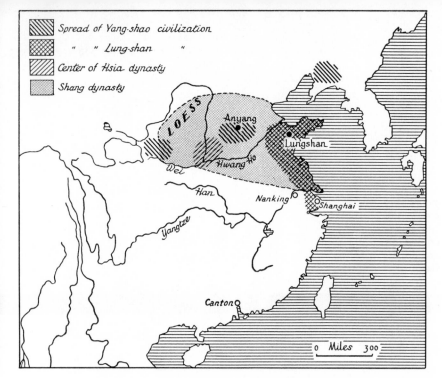

Map legend:
- Spread of Yang-shao civilization
- " " Lung-shan "
- Center of Hsia dynasty
- Shang dynasty

LOESS
Anyang
Lungshan
Wei
Hwang Ho
Han
Nanking
Shanghai
Yangtze
Canton

0 Miles 300

churia, a western civilization in what is now the province of Szechwan, and a southern civilization, of slightly later date, in the present-day Kwangsi province. There may have been another civilization of the same period in the heartland of China, the remains of which have not come to light. It seems more probable, however, that the earliest civilizations arose around the margins of China, as these remains suggest, and later merged to form the entity that we know as China.

"China"

Two stages leading to the emergence of this entity have been revealed by archaeological investigations. Both belong to the Neolithic Age.

The first is the so-called "Yang-shao" civilization. This seems to have flourished over a considerable period of time and to have extended from what is now Kansu, in the west, eastward to what is now southern Manchuria. The distinguishing mark of this civ-

ilization is its painted pottery, which shows great beauty. In shape and decoration, it closely resembles specimens that have been found in Persia, on the western edge of the Central Asian steppe, and in southern Russia. It also shows similarities with the oldest pottery found in America, which comes from Guatemala.

The second Neolithic civilization in the heartland of China takes its name from Lung-shan, a place in modern Shantung province, where the first findings were made. Other sites of this civilization have been discovered in Shantung, Honan, and Anhwei provinces and near Hangchow in Chekiang. At central Honan sites, where both Yang-shao and Lung-shan overlap, the former is known to be the older. The pottery of the Lung-shan is not the same as that of the Yang-shao; it is characterized by a lacquer-black shard that is sometimes as thin as an eggshell.

The Lung-shan people lived in villages or towns on the tops or slopes of hills close to river valleys. Often their settlements were so close together as to be within sight of one another. Their houses were made of pounded earth, covered with a slip of chalk and furnished with a heatable bed—features that still survive in northern China. Their domesticated animals included the dog, the pig, the sheep, and the horse. One of their customs, which has survived in China and Mongolia, is a method of divination making use of the shoulder blades of animals. They also used incised signs that resemble characters in later Chinese writing.

Myths and Culture-heroes

Out of the dim and unrecorded dawn of Chinese culture, there has come down to us a body of myths and legends that give us some notion of the earliest institutions of Chinese society and the ideals of leadership portrayed by the culture-heroes. These myths and legends give us a view of a stage of civilization when man was still a child of nature, when no social order existed, when people knew their mothers but not their fathers,

garbed themselves in furs and rushes, and lived in tents.

Then appears Fu-hsi, the first civilizer, whose name has to do with cooking and the kitchen. He is portrayed as the first hunter and fisher, and the first to tan the hide of the pig for leather. To him is also attributed the introduction of the social institution of marriage and the ceremonies for initiation into adult life.

The second culture-hero of the age of myths is Shen-nung, the divine husbandman, who is also known as Yen-ti, the Lord of Fire. To him is attributed the use of the hoe and the wooden plow and the introduction of organized trade. He is usually depicted bearing an ox head. This seems to suggest a prehistoric migration from a cattle country in the west, spreading to the east and south.

The third culture-hero is Hwang-ti, the Yellow Lord or August Lord. Hwang-ti later became the patron saint of Taoism and was widely worshiped. For this reason, the cultural innovations attributed to him are

Modern Provinces of China

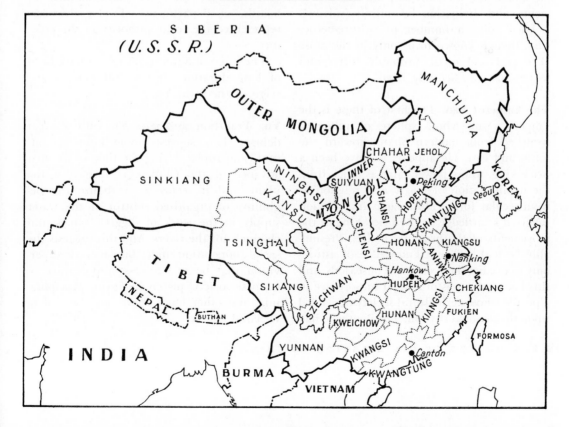

Pre-Bronze Age Pottery—painted black and brown, dating from before 2200 B.C. Such pieces are presumed to have been funeral vases, and some have been found with grain inside. (Mary Edwards and Norman Donant, photographers)

especially numerous. They include the planting of the seven kinds of grain, the well, the house, pottery, the bow and arrow, coinage, the pestle and mortar, boats and oars, clothing and shoes, the calendar, musical instruments, and divination by milfoil (yarrow).

Then come a number of culture-heroes who, though known to us only in the guise of legend and myth, probably correspond to persons who actually lived.

The Emperor Yao. The first of these is the Emperor Yao, whose sphere of influence stretched from modern Shansi toward the south and east. He appears to have been a priest-king, whose power came as much from the manipulation of magic and religion as from secular force. This magic and religion involved knowledge by the priest-king of the movements of the heavenly bodies. Presumably he had sufficient knowledge of astronomy to predict the recurrence of seasons, and this knowledge was of crucial importance to a people whose agricultural society depended upon the seasonal rhythm. The man who had

access to the secret knowledge permitting prediction of this kind would be at once a priest and a ruler. From the earliest known times, the rulers of China have always reserved to themselves the prerogative of calendar-making, and they have required those who accepted their rule to accept also their calendar.

The Emperor Shun. At the eastern border of his realm, Yao must have collided with another civilization, the culture-hero of which was Shun. This may have been the Lung-shao civilization. Tradition relates that Yao had need of help to cope with the Miao tribes, who were apparently aboriginal groups living in scattered areas of Yao's domain. The warrior Shun came to Yao's aid, but then established himself as a joint ruler with Yao and ultimately reduced the latter to the status of a subject.

With Shun, new religious conceptions and a strict political organization took the place of the priest-kingship of Yao. An anthropomorphic deity, Shang-ti, and six other gods were recognized, and political administration, which hitherto had been given over to helpers of Yao, was placed under six boards, or departments. Twelve overseers represented the royal authority in the provinces.

The reign of Shun seems not to have been of long duration. It was followed by the reign of the great Yü.

Yü. Tradition associates Yü with a great deluge. This suggests some kind of natural catastrophe during the time of the first advance of the Chinese culture into the plain, and it seems to symbolize the beginning of organized control of the water supply in the work of digging canals and channels for the rivers. And this suggests the social cooperation under bureaucratic supervision that became an essential feature of Chinese society, just as in Egypt, Mesopotamia, and other lands it was an essential of Oriental society.

The Hsia Dynasty

Yü is traditionally called the founder of the first Chinese dynasty—the Hsia—about the end of the third millennium B.C. At this point the age of myth and legend blends into the beginning of the historic period, for, though historians cannot verify the existence of the Hsia dynasty, they have ample evidence of a Hsia state. This had its center south of modern Shansi and extended southward into central and northern Honan. Its cultural influence spread still farther, probably reaching to the northeastern limit of China.

The rulers of this area seem to have exercised full power as secular rulers for only a few generations. Apparently the third Hsia sovereign was deposed by an eastern barbarian, and thereafter the heads of the clans or tribes took over the management of the government. One of these chieftains, known as the lord protector, became the secular representative of the ruler, while the latter retained only priestly functions. The principal of these functions was the making of the calendar, which remained a magic or religious secret. As evidence that this secret rested upon sound astronomical knowledge, we may note that over 1000 years later, Confucius was so favorably impressed by the Hsia calendar that he recommended a return to the use of it.

Gradually the Hsia dynasty lost its priestly authority as well as its secular power. One reason for this was, probably, that the calendar was not revised so as to compensate for its inaccuracies, and eventually it no longer rightly predicted the seasons and movements of the heavenly bodies. Moreover, foreign religious practices had been penetrating the palace under one of the last of the Hsia rulers. Shamanism—the primitive religion, in which the unseen world of gods, demons, and ancestral spirits is believed to be responsive only to the shamans or medicine men—coming from the north, had always been accepted by the people, but now the king was involved. Dances and songs in the very palace of the priest-king, led by young and slim girl-priestesses, would naturally lessen the awe of the people for a king whose power was supposed to come from the stars in the heavens.

Nor was this all. This same king, K'ung-chia, is said to have quarreled with the lord protector, who was one of the most powerful of the clan chieftains. The consequence was that this lord protector, Li of Shang, after subjugating the other clan chieftains, deposed the last Hsia sovereign and took the throne himself.

The Shang Dynasty

As king, Li of Shang is known as T'ang the Completer. The period of his reign seems to have been about 1500 B.C.

The traditions relating to this new Shang dynasty are quite different from those of the previous Hsia. They suggest that matriarchal elements now came to the fore within society. Thus in religion, the female element became prominent, for example, the spirit of the Earth, She, which was regarded as female, took precedence over the spirit of Heaven, which was regarded as male. Moreover, the succession to the throne now passed from the king to his brother rather than, as under the Hsia, from the king to his son. The new pattern is also characteristic of a matriarchate.

The area over which the Shang ruled was extensive. From a center in Honan, it reached westward to comprise at least central and southern Shansi, and Shensi; to the south, it took in modern Hupeh as far as the Yangtze River and perhaps beyond; eastward, it included present-day Anhwei, Kiangsu, and Shantung; northward, it stretched over the larger part of Hopeh, including Peking, and into Korea.

Such a large area required a new kind of political organization, with a greater delegation of power. Hence the Shang did not

Ceremonial Covered Bronze Vessel—twelfth century, B.C., late Shang dynasty, 14³⁄₁₆ inches high. Such vessels were used for wine. They were cast by the so-called "lost-wax" method. (Courtesy of the Smithsonian Institution, Freer Gallery of Art, Washington, D. C.)

make use of overseers in the conquered countries, nor did they rely upon the swords of their lords protector. Instead they left the native princes in their own territories, requiring them to appear at court from time to time and pay tribute. In this way they created a political structure that came close to being "feudal," although it was not quite the same as the feudalism that later emerged in Europe.

Two independent traditions give the names of thirty successive Shang rulers, and archaeological findings confirm most of the names in the listing. But the sources diverge in regard to the dates. According to traditional dates, the Shang dynasty lasted from about 1766 to about 1122 B.C., but many modern historians believe that the period should be dated from about 1523 to about 1027 B.C.

The Culture of the Shang Era

Archaeological excavations have produced a wealth of material on the culture of the Shang era. Much of this material is in the form of oracle bones, for the Chinese, like the Greeks and other early peoples, sought advice from oracles.

Much earlier, in the Lung-shan civilization, the custom had developed of taking the bones from the shoulder blades of various animals and heating them in a fire, then giving a divinatory interpertation to the cracks that appeared in the bones. This custom also appeared among the Shang people, who made use of tortoise shells as well as bones. It was their practice, moreover, to write questions and sometimes the answers on the oracle bones. The tens of thousands of such bones which have been discovered therefore provide us with a large store of written documents. And since questions were often addressed to the oracle by the kings, the names of the kings are thus recorded. Private persons also made use of the oracles, and their questions give us a notion of the problems that arose in everyday life. Often the questions concerned the prospects for the harvest or relations within the family and among neighbors.

Excavations have also brought to light at modern Anyang the remains of the city that was the capital from the time of the nineteenth Shang sovereign until nearly the end of the dynasty. The city seems to have been densely populated and to have been walled about on those sides where natural protection was lacking. The gates resembled those used on modern Chinese cities, even to the tower rising above the gate.

The houses of the city are built on the same pattern as the modern Chinese house— a framework of columns and rafters on a stone plinth, with a terrace of pounded earth, often covered with tiles or mats. The walls of pounded earth served only as a protection against the weather, not as a support to the roof. Some of the houses are rather large, measuring as much as 100 feet in length and 30 in width. Usually they faced east or west, not south, as do most Chinese houses of today.

The burial places show that the coffins of the dead were put in wooden dolmens. This is unlike the custom of the Hsia, who placed the bodies of their dead in a crouching position in sepulchral urns.

The numerous animal bones give an indication of what animals were hunted or kept under domestication. Among the animals of the hunt were tigers, panthers, bears, hares, tapirs, badgers, stags, and monkeys. The domestic animals were the dog, pig, sheep, goat, ox, water buffalo, horse, monkey, and perhaps the stag. Horses were not used for riding but for drawing chariots, which were well made and intricately ornamented.

Rice, wheat, and millet were the cereals grown. Textile plants were also cultivated, but nothing remains of the cloth that was made. However, spindles have been found, and ornaments of stone and metal that presumably were used on clothing. The pottery is not of so good a quality as that of earlier periods, though kaolin was being used in making it and occasionally glazes were produced. Its deterioration was probably due to the use of bronze for the better grade of utensils. Apparently metal and shell were used as money, which indicates commerce above the level of barter. The weapons in use included bone and metal knives, bows and arrows (the latter having arrowheads made of stone, bone, or metal), swords, and lances.

The craftsmanship of the Shang period sometimes attained an excellence never surpassed or even matched. This is especially true of the work done in bronze and the carving of jade. Also notable are the carvings in wood and bone, and sculpture in marble and other kinds of stone, including animal figures larger than life size. Painting was devoted to the decoration of walls and columns.

THE CHOU DYNASTY

As the Shang dynasty began to decline, a new power arose in the west. This was the Chou clan, whose domain was in the region of the Wei River Valley in Shensi. Ultimately the head of this clan deposed the last Shang sovereign and established the new Chou dynasty.

Chou Feudalism

The new dynasty imposed on Chinese society a political structure that is known as Chou feudalism. This has features in common with the feudalism that developed in the west, but it also has features that are specifically Oriental. These distinctive features arise from the fact that in China, as in other Oriental lands, agriculture depended on irrigation, as it never has in Europe, and irrigation required a large degree of social cooperation and bureaucratic regulation. Hence Chou feudalism involved more political organization than was characteristic of western-type feudalism.

The feature that is common to China under the Chou dynasty and to other lands under a feudal regime is the human relationship known as vassalage. In Chou China, as in other feudal lands, a young nobleman customarily attached himself to a prince or future prince, and each was bound by honor to respect the tie between them, regardless of what vicissitudes might arise. The loyalty of each to the other, which was designated as *chung,* soon became one of the cardinal virtues. It was considered to have a binding force stronger than that which arose in any other relationship—stronger than even the duty of the son to his parents. The vigor of this conception is shown by a story from the Chou period: A man bound in vassalage to a prince was asked by his lord to induce his two sons, who were vassals of the rebellious son of this prince, to leave the son and, like their own father, give service to the prince.

But rather than ask his sons to commit a breach of loyalty to their own lord, the father committed suicide.

Each of the succeeding kings of the Chou dynasty invested local rulers with the power to govern a specific territory, which became his fief, on condition that the ruler give the king his loyalty as a vassal. The men to whom were given the larger fiefs were known as *hou*—feudal lords or princes. After their death, they were customarily given the honorific title *kung,* which is ordinarily translated as *duke.* Both terms are therefore used to refer to these principal vassals of the king.

The duties incurred by the holder of a fief were those characteristic of a feudal situation. Among them was the duty of the vassal to appear at court on certain occasions and to render military assistance to the king when the need arose—for example, when invaders presented a grave threat to the frontier, or when the aboriginal peoples within the empire broke out in rebellion. Various occasions called for the presence of the vassal at the court. Vassals were always summoned at the time when a new king succeeded to the throne or when religious rites of great importance were conducted. From time to time, also, they were required to appear in order to report on the situation in their fiefs.

The feudatories were also expected to send tribute to the royal court. The tribute, however, was not a regular tax but a personal gift of the vassal, meant as a token of his loyalty. Usually it consisted of some article of luxury or an exotic product of a certain area. When a prince failed to send tribute to the court, this was not a breach of the feudal relationship, but the failure would give rise to doubt of his loyalty. If such a suspicion were corroborated by other evidence, the king could take the fief away from the vassal or send out a punitive expedition. Besides gifts of this kind, meant as tokens of loyalty, vassals sometimes made contributions in the form of labor forces that the king could use in the building of royal palaces, defense works, or roads and bridges.

Apart from the obligations that have been mentioned, the feudal lords were completely free to rule as they chose within the areas of their fiefs. They could add to their holdings by conquering new territory outside the borders of the empire, and they could secure the services of a lesser lord, to whom they would give over part of their lands as a sub-fief and from whom they would exact loyalty. The feudal princes did not, however, have any official position in the court or a voice in the choice of the successor to the king. Sometimes, to be sure, a prince or several of them in alliance might interfere in the succession or the affairs of the court, but such action was never regarded as within their right.

Those who held official positions in the court made up a group known as the *ta-fu.* This group was recruited from the same social stratum that included the great fief-holders, but the latter were not part of the *ta-fu.* This officialdom had much more power and prestige than did the court of the kings in Europe during the feudal era. The reason was that the government had a large role in the economic life of China as well as in the management of war and diplomacy, and the men who became officials of the court ordinarily began their careers in lower positions in the public administration, rising to higher offices as they demonstrated their proficiency. Men of ability were much in demand and were well paid.

Below the group of great feudal lords and high officials was the class of knights, or *shih.* In the Chou society the knight was not a minor nobleman, living on land of his own, like a small-scale model of the great lord. He was wholly dependent on the lord whom he served. The service that he rendered might be military, but it was not necessarily so, for some knights held positions in the lower and middle levels of officialdom. Serv-ice of this kind involved knowledge of the traditions and religious scriptures. From among the knights, therefore, were recruited not only scribes and recorders but also phi-losophers, and eventually *knight* became synonymous with *scholar.* The self-assurance and social prestige of scholars in China is owed, in part, to their historical association with knighthood.

Chou Economy and Society

At the bottom of the social scale were the peasants, who made up the mass of the people. Their position is indicated by an early Chinese adage: "The superior man uses his mind, the commoner uses his body. He who uses his mind rules, he who uses his body is ruled. He who rules feeds on others, he who is ruled provides food for others." This gives a concise statement of the burden that lay upon the peasant.

The burden involved services of several kinds. The most important was service on the lord's demesne, for the peasants were obliged to work the lord's land as well as their own. And only after they had finished with the work for the lord were they free to cultivate the land that they tilled for themselves. Another service was *corvée* labor. This meant that each year every adult male had to give a certain amount of work for whatever purposes his lord might indicate. Usually this labor was used in building palaces and cities, stockades and other defense works, and projects for irrigation and flood control. In times of emergency the peasants might also be conscripted for military service.

The peasants were regarded as part of the fief that was given to a prince. They were not permitted to leave the land or to sell the parcel allotted to them for their particular use. They were free, however, to sell or barter whatever they raised on their own land, except for a stipulated contribution to the lord. And the lord was supposed to "love the

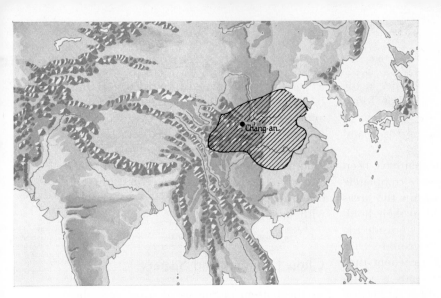

people"—that is, to show consideration for their needs and to protect their property.

The peasant families provided for nearly all their own needs. They raised their own food, made the textiles that they used for clothing, and fashioned most of their own tools and utensils. A certain amount of barter developed among the families of each village, but artisans and traders did not form a separate class of importance in the village.

A small number of merchants and artisans lived by supplying luxury goods for the courts of the various lords and the king. But this market was not large enough to support a class of traders and craftsmen and hence to make this group a separate social force.

Chou Administration

The first generation or two of the Chou dynasty saw the working out of the feudal pattern of government that has been described above, and for some time thereafter the system worked well, as long as the Chou rulers took heed to protect the northern and western borders of the Empire against the menace of the steppe peoples living beyond. But the burden of defending the frontier imposed a severe strain on the royal government, and after the ninth century B.C. the effectiveness of Chou rule declined. By the

time of the reign of King Yu (781–771 B.C.) the dynasty had been so weakened that the border defenses were unmanned. This permitted barbarian peoples from the west to sweep in upon the Empire, raid the capital, and kill the king. The death of King Yu in this manner, in 771 B.C., marks the end of Chou rule and of the Chou system of feudalism.

Chou Arts and Crafts

Despite its ignoble end, this period saw great advances not only in institutional and political life but also in the arts and crafts. The outstanding work of the early Chou period was in bronze and jade. This was the continuation of a tradition that had begun in the time of the Shang, but the work done under the Chou shows more simplicity of form and a more natural flow of line rather than the decorative luxuriance of the Shang period. The craftsmanship of the early Chou succeeded better in expressing the sacramental spirit of the great religious and political rituals in which the bronze and jade works of art were intended to be used. Lacquer objects also were made for ceremonial or household use (p. 338) although most of these pieces appear to date from the fifth to third century B.C., the so-called "Late Chou" period.

Chou Literature

Three works of literature survive from the early Chou era. The first of them is the *Book of Changes,* a manual for divination, principally by the manipulation of stalks of milfoil. The second is the *Documents Classic* or *Book of Documents,* which is a handbook of political rhetoric. It includes speeches delivered by kings and other political figures at historical occasions of epochal importance. The third is the *Book of Poetry,* which includes ritualistic hymns, odes and ballads extolling the great culture-heroes, lyrics of the aristocracy, and some popular songs.

Thus the range of early Chinese literature includes the philosophical—if the ideas expressed in the *Book of Changes* may be called philosophy—the politico-historical, and the poetical. It does not include manifestations of religious thoughts and attitudes except by implication; nor do we find any great epics, such as those that form the earliest body of literature in many other civilizations.

AN AGE OF TRANSITION, 771–221 B.C.

The ruling house of Chou never recovered its former position after the events of 771 B.C. But this date marks more than just a crisis in the dynasty, for it is also an index of changes in the Chinese economy and social structure.

The Rise of a Money Economy

In the economic field, these changes included a greater use of money as a medium of exchange. Money had been used before, in prefeudal as well as feudal China, but previously the cowrie shell had been the principal measure of value. In the new period copper coins appeared and attained great importance.

The development of a monetary economy brought about further economic rearrangements. A notable result was that land gradually became a form of property that could be sold and bought, and that the peasant was no longer attached to the land as though part of it. As land began to change hands with more ease than before, the holding of large estates was no longer confined to members of the topmost group in the feudal hierarchy.

The increasing use of money also led to the emancipation of the trades and crafts.

Hitherto these occupations had been a form of service to feudal lords. Now, with the growth of commerce, free merchants and free craftsmen emerged as a social class distinct from the peasantry and from the aristocracy.

It was not long before a new monetary aristocracy arose. Recruited mainly from among emancipated merchants, this monetary aristocracy became a threat to the feudal class, whose position rested upon land ownership and respect for tradition whereas the merchants gave voice to a more rationalistic outlook on social and economic mat-

Chinese Dynasties and Periods, 1766 B.C.–A.D. 220

Shang	?1766–1122 B.C.
Chou	1122–249
Period of the Spring and Autumn Annals	c.722–481
Period of the Warring States	481–206
Eastern Han	206 B.C.–A.D. 25
Western Han	A.D. 25–220

ters. Gradually the old feudal aristocracy found itself compelled to share both political power and social position with this new group.

Though benefiting the artisans and merchants, the changes that came about with the transition to a money economy had disastrous effects on the peasants. As the tie between the peasant and the land was loosened, the peasants often were obliged to leave their native villages, many of them forming roving gangs of bandits that terrorized the countryside.

Political Change

Rationalization in the field of economics was paralleled by rationalization in the field of political organization. Gradually the feudal system, based on the delegation of power, was replaced by an administrative system more effectively and uniformly directed from the center. Thus the states were no longer divided into fiefs, governed by feudal vassals, but into administrative units that were staffed by officials of the central government. This new system developed only slowly, and it was established in some parts of the country sooner than in others. But those states that first made the change gained much greater power, and ultimately, therefore, the new system was generally adopted.

Government intervention in economic affairs also increased during this period. Often this took the form of public works for irrigation, on a larger scale than ever before. Another form was the establishment of a government monopoly of the production and distribution of iron, which the Chinese began to use about 500 B.C., and of the mining and distribution of salt.

In view of these new circumstances, the house of Chou, whose position was based on the old traditions of feudalism, could not regain its former vigor. The barbarians who had invaded the kingdom had taken over the larger part of the royal domain—that is,

the portion of the kingdom that was under the immediate control of the dynasty and not held as fiefs of the great feudal lords. Then, when the barbarians were at last driven out, these lands were not restored to the royal domain but were taken over by the rulers of Ch'in, one of the most "modern" states of the time. What remained of the old royal domain was hardly enough to support the royal household, certainly not enough to give the dynasty political and military supremacy over the feudal princes.

Yet the Chou dynasty did not disappear for another five centuries. The reason for its survival was that its position did not depend solely upon military and economic power but also on its spiritual leadership; the dynasty was also a royal priesthood, and as such, it remained a symbol of national unity. The states that made up the kingdom continued to show respect for the king in his role as a priest and a symbol of unity, and they even went so far as to strengthen the ritual authority of the king. To give more substance to the idea of the unity of the land, the states from time to time held conventions, or congresses, over which the king presided. At these meetings, problems of national interest were discussed, and measures were taken to punish the states that were deemed to be acting against the common good.

But these means for attaining unity were far from effective. Feuds among the states soon broke out into warfare, and before long the larger states were swallowing up the smaller ones while continuing to struggle among themselves. In this situation the so-called "outer states"—those that had not in the beginning belonged to the Chou Empire —were at an advantage, because their more remote location permitted them to stay aloof from the warfare when this was to their interest and to intervene only when it served their purposes. Notable among the states that gained this advantage were Ch'in in the west and Ch'u and Wu in the middle and lower Yangtze Valley.

The Great Chinese Philosophies

The changes that we have been considering in political practice and social climate were not without profound effect on Chinese thought, because these changes forced the Chinese to take stock of their traditions and either abandon them or adapt them to the new atmosphere. So challenging was this intellectual problem that the last centuries of the Chou dynasty became the most creative period in the history of Chinese philosophy.

Taoism. Those intellectuals who endeavored to retain as much as possible of the old traditions are known as Taoists. This name comes from *Tao*, the general principle that they made their guide, which may be translated as the "way of Heaven" or "natural law."

Their interpretation of this principle led the Taoists to withdraw from political affairs and even from organized social life. They devoted themselves to simple activities, such as farming, and many of them eventually became hermits, giving themselves over to a mystic contemplation of nature.

The "Legalists." Other schools of thought took over the basic conception of *Tao*. Notable among these were the "Legalists," who made the Taoist principle of natural law into a rationalistic legal principle, applied to politics. In their view, social phenomena as well as natural phenomena should conform to a logical pattern. Hence the laws of government should rest upon reason, not merely on the customs of past ages.

The School of Mo Ti. Like the "Legalists," the thinkers of the school of Mo Ti (*c.*468–*c.*382 B.C.) were champions of reason, and their handbooks of logic bear comparison with Aristotle's. But in the Mohist system of ideas, reason was put to the service of principles of a moral character, and this position has an emotional strength that makes it verge upon becoming a religion. For Mo Ti, the main principles that men should honor are universal love and mutual help. "He who has surplus strength should work for others. He who has surplus wealth should share it with others." The utopia he outlined was a world in which universal love reigns supreme, and economic and social problems are easily solved. To those critics who argued that the ideal of universal love is hard to attain, he answered:

To lay siege to a city, to fight on the battlefield, to make a reputation for oneself by sacrificing one's life, these are things that are hard to attain. But if you encourage people with the right words, they will do it. How much more would that be the case with universal love and mutual aid: He who loves the people will be loved by the people. He who aids people will be aided by people. Is that really so hard to attain?

The diversity of the systems of thought that have been mentioned so far is a reflection of the diversity of political and social developments during this period. The degree of abstraction that is to be found in many of these systems shows a desire to solve human and social problems from a detached point of view. Yet they were all doomed to failure, because, to be successful, any system would have to take into account both the continuing force of Chinese tradition and the realities of Chinese institutional development at the time.

Confucianism. The system that came closest to achieving this synthesis was Confucianism. Confucius (*c.*551–*c.*479 B.C.) once said of himself that he was not a creator, only a preserver of tradition. This is true in the sense that he succeeded in preserving those parts of tradition that could be made to conform to the historic developments of the new age. He may be compared to the great prophets of the Old Testament, seeing the doom toward which the age was moving, but knowing the solutions through which this doom might be averted. In his view, the social life of man could not be organized by abstract principles or by political devices. It was man himself, Confucius believed, who must work out his own destiny. Hence the development of the human personality was the key to the Confucian system, and education, which involves the formation of personality, was of central importance.

Personality, as this conception appears in Confucianism, must not be confused with individualism. The individual was of interest to Confucius only insofar as he performed social duties. The education that Confucius advocated was not intended, therefore, for the development of the individual's own bent, but to make him into a gentleman—a man, as Confucius conceived him, who is destined for social leadership and whose moral training is of more importance than his technical skill. The gentleman, as Confucius thought of him, should combine all the qualities that are essential to social order, and in his personal conduct he should set an example which becomes the model of social habits and customs.

Confucianism did not at once prevail over the rival philosophies, but after several generations it did become the leading ideology of Chinese society. Eventually it became the orthodox ideology of imperial China.

Mencius. Hardly less significant than Confucius in the history of Chinese philosophy was Meng-tze, or Mencius (*c*.371–*c*.288 B.C.), whose book, called *The Book of Mencius*, became one of the great Chinese classics. Mencius, like Confucius, was interested in the good life, and he believed that it could be best promoted by good government. Mencius, who was a pacifist, was therefore especially interested in the training of princes in the business of governing well. Like Plato, he believed that rulers should be men of intellect, or philosophers. He believed that kings must maintain the confidence of their people; when a ruler lost that confidence, he lost the "mandate of Heaven"; at that point the people had the right to depose him.

The various schools of philosophy that arose toward the close of the Chou era profoundly affected Chinese civilization from that time forward. The writings of Confucius and Mencius came to be incorporated into the "Chinese Classics" and to contribute a sort of central thread in all the subsequent development of Chinese culture.

CH'IN AND HAN: THE FOUNDING OF THE CHINESE EMPIRE

During the last two centuries of the Chou period, the princes of one of the great fiefs, Ch'in, rose to such prominence and power that in 256 B.C. they challenged the Chou dynasty. A generation later, in 221 B.C., the ruler of the Ch'in assumed the title of Shih Hwang-ti—First Emperor—suggesting that his reign marked the beginning of a new era.

The Ch'in State

The location of Ch'in, on the northwest frontier of China, helps explain its success.

For this was a region exposed to barbarian attacks, and in self-defense, the Ch'in rulers had to adopt some of the military tactics and weapons of the barbarians. Thus they reorganized their army to make it a more mobile force, trained to fight on horseback. It proved a match for the barbarians and much more than a match for other Chinese armies, which still used chariots. The location of Ch'in had another advantage, in that Ch'in was too far off to become deeply involved in the destructive rivalries of the other Chinese feudal states and thus waste its strength.

Ch'in had been fortunate, too, in having able advisers and administrators, who introduced a number of innovations that strengthened the government. No new fiefs were granted after the middle of the third century B.C., and the feudal system gradually died out. An extensive irrigation system, which is still functioning, was built in Szechwan in the third century B.C., and when occasion arose, population was transferred to places where there was need of more labor for public works or soldiers for defense needs.

After gaining the imperial throne, the rulers of the new dynasty introduced throughout China the reforms that had earlier been made in their own fief. Thus feudal tenure of land generally disappeared in favor of private ownership, while the provincial government was placed under bureaus and departments responsible to the emperor. Strict laws and severe punishments kept both the officials and the populace under control. As another measure insuring uniformity, a single script was made official throughout the entire country. This was not a new script, but it now came into universal use for the first time, and ever since then China has retained a single, universal system of writing, although the spoken language has varied from place to place.

The Burning of the Books. Later Chinese scholars have been critical of the Ch'in dynasty because its policy was to discourage scholarship. The reason for this attitude was political, since scholars, who were taught to revere tradition, would be critical of a new dynasty that broke with the customs of the past and set up for the first time an authoritarian, centralized state. Accordingly the Ch'in leaders ordered the burning of all books that might prove dangerous. Among those destroyed were the *Shih Ching* (*Book of Odes*) and *Shu Ching* (*Book of History*), which were the basis of the Chinese classics, the works of those political philosophers whose writings put feudalism in a favorable light, and the histories of all feudal states. Exempted were the official archives and works on medicine, divination, agriculture, and arboriculture.

However, the damage done to learning was not irreparable. Many of the proscribed books were hidden away by scholars, and in the later Han dynasty a zealous search was made to recover them. In the outcome this served to increase the Chinese zest for collecting records of the past and resulted in a greater respect for scholars, which became part of the Chinese heritage.

Public Works. The Ch'in leaders launched an ambitious program of public works. The most notable item in it was the construction of the Great Wall of China, which provided for the first time an effective barrier against the barbarians to the north. This imposing wall, built with the toil of thousands of impressed laborers, was kept in repair and extended by later monarchs. Parts of it are still standing—mute testimony to the engineering skill of its early builders. Other items in the

Chinese Characters—Shang and Chou. The one-character Shang inscription (*left*) appears inside the twelfth-century B.C. vessel pictured on page 344 and also inside its lid. The Chou inscription (*right*) was found on a bronze of the middle fifth century B.C. (Courtesy of the Smithsonian Institution, Freer Gallery of Art, Washington, D.C.)

The Great Wall. (Philip Gendreau, N.Y.)

program involved the destruction of the old walls around some of the feudal states, the building of broad, tree-lined roads that led from the capital to the borders of the Empire, and the construction of canals, notable among which was the canal linking the Yangtze and the Hsi (West) rivers.

Other measures gave further expression to the Ch'in desire for uniformity. For example, a decree prescribed that all carts throughout the Empire were to be built with the same distance between the wheels. Similarly an attempt was made, with partial success, to establish standard units for the measurement of weight, size, and capacity. An endeavor to provide uniform currency caused the disappearance of precious stones, shells, and tin as mediums of exchange, but its success was not great enough to establish uniform values for the various gold and bronze coins that continued to circulate throughout

the land during this period of the Ch'in.

The efforts of the rulers to make China economically stable were doomed to disappointment. Though the private ownership of land was introduced and the peasants were thus freed from their feudal lords, the small farmer was under an economic pressure that frequently forced him to yield his plot to more affluent neighbors. Much of this economic pressure was due to the increasing burden of taxes, which inevitably increased in proportion to the rising public expenditures for public works, the building of palaces and parks for the court, and the maintenance of large armies. The latter continued to be a drain on the treasury even after the dynasty had accomplished the unification of the country, for the Ch'in undertook the conquest of a number of new territories, in what is now Fukien, Kwangtung, Kwangsi, and also Tonkin in northern Indochina.

The Han Dynasty

After Shih Hwang-ti died in 210 B.C., his dynasty soon collapsed. His successor was unequal to his tasks; critics became more articulate, and there was discontent because of the high taxes, the use of forced labor, and the harsh laws. Within three years, revolts broke out, in the course of which the capital was burned and other cities were sacked. By 202 B.C. a man of peasant origin, Liu Pang, rose to leadership of one of the rival armies that were contending for supremacy, and shortly he emerged as the founder of a new dynasty, the Han.

The Han dynasty lasted until about A.D. 220, with a short interregnum from A.D. 9 to 23. So long was its span and so great were its achievements that the Chinese have often referred to themselves as "the sons of Han." For a time the feudal system was restored, because at first the central government lacked the power to make good its rule over the local rulers. But a close watch was kept on the feudal princes, and the administrative structure that the Ch'in had built up was not allowed to disappear. Eventually measures were taken to shift back from a feudal regime to one of centralized government. In 127 B.C. a decree was issued that limited the inheritance of the oldest son to one half the fief, the remainder to be distributed among the other sons. This led to a gradual shrinkage in the size of fiefs, and no large new fiefs were created.

At first the Han were as suspicious of scholarship as the Ch'in before them. But soon the laws against scholarly activity were not enforced with vigor, and they were repealed shortly after the beginning of the second century B.C. An intensive search was then begun to discover copies of works that had survived the destruction of books under the Han, and schools were established for the study of classical texts.

This revival of scholarship established the primacy of Confucianism in Chinese intellectual life. It became the basic philosophy of the state throughout later centuries, and a knowledge of the books known as the Confucian classics came to be the basis of the examinations for appointment to the civil service.

Public Works of the Han. Like the Ch'in, the Han rulers engaged in an extensive program of public works. The Great Wall was kept in repair, and additions were made to it. More irrigation systems were built, and further work done in the building of dikes and canals. A large capital city was built at Ch'ang-an, and when that was destroyed in the course of fighting during the interregnum of the first century A.D. a new capital was established, farther east, at Loyang. The

Pottery House Model—Han Dynasty. Such models, intended for tomb burials, provide much of our knowledge of Han architecture, since no structure survives from that period. In such a house, domestic animals were kept in the court and first floor, while the living quarters were above. (Nelson Gallery and Atkins Museum [Nelson Fund], Kansas City, Mo.)

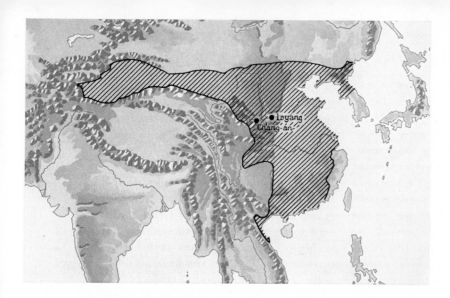

labor and money required to build these cities, with their gardens, palaces, homes, and government buildings, was a heavy burden on the treasury. This burden could be borne without undue strain at times when the land was prosperous, but when hard times came, it produced a critical problem.

The Han Empire

The era of the Han dynasty has sometimes been called the Imperial Age. While the great achievement of the Ch'in had been the unification of China, the endeavor of the succeeding dynasty was to extend Chinese rule over new territories, and ultimately the Ch'in thus created an empire almost as large as that of the Romans. One reason for this expansion was the need of the Chinese to protect themselves against the Hsiung-nu in the north. These were a barbarian people, probably the same as those known to Europe as the Huns. They had been held in check by the Ch'in rulers, but in the early days of the Han dynasty, they broke into the Hwang Ho plain, and only by a conciliatory diplomacy was an uneasy peace with them achieved.

In the reign of Wu Ti (140–87 B.C.) an attempt was made to drive back and defeat the Hsiung-nu. As part of this endeavor, a mission was sent to another barbarian people, the Yüeh-chih, in the hope of enlisting their aid against the Hsiung-nu. This hope was disappointed. However, most of the kingdoms in Central Asia were induced to recognize the suzerainty of China and send diplomatic missions to the Han court.

In the confusion attendant on the interregnum, the Hsiung-nu renewed their pressure, and again the rulers of China were impelled to enlist the aid of peoples to the west. This eventuated in Chinese control of present-day Turkestan and many small kingdoms westward as far as the Caspian Sea. For a time even the kingdom of the Kushans, in northern India, sent tribute to the court of the Hans.

The Han rulers also turned their attention to the northeast, moving into southern Manchuria and northern Korea. Colonists were transported to these regions, and an administrative capital was established near modern Pyongyang. This settlement grew and prospered, remaining under Chinese control throughout Han times. From this center, Chinese cultural influence spread to southern Korea and Japan.

In the south the Han succeeded in establishing their control over all of what is now China and into Tonkin and Annam in Indochina. Thus the Han Empire included much more than China itself.

The Spread of Chinese Culture. This extension of Chinese rule and political influence had far-reaching effects, for it led to the introduction of Chinese cultural patterns among the less-advanced peoples of Annam and Tonkin, southern Manchuria, northern Korea, and Central Asia. At the same time it added to Chinese knowledge of lands beyond China's borders. In the later Han period the Chinese even became aware of, and traded with, the far-off Roman Empire.

Trade with the West. Another result of China's expansion was the opening up of new routes of trade (pp. 214–215). To the ports of Annam, which now formed part of the Chinese Empire, came goods, traders, and envoys from the lands of southeastern Asia, India, Syria, and even the Roman Empire. Trade also passed along routes through the mountain passes from Yunnan to Burma, and across Central Asia, through Turkestan, to the peoples of the west. Most of the articles that passed in this trade were those having large value and small bulk. Among them were silk thread and silk cloth, iron, skins, cinnamon, and rhubarb, jade, glass, amber, precious stones, and horses.

But not all the consequences of this imperial expansion were favorable. The Han treasury incurred heavy expenses for waging military campaigns to conquer new territories and to defend them, for protecting trade routes, administering conquered areas, and sending presents to foreign rulers. These expenses required an increase in taxes, which, in turn, produced dissension among the populace.

Economic Problems. The schemes of the government for raising revenue were various. A principal source of income was the tax on land. At times, this tax was so high that it took three quarters of the produce of the land, but at other times it was so low as to be negligible. There were also, at times, a poll tax and taxes on vehicles and boats. Another source of revenue was the granting by the government, for a price, of rights giving private persons monopolies of the sale of such articles as salt and iron. For a time the right to mint coins was granted to private persons on the same basis. Titles of official rank were also sold.

In order to stabilize prices and insure a steady flow of produce to the capital, the Emperor Wu Ti instituted a practice known as "leveling." Goods of which there was a surplus were bought by agents of the government and sold when scarcity later threatened to raise the price. This tended to even out the prices and to prevent speculation. The same aim was served by the practice that permitted the provinces to pay taxes in kind, choosing for this purpose whatever goods were most abundant. This produce was then transported to other provinces where it was most needed.

Gilt Bronze Panda—Han Dynasty. Han sculpture in the round is a rarity, and the realism of this small panda is unusual in Oriental art. It is possible—but debatable —that the art of Hellenistic Greece found its way across Central Asia to influence the Chinese. Since religious subjects demanded traditional symbols, it may be that sculptors found freedom of expression in such animal forms. (Collection City Art Museum of St. Louis)

Chinese Plane Sundial—found in a third-century B.C. tomb at Loyang. This Han sundial is of gray limestone, about eleven inches square and one inch thick. The gnomon is missing, and there is no base, but it is assumed that the dial would be tilted on a base. The circle is graduated for 100 sections with radii lines number 1 to 69 incised from the circle to the center, number 35 being due north if the dial should be tilted from the south, or due south if a double gnomon should be used. (From "An Ancient Chinese Sun-dial" by W. C. White and P. M. Millman, courtesy of the Royal Ontario Museum, Toronto)

CULTURE IN THE AGE OF THE CH'IN AND HAN

While the Ch'in and Han period is characterized as the age of the imperial state, it was not without significance in the history of Chinese social and intellectual life. With the gradual re-establishment of Confucianism as the basic philosophy of the state, great attention was paid to the resurrection, editing, and reinterpretation of the classics. In the first century B.C. scholars produced China's first comprehensive bibliography, listing almost 700 works of poetry, divination, philosophy, astronomy, military science, and medicine.

Memoirs), included almost all the historical documents then known. It became a model for all subsequent Chinese historians. His work was later brought down to date, and extensive histories were written of each succeeding dynasty.

Other important literary works also appeared during the Han era. Among them were a number of treatises on philosophy and China's first substantial work in lexicography. New editions of the classics were brought out, written in the script that had become standard and on paper rather than on the silk, which had been used hitherto.

Literature

The Han period witnessed the appearance of China's first real historians, of whom Ssŭ-ma Ch'ien (138–85 B.C.) was the most eminent. His work, the *Shih Chi* (*Historical*

Science

Important scientific studies were made, and for a time, China seemed destined to develop a scientific spirit. Accurate sundials were devised, and a calendar, based on the phases of the moon, which remained in official use until 1927. As early as 28 B.C. the Chinese began to observe and record sunspots, and they calculated with remarkable accuracy the time required for a revolution of the moon. In the latter half of the first century A.D. the astronomer Wang Ch'ung made the bold assertion that eclipses of the sun and the moon are natural phenomena, having no relation to politics. This ran counter to the orthodox scholarly view that they were manifestations of Heaven's displeasure and a warning to the emperor to mend his ways. In a book entitled *Critique of Opinions,* Wang Ch'ung decried superstition and ignorance and advocated rational thinking and the observation of facts. However, the turmoil at the close of the dynasty and the opposition of traditional scholars to such radical ideas were sufficient to check the growth of the scientific spirit.

Philosophy and Religion

Taoism, which was probably more influential than Confucianism at the beginning of the Han dynasty, suffered after 141 B.C. as the result of an imperial edict requiring the dismissal from office of all who were not Confucianists. Taoism did not disappear, however, and later underwent a revival. Early in the second century A.D. the Taoists persuaded the ruler to repeal the ban imposed in 141 B.C., so that they could enter government service.

Buddhism was introduced into China at some time near the beginning of the Christian era. The date is not known, nor the route by which it came, but presumably the Chinese became acquainted with it while they were engaged in their imperial ventures in Central Asia. Not until a later period, however, did Buddhism gain a significant prestige in China. Its rise to prominence will therefore be discussed in the next chapter.

Han Art

Less is known about Ch'in and Han art than that of later periods, because much of it was destroyed when the capital cities were burned. What little has survived gives reason to believe that painting continued in this era. Specimens of pottery have been found, some of which are glazed. Han artists also continued the Chou tradition in bronzes, in a style characterized by simplicity and elegance. Lacquer-ware seems to have been common, for Han pieces have been found not only in China proper but wherever Chinese colonies existed.

Sculpture. Although there are some examples of sculpture in the round (p. 357), Han artists probably favored work in low relief, carved in stone. This sculpture sometimes depicts scenes from mythology, but more frequently records events in the life of the person whose tomb the artist decorated. The figures, especially of animals and birds, while not so massive as those of the Chou, show skill in the representation of line and movement. Also found in tombs are simple clay figures of houses, animals, and utensils as well as of figures of the friends and family of the deceased, entertainers, soldiers, officials, and servants, all of whom would accompany him in the afterworld.

The Han Achievement

Little is known of the life of the average man during this Imperial Age, except that he was preoccupied with the problem of making a living—ordinarily by agriculture. There were times when he prospered, but there were many occasions when he suffered from high taxes and forced labor. When conditions became intolerable, he would desert his land and turn to banditry, as during the closing days of the Han period.

The Han set the pattern of Chinese life for centuries to come. Steering a middle

Men in Conversation—detail from a Han painting (third century A.D.) on hollow bricks, excavated from a tomb near Loyang. The entire painting presumably represents an animal fight at Shanglin, the imperial park at Shensi. Here we see men spectators, standing aloof, while another section shows the ladies busily gossiping. What has been called the Chinese genius for spacing is already evident in this detail. (Courtesy of the Museum of Fine Arts, Boston)

course between the decentralization of the feudal era and the harsh autocracy of the authoritarian Ch'in, the Han rulers estab- lished a form of government that remained the basic political pattern of China from their time until the Revolution of 1911.

Suggestions for Further Reading

Source Materials

Anthologies

E. R. Hughes, *Chinese Philosophy in Classical Times* (New York, 1942).

Selected translations from all the more impor- tant philosophical works of the Chou era.

Lin Yutang, *The Wisdom of China* (London, 1941), pp. 567–1101.

Excellent selections from Taoism, *The Book of History,* the Confucianist writers, and later Chinese poetry and tales.

A. Waley, *Three Ways of Thought in Ancient China* (London, 1939).

Translations from late Chou Confucianism,

Taoism, and Legalism, with excellent intro- ductions.

R. Warnock and G. K. Anderson, eds., *The World in Literature* (Chicago, 1950–1951), Volume I, pp. 17–22.

Selections from the *Analects* of Confucius and from *The Book of Songs.*

Contemporary Writings

H. Dubs, trans., *History of the Former Han Dynasty by Pan Ku* (2 vols., Baltimore, 1938, 1944).

A critical translation of the work of a famous Han historian with annotations.

E. M. Gale, trans., *Discourses on Salt and Iron: A*

Debate on State Control of Commerce and Industry in Ancient China (Leiden, 1931).
Translation of a record of the great debate in 81 B.C. over the wisdom of the state monopoly of salt and iron.

Shih ching, The Book of Songs; translated by A. Waley (Boston, 1937).
The Book of Songs put into beautiful English.

Shu ching, The Book of Documents; translated by B. Karlgren (Stockholm, 1950).
The most up-to-date translation of *The Book of Documents.*

N. L. Swann, *Food and Money in Ancient China* (Princeton, 1950).
Complete text and translation of this part of the *History of the Former Han Dynasty.* Supplementary material by the translator on several aspects of Early Han economy.

R. Wilhelm, *The I Ching or Book of Changes;* translated by C. F. Baynes (2 vols., New York, 1950).
Translations of *The Book of Changes* with additional notes.

Secondary Works

D. Bodde, *China's First Unifier, A Study of the Ch'in Dynasty as seen in the Life of Li Ssŭ* (Leiden, 1938).
Story of the chief adviser to the Ch'in ruler, Shih Huang-ti.

D. Bodde, *Statesman, Patriot and General in Ancient China* (New Haven, 1940).
Biographies of three leaders of the Ch'in dynasty.

H. G. Creel, *The Birth of China* (London, 1936).
An account of the earliest stages of Chinese history, based on written as well as archaeological sources.

J. Needham, *Science and Civilization in China* (London, 1954), Volume I.
The first of seven volumes on Chinese science. An unusually important and valuable book.

R. C. Rudolph and Yu Wen, *Han Tomb Art of West China* (Berkeley, 1951).
A well-written and carefully illustrated description of bas-reliefs of two sandstone-cliff cave groups in Szechuan.

J. K. Shryock, *The Origin and Development of the State Cult of Confucius* (New York, 1932).
Traces the influence of Han rulers on the creation of Confucianism as a state cult.

N. L. Swann, *Pan Chao, Foremost Woman Scholar of China, First Century* A.D. (New York, 1932).
A scholarly and readable account of one of China's distinguished women, valuable also for its description of the era.

R. L. Walker, *The Multi-state System of Ancient China* (Hamden, Conn., 1953).
The political history of middle Chou times.

C. M. Wilbur, *Slavery in China During the Former Han Dynasty* (Chicago, 1943).
Describes society of the period, the various types of slaves, the status of the slaves and the owners, the method of freeing slaves.

R. Wilhelm, *A Short History of Chinese Civilization;* translated by J. Joshua (New York, 1929).
An understanding account of Chinese civilization up until the Sung period.

Atlas

A. Hermann, *Historical and Commercial Atlas of China* (Cambridge, Mass., 1935).
Best atlas for all periods of Chinese history.

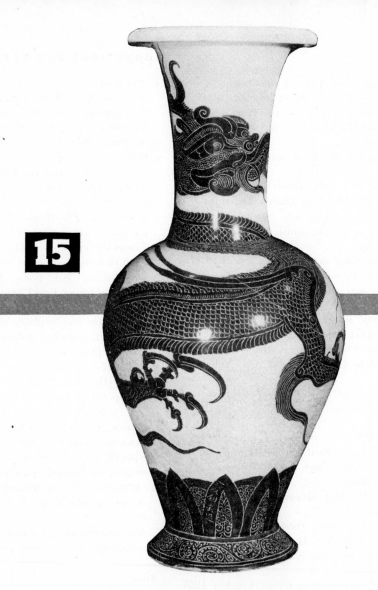

15

China's Golden Age

Porcelain Vase—Northern Sung, twelfth century. Among the many triumphs of the Sung dynasty potter, the most magnificent decorated pieces are the Tz'u-chou wares ornamented with painted and carved slip. (Nelson Gallery and Atkins Museum [Nelson Fund], Kansas City).

When the Han dynasty at last disappeared, after having given China a unified rule for almost four centuries, an age of disorder ensued. This period of political confusion lasted from the third to the seventh centuries A.D. It thus provides a contrast to the period of disorder in the western world, which began with the decline of the Roman Empire and which lasted much longer and was more destructive.

The immediate sequel to Han rule was the emergence, after A.D. 220, of three separate kingdoms—Wei, north of the Yangtze River, Wu, in the south, and Shu, in the west. After forty years of warfare Wei defeated the other two kingdoms and established a new dynasty, the Chin. This dynasty maintained an uneasy and undistinguished existence until A.D. 420, when it disappeared. The next century and a half was a time of extreme confusion. The area south of the Yangtze passed under the rule of a succession of Chinese kingdoms, while various non-Chinese kingdoms held the region north of the Yangtze. But the diverse peoples of these northern kingdoms—Turkic, Mongol, and Tungusic—were never able to unite, nor did any of them become strong enough to overcome the Chinese dynasties to the south.

During these three and a half centuries of political confusion, large numbers of Chinese migrated to the south, settling among the non-Chinese tribes who were established there. This migration brought about the diffusion of Chinese culture among the less-advanced peoples with whom the Chinese newcomers mingled, and it thus insured the survival of the Chinese way of life south of the Yangtze. In the north, too, Chinese cultural traditions persisted, even though non-Chinese peoples held political dominance; indeed, after a time, the invaders were assimilated. Despite the breakup of the old Han Empire, therefore, China continued to have a common pattern of culture.

The disorder began to abate toward the close of the sixth century, when Yang Chien, a Chinese official of one of the northern kingdoms, deposed the ruler, killed the rival claimants to the throne, and in 589 conquered the lands south of the Yangtze. The Sui dynasty, which he established, lasted until 618.

Despite its short reign, the Sui dynasty was of large importance. Not only did it reunite China under a single rule, but it ex-

tended the frontiers to include Formosa, Annam and Champa in Indochina, and Kansu in the northwest. The administration of the empire was again centralized, a vast program of canal building was inaugurated to improve communications, and numerous cities, including three capitals, were rebuilt with more extravagant plans.

But the Sui attempted too much. The heavy expenses of the government necessitated high taxes, which led to unrest. Especially damaging to the regime were four successive attempts—all in vain—to conquer Koguryo, a kingdom that included the northern two-thirds of Korea and southern Manchuria. By the time the Turks launched a new attack from the north, there was enough dissatisfaction within the country to support an insurrection led by Li Yüan, who claimed relationship with both the Sui rulers and the Turks. In 618 Li established the dynasty known as the T'ang, which many Chinese regard as the most brilliant of all the Chinese dynasties.

THE EMPIRES OF THE T'ANG AND THE YÜAN (MONGOLS)

The T'ang dynasty (618–906) was consolidated by Li Shih-min, the son of Li Yüan, who forced his father to abdicate in 626 and assassinated two of his brothers in order to make his own position more secure. His vigorous personality and great ability made Li Shih-min one of the foremost of all Chinese emperors. After his death in 649, one of his concubines became the wife of the succeeding monarch. Soon she took over the direction of affairs, and when her husband died she ruled in her own right as the Empress Wu. One of the few woman rulers of China, she became the second of the three greatest figures in the T'ang dynasty. The third was one of her grandsons, usually known as the Emperor Hsüan-tsung, who reigned from 712 to 756.

During the reign of Hsüan-tsung, the T'ang Empire reached its zenith. In expanse, riches, and power, it was the equal of the Moslem Empire of the Arabs, and it produced some of China's greatest artists and literary figures. But after this reign, the dynasty brought forth no more great rulers, and a slow deterioration set in. The dynasty came to an end in 906, when provincial generals defied the authority of a weak emperor.

The T'ang Administrative System

Under the T'ang, the old system of examinations for the civil service was revived, and a steady supply of capable administrators was thus assured. The Confucian classics remained the basis for these examinations, and schools were maintained at government expense for the study of these works, as well as other studies in history, philosophy, poetry, mathematics, and calligraphy. The schools established in the great capital city of Ch'ang-an attracted scholars from most of the countries of Asia.

To provide for an adequate flow of revenue to the state and perhaps also to gain popular support, the land was redistributed with the apparent intention of equalizing the holdings. This aim was not completely attained, however, for the tendency toward the formation of large estates continued and even accelerated during the closing years of the dynasty.

Taxes were of various kinds—an income tax levied on those who lived in cities, a tax in kind paid by farmers, a labor tax, which sometimes could be paid in silk, and excise taxes on certain commodities. Additional revenues were derived from state monopolies, especially those on salt and iron. Though a considerable portion of the population—princes, nobles, the host of officials—and the monasteries paid no taxes, the revenues proved adequate, at least in the first half of the dynasty, to maintain the government, including the armed forces, and to provide for the building of the beautiful T'ang capital, Ch'ang-an. With a cosmopolitan population close to 2,000,000, this was one of the grandest cities in the world at that time, and it became a model for other countries, especially Japan.

The T'ang rulers extended the system of canals begun by the Sui, especially the canal connecting the Yangtze with the capital. These canals, together with the good roads, made it possible for travelers and traders to move with comparative ease throughout the vast empire. Foreign commerce, as well as domestic, was of importance. Much of this trade passed through the port of Canton, where the government permitted foreign merchants to establish headquarters and to manage their own affairs under a leader responsible to the Chinese officials for the good behavior of his fellows.

Besides establishing their position at home, the T'ang rulers engaged in a program of foreign expansion. At first they had much success, building an empire more extensive than that of the Han dynasty and making their court as splendid and awe-inspiring as was the court of Louis XIV at Versailles centuries later. About the middle of the eighth century, however, their power was challenged by the Arabs, who began to penetrate into Central Asia, and eventually the T'ang had to acknowledge the primacy of the Arabs in this area.

During the last century and a half of their reign, the T'ang rulers were faced with internal rebellions, which became more frequent and more serious as time went on. To cope with these, the dynasty was forced to call upon the help of foreigners, principally Turks, Uigurs, and Arabs, and of local military leaders. But the latter soon established virtual independence, disregarding court orders and waging war among themselves.

In 906 one of these local rulers deposed the last T'ang emperor. But since this rebel was unable to establish his power outside the immediate environs of the capital, the Empire broke up into a number of separate kingdoms. For the next fifty-five years, there were five rival dynasties in the area north of the Yangtze, and ten "kingdoms" headed by military leaders in the south.

The Kingdoms of the Sung and the Chin

A first step toward the restoration of order was taken in 960, when one of the warring generals established a new dynasty, generally

The Mongols

known as the Sung. This new kingdom was unable, however, to maintain its power over the north. Eventually it was pushed south of the Hwai River (about midway between the Yangtze and the Hwang Ho) and was henceforth known as the Southern Sung. Meantime the Ch'i-tans, a Mongol pastoral people, had established themselves in southern Manchuria and the northern part of China. Their kingdom of Liao was subsequently taken over by the Ju-chen, a Tungusic people from the northern area around the Amur River. This Ju-chen kingdom, known as Chin, became the foremost power in northern China, while the Sung continued to hold the south. Still a third kingdom, Hsi Hsia, arose in the northwest, under the rule of the Tangut, a Tibetan people who had migrated northward and had begun to assimilate Chinese culture.

As these kingdoms were arising out of the disorder following the disappearance of the T'ang dynasty, the Mongols were beginning their rise to historical prominence. During the twelfth century these tribesmen, living east and south of Lake Baikal, had occasionally intervened in the wars between the Ch'i-tans, the Sung, and the Tangut. About the end of the century they were organized into a formidable confederation by a ruthless and capable leader, who took the title of Genghis Khan (perfect warrior) after he had conquered Mongolia in 1206 and established his capital at Karakorum.

Turning his attention to China, Genghis Khan soon forced the Tangut to recognize his supremacy. Then he proceeded against the Chin kingdom, capturing its capital, Yenching (Peking), in 1215 and forcing its government to withdraw south of the Hwang Ho. Thereafter his attention was diverted for a time to his western campaigns, leading to the invasion of southeastern Europe. Upon his return, he led a successful attack upon the Tangut Hsi Hsia kingdom in 1227, but he met his death in the course of the fighting. His immediate successor, Ogotai, combined with the Sungs in a campaign against the remaining Chin territory, which fell under Mongol control in 1234.

The Mongol Empire

Under Kublai Khan, who became their leader in 1260, the Mongols again turned westward, advancing deeper into Europe and overthrowing the Abbasid caliphate in Baghdad. On their return they conquered the kingdom of Nan Chao, in present-day Yunnan, forcing its inhabitants, the Thais, to migrate southward into what is now Thailand. Then the Mongols, moving into Tonkin, were in a position to approach the Sung Empire from the south and to complete its conquest in 1279.

For the first time in its history, all China thus passed under the rule of an alien conqueror. At first it seemed destined to be merged with the other lands under Mongol rule, becoming a province in a vast new empire, for Kublai Khan remained the nominal head of all the Mongols. However, his rule in the west was contested, and China therefore became the area of his main interest. Hence the outcome of the Mongol conquest was the reuniting of China under a new Mongol dynasty, which took the name of Yüan. Its capital was established at Yenching, renamed Shun-Tien Fu (known as Cambaluc to European traders) and renovated and completed under Kublai Khan.

Kublai Khan made a number of attempts to extend his rule over other lands. Korea passed under his control, but his two endeavors to invade and conquer Japan ended in failure. In southeastern Asia he met with partial success. Though he tried to force the kings of Annam and Champa to acknowledge his supremacy, he had to content himself with only a vague suzerainty over them. In Burma his armies won victories, but he could not establish a permanent domination. An invasion of Java had to be abandoned, owing to the adversities of the climate and heavy casualties in the fighting.

Though these ventures of Kublai Khan to broaden his empire met with but limited success, the Mongol period saw China enter into closer relations with foreign lands. Since all the Central Asian trade routes were in Mongol hands, travelers and traders could very easily pass eastward into China. And because the Mongol rulers of China were reluctant to make use of Chinese as officials in their government, foreigners were assured of a warm welcome in the Yüan capital. Throngs of artists, engineers, merchants, scholars, and religious leaders therefore made their way into China. The most famous of the foreigners who lived in China in the Mongol period was the Italian Marco Polo.

Gradually the Mongol rule weakened. The successors of Kublai Khan were not so capable as he, and under weaker rulers the quality of the officialdom deteriorated. Foreign traders drained the country of its wealth, and increasing inflation brought hard times. Natural calamities worsened the situation in the middle of the fourteenth century, leading to the emergence of a number of secret societies that aimed at rebellion and the overthrow of the alien dynasty. One such attempt attained its aim in 1368, when the last Mongol ruler was driven from the capital. Though the Mongols subsequently tried to invade China, they did not succeed, nor did they ever again become a serious threat.

The Mongol (Yüan) Empire

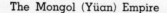

Shun-Tien Fu
(Peking)

CHINESE ECONOMIC LIFE DURING THE GOLDEN AGE

Agriculture

Throughout all these political changes, agriculture remained the economic basis of Chinese civilization. The records do not give a clear picture of the life of the Chinese peasants, but it is known that they lived in villages, which usually were surrounded by walls for protection, rather than in houses dispersed through the countryside.

Though individual ownership of land seems to have been common, there was a constant trend toward landlordism and tenancy. When the government was strong, small landowners were usually able to keep their plots, but when the administration became weak, their plight was grave. Some of the peasants would be forced to turn over their land to religious organizations in return for protection, while court favorites would obtain estates as gifts of the emperor at the expense of small landowners. As taxes and other burdens mounted, the poorer farmers would have to sell out to larger landowners or merchants who wished to invest in land. Or they would fall into debt, eventually forfeiting their land to the money-lenders.

Occasionally the government took steps to counteract this trend. For example, in the early years of the T'ang dynasty, a program was adopted by which all farmers were made tenants of the state; in effect, the land was thus nationalized. An attempt was then made to redistribute the land in holdings according to the size of the family. But measures of this sort were never pushed through to achievement.

Tea and Silk. A number of new crops were developed in this period. Among them was tea, which was used as a beverage as early as the third century. Tea gained a wide vogue in south China by the seventh century and in the north by the eighth or ninth. No other people have used tea so long as the Chinese or developed so discriminating a taste for it.

Associated with agriculture was the manufacture of silk, because, in areas where the mulberry trees grew, farmers raised cocoons as a kind of crop. Some peasants spun thread from the cocoons, but others sold them to buyers from the towns, who completed the process of making silk. This was a thriving industry, since half the population wore garments of silk, and the largest of the silk

The Famous Scroll of the *Silk Beaters*—copy by the Sung Emperor Hui Tsung (1082–1135) of a painting by the T'ang artist Chang Hsüan. From right to left, ladies are beating, winding, and ironing silk. The scroll, painted on silk in full color, measures slightly

factories is reported to have employed thousands of workers.

Cotton seems to have come into general use by the tenth century. Usually the cotton was spun by the wives of the peasants who grew it. Some was used by the family for its own needs, and some was sent to market.

The Porcelain Industry

Another product that appeared in this period was porcelain, and its manufacture also became an important industry. Though pottery had been known since prehistoric times and had been made by many other peoples besides the Chinese, porcelain was invented by the Chinese alone, and no other people has ever equalled the skill of the Chinese in its manufacture. There is an early reference to porcelain in the third century A.D., but the first real description of it dates from the middle of the ninth century, when an Arab merchant reported that the Chinese made bowls of a certain kind of clay, as thin as glass and almost transparent. No doubt, the general acceptance of tea as a beverage in T'ang times stimulated the use of porcelain,

and dishes and cups of this ware became common. But the finest porcelain was regarded as a work of art and was made for the imperial court (p. 362).

The Cities

The manufacture of porcelain and silk developed into industries of some importance, but as a rule the villages, in which lived most of the population of China, provided their own necessities. As a result, cities never grew to large size. The T'ang capital, Ch'ang-an, is a notable exception. Certain seaports, such as Canton and Hangchow, although centers of dense population, were far smaller than Ch'ang-an. But urbanism never became a characteristic of the Chinese civilization, and agriculture remained the principal economic pursuit.

The Irrigation System

The conditions of Chinese agriculture were such as to necessitate constant attention to irrigation and flood control. For the most

over 57 inches long and 14½ inches high. Placement of the figures and use of empty spaces makes this one of the finest examples of composition in Chinese painting. (Courtesy of the Museum of Fine Arts, Boston)

The Wounded Horse with the General—one of the stone reliefs from the tomb of the Emperor T'ai Tsung (618–649), known also as Li Shih-min (p. 364), that depict the emperor's favorite battle chargers. (From Collections in the University Museum, Philadelphia)

part, the rivers of China flow across broad plains, and as silt is deposited on the bed of the river, its level tends to rise. Hence dikes are needed to keep the river from overflowing its banks in time of high water and thus ruining the farmlands of the plain. The same dikes can be used to control the flow of water into the irrigation ditches that bring water to the fields when needed.

The Chinese had early developed efficient systems of irrigation and flood control, but the dikes and ditches were not always kept in good repair. When a new dynasty took over the government, it would usually attend carefully to their upkeep. But as the dynasty eventually declined, public works would often be neglected, with tragic consequences.

The building and maintenance of canals —as an avenue of transportation as well as an aid to irrigation—was another important function of the government. Notable among the canals was the one connecting the Yangtze and the Hwai rivers, constructed in the fourth century, and the system called the Grand Canal, linking the Yangtze with the Mongol capital at Cambaluc. At one time canal building occupied about 3,500,000 impressed laborers and another 2,000,000 auxiliaries.

Foreign Commerce

Foreign trade played an important role during most of this period. Much of this passed along the overland routes through Central Asia, even when these routes were not under Chinese control. Silk, exported from China to the Byzantine Empire, was the main article in the overland trade. So avid were the Byzantines to obtain this luxurious textile that it was reputed to be worth more than its weight in gold. Silkworm eggs, it is said, were smuggled out of China in a bamboo tube and taken to Constantinople about the middle of the sixth century. Whether this is true or not, the silk trade began to decline about that time as Europeans learned to produce their own silk. Later, during the time of the Crusades, the silk industry spread into western Europe.

Meanwhile there was also a great Chinese commerce by sea. Until the seventh century much of this trade was conducted by Indians, coming from the numerous Indian colonies in southeast Asia. But by the beginning of the T'ang dynasty most of China's sea trade was in the hands of the Arabs, who made use of the southern port of Canton. In the Sung period Chinese traders began to build ships and venture into southeastern Asia, and this traffic continued into Mongol times. Eventually the Chinese overseas trade reached as far as India and Ceylon, though it was difficult for the Chinese to break into the maritime trade west of Malaya, which was largely an Arab monopoly.

Besides silk, the principal Chinese exports were porcelain, paper, gold, silver, and copper coins. The most prominent items in the import trade were spices, jewels, aromatic and hard woods, incense, ivory, fine textiles, and medicines. As the value of imports tended to exceed that of exports, the unfavorable balance put a drain upon China's store of gold, silver, and copper coins, which were sent out of the country to pay for the imports. This problem had assumed alarming proportions in the time of the Sung, but it became still more serious in the Mongol period, when foreign traders were given a privileged position. As a rule the foreign merchants paid no taxes, and the profits they made in China were sent back to their own countries. Moreover, large numbers of foreigners became government officials under the Mongol dynasty, and many of these were given large grants of land as a reward for their services. The wealth that they received from their estates was also sent back to their homeland.

The Chinese Fiscal System

In order to meet the crisis created by this drain of wealth, the Mongols resorted to an increasing use of paper money. Though paper money was used as early as the T'ang period, it did not become a common medium of exchange until about the middle of the tenth century, when merchants began to use slips of paper as bills of exchange in place of heavier metals. Then the Sung emperors established a government office for the issuance of paper money. As the political troubles of the dynasty increased, an exces-

sive amount of currency was put out, leading to a decline in the value of the money and a serious rise in prices. The Mongols restored the value of the currency during the early part of their rule, but in their last years the terrible disaster of inflation was repeated. The ensuing economic crisis helped create the dissension that led to the overthrow of the Mongols in 1368.

A tax on land provided the principal revenue of the government. Generally this tax was levied according to the plan that was used during the T'ang dynasty. Land was assigned by the government to all persons over eighteen years of age. In return for the grant of land, the tenant was required to furnish a stipulated amount of rice or silk or fourteen ounces of silver. In addition, each tenant was required to contribute twenty days of labor on public works. These levies were reduced when times were hard or for tenants who were given less desirable land.

Boats were used to bring to the capital the grain that was given over to the government as a tax. The cost of transporting the grain used up a considerable portion of its value, for it required a large number of boats and much manpower and there was little cargo for the boats on their return trips. A portion of the grain reaching the capital was distributed among the officials and nobility of the court who received their income according to a scale based on the amount of grain produced on a given acreage of land. For example, the largest income thus allotted was the amount of grain produced on a plot of about 600 acres.

Merchants and other inhabitants of the towns were classified in nine grades according to their property, and taxes were assessed accordingly. These taxes were usually paid in *cash*—the *cash* being a small coin, 1000 *cash* having about the same value as one ounce of silver. There were also transportation taxes, levied on both goods and passengers, and sometimes taxes on wine and tea. Other revenues came from monopolies of the sale of salt, iron, and copper, and the minting of money.

In periods when the government was weak, a disproportionate burden of the taxes was commonly put upon the small farmer, because large landowners and court favorites could induce the government to declare their lands tax exempt. Frequently the burden of taxes on the small farmer forced him into debt, and often he lost his land to the moneylenders. This kind of abuse in the collection of taxes inevitably led to general discontent and helped put an end to the dynasties that had become incompetent.

Wang An-shih. When economic troubles seemed unbearable, reformers sometimes appeared. One of the most famous was Wang An-shih, who served as minister to a Sung emperor from 1068 to 1076. Wang devised a series of reforms to aid agriculture and reduce, if not eliminate, usury. He ended the costly process of transporting all the grain tax to the capital and, instead, had grain collected within a province. After filling local needs, the surplus was transported to localities where there was a scarcity and sold or stored in government granaries. Another reform was a loan to the farmer in the spring, to be repaid after the harvest in the fall at a low rate of interest. As further relief for the farmer, the compulsory labor service was abolished. Public works were completed with labor paid from a special tax on all citizens, including townsmen, levied approximately according to wealth. By these devices Wang expected to increase the amount of land under cultivation, stabilize prices, weaken the pernicious hold of the moneylenders upon the farmers, and distribute the tax burden more equitably, believing that in the long run the government itself would benefit by increased revenues.

Though Wang maintained that he was merely using ideas that had been advanced by others as long before as the Han dynasty, naturally his reforms aroused opposition from the landed gentry, the merchants, and the moneylenders. Abuses also crept in as "loans" became compulsory under corrupt officials. He was forced out of office and a few years after the death of the emperor his reforms were repealed. The resulting agricultural crisis undermined the position of the Sungs and remained to plague future dynasties. Yet Wang's administration had given evidence of the ability of Chinese leaders to work out solutions for their problems.

SCIENCE IN THE GOLDEN AGE OF CHINESE CULTURE

Closely related to economic growth were important developments in science, for though some of these were wholly the work of Chinese genius, others were a result of contacts through foreign trade with Central and West Asia, India, and Southeast Asia.

Alchemy and Medicine

Prominent in early Chinese science was the study of alchemy, which became important after the middle of the second century A.D. Much of this work in alchemy was an outgrowth of Taoism, which will be discussed on page 377, and because scholars held Taoism in low esteem, interest in this field was confined mainly to men of "low origin." This is regrettable, because an interest in alchemy was often the beginning of a scientific interest in chemistry, and if the best minds of China had turned to this field, more progress might have been made in developing a scientific method and spirit.

Yet some evidence of a scientific interest, even among Taoists, is to be found in the field of medicine. A *materia medica,* written by a Taoist in the third century, includes a long list of medicines and directions for preparing various remedies. It was revised and amended several times during the following centuries. Indian works on medicine were brought to China by Buddhist missionaries and, after these works were translated from Sanskrit into Chinese, they were widely studied even by Chinese scholars who did not accept the Buddhist religion. During the Sung period the Chinese discovered a method of inoculation against smallpox, and in the fourteenth century, chaulmoogra oil, obtained from the seeds of the East Indian chaulmoogra tree, was used in the treatment of leprosy.

Mathematics

The study of mathematics was advanced by the translation of Indian treatises brought to China by Buddhist missionaries. The Chinese themselves soon made important contributions of their own. The first approximately correct calculation of the value of *pi* was made in the fourth century by Tsu Ch'ung-chih. In the thirteenth century the Chinese began to use the abacus, soon demonstrating a remarkable proficiency in the mastery of this device, and about the same time they took over from the Indians the use of the zero. It is possible that one of the greatest of the Chinese mathematicians of this era, Kuo Shou-ching, developed spherical trigonometry in connection with his study of astronomy and his work in engineering.

Geography and Metallurgy

As a result of their growing skill in mathematics and their increasing knowledge of foreign lands, the Chinese became outstanding geographers and mapmakers. As early as the third century rectilinear divisions were used on a Chinese map, and by the thirteenth century Europe, Asia, and Africa were all shown on a single map.

As early as the fourth century the Chinese made use of coal as a fuel. In this, they were far ahead of the peoples of the western world, for when Marco Polo visited China in the Mongol period, he brought back to Europe the astonishing news that out of their mountains the Chinese dug a kind of black stone that would burn like charcoal, giving a heat that would last overnight. The Chinese also achieved skill in metallurgy, and as early as the eleventh century, they were able to combine copper, lead, and zinc in the proportions desired, as is shown by

A Chinese Abacus. Although the date of this is not known, little about the abacus has changed since it was first used by the Chinese. (International Business Machines Corporation)

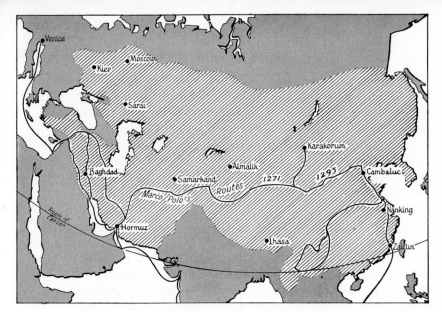

The Route of Marco Polo through the Mongol Empire

the standardized mixture of these metals in Chinese coins. Not until the eighteenth century did the Europeans learn how to refine zinc; when they did they borrowed the technique from the Chinese.

The Compass

One of the most remarkable Chinese inventions was the compass. As early as the eleventh century it was known that a steel needle, after being rubbed against a lodestone, would point to the south, and it was also known that the needle would deviate a little from true south. At first the device was used by geomancers for picking the location of graves, but by the early twelfth century, it was used in navigation on the seas. The Arabs probably took it over from the Chinese and introduced it to the Europeans. Not until several centuries later did the Europeans understand the principle of magnetic deviation.

Gunpowder

No less renowned is the Chinese invention of gunpowder. This was first used during the T'ang dynasty, but only in the manufacture of firecrackers, which were used on festive occasions. In the twelfth century a kind of grenade was used in warfare, and other explosive weapons were used against the Mongols in the thirteenth century. Gunpowder made its appearance in Europe a little later, but historians have not established whether it was independently invented in Europe or taken over from China.

Paper and Printing

Another important Chinese invention was paper. The technique of its manufacture was perfected by Ts'ai Lun in A.D. 105 during the Han dynasty. In subsequent centuries the Chinese developed many uses of paper, including wallpaper. From China the technique of papermaking spread into Central Asia, whence the Arabs brought it to the western world.

Related to the use of paper was the invention of printing. The first step in this evolution was the use of seals, made of stone, metal, or clay, which were inked and then pressed against paper or other writing materials. Next came the use of wooden blocks the size of a page, on which were carved a large number of characters. Eventually individual characters were carved on small pieces of wood, making movable type, and these pieces were assembled to make the page. The first printed book known—a sacred Buddhist text—dates from A.D. 868. By the next century printed texts of the major classics, running to 180 volumes, were available, and by the eleventh century, printing by movable type was in use.

Block printing is known to have spread westward from China as far as Persia, and playing cards printed in China were used in Europe before printing was developed there. But it has never been proved that the Europeans learned the process of printing from the Chinese rather than inventing it for themselves.

THE GREAT RELIGIONS OF CHINA

The three great religions of China are Confucianism, Taoism, and Buddhism. The last of these came to China from India, but the other two are of Chinese origin.

Confucianism

There is room for debate as to whether Confucianism should be regarded as a religion. The teachings of Confucius himself are concerned mainly with rules of morality rather than with an afterworld or a supreme being. However, some of the followers of Confucius later began to render honor to his memory in a manner that resembles the worship of a deity, and similar respect was also given to some of his foremost disciples. We need not settle the question as to whether these ceremonies indicate that Confucianism became a religion after the death of Confucius and despite his intention, but we note, at any event, that Confucianism has had a pervasive moral influence upon Chinese thought that makes its role comparable to that of a religion.

After the collapse of the Han dynasty in A.D. 220, Confucianism declined in repute, and the written examination system, which was based primarily on the Confucian classics, broke down. This made room for the introduction of Buddhism and the growth of Taoism. Yet Confucianism did not die out, and when China was reunited under the Sui and the T'ang, the examination system was re-established substantially as it

had been under the Han, and Confucian scholars were restored to official positions in the government. Though many of the T'ang emperors were patrons of Taoism, Confucianism continued to regain prestige and in the Sung period almost overwhelmed Taoism and Buddhism. In the latter part of the Sung dynasty there was a re-examination of Confucianism, out of which grew a new interpretation—neo-Confucianism—which will be discussed presently.

Buddhism

Buddhism entered China during the Han dynasty, but it did not become a major Chinese religion until the next period—the four centuries of confusion that followed the collapse of the Han. Then, as China entered into contact with India and with Central Asia (to which Buddhism had spread), merchants, missionaries and scholars came to China in such large numbers and received so warm a welcome that China seemed on the verge of becoming "Indianized." The number of Chinese Buddhists increased at such a rapid rate that by the fifth century they comprised, in some areas, nine tenths of the population.

Scores of Chinese scholars traveled overland or by sea to India, where they visited monasteries and temples, conferred with Indian scholars, collected texts, studied Sanskrit, returned to China, wrote accounts of their travels, and spent years translating

Head of Buddha—from the Yün-kang caves, fifth century, Northern Wei Period. Some of the earliest Buddhist sculpture in China is found in great rock-cut temples in north Shansi province much like their Indian models (p. 320). The long slim head with arched eyebrows and archaic smile are typical of the period. (Nelson Gallery and Atkins Museum [Nelson Fund], Kansas City)

Buddhism introduced some ideas that were alien to the native Chinese outlook upon life. Among these were asceticism, the celibacy of monks and nuns, the sanctity of animal life, pity for the suffering of other human beings, the transmigration of the soul, and the notion that a righteous person might become the savior of his fellow men. The concept of *Nirvana* never made a deep impression on Chinese thought, and the idea of *karma* became the topic of a running debate between the Buddhists and the Confucianists and Taoists. The Buddhists believed that a man would make his own fate, either winning salvation by faith and good behavior or incurring a punishment in one or more hells. The non-Buddhists, on the other hand, looked upon fate as something predetermined, which a man could not change and should learn to accept.

As might be expected in a country where there was generally a spirit of religious toleration and a considerable freedom of thought, many diverse sects developed among the Chinese Buddhists. One of the most popular was the school of the Ch'ing T'u, or Pure Land. According to this sect, there were many Buddhas, who had attained supreme enlightenment and then passed on to the Pure Land, or Western Paradise. Because they had earned a surplus of merit, they would give help to those who invoked their name and asked their aid. Another sect was the Ch'an—which also appeared in Japan, where it is known as the Zen. This sect placed an emphasis upon meditation, though it also recognized the importance of good works and asceticism. Later it stressed the significance of sudden enlightenment, or spontaneous conversion. The school of the T'ien-t'ai, which placed great emphasis upon the intensive study of the sacred scriptures, had an appeal to the scholarly classes. Still another sect, the Chên-yen, or True Word, gave expression to the Chinese interest in rituals and symbols. It appealed to some Chinese because it made a place for the traditional rites of ancestor worship

the sacred texts and adding commentaries. Notable among them was Fa-hsien, who set out in 399, traveling through Turkestan and Afghanistan on his way to India, where he lived for several years. From Ceylon he set sail for home on a foreign ship, at one time in the journey out of sight of land for seventy days. Eventually, after an absence of fifteen years, he reached China. Another traveler, Hsüan-tsang, was absent from China from 629 to 645, making the round trip by land through Central Asia. He translated an enormous number of sacred scripts into Chinese. I-ching, who made a voyage to India and resided there from 671 to 690, prepared, in addition to his translations, a Sanskrit-Chinese lexicon.

and provided experts who could "rescue" souls at funerals.

While winning over some of the Chinese, Buddhism provoked strong opposition among others. Non-Buddhists were critical of the Buddhist emphasis upon the salvation of the individual rather than upon his obligation to the family. They were also critical of the enormous wealth that was accumulated by the Buddhist temples and monasteries, and they looked with disfavor upon the Buddhist nuns, who did not perform a woman's proper function (bearing children), and the Buddhist monks, who evaded the obligation of military service.

On occasion this antagonism led to attacks upon the Buddhists. The most serious of these occurred between 842 and 845, when monks and nuns were killed, Buddhist buildings destroyed, and most of the Buddhist clergy forced to take up secular vocations. Thereafter Buddhism entered into a slow decline. However, waves of persecution such as this were never so serious as in Europe, and there were no great religious wars. Buddhism did not disappear, as it did in India, though it never regained its former prestige and power.

The Revival of Taoism

Though its origins date back to the late Chou dynasty, Taoism, the third great religion of China, did not reach its full flower until about the same time as Buddhism. In the Han period the Confucian scholars had taken a scornful view of the magical rites of the old folk religion and had spurned the mysticism of the *Tao-te-ching*, the Taoist classic. But magic and mysticism continued to have a popular appeal, and Taoism, therefore, had won favor with those who were not satisfied by the ceremonials and philosophy of Confucianism.

Shortly after the fall of the Han dynasty there had appeared a group of Taoist scholars who referred to themselves as "the Seven Sages of the Bamboo Grove." These scholars did much to revive interest in Taoism by ridiculing the formalism of the Confucianists, which they regarded as encouraging hypocrisy. Sometimes their behavior was so dramatic as to be sensational. One of them, for example, always carried a jug of wine and was accompanied by a servant bearing a spade, with which to bury the scholar instantly, without rites, wherever he might die. But these Taoists also devoted themselves to serious labors, writing commentaries on Chuang-tzu and teaching the virtues of the simple life, in harmony with the rhythm of nature. When Taoists became government officials, as sometimes happened in the four centuries of confusion after the close of the Han era, the doctrine of the simple life had to be modified, for a role in public affairs did not accord with the virtues of inaction and the avoidance of effort. Accordingly, Taoist teachers of the third and fourth centuries began to argue that inaction did not mean withdrawal from life, but a kind of life marked by spontaneity and tolerance, a preference for *laissez faire* as against artificial rules of conduct.

By T'ang times the Taoists had absorbed a religious group that had arisen in the

Pottery Pilgrim Bottle—T'ang dynasty. Probably the finest example yet found of Yüeh ware, the *pi sē* or secret ware of princes of Yüeh. (Courtesy of Museum of Fine Arts, Boston)

second century. This group had taken over the term *Tao* and used it as the name of a supreme power governing the entire universe. Its inspiration came from the teachings of Chang-ling, who seems to have been influenced by the Zoroastrian religion of Persia and to have proclaimed himself Heaven's Apostle—T'ien Shih. When this group merged with the Taoists, the head of the Taoists took over this title. Foreigners sometimes spoke of him as the Taoist pope. The title remained in use until 1927.

In some respects Taoism imitated Buddhism. For example, the Taoists established monasteries—though these admitted both men and women and did not require the practice of celibacy. Taoists also held out the hope of immortality, matching the Buddhist teaching of a future paradise.

Taoism came under attack because of the laxity in some of the monasteries and also because of the attention it paid to mystical and magical rites. The censure increased during the renaissance of Confucianism in the Sung dynasty. Although the early Mongols tolerated and even encouraged Taoism, its priests found themselves on the losing side in a great controversy with the Buddhists near the middle of the thirteenth century. Asked to discontinue their activities, the Taoists refused. Thereupon Kublai Khan ordered part of their property confiscated, and in 1258 he decreed the burning of all Taoist books. Despite this blow, which was a great tragedy for China as well as Taoism, the religion survived as an underground movement and eventually helped to effect the overthrow of the Mongol dynasty.

The Confucian Revival

Though quiescent during the period of the ascendancy of Buddhism and Taoism, Confucianism never died out. And in the time of troubles that came with the decline and collapse of the T'ang dynasty, it underwent a marked revival. The teachings of Confucius, which stressed the duty of the individual to society, seemed more appropriate to the needs of this age than did the Taoist and Buddhist emphasis upon the individual as an end in himeslf.

But for the needs of this age, more was required than the mere memorizing of the Confucian classics. The basic principles of Confucianism had to be reinterpreted and revised, in order to make possible an intelligent application of them to the new situation. Accordingly, a number of scholars in the Sung dynasty undertook countless discussions, in the light of Confucian teachings, of the problems of the nature of man, human society, and the universe.

Chu Hsi. The generally recognized leader of this renaissance of Confucian thought was Chu Hsi (1129–1200). As a young man, he was a student of both Buddhism and Taoism, but neither satisfied him, and accordingly he turned to the study of the Confucian classics. Gifted with an unusual ability to synthesize, Chu Hsi produced an interpretation of Confucianism that, though nominally opposed to Buddhism and Taoism, contained elements of both. Central to it was the belief that the universe is governed by natural law and that man will do well to seek to obey the laws of nature.

In his own time Chu Hsi was severely criticized, but soon after his death his works won official approval, and for some seven centuries they remained the standard exposition of Confucianism. His influence represented a victory for the school that believed, among other things, in the economic policy of *laissez faire*, which was to serve most of the succeeding dynasties.

Other Religions

Several other religions besides Buddhism were to enter China from foreign countries in the period from the end of the Han to the end of the Mongol rule. One of these was Nestorian Christianity, which seems to have been introduced early in the seventh century by a missionary from Central Asia. It won few converts among the Chinese, however, and it all but disappeared during the T'ang religious persecutions in the middle of the ninth century. Some Nestorian Christians figured among the foreign officials who served at court under the Mongol dynasty, but with its downfall even this vestige of Christian influence was wiped out.

Manichaeism was brought into China by Persians, probably about the end of the seventh century. It won some acceptance among the Uigurs, but scarcely any among the Chinese themselves. There is also evidence that there were Jews at Canton in the ninth century and in Honan during Sung times. As a religion, however, Judaism made little impression, and the Jews who settled in China were eventually absorbed into the Chinese population.

Islam was slightly more influential, but just when it entered, by what route it came, and by whom it was introduced is uncertain. As early as T'ang times, there were Moslem communities of Arab traders in Canton and other seaports, and Moslem influence was established in Central Asia as early as the late seventh century. But not until the Mongol period was there a substantial number of Chinese Moslems. These appeared in Yunnan province, where they were perhaps the descendants of Moslem soldiers in the Mongol armies; in Kansu province, where they became a majority of the population; and in nearby Shensi province, where they remained a minority. Their readiness to regard all Confucianists, Taoists, and Buddhists as infidels did not endear them to their neighbors, and few Chinese became converts to the Moslem religion. But as long as Islam remained strong in Central Asia, its influence in China did not disappear.

THE GOLDEN AGE OF CHINESE LITERATURE

The respect in which the Chinese have traditionally held scholarship has been a stimulus to the production of an abundant literature on varied topics. Aided by the invention of paper and later of printing, this literature has always been widely disseminated, and much of it has been preserved. During the period ending with the Yüan dynasty, most of it was written in the classical language, which was used only by scholars. However the language was not in danger of becoming sterile, for it was constantly enriched by the contacts of the Chinese with foreigners, especially the Indians. From Sanskrit, for example, the Chinese took over thousands of new words and ideas. Moreover, scholars devoted much attention to the study of language, compiling huge dictionaries and lexicons, such as the Chinese-Sanskrit lexicon of the seventh and eighth centuries.

History

Historical writings are among the most numerous of Chinese literary works, for the Chinese have always held history in high regard. Using as a model the work of the great Han historian, Ssŭ-ma Ch'ien, historians kept careful and detailed records of the events of all the succeeding dynasties. Outstanding were those of the Sung period, when, for example, Ssŭ-ma Kuang wrote a monumental work covering the period from the closing years of the Chou dynasty to the middle of the tenth century. Chinese officials themselves wrote memoranda and memorials to the court on a variety of subjects and also records of their decisions and actions. Since most officials were also scholars, these documents were usually well written; they provide the modern historian with valuable source materials.

The Literature of Science

A number of literary works treated matters of science. Among these were treatises on agriculture, sericulture, geography, medicine, mathematics, astronomy, and handicrafts. The works on agriculture included, for example, information on plowing, kinds of seeds, methods of planting and reaping, irrigation, types of implements, and the care and breeding of cattle.

Related to these are the compendiums and encyclopedias that were occasionally written at the order of the ruler. One of these, compiled at the order of a prince of the kingdom of Wei just after the collapse of the Han dynasty, is reputed to have contained 8,000,000 words.

Religious Literature

Religious writings made up a large part of Chinese literature. In addition to the Sanskrit works imported from India, which were translated by Chinese scholars, there were collections of sacred Buddhist scriptures. The first comprehensive collection was the *Tripitaka,* written in A.D. 517. Later editions of this work included new material, and by the end of the tenth century it comprised 5048 volumes. Also notable were the *Jataka Tales,* or stories of the birth of the Buddha, which were first translated about the middle of the third century. Buddhist scholars, in addition, prepared biographies of leading Chinese and foreign monks, and various smaller works intended for the general public.

Perhaps in imitation of the Buddhists, the Taoists also compiled a body of sacred scripture, including numerous commentaries on the *Tao-te-ching* and the works of Chuang-tzu. Much controversy developed around a Taoist book of the fourth century, *The Conversion of the Barbarians,* in which the author maintained that Lao-tze had traveled from China to India and become the teacher of Buddha. This outraged the Buddhists, who contended that Buddha antedated Lao-tze by two centuries and therefore could not have been his pupil. The dispute became so heated that more than once the *Conversion* was put under a ban.

Confucian writers were also prolific at times throughout this period. The classics were reissued in numerous successive editions, and occasionally they were carved on stone tablets, as, for example, at the University of Ch'ang-an.

The Chinese Poets

The Chinese produced no great epics like those of the Indians or the Greeks, and in in the period ending with the collapse of the Yüan dynasty, prose fiction was regarded as beneath the notice of the scholar and left to popular writers and the professional storytellers who wandered from village to village. In lyric poetry, however, there were significant achievements in this era. Indeed the best of all Chinese poetry was written during the T'ang dynasty, when Confucianism was too weak to exercise a restraining influence. Moreover the Buddhist and Taoist penchant for meditation and love of nature quickened the imagination of those scholars who were poets, and the conditions of peace, order, and prosperity that prevailed under the T'ang provided a favorable environment for cultural interests.

Li Po. Among more than 2000 T'ang poets whose names have survived, Li Po (*c.*700–762) was one of the most renowned. Though married, he found it impossible to settle down in a domestic routine, and, after studying for a time with a Taoist priest, he became a wanderer, devoted to the pleasures of wine and poetry. Introduced at the imperial court and given a sinecure, he joined a congenial group who referred to themselves as the "Eight Immortals of the Wine

Cup." But as a result of intrigue, Li Po was ousted from the court and obliged to resume his wanderings. Legend attributes to him a romantic death: while boating, he reached out to embrace the moon's reflection on the water, toppled from the boat, and drowned.

The poetry of Li Po is generally gay, often humorous, and marked by a feeling of harmony with nature. Often, too, it is deeply meditative and philosophical. As, for example, in

My Wish

The Yellow River flows toward the Eastern Ocean,
The sun sinks toward the western sea.
Like time, the water flows forever.
They never cease their flowing!
The Spring disappears with my youth,
The Autumn arrives with my white hairs.
The life of man is shorter than that of the pines,
Oh, that beauty and strength might never fade,
That I might mount upon some celestial dragon
And breathe the essence of the sun and the moon,
That I might be immortal!

Tu Fu. Tu Fu (712–770), another of the "Eight Immortals of the Wine Cup," is regarded by many Chinese as superior to Li Po. Though his poetry was not so spontaneous, it shows a deep insight into suffering and tragedy. For example:

The Wind Snatches Away the Roof of My Cottage

In the course of the eighth moon, the autumn marches on,
The fall wind scolds.
It snatches away three layers of my thatch-roof.
They fly away, across the river and scattered everywhere;
Some catch on the branches of the trees,
Others are drowned in the flowing of the water.

In a moment, the wind is calm, but the clouds are black,
The laden autumn sky is lost in shadow.
The old covers of my bed are cold as iron,
And the children, going to bed, rip them.
My cottage is open to the sky;
Around the bed, not a spot is dry;
The rain, fine as silk, falls endlessly.
In this troubled time, I hardly sleep;
The humid night seems endless.
Oh, that one might stand firm as the mountain
Against the rain and the wind!
Alas! When will such a home appear before my eyes?
Could this my dream but be realized,
I should be happy,
Even though my cottage were in ruins
And I were to die of cold!

Po Chü-i. A third great T'ang poet, Po Chü-i (772–846), lived a little later than Li Po and Tu Fu. Unlike them, he had a distinguished career both in the capital and in the provinces, writing poetry only in his leisure. Though an orthodox Confucianist, he gave more attention to content than to form and believed his poetry should be understood by all. To test its clearness, he is reputed to have read his poems to an old country woman, revising them until she understood. His romantic poems were popular with his contemporaries of all walks of life.

During the Sung dynasty most poetry was written by scholars who were also officials. Consequently they looked upon poetry as a hobby rather than a vocation. In the Mongol period, however, when Chinese scholars were shut out of government service, many of them turned to the writing of drama and poetry. Some of their verses were written in the vernacular, and the language of poetry thus came closer to the spoken tongue than did the language of written prose.

Chinese Music

In early forms Chinese music and poetry were so closely related as to be nearly identical. Because the Chinese language consists of monosyllables, each of which depends for its meaning upon the tone in which it is spoken, Chinese speech itself contains the basic elements of music—stress, rising and falling tones, and relative pitch. The natural music of the language thus suggests the melodic outline.

Shên Yüeh, a fifth-century poet, is a figure of crucial importance in the development of Chinese music into a separate and formal art. Though Chinese music originated much before his time, Shen Yueh became the first to define the musical values of the language in such a manner as would permit the composition of music to evolve rules of its own. His role in the history of Chinese music is comparable to that of Bach in European.

In Chinese music, unlike European, melody became much more important than harmony. This was owing to the close association between music and poetry, because in Chinese poetry, the artistry of the poet depended mainly upon the balance of the tones used in the words that he chose, since the sequence of these tones formed the melodic pattern. And because of the association of music with verse, music, like poetry, entered into a decline.

However, music was not wholly bound up with poetry. In ancient times it was used as an accompaniment to dances, which formed part of religious ceremonies and sacrifices. Gradually the dance also developed into a form of popular entertainment, separate from religious occasions. Likewise, instrumental music became a form of art and entertainment in its own right, reaching its highest development in the T'ang dynasty. In the reign of Emperor Hsüan-tsung (712–756) an orchestra was used at state ceremonies to celebrate victories, and a large festival orchestra is said to have comprised 10,000 musicians, who performed upon 300 different kinds of instruments. The music of the orchestra is described by Chinese historians as having been so melodious that the birds sang and the animals danced.

The Chinese Drama

Theatrical performances also made their appearance during the T'ang period. These were not a popular entertainment but a pastime of the court. Emperor Hsüan-tsung has come down in history as the patron of Chinese drama, and the Pear Garden—a kind of dramatic academy that he maintained at his court—has become a symbolic name for the theater.

But the drama did not become a full-fledged art until the Yüan dynasty, when Chinese intellectuals, barred from official posts and discouraged from the study of the classics, turned their talent to the writing of plays. These were written for the entertainment of the cultured Chinese—not for the Mongol conquerors, whose taste ran to juggling and similar feats of physical skill. The themes of the plays were drawn from history and from Confucian, Buddhist, and Taoist sources, and the presentation usually consisted of four acts. Each act used a single keynote and featured one singer—the hero or heroine—who was considered the host, while the other members of the cast were guests. Music was an integral part of the play, providing an accompaniment to the rhythmic gestures and dances of the actors and sometimes providing musical themes that would express appropriate moods or sentiments. So important was the role of music that Chinese plays should be compared with European opera.

As the drama became a serious art in the Mongol era, it also won a wide audience. Ever since, the Chinese people have retained a liking for the theater, and the drama has remained one of their important arts.

THE ARTS OF THE GOLDEN AGE

Calligraphy

The brush, too, has been a medium of the Chinese poetic genius. The written characters of a poem, each representing a word, must not only sound right; they must look right. A line of poetry should have a balanced appearance, and the manner of the writing should itself suggest the meaning.

For this reason the Chinese have always valued good calligraphy, or the skillful painting of characters with brush and ink. Scrolls depicting the work of famous calligraphers are prized as highly as paintings, and examples of their writing are studied as models. Treatises have been written on the fine points of this art, and its rules recognized as canons.

Painting

Poetry and calligraphy are thus closely related to Chinese painting. The painter makes use of the same materials—brush, ink, and paper or silk—and, as in writing, his execution must be swift and sure, with no erasure.

Because the painting must be done with a few quick strokes, the artist must make clear in his mind before he begins just what he wishes to reproduce. Though it takes but a few moments for him to make the strokes, his work is not hastily done, for he must spend much time studying the scene that he wishes to paint and meditating on its inner meaning. Because he does not paint what he sees but what he thinks, he must be a man of penetrating intellect as well as an expert in the use of the brush.

Example of Sung Calligraphy. Two lines from a poem by Su Shih (1036–1101), written by the Emperor Hsiao Tsung (1127–1194), one of two album leaves. The poem has been translated as

The wind beating against the cliffs all day, Wafts the boats on.

(Courtesy of the Museum of Fine Arts, Boston)

盡日舟行擘岸風　平生慣是連江雨

Detail from *Clear Weather in the Valley*—landscape scroll by Tung Yüan, Sung dynasty, late tenth century. Landscape painting was one of the great artistic achievements of the Far East, and this scroll is one of the best in western collections. Tung Yüan, also known as Tung Pei-yüan, painted in several styles—here in ink and light color on paper. (Courtesy of the Museum of Fine Arts, Boston)

Most Chinese pictures, like poems, were painted on scrolls, which could be hung up, studied and admired for a while, and then put away until another time. A collection of paintings was not kept permanently on display, as in our art galleries, but was treated as we would treat a library of books.

The three great religions all had an impact on Chinese art. Confucianism, by its emphasis upon the past and its concern for social values and family relationships, led to an interest in the painting of famous persons and historical scenes. Buddhism inspired the representation of bodhisattvas (potential Buddhas) and the Buddha himself, for these serene and compassionate figures were be-

lieved to give help to others seeking the way of self-enlightenment. Taoist mysticism and magic contributed to Chinese art a certain ethereal spirit, a love of nature, and a consciousness of the insignificance of man. The Taoists, who regarded silence as a virtue, may also have been responsible for the artistic use of empty space, which is an eloquent feature of many Chinese paintings.

Wu Tao-hsüan. Although almost nothing remains of T'ang paintings, the generally recognized master of all Chinese painters was the eighth-century T'ang artist Wu Tao-hsüan (known also as Wu Tao-tse), who worked part of the time at court under the patronage of Hsüan-tsung, during whose reign the art of poetry, too, reached its height. Among his achievements were more than 300 Buddhist frescoes. He was noted for his originality, imagination, and the lifelike quality of the people he painted. Most of his paintings were destroyed during the An Lu-shan rebellion of 755, and the few that survived into Sung times were destroyed during the warfare of the latter half of the dynasty.

because it was believed that in the after-world a man would be served by the same persons who had served him in life, and the effectiveness of their service would be determined by the perfection of their likeness

Kneeling Bodhisattva—eighth or ninth century, T'ang dynasty. After the return of Hsüan-tsang (p. 376) with his group of images, Chinese art showed a strong Indian influence. (Courtesy of the Fogg Art Museum, Harvard University)

Chinese Sculpture

Chinese devotion to the art of painting had no counterpart in sculpture. One reason for this was that Chinese were never much interested in the representation of the human figure—their painters preferred landscape scenes. Another was that most artists, being also scholars, considered the brush rather than the chisel the proper tool for the expression of their ideas.

Nevertheless, the prevalence of Buddhism—a foreign influence—provided some incentive for the carving of such figures as Buddhas and bodhisattvas. This kind of sculpture first appeared in the fourth and fifth centuries, when the northern part of the country was controlled by non-Chinese peoples and Buddhism was spreading rapidly. At first this art showed a strong Indian influence, especially in the general pose of the figure, the position of the hands, and the clothing. In their early efforts Chinese sculptors seem to have regarded the human form as little more than a block on which to carve the draperies, but by the time of the T'ang, they were showing more concern for the figure itself. And in their sculpture, as in painting, the characteristic Chinese sense of rhythm was evident.

The T'ang dynasty is also noted for the perfection of the small figures, made of clay pressed in a mold, that were placed in tombs. These figures were made with great care,

in these statuettes. Among them are to be found the images of camel drivers from Central Asia, Syrian singers and actors, and jugglers from India—evidence of the large number of foreigners who lived in China during this time. Likewise, the number of entertainers, mounted horsemen, and various kinds of serving men and women gives an indication of the size of the households of the wealthy classes.

Chinese Architecture

Since most Chinese buildings were made of wood or other perishable materials, little remains of the architecture of this period. The beautiful pagodas that dotted the landscape—some within temple grounds, others built as memorials—were a Buddhist influence. They were the Chinese interpretation of the Indian *stupa*. They always had an odd number of stories (since odd numbers were propitious), and usually they were octagonal. Another architectural characteristic, which may have developed from the gateways to Buddhist temples, was the *pailou,*

a ceremonial gateway made of stone, or of wood, with a tiled roof.

Although nothing remains of the imposing T'ang capital at Ch'ang-an except for part of its walls, we have a description of this city which reports that it had the form of a great rectangle, about six miles long and five miles wide. Broad streets divided the city on the pattern of a gridiron, and a main road led to the imperial palace in the northern part of the city. It was surrounded by a wall, pierced by gates at the main entrances and surmounted by guardhouses at regular intervals. You can gain a further notion of its magnificence from modern Peking, which was modeled after C'hang-an. This T'ang city also served as a model for the Japanese capitals, first at Nara, then at Kyoto.

Then, as now, the typical home of the rich Chinese was built around an inner courtyard, which often included a rock garden with a miniature lake, streams, hills, paths, and bridges. Sheltered in this courtyard, the family could preserve the illusion of retiring to the mountains to commune with nature and thus gain inner strength and calm contentment.

Suggestions for Further Reading

Source Materials

Anthologies

F. Ayscough and A. Lowell, eds., *Fir Flower Tablets (Boston, 1921).*
An excellent collection of translations of Chinese poetry.

C. H. Hamilton, ed., *Buddhism, a Religion of Infinite Compassion* (New York, 1952).
Selections from Buddhist scriptures, with commentaries by Hsüan Tsang and other writers.

Lin Yutang, *The Wisdom of China and India* (New York, 1942), pp. 867–1101.
Selections from the great Chinese poems, tales, wit and humor, and proverbs.

A. Waley, *Translations from the Chinese* (New York, 1941).
A collection of translations of the best Chinese poets, chiefly of the Golden Age.

R. Warnock and G. K. Anderson, eds., *The World in Literature* (Chicago, 1950–1951), Volume I, pp. 22–27.
Selections from the poems of Li Po and Tu Fu.

Contemporary Writings

Kuo Jo-Hsü, *Experiences in Painting;* translated by A. C. Soper (Washington, D. C., 1951).
Full Chinese text of this eleventh-century history of Chinese painting, with an excellent, complete translation. Contains explanatory notes by the translator on a wide variety of subjects related to painting.

Marco Polo, *The Adventures of Marco Polo,* edited by R. J. Walsh (New York, 1948).
A fascinating description of China under the Mongols by the most famous of European travelers.

E. O. Reischauer, ed., *Ennin's Travels in T'ang China* (New York, 1955).
An eyewitness description by a Japanese traveler of China during its Golden Age.

Secondary Works

W. Bingham, *The Founding of the T'ang Dynasty; The Fall of Sui and the Rise of T'ang* (Baltimore, 1941).
An examination, based on Chinese sources, of the factors that caused the fall of Sui and enabled the founder of T'ang to overcome his many rivals. Excellent case study of the fall of a dynasty.

L. Binyon, *The Spirit of Man in Asian Art* (Cambridge, Mass., 1936).
A series of lectures delivered at Harvard University by the well-known British critic. Lectures one and three discuss especially the influence of Taoism and Buddhism on Chinese art, principally in T'ang and Sung dynasties.

Chi Ch'ao-ting, *Key Economic Areas in Chinese History as Revealed in the Development of Public Works for Water-Control* (London, 1936).
A study that shows the relation between measures for water control and political power, and the shifting of important economic areas from one dynasty to another.

H. S. Galt, *A History of Chinese Educational Institutions* (London, 1951), Volume I.
This volume, based on Chinese sources, carries its subject from the beginning to A.D. 960. It also contains material on persons and events of each period.

A. Herrmann, *Historical and Commercial Atlas of China* (Cambridge, Mass., 1935).
Best for all periods of Chinese history.

Huang Siu-chi, *Lu Hsiang-shan, a Twelfth-century Chinese Idealist Philosopher* (New Haven, 1944).
A study of the thought of an opponent of Chu Hsi. Based on source materials, this study is clear and objective.

W. Hung, *Tu Fu, China's Greatest Poet* (Cambridge, Mass., 1952).
A biography of the great T'ang poet and a lively account of the time in which he lived. Includes many excellent examples of his poetry.

E. A. Kracke, *Civil Service in Early Sung China, 960–1067* (Cambridge, Mass., 1953).
An analysis of the structure of the Chinese civil service from the emperor down to local officials. A detailed study including types and procedures of examination, appointment and promotion of officials.

Lin Yutang, *The Gay Genius: The Life and Times of Su Tungpo* (New York, 1947).
A biography of the Sung poet, essayist, calligrapher, and statesman. Also good for the story of his family, his friends, and his political enemies.

G. Rowley, *Principles of Chinese Painting* (Princeton, 1947).
Designed primarily for those "who look upon the art of Asia for the first time."

P. M. Sykes, *The Quest for Cathay* (London, 1936).
The Polo brothers, including Marco, and other explorers. Includes short extracts from the accounts of John of Plano Caprini and William Rubruquis.

A. Waley, *The Life and Times of Po Chü-i* (New York, 1950).
The best English language biography of this famous T'ang poet. Contains valuable information on the society of which he was a part and the institutions of his time.

H. R. Williamson, *Wang An Shih, a Chinese Statesman and Educationalist of the Sung Dynasty* (2 vols., London, 1935–1937).
The most extensive work on the eleventh-century reformer and scholar. Includes a description of his attempts to invigorate the weakening Sung dynasty and an examination of the argument of his chief contemporary critic.

K. A. Wittfogel and Feng Chia-sheng, eds., *History of Chinese Society: Liao (907–1125)* (Philadelphia, 1949).
A detailed study of Chinese society: its economic and social organization, political institutions and practices. Describes techniques for ruling Chinese, which were followed by later invaders of China.

Recordings of Chinese Music
Chinese Classical Music (Folkways 12, 802).
Music of the Orient (Decca DX-107).

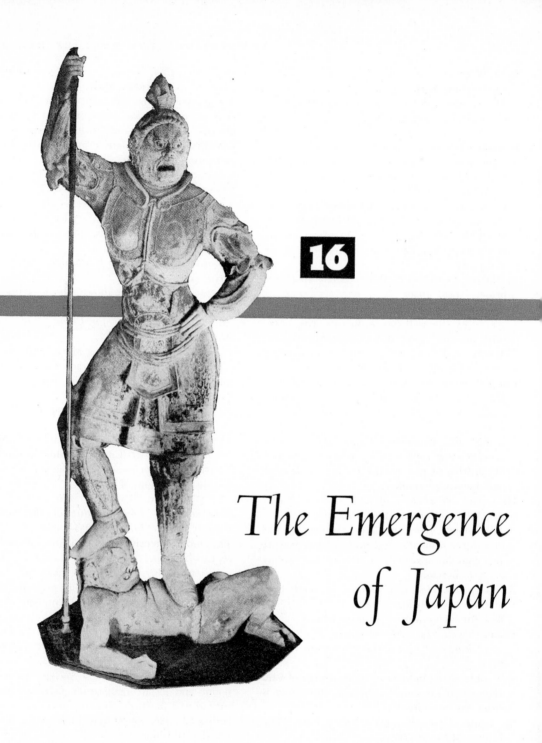

16

The Emergence of Japan

A Guardian King of the Buddhist Heavens—Todaiji Temple. In the Nara period (p. 398) the image of Buddha was placed on an elevated platform, guarded at the four corners by demigods in warrior attire.

A sign of the greatness of T'ang China was the spread of Chinese civilization in the T'ang era to the lands near by. It is not surprising that Chinese culture was introduced into Annam and Korea, since these were tributary states, acknowledging Chinese suzerainty. But it is significant that Chinese culture was also adopted in Japan, which did not pass under Chinese political dominance. In all these countries the Chinese ideograph became the basis of the written language and thus of intellectual and cultural development, while the writings of Confucius and Chinese translations of Buddhist texts became a dominating influence in religion and ethics.

No country is more in debt to China than is Japan. So great have been the borrowings of the Japanese—first from the Chinese and later from the west—that the Japanese are often scorned as mere imitators. But this is unjust, because the Japanese have taken from foreign civilizations only those elements that fitted their needs and environment. The resulting combination has been unique, and Japan today represents a distinctive civilization of great interest and of much importance.

JAPAN IN EARLIEST TIMES

Japan consists of four large mountainous islands and many smaller ones. Kyushu, the southernmost of the great islands, and Honshu, the largest and most important, seem to have been the sites of the earliest settlements; Shikoku was somewhat off the routes used by those who first came to the islands, and Hokkaido, the northernmost island, was not settled and developed until the late nineteenth century. Of the nearly 1000 small islands, many are still unoccupied. Early Japanese history thus centers on the islands of Kyushu and Honshu.

The four big islands together have an area about equal to the state of California. Their backbone is a range of volcanoes, which often cause serious earthquakes. Since the mountains are not suited to farming, most of the people live in the valleys, which are among the most densely populated areas in the world. Although the terrain has some disadvantages, the climate of Japan is favorable. Temperatures are moderate, and rainfall is abundant. Fish are plentiful in the warm coastal waters, and the many harbors and inlets provide shelter for fishing boats. Almost alone among the peoples of the Orient, the Japanese have always been seafarers.

The Ainu

The earliest inhabitants of Japan (so far as is known) were a short, hairy people known as the Ainu, who probably were distantly related to the Caucasian race. They were a rude and primitive people, supporting themselves chiefly by hunting. As other peoples arrived in the islands, the Ainu were driven to the north, where a few of them still survive, living in small communities that are preserved by the Japanese government as tourist attractions. Undoubtedly many of the Ainu intermarried with their conquerors, for many of the Japanese are, like them, swarthy and hairy.

The Early Japanese

The earliest Japanese came from northeastern Asia in a series of migrations before the Christian era. Another group of immigrations seems to have come from southern China, moving by way of Formosa and the Ryukyu Islands to southern Japan. Though much doubt remains concerning this latter stream of migration, it offers an explanation of some similarities between the Japanese and their southern neighbors. Like them, the Japanese are short of stature. Moreover the houses of the Japanese are more like those of southern Asia than those of China, for they are best suited to summer living and give poor protection against the severe winters of some parts of Japan. The Japanese house is made of wood and stands several feet above the level of the ground. Its wall

space is largely given over to sliding wooden panels of lattice design, to which rice paper is glued. In summer the panels can be removed, making possible a maximum of outdoor living. In winter, however, these panels admit drafts of cold air, the floor becomes damp, and the heating, which is provided by a brazier of charcoal, is inadequate.

The immigrants coming from the south were less important in Japanese history than those who came from northeastern Asia by way of Korea. These seem to have been warriors who were accustomed to fighting on horseback. Related to the marauders who beset the Chinese, they knew the use of iron, and their better weapons and more advanced state of culture gave them a great advantage over the primitive Ainu. They brought with them bronze mirrors and ornaments made in the shape of a comma—artifacts that have also been found throughout Manchuria and Korea. In Japan they became symbols of imperial rule.

These invaders came in small groups, probably based upon tribal organization, and each successive group attained a measure of control over a specific region. By the time of the Han dynasty in China—probably by the first century A.D.—the most important of these groups of warriors were located in northern Kyushu and in the Yamato region of southeastern Honshu. From Yamato came the imperial Japanese clan and the myths of divine origin that grew up around it.

The Clan Period

The period that preceded the adoption of Chinese civilization in the sixth century A.D. is often referred to as "the period of the clans." Social and political institutions reflected the tribal organization of the settlers who had come into Japan in the preceding centuries. Ties of blood relationship, which were supposed to be the basis of the tribe, were especially important in early times, because of the stress upon the family and the

constant preoccupation with warfare. Moreover, the many valleys and inlets of Japan
provided an environment suitable for a de-
centralized society, and since agriculture did
not require elaborate irrigation works, as in
China, there was no pressing need for a
large-scale social and political organization.
As a rule, therefore, each clan, comprising a
group of warriors bound together by real
or fancied ties of kinship, held control of a
particular valley. Within that area the individual's social position and prestige depended on his status in the clan. This kind
of society was rigidly hierarchical.

The clan itself did not include all the inhabitants of an area, but only the upper
classes. Beneath them were groups of workers
organized into guilds. These included captives taken in the wars of invasion, other
captives and artisans who had been brought
along from Korea, and the Ainu. Their
status was virtually that of slaves, for the
members of each guild, or *be*, were held in
bondage, and their children were obliged to
follow the same pursuits as the parents.
Thus the *be* conformed to the general pattern of family and hierarchy on which the
ruling class was organized.

We know very little about the life of these
early Japanese. From the comments of some
Chinese traders and missions who visited
the islands, we can gather that they lived
in crude houses, ate with their fingers, and
had little notion of obedience or loyalty.
These observations are naturally somewhat
disparaging, because they were written for
a Chinese audience that looked down upon
the Japanese as barbarians. From other
sources we have reason to believe that by
the fourth and fifth centuries A.D., the primitive clan organization was inadequate for
the needs of Japan. The members of the
be no longer were kept under so tight control as previously; the family associations,
which were the basis of the clans, were
growing looser; and even the imperial clan,
which was the greatest of them all, was being
infiltrated by competing groups.

Shintō

To check the disintegration of the clan
system, the imperial clan made use of a religious mythology known as Shintō, or "the
way of the gods." This name, derived from
the Chinese, was given by the Japanese to
their native religious beliefs after Buddhism
made its appearance in the islands in the
sixth century, presenting a challenge to the
older forms of worship.

In origin, these beliefs were little more
than crude, animistic traditions of nature
worship. *Kami*, the word ordinarily used
for *god* in Japanese, at first meant only
unusual, striking, or *awe-inspiring.* Unusual
waterfalls, precipices, and placid seas could
all suggest qualities of the unseen and

Haniwa Armored Man—terracotta figure from
a pre-Buddhist burial mound. (Courtesy of Pageant of *Japanese Art*, Vol. III, plate 2.)

supernatural, and the word for *unusual* would thus take on a religious connotation. The early Japanese peopled their beautiful islands with spirits. Thus numerous shrines were established on Mount Fuji, and one of the most celebrated Shintō shrines is to be found on the shores of the beautiful Inland Sea.

In the clan period each clan had its own *kami,* identified with the area that the clan ruled. Each shrine had its own priesthood, which was associated with a given clan. The priests of the Yamato area in Honshu gradually assumed a primacy over their rivals, and from this group sprang the imperial family of Japan. From the first, this family combined supernatural claims with the support of powerful political forces in the Yamato area. These advantages, together with the traditional Japanese respect for heredity, have made it possible for the imperial

family to maintain an unbroken line of succession down to the present day. To be sure, the fortunes of the imperial family have undergone many vicissitudes—for long periods, the emperor has had little power; sometimes emperors have been assassinated; and one emperor was so destitute that he was forced to sell souvenirs of his handwriting. Nevertheless the imperial family never died out, and the Japanese are proud that their rulers can trace their descent to the dawn of Japanese history.

The Shintō mythology owes its present form to the fact that it was transmitted by the imperial family, which used this mythology for political purposes. It consists of several cycles of myths, which explain the creation of the world and of Japan through the actions of various gods and goddesses. The crucial portion of these myths, which is the portion explaining the origin of the Japanese homeland, depicts the islands as the offspring of a cosmic god and goddess. The islands are therefore of divine origin, and their rule was assigned by the sun goddess to her grandson. In turn, his grandson was the Emperor Jimmu, under whom were undertaken the first great campaigns against the Ainu.

These myths were obviously designed to give prestige to the imperial family, since they provided the basis for the emperor's claim of divine descent. Until the Japanese defeat in 1945, schoolchildren in Japan were required to accept them as the true account of the origins of the Japanese state. The tradition based on these myths assigns 660 B.C. as the date of the accession of Jimmu, the first emperor. But this date is probably much too early, for it makes it necessary to ascribe to his successors reigns of inordinately long periods, in order to bring the account down to the eighth century A.D., when the first histories were compiled. Historians today place the beginning of Jimmu's reign about 30 or 40 B.C.

Primitive Shintō had little of ethics or moral teachings to offer its followers. It involved no sense of sin or guilt, but only pollution. Its ceremonies therefore stressed purification through washing. The greatest offenses were those that prevented the normal production of food, and the earliest specimens of Japanese literature are ceremonial prayers offered by the emperor, which seek to appease the divine wrath and assure good harvests.

Since the early Japanese generally accepted the Shintō beliefs, presumably the imperial clan, to which the Shintō myths attributed a divine origin, had primacy over the other clans. Probably this primacy was greatest in the area controlled by the Yamato group, whose spiritual authority centered in the great shrine at Ise. But the pre-eminence of the imperial clan did not go unchallenged. Competing clans began to try to share the imperial power, and new Shintō priesthoods contested the spiritual leadership of the imperial family, whose power was originally that of a priesthood. Moreover, the introduction of Buddhism presented new problems for the imperial family. Thus, by the sixth century A.D., a crisis had arisen in Japan, out of which was to come a series of reforms and innovations strengthening the imperial clan.

THE ROLE OF KOREA IN EARLY JAPANESE HISTORY

Korea played a tremendously important role in the early history of Japan by serving as the link between the island people and China. Because it was close to China, Korea soon passed under Chinese rule, while the sea provided Japan with natural barriers against Chinese invasion. Yet the Japanese were in constant contact with Korea, and from Korea, Chinese civilization was transmitted to the islands.

Like Japan, Korea is mountainous, but its climate posed a sterner challenge to the immigrants from northeastern Asia. Generally the northern part of the country is too cold to permit the cultivation of rice. For this reason the main center of population in modern times has been in the warmer plains of the south. In early times, however, northwestern Korea was the cultural center of the peninsula, because this region was in close touch with China.

The Chinese Colony at Lolang

One factor in the spread of Chinese influence into Korea was the harsh rule of the first Chinese emperor, Shih Huang-ti (c.249– 210 B.C.), who imposed enormous exactions of labor and treasure for such projects as the Great Wall. To escape this burden, it appears that many Chinese fled to Korea.

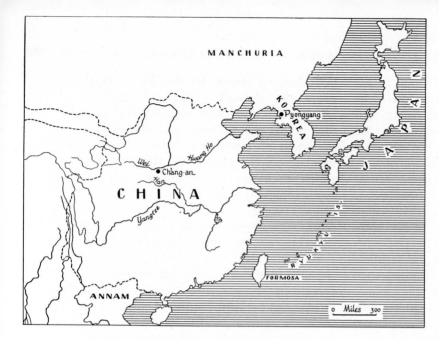

The Far East
about 200 B.C.

But not until the Han dynasty did the Chinese attempt the conquest of northwestern Korea. In 108 B.C. the colony of Lolang was established, with its capital at the site of the present city of Pyongyang, which is now the capital of North Korea. Excavations at the site of Lolang, which became a great metropolis, have unearthed numerous weapons, much lacquer, jade, pottery, and many coins and mirrors. These remains indicate that the Chinese introduced their arts and crafts into this colony. Moreover, the Han rulers established an orderly administration, similar to that which they organized in China itself. The Han emperors were not able to maintain their hold in northwestern Korea for more than a century, but even after their support was withdrawn from the colony, the Chinese culture continued to spread throughout the peninsula.

Korea's Relations with Japan and China

After the fall of the Han dynasty Korea was divided among three competing states. The northernmost of these, Koguryo, lasted into the seventh century A.D. Southern and central Korea were divided between two other states: Paikche, on the southwest coast, and Silla, on the southeast coast. For a time a fourth state—Mimana—served as a mainland outpost of the Yamato warriors of Japan.

The constant warfare of these early kingdoms in Korea was of great importance to Japan. For in 552 the king of Paikche, hoping to get Japanese help against the rival kingdom of Silla, sent a small Buddhist image to the emperor of Japan. With it was sent a message indicating that the religion which this idol represented was singularly beneficial. This incident is generally taken as the beginning of the introduction of Buddhism into Japan—although Buddhism was probably known in Japan prior to 552 and did not become important until later.

The Japanese did not respond to the appeal of Paikche for aid, and in successive wars the fortunes of this small kingdom steadily failed. Eventually it was conquered by the Chinese, when, under the T'ang dynasty, China resumed its imperialistic expansion into Korea. When Paikche fell, many of its scholars and artisans fled to Japan to avoid being carried off to China. This migration was of great significance, because the

Korean scholars who settled in Japan brought with them knowledge of Chinese writing and of the works of both Confucius and Buddha. Thus these scholars did much to prepare Japan for a closer contact with China.

Korean Culture

Korea's nearness to China was both an advantage and a misfortune. It made possible, on the one hand, Korean assimilation of the more advanced Chinese culture. But this, on the other hand, inhibited the growth of a native Korean culture.

Japanese historians argue that the harm outweighed the good. They say that Korea developed an "inferiority complex," and that this caused the Koreans to become more Confucian than the Chinese themselves. For example, the Korean white dress and tall hat, which is not at all a practical kind of costume, resembles the mourning garb of a Chinese Confucian. The Japanese believe that they were more fortunate than the Koreans, because they were not so close to China. They feel that they were able to take over from the Chinese whatever they regarded as valuable for them, while they were also able to maintain a culture of their own, distinct from that of the Chinese.

Yet the Koreans certainly drew much benefit from their close connection with China, and Korea made a more rapid cultural advance than did Japan. Its artisans, painters, and potters were renowned throughout the Far East. Korea led the world in the development of printing from movable type, and Korean merchants roamed the seas of Asia long before the Japanese did. Indeed, for a time Korean ships were probably more numerous than those of China in Asian waters. Early Japanese travelers sometimes posed as Koreans when they had occasion to visit China, since the Chinese regarded the Koreans as far more "civilized" than the Japanese.

Kannon Bosatsu—an attendant Buddhist wooden image that shows a strong Korean influence. (Courtesy of *Pageant of Japanese Art,* Vol. III, plate 5)

THE CHINESE IMPACT ON JAPAN

Buddhism in Japan

The Buddhist image that the king of Paikche sent to the emperor of Japan in 552 provoked a bitter struggle as to whether or not Buddhism should be tolerated in Japan. Families that had vested interests in the Shintō rites and ceremonies regarded the new religion as a threat to their importance, while other families favored Buddhism because it afforded a means of challenging the established interests. For a time Buddhism served chiefly as an issue of contention for the upper classes, and only gradually did it begin to spread among the common people.

After some vicissitudes, the new religion found strong supporters in the prominent Soga family at the Japanese court. As Buddhist monasteries grew up and the number of believers increased, the prestige of the Soga family rose in proportion. Finally the imperial family itself took up the new religion, becoming devoutly Buddhist by 600.

Prince Shōtoku, who headed the government from 593 to 622 as regent for a woman ruler, was among those primarily responsible for the spread of Buddhism in Japan. To better his own grasp of the new faith, he studied the sacred writings of Buddhism and also became learned in Confucian writings. A set of seventeen maxims that he issued in 604 urged the officials to observe harmony, Buddhism, ceremony, faith, diligence. Although this document, sometimes known as a constitution, indicated that the ruling classes were not following such values, it also shows that the imperial family was beginning to see in Chinese civilization certain values and institutions that might be used to further its own political aims.

Japanese Missions to China

In 607 Prince Shōtoku sent the first Japanese embassy to China. This was an event of tremendous importance, because it meant that from then on Japanese scholars and officials who had seen the Chinese system in operation would be available for advice and planning in Japan. So far as concerns diplomatic relations between the two countries, however, the first embassy had little success. The Japanese envoys brought with them letters bearing the greetings of the ruler of the Land of the Rising Sun, addressed to the emperor of the Land of the Setting Sun. Despite the condescending tone of these greetings, the Chinese courtiers decided that the Japanese mission might be received at court, since the discourtesy of the letters arose presumably from Japanese ignorance rather than intentional affront.

This mission—the first of a series of twelve—marked the beginning of the first great period of Japanese borrowing of Chinese culture. That period was to continue until about the middle of the tenth century, by which time changes in both China and Japan caused the Japanese to feel that they had little further to learn from their neighbors.

An important feature of the missions that the Japanese sent to China was the inclusion of students in the official entourage. These students usually stayed in China for a long period, often coming with one mission and returning with another. Many of them were Buddhist monks, and from their numbers were drawn nearly all the great Buddhist leaders of early Japan.

In addition to studying Chinese translations of Buddhist texts and observing the religious organization of Chinese Buddhism, these students took close heed of Chinese political institutions. They were deeply impressed by the power of the centralized Chinese state and dazzled by its wealth. To some of them, Chinese political grandeur was probably no novelty, for many of these students were Chinese or Koreans who had made Japan their adoptive homeland, or they were the descendants of Chinese or Koreans who had only recently migrated to Japan. But whether they became acquainted with China for the first time or simply renewed an earlier acquaintance, they tried, on their return to Japan, to reproduce in Japan the advantages of the Chinese system of government.

When the first group of such students returned to Japan in 640, after a lengthy absence, they found that conditions in Japan were in an even worse state, as compared with China, than when they had left. Under Prince Shōtoku, some advance had been made toward the centralization of political power, but this gain had subsequently been lost, for the great Soga family had so increased its political influence as to present a grave threat to the imperial family. Already the Soga were referring to their children as princes, and they seemed nearly ready to depose the emperor and seize the throne. It was to block such a development that the great Taika Reform of 645 was planned and executed by students who had returned from China.

The Taika Reform

The Taika Reform of 645 was one of the great turning points in Japanese history. It ranks in importance with the Meiji Reform of 1868, which saw the adoption of western institutions. Involved in the Taika Reform was a struggle between the imperial family and the Soga family, and this struggle had religious implications, because the Soga made use of its sponsorship of Buddhism as a means of gaining political influence. However, the defeat of the Soga did not mean a revival of Shintō, as opposed to Buddhism. Instead, Buddhism was wrenched from the hands of its Soga protectors.

But the Taika Reform had much broader significance than simply the victory of the imperial family over a rival family. It involved also the introduction of Chinese political institutions, as a means of bolstering the prestige and power of the imperial family. This meant sweeping changes in Japanese social and political organization and an enormous increase in the influence of Chinese culture.

The first great step in the reform was in the direction of more effective political centralization. To this end, the political role of the clans was abolished, and the land was divided, as in China, into provinces, each under the administration of a governor. The emperor, however, did not have strength enough to appoint whomever he chose as governor. In many cases he was obliged to name as governor the head of the clan that formerly had dominated the region. Hence the new system did not achieve so great a degree of centralization as in China. It was most effective in those regions where the court had large prestige and power. This meant, chiefly, the broad plains of the modern Osaka-Kyoto area, northern Kyushu, and the coastal regions between these points.

The centralization of administration required fiscal reform, since the central government had need of greater revenues. Accordingly the Taika reformers boldly strove to adopt the system of a tax on land that was used in T'ang China. The land was declared to be the property of the emperor, and peasants were given plots to cultivate. Since land was presumed to be held only by grant of the court, the government had the right to take a portion of the produce of the land as a tax. Moreover, the government was supposed to redistribute the land periodically—to prevent private persons from assuming proprietary rights and to give more land to large families, which had greater need of it.

In practice this system did not work out as intended, because the imperial family was not able to tamper with the landholdings of those families upon whose support it must depend. Whatever the law said, such families treated their lands as though they had full ownership of them. Furthermore, serious practical difficulties arose in redistributing landholdings, for the ruggedness of Japanese terrain meant that fields of the same size did not necessarily have the same value. This was a situation quite unlike that in the broad plains of northern China, which were irrigated by state-controlled water works. On the Kyoto Plain, however, where Japan's early capital cities were located, this problem was not so serious. It was in this region, where the political control of the court was strongest, that the new system of taxation was most effective.

The Capital and the Court

The Japanese students who had visited China in the years preceding the Taika Reform had been greatly impressed by the size and splendor of Ch'ang-an, which was the western capital of China under the T'ang dynasty. As part of the endeavor to use Chinese political institutions to strengthen the imperial government the leaders of the Taika Reform sought to build a comparable city in Japan, to serve as the capital of the imperial government. Nara was first chosen as the site, and the building of a city was begun there in 710. But before this city was completed, the site of the capital was moved, in 794, to Heian-kyō, the modern Kyoto.

Both cities were laid out with great thoroughfares running from north to south and from east to west, at regular intervals, and the blocks thus marked out were subdivided by smaller streets, also in a regular pattern. The Buddhist temples in these cities, among the oldest wooden buildings still standing, show the technical ability and religious fervor of early Japan.

But the Japanese did not as yet have need for cities of this size, and neither Nara nor Heian-kyō was ever finished as planned. Commerce was on too small a scale to give economic support to large cities—though Chinese coins were imported in the hope of encouraging trade—and the government was not strong enough to create a real need for a great administrative center.

Nor was there real need for the elaborate ranks of officials that were set up. They were given titles that implied central control of all Japan, and an appropriate costume was prescribed for each rank—from scribe to minister—as at the Chinese court. But only those who served in the court itself or the administration of the region near the capital had duties of practical importance.

Despite the obvious shortcomings of the new political institutions, a great deal was achieved by the Taika Reform. The authority and prestige of the imperial family were raised to such heights that it was never again seriously challenged. And the elaborate codes of law and tables of rank for the various officials of the government continued to remind the Japanese of the aspirations and prerogatives of the court, even at times when its actual power was in eclipse. Some of these titles of rank were used again, more than ten centuries later, when a great new series of reforms was inaugurated in 1868.

Japan's Debt to China

The political and institutional forms that were taken over from China in the Taika Reform were not the most important of the Japanese borrowings from China. Indeed, this reform was only a single incident in the long process of assimilation by which the Japanese adapted the culture of China to their needs.

Of much larger and more lasting importance was the adoption of the Chinese system of writing. The early Japanese had no written language of their own; their myths and legends were committed to memory and handed down by word of mouth. By the fourth century A.D. some knowledge of Chinese writing had reached Japan. This knowledge, probably, was brought over by Koreans and Chinese who either voluntarily migrated to Japan or were taken as captives when the

Japanese intervened in the warfare in Korea. During the fifth and sixth centuries a small but growing number of Japanese scribes learned to read Chinese. But this achievement, important though it was, did not solve the greater problem of using Chinese characters for the writing of Japanese.

It is unfortunate that the Japanese had to use the Chinese written language as a model for their own, for the two languages are quite unlike. The Chinese spoken language uses only words of one syllable, and each character in the written language signifies a word referring either to an idea or a thing. But the Japanese language is polysyllabic and agglutinative—complex words have grown from simpler ones. For example, the Japanese word for heart is *kokoro*, while the Chinese word is *shin*. The Japanese therefore had two choices: they could either use the Chinese character for heart, giving it the Japanese pronunciation instead of the Chinese, or they could use the Chinese character for heart as the phonetic symbol for the sound *shin*, whenever that syllable occurs in a Japanese word. Innumerable problems and ambiguities arose until the Japanese decided how to systematize their usage. In early Japanese texts proper readings can be determined only by the context in which the Chinese character appears.

The task of adapting Chinese writing to their uses was made harder because the Japanese were especially anxious to read and master Chinese translations of Buddhist writings. But the Chinese themselves had encountered a grave problem in seeking equivalents in their own language for the terms that they were translating from Sanskrit. Not all these words had equivalents in Chinese, for some were the proper names of persons or sacred places, such as mountains, and some were magic incantations—virtual mumbo-jumbo. Pity the Japanese scholar laboring over these texts, as he sought to discover how to write in Japanese a word appearing in a Chinese character, which itself did not refer to a Chinese word but to an Indian proper name or a magic word in Sanskrit (see p. 400).

Gradually Japanese scholars worked out a system whereby certain Chinese characters were uniformly used as phonetic symbols. Later these characters were abbreviated into new forms called *kana*. These did not supplant the characters taken over from Chinese, and in modern Japanese writing the root of a noun or a verb, ordinarily, is represented by a Chinese character or a compound of characters, while the suffixes, verb endings, and connective words are indicated by means of *kana*.

The system of writing thus worked out is comprehensible but cumbersome. It requires long years of study to memorize the characters and their various meanings—time that otherwise could be devoted to more valuable

The Priest Ganjin—Japanese portrait sculpture in wood. Ganjin was a Chinese priest of the T'ang period, who went to Japan in 753 to spread the Buddhist doctrine. (Courtesy of *Pageant of Japanese Art*, Vol. III, plate 26)

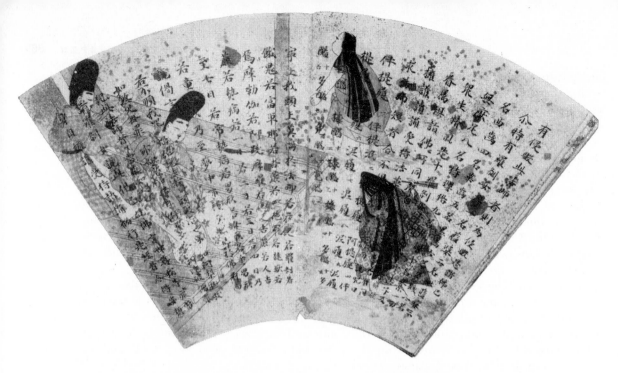

The *Lotus Sutra* and Genre Paintings on the Face of a Fan—Heian Period (p. 402) or later. The teachings of the *Lotus Sutra* are the basis of the Tendai Buddhist sect (p. 407). Here, in Chinese characters, a section of the *Sutra* has been superimposed on block prints that have been colored. These genre paintings depict scenes from the life of the people and have no relationship to the text of the *Sutra*. Genre painting had its beginnings about the twelfth century. (Courtesy of *Pageant of Japanese Art*, Volume I, plate 25)

learning. The number of characters that a person can use is proportional to the amount of time he has devoted to the study of the written language. Popular literature and newspapers require mastery of relatively few Chinese characters, but educated Japanese are expected to know many thousands.

Confucianism

One of the great benefits of the Japanese writing system, based as it is on Chinese characters, was that it permitted Japanese students to gain ready access to the Confucian classics. These Chinese texts soon became the required reading of all educated persons in Japan, and they remain an essential part of the Japanese outlook on the world. To be sure, not all parts of Confucianism were equally attractive to the Japanese. For example, the idea of selecting officials by scholarly examinations, rather than by lineage, did not win much vogue in a Japan that was still highly conscious of family and hierarchy based on birth. Nor did Mencius' suggestion of the right of rebellion win wide approval. Yet the Japanese did respond favorably to the Confucian teachings of graded love, the harmonious ordering of social relations, and, above all, loyalty. These formulations of ideas already implicit in their own tradition became for the Japanese the most important parts of Confucianism. Until the end of World War II and the American occupation of the islands the Japanese government continued to make the Confucian teachings of harmony and loyalty a part of the instruction given in the public-school system.

Buddhism

Along with the Confucian classics, Japanese students imported and studied Chinese editions of the Buddhist scriptures. The text that had the most influence in Japan was the *Lotus Sutra,* which is probably the purest statement of the *Mahayana* school of Buddhism.

Since Confucianism came into Japan at the same time as Buddhism—and at a time when Buddhism was held in high esteem in China—there was never a grave conflict between the two creeds. In China the scholar class had been hostile to Buddhism, because the social and political influence of this class came from its knowledge of the Confucian classics. The scholars feared that the spread of Buddhism would mean a lessening of the respect given to Confucianism, with its emphases on family and state, and the T'ang dynasty scholar-officials persuaded their emperor to persecute Buddhism for political rather than religious reasons. In Japan, however, Buddhism was regarded as part of the Chinese civilization, and it was given the respect shown to all things Chinese. Not until a much later date did Confucian scholars in Japan become hostile to Buddhism.

As for Shintō, it was much too crude to offer effective opposition to either Confucianism or Buddhism. It did not disappear, nor did the emperor cease to perform the proper ancestral rites and invoke the traditional deities, but the pre-eminence of the native religion was no longer unchallenged. Those Japanese who came under the influence of Confucianism or Buddhism did not, as a rule, regard these new bodies of thought as conflicting with the old religion, nor did the Shintō leaders choose to provoke a conflict. On the contrary, they were generally conciliatory, recognizing that they must move with the times. Not until the seventeenth and eighteenth centuries did a sharp split appear between those who upheld the native religion and those favorable to the new.

Buddhist Art in Japan

Nothing about Buddhism made a stronger appeal to the Japanese than the rich art in which it was expressed, and few elements of Chinese culture found a greater response than works of pious Chinese and Korean craftsmen.

The temples built at Nara and Kyoto are, in fact, among the best extant examples of T'ang temple architecture. Built with a fine sense of strength, balance, and grace, they must have seemed to the Japanese of the seventh century an obvious proof of the superiority of the Chinese civilization. Also notable is the great statue of Buddha that was dedicated at Nara in 752.

Painting drew inspiration from the large number of Buddhist deities and the richness of Buddhist imagery. Especially celebrated are the paintings on the walls of the Horyūji Temple near Nara, depicting Buddhist scenes and deities. Paintings such as these show the otherwordly and metaphysical detachment characteristic of Indian Buddhist art.

Japanese Buddhist sculpture is deservedly famous. Because of the lack of stone suitable for carving, sculptors were restricted to wood (pp. 395, 399). But this medium permitted a fluidity of treatment and a delicacy of line seldom equalled in the sculpture of other lands.

In taking note of these various ways in which the Japanese were indebted to the Chinese, we must not be tempted to exaggerate the role of Chinese culture in the life of Japan. Nara and Heian-kyō became little oases of Chinese civilization, but even there important parts of the Chinese political system were omitted. In poetry, the Japanese owe little to the Chinese. And outside the capital cities the Chinese influence was probably very slight indeed. Most of the people continued to live in the same kind of houses as before, to grow the same crops in the same manner, and to observe the simple ceremonies of the old Shintō worship. And in many areas, the old clan heads, now governors, held political power much as before, despite efforts to establish a centralized administration.

Phoenix Hall of Byōdō-in. Originally a villa of Fujiwara Yosimichi, Byōdō-in was converted into a monastery in 1052 and this hall built in 1053. Its shape is copied from the Buddha's palace in pictures of the Amida Paradise. The building is planned symmetrically but appears symmetrical only when an observer on the opposite side of the pond is directly in front of it. (Courtesy of *Pageant of Japanese Art*, Vol. VI, pl. 11)

JAPAN IN THE HEIAN PERIOD

By the time when the capital had been moved to Heian-kyō in 794, the first flush of enthusiasm for Chinese models had begun to subside. For many years more the court continued to send missions to China, but the main task now became one of adapting Chinese models to Japanese needs and thus assimilating what had already been taken over.

Heian-kyō means "Capital of Peace and Tranquility," and the period from 794 to 1100 is known as the Heian Period. During this interval the Japanese court developed a distinctive way of life that deserves close study, for seldom in history has so much importance been attached to the forms of social behavior. The business of the courtiers was not politics but the proper observance of ceremony and the cultivation of art and literature—the routine of living itself became the highest of the arts. It is not surprising, therefore, that the Heian Period became the "Classical Age" of Japanese cultural life.

Court and Country

During the Heian Period the incomplete and uneven absorption of Chinese civilization produced a sharp division in Japanese society. While the courtiers and officials in the capital city devoted themselves to mastery of the arts and of literature, in the more remote sections great private holdings in land were gradually building up. Although these private estates were owned by court nobles and temples, their managers became a new class of squire-knights, who were to replace the more highly cultured aristocrats after the end of the Heian Period.

We have noted that the centralization of power that was the goal of the Taika reformers was never completely successful. In many outlying districts the edicts of the emperor received little more than perfunctory observance, and, before long, scarcely even a nominal compliance. The weakness of the central government was worsened, moreover, by the practice of giving large grants of land to favorites of the court, for this meant that the government lost the income of these lands. Likewise, generous gifts of land were often made to Buddhist temples. This practice was in contrast to the custom in China, where it was an accepted principle that the emperor should not give lands in perpetuity —though he might assign an estate to a favorite to be held for a limited period of time.

In the Heian period in Japan one family, the Fujiwara, benefited most notably from the grant of estates. This family was related to some of the Shintō leaders who had helped plan the Taika Reform. Because of this kinship the Fujiwara had become special favorites at the court. Gradually their influence at the court increased until they had few rivals. By the middle of the ninth century members of this family gained what amounted to an hereditary right to the office of *Kampaku,* or chancellor. Thereafter, the chancellor saw to it that the sons of the imperial family ordinarily married women of the Fujiwara family, and often the heir apparent to the throne was a grandson of the chancellor. Commonly the chancellor would persuade the emperor to retire at an early age—which he was usually glad to do, since his office required him to observe a burdensome ritual—and thereupon a Fujiwara grandson would become the nominal ruler, with his maternal grandfather as regent. In such a situation the Fujiwara were never tempted to overthrow the dynasty, no matter how great their power grew, because they could hardly have improved their position by doing so.

But the influence of the Fujiwara was not confined to the court; it also extended to remote parts of the realm. As special court favorites, the Fujiwara received more tax-free estates, or *shōen,* as they were called, than any other family. *Shōen* could be accumulated by a variety of means. They were given as rewards for special services or as payments for official duties. In addition, tax-free status was often given for fields newly cleared and brought into cultivation. Persons in humble station who owned land usually found it wise to present their *shōen* to great personages, having influence at court, who would, in return, permit the original owners to remain on the land as agents or intendants. And since no other family at court could match the prestige and power of the Fujiwara family, their holdings rose steadily. As part of the bargain, the managers of estates were obliged to send shares of the estates' production to their protectors, thus adding further to the riches of the Fujiwara.

Much of Japan was brought under cultivation in this manner. And since most of the areas thus developed were at some distance from the capital, they were the areas which soonest broke loose from central control, once the prestige of the court began to wane.

Another potential threat to the power of the central government arose from the need for military action against the Ainu, for these aboriginal inhabitants of Japan were not decisively defeated until the ninth and tenth centuries. In the interest of more effective measures against them, the court created a new office—*Sei-i-tai-shōgun,* or "Barbarian-subduing Generalissimo." Eventually this became the title of the military rulers who usurped the power of the emperor. Though the *shōgun* did not gain political power until the twelfth century, the problems of frontier fighting were such that from the first the military leaders in the field had a considerable degree of independence.

Until the twelfth century, however, the courtiers at Heian-kyō retained their prestige and the outward appearance of authority. The broad avenues of the capital were filled with palanquins and processions of officials, resplendent in their robes of office and proud of their titles. But their titles meant little, for often the governors and other officials did not even leave the capital to challenge the intendants—or managers—who administered the estates of the great magnates. Instead they chose to live in splendor in the capital.

Heian Literature

Seldom has a capital been so completely separate from the countryside in culture, interests, and tastes. While the intendants in the provinces were developing and administering their estates, the courtiers in Heian-kyō were occupied in frivolous pursuits—lovemaking, versification, and ceremony. So intense was their devotion to literature that much of what they wrote seems overrefined and overerudite, crowded with allusions that only the initiates could catch. Much of the literature that they prized most highly has been lost or forgotten. In poetry and in the diaries and novels of court ladies, however, the Heian courtiers produced notable works of literature.

The Writing of History. The official histories written in the Heian Period have retained an important position in Japanese literature. These histories were written in the Chinese manner, for in China, as already noted, each dynasty kept a day-by-day chronology of its deeds and compiled an account of the reign of the preceding dynasty. In Japan the imperial court was especially anxious to make a record of its achievements and establish its prestige. Accordingly, official bureaus were set up for the writing of works of history. In 720 appeared the *Nihon Shoki,* or *Chronicles of Japan,* which became the first of a succession of official histories. Chinese in style as well as language, it sought to account for the origin of the imperial family, and, like another work which is dated 712, the *Kojiki,* or *Record of Ancient Things,* it established the spurious date of 660 B.C. for the accession of the Emperor Jimmu. This date seems to have been chosen because it would give the Japanese dynasty the great prestige of age. In addition, it also satisfied a Chinese belief that events of outstanding importance came at intervals of 1260 years.

Poetry. The Heian-kyō courtiers tried their hand at writing Chinese poetry, but their work has little merit. The poetry written in Japanese, on the other hand, is a remarkable achievement, which owes nothing to Chinese models.

The characteristics of Japanese poetry derive from those of the Japanese language. Since Japanese words have no accent, Japanese poetry does not depend upon meter in the same sense as does English verse. Nor does it make use of rhyme, for every syllable in the language ends with a vowel, and since there are only five vowels, there are only five possible rhymes. Instead of rhyme or stress, the basis of Japanese poetry is the number of syllables in a line. The favorite verse forms have been lines of five syllables, alternating with lines of seven syllables. In the Heian Period the favorite short poem had a total of thirty-one syllables, arranged in lines of five, seven, five, seven, and seven syllables. In later times poets made the form still shorter, comprising lines of five, seven, and five syllables, or a total of seventeen syllables in the entire poem.

Since Japanese words are polysyllabic, this means that not much can be stated—but a great deal must be suggested. The early short poems of thirty-one syllables usually suggested a scene of nature and a season, with a deft turn relating this to the poet's emotion. The later poems of seventeen syllables could only give the merest whiff of an idea. Such rules place a severe restraint upon the poet—he cannot, for example, attempt the treatment of a theme of epic proportions. The great majority of the poems deal with love and nature in a melancholy tone. Poems so short and cryptic require much of the reader, who must respond to the poet's suggestion and provide much of the meaning of the poem out of the resources of his own imagination. And they lose much of their charm and subtlety in translation.

The economy of phrase required in Japanese poetry inevitably led to conventionalism, by which a single word would connote a season, and a season would suggest an emotion. For example, such words as *haze, melt-*

ing snow, or the *nightingale* suggested spring or such emotions as eagerness and anxiety lest the beauty pass unseen or unheard, while *falling leaves* and *wind* signified winter and melancholy.

These examples are typical of the early poems of thirty-one syllables:

Fall gently,
O rain of spring!
scatter not
the cherry blossoms
until I have seen them.

To what shall I compare
this life of ours?
It is like a boat
which at daybreak rows away
and leaves no trace
behind it.

The later poems of only seventeen syllables are even less explicit:

In a morning-glory
today I seem to see it
—my life!

An old well!
the frog leaps
—the sound of the water.

The composing of poetry was an honored pastime at court, and various emperors ordered the compilations of the best works written in their reigns. The first of these anthologies, the *Manyōshū,* was compiled at Nara in 759. It contains 4496 poems, each bearing the date of its composition. Another anthology, the *Kokinshū,* which appeared in 905, runs to twenty volumes, containing 1100 poems. As the Heian Period progressed, the writing of poetry became an ever-greater preoccupation of the court nobles, ministers of state, and their ladies. But the freshness of invention that characterized the works of the early anthologies gave way to a greater concern with rules, forms, and conventions, and emotion was supplanted by elegance.

More and more the poets tended to complain in high-flown language that the times did not measure up to their idealized and conventionalized version of the glories of nature.

Diaries. The ladies of the court had a role of considerable importance in the development of Japanese literature. Of special interest are their diaries. These wonderfully human documents tell us much about court life, and they give an indication of the degree to which taste was refined. The proof of breeding, as it appears from these diaries, consisted of such matters as a man's ability to express his emotions in a graceful phrase or to choose just the right color of paper on which to write his poems or to pick out the proper blossom to be sent with the poem to his lady. As an indication of how exacting were the standards of taste, we quote the comment Lady Murasaki wrote in her diary of one of the other ladies present at a court ceremony: "One had a little fault in the color combination at the wrist opening. When she went before the Royal presence to fetch something, the nobles and high officials noticed it. Afterward the Lady regretted it deeply. It was not so bad; only one color was a little too pale."

The Tale of Genji. The greatest prose work in Japanese literature is a novel written in the tenth century by Lady Murasaki while she was lady-in-waiting to the empress at Heian-kyō. Its hero—Prince Genji, "the shining one"—is Lady Murasaki's conception of the perfect courtier. Around him the author wove with masterful skill a series of episodes dealing with life in the inner court circle. The tone of the novel is melancholy and romantic. It includes striking discussions of psychology, of painting, and of literature, and it is certainly one of the world's first great novels.

Although the work has little plot, it presents a wealth of characters—thirty main ones and 300 others of lesser importance—and thus it gives a panoramic view of the range of

Detail from Image of Fudō Myōō—the famous "Red Fudō" of Mount Kōya. Myōō is the foremost of the Five Enlightened Kings, who are especially revered by Tendai (or Esoteric) Buddhists. A manifestation of Dainichi and a powerful conqueror of evil, Fudō is shown in many frightening aspects. According to tradition, a priest of the Tendai sect saw Fudō in a vision and later had the apparition drawn in blood from his own head. The result was this painting on silk. (Courtesy of *Pageant of Japanese Art*, Volume I, plate 9)

personalities at the court. Each is vividly portrayed, and each stands apart from the others. In such points as the skillful choice of the proper season to match the emotion in a given scene, the author demonstrated her mastery of the forms and moods of the Heian society, and the artistic merits of her work are such that it has always held a prominent place in Japanese literature.

The novel also has interest for what it shows of the weakness of the Heian court society. The author, like her characters, regarded the capital as the sole haven of culture and contentment, while the countryside appears as a land of barbarism—redeemed only by the beauties of Nature. Thus when Genji falls into temporary disgrace, his exile from the court is treated as though it were an unbearable punishment, because it means his separation from the center of refinement and graceful living.

Another interest of the novel is its revelation of the role of Buddhism in the court. Though Buddhism seems not to have influenced the courtiers to lead religious lives, its ceremonies and rituals were an important part of daily court life. And the Buddhist emphasis upon the transitory nature of life seems to have harmonized well with the poetic Japanese approach to nature. The mood of wistfulness and vague melancholy that is characteristic of Japanese literature is an artistic expression of an attitude that Buddhism approved.

Religion

During the Heian Period Buddhism probably had little influence outside the court. For the most part the Japanese Buddhists at this time were concerned with the metaphysical and philosophical disputes typical of Indian Buddhism, and these disputes were of little interest except to scholars or courtiers who fancied themselves scholars. Moreover, only a man with leisure and wealth could afford to repair to Buddhist retreats or finance expensive religious ceremonies for the benefit of those dear to him.

However, the founding of two new Buddhist denominations in this period prepared the way for a wider diffusion of the Buddhist message. One of these, the Tendai denomination, was the Japanese branch of a denomination that had originated earlier in China. It was introduced into Japan by a Japanese monk named Saichō, who went to China in 802, returning to his homeland three years later to set up a new temple and school. Though he encountered opposition

during his lifetime from the older, established priesthood of Nara, he was honored by the emperor after his death and accorded the title of National Teacher.

The chief features of the Tendai denomination derived from the basic idea that study, contemplation, and good works are all efficacious means of attaining the Buddhist truth. Tendai thus made an appeal to persons who favored any one of these forms of religious devotion. In another sense, too, Tendai took a broad view, for it taught that not only human beings but also beasts, plants, and even inanimate things might attain to Buddhahood. This teaching gave a still larger meaning to the Buddhist virtues of kindness and compassion.

The other sect was Shingon, or True Word. It, too, was brought to Japan by a monk, Kūkai, who, like Saichō, had spent three years in China and was honored on his return with the title of National Teacher. Shingon appealed especially to the court nobles, for it placed much importance in elaborate and forbidding esoteric ceremo-

Detail of a Caricature of Birds and Beasts—from the first of four paper scrolls in black and white, late Heian Period. Opinions differ as to the intended meaning of the scrolls, but they are often explained as satirizing the life of the monks. (Courtesy of *Pageant of Japanese Art*, Volume I, plate 27)

nies. This sect had much influence upon art, because its rich and varied imagery and rituals provided new subjects for painters. Its graphic conception of the cosmic order—the *mandara*—had much the same role in Japanese art as the Christian vision of the Last Judgment did in the religious art of the west.

Shingon and Tendai did not compete with each other so much as both did with the older Nara sects, which they eventually conquered. The temples, schools, and monasteries of these new denominations, like those of the older, were generously endowed with grants of land, and ultimately they gained a power that overshadowed that of the court.

Disintegration of the Heian State

By the year 1000 the Heian-kyō court was suffering the consequences of its ill-advised generosity in making gifts of tax-exempt land. By that time such grants had reduced the income of the court while increasing the economic strength of the new rural interests in the countryside.

To check the shrinkage of its revenues, the court was forced to increase the exactions upon those areas that remained subject to taxes. But this caused numbers of peasants and artisans to migrate from the regions where taxes were severe to areas where the landholders were exempt from taxes, since in those regions the common people also fared better. Thus the outlying regions became the areas of most vigorous economic growth, while the capital and the areas under its sway suffered economic decline.

This process of decentralization was not unwholesome, for it meant that the knowledge and skill that previously had been monopolized by the court were more widely diffused. Not only did peasants and artisans migrate to the areas of economic growth, but, also, young warriors and the Buddhist clergy moved. By the time when the warriors from the provinces took over political power

at the capital, they were much more civilized than the rude fighting men who had been their ancestors but a few generations earlier.

The gradual decline and growing weakness of the Heian-kyō government were reflected in its inability to control feuds among rival groups of Buddhist monasteries, which often caused disorder in the capital. Lacking the power to compel these monasteries to obey its decrees or to suppress the disturbances that they created by their quarrels, the court appealed to the Fujiwara for advice and help, and the Fujiwara called upon the managers of their estates to send troops to the capital to maintain order. These worthies, long accustomed to keeping order in the provinces which they administered, responded readily to the summons. But once they came into the capital to quiet the Buddhists, they chose not to return home and continue sending tribute to the Fujiwara. Instead, after another half-century of strife, they took political power into their own hands.

In the wars and unrest that accompanied this crisis, many a Heian-kyō courtier was convinced that a new dark age was beginning. No longer were the times such as would permit the continuation of the elaborate and refined life of the court and the temples of the capital. But civilization did not perish; instead the new age meant a wider extension of civilization. For as the Buddhists realized that never again would men have the leisure to devote to the elaborate ceremonies of Shingon, they turned themselves to the propagation of a simpler religious message, better suited to the needs of the common people, in an age of fear. And as scribes and scholars found themselves deprived of their posts at court, they took up the task of educating the military men who were now their masters. The civilization which replaced that of Heian-kyō was not so glamorous or so dazzling, but it was sounder and stronger, and it was destined to prove more enduring.

Suggestions for Further Reading

Source Materials

Anthologies

W. T. de Bary, *Readings in Japanese Thought* (New York, 1957).

A new work that provides the best coverage of early Japanese political, moral, and philosophical thought.

D. Keene, *Anthology of Japanese Literature: Earliest Era to Mid-Nineteenth Century* (New York, 1955).

The best anthology, with good examples of all early literary forms.

A. Miyamori, trans., *Masterpieces of Japanese Poetry, Ancient and Modern* (2 vols., Tokyo, 1936).

A large anthology which gives each poem in romanization, in translation, and is annotated throughout.

Nippon Gakujutsu Shinkokai, *The Manyoshu. One Thousand Poems Selected and Translated from the Japanese* (Tokyo, 1940).

Translations of part of the oldest anthology, compiled by imperial order in the eighth century, together with a helpful introduction which discusses the society of Nara times.

Contemporary Writings

Diaries of Court Ladies of Old Japan; translated by A. S. Omori and K. Doi (Tokyo, 1935).

Translations of three famous diaries of the eleventh century, including that of Lady Murasaki.

Sei Shonagon, *The Pillow-book;* translated by A. Waley (New York, 1953).

Superbly translated selections from a court lady's diary, with helpful introductory comments.

Murasaki Shikibu, *The Tale of Genji;* translated by A. Waley (Mentor edition, New York, 1955).

An excellent translation of the most famous Japanese novel.

Secondary Works

M. Anesaki, *History of Japanese Religion, with Special Reference to the Social Life of the Nation* (London, 1930).

An excellent introduction to the role of religion in Japanese society.

E. F. Fenollosa, *Epochs of Chinese and Japanese Art, an Outline History of Asiatic Design* (2 vols., New York, 1921).

An early work, handsomely illustrated, which seeks to relate art to the society in which it developed.

L. C. Goodrich, ed., *Japan in the Chinese Dynastic Histories: Later Han through Ming Dynasties;* translated by R. Tsunoda (South Pasadena, 1951).

Translations, with notes, of the sections pertaining to Japan in early Chinese histories.

G. J. Groot, S.V.D., *The Prehistory of Japan* (New York, 1951).

The most recent and authoritative survey of findings in archaeological sites.

D. Keene, *Japanese Literature: An Introduction for Western Readers* (Wisdom of the East Series, London, 1953).

Stimulating and readable essays on Japanese prose, poetry, and theater.

H. Minamoto, *An Illustrated History of Japanese Art;* translated by H. G. Henderson (Kyoto, 1935).

A basic, heavily illustrated account by a Japanese authority.

E. O. Reischauer, *Japan Past and Present* (New York, 1946).

By far the best introductory survey of Japanese history.

G. B. Sansom, *Japan: A Short Cultural History* (New York, 1943).

The best general history, covering Japan from earliest times to the nineteenth century.

PART III

The Atlantic Civilization: The Feudal Era

In A.D. 476, when the German king Odoacer made himself master of Rome and thus wiped out the last vestige of Roman political power in the west, that part of Europe that lay west and north of the Alps was one of the relatively backward areas of the world. In this region, to be sure, a pastoral culture had been developing ever since the time of the cavemen of the Paleolithic and Neolithic ages. And the Romans had brought an advanced civilization into Spain, Gaul, and England. But with the decline of Roman authority in western Europe, that Roman civilization had broken down.

For the next five hundred years, moreover, western Europe was to be overrun by successive hordes of barbarians from Germany, central and northern Europe, and even western Asia. In the disorder that ensued, such settled civilization as had survived the passing of Roman rule was to a great degree submerged. In these centuries of chronic warfare and upheaval, the peoples of western Europe had little chance to build a civilization rivaling the splendors of Rome or Greece or comparable to those that still endured from ancient times in India and China.

Yet out of these troubled centuries there emerged, about A.D. 1000, a new civilization that—though it inherited much from the prehistoric cavemen and the Gauls, from the Greeks and Romans, and from the Germanic barbarians—was essentially different from every other civilization in history. As it grew, this new "European" or "western"

civilization was to pass through a succession of phases of development—feudal-agrarian, commercial, and industrial. In the course of this evolution its political institutions were to grow through the original feudal forms into the characteristic national state. Characterized in the Feudal Era by a western form of Christianity, its religious unity was eventually to be broken up by the appearance of many dissident forms of Christianity that paralleled the appearance of the territorial states and, largely as a matter of expediency, suggested the validity of the principle of religious toleration. Its first great intellectual achievement was the formulation of a new and characteristic philosophical synthesis called Scholasticism; but its intellectual life was gradually to evolve out of the authoritarian Scholasticism of the Feudal Era into a new intellectual outlook characterized by secularism, humanism, and, above all, the perfection of the intellectual instrument called science.

As it passed out of the Feudal-Scholastic culture of its first settled era into the secular, national, and scientific culture of its Commercial Era, this western civilization was to burst the bounds of geographic limitation to Europe and reach out—driven chiefly by commercial-capitalistic motives—to explore and exploit the other areas of the globe, both the formerly known, in India and Asia, and the formerly unknown, in Africa, Australasia, and the American hemisphere. Then, with the exploration and exploitation of the

Eurasia in 800

"new world," Europeans themselves were to move overseas—taking with them their religion, their literature, their art, and their economic, social and political forms and ideas—to found little Europes in the western hemisphere, in Africa, and, eventually, in Australia and New Zealand. This expansion of the "western" civilization into new lands would mean such a territorial spreading of its basic features around the Atlantic, and such a growth of new variants of the basic European pattern of civilization, as to justify us in calling this new community of "western" societies an *Atlantic* civilization, to

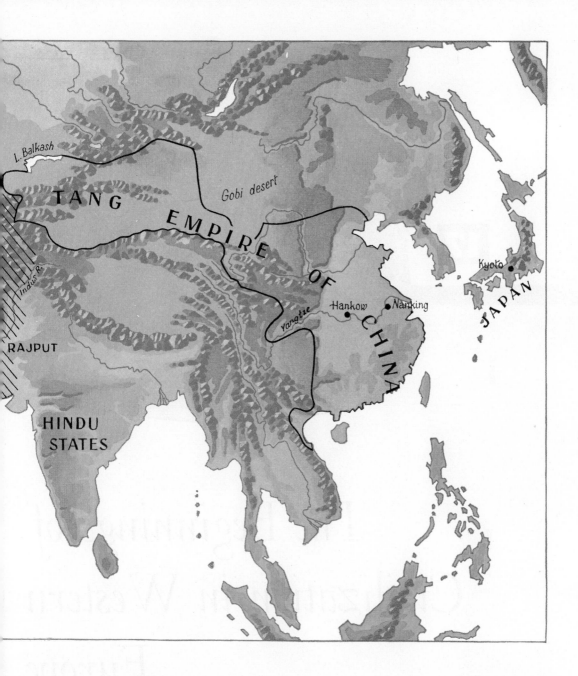

distinguish it from the older civilizations of the Mediterranean, of India, or of China and Japan.

In its contacts with these older civilizations the young and vigorous Atlantic civilization was to influence them very little at first. But its "westernizing" influence was to grow; and the mere establishment of economic, religious, and political ties between the west and the east was the beginning of a network of ties and relationship that would eventuate, in the nineteenth and twentieth centuries, in the formation of a veritable community of the world.

17

The Beginnings of Civilization in Western Europe

Barbarian Chieftain's Helmet—Frankish, sixth century. The shape is Asiatic, but the gilded embossed pattern shows the influence of Christian art. (Courtesy, Metropolitan Museum of Art)

The beginnings of human culture in western Europe go far back into the Paleolithic Age. In the course of its own growth, this culture developed to the stage of the Neolithic and then the Bronze Age, before it was submerged in the more advanced civilization that Rome introduced into western Europe from the lands around the eastern shores of the Mediterranean. But this civilization all but perished with the passing of Roman rule, and the civilization that we know as "European" represents a continuous, if uneven, growth from the pre-Roman Stone Age culture of western Europe. It has borrowed much from other civilizations, but in origin it is European. Its history therefore begins long before the time of the Roman Empire.

THE PEOPLES OF WESTERN EUROPE BEFORE THE ROMAN ERA

The Northwest European Plain

The matrix of civilization in western Europe was the broad, rolling plain that lies between the Elbe River on the north and the Pyrenees Mountains on the south. The British Isles, which have a similar terrain and climate, may be regarded as forming part of this same region. It is a land of fertile soil and plentiful rainfall. In ancient times it was heavily forested and well provided with wild game, and the earliest known cultures in the region were those of forest peoples.

South of the Pyrenees lies the Iberian Peninsula. For the most part it is a high, semi-arid plateau. Except in the northwest its soil and climate are more like those of North Africa and the Mediterranean countries than the Northwest European Plain. Despite these differences, however, the peoples and cultures of the peninsula at the dawn of historic times were closely related to those of the Northwest European Plain, because most of the successive waves of migration that swept into western Europe also spread southward across the Pyrenees.

The earliest of these migrations of which we have knowledge was a wave of invasions about 1000 B.C. The newcomers were an Indo-European people called the Celts, who mingled with an earlier stock already established in both the plain of western Europe and the Iberian Peninsula. Apparently the Celts introduced the use of iron, for the earlier settlers had known only bronze. The Celts seem also to have brought with them the custom of burying the dead in stone crypts, covered by tumuli or mounds of earth. From this and other evidence we know that they settled over a wide area, for their remains have been discovered in Portugal as well as Scotland and Ireland. Presently, between 1000 and 500 B.C., a highly sophisticated and generally sedentary culture appeared throughout both the Iberian Peninsula and the region that the Romans later called Gaul—that is, the area between the Rhine River and the Pyrenees.

The Gauls

Gaul was the center of this emergent civilization. Its society was based upon the grouping of families into clans and clans into tribes. In turn, the tribes banded together into federations that are sometimes spoken of as "nations," although this is not a strictly correct use of the term. The leaders of the tribes were elected, as were the heads of the federations, and in each federation there was an assembly made up of tribal chieftains and the heads of clans and families.

Agriculture was the basis of the economy. Wheat and other grains were raised, and domestic animals, such as sheep, horses, pigs, and cattle, were common. Trade was well advanced, and by 500 B.C. tin mined in Gaul was being shipped to the eastern Mediterranean.

The religion of the Gauls, which was of supreme importance in their culture, was administered by priests known as the *Druids*. This religion was a kind of animism, which peopled the world of nature with supernatural spirits. These deities were regarded as cruel and capricious, and human sacrifices became a common feature of the ceremonies performed to appease them. From their control of these rites, the Druids gained a power rivaling that of the great military and tribal chieftains. They were also the guardians of learning. From the Greeks they discovered how to read and write—the Gauls had no written language of their own—but in connection with their religious rites they had made some rudimentary observations of natural phenomena that may be considered as the beginnings of scientific knowledge.

The Celto-Iberians

The culture of the peoples south of the Pyrenees was generally similar to that of the Gauls, yet it showed some notable differences. Because the peninsula was semiarid, the culture traits of this area were not those of a forest people. Many of the traits resembled those of the peoples of North Africa, for Spain formed a cultural bridge between Africa and the Mediterranean, on one side, and the Northwest Plain on the other.

As in Gaul, agriculture was the principal economic pursuit. But among the crops raised were some, such as figs, dates and olives, that are not grown in northern Europe but are common to the warmer lands of the south. Mining was also important. The principal products of the mines were iron, tin, copper, silver, and salt.

Iberian society centered in the family, which was generally monogamous, but tribal organization was of some importance. As in Gaul, religion featured a number of nature deities, including a mother-goddess symbolizing fertility, and worship of the sun and the moon. Even in that remote past, too, as at the present time, the people of the peninsula were fond of singing and dancing, and each region developed songs and dances of its own.

Like Gaul, then, the peninsula was the home of a fairly sophisticated and advancing preliterate culture that, by 500 B.C., seems to have been on the verge of achieving the fullness of civilization. The ultimate step in the transition was taken—first in Spain, then in Gaul—when traders and colonists from the eastern Mediterranean made their appearance in these lands.

WESTERN EUROPE IN THE ROMAN ERA

The Phoenicians and the Carthaginians

The earliest of the peoples of the eastern Mediterranean to "discover" western Europe were the Phoenicians. These intrepid traders had passed through the Straits of Gibraltar about 1100 B.C. and had planted a colony at Cadiz, which soon became famous for its export of silver and tin. Later the Carthaginians founded colonies along the Mediterranean coast of the peninsula and, about 500 B.C., took Cadiz from the Phoenicians. In the third century B.C. the Carthaginian general Hamilcar Barca conquered most of the Iberian Peninsula and the Balearic Islands and made these lands into an outpost of the Carthaginian Empire. This empire was not destined to endure for, as we have seen (p. 172) in the last two decades of the third century B.C. the Romans drove out the Carthaginians and ultimately, in 133 B.C., emerged as the masters of the land that they called "Spain."

The Romans in Spain

Soon Spain was thoroughly Romanized. The centralized Roman rule was extended throughout the peninsula except for the Basque country in the northwest; Roman law became the law of the land, and Latin became the official language. Roman buildings, theaters, roads, and aqueducts appeared in the larger cities, and great estates were established in the countryside. Under this Roman regime, Spain prospered more than ever

La Dama de Elche. This remarkable stone head, sometimes identified with the Virgin, is probably one of the earliest examples of Iberian sculpture. (Prado Museum, Madrid).

before, and a number of natives, after gaining a Latin education, achieved distinction in the Roman Empire. Among them were Seneca, Martial, and Quintilian as well as several emperors.

Roman rule lasted until A.D. 409, when the Suevi and the Vandals swept into Spain in the first wave of the Germanic invasions. Soon after them came the Visigoths, who entered the peninsula in 419. Their kingdom in Spain, with its capital at Toledo, lasted until 711, when it was overthrown by the Moslems coming in from North Africa.

The Greeks at Marseilles

Meanwhile a similar process had begun in Gaul where, about 600 B.C., a group of Greeks from Asia Minor had founded the city of Massilia. Marseilles, as this city is now called,

soon became a great and prosperous market for such Gallic products as carved wood, iron, tin, foodstuffs, and wine. From the Greeks established in this outpost, the Gauls learned the use of a written language and coined money.

Exposed to the constant menace of the Gauls, the Greeks of Massilia in 125 B.C. appealed to the Romans for aid, and a Roman army was dispatched across the Alps. After defeating the Gauls in the valley of the Rhône, the Romans established a base of their own at Narbonne and took Massilia under their protection as an "allied" state. The Greek colony kept this status until the Romans conquered the rest of Gaul, whereupon it was merged with the larger Roman domain.

The Roman Era in Gaul

The Gallic campaigns of Julius Caesar between 59 and 51 B.C. made Gaul a Roman province, as it was to remain for the next five centuries. Roman rule was also extended into the southern portion of Britain, but it was never so secure in that remote land as in Gaul, nor did it last so long.

Under the Roman regime the tribal organization of the Gauls was swept aside. In its place the Romans established a political organization based on residence rather than kinship. The whole of Gaul was divided into four administrative areas, and Roman law was applied in all four. However, the laws were adapted to the customs of the Gauls, and the natives were given some voice in their government through a council that met in Lugdunum (Lyons), the center of Roman administration for all Gaul.

For the most part, the Roman rule represented an advance from a primitive to a civilized kind of social organization. But not all the Roman innovations were a clear social gain. Among them was slavery, which was not common in Gaul until the Roman era, and the form of bondage characterized by the *colonus*—the peasant who was obliged to remain on the land that he cultivated.

Like Spain, Gaul prospered in the Roman era as never before. Agriculture thrived and expanded, and industries developed to the point where Gaul was exporting pottery, glass, hardware, and textiles as well as grain and wine.

The culture of Gaul was also largely Romanized. The Roman deities took the place of the nature gods of the Druids, and Latin became the language of the educated classes. Among these were the Gallic merchants and what remained of the old Druidic priesthood, as well as Roman officials. Through Latin literature, the upper classes among the Gauls gained some knowledge of Greco-Roman science and engineering and also of

other elements of the Mediterranean cultural heritage.

Yet this remained an alien culture, borrowed by the Gauls or imposed upon them. When the power of Rome began to decline, the civilization that the Romans had introduced also began to fade. When the German barbarians overran Gaul in the series of invasions that began in the third century A.D., the Gauls reverted to a more primitive level of civilization. Not until after five or six centuries of disorder did a new civilization arise in western Europe. And though this owed much to Rome—for the Celtic peoples of Gaul and Spain never forgot *all* that the Romans had taught them—it owed still more to the native genius of the peoples of western Europe.

The Provinces of Gaul

THE EARLY GERMANS

During the period of the Roman rule in Gaul and Spain, the area east of the Rhine and north of the Danube was inhabited by a number of Germanic tribes. The Romans never conquered these peoples, who kept up a constant pressure upon the northern borders of the Empire. Eventually, when Roman power crumbled, the Germans overran western Europe.

Germanic Institutions

The largest social and political unit among the Germans was the tribe. Among those tribes known to the Romans were the Alemanni, Goths, Franks, Vandals, Teutons, and scores of others. Customarily the Romans used the word *Germani* for the entire race, comprising all the tribes, and *Germania* for its homeland. The various tribes shared a common language, which is one of the numerous Indo-European tongues and they shared a common religion. Otherwise the Germans were not united, and there were wide differences among the tribes.

Among the Germans, like other primitive peoples, the basis of the tribe was supposed to be a bond of kinship among the families that it comprised. Yet the tribes were so large that this kinship must have been fictitious. Nevertheless, the supposition that members of the same tribe were kinsmen of one another was of great importance, because the basis of tribal law was *personal*, not territorial. In other words, the laws of the tribe governed all persons who belonged to the tribal group, not all persons who inhabited a specific place. In the great age of their migrations tribes would move over distances of many miles. When the tribe settled in a new homeland, it would not regard as members of the tribe whatever other peoples might happen to inhabit the place where the tribe now was settled. This principle of the "personality" of law, derived from Germanic custom, was to have much practical significance in the Feudal Era of western European history; not until after long centuries was it wholly supplanted by the newer idea of the "territoriality" of law.

Some tribes—though not all—had kings, but the office was never one of large importance. The king was not the leader of the tribe in time of war, since, at the start of each campaign, military command was given to a man specially chosen for this honor because of his valor. Nor was the king the source of law, for the laws of the tribe were based on custom that no one could alter. When a man committed a wrong against a tribe—for example, if he showed cowardice in battle—it was the priest who condemned him, not the king. And when a man committed a wrong against another individual, it was left to the man who had suffered the wrong to gain redress, or to his kinsmen, if he had been slain. The custom of the tribe prescribed what redress was due for each kind of wrong. For instance, a man who killed another was supposed to pay the surviving kin an indemnity of a specified value. This was called *wergeld,* or "man money," and the amount varied according to the rank of the slain man. But the king had no power to force a wrongdoer to pay *wergeld,* and the tribe as a whole did not concern itself with such matters.

The ultimate source of authority in the tribe was the assembly of all the freemen. This assembly selected the king (if any), usually from among a deceased king's descendants, the military leaders, and the lesser chiefs of the tribe. It also deliberated on such issues as making war or peace. But it did not have "legislative" functions in the modern sense, because, as we have noted, the law of the tribe consisted of the customs handed down from the immemorial past.

Another tribal institution is of interest because of its connection with the beginnings of the later European feudalism. This was the *comitatus,* or *Gefolge,* which was a group of young warriors who voluntarily associated themselves with a leader renowned for his valor and skill in warfare. The younger men would give him their obedience and loyalty, and he, in return, would promise them a share in the plunder to be gained in the course of their fighting together and would provide them with arms and subsistence.

Economic Life

Scholars know little and argue much about the economic life of the early Germans. Agriculture, it is clear, was their main source of livelihood, and private persons, it is also certain, did not have anything like outright ownership of the land. Their settlements usually took the form of what is called the *nucleated vil.* This means that the houses were grouped together in a compact village, with the fields outside the village. Assimilated with the forms derived from the Roman villas, the nucleated vil in the Feudal Era became the basis of the manor, or seignury, in which the peasants labored as serfs under the domination of the lord.

The social organization of the tribe was complex. At the top was a nobility, and generally a nobleman was a large landholder. Thus social prestige was linked with economic privilege. For the most part this nobility was hereditary, but membership was not exclusively determined by birth, and men of vigor could gain admittance to the nobility.

Below these magnates were the non-noble freemen. Most of the Germans belonged to this rank. Ordinarily, the freemen held tracts of land, but some did not and these were obliged to work for the others as tenants, tilling the land as sharecroppers. Below the freemen were a class of men neither free nor slaves, who were bound to the land. Such a German was called by Roman writers a *litus.* His status was much the same as that of the Roman *colonus,* the Roman peasant who was also bound to the land. This form of bondage, common to the *litus* and the *colonus,* was the source of the institution of serfdom that prevailed throughout western Europe in the Feudal Era.

Culture and Religion

The general cultural level of the Germanic tribes is indicated by their use of metal implements, wheeled vehicles, and garments of woven cloth as well as animal skins. But at the time of their great migrations they were without a written language. The earliest work written in a German language was a translation of the Bible, made in A.D. 340 by an Arian missionary named Ulfilas.

The religion of the Germans was animistic. The names of some of their gods survive in English names for the days of the week. Thus Wednesday perpetuates the name of Wodin, the great father of the gods, and his son Thor, the god of thunder, gave his name to Thursday. Sacrifices were offered to the gods, and the priests who conducted these rites became a privileged caste. Commonly, religious ceremonies were held out of doors, because of the special reverence given to trees and groves. Reminiscent of primitive German religious rites are the custom of decorating a tree at Christmas and the children's hunt for Easter eggs.

Christian missionaries began to penetrate the German world as early as the fourth century, but those who won success at first were heretics of the Arian persuasion (p. 233). The first large Germanic group to be won over to Roman Catholicism was the Frankish nation, whose king, Clovis, was baptized late in the fifth century.

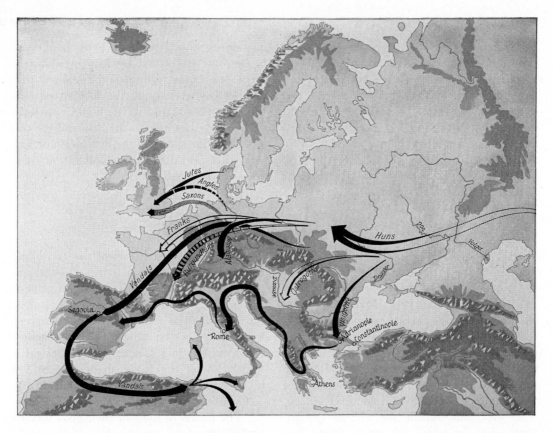

The Barbarian Invasions

THE GREAT MIGRATIONS

The Prelude to the Migrations

During the long centuries of the *Pax Romana* the German frontier was efficiently policed by the Roman legions, as was the frontier across the north of Roman Britain, protecting that province from the Celtic tribes of what is now Scotland. But as the Roman Empire entered into its decline, the morale of the army began to sag. To bolster the frontier forces, the emperors began to admit German tribesmen into the legions. By the fourth century whole bands of German tribal warriors, under their own officers, were accepted by the Romans as *foederati*, or military allies. These bands of Germanic allies were permitted to establish settlements along the border on the Roman side in return for their aid in defending the frontier against those tribes remaining on the other side. This practice was a grave omen of the decline of Roman power, but so long as the Romans kept control of their Germanic allies, there were no mass migrations of Germans into the Empire in defiance of Roman wishes.

In the fourth century, however, the floodgates burst, and Germans began to pour across the border in such numbers as to overwhelm the Empire. In some regions the Romans made a vain attempt to stem the tide, but elsewhere, recognizing that resistance was hopeless, they saved their pride by treating the invaders as "allies" whom they were permitting to settle on the soil of the Empire. Sometimes the Germans were willing to accept this fiction and profess their recognition of the overlordship of the emperor. But, in point of fact, their tribal kings became the actual rulers wherever their tribes settled.

In the midst of these invasions, the West Roman Empire disappeared. We cannot set a date for its close, since the decline of imperial rule was a gradual process. But as a sign of its passing, we may note the dramatic occurrence in A.D. 476, when the German chieftain named Odoacer deposed the last Roman Emperor, Romulus Augustulus. This marked the end of the unbroken succession of Western emperors that had begun in 27 B.C. with Augustus Caesar.

The Pattern of the Migrations

So complete was the collapse of the imperial resistance that the movement of the Germans into the Roman Empire is better described as a migration than an invasion. This migration became large scale in the fourth century, and it continued through the fifth and sixth centuries. It was not a matter of an armed incursion of warriors but a movement of population, for the warriors brought with them their women and children and sometimes even their herds of livestock. Though a tribe might wander about for two or three generations before settling down in a new homeland within the Empire, it would nevertheless continue to hold together as a complete social organization.

When the tribe at last settled down again, the Germans would usually take a portion of the land for themselves—often a third or a half. But the newcomers, never more than a minority of the population, were far outnumbered by the natives. Gradually the native Romanized Gallic population merged with the Germanic invaders, the larger landowners mingling with the German nobles, while the peasants of native stock blended with the lower classes among the Germans. In the course of this merger the Germans were to some degree Romanized, since the culture of the peoples of western Europe was now more Roman than Celtic. Yet the Germans contributed elements of their own culture to the new civilization that later arose in those regions that had once been the Roman provinces of Spain, Gaul, and Britain.

Wherever they settled, the German conquerors established new kingdoms. But these were not of the same kind as the tribal kingdoms that had arisen among the Germans before their migration into the Empire. In the older kingdoms the office of king had been a position of honor but not of power. In the new kingdoms now formed, where the Germans lived at first as a race of conquerors among a large mass of non-German natives, the king took on a role comparable to that of a war leader, whose commands required obedience. Often, too, he was the head of a *comitatus,* or *Gefolge.* And, since he was not merely the leader of his own people but also the master of a conquered populace, he could not avoid assuming something of the impersonal authority that formerly had been exercised by officials of the imperial government.

Yet the Germans were still too primitive in their thinking to grasp the Roman conception of law. As we have seen, they thought of law as personal rather than territorial; the law governing an individual was determined by the group to which he belonged, not by the place where he resided. As a general rule, therefore, the Germans sought to perpetuate their own tribal law in matters concerning Germans, while they tried to enforce Roman law in matters concerning the Romanized native population. Thus Roman law did not wholly disappear, but it survived only in a debased form, as though it were nothing more than the "tribal custom" of the conquered peoples of western Europe.

The Dark Ages

With the setting up of the Germanic kingdoms, Europe entered into the period known as the Dark Ages. It is given this name because for some centuries Europe was almost without a civilization—the civilization of Rome almost disappeared in the course of the Germanic migrations, and not until after a prolonged interval of confusion and disorder did a new civilization emerge. It is not possible to set precise limits to this period, but generally it is taken as extending from the fourth or fifth to the seventh or eighth centuries.

One reason for the cultural decline of the Dark Ages was the upheaval resulting from the inrush of the Germanic people. Civilization represents the sum of all that a people accomplishes above the task of securing a bare livelihood; it is therefore a product of leisure and wealth, for it depends upon the time and means available after the brute needs of existence have been met. But the period of the Germanic migrations was a time of chronic warfare and a precarious scramble to seize wealth or protect it against seizure; and in such a situation, men were far too preoccupied with the problem of survival to devote themselves to intellectual and artistic pursuits.

But this was not the sole misfortune of the times. The collision of the Romans and the Germans occurred at a time when the civilization of the Roman Empire, as well as its political power, was in decline. Had the Germans entered the Empire earlier, when the civilization of Rome was at its prime, the Germans would probably have become as Romanized as the Celts of Gaul and Spain. But, as it happened, they made their entrance at a time when the Romans were in the course of forgetting their cultural heritage. The shock of the Germanic incursion thus served to hasten a breakdown of culture that had begun some centuries before.

THE EARLY GERMANIC KINGDOMS

The Visigoths

Prominent in the first waves of the Germanic migrations were the Goths. These comprised two groups: the Visigoths and the Ostrogoths. Both groups seem to have made their home in the far north of the German world —a part of Sweden is still known as Gotland. But their first contact with the Roman Empire was on the lower Danube, on a portion of the frontier within the domain of the East Roman or Byzantine Empire.

In 375 the Visigoths appealed to the Emperor Valens for permission to enter the Empire in order to escape the harassment of the Huns. With his approval, they settled in the Roman province of Moesia, in what is now Rumania. But disputes arose out of their dealings with the grafting Roman officials of the province, and the Visigoths soon began to move westward. To check their marauding, Valens led an army against them, but his troops were defeated at Adrianople in 378, and the emperor himself was killed. This was a dramatic moment, for it was the first time in many centuries that Roman legions were defeated within the borders of the Empire.

The successor of Valens made peace with the Visigoths, recognizing them as "allies" with the right to settle within the Empire and promising them a payment of money. But a later emperor failed to make the promised payment, whereupon the Visigoths, under a bold and vigorous leader named Alaric, resumed their westward march. After some years of restless wandering in northern Italy, in 410 the Visigoths captured and pillaged Rome.

Though the news of their sack of Rome shocked the whole imperial world, the Visigoths did not long remain in the capital, for what they wanted were broad and fertile lands on which to settle. Pushing on toward the west, they discovered at last a suitable new homeland in southern Gaul and northern Spain. There they established a kingdom, with its capital at Toulouse, reaching across the Pyrenees. This was the first Germanic kingdom on Roman soil. Though another Germanic people, the Franks, in the sixth century dispossessed the Visigoths of the portion of their kingdom that reached into Gaul, the Spanish portion endured as a Visigothic kingdom until the Moors conquered Spain in the eighth century.

The Vandals

Soon after the Visigoths began their wanderings across the West Roman Empire, another group of tribes known as the Vandals pressed westward across the Rhine into Gaul. Subsequently they moved into Spain but were driven onward as the Visigoths advanced across the Pyrenees. In 429 they crossed the Straits of Gibraltar into North Africa, where they established a new Vandal Kingdom with its capital at the site of ancient Carthage.

Presently the Vandals became a Mediterranean naval power. So extensive were their raids upon the coastal towns of Sicily and the Italian mainland that *vandalism* has become a synonym for destruction. In 455 one of of their expeditions descended upon Rome —its second pillaging by barbarians.

The Vandal kingdom of Africa lasted for about a century, until the great Byzantine emperor Justinian undertook to reconquer the lands of the western Empire. In 533 his general Belisarius landed in Africa and within a few years he had destroyed the Vandal kingdom. But the Byzantine Empire held this region for only a little more than a century, and by 700 the Moslems controlled the entire African coast as far as the Atlantic Ocean (p. 275).

The Huns

In the midst of these Germanic migrations, the Huns made their appearance. These were not Germans but a people of Central Asia. Their fierce onslaught terrorized the Germans as well as the Romans, for the Huns were ruthless warriors, and their horsemanship was the best ever seen. So horrible was their reputation for murder, rape, and plunder that the mere mention of their name caused men to shudder—even in an age when the ravages of warfare were a commonplace occurrence.

After ravaging the region along the Danube, the Huns entered Italy and in 452 appeared before the undefended gates of

The Barbarian Kingdoms about A.D. 526

Rome. Tradition relates that Pope Leo I went out to meet Attila, the great Hun leader, and persuaded him to spare the capital. This seems hard to believe, since Attila—"the Scourge of God"—was not a Christian, but in any event the Huns turned northward without sacking Rome. A year later Attila died, and his army seems to have broken up, for thereupon the Huns disappeared from western history.

The Ostrogoths

At the time when the Visigoths were filtering into the lower Danube Valley, the Ostrogoths were established in the southern part of what is now Russia. As the Visigoths moved westward, the Ostrogoths pressed in upon the borders of the Byzantine Empire, receiving permission to settle within it. But to insure their good behavior the imperial government required them to send the sons of some of their leading magnates to Byzantium, where these young princes would be kept as hostages.

One of these Ostrogothic princes was destined to win fame as Theodoric the Great. Growing up as a hostage at the court of Constantinople, Theodoric acquired a veneer of Byzantine culture and a considerable political acumen. Presently he proposed to the Emperor Zeno that he be permitted to lead the Ostrogoths into Italy, where at that time the Visigoths were established. We have already noted that in 476 the Visigothic king Odoacer had deposed the last emperor of the west, Romulus Augustulus, and no one had succeeded to the vacant throne. Theodoric promised that, once he had defeated the Visigoths, he would re-establish imperial authority in Italy, acting in the name of the Byzantine emperor.

The emperor readily agreed to this plan. Not only did it hold out the hope of increasing his prestige, but it gave promise of removing the threat of the Ostrogoths, who were then established too close to Constanti-nople for comfort. Accordingly, Theodoric led his people into Italy in 489, and in 493 he defeated and killed Odoacer. Thereupon he set up the Ostrogothic kingdom of Italy, with its capital at Ravenna.

In this new realm, Theodoric the Great ruled the Ostrogoths as their own king, governing the larger mass of the Italian populace as the vicar of the Byzantine emperor. Actually, however, he was an independent monarch ruling the entire Italian Peninsula, for his role as an imperial vicar was little more than a fiction.

Theodoric the Great was the most enlightened of the Germanic kings of his time. He himself was a man of some education and culture, and among the Roman nobles in his realm were some men whose writings were among the most impressive of the time, although much inferior to the literature of earlier ages. Foremost of these were the philosopher Boethius (c.475–525) and the historian Cassiodorus (c.480–c.575). But when Theodoric died in 526, his successors proved unequal to the task of maintaining order, and this gave occasion for the Emperor Justinian to undertake his program for reconquering the west and reuniting it with the eastern Empire. In 540 Belisarius turned from Africa, after mastering the Vandal kingdom there, to launch a campaign in Italy. This venture was brought to a successful conclusion by Narses, who took over command from Belisarius and completed the destruction of the Ostrogothic kingdom in 555.

Germanic Kingdoms in Britain

Even the remote and isolated Roman outpost of Britain suffered the same Germanic inundation that swept over the rest of the Empire. Though Britain had been a Roman province for four centuries, the Roman legions were withdrawn from the island in 410, because of the greater need of them elsewhere in the hard-pressed Empire. Left defenseless, the island was assaulted by successive waves of German invaders during the second half of the fifth and first half of the sixth centuries. These invaders were drawn from three Germanic peoples—the Angles, the Saxons, and the Jutes. However, not all the members of these tribes took part in the migration to Britain, for most of the Saxons remained in Germany, and so did at least some portion of the other tribes. Nevertheless, the number of Germans who reached Britain was large enough to overwhelm the Celtic population. Except in Wales and Scotland, to which some of the Celts fled for refuge, the Anglo-Saxon stock became the dominating strain in the racial mixture of the modern English people.

The invaders of Britain came from tribes that were among the rudest and least civilized of the Germanic peoples, and none of them was Christian at the time of migration. Though Christianity may have made some progress in Britain under the Roman regime, no trace of it remained after the Germanic invasions. In 597, however, a Roman monk named Augustine—not to be confused with the greater Augustine who was Bishop of Hippo—landed in England and soon converted King Ethelbert of Kent, the ruler of one of the numerous small kingdoms that the invaders had established. The first English bishopric was established in the Kentish town of Canterbury, and, thereafter, Christianity spread rapidly through the rest of England.

Eventually the various Germanic kingdoms in England were united under the rule of the kingdom of Wessex. But for a long time the Anglo-Saxon conquerors of England were harassed by still other invaders of the island—the Danes and other Norsemen, coming from Scandinavia. And in 1066 the rule of England was taken over by William the Conqueror, the Duke of Normandy, a descendant of Scandinavian marauders who had earlier settled on the coast of France across the English channel from England. This Norman conquest ended the Anglo-Saxon period of English history, and there-

after England was drawn into the main stream of the history of the new European civilization.

The Roman Pharos, or Lighthouse, at Dover. Three hundred and eighty feet above the English Channel stands the earliest surviving Roman structure in Britain, built not later than A.D. 50. The pharos was originally 80 feet high and was topped with a beacon. (British Information Services)

THE KINGDOM OF THE FRANKS

The Frankish People

The greatest of the Germanic heirs of the West Roman Empire were the Franks. From their homeland on the lower Rhine, they gradually extended their rule until it took in all the territories of the Roman Empire in western Europe except Spain and Italy. In addition, they gained great new territories in Germany that had never known Roman rule. Though a Germanic people, whose kingdom was the beginning of the first German empire, they established the first great kingdom in what was to become France, and that land still bears their name.

Unlike such other Germanic peoples as the Vandals or the Goths, who migrated from their original homeland and set up new kingdoms in other lands, the Franks never undertook a mass migration. At their earliest appearance in history, they inhabited the region where Germany, Holland, and Belgium now come together. And throughout the great age of migrations this remained an area of Frankish settlement. But from this base the Franks gradually extended their rule, until at last their realm included all the other Germanic kingdoms on the mainland of Europe.

Clovis

This process of expansion began under a line of Frankish kings known as Merovingians—the name comes from Merovech or Merovius, the semilegendary founder of the house. The most famous of the Merovingians was Clovis (481–511), who in 486 defeated the last Roman governor of Gaul. Ten years later Clovis was converted to Christianity. His conversion was an event of crucial importance for, unlike most of the other German rulers, Clovis was not won to Christianity by Arian missionaries. Because he was orthodox, Clovis was looked upon with spe-

cial favor by the pope, and his successors benefited from what amounted to an alliance with the growing power of the Roman bishops. This alliance was to prove a large advantage to the Franks in their struggles with rival Germanic peoples.

At the death of Clovis in 511 his kingdom included all northern and central Gaul and reached well across the middle and lower Rhine into what is now Germany. Though the sons of Clovis partitioned the kingdom so that each could have a realm of his own —this was an unwise practice to which the Frankish rulers remained addicted—these sons added greatly to their heritage, for they and their successors brought the rest of Gaul under Frankish rule and secured new gains in Germany.

Charles Martel

The later descendants of Clovis proved to be weaklings, known as the *rois fainéants*—or "do-nothing kings." Yet the Frankish realm did not weaken, even under these ineffective kings, for strong-willed ministers took over the exercise of the king's powers. These ministers held the office of "mayor of the palace." The greatest of them was a man known as Charles Martel—the Hammer—who gained the office in 714 and held it until his death in 741.

The principal problem that Charles Martel had to face was the Moslem threat. In 711 the Moslems had begun their invasion of Spain, and soon thereafter they had destroyed the Visigothic kingdom north of the Pyrenees. Pressing onward into southern Gaul, they seemed destined to overrun the whole of western Europe. But in 732 the Franks under Charles Martel brought their advance to a stop in the great battle of Tours. Though the Moslems continued for some while to hold the region of Gaul south of Tours, they never advanced farther northward, and eventually they were driven back into Spain.

In the course of his campaign against the Moslems, Martel was forced to introduce changes in his army that were to prove of great importance. The Moslems fought on horseback, and the force of their cavalry attacks was the secret of their success as warriors; the Germans, like the Romans, relied mainly upon foot soldiers, using horsemen only as auxiliaries. To meet the Moslem threat, the Germans were therefore obliged to make much larger use of cavalry than ever before.

This change to a reliance upon mounted soldiers had far-reaching social implications. Hitherto the freemen of the tribes had been warriors who provided their own weapons and served without pay. The nobles and other large landowners could afford horses of their own but the common soldiers, who were not rich enough to do so, were obliged to fight on foot. In order to obtain the services of a larger number of horsemen, Martel therefore made grants of land to fighting men who otherwise would be too poor to serve as cavalry. This was not a new practice, but Martel made more such grants than hitherto. After his time the role of the foot soldier became secondary to that of the knight, or horseman. Thus military service became—as it was to remain throughout the Feudal Era —a privilege of the upper class rather than a burden upon the common man.

Pepin the Short

On the death of Charles Martel in 741, two of his sons succeeded to the office of mayor of the palace. One of these brothers died in 747, leaving the other, known as Pepin the Short, to exercise the powers of the office in his own right alone.

But Pepin the Short was unwilling to remain the minister of a "do-nothing" king. He wished to obtain the title of king for himself, since he, like his forebears, had the actual power of a king. His candidacy for the throne had the support of the bishops, whose favor he curried, and of the nobles, whom he either persuaded or compelled to give their approval. In November 751 the magnates of the Frankish kingdom met in an assembly at Soissons and voted the deposition of the last Merovingian king. Thereupon Pepin was raised upon a shield by his warriors, according to an ancient German custom, and was anointed by a bishop as King Pepin. The new line of kings, of which he thus became the first, is known as the Carolingian house. Its name comes from Charlemagne, or Charles the Great, who was the son of Pepin the Short and the most illustrious of its rulers.

Though acclaimed and anointed as king, Pepin the Short was eager to have his new title recognized by the pope. And as it happened, the pope had need of Pepin's help— for at this time a new group of Germanic invaders, the Lombards, were moving into northern Italy, and the pope was fearful of their power. Accordingly Pope Stephen II betook himself to Metz, where he met Pepin and his court, and in January 754 he anointed the king once again. At the same time he

Merovingian Chalice and Its Paten of Gold— discovered in Saône-et-Loire in eastern France. (*Bibliothèque Nationale*)

secured from Pepin the promise that the Frankish king would intervene to protect him against the Lombards and would give to the papacy the rule of the lands held by the Lombards.

Within two years Pepin kept his promises. After defeating the Lombards, he took with him to Rome the keys to the towns in northern Italy that he had captured. These he placed upon the tomb of St. Peter, together with a document conveying to the pope and his successors the rule over the conquered Lombard lands. By this deed, known as the Donation of Pepin, the bishops of Rome gained an extensive new domain, stretching diagonally across Italy from below Rome to the northeast corner of the peninsula.

CHARLES THE GREAT AND THE CAROLINGIAN EMPIRE

Charles, son of Pepin the Short, became the sole king of all the Frankish lands in 768. He was the greatest monarch of his time and one of the greatest in the whole of European history. In France he is known as Charlemagne—the name in French is a contraction of *Carolus Magnus,* which is the Latin for Charles the Great—and every French schoolboy is taught to think of him as one of the heroes of early French history. In Germany he is known as Karl der Grosse, and every German schoolboy is taught to think of him as one of the heroes of early German history. We need not be surprised at this, for the importance of Charles the Great transcends national boundaries.

We know more about Charles than about most of his predecessors because his biography was written by Eginhardus, or Einhard, a court secretary, who had a chance to observe him during the last years of his reign. Einhard describes Charles as a man of large stature, more than six feet tall, with fair hair and mustache, a long nose, and a merry face. He was a man who lived with gusto. Though he had several wives in succession, he also had a number of mistresses who bore him several illegitimate children. He was so attached to some of his daughters that he never permitted them to marry. So unrestrained was his affection for them that they also bore him illegitimate children—or grandchildren. Though temperate in his use of wine, he was fond of good eating and found it hard to observe religious fasts, which he thought were bad for his health. Nevertheless, and despite his moral lapses, which at times he seemed to repent, he won such fame as a warrior for Christianity that he came to be venerated as a saint.

Charles the Great's Policy in Italy

In his dealings with the pope, Charles showed more firmness than had his father. But when the Lombards began to recover from the defeat that Pepin had inflicted upon them and once more became a menace to the papacy, Charles led an army into Italy and crushed them for all time. Thereupon he confirmed the Donation of Pepin—though he also made it plain that he intended to exercise the ultimate power in Italy as well as elsewhere in his domains.

Conquests in Germany

In the course of a series of wars that lasted throughout his reign, Charles extended his rule over most of what is now Germany. This was an occurrence of much significance, because the Roman Empire had never included the lands east of the Rhine and north of the Danube, and, consequently, until this time the German peoples who still remained in the Germanic homeland had never undergone Roman or Christian influence. Only in the age of Charles the Great did they begin to share in the new European civilization, in which Roman and Christian traditions mingled with the Germanic heritage.

Campaigns in Spain

In 778, when a revolt broke out within the Moslem Emirate of Córdova, Charles the Great took advantage of the occasion to lead an army across the Pyrenees into Spain. His immediate aim was to drive the Moslems farther south in Spain, thus making more secure the borders of his own kingdom; his larger hope was to reconquer the whole of Spain for Christendom. In neither did he succeed. After a long and vain siege of the Moslem stronghold of Saragossa, Charles had to turn back to France. In the course of withdrawal through the Pyrenees, the Basques fell upon the Frankish army in the pass of Roncesvalles, inflicting heavy losses upon the retreating Christians. This disaster was later commemorated in the *Song of Roland,* the first great epic in the French language. In a second venture into Spain, 801, Charles fared a little better, conquering the region between the Pyrenees and the Ebro River and organizing there a buffer state that would protect his southern frontier.

Revival of the Roman Imperial Title

By the end of the eighth century Charles was the master of western Europe. His kingdom extended from the North Sea to the Pyrenees and the center of Italy, and from the Atlantic Ocean to the eastern limits of the German lands. In point of fact, he was more than a king, and on Christmas Day of the year 800 he was crowned and acclaimed as emperor, the successor to the rulers of the West Roman Empire.

Historians are not sure whether the initiative for reviving the Roman imperial title came from Charles or from the pope. In November 799 Charles had gone to Rome to investigate a dispute that involved Pope Leo III. The manner in which Charles handled the investigation was such as would win for him the gratitude of the pope and so was his ultimate decision. Two days later, on December 25, Charles attended a solemn mass in St. Peter's. As he was rising from his knees, according to his biographer Einhard: "Pope Leo placed a crown upon his head, and all the Roman people cried aloud, 'To Charles Augustus, crowned of God the great and pacific Emperor of the Romans, life and victory!'" Einhard adds that the pope's action was not pleasing to Charles, who de-

Charlemagne's Empire

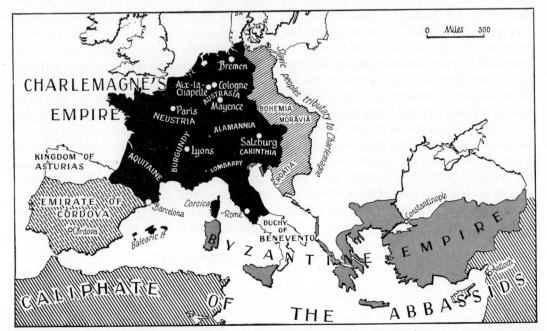

Charlemagne at the Head of His Army—a nineteenth-century wood engraving from François Pierre Guillaume Guizot's *A Popular History of France*

clared that he would not have entered the church on that day, although it was a great festival, had he been able to foresee the pope's intention. However that may be, the imperial coronation of Charles was an eloquent indication that the idea of the Roman Empire had not died out in the minds of the men of western Europe.

Despite his new title, Charles remained the ruler of a Germanic kingdom quite unlike the Roman Empire of ancient times, and its social and cultural life was far inferior to that of the sophisticated civilization over which the earlier Roman emperors had presided. Yet we cannot hold Charles accountable for the shortcomings of his empire as compared to that of Rome, for the restoration of a government and a civilization in western Europe comparable to that of the Roman regime at its best was a task far greater than any one man could accomplish. What Charles did achieve was creditable enough, because he brought to a wide area of Europe a greater measure of political order than had been known for several centuries.

Charles' Religious Ideal

Charles conceived of himself as the Christian emperor whose duty it was to establish the kingdom of God on earth. His conception of that kingdom suffered from his own intellectual and moral limitations, which were those of a crude age, but he was a devoted reader of the Church Fathers and other theologians whom he took as guides. Einhard reports that his favorite work was St. Augustine's *City of God*. We may wonder how well Charles understood the subtle reasoning of the great doctor, but we may be sure that he grasped the main idea that Augustine set forth: that mankind is divided between those who belong to the realm of the godly and those whose loyalty is given to an earthly city. And Charles saw himself as the protector of the realm of the godly.

Because of his theocratic conception of his office as a Christian emperor, Charles took it upon himself to dictate the appointment of bishops and exercise a decisive influence in the choice of the popes. Likewise he concerned himself with countless questions of ecclesiastical discipline, established rules of the education of the clergy and for the furtherance of dignity and uniformity in church ritual and hymnody, and supervised the government of monasteries. Indeed, no question of religious belief or practice was outside the scope of his concern, as he conceived of his responsibilities.

Secular Government

In his secular government Charles did not fundamentally change the governmental machinery that he had inherited from the Merovingians, but he appreciably improved its efficiency. At the center of his government he continued to use the same household officers found in the palace of the Merovingian kings, but during his reign their functions became more like those of ministers heading administrative departments than like personal attendants of the king. As the representatives of the king in local administration, he continued to make use of the counts, but he instituted new measures to check the abuse of their power and to mark out more clearly the boundaries of the counties.

As in the Merovingian period, the counts were ordinarily appointed for life and were given estates for their personal support. Commonly the counts sought to transmit their office to their heirs and to add new lands to those assigned them. And because communications were difficult, they had a large degree of independence in the use of their political power. Thus they tended to become local magnates rather than agents of the central power. To counteract this development, Charles created officers of a new rank, called *missi dominici,* or "messengers of the lord." These were traveling counts, whose duties were to ride through the various counties on tours of inspection, check on each local count's administration, and either deal with abuses on the spot or report irregularities to the king. Usually Charles sent out these traveling counts in pairs—one

a layman and the other a churchman—so that each would keep watch on the other, while both kept watch on the local counts.

Thus Charles was assisted in local government by three kinds of counts—the ordinary count (*comes, Graf*), administering a county or *gau;* the count of the march (*comes marchiae, Markgraf*), governing a march, or county, located on the border and therefore of special military importance; and the traveling counts (*missi dominici, Sendgrafen*). Some subdivisions of the realm were called duchies and were under the administration of dukes. In earlier times the title of duke had signified an office of military command rather than of local administration, but by the time of Charlemagne it had lost this special meaning. Eventually *duke* came to mean a higher rank than *count.*

The Capitularies

In the age of Charles the Great no one supposed that the king was the supreme lawmaker in his realm, for law was understood to have its origin in the customs handed down from the past, and the king did no more than enforce these customs. However, the customary laws of the Germans, arising out of the needs of a relatively small and simple tribal society, proved inadequate for some of the needs that arose in the administration of the huge realm over which Charles now presided. Hence Charles was obliged to issue a great number of edicts, many of which we would consider as new laws. These edicts are known as *capitularies* —from their arrangement according to chapters (Latin: *capitula*). A notable capitulary is the one creating the office of *missi dominici.*

Carolingian Economic Life

The economic life of the Carolingian Age was almost wholly confined to the pursuits of the self-sufficient agricultural village. A

One of Charlemagne's Ivory Chessmen. An ancient importation from the Orient, chess was the most popular indoor game of medieval noblemen. (*Bibliothèque Nationale*)

tory of farm implements should be sufficient, so the steward was told, so that no one would have to borrow tools from a neighbor. Included in the long list of agricultural products for which the steward must account were hogs, hay and grain, wine, beer, nuts, fruits and vegetables, eggs, fish from the fishpond, honey, firewood, and such by-products as horns and hides. Facilities must be available for soapmaking, woodworking, shoemaking, metalwork, and the fashioning of swords. For such work the steward was required to have a staff of artisans. Cloth was made by women of the serf class.

The "Carolingian Renaissance"

As the emergence of a strong government brought a semblance of order in social and economic life, intellectual and cultural activity began to revive. Though the achievements of the Carolingian Age in this field are not to be compared with those of the Classical period, they were so far in advance of the Merovingian period that historians sometimes speak of the "Carolingian Renaissance." Charles himself was interested in education and established schools for boys at several of his more important residences. Boys of humble station were often admitted to these "palace schools," and teachers were brought there from all over Europe. Charles also invited men of letters to his court. The most famous of these was an Englishman, Alcuin of York, some of whose writings on grammar and philosophy have survived.

In music the Carolingian Renaissance saw the spread of the Gregorian chant throughout the churches of Latin Christendom. In this period, too, the organ was introduced into western Europe from the east. Though in the east the organ was used for secular music, in the west it came to be identified with religious services. In popular music the fiddle and bagpipes came into prominence, while Moorish influence is found in increasing use of castanets and tambourines.

revealing picture of these villages is provided by one of Charlemagne's *capitularies* that deals with the management of the royal villas —that is, the manorial villages or farms belonging to the king. Though presumably these villas were more pretentious than those of men of humbler rank, life must have been much the same in other villages.

From the instructions given to the steward (who was obliged to account to the king for the management of the villa), one gathers that the furnishings of the manor house included tables and benches, beds with adequate blankets, pillows and linen, and a large store of kitchen utensils. The inven-

Charles' Successors

Charles the Great died in 814. His intention was to divide his realm among his several sons but, as it happened, only one of these outlived him. Hence the whole realm passed to the survivor, Louis the Pious.

But at the death of Louis the Pious, the Frankish Empire was divided among Louis' three sons. The imperial title passed to the eldest of them, Lothair, who was also to receive a portion of the Carolingian realm, while a separate kingdom in Germany was provided for the second son, called Louis the German, and another, in France, for the youngest, Charles the Bald. In the hope of despoiling Lothair of a portion of his inheritance, the other two brothers combined against him, and warfare broke out among them. At its conclusion in 843, an agreement was made in the Treaty of Verdun by which Lothair kept the title of emperor, with rule over the Frankish domains in Italy and over the lands between the Rhône and the Rhine rivers as far as the North Sea.

Thus the huge realm of Charles the Great was broken up into three new kingdoms. Two of these were to endure: the kingdom of Charles the Bald was to become the kingdom of France, and the realm given to Louis the German was to evolve into the first political organization embracing the whole

of what we know as Germany. The dream of a great empire that would include all western Europe was to persist for centuries longer, but no one again was to come so close to realizing this dream as had Charles the Great.

||||||||||||||||||||||||||||||||||||||||||||||||||||||||||||||||||||||||||||||||||

Rulers of the Frankish Kingdom, 481–987

Merovingian Dynasty

Clovis	481–511
(Charles Martel	714–741)

Carolingian Dynasty

Pepin the Short	(751–768)
Charles the Great	768–814
Emperor of the Roman Empire	800
Louis I (the Pious)	814–840
Charles II (the Bald)	843–877
Louis II	877–879
Louis III ⎫ joint rulers Carloman ⎭	879–882
Carloman	882–884
Charles III (the Fat)	885–887
Charles III (the Simple) *	893–923
Louis IV	936–954
Lothair	954–986
Louis V (the Sluggard)	986–987

* From 888 to 898 Odo (also known as Udace), the first of the House of Capet, was king or contender for the throne; in 922 Robert of Burgundy was declared king, but he was killed in battle the following year, and during 923–926 Raoul of Burgundy was king.

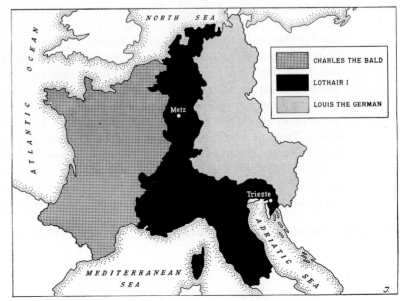

Division of Charlemagne's Empire

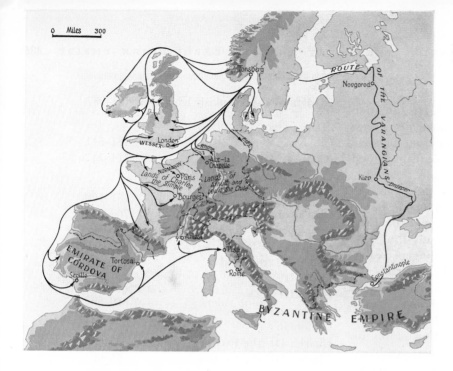

THE "AGE OF IRON"

As the Carolingian Empire disappeared, a new age of invasions began, and once more Europe was reduced to chaos. By the beginning of the tenth century Europe was at its nadir, as dark or darker than in the worst centuries before the reign of Charles the Great. So brutal was this era that it well deserves to be known as the "Age of Iron."

The Norsemen

The invaders who brought this new turmoil to Europe were a Teutonic people, related to the Germanic tribes that had figured in the earlier migrations of peoples in the fourth through the sixth centuries. Their homeland was in Scandinavia, far removed from all Roman influence and outside the scope of Frankish power under Charles the Great. They are known in history, variously, as the Norsemen or Northmen or Vikings.

Inhabiting a cold and mountainous region, ill-suited to agriculture, the Norsemen had early turned to fishing as their principal source of livelihood. Gradually they had also turned to seafaring ventures that sometimes were in the nature of commerce but as often were simply piracy. Their ships, propelled by both sails and oars, were the swiftest in Europe, and their voyages the most daring since the time of the Phoenicians. During the ninth and tenth centuries there was scarcely a region in Europe where they did not make an appearance, usually as savage raiders. Charles the Great came in contact with them while conquering northern Germany, and as a bulwark against them he had organized the Danish March, which gave its name to Denmark. But even the great Charles, had he lived, probably could not have held back the Norse invasions that plagued the whole of Europe after his death.

The record of the Norse expeditions is all but incredible. Five centuries before Columbus, a Viking band under Lief Ericson crossed the Atlantic, establishing settlements in Iceland and Greenland and making explorations in North America. Other Norse raiders ravaged England, Scotland, Ireland,

and the smaller islands, and for a long time Danish and Norwegian kingdoms ruled portions of these lands. Their ventures along the western coast of Europe brought them to the Straits of Gibraltar, through which they passed into the Mediterranean to raid both the coast of North Africa and the Mediterranean shores of Spain, France, and Italy. But most frequently it was the Atlantic coasts of France and Germany that suffered from their attacks, since these regions were closest to the home of the Norsemen in Scandinavia.

Eastern Europe, as well as western, was exposed to their power. Swedish adventurers passed over the northern coasts of Russia, then along the rivers of Russia to the Black Sea and as far as Constantinople. In Russia they founded trading towns at Novgorod and Kiev (about 862), and from the ranks of Swedish adventurers came the first princes of Russia.

The Norsemen in France

Of special importance were the incursions of the Norsemen in what is now France. The Seine River gave them easy access to the interior of northern France, and Paris was sacked by them three times in the ninth century. The Loire led them to the heart of central France, and the Garonne brought them inland as far as Toulouse in the southwest.

The weakling kings who succeeded Charles the Bald could not defend their lands against these invaders. Even had the kings been more energetic in seeking to organize a defense, it would have availed nothing. The noble magnates of the kingdom would not submit to the king's leadership, preferring to preserve their political independence and improvise defenses for themselves. Among these magnates, the counts of Paris stood out as being especially vigorous in meeting the menace of the Norsemen. Eventually one of the counts of Paris was to depose the last of the Carolingian kings of France and take the throne himself.

Before this came to pass, however, the Carolingian king Charles the Simple took a momentous step in the hope of forestalling further Norse depredations. In 911 he made an arrangement with Rollo or Rolf the Norseman, the leader of a band that was making raids along the Seine. By this agreement Rollo was given the title of duke and permitted to settle in the region that came to be known—because the Norsemen lived there—as Normandy. Rollo, who now became a Christian, acknowledged the king of France as his overlord. Thus Charles the Simple hoped to gain an ally who would help him check both further Norse invasions and the rising power of the Count of Paris.

Duke Rollo made his capital at Rouen, which eventually became one of the busiest and most beautiful towns of northern France. One of his descendants was that Duke of Normandy whom the French call William the Bastard and whom the English call William the Conqueror. It was he who invaded England in 1066 and seized the English crown from the last Saxon king. Other descendants of Rollo also kept up the ancient Norse habit of adventurous wandering. In the eleventh century a band of Norman knights invaded southern Italy and Sicily and set up in this region a new realm known as the Kingdom of the Two Sicilies.

The "Holy Roman Empire"

Germany also suffered from Norse incursions, because the Rhine and other rivers flowing into the North Sea made it possible for these seafaring raiders to venture far inland. As in France, too, local magnates gained greater independence as they organized the military defense of regions under attack.

When the last Carolingian king of Germany died in 911, the strongest of these local magnates was the Duke of Franconia, who was chosen by the other leaders to succeed to the Carolingian German throne. From that time on the German Monarchy was elective, and after 962 it bore the name of "the Holy Roman Empire." It gained this name when Otto the Great was crowned as emperor by the pope in a manner reminiscent of the coronation of Charles the Great. Otto had even less right than Charles to be called a "Roman" emperor for, whereas the word *Roman* implied the head of a universal realm, Otto's rule actually extended over only Germany and Italy. It was to prove a misfortune for Germany that its rulers bore this grandiose title, because it encouraged them to keep an interest in Italian affairs on the ground that a "Roman" emperor should at least have a foothold in Rome. And while the German emperors were involved in Italy, their attention was distracted from the task of building a strong central government in their homeland. Yet the memory of the Roman Empire commanded so much respect that in the age of Otto the Great this title seemed to convey great dignity to the German ruler. It remained in use until 1806.

The Kingdom of France

Eventually France was to outdistance Germany in the development of a strong central government, though the German rulers were to have the more resplendent title. But in the ninth and tenth centuries the French kingdom suffered as much as the German from the decentralization of political power. The later kings of the Carolingian line were reduced to a shadowy position, since their actual power was limited to the environs of their capital at Laon. Elsewhere local magnates, such as the counts of Paris and the dukes of Normandy, ruled their domains with little or no regard for the king. Nor were the Carolingians even allowed to keep their title without dispute, because in 888 the French nobles deposed the king and gave the throne to Odo, or Udace, Count of Paris. At his death, the Carolingian house recovered the rule and kept it until the last king of that line died in 987. Thereupon the bishops and nobles of northwestern France again chose a Count of Paris, Hugh Capet this time, as the new king. His descendants were to hold the throne until the nineteenth century.

The beginning of this new Capetian dynasty was unpromising, because at his accession the power of Hugh Capet was limited, for all practical purposes, to his ancestral domain, the county of Paris. But Hugh and his successors were never distracted from the task of building a strong, centralized monarchy, as the German monarchs were by the dream of building a universal empire.

Suggestions for Further Reading

Source Materials

Anthologies and Collected Documents

G. H. Knoles and R. K. Snyder, eds., *Readings in Western Civilization* (rev. ed., New York, 1954), pp. 216–236.

Selections from the Roman historian Tacitus' description of the customs of the Germans and from Eginhard's *Life of Charlemagne.*

J. H. Robinson, ed., *Readings in European History* (2 vols., Boston, 1904), Chapters II–VIII.

An excellent selection of short documents illustrative of life in the period of the Germanic invasions and the Frankish Kingdoms.

O. J. Thatcher and E. R. McNeal, *A Source Book for Mediaeval History* (New York, 1905).

An excellent collection of documents illustrative of the history of Europe in the Feudal Era.

Contemporary Writings

Augustine, Bishop of Hippo, *The City of God.*

There are many editions of this classic statement of the Christian philosophy of history. It is difficult reading.

Boethius, *The Consolation of Philosophy.*

There are many editions of this classic by one of the last great philosophers of the Greco-Roman civilization.

Einhard, *Early Lives of Charlemagne by Einhard and The Monk of St. Gall;* translated by A. J. Grant (London, 1905).

Standard texts of two contemporary accounts of Charlemagne's life and career.

Gregory of Tours, *History of the Franks*, edited by D. M. Dalton (Oxford, 1927).

A classic—the best contemporary history of the age of the Franks, especially Charlemagne.

Tacitus, *Germania.*

A classic description of the Germanic tribes by a great Roman historian. Available in many editions.

Secondary Works

R. F. Arragon, *The Transition from the Ancient to the Medieval World* (New York, 1936).

An interesting survey of the changes in European civilization that took place between the end of the Roman dominion and the formation of the new "western" civilization.

S. Dill, *Roman Society in Gaul in the Merovingian Age* (New York, 1926).

An excellent study of Merovingian society.

A. Dopsch, *The Economic and Social Foundations of European Civilization* (New York, 1937).

An important study; corrects older, somewhat exaggerated accounts of the extent of the "collapse" of the west after the withdrawal of Rome.

E. S. Duckett, *The Gateway to the Middle Ages* (New York, 1938).

A survey of the cultural life of the barbarian kingdoms.

A. Guerard, *French Civilization from its Origins to the Close of the Middle Ages* (New York, 1921).

An excellent, older survey of the earliest history of civilization in western Europe.

M. L. W. Laistner, *Thought and Letters in Western Europe, A.D. 500–900* (New York, 1931).

A scholarly survey; very valuable.

J. L. La Monte, *The World of the Middle Ages; A Reorientation of Medieval History* (New York, 1949).

Makes the Byzantine Empire and the Moslem caliphates the central theme of the early Middle Ages (to the fourteenth century).

F. Lot, *The End of the Ancient World and the Beginning of the Middle Ages* (New York, 1931).

A fine survey of the history of the west in the period between the withdrawal of Rome and the establishment of feudal society.

H. S. L. B. Moss, *The Birth of the Middle Ages, 395–814* (Oxford, 1935).

A good survey of the decline of Roman power in the west and the establishment of the barbarian kingdoms.

J. W. Thompson, *An Economic and Social History of the Middle Ages* (New York, 1928).

A standard dependable survey.

D. Whitelock, *The Beginnings of English Society* (Harmondsworth, England, 1952).

A good survey of Anglo-Saxon England.

18

The Political
Institutions
of the Feudal Era

A Knight in Armor—about 1400, Italian. This late medieval type of armor is composed of large plates, shaped to fit the body, then covered with red velvet. Covering armor with fabric was done only by the guilds of Linen Armorers, who were also tailors. (Courtesy of the Metropolitan Museum of Art)

Most people living in western Europe in the centuries between the death of Charles the Great (814) and the Norman conquest of England (1066) had reason enough to think of political disorder and constant warfare as the normal conditions of human life, which might endure forever. Yet by the beginning of the eleventh century western European society was achieving a considerable degree of political stability, and this achievement marked the dawn of a new era. What brought about this political stability was the development of a set of institutions known as *feudalism,* and the new period in European history is therefore called the Feudal Era. It was in this feudal period and within the framework of feudal institutions that the new civilization of western Europe took shape.

(This era is also known as the "medieval period" or the Middle Ages. But these terms are misleading, because this was a creative epoch, not a mere intermission between ancient times and the modern age. The term *Feudal Era* is more appropriate, because feudalism was the characteristic form of social and political organization in this stage of European development.)

FEUDALISM

The feudalism of western Europe comprised a number of complex and diverse practices that evolved over a long period of time and took different forms in different places. For this reason, it cannot properly be called a "system," or can a precise date be assigned for either its beginning or its disappearance. We can speak of the epoch from the eleventh through the thirteenth centuries as the Golden Age of Feudalism, but some of its practices appeared much earlier, and some did not die out until much later.

The Origins of European Feudalism

The general characteristic of feudalism was that those persons who possessed landed estates also exercised political power. This is in contrast to the modern social order, in which all political power is concentrated in a government, and those who own land and those who do not are equally subject to the laws of the government. Feudalism arose in Europe at a time when there was no strong government, and it declined in proportion as the kings increased their power and established effective central government.

Some of the practices of feudalism had begun to develop even before the German migrations started. As the Roman government ceased to exercise effective control over the provinces, the owners of some of the *latifundia,* the large landed estates, began to rule their holdings virtually as they pleased. Then, when the Germanic tribes invaded western Europe, the strongest of the Germanic warriors tended to merge with the large landholders of the Roman era to form a single new class of landholding magnates.

These magnates became a military élite. One reason for this was that the German warriors who merged with the landowners of the Roman regime perpetuated their tradition of warfare. Another reason was that warfare came to be an expensive vocation. In the preceding chapter we noted that by the time of Charles Martel foot soldiers were displaced by cavalry, but only a man who owned estates of some size could afford to provide himself with a horse and armor. This linking of land ownership with the vocation of the mounted warrior became one of the features of feudalism.

Still another factor in the growth of feudalism was the decentralization of political power in the reign of Charles the Great, whose realm took in nearly all western Europe. Charles had done his best to prevent the counts from gaining independence of the central government. But his best was not enough, and the counts succeeded in making their office hereditary and keeping possession of the estates that had been assigned to them. The breakdown of the Carolingian Empire thus endowed these landed magnates with "a piece of government," a portion of the political power once claimed by Charlemagne.

Lord and Vassal

Feudalism, in the proper sense of the word, involved only persons of "noble" status. In such a kingdom as France, for example, only a few thousand persons were engaged in feudal relationships. These were the persons who controlled the wealth and military power of the land, but the population also included millions of peasants and tens of thousands of merchants and artisans living in the towns. The latter were often under the jurisdiction of a feudal lord, but because they were not of noble birth, they could not participate in the feudal relationship that linked lords and vassals.

A feudal lord was the holder of a *fief*. Usually the fief was a landed property. It might be as large as a kingdom or as small as a single village. Thus a feudal lord might be a king or a duke, holding a great domain, or he might be a simple knight, whose fief consisted of but a small manor, comprising a house for the lord, a church, and the habitations of some scores of peasants who tilled the land of the manor. Occasionally a fief might take some other form. For example, it might involve the right of a lord to collect tolls from persons making use of a bridge, or it might involve another kind of privilege which would provide him an income. Normally, however, the fief was a piece of land.

Nearly every feudal lord owed allegiance to another lord, who was called his *suzerain* or overlord, while still other lords, known as his *vassals,* gave him their allegiance. The King of France, for example, was the overlord or suzerain of all the great dukes, counts, and other nobles in his realm who held their fiefs directly as vassals of the king. In turn, these great lords were the suzerains of other feudal lords, who were their vassals. This progression continued down to the lowest rank in the feudal order, comprising those knights who had no vassals beneath them.

We must not picture this feudal hierarchy as a neat and orderly pattern, like the table of ranks in an army, running from general down to lieutenant. Though titles of nobility implied degrees of dignity and social prestige, ranging from king to duke, count, viscount, baron, and knight, a lord's position in the feudal hierarchy did not always correspond to the rank that his title suggested. Moreover, a lord was usually involved in a number of feudal relationships, being both the vassal of several suzerains and the suzerain of several vassals. For instance, William the Conqueror was at once King of England and Duke of Normandy. As King of England, he was independent of the King of France and equal to him in social prestige, and all the great feudal lords of England were his vassals. As Duke of Normandy, William was a vassal of the King of France, holding Normandy as a fief of the French crown. Furthermore, in the case of some of the feudal lords who held lands in England as vassals of the King of England and lands in France as vassals of the Duke of Normandy, William was their suzerain in both lands. Feudal relationships, it is evident, were not a neat pyramid, but a crazy-quilt.

As a rule, the relationship of vassal and suzerain was hereditary. If the Viscount of X held a particular fief as a vassal of the Count of Y, the eldest son of the Viscount would succeed him as vassal, and the eldest son of the Count would usually become, at his father's death, the suzerain of the Viscount. Over a long period of time, however, families die out. Whenever this happened, the same feudal relationship would continue in respect to a specific fief, but a new family would assume the status of vassal or suzerain.

The Duties of Lords and Vassals

The relationship between a vassal and his suzerain imposed duties upon each of them. The simplest description of these duties is that the overlord owed protection to his vassal, while the vassal owed service to his overlord.

The vassal did not "own" the land that made up his fief—that is, he did not have an outright ownership in the modern sense. Rather, he "held" the fief on condition of performing certain services, which usually were military. As long as he performed these services, he continued to hold the fief, and his heir had the right to inherit it. Likewise the overlord was obliged to protect the vassal in the possession of his fief—even, if need be, calling upon others of his vassals to help him protect a vassal whose fief was under attack. As long as the vassal performed his

A Medieval Castle and Its Town. Although the photograph is modern, the scene has changed little since the nobles of the de Luynes family built their medieval castle on a hilltop in France. In the background, beyond the castle, are a chapel and the manor fields. In the foreground is the small town with its cemetery. (Courtesy of the French Government Tourist Office)

duties to the overlord, the latter was obliged to furnish him protection in return. The relationship between them was contractual and reciprocal.

The nature of the overlord's obligation was simple—he was to help defend a vassal who was threatened by some other feudal lord. The duties of the vassal were more diverse, and they varied at different times and in different places at the same time. Certain obligations, however, were nearly universal.

The foremost of the vassal's duties was military service, because a feudal lord had the right to summon his vassals to fight for him in time of war. But this right was not unlimited. Usually the vassal could be required to fight for a total of forty days in a year. When this time was up, the vassal had the right to return home, even though his overlord might still be at war. Sometimes a lord could call upon his vassal to bring with him whatever other lords were his vassals. But this was not always his right, for one of the maxims of feudal law held that "the vassals of a vassal are not the vassals of their suzerain's overlord."

In addition to military service, the vassal might be required to make gifts of money to his overlord. These were called *aids*. Ordinarily these gifts were due on three occasions: when the overlord's eldest son came of age and was knighted, when his eldest daughter was married, and when the lord himself was taken captive and held for ransom. Except in these circumstances, however, the overlord could not require his vassal to give him money. This limitation was of large importance, because it meant that, under feudal law, even kings had no right to levy taxes. Like any other feudal lord, the king was supposed to "live of his own"—that is, from the income of his own manors and whatever other income he might gain according to feudal law from those lords who were his vassals.

A third obligation of the vassal was his duty to "sit in counsel with his lord." This meant that the vassal must respond when

the overlord summoned all his vassals to meet as a court of justice, for, whenever either a suzerain or a vassal accused the other of a breach of his feudal obligations, all the vassals of the lord assembled to hear the dispute and render a decision.

Certain other prerogatives of the overlord require mention. Among these was the right of forfeiture. This meant that if a vassal broke or ignored his obligations to his lord, the latter could take away his fief and either keep it himself or assign it to another vassal. Another was the right of wardship, by which the overlord would administer a fief and take a share of its income if his vassal should die without a male heir or leaving a son who was a minor. Still another prerogative was the right of administering justice. All lords had the right to hold a court of justice for settling disputes among their vassals or between the lord and a vassal. But some lords also had the right to administer justice over all persons, not only their vassals, who resided within the area of their fief. This is in contrast to the modern idea that the administration of justice is the exclusive prerogative of the central government. Only great lords had this right in the feudal period, but they stoutly defended it against the king, because the fines that they imposed were an important source of revenue.

The Ceremonies of Feudalism

We have noted that by the great age of feudalism, the status of the vassal was hereditary, and the eldest son of a vassal had the right to succeed to the holding of a fief when his father died. Nevertheless, the idea also persisted that the overlord conferred the fief on the vassal, for the vassal not only inherited property but an obligation of personal loyalty to his suzerain. Hence ceremonies developed to symbolize this personal tie. These ceremonies included the *investiture*, by which the lord made a symbolic gesture—perhaps handing the vassal a clod of earth—to show that he was bestowing the fief upon him; *homage,* by which the vassal declared himself to be the "lord's man"; and *fealty,* by which the vassal swore a sacred oath to be true to his obligations as a vassal.

Private Warfare

One of the characteristics of the feudal period was the prevalence of private warfare. When a dispute arose between feudal lords, more often than not it was settled by warfare between them. Even when a court of justice decided that one of the parties was in the right and the other in the wrong, the one who had right on his side was obliged to summon his vassals to help him enforce the decision, since it was the function of the court only to render a decision, not to take measures against the wrongdoer. But often these wars were begun on the flimsiest of excuses, with little or no pretense that a wrong had been done, and frequently a lord would attack another in defiance of his solemn vows as a vassal or his pledge as a suzerain. What was worse, the warfare among the lords wreaked great hardship upon the common people, who were not parties to the dispute but were often slain in the course of the fighting or saw the fields laid waste and the crops ruined.

The Life of the Nobility

For all his privileges, the everyday life of the feudal lord was not such as modern men would envy. His home, which by the eleventh century was usually built of stone, was designed to withstand attack but not to provide comfort. The rooms were damp and chilly, being heated in winter only by fireplaces, and were scantily furnished. Though the meals of a prosperous lord were heavy with meat, fruits and vegetables were available only in season, since there was no way of refrigerating or preserving them.

The life of the noble women in the Feudal Era was wholly confined to the home. Their time was spent in prayer, needlework, childbearing, and the management of the house. Because marriages had much bearing upon feudal relationships, the father always arranged his daughter's marriage. Frequently girls were betrothed in infancy, and commonly they were married at fourteen or fifteen. Yet women were treated with much respect, and though it was a rare exception, sometimes women managed fiefs and even made war.

The upbringing of the boys of noble families was designed to fit them for a role in a world of chronic warfare. Reading and writing were not part of their education, since these attainments would be of no use to them, but they were well trained in the use of arms and taught the sport of hunting, which is the appropriate recreation of a fight-

Detail of "Hunt of the Unicorn"—a tapestry. Hunting was a sport but also a necessity, for meat was the staple of Feudal Era meals. (Courtesy, Metropolitan Museum of Art)

Here begynneth the knightes tale—an illustration from one of the earliest editions of Chaucer's *Canterbury Tales* (p. 539), c.1491. (New York Public Library, Rare Book Room)

ing man. The eldest son was also prepared for the task of managing the fief that he would inherit. Since normally the younger sons had no inheritance, they were obliged to make their own fortunes. Usually they took service as men-at-arms in the retinues of kings or great noblemen. The feudal world was no place for a weakling or one who was bookishly inclined. A young man who had no taste for the strenuous life did well to enter the Church.

The Art of War

The military art of the Feudal Era was chiefly concerned with the cavalry. Both horse and rider were fitted with armor. In the Carolingian days, the armor was usually made of leather, with iron reinforcements, but by the great age of feudalism, it was made of innumerable links of iron chain.

Not until near the close of the Feudal Era did this chain armor give way to armor made in plates. As the armor became more elaborate, its weight increased. Eventually this proved to be a serious disadvantage, for a knight who was knocked off his horse could not remount, and he would then be nearly helpless.

A helmet and shield completed the defensive armament of the knight. The shield was usually made of leather-covered wood, studded and braced with metal, because it would be too heavy if it were wholly made of metal. The knight's offensive weapons ordinarily included a long lance, with which he strove to unseat his opponent, and, for use at close quarters, a heavy sword, a battle-ax, or a mace (a metal-headed club).

Since the horsemen were all noblemen who were not in the habit of obeying orders, discipline was loose, and strategy and tactics were rudimentary. In a battle in the open field, both forces charged at each other with tilted lances, each knight hoping to unhorse his adversary. Those who were knocked to the ground as the two forces met were usually finished off by the sword, though the more fortunate were taken captive, to be held for ransom. Those who remained on their horses continued the fight in individual combats, each pair of knights slashing at one another with swords or maces until one was gravely wounded or killed.

Siege warfare, however, was more important than fighting in the open field. Sometimes an attempt would be made to storm the beleaguered castle, and battering-rams or other devices might be used to make a breach in the walls surrounding the castle or to force open the gates. But ordinarily a castle could not be taken by storm, so the siege usually meant a blockade, the attackers hoping that the defenders would be starved into surrender. To hasten this outcome, the attackers often would burn the crops in the fields surrounding the castle, and sometimes would kill those peasants who had not been given refuge within its walls.

Late in the Feudal Era foot soldiers made a comeback. English archers, using the longbow, turned the tide against the French in the famous battles of Crécy (1346) and Poitiers (1356) during the Hundred Years' War. On the continent more use was made of the crossbow. This was heavier and more powerful than the longbow, and often it was equipped with a mechanical device for drawing the bowstring. So great was its force that the arrow of a crossbow would pass through an armored knight or his horse.

Another weapon that gave advantage to the foot soldier was the pike. This was a spear, twelve feet or more in length but light enough to be carried by a man on foot. In battle, pikemen were ranged in several ranks, their pikes thrust forward to make a solid hedge of sharp spears. Horsemen found it impossible to break through such a phalanx.

The increasing use of archers and pikemen gave an advantage to kings in their struggle to force the feudal lords into obedience. Once the king could hire foot soldiers, he no longer had to depend for his military power upon the services of his vassals. And once the king had the means to impose his will upon the feudal lords, instead of being at their mercy, the age of feudalism was over.

Chivalry

As the Feudal Era was coming to its close, the aristocratic fighting class developed an elaborate code of conduct and behavior, which is known as *chivalry*—from the French word *chevalier* (horseman, *i.e.,* a knight). It is ironic that the rules of knighthood were thus formulated just at the time when the knights were losing their former power.

At the outset of the Feudal Era a young man became a knight by the simple fact of taking up arms and fighting against his father's enemies. Once he became a feudal lord, he fought, pillaged, and ruled his domain quite as he pleased. But by the fourteenth century a young man was expected to go through an elaborate rite of initiation before he was recognized as a knight. In some countries the king insisted that he alone had the power to confer the title of knighthood, though any young man born to noble rank would have the right to require the king to bestow the title upon him. At the time of his being knighted, the young man would take a solemn oath to uphold his honor, preserve his fidelity, and use his power as a warrior in the service of the weak.

As part of this process of regularizing feudal usages, a definite order of precedence was established for the various titles—duke, count, viscount, baron, and others. And special "orders of knighthood" were established in most countries as an exceptional distinction, given only to certain noblemen, often as a recognition of their personal merit. Typical of these were two English orders that still survive—the Knights of the Garter and the Knights of the Bath.

Surrender of a Town—This German woodcut, 1514–1516, shows an army of mounted knights receiving the surrender of the kneeling townspeople, with other mounted knights in the background. (Courtesy of the Metropolitan Museum of Art)

Bishop Odo of Bayeux on the Eve of the Battle of Hastings. At left, Odo says grace at table; in the center Odo and William hold a council of war. Another scene, similar to that on page 456, shows Odo, dressed as a soldier, with a mace cheering on his troops. This scene is from the Bayeux Tapestry—which is not a tapestry but an embroidery on linen—that was commissioned for the nave of Bayeux Cathedral. (Victoria and Albert Museum)

The Church and the Feudal Order

Feudal relationships were not confined to members of the aristocratic fighting class but also involved the Church. The reason for this was that the Church held a large portion of the land in all countries of Europe, since land was virtually the only form of wealth in the Feudal Era. But the possession of land was virtually impossible except within the framework of feudal relationships. Consequently the officers of the Church—bishops, abbots, and others—had to accept some of the obligations of vassalage as the condition of their holding the lands from which the Church derived its income, and usually they also stood as suzerains to feudal lords who held land from them as their vassals. Hence some bishops were great feudal magnates as well as ecclesiastic officials. This was especially true in Germany, where the archbishops of Mainz, Trier, and Cologne ruled huge domains, but it was also true in France.

This situation led to grave abuses. Churchmen were forbidden to marry, and, though some of them kept mistresses and begat illegitimate children, they could not have legitimate heirs. When a bishop or abbot died, his successor was elected, according to church practice, by the clergy of the cathedral or the monks of the abbey. But frequently the overlord interfered in the election, seeking to dictate the choice of the new bishop or abbot, so that the fief would be held by a vassal who would be subservient to the overlord. Often the overlord would thus give the bishopric or abbey to a young man of noble family who was not in line to inherit his father's fief. Often, too, the man who was made into an officer of the Church in this manner had little or no sense of religious dedication, and many were morally lax, even dissolute. All too commonly they made use of their feudal power for the advantage of their overlord or their kinsmen or to win domains for their illegitimate children or simply for their personal aggrandizement, rather than in the interest of the Church.

In the early Feudal Era the papacy itself was not free from corruption of this sort. But from the eleventh century on a series of popes undertook to check the abuses that had arisen from the interference of feudal lords in the choice of bishops and abbots. This led to bitter struggles between the popes and the kings of France and Germany, because these monarchs, who were constantly striving against their unruly vassals, wanted to make sure that at least the fiefs of the Church would be held by men on whom they could rely. There was logic on both sides: the pope wanted a dependable churchman, and the overlord wanted a dependable vassal.

But even when there was no outside interference in his election, the bishop or abbot could not avoid involvement in secular problems, for as a feudal lord he exercised many of the functions that are now the prerogative of the government. Like other great feudal magnates, he administered justice in his fief, and though the bishop himself was forbidden to wage war, since no churchman might shed blood, he was often obliged to send his vassals into battle, either to defend his fief against attack or to render aid to his overlord. Some of the less-scrupulous bishops would sometimes disregard or circumvent the prohibition that was supposed to keep them from fighting in person. One such was Odo, Bishop of Bayeux, who was a brother of William the Conqueror. To sate his taste for warfare without violating the letter of the law, Odo went into battle armed with a leather-covered club, since with this he could crack a foeman's skull without shedding blood!

The Church was also involved in feudalism in another manner, which is more creditable. As the guardian of morals, the leaders of the Church kept up a constant effort to mitigate the brutality and wanton destructiveness of feudal warfare. Thus the Church proclaimed the idea of the "Peace of God," which held that certain persons and places should be secure against the menace of war. By a series of Church decrees, the gravest penalties were imposed on any fighting man who should inflict damage upon a monastery, nunnery, or church building or should violate the person of a priest, monk, or nun. Later the same protection was extended to all women and children, peasants, merchants, and virtually all other noncombatants. Though these decrees were often violated, they had some beneficial effect.

The "Truce of God" was a similar conception. This meant that warfare should be suspended at certain times when men's minds should be upon religious observances. These periods included certain days of the year set aside for religious vigils, the week end (from Thursday to Monday), and the whole of the Lenten and Advent seasons.

Like the idea of the "Peace of God," this conception of "open" and "closed" seasons for warfare remained a moral principle, which men did not often respect. But it brought about some measure of improvement in the situation.

The Manor as a Political Unit

It must be remembered that the feudal regime we have been discussing involved only the upper classes of society. Beneath them were the millions of "ignoble" persons. Some of these were the merchants and artisans living in the towns; others were free farmers who owned their own land and worked for themselves, much as the peasants of Europe do today. But the great mass of population in the Feudal Era was made up of agricultural laborers who lived and worked on the manors held by feudal lords.*

* For the manor—or seigneury—as an economic and social institution, see the next chapter.

Twelfth-century Norman Knights and Peasants —as depicted in Guizot's *History of France*.

For these masses of working people, the lords of the manors—the *seigneurs*—were the political rulers, and their political power over the human beings in their charge was well nigh absolute. Each seigneur made the rules and regulations, such as they were, governing the behavior of the non-noble persons on his manor. To be sure, custom or "customary law" protected the serfs and villeins from abuse, and even in the serf-seigneur relationship there was a contractural obligation binding the seigneur as well as the serf. The serf was bound to the land, for example, and if he left it his seigneur might punish him. But the seigneur could not legally remove the serf from the land, either, nor could the seigneur deprive him of the right of his dependents to remain there.

Yet for all practical purposes the seigneur was both lawmaker and judge for the people of the manor. For non-noble persons, the seigneur held a court which was called the *court leet*—that is, for leet-men; for persons of noble rank, he held the *court baron*—

that is, court for the knights or others of noble birth. In the latter courts, as juries came to be used, no one of non-noble status could be a member of a jury: it was one of the feudal privileges of a noble that he must always be tried, when he was accused, by a jury composed of men of a rank equal to his own—his "peers."

The manor was thus a political institution, in the sense that it was the lowest and the basic unit in the structure of government. For the noble vassal in the feudal system, the personal and contractual relationships between lord and vassal tended to ameliorate the arbitrary nature of the lord's authority; for the masses of serfs and other workers, the political authority of the lord of the manor was practically absolute. They had absolutely no voice in their government —no one ever dreamed of such a thing—and the seigneur was the only governor they knew. Even though they might have heard of the king, unless they happened to be on one of the king's own manors, his authority over them was practically nil.

THE FEUDAL MONARCHIES: FRANCE AND ENGLAND

For about seven centuries—from the time of Charles the Great to the middle of the fifteenth century—the manor remained the basis of the social and political organization of Europe. The manor was the community within which were embraced most of the common people, and it was also the basis of the elaborate feudal relationships among the upper classes. Yet in the midst of the great age of feudalism, about the beginning of the twelfth century, a new system of political organization was taking shape. This was a system of regional or "national" integration. It represented a force for centralization, as compared with feudalism, but it also marked the breakup into smaller communities of the great international community of Christendom, to which the Roman Catholic

Church sought to give an organized expression.

This development came about through the struggle of certain dynasties of feudal kings for a preponderance of political power over their feudal vassals. It meant a shift from the personal relationships of feudalism to the more impersonal concept of a government that would exercise exclusive and unlimited power over all persons living within the bounds of the kingdom.

The struggle of the kings for political supremacy occurred in all the countries of western Europe, but the clearest examples of the process were in France and England. In these countries the kings attained a nearly complete success, and their kingdoms became the greatest of the modern states.

The Capetian Kings of France

The Carolingian line in France was supplanted by a new dynasty (p. 438), when Hugh Capet, Count of Paris, was crowned king in Reims cathedral on July 1, 987. He is described as "King of the Gauls, the Bretons, the Normans, the Aquitanians, the Goths, and the Gascons." This title seems to suggest a rule over a large part of what we know as France, but actually it meant little more than a ceremonial recognition of the royal dignity by the great barons who ruled the various feudal subdivisions of France. Centuries were to elapse before the Capetian kings would be able to give practical expression to their authority outside their own feudal domains. In the time of Hugh Capet, these domains included little more than the Île de France, the region around Paris. But eventually they were to extend their authority over one after another of the great baronial domains, until at last the whole of France was under their rule.

Notable progress in this direction was made under Louis VI (1108–1137), called Louis the Fat. His reign saw the beginning of an alliance between the king and the merchants. This was an era of the rapid growth of commerce, and the merchant class was anxious to gain a measure of freedom from the capricious exactions of the feudal lords. By granting charters to the towns where the merchants settled, giving them the right of self-government, the king gained the support of the townsmen against the intractable barons.

Louis' greatest stroke, however, was the marriage that he arranged between his son, the future Louis VII, and Eleanor of Aquitaine. The latter was the daughter of the Duke of Aquitaine, who had no male heir. Consequently she was to inherit his great fief, the largest of all the fiefs in France and larger than the king's own domain. This marriage gave promise that this huge area would be brought under the king's rule. Unhappily, the promise was not to be fulfilled.

Louis VII (1137–1180) had been born a younger son, and, since he was not due to inherit the crown, he had been given a clerical education and destined for a post in the Church. The death of his older brother made him the successor to the throne, but he was not prepared for this responsibility, either by education or by temperament. His wife, Eleanor of Aquitaine, is said to have complained that she "thought she had married a king, but found she had married a monk." Louis was no better pleased with the marriage than she, and in 1149 he had the marriage dissolved.

Their divorce was a catastrophe for France, because Eleanor promptly remarried. Her second husband was Count Henry of Anjou, who was also Duke of Normandy and Count of Maine. And in 1154 her husband inherited the throne of England, where he became King Henry II. Thus the vast domain of Aquitaine was detached from the domain of the French kings and, what was worse, became one of a number of fiefs in France held by the king of England.

Some of the damage was repaired by Philip II (1180–1223), the son and successor to Louis VII. Known also as Philip Augustus, he became one of the greatest of French kings. He had none of his father's extreme piety, but he was a shrewd, calculating, and unscrupulous statesman, who devoted himself wholly to the task of extending the royal authority. By a combination of warfare and intrigue, he eventually succeeded in reducing the holdings of the English kings in France to about one fourth of the area that Henry II had held. The lands that he wrested from the English kings he added to his own domain, and so greatly did he increase its size that he is sometimes called the founder of modern France.

The work of enlarging the royal domain was continued under Louis IX (1226–1270), who is also known as "Saint Louis" because he was eventually canonized by the Roman Catholic Church. Famed in legend as a scrupulously just ruler, Louis IX proclaimed the

Blanche of Castile and Her Son St. Louis—as they appear in an illuminated manuscript, c.1226–1234. (Pierpont Morgan Library)

the sovereignty of the king to a much greater degree than had been characteristic of the feudal conception of customary law. Philip the Fair was influenced by this neo-Roman attitude toward the royal power, and he exploited it fully during his reign.

Dramatic evidence of the growth of the king's power was given in the outcome of a struggle bewteen Philip the Fair and the papacy. This quarrel arose out of the king's constant need for more money. The growth of the royal bureaucracy required more revenue than the king received from feudal dues and the other sources available to him. To solve the problem, Philip undertook to impose taxes upon wealth of the Church. This brought forth an outraged protest from Boniface VIII, the reigning pope, who forbade the clergy to pay taxes to a secular ruler without the pope's consent. Philip promptly replied with a royal decree forbidding the sending of money or other wealth out of the kingdom without the king's consent. Thus he shut off the revenues that were sent to Rome by the French clergy.

Though the dispute was temporarily settled by a compromise, Boniface never forgave Philip for challenging his authority, and in 1300 he issued a decree, entitled *Ausculta fili,* in which he asserted that the pope was supreme over all earthly rulers. When copies of this decree reached France, Philip had them burned, and the quarrel was on again.

As a move to rally public opinion to his support, Philip then convened a meeting of the Estates General in 1302. This institution was an outgrowth of the court that the king customarily held as a feudal lord, to which were summoned the foremost vassals of the king, including bishops and abbots. But to this meeting Philip also invited representatives of the chartered towns of the kingdom. For this reason, the meeting of the Estates General of 1302 was of special significance, because it transformed that institution from a feudal assembly into a national body comparable to the English Parliament.

principle that appeals could be made to the king from the decisions of all feudal courts. Though severe in his punishment of heresy and blasphemy, in other respects he was the most humane and enlightened ruler in a cruel age, and when he died in 1270, he was greatly mourned by his people.

Philip IV (1285–1314), known as Philip the Fair, was the next great king of France. He built up the royal administration by greatly increasing the staff of lawyers and officials, drawn mostly from among the townsmen. Many of his advisers had been trained in the principles of Roman law, the study of which was reviving at this time. Since Roman law had been based upon the assumption that the emperor was the supreme source of law, their studies led them to exalt

On his side, Boniface also took action to strengthen his position. This took the form of a new papal decree, entitled *Unam sanctam,* which expressed in more vigorous terms than ever before the principle that the spiritual power of the pope was supreme over the temporal power of kings and other secular rulers. Moreover, he threatened to excommunicate Philip if the latter did not submit. This threat so provoked Philip that he sent his minister Nogaret to Italy to intimidate the pope. In September 1303 Nogaret stormed into the presence of the aged pontiff, who was at the town of Anagni, seized the pope, and handled him violently. A popular uprising in the town forced the release of Boniface, but the pope never recovered from the shock of this "terrible day at Anagni," and shortly afterward he died. The successor chosen to replace Boniface VIII as pope lived only another nine months. Thereupon Philip's agents brought about the election of a French churchman, Clement V.

Under pressure from Philip, in 1309 Clement moved the papal court from Rome to the town of Avignon, a small papal fief in the south of France. This was a grave blow to the papacy, for the rest of Europe regarded the papacy as now captive to the French king. But it gave striking proof of the enormous increase of the French king's power.

The Hundred Years' War

Much of the gain made up to the time of Philip IV was wiped out soon after his death. In 1328 the direct line of the Capetians died out, and the crown passed to Philip of Valois, who was the son of a brother of Philip IV. And with the accession of this Valois king, Philip VI (1328–1350), a war broke out between the French and English kings. This war went on for more than a century—from 1337 to 1453—though the fighting subsided from time to time during periods of uneasy peace. In the course of this war new disasters came upon France.

The immediate occasion for the outbreak of the war was the assertion by the English king, Edward III, of his right to inherit the throne of France on the extinction of the Capetian line. Edward had some basis for this assertion, since his mother was a daughter of Philip IV. However, the French custom excluded women from the line of succession to the throne, and therefore Philip VI, in the French view, had the better right.

Other issues were also involved. Apart from his claim to the French throne, Edward III had an interest in France because of his hope of recovering the fiefs that once had been held by Henry II (both in his own right and as the husband of Eleanor of Aquitaine) but had since been taken by the later

Kings of France, 987–1483

Capetian Dynasty

Hugh Capet	987–996
Robert II	996–1031
Henry I	1031–1060
Philip I	1060–1108
Louis VI (the Fat)	1108–1137
Louis VII	1137–1180
Philip II (Augustus)	1180–1223
Louis VIII	1223–1226
Louis IX (St. Louis)	1226–1270
Philip III	1270–1285
Philip IV (the Fair)	1285–1314
Louis X	1314–1316
John I	1316
Philip V	1316–1322
Charles IV	1322–1328

Valois Dynasty

Philip VI	1328–1350
John II	1350–1364
Charles V	1364–1380
Charles VI	1380–1422
Charles VII	1422–1461
Louis XI	1461–1483

Capetians. Moreover, the English were eager to give help to the townsmen of Flanders, who were rebelling against their feudal lord, the Count of Flanders. The reason for the English interest in this rebellion was the large amounts of raw wool exported from England to supply the weaving industries of these prosperous Flemish towns. Since the Count of Flanders was a vassal of the King of France, Philip VI was aiding him in his endeavor to put down the rebellion, and the English were unwilling to have the Flemish towns pass under French dominance.

Fighting was on a small scale until 1346 when Edward landed in Normandy with an army that was exceptionally large by the standards of the time. As the English fought

their way inland, menacing Paris, Philip called out all the forces that he could muster for the defense of his kingdom. On August 26, 1346, the two armies met at Crécy, in Picardy, in the greatest battle fought in western Europe up to that time. The French army presented what seemed an invincible array of armored and mounted knights, but the English had a strong force of archers—who could be recruited in larger numbers than knights, since their weapons and equipment were much cheaper. As it turned out, the English archers were more than a match for the French knights, who fell by the thousands under the showers of deadly arrows. The battle ended with the worst defeat the French had ever suffered.

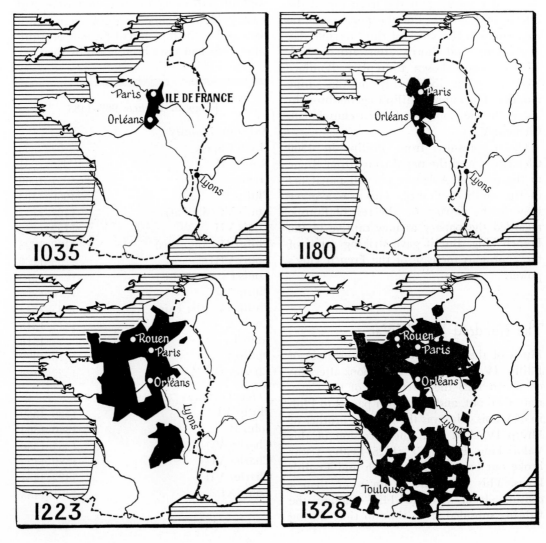

After their victory at Crécy, the English kept the upper hand for more than ten years, but, though they won another resounding triumph in the great battle of Poitiers in 1356, they did not bring the war to a decision. Thereafter the French turned to guerrilla warfare with increasing success, until by 1380 the English were pushed back to the coastal towns of Calais, Cherbourg, Brest, Bordeaux, and Bayonne. Had not civil war and intrigue hampered the French at this point, they might have finished expelling the English from their country. The English took advantage of the disorder within France to push another offensive and seemed in a fair way to re-establish their hold upon a large part of the country, when, while they were besieging Orléans, the French were electrified by the appearance of a young girl, Joan of Arc (1412–1431), who assumed leadership of the French army and led it to victory.

By her appeal to religious fervor and patriotic pride, Joan of Arc restored the flagging spirits of the French and inspired superstitious misgivings among the English. Consequently, when she fell into the hands of the English as a result of treachery on the part of some of her countrymen, the English caused her to be condemned as a witch and burned at the stake.

Her death, however, had the opposite effect from that intended by her captors. Instead of losing heart, the French were stirred

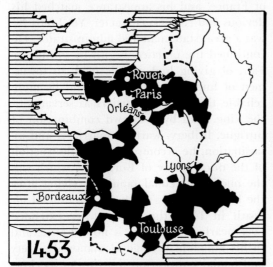

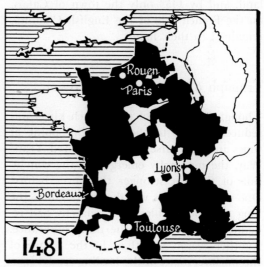

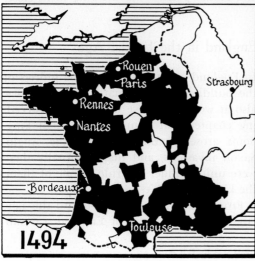

The Evolution of France

The Battle of Hastings. The Bayeux Tapestry is our best authority on arms and armor of the period. A fully armed knight wore a shirt of mail reaching to the knee, called a hauberk or byrnie. The helmets were conical, with a nose piece. The main weapons were the sword and the lance. Compare this eleventh-century equipment with that of the knights on pages 440, 446 and 447. (The Bettman Archive)

to new efforts to drive the English from their land, and by 1453 only the town of Calais, on the French side of the English Channel, remained in their hands.

Triumph of French Royal Power

Though the power of the French kings was reduced almost to the vanishing point at times in the course of the Hundred Years' War, the monarchy emerged at the conclusion of the war stronger than ever before. One reason for this was that throughout the long time of troubles the monarchy had remained the symbol of the unity of France. Another reason was that, in the course of the warfare, many of the leading feudal families of France had been ruined or killed off. Still another was that the Estates General had become accustomed to granting the king the right to levy taxes and raise troops on the ground of a grave emergency—and this emergency had become chronic. Thus France had become habituated to the king's exercise of fiscal and military functions beyond the role normally given him under the customary law of feudalism.

Under Louis XI, who ascended the French throne in 1461, the process of establishing monarchical absolutism reached its culmination. Short, bandy-legged, shifty-eyed, he was the least prepossessing of all the kings of France, and his appearance matched his devious and ruthless character. Yet Louis XI was a great statesman and administrator. He continued the practice, begun by Philip the Fair, of giving high public office to townsmen of humble birth, who would be more reliable than noble courtiers as servants of the king. And by a shrewd combination of intrigue, bribery, warfare, marriage, and assassination, he accomplished the destruction of the ducal house of Burgundy, which was the one great feudal family surviving after the Hundred Years' War. By the time of his death in 1483, the royal power extended over nearly all of what is now France, and in his kingdom the age of manorial society and feudal politics was drawing to its close.

England in the Feudal Age

In England, meanwhile, the same process of the building up of monarchical power was also at work. We have noted in the preceding chapter that a number of small kingdoms arose in England after the Anglo-Saxon invasions, and that eventually these were united under the rule of one of them, the kingdom of Wessex.

From the eighth century onward this new Anglo-Saxon kingdom of England was subjected to the raids of the Norsemen. And in 1016 the king of Denmark, who had already conquered the neighboring kingdom of Norway, not only invaded England but occupied it, taking the throne for himself. Thus England became part of a Scandinavian empire. But this period of Danish rule ended in 1042, when an heir of the native house of Wessex regained the throne. This was Edward the Confessor (1042–1066), so called because of his piety.

Edward the Confessor died without heirs. At his death, the nobles of the realm chose one of their own number as his successor. But the accession of this new king, whose name was Harold, was challenged by William, Duke of Normandy, on the ground that Edward the Confessor had promised him the succession. To enforce his claim, William gathered a band of Norman warriors and invaded England. Harold raised an army to repel the invasion, and the two forces met at the famous battle of Hastings on October 14, 1066. Harold lost his life as well as the battle. After the battle, the Normans overran England.

The Norman conquest was one of the great turning points in the history of England. First, it meant the establishment of a much closer connection than ever before between England and the rest of Europe, for William the Conqueror and his successors continued to have large feudal holdings in France, and the king and his ministers were as much at home on one side of the English Channel as on the other. Second, it meant the establishment of a more centralized government than ever before. William himself was a man of exceptional vigor, who owed his prominence solely to his own ability and force of character. Being of illegitimate birth, he had had to fight to make good his succession to the duchy of Normandy before his attempt at the English throne. And by conquest he had also gained the French fiefs of Brittany and Maine. Once he became king of England, William was not the kind of man to permit his rule to be challenged. And since the realm was his by virtue of a conquest, he was free to reorganize the pattern of feudal relationships in such a way as to assure the supremacy of the king over his vassals.

In this reorganization, William dispossessed a number of the feudal lords of the Anglo-Saxon era and gave their fiefs to Norman retainers who had helped in the conquest of the island. Others were allowed to keep their fiefs, but only by the grace of the king. Thus both the old Anglo-Saxon nobility and the newer Norman nobility were obliged to acknowledge that their position as feudal lords was dependent upon the favor of the monarchy. Morover, William saw to it that no nobleman, either Norman or Anglo-Saxon, would possess feudal holdings large enough to enable him to withstand the power of the king—as William

The Tower of London—begun by William the Conqueror about 1078, is a massive, stone fortress, with walls 11 to 15 feet thick (British Information Services)

The Angevin "Empire"

himself, holding the great fief of Normandy as a vassal of the French king, was able to defy his overlord.

William also took measures of much significance affecting the Church. He appointed capable men to high ecclesiastical office —such as Lanfranc, who became archbishop of Canterbury—and he generally tightened up discipline in the English church, which had grown somewhat lax in the Anglo-Saxon era. However, William was not disposed to admit the supremacy of the pope over secular rulers. When Pope Gregory VII sought to

have William acknowledge that he held the realm of England as a papal fief, William stoutly refused. Furthermore, he put into English law three important provisions limiting the power of the pope over the English church. By these provisions, the king's permission was required before any papal decree could be promulgated in England, before a council of churchmen of the realm could be convened, and before the sentence of excommunication could be imposed upon any English baron. Later kings were not always able to uphold these provisions against the strongest of the popes, but generally the English church remained freer of the papal domination than the churches in other countries of Europe.

The "Angevin Empire"

Among the successors of William the Conqueror, one of the most notable was Henry II (1154–1189), the founder of the new house known as the Plantagenet. Henry was the heir to the French fiefs of Maine and Anjou as well as Normandy, and he was the husband of Eleanor of Aquitaine after the dissolution of her marriage to the King of France. Henry II thus held much larger possessions on the continent than the whole of the English kingdom. So vast were his domains that they are often referred to as the "Angevin Empire." Because England gave Henry II the title of king, while elsewhere his status was that of a vassal to another king, we are likely to think of him as an English king who held big fiefs on the continent. However, Henry himself gave more attention to his holdings on the continent than to his island kingdom, and we might better think of him as a great French lord who happened also to hold the modest kingdom of England.

Henry II was succeeded by his third son, who is known as Richard Lionheart. Though he was a romantic and heroic example of the ideals of chivalry, Richard was an ineffectual king. His brother John, who succeeded him, was even worse. Both these rulers fell victim to the wiles of Philip II of France, with the result that most of the Angevin holdings in France were lost.

Magna Carta

So gross was the misrule of King John that the nobles rose in rebellion and forced him in 1215 to grant a document known as Magna Carta, or the Great Charter. In this document John promised to respect a number of limitations upon his power as king. At the time this represented a step backward, since the great need of England in that age was for a strengthening of the royal power in order to terminate the disorder of feudalism. In later times, however, these restraints upon the king came to be prized as a guarantee of the liberties of the English people. For this reason, Magna Carta is regarded as a document of the greatest historic importance.

Its main provisions were these: (1) The Church was guaranteed all its "rights and liberties" as established in the law of the land. (2) Barons and all other feudal tenants were promised that there would be no exactions of dues and duties beyond those of customary feudal law. (3) Special grants of aid could be obtained from the baronage only by the consent of the Great Council, which was the assembly of all the feudal lords who were vassals of the king himself. (4) The rule of law was recognized as forbidding capricious arrests and extortions by the king. The terms of this guarantee were:

39. No freeman shall be seized, or imprisoned, or dispossessed, or outlawed, or in any way destroyed, nor will we commit him to prison, excepting by the legal judgment of his peers, and by the laws of the land.

This guarantee extended not only to feudal barons but to every freeman. It became the basis of the rights that the English and Americans call "due process of law," and for seven centuries it has been cited as an assurance against arbitrary arrest or punishment at the whim of rulers and governments.

The Creation of Parliament

Though John agreed to the limitations on his power that were specified in Magna Carta, he did not live up to his word. As a result, England was again plunged into civil wars. After many years Simon de Montfort emerged as the leader of the barons in the struggle against Henry III (1216–1272), John's son. After defeating this king in battle, Montfort took over control of the government, and in 1265 he summoned an assembly of his supporters that became the ancestor of the English Parliament. This assembly, known as "Simon de Montfort's Parliament," was an outgrowth of the earlier institution of the Great Council. This Parliament included, like the Great Council, all the principal vassals of the king, but it also included, as the Great Council had not, two knights from every shire and representatives of the towns.

This practice continued in the reign of Edward I (1272–1307). Especially notable was the Parliament that this king convened in 1295. It became known as the "Model Parliament" because its organization set what was to be the pattern for later Parliaments and because the king agreed, at the time of its meeting, that its consent was necessary for extraordinary grants of money. The principle was stated in these terms: "That which touches all should be approved by all." Thus the king acknowledged the right of Parliament to a regular voice in matters of government.

As in France, Parliament consisted of three "estates": the barons, the clergy, and representatives of the lower orders. In France these three estates formed separate chambers in the Estates General. In England, however, the lay and ecclesiastical

Kings of England, 1042–1509

Anglo-Saxon

Edward the Confessor	1042–1066
Harold II	1066

Norman

William I (the Conqueror)	1066–1087
William II (Rufus)	1087–1100
Henry I	1100–1135
Stephen	1135–1154

House of Plantagenet

Henry II	1154–1189
Richard I (Lionheart)	1189–1199
John	1199–1216
Henry III	1216–1272
Edward I	1272–1307
Edward II	1307–1327
Edward III	1327–1377
Richard II	1377–1399

House of Lancaster

Henry IV	1399–1413
Henry V	1413–1422
Henry VI	1422–1461

House of York

Edward IV	1461–1483
Edward V	1483
Richard III	1483–1485

House of Tudor

Henry VII	1485–1409

lords sat together as one chamber, called the House of Lords. The other chamber comprised, as in the Model Parliament, two knights from each shire and two burgesses each from certain towns. It came to be known as the House of Commons. This does not mean that it represented "the common people"; the knights and burgesses were present as the spokesmen of corporate communities—the country gentry and the merchants of the towns—while the lords of the upper chamber sat in their own right, not as representatives of others.

The Wars of the Roses

During much of the fourteenth and fifteenth centuries, as we have noted, the English kings were preoccupied with intermittent campaigns in France known as the Hundred Years' War. England itself was untroubled in this era, while France was reduced to ruinous disorder. But just as the war in France was coming to its end, civil strife broke out in England. This series of domestic upheavals is known as the Wars of the Roses, because one of the factions took a white rose as its emblem, while the other took a red one. Those bearing the white rose were the Yorkists, a faction of nobles in rebellion against the king. The red rose was the badge of the Lancastrians, or the supporters of the king. After several decades of conflict, the struggle was ended in 1485 with the victory of Henry Tudor, one of the Lancastrians, who gained the throne as Henry VII and became the first of the Tudor line of English kings. His reign marked the dawn of a great new era and the beginning of the modern history of England.

THE HOLY ROMAN EMPIRE

The monarchy that arose in Germany during the feudal period bore the name of the Holy Roman Empire of the German Nation. It was a strange and misleading title, for as the great French cynic Voltaire later remarked, it was "neither holy, nor Roman, nor an empire," although it did include many of the most important regions of Italy. And if this monarchy had been, as its name implied, a continuation of the Roman Empire of ancient times, it would have been a state embracing many nations, not merely the German nation. The title bears witness, however, to the haunting persistence of the idea of the Roman Empire centuries after the disappearance of Roman rule in western Europe.

Otto the Great was the German ruler who revived this title in 962, but neither he nor his successors had any practical authority, despite their title, over the western European nations of France, England, and Spain. Their realm was limited to Germany and Italy. Even in these lands, the effectiveness of their rule was slight, for under the feudal regime political power was not centralized but dispersed among hundreds of feudal lords. In Germany the most important of these were the great bishops—notably, the archbishops of Mainz, Trier, and Cologne—and the rulers of six large feudal domains known as *stem-duchies*. Otto the Great was himslf one of these stem-dukes, ruling Saxony, and even after his assumption of the title of emperor, his practical influence came mainly from his possession of this domain.

In 1025, on the death of the last descendant of Otto the Great, the magnates of the Empire elected Conrad of Franconia, the ruler of another of the stem-duchies, to succeed to the imperial title. For a century thereafter the crown remained in this Franconian house, most of whose members were exceptionally capable.

The Investiture Controversy

The chief development under the Franconian emperors was a dispute with the papacy over the issue of who was to control the selection of German bishops. This is known as the Investiture Controversy.

Its origin was in a movement for the reform of the papacy, which had fallen into moral decay during the early centuries of the Feudal Era. This reform was begun by Otto the Great and carried on by his successors, who succeeded in taking the choice of the pope out of the hands of the leading families of Rome and made it a matter of dictation by the German emperor. In the short run this was an improvement, for the Roman families who formerly controlled the election of the pope had made the office of the pontiff a source of corrupt advantage for themselves. But, in the long run, it was to produce new discord, for once the papacy passed back into the hands of men of high moral purpose, devoted to religious ideals, these churchmen would naturally protest at the interference by the German emperors in the selection of the popes and at the interference by other secular rulers in the choice of bishops and abbots.

In 1073 the leader of these reforming churchmen gained election as pope, taking the name of Gregory VII. Thereupon the new pope undertook to establish the principle that only a representative of the pope had the right to invest a bishop or abbot— that is, to confer upon him the religious authority of his office. This would mean that the pope would have the decisive influence in the choice of the candidate for the leading church offices. But since, as we have seen, bishops and abbots were feudal lords as well as church officers, this would mean that the pope would control the selection of the men who were to exercise large influence as vassals of secular rulers. All over Europe secular rulers challenged this claim of the pope, insisting upon their own right to induct into office the men who, as bishops and abbots, were to be their vassals.

The struggle was fought with exceptional bitterness between the pope and the German emperor. No sooner did Gregory VII issue his decrees against the investiture of bishops by laymen than Henry IV, who was the German emperor at the time, made plain his refusal to respect the papal edicts. Promptly the pope excommunicated him and declared that Henry's vassals were freed from their oaths of allegiance to him. This gave the signal for rebellions to break out all over Germany. Finding it impossible to cope with the problem of civil war while under the papal ban, Henry IV was forced to make a humble submission. The circumstances of his capitulation were dramatic, for Gregory VII made the German emperor wait for three days outside the castle of Canossa near Parma, Italy, where the pope was staying at the time, before he would grant forgiveness and rescind the excommunication.

Within a few years, however, Henry resumed the struggle, invading Rome with an army and forcing Gregory to flee. Though Gregory died in exile, Pope Urban II, who soon succeeded to the papal power, struck back at the emperor, encouraging the German feudal lords to rise up once again in rebellion. In the course of this rebellion Henry IV was deposed in favor of his son, who became Henry V. Like Gregory VII, whom he had warred upon, the former emperor died in exile.

The Hohenstaufen Emperors

After the death of Henry V in 1125, the succession of the Franconian line ran out. The great magnates of Germany, who were by this time commonly known as the "Electors" of the Empire, then turned to the Duke of Saxony, who became Emperor Lothair II. He lacked a son, and his son-in-law, Henry the Proud, was so powerful and able a man that the Electors, tiring of strong rulers who put curbs upon them, turned for their next choice to the Hohenstaufen family of Swabia.

This was the beginning of a long dispute between two factions, the Guelfs and the Ghibellines. The Guelfs were the family and partisans of the disappointed candidate, Henry the Proud, while the Ghibellines were the family and supporters of the Hohenstaufens. In later centuries the partisans of the popes—the natural enemies of all German emperors—were loosely called "Guelfs," while the imperial partisans were called "Ghibellines." The feud was thus carried on in Italy as well as Germany, and in Italy it became involved in issues of local politics, with little or no bearing on the quarrel that had given rise to the two factions.

The first Hohenstaufen emperor was Conrad III, but he is of less interest than his son, the famous Emperor Frederick Barbarossa—Red Beard—who ruled from 1152 to 1190. He was one of the greatest of all the imperial rulers and became the most popular figure of German legends dating from the Feudal Era. He made a heroic endeavor to live up to the pretensions of a supreme and absolute rule that his title as Roman Emperor implied. But he met with stubborn resistance, not only from the papacy and the German feudal lords, who had earlier contested the emperor's power, but also from the cities and towns of northern Italy, which in this age were growing rich and powerful and were unwilling to submit to the rule of a German monarch from the other side of the Alps. Though Frederick Barbarossa never gained the triumph he sought, his valiant exertions impressed his name upon the romantic imagination of Europe in his time. And the manner of his death was such as to add to the tradition, for he was drowned in a river in Asia Minor while leading one of the Crusades.

Frederick Barbarossa was succeeded by his son Henry VI, who ruled only seven years. Then ensued a period of confusion, during which Innocent III, one of the mightiest popes of the Feudal Era, sought to dispose of the imperial succession according to his view of the best interest of the Church. At length, in 1212, he named as king a boy who was to win renown as Frederick II, who became emperor in 1220.

As a boy and young man, Frederick II was the docile creature of Innocent III. But after Innocent's death, succeeding popes had bitter cause to regret Innocent's choice of Frederick as emperor, for Frederick was to give the papacy more trouble than any other lay ruler in Europe.

Frederick was of German descent on his father's side, but his mother was Constance, daughter of the Norman kings who had made themselves masters of Sicily. In his education, tastes, and associations, Frederick was much more Italian than German. His outlook also showed the influence of his contact with the many Moslem men of learning who lingered in Sicily even after the Moslem rulers of the island were driven out. Indeed, Frederick seems to have been not merely the most cultivated ruler of the Feudal Era but the most skeptical. Whereas other rulers who fought the papacy as a rival political institution remained faithful to the religious doctrines of the Church, Frederick apparently scorned the church creed as well as the political pretension of the pope. Living by preference in Italy, he aided Moslem and Jewish scholars and scientists, delved into alchemy and astrology, and seemed so scandalously preoccupied with infidel learning that he was reputed to be a magician. In legend he became known as *Stupor mundi*—the "wonder of the world." Despite his personal skepticism, he savagely —and cynically—enforced the most cruel edicts against heresy in Italy for political reasons.

In his youth Frederick had promised Innocent III that he would regard the pope as the feudal overlord of his Sicilian kingdom and that he would never unite Sicily with the imperial domains in northern Italy and Germany. But he resisted with arms every attempt of the popes to enforce this agreement, and by the time of Frederick's death in 1250 the Italian Peninsula was irreparably broken into fragments—the Sicilian kingdom in the south, the states of the Church in the middle, and a congeries of city-states in the north, which became practically independent as the imperial authority over them weakened.

Frederick was succeeded in 1250 by his young son Conrad IV. This youth was no match for the papacy, which for half a century had been hoping to destroy the Hohen-staufen family. Soon the pope set up a rival emperor in Germany, and Conrad was hounded to his death in southern Italy in 1254. Then followed a period, from 1254 to 1273, when there was no emperor at all. This interval is known as the Great Interregnum.

The Hapsburg Emperors

But the German world grew uncomfortable without an Emperor. Little as the feudal lords were inclined to obey him, they were

||||||||||||||||||||||||||||||||||||||||||||||||||||||||||||||||||||||||||||||||

Holy Roman Emperors, 962–1558

Saxon Dynasty

Otto I	962–973
Otto II	973–983
Otto III	983–1002
Henry II	1002–1024

Franconian (Salian) Dynasty

Conrad II	1024–1039
Henry III	1039–1056
Henry IV	1056–1105
Henry V	1105–1125
Lothair II (Duke of Saxony)	1125–1137

Hohenstaufen Dynasty

Conrad III	1138–1152
Frederick I (Barbarossa)	1152–1190
Henry VI	1190–1197
Philip of Swabia	1198–1208
Otto IV	1209–1215
Frederick II	1220–1250
Conrad IV	1250–1254

Interregnum	*1254–1273*

Hapsburg, and Other Minor Dynasties

Rudolf I (of Hapsburg)	1273–1291
Shifting of succession from one minor dynasty to another	1291–1437
Albert II	1438–1439
Frederick III	1440–1493
Maximilian I	1493–1519
Charles V	1519–1558

||||||||||||||||||||||||||||||||||||||||||||||||||||||||||||||||||||||||||||||||

Holy Roman Empire under the Hohenstaufen

lay in what is now a part of German-speaking Switzerland.

For a man chosen in the hope that he would prove ineffectual, Rudolf showed surprising vigor. His principal achievement was in defeating Ottokar, King of Bohemia, a Slavic conqueror who had gained control of a large part of what is now Austria. After defeating Ottokar, Rudolf himself became Archduke of Austria, and this domain became the basis of the feudal power of the Hapsburg family. In later centuries the Hapsburgs added other territories to their personal possessions and thus became one of the greatest families in Germany. Ordinarily they also held the imperial throne, though at times it was given to members of other families. But their power was largely derived from their own domains rather than from the office of emperor.

The dynasty founded by Rudolf of Hapsburg had an amazingly long life. Usually as Holy Roman emperors, and always as hereditary rulers of the ever-expanding family fief of Austria, the Hapsburgs reigned until 1918. In 1806 Napoleon declared that the Holy Roman Empire had "ceased to exist," whereupon the Hapsburgs changed their title to emperor of Austria and, later, of Austria-Hungary. In that capacity they continued to rule until the Austro-Hungarian monarchy collapsed following defeat in World War I. Heirs of the family survive today.

Until long after the close of the Feudal Era in other countries, "Germany" did not form a state having a single supreme government, but remained a geographical expression referring to some hundreds of domains large and small—kingdoms, principalities, duchies, counties, free cities, and others. As a matter of courtesy the rulers of these lands acknowledged the emperor as their superior —in the sense that he held a more resplendent title than theirs. But for all practical purposes, the rulers of each of these domains was independent of the Holy Roman Emperor, and the rule of the latter was confined to those lands that he held in his own name.

obsessed by the tradition that they should have over them a ruler bearing the great Roman title. And as the Interregnum dragged on, the papacy gained confidence that no future emperor would dare defy its authority. So by 1273 the reigning pope agreed with the German Electors that it was time to choose a new emperor.

This time the choice did not fall upon one of the stem-dukes, because one of these great magnates might be tempted to make effective use of his position as the titular head of the Empire. Instead the election was given to an obscure German nobleman, Rudolf of Hapsburg, whose modest domain

THE POLITICAL THEORY OF THE FEUDAL ERA

At the beginning of the Feudal Era in western European history, there was no effective centralized political authority anywhere. Nor was there any recognizable body of theory to advocate any such authority. By the end of that era, however—by the time, say, of Louis XI of France and the Tudor kings of England—the theoretical core for the modern integral sovereign state was well thought out, well stated, and nearly complete.

The first theoretical writings on political power were by-products of the quarrels between popes and the emperors (and kings). The monarchs who clung to the royal office managed to do so, usually, because they were strong enough to assert themselves over other feudal potentates. As strong men they also had to assert themselves against the great universal power, the Church. At the

beginning, all the weighty theorizing was on the side of the Church whenever the popes quarreled with kings, because the arguments were penned by theologians. In theory, the early political doctrine rested upon the idea of "two swords"—that of the Church and that of the king—both delegated by God for the exercise of authority in the two spheres, spiritual and temporal. But, of course, the two spheres overlapped. As monarchs grew in power, quarrels with the Church over disputed areas of authority grew in intensity.

The Investiture Controversy, which began in the eleventh century over the selection of bishops, was productive of much pamphleteering by churchmen exalting the claims of the pope over those of the king. Because the pope had the "power of the

Europe about 1100

keys," he had jurisdiction over morals. Almost every political question had a moral angle; so there was practically no political question on which a powerful pope could not claim to discipline an allegedly erring king. The popes in these struggles freely used the spiritual weapon of excommunication. This was intended to have practical consequences, because the subjects of an excommunicated king were supposed to be freed from their allegiance to him. This weapon was used with great effectiveness by Gregory VII against the Emperor Henry IV in 1077 and by Innocent III against King John of England in 1209. The first comprehensive theories of "the State" as we know it today emerged from these controversies.

John of Salisbury

John of Salisbury (1120–1182) was an Englishman who taught at Chartres, in France, where he was distinguished for his knowledge of the ancient Latin classics. In political theory he was the author of a book called the *Polycraticus*. It is very pro-papal in exalting the superiority of the "priest over the prince," but this prejudice has an interesting consequence. He defines a prince who intrudes on church authority as a "tyrant," and says that, if there is no other remedy, the killing of such a tyrant is justified. This argument about justifiable tyrannicide was to recur in political theory for many centuries.

Thomas Aquinas

By the thirteenth century the rediscovery of ancient Roman law and the reading of Aristotle's *Politics* gave men a sophisticated view of the political state unknown to the cruder theories of early feudalism. The Aristotelian doctrine is made very clear by Thomas Aquinas (*c*.1225–*c*.1274), who wrote a special work in political theory: *De regi-*

mine principum (*On the Rule of Princes*). Aquinas starts with Aristotle's dictum that man is a social creature, and that a superior coercive power is necessary for the common good. This power originated, Thomas thought, in primitive patriarchal headship, but it is now delegated to a prince or head. Thomas taught that although all political authority is ultimately from God and is inferior to spiritual power, God may delegate it through "the people." It is easy to misunderstand Thomas's reference to "the people"; he actually had in mind the "estates" of ecclesiastical, feudal, and communal representatives of a minute fraction of the population. But the important point is that the prince is theoretically elective even when a hereditary succession is tolerated. The king's authority is of divine origin, but his personal claim to exercise it is not. He loses his right to it by "tyranny." Although Thomas seems to shrink from the frank tyrannicide advocated by John of Salisbury and is not clear on just what to do in such a case, his implication is clear: a tyrannical prince loses his claim to power.

This theory of a king's position was strengthened by the study of Roman law. Although the ancient Roman emperors of the last imperial centuries were about as absolute as monarchs can be, the theory of their power in Roman law was that it was of popular origin. The famous principle expressing this is contained in the *Institutes* of Justinian: "What the prince had pleased to ordain has the force of law, since by a regal law enacted concerning his imperium the people had conceded to him and conferred upon him the whole of its imperium and power." Later Roman emperors has tended to concentrate on the first clause ("What the prince had pleased . . .") and to forget about the rest of the text, and so did the western European kings advised by lawyers trained in the revived Roman law. But philosophers, such as Thomas Aquinas, never ceased to insist that the royal power was a delegated authority.

In the later Feudal Era the kings grew so strong that they defied popes with impunity. Philip IV of France treated old Boniface VIII in 1303 with a high-handedness in dramatic contrast with the great days of papal power under Gregory VII and Innocent III. Subsequently, the "Babylonian Captivity" of the French popes at Avignon (p. 504), and the later scandal of a Christendom divided in allegiance between two and three popes, all contributed to a great loss of papal prestige. This was reflected in later political thought. In the fourteenth century there began a strong line of anti-papal theory that, for the first time in the Feudal Era, philosophically exalted the secular over the ecclesiastical power.

Dante, Dubois, and Marsiglio

Dante Alighieri (1265–1321), for example, who is much more important in the history of literature as the first and greatest poet in the Italian vernacular, was also embroiled in political controversy. In the perennial quarrels of Italian city politics, he was a "Ghibelline" or member of the pro-imperial party, opposed to the "Guelfs" or pro-papal party. In defense of the emperor against the pope he wrote a book, *De monarchia (On Monarchy)*, which vigorously defended the independence of the imperial authority by argument drawn from the kings of the Old Testament, from Roman history, from Aristotle, from allegories about the sun and the moon, and from all the logic and indignation that he could mix.

Pierre Dubois (1255–1321) was a counselor of Philip IV of France in the bitter quarrel with Boniface VIII. He is interesting as the new type of royal counselor, a layman trained in Roman law. Such advisers were beginning to replace the churchmen of an earlier day at the royal courts. Dubois denounced the claim of the papacy to temporal power in Italy and urged the pope to transfer all such claims to the king of France.

Likewise all clerics should transfer their secular holdings to secular persons. The pope and his clergy could thereby concentrate their attention on spiritual affairs. The French king, in turn, could use the clerical wealth for establishing his hegemony in Europe—which Pierre, as a good French patriot, thought to be the best possible arrangement for Christian Europe. He in no sense questioned the purely spiritual authority of the Church and the clergy, but he advocated, for example, the idea that a great many priories and nunneries should be turned into schools for boys and girls.

Marsiglio of Padua (1270–1342), was an Italian priest who combined experience in the practical politics of the Italian cities with a term as rector of the University of Paris. His most famous work was his *Defensor Pacis (Defender of Peace)*, which is a classic of political theory because it clearly foreshadows the end of the universal papal hegemony of the Feudal Era and the beginning of the system of modern sovereign states.

Following Aristotle, the *Defensor Pacis* defined the state as an organization to secure a peaceful, orderly and prosperous society. Older writers, such as Aquinas, had found this compatible with religious ends, but Marsiglio underscored the point that the state had nothing to do with the salvation of souls. The state is not concerned with purely spiritual affairs. But it is very much concerned with the visible Church. Churchmen are residents within the state; their property is like other property, involved in relationships requiring regulation by law. Therefore the persons and the property of churchmen should be completely subject to the state. The Church has no right to its own system of law and its own courts, independent of those of the state, or to the exercise of any coercive power whatever.

This is an extreme assertion for the fourteenth century—and a very radical reversal of older doctrines that regarded the secular power as subject to the ecclesiastical power.

Marsiglio does not deny the spiritual dignity of the clergy—he is personally a "believer" —but he categorically denies the right of any spiritual authority to dictate to the secular power. In a sense he anticipates the later doctrine of separation of Church and state, and even goes beyond it by the vehemence of his insistence on the strict control of clerical persons and property by the state.

This was radical enough for the age, but Marsiglio went even further. For even within the church itself, he thought, there was no rightful claim to the exercise by the pope of supreme spiritual power. He thought that the popes had usurped the religious authority that once and rightfully belonged to the whole body of the faithful (*universitas fidelium*). A council including laity as well as clergy should be the supreme spiritual authority, of which the pope should be the mere executive officer with delegated and limited power. This is the theoretical foundation for the "Conciliar Movement" of the next century, which for a time challenged the power of the popes. This movement eventually faded out of Catholic history; accordingly, Marsiglio failed to weaken the power of the pope within the Catholic Church. True, Marsiglio's challenge to the pope's religious authority, like the developing challenge to the pope's political au-

thority on the part of secular monarchs, was a symptom of another force that was at work deep in European society toward the weakening of papal—even Roman Catholic —authority, a force that would drastically challenge that power during the Protestant Revolt.

Marsiglio's book has great importance apart from its elements of religious controversy. His conception of the state envisions a strictly limited monarchy. He prefers the localized responsibility of monarchy to other forms of government, but the monarchy should be elective, as it was in the Holy Roman Empire. The king is the administrator and executor of the laws; he should not make them. That power belongs to what Marsiglio calls the "legislator." This is a collective term for "the people." He did not mean modern democracy, of course— that would be too much to expect in the fourteenth century even from a radical such as Marsiglio; he meant the "better" citizens —the wealthy, well-born, and wise. This collective legislator should act by majority vote.

In political theory Marsiglio obviously signaled the approaching end of the Feudal Era—as his colleague William of Ockham, to be noted presently (p. 530), did in theology and metaphysics.

Suggestions for Further Reading

Source Materials
Anthologies and Collected Documents
F. Le V. Baumer, ed., *Main Currents of Western Thought* (New York, 1952), pp. 71–84.
  Good selections from the political and social writings of John of Salisbury, Thomas Aquinas, and Dante.
Columbia College, *Introduction to Contemporary Civilization in the West* (2 vols., New York, 1946), Volume I, pp. 1–19.
  Documents illustrative of feudal relationships (including Magna Carta) and of the relationships between Church and state (including *Unam Sanctam*).

G. H. Knoles and R. K. Snyder, eds., *Readings in Western Civilization* (rev. ed., New York, 1954), pp. 239–249.
  Good samples of manorial and feudal documents, and the text of Magna Carta.
J. H. Robinson, ed., *Readings in European History* (2 vols., Boston, 1904), Chapters IX–XIV.
  Documents illustrative of feudalism, of the development of monarchies, and of the conflict between Gregory VII and Henry IV.
O. J. Thatcher and E. R. McNeal, *A Source Book for Medieval History* (New York, 1905).
  An excellent collection covering nearly all aspects of life in the Feudal Era.

Contemporary Writings

J. de Brakelond, *Chronicle;* translated by H. E. Butler (London, 1949).

A contemporary description of life in a monastery in feudal England.

Dante Alighieri, *De Monarchia (On Monarchy).*

One of the classic treatises on government from the feudal period of western history.

J. Froissart, *The Chronicles,* edited by H. P. Dunster (New York, 1906).

The classic contemporary account of the Hundred Years' War.

John of Salisbury, *Policraticus.*

Described in text.

Marsiglio of Padua, *Defensor Pacis (Defender of the Peace).*

Described in text.

Secondary Works

G. Barraclough, ed., *Medieval Germany, 911–1250* (Oxford, 1948).

Essays by German historians.

E. M. J. Perroy, *The Hundred Years' War* (London, 1951).

A standard, up-to-date work.

C. Stephenson, *Medieval Feudalism* (New York, 1942).

One of the best works on the subject.

J. W. Thompson, *Feudal Germany* (Chicago, 1928).

The standard work on Germany in the Feudal Era.

B. Wilkinson, *The Constitutional History of England, 1216–1399* (New York, 1952).

A standard, up-to-date account.

19

The Economic Life of Feudal Europe

Coat of Arms of the Coopers' Guild—
from a stained glass window, Germany,
fifteenth century. (Courtesy of the Metropolitan Museum of Art)

Most of the population of Europe during the Feudal Era lived in small manorial villages and gained a livelihood from agriculture. This pattern of social and economic life represented an advance over the semi-nomadic existence of the Germanic tribal peoples in the age of their great migrations. Moreover, during the Feudal Era considerable progress was made in the methods of agriculture. For example, the practice of allowing one half the arable land to lie fallow was abandoned in favor of a system of three fields, by which two thirds of the land was kept in production. Nevertheless, the manorial society remained on a lower level of economic development than the urban society of the earlier Roman regime. This was so because feudalism required each village to provide for nearly all its own needs, which meant that nearly all labor was devoted to agriculture rather than to commerce and industry.

During the Feudal Era, however, trade gradually gained in volume, and eventually towns sprang up amid the manorial villages. By the close of this age a small but important part of the population was earning a livelihood by commerce and industry, and Europe generally was as prosperous as in the time when Rome was at the peak of its greatness. This economic revival was going on at the same time that the kings of England, France, and some other countries were re-establishing political order, and both forms of social progress were of equal importance.

THE MANORIAL ECONOMY AND SOCIETY

The manor was the basic unit of economic life in Feudal Europe. Its size varied, but at the smallest it was large enough to provide for all of its basic needs. It included a residence for the lord who was its master, a large farm for his support and the support of the people who labored on it, a cluster of workshops for the maintenance of the house and farm, and a parish church. The number of inhabitants might be scores or hundreds.

The land of the manor would include a pasture area, sometimes a piece of forest to

Plowing and Harrowing—from the *Luttrell Psalter,* an English illuminated manuscript, c.1340. (Courtesy of British Museum)

provide wood for fuel and building material, and arable land on which were grown staple cereals. The arable land, which was cultivated by serfs or tenants, was divided into a great number of strips. The produce raised on some of these strips was earmarked for the lord and that from others for the priest. The remainder was for the serfs or tenants, who did all the work.

Status on the Manor

If the lord resided on the manor, he managed it himself. But often a lord would have a number of manors, residing on one of them and leaving the others to the management of a steward or, if the manor house were a castle, a man-at-arms known as the castellan. In the manor house would also reside a number of domestic servants and perhaps men-at-arms. But most of the population of the manor was made up of agricultural laborers. Their status was that of either a serf or a free tenant.

The status of the serf was one of limited bondage. Unlike a slave, he was not a mere chattel, with whom the lord could do as he pleased, because, by customary law, the serf had rights that the lord was supposed to respect. Yet, unlike a free man, the serf was obliged to remain on the manor where he was born and to perform for the lord certain duties that custom prescribed. Thus

he was required to till those strips in the cultivated fields that belonged to the lord, to do other domestic and farm chores for the lord, and to give the lord a portion of any income that he gained from any source. At the serf's death, the lord usually levied an inheritance tax before the serf's heir took over his father's cottage and belongings.

There were also some free tenants who worked on the land. They gave a portion of the harvest to the lord as a rent, and kept the rest for themselves. The routine of the free tenant's work was much the same as that of the serf, but his status was comparable to that of a sharecropper nowadays. He was free to leave the manor if he chose, and whatever property he accumulated belonged wholly to him. As a rule, the free tenant did not wish to leave the manor on which he grew up, while serfs were often tempted to escape from their bondage by running away. For this reason, the lord often gave serfs their freedom, in order to keep them from running off, since he had need of their labor. In the early Feudal Era, serfs were a large proportion of the population—perhaps half. But gradually their number dwindled, and by the close of the period, nearly all the peasants in western Europe were free men. Yet vestiges of serfdom lingered in France until the Revolution of 1789, and in Germany until 1848, while most of the population of Russia was made up of serfs until as late as 1863.

The serf's lot was hard but not without relief. His dwelling was little better than a hovel; his clothes were of battered leather and worn rags; and his food was a monotonous diet of bread and cheese, with little meat, vegetables, or fruit. But the burden of his work was lightened during the winter, after the harvest and before the spring planting, and even in the summer the numerous religious holidays gave him frequent respite from his toil. On such occasions as harvest festivals and market days, the serfs and peasants indulged in dancing, games, and what feasting their meager means permitted. And though the serf was not free to leave the manor, he was at least assured of a livelihood, for he could not legally be denied the right to till the land and reap a portion of the harvest for himself.

Farming Methods

The people of the Feudal Era had little knowledge of scientific agriculture, but their farming methods were not ill suited to their needs. In the earlier centuries of this era, the arable land of the manor was ordinarily divided into two fields. Each year, in alternation, one of these fields was cultivated and the other was allowed to lie fallow, so that it could recover its fertility. This practice checked the exhaustion of the soil, but it meant that only half the land could be put to productive use in any one year. Gradually this "two-field system" was supplanted by the "three-field system." Under this newer system, the arable land of the manor was divided into three fields instead of two. One was planted with an early crop, such as barley or oats, another with a late crop, such as rye or winter wheat, and the third was left fallow. This system meant that only a third of the land, instead of a half, was kept out of production. And it also meant that the manor would reap two harvests each year, one in the early summer, the other in the late fall or early winter.

Each cultivated field was divided, as we have noted, into numerous strips, each strip only a few furrows in width but as long as the field. Some of these strips were assigned to the peasants, while others were worked for the benefit of the lord and the parish priest. But, ordinarily, all the serfs worked together as a gang rather than each tending to his own strips. One reason for this was that the plow used at this time was heavy, requiring several oxen to draw it and a number of men to steady and guide it. Hence no one man could plow alone.

The Lord's Income

The main source of the lord's income was the harvest of those cultivated strips that were earmarked for his use. But the lord had numerous other kinds of income from the manor. In addition to their obligation

Sowing and Reaping—from the *Luttrell Psalter*. The illuminations in this manuscript show many phases of rural life. (Courtesy of British Museum)

to cultivate his strips and give him the harvest from them, the serfs also had to give the lord a portion of the produce of their own strips—a kind of rent payable in kind. Moreover, they were obliged to provide a certain amount of unpaid labor, called the *corvée,* for whatever work about the estate, such as digging or building, he might want done. The serfs and tenants were further required to make use of the flour mill and bake oven that the lord provided and to give him a share of the flour and bread. Besides these exactions the lord had the right to impose an annual tax, called the *taille,* and an inheritance tax whenever a serf or tenant died.

A rapacious lord thus had the opportunity to take away from the serfs and tenants virtually everything they produced or possessed. And if he chose to do so, they had no redress, because the only court to which they could appeal for protection was the manorial court, over which the lord himself presided. However, a lord would seldom make such use of his prerogatives as would ruin the serfs and tenants, for the simple reason that he depended on their labor for his own income. Just as he would not overwork a horse or let his cattle starve to death, he would not mistreat the serfs and tenants to such a degree that they would run away or lack the strength to do their work.

THE REVIVAL OF TRADE

In the anarchy of the early Feudal Era, the slowing down of commercial activity, which had begun under the Roman Empire as early as the second century, went steadily on. Towns, naturally, continued to shrink both in numbers and in size, as their sources of livelihood dried up. By the fifth century the exchange of natural and manufactured commodities had been reduced to a trickle. During the Carolingian period trade, both foreign and internal, continued to be only a small-scale operation, without any noticeable change for better or for worse. Not for another two centuries were conditions again to be favorable for the resumption of trade. Certain very important basic adjustments and improvements had first to be made in the economic and political spheres.

During the universal confusion of this "Age of Iron," men sought shelter in the haven of the manor, and each manor had to provide for its own needs. Most of the once great cities of the West Roman Empire declined into mere ruins, in which the few impoverished descendants of the prosperous townsmen of antiquity filched the stones from ancient monuments and temples to build their hovels. A striking example of this urban decline was Rome itself, which in its time of greatness had numbered several million inhabitants but contained only a few thousands by the ninth century.

Trade in the "Age of Iron"

Even in the "Age of Iron," however, there was a trickle of trade in Europe, because no manor was ever able to provide for all its wants. For example, salt is a necessity in the diet of human beings and domestic animals, but salt is not to be found everywhere. Those villages that had no salt were forced to obtain it from outside. Likewise spices were in demand, because of their use in the preservation of food. Wine was also widely consumed, although it could be produced only in limited areas of Europe. Moreover, the people of Flanders (modern Belgium) early acquired exceptional skill in the weaving of woolen and linen cloth, and the products of their looms were distributed in far-off regions even as early as the tenth century.

But this small volume of trade during the "Age of Iron" was not sufficient to bring into being a new social class. It was handled by itinerant peddlers, who wandered from one manor to another. Their casual visits were sufficient to cope with the problem of economic exchange, for the simple reason that exchange was not characteristic of the economic life of the manor. Even if the people of the manor had wished to obtain more goods from outside their own village, they could not have done so, because the manor produced little more than enough for its own needs and had little surplus to trade for the products of other villages or towns.

Trade with Byzantium

More important during the early Feudal Era than the trickle of trade within western Europe was the revival of commerce between western Europe and the Byzantine Empire. This trade had shrunk since ancient times, especially after the rise of Moslem seapower in the Mediterranean, but it never quite died out.

The Italian port cities were the chief beneficiaries of this eastern trade. Their location gave them an advantage, as did the traditions of commerce that persisted from earlier days. And during the early Feudal Era they escaped the worst of the disorder prevailing farther north in Europe. In antiquity the ports of northern Italy were less important than those of the southern end of the peninsula and the island of Sicily. The Moslems, however, interfered with access to these ports for long intervals in the ninth century and later. Consequently, Italian maritime trade shifted to the cities on the peninsula's northern coasts.

The greatest of these cities was Venice, situated on the northern curve of the Adriatic and the most secure from the menace of Moslem sea raiders. The Venetians were known throughout the Feudal Era as the most astute businessmen in Europe, and the great fleet of armed galleys that assured the defense of the city made Venice the first important naval power in Europe after the fall of the West Roman Empire. Other northern Italian seaports—notably Genoa and Pisa—were rivals of Venice in the Mediterranean trade, and all of them fought innumerable engagements against the Moslem fleets, which for a time seemed about to make the Mediterranean into an Islamic lake. But the merchants of Venice did not scruple to trade with the Moslems whenever circumstances allowed. Nor did they hesitate to pillage the fleets of rival Italian cities when this proved profitable. Considerations of religion were of much less importance than the chance for profit, and the line between piracy and legitimate business was thinly drawn.

This west-east commerce was kept going, even during the earliest centuries of the Feudal Era, because the Byzantine Empire provided an insatiable market for foodstuffs and raw materials. A highly civilized and densely populated community, such as Byzantium always was, has a constant and pressing need for staple imports, which must be paid for with exports. No matter how great the risk, Italian seafarers could never resist the temptation of the immense profits to be made by bringing to this eastern metropolis the fish, salt, grain, wine, and other bulk staples produced in western Europe and carrying back spices, dyes, perfumes, and the luxury wares made by the artisans of the east.

This continuous business intercourse with the most highly civilized corner of the European world helped to maintain the cultural life of the Italian cities at a higher level than the rest of western Europe. Consequently, while most of Europe was still in the darkness of the tenth century, Venice was a remarkably advanced community. Venice was never long afflicted with powerful landed barons; its rulers and social leaders were its merchant princes, who made up a patrician aristocracy of business wealth.

Since the income of the Italian merchants depended upon the volume of their im-

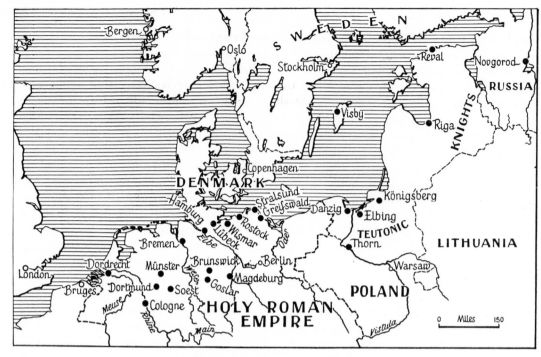

Cities of the Hanseatic League

ports and exports, they were impelled to widen the scope of their activities in order to increase their profits. Hence they sought to develop new markets north of the Alps for the goods that they imported from the east. From these regions, in return, they obtained new supplies of goods for export. Thus Italian "salesmanship" became an important stimulus to the revival of trade throughout feudal Europe.

Entrance of Germans into Commerce

At the northern end of the trade routes across the Alps, there arose a number of commercial towns that became centers for the distribution of goods from the south and the accumulation of products of the northern areas, destined for shipment southward. The earliest trade route across Europe from north to south was the so-called "Varangian route" (p. 436) across what is now Russia, from Scandinavia to Constantinople.

Originally trade along this route was in the hands of the Swedes, but eventually German traders took it over. And when, because of tribal disturbances among the Slavs, the Varangian route was gradually closed, the Germans deflected the trade of northern Europe westward through the Baltic Sea. Their traders called at the ports of Britain and Flanders to exchange merchandise with Italian traders coming up from the south. The Flemish port of Bruges soon became one of the most famous commercial centers of Europe, and the profits of trade were added to those gained through the sale of the products of the Flemish cloth industry.

The Hanseatic League. The most important north German ports were Danzig, Stettin, Lübeck, Hamburg, and Bremen. Merchants from these towns maintained permanent agencies in Bruges, London, and other foreign ports, and, to protect their far-reaching commercial interests, these German cities banded together in a trade association known as the Hanseatic League. For a time the Hanseatic League was a formidable power in northern Europe, and the cities belonging to it exercised considerable influence in the politics of the Holy Roman Empire.

By the middle of the eleventh century the vigor of the reviving commerce of western Europe was unmistakable. By then, too, the worst of the political anarchy of the "Age of Iron" was passing, as the abler kings and some of the greater feudal lords had succeeded in establishing some measure of political order. Western Europe was still far from achieving stability, but it had reached the bottom of its decline and was beginning the upward climb. Then, at the close of the eleventh century, came the Crusades, which provided a tremendous new stimulus to the economic revival that had begun in the previous two centuries.

The Crusades

The Crusades were a series of military expeditions to the Near East for the ostensible purpose of recapturing Jerusalem and its environs from the Moslems. In the middle of the seventh century the Arabs had overrun Palestine and Syria and had detached these lands from the Byzantine Empire

The Crusades

First	1095–1099
Second	1147–1149
Third	1189–1192
Fourth	1202–1204
Children's	1212
Fifth	1217–1221
Sixth	1228–1229
Seventh	1248–1254
Eighth	1270
Ninth	1271–1272

(p. 274). To pious Christians, it seemed blasphemous for the Moslems to hold possession of the land where Christ had lived and died and where his tomb remained. But the East Roman Empire was not strong enough to drive the Moslems out of Palestine, and for four centuries nothing was done to right this supposed wrong.

The religious motive was certainly the chief factor inspiring the First Crusade, which was launched by Pope Urban II in 1095. But even at the start, other motives also had much influence. Some of those who took part were hopeful of conquering rich

Markab Castle—standing guard over the village of Banias in Syria, on the edge of the Mediterranean. An Arab castle, Markab fell to the Crusaders in 1117, and from 1186 to 1285 it was commanded by the Knights Templars. (Arab Information Center)

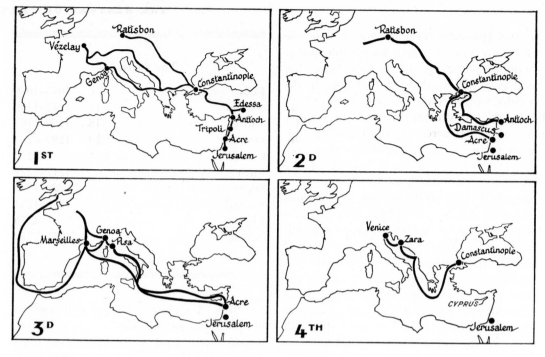

The Crusades—First, Second, Third, and Fourth

fiefs for themselves in eastern lands; others were moved simply by the love of adventure; and perhaps still others asked no more than an excuse for a vacation from their wives. As time went on, the most important motive came to be that of the Italian merchants, who saw in the Crusades a chance of building up a stronger position in the Near East, to the advantage of their commerce. By the time of the Fourth Crusade (1202–1204), the religious interest in the movement was negligible, and many of those who took part were stirred by the same ideas as those who set out in modern times to win new empires in far-off lands.

Indeed, the Fourth Crusade has been nicknamed "the businessmen's crusade." So little did religion count in it, so plain was the economic motive, that the Crusaders made no attempt to fight against the Moslems in Palestine but instead turned against the Christian stronghold of Constantinople. Entering the eastern metropolis by force of

arms, the Crusaders set up a government of their own, known as the Latin Empire of the East, which lasted for fifty years (see chronology, p. 264). Meantime the Venetian merchants and shipowners reaped a handsome profit, for the new government granted them valuable trade concessions in return for their help in transporting the invaders to Constantinople.

Despite the failure of the Crusades to attain their avowed purpose of driving the Moslems out of Palestine, the expeditions had important consequences for western Europe. On their return from the exotic centers of the Byzantine and Islamic cultures, the veterans of the Crusades brought with them a taste for the amenities of life that they had discovered for the first time during their sojourn in the east. Thus the market for luxury goods in western Europe was tremendously increased, and, to meet this demand commerce increased to an unprecedented volume.

The Merchants

As trade increased, so did the number of persons who made their living from it. Thus a new social class, made up of merchants, came into being. The question of where these merchants came from presents an obscure but challenging historical problem.

With rare exceptions, they were not recruited among the upper classes. Churchmen seldom turned to business as a vocation, for they were forbidden to do so, and generally the Church looked upon trade as fraught with temptations to sin and therefore dangerous to the soul. Some of the early merchants came from the baronial class, especially its lower ranks. A knight without a fief or a younger son without prospect of a landed inheritance might turn to trade for a livelihood. But this was uncommon, because the man "in trade" was considered to be far inferior in status to the meanest of noblemen. This attitude persisted throughout the Feudal Era and well into modern times; some vestige of it lingered on until as recently as the nineteenth century.

It is apparent, then, that most of the earliest merchants moved upward from a lower class rather than downward from a higher. Yet they were not ordinarily recruited from among the mass of serfs and free tenants who were the bulwark of manorial society. They came, perhaps, from the fringe of "floaters," sloughed off from the tight little manorial groups of serfs and tenants. These comprised persons of humble birth who had no place of their own in a manor. Most of them lived as vagabonds, sometimes finding work as itinerant harvest hands, sometimes begging for their food and shelter, often resorting to crime.

But it is a tenable supposition that some of the more resourceful individuals of this sort would turn to pack-peddling. In his wanderings such a man might notice that a certain village had a good harvest, while another, not far distant, was bringing in a poor crop. After working as a harvest hand

in the village where the harvest was abundant, he might take his pay in the form of a quantity of grain or some other kind of produce. Then he could carry this store to the village where the harvest was inadequate, selling it at a profit and thus amassing the capital for another trading venture on a larger scale.

Some such evolution would account for the origin of many of the early merchants of the interior of Europe, apart from those in the Italian cities and the few other places where business had never ceased to be a normal vocation. In the later centuries of the Feudal Era, when the merchant class was large and prosperous, most of its members were born into it. Then the merchants tended to become another stratified group in the social order—the "middle" class between the upper classes of noblemen and high ecclesiastical dignitaries and the bottom stratum comprising those who worked

The Merchant George Gisze—portrait by Hans Holbein, the Younger (p. 590), of the representative in England of several Hanseatic houses. The painting was made in 1532 and shows north German dress and objects of that period. (*Photographische Gesellschafte*)

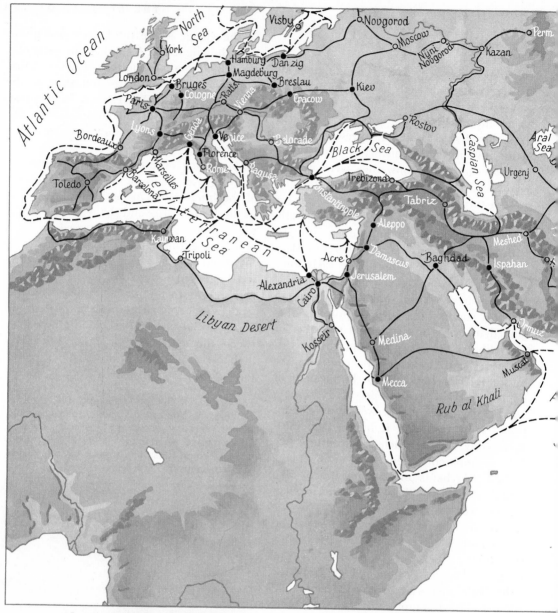

Land and Sea Routes of Medieval Commerce in the Thirteenth Century

on the land. Yet this "middle" class never became so exclusive as the hereditary nobility and the clergy, and persons of humble birth continued to rise into it. Moreover, the class as a whole continued to gain greater riches, influence, and power, until ultimately —much after the close of the Feudal Era— it was to dislodge the upper classes from their social and political pre-eminence. It was thus to become the chief instrument of social progress and democratic political revolution.

The Hazards of Commerce

However splendid was the future of the middle class in the centuries to come, the lot of the merchant in the Feudal Era was one of hard work and innumerable hazards.

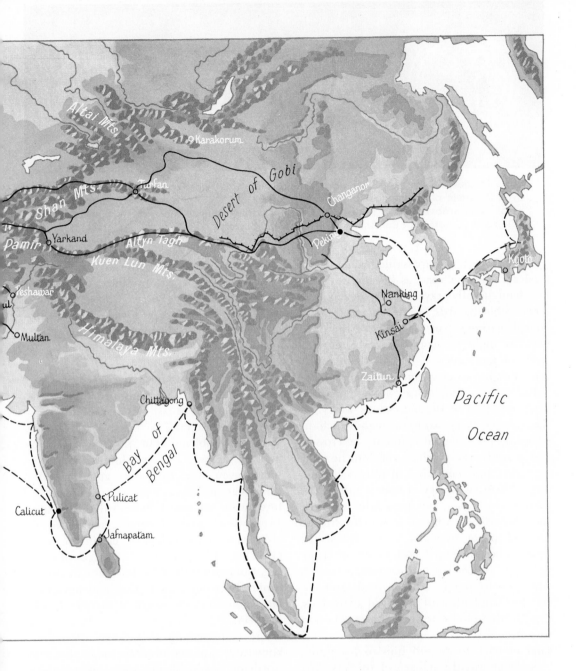

Even after centers of trade were established in towns, a trader had to travel constantly, both to obtain supplies of raw materials and to bring his wares to market.

If possible, the merchant traveled by boat, and for this reason, most inland towns grew up along rivers. But at times he could not avoid travel by land. For overland transportation, merchandise was loaded on the backs of pack animals or in cumbersome wagons. The roads, however, were mere dirt tracks, because the paved highways of the Roman Empire had long since crumbled into ruin. When the roads were dry, they gave up clouds of choking dust, and when they were wet, the wagons would sink hub-deep in the mud. Bridges were few, and often unsafe. Where there was no bridge, the merchant would have to ford the river, but at times of high water the ford would be

481

Two Medieval Coins. The German silver bracteate (*left*) was issued by Bishop Ulrich von Reinstein of Halberstadt between 1149 and 1160. The florin (*right*) was issued in 1252. On its obverse is a portrait of John the Baptist and on the reverse, the lily of Florence. (Courtesy of the American Numismatic Society)

dangerous, if not impassable. Whether he used a river or a road as his highway, the merchant usually traveled only in daylight. The visible hazards of the day were great enough without courting those of the darkness. At night he would seek shelter at a castle or monastery, if he could not find a miserable inn to give him lodging.

Bad roads and worse accommodations were only part of the merchant's worry. At the gate of every town through which he passed, at every feudal boundary he crossed, and at nearly every bridge and ford he used, he had to pay some kind of toll or customs duty. These lawful levies took a substantial share of his profit, but he might well lose the whole of his capital, if not his life, to the swarms of brigands who infested the roads. These included both common criminals and "robber barons," or ruffian knights whose castles dominated the roads and rivers. Not content with legalized extortions, these lords would often send their retainers to pillage a traveling merchant or use some kind of trick to despoil him of his wares.

So great was the danger of robbery that merchants seldom traveled alone. Usually they banded together and hired armed guards of their own. To these bands would cluster numbers of pilgrims, ecclesiastics traveling on the business of the church, vagabonds, and others obliged to travel for personal reasons. Because of the need for forming groups in the interest of mutual protection, merchants ordinarily traveled on certain routes at certain times, when other merchants would also be using that route. As a rule they did not travel at all during the winter when the roads were all but impassable.

Chaos in Coinage and Measures. When the merchant had run the gamut of the hazards of the road and at last had arrived at a market town or a fair, he faced a whole new series of problems. The process of buying and selling was far less simple than it is today, even after the buyer and the seller came together. Money was scarce, and therefore barter was easier than dealing for cash. Even when money became generally available, its value remained uncertain, for most great feudal lords assumed the right of coinage. Commonly these lords sought to realize profits by issuing coins that had a greater face value than the worth of the metal used in them.

Great shrewdness and much specialized knowledge was required to judge the true worth of a coin. Hence some men made a profession of exchanging money. A merchant unsure of the value of a coin offered to him in payment for merchandise would take it to a money-changer to have it appraised. At a great fair, to which merchants would come from all over Europe, the money-changer would thus have to assess the value of coins of a bewildering variety, some of them minted in far-off lands. Eventually certain coins won a wide reputation as being trustworthy, and they came to be a standard of value. Such were, for instance, the florin, coined in Florence; the *livre tournois,* which was one of the most respectable of the coins issued in France; and the English pound sterling, so-called because it represented one pound of sterling silver pennies.

A similar problem arose from the lack of standards of weight and measurement. These varied widely from one locality to another, and even when the same unit was used in many regions, it was seldom capable of exact measurement. For example, a "foot" was taken to be the length of a human foot. But since human feet are not of a uniform length, there would be considerable variation in the size of two pieces of cloth, each measuring three "feet" in length.

The Fairs

Despite all these difficulties, trade continued to grow in volume. A sign of its growth was the rise to prominence of a great number of fairs in all the countries of western Europe. These fairs served as the principal places of business transactions before towns developed to such size as to supersede them.

Originally the fair was a gathering of merchants, who would meet at the same place each year at a time established by custom. There they would buy from one another, to replenish their stocks, and would sell their wares to the gentry and villagers of the vicinity. Many of the fairs lasted several weeks, and some were held at the same place on two or more occasions in the same year. Eventually some fairs, such as those of Champagne, a region in northern France, became year-round attractions.

The site of the fair was usually a strategic spot on a well-traveled road, at a crossroad, or at the junction of two rivers. In a meadow near the protective walls of a large castle or monastery, the merchants would set up their booths and do business for the duration of the fair, moving on to another place at its close. Inevitably many disputes arose over business transactions at the fairs, since these involved traders coming from different regions. These disputes could not be settled in the usual feudal or royal courts, because the laws administered in these courts was based upon custom, and in the early centuries of the Feudal Era trade was so new and uncommon that custom did not provide guidance for the settlement of some of the problems arising out of commercial dealings. So the merchants at the fairs usually settled their business disputes in courts of their own. In England, these were known under the name of "Courts of Pie Powder." The phrase seems to have been a corruption of the French *pied poudreux*—"dusty foot" —which was a nickname for the road-plodding merchant. From these courts there gradually developed a new body of customary law, known as "Law Merchant," for the administration of commercial justice at fairs and, later, in towns.

The hubbub of the fair was a pleasant entertainment in itself, but side shows and concessions furnished a further source of amusement—for along with the merchants came animal trainers, whose performing bears amazed the rustics, freaks, contortionists, jugglers, and other concessionaires. Thus the atmosphere of the fair was not unlike that of a circus arriving in a small, rural town in our own time. It provided a welcome interruption in the monotonous routine of the manor-bound villagers. In pictures dating from the great age of fairs may be seen the villagers frolicking, getting drunk, and engaging in heavy-handed amours. And from sermons dating from the same period, in which moralists denounced the fleshly temptations of the fair, we have further evidence that the manorial rustic found in it a relief from the burdens of tenant life on the manor.

Carcassonne—medieval walled city. A stronghold of the Albigensians (p. 514), it was taken by Simon de Montfort in 1209. (Courtesy, French Government Tourist Office)

The Rise of Towns

As commerce gained in scope, towns arose all over Europe. The mark of a town was that most of its people earned their living from the exchange of goods or the production of goods destined to be sold. As the population grew, a town came also to include lawyers, doctors, public officials, teachers, and other members of the professional segment of the middle class as well as merchants. A village, in contrast to a town, was an agricultural settlement, and nearly all its population was made up of persons who worked on the land.

The oldest towns in the Feudal Era were those that never ceased to be trading centers, even in the Dark Ages. Such were the Italian seaport towns, some other seaport towns on the Mediterranean—Marseilles and Barcelona, for example—and on the shores of the North Sea and the Baltic, and a certain number of towns located on rivers, such as Cologne and Paris.

Other towns took their start at some time during the Feudal Era. Some of these arose at the site of a cathedral, while others developed outside the walls of a castle. In French, a fortified place was called a *bourg*, in German, *burg*. Hence the men living in towns outside a castle came to be known in French as *bourgeois*, in German as *burger*. The English equivalent is *burgher*, from the word *borough*, which originally signified castle or stronghold. The French word *bourgeoisie*, derived from *bourgeois*, is often used in English, for want of a better term, as the name of the middle class, comprising business and professional people.

Since towns derived their livelihood from commerce, trade routes determined their location. Hence the greatest towns in Italy were seaports, such as Venice, Genoa, and Pisa. Rome was an exception to the rule, for its importance arose from its role as the home of the papacy rather than from commerce. Other cities gained their vigor from the overland trade, passing through northern Italy to the lands across the Alps. Among these were Florence and Milan. Throughout the Feudal Era northern Italy remained the most urbanized region of Europe, with Flanders as an increasingly close second.

Proceeding northward from Italy, the merchant travelers crossed the Alps into Germany by way of the Brenner Pass and the St. Gotthard Pass. From the Brenner Pass the main routes led to Innsbruck, Augsburg,

Ulm, Ratisbon, Nuremberg, Erfurt, Leipzig, and Magdeburg, and thence to Lübeck and the great Hanseatic towns of the north. From the St. Gotthard Pass the traveler would continue into the Rhine Valley toward Basel, Strasbourg, Spires, Worms, Mainz, Frankfurt-am-Main, Coblentz, and Cologne. From Cologne a road led on to Bruges and the other towns of Flanders.

The leading towns of the north German coast were linked together, as we have noted, in a commercial association known as the Hanseatic League. Among them were Bremen, Lübeck, Stettin, and Danzig. Others were taken in, until by 1350 the League comprised ninety towns, including such inland centers as Magdeburg, Berlin, Brunswick, and the great Rhine port of Cologne. During the fourteenth century the cities of the Hanseatic League nearly monopolized the trade of northern Europe. Offices and warehouses of the League were maintained not only in such trading centers as London, Bruges, and Stockholm, but even as far off as Novgorod, in Russia.

So numerous and rich were the Flemish towns that the whole of Flanders seemed to be a single, huge market place. The greatest of the Flemish cities was Bruges, a river port close to the sea but protected against offshore storms. It became the meeting point for the exchange of goods from northern and southern Europe, for to its docks came ships from Venice and other Italian towns and those from the Hanseatic cities and other ports of the Baltic and North Sea regions. Moreover it was a terminus for overland routes from northern France and for the river traffic along the Rhine. Other Flemish towns grew rich as suppliers of woolen and linen cloth. Among these were Ghent, Antwerp, Ypres, Brussels, Louvain, and Tournai.

In France the pattern of the navigable rivers often determined the sites of great towns. From Marseilles, which was the main French port on the Mediterranean, trade passed northward along the Rhône as far

as Lyons. From Lyons a main route continued to Paris. The overland route from Italy proceeded into France by way of the Great St. Bernard Pass, continuing past Lausanne, Besançon, Dijon, and Troyes to Paris. Paris itself owed its first importance to the fact that it was a political capital. But it also gained advantage from its location on the Seine at a point where several overland routes intersected and crossed the river, for seagoing vessels could navigate the river upstream as far as the capital. Its maritime importance is commemorated by the ship on the official seal of Paris. But not all its trade was water-borne. Much of it came overland from Flanders, the Channel ports, and the center and south of France.

In England the main trade routes led from the seaports to the interior. Like Paris, London flourished because it was both a sheltered river port, with access to the sea, and a political capital. The entire English coastline was dotted with other busy harbors. Among them were Hull, Yarmouth, Ipswich, Sandwich, Dover, Portsmouth, Portland, Plymouth, Bristol, and Chester. The larger inland towns lay along the main routes from north to south and from east to west. These included Northampton, Stamford, Boston, Leicester, Shrewsbury, and Lincoln. The great fortified town of York dominated the highway leading to Scotland by way of Newcastle and Berwick.

Life in the Towns

A number of European towns have shown few outward changes since feudal times. Best known of these are Carcassonne in France and Nuremberg in Germany. From the walls and buildings erected in these towns in feudal times, we gain an impression of what everyday life must have been like in towns of Europe eight or ten centuries ago.

For defense, the town was always surrounded by a wall. Because the walls set bounds to the outward growth of the town, the buildings inside crowded upon one another. Because space was at a premium, the streets were narrow. Often the law provided that the street must be wide enough to permit a man on horseback to ride down the center, holding a lance crosswise of the street. This was far from a generous measure, but the builders encroached upon even this narrow width by having the upper stories of their houses overhang the street. And since the houses commonly rose to a height of four or five stories, this meant that the sun scarcely ever reached the lane below.

The streets were filthy. Seldom were drainage sewers provided, and garbage was tossed on the ground or the pavement to be scavenged by the dogs, cats, pigs and rats that roamed the town. The rotting refuse gave off a constant stench, and, what was worse, it also was a cause of both endemic and epidemic diseases. The most famous of the epidemics, the "Black Death" of 1348–1350, is said to have taken the lives of one third the population of western Europe. It seems to have been the disease now known as the bubonic plague, which is associated with filth because it is spread by fleas that infest rats. Apart from such epidemics, diseases spread by polluted water and tainted food must also have taken a heavy toll. Probably more than half the children born in the towns died while infants. The people of the town paid a severe price, it is evident, for the privilege of living within its walls.

There was no distinction between a business section and a residential section. Nearly every townsman who was prosperous enough to own a house was a businessman of some kind, and ordinarily his home was also his place of business. At first houses were made of wood, with thatched roofs. But houses of this sort easily caught fire, and the flames quickly spread. So from the end of the twelfth century the houses of the well-to-do were usually built of stone or brick, as were most of the public buildings. In many areas, particularly southern Europe, tiles were used for roofing instead of thatch or wood.

With the flourishing of commerce, wealth brought luxury into the homes of the more prosperous town merchants. In the fourteenth and fifteenth centuries, the mercantile patrician filled his house with tapestries, fine rugs, gold and silver ware, and expensive dishes. With these amenities in his snug house, he lived in more comfort than did the rural baron, who was his social superior. So obvious were the comforts to be had in a good town house and so interesting were the contacts to be made in town that the upper provincial nobility and the higher ecclesiastics began to acquire dwellings in the cities, which they occupied for part of the year.

At night the townsman did well to take advantage of the comforts of his home, for it was not safe to venture outside. The unlighted streets were the haunt of homeless vagrants and cutthroats, and there was no police except for the "watch," consisting of a few guards whose duties were to see that the gates were secured at night and to keep a lookout for surprise attacks upon the town itself. On the rare occasions when the respectable townsman had need to go out at night, he took his manservants with him, carrying torches and weapons. If he should be set upon and robbed or murdered, the town officials would make little effort to apprehend the persons who committed the crime. They would, to be sure, inflict severe penalties on a lawbreaker, once the criminal was caught, but it was up to the victim or his kinsmen to discover the assailant.

By day the main street of the town was an entertaining scene of bustle. In the shops along the streets there was a hum of business as the merchants and their customers haggled over the sale of bread, meat, vegetables, spices, wine, salt, cloth, shoes, gloves, weapons, housewares, and countless other commodities. In the streets the humbler vendors hawked their odds and ends of second-hand goods and refreshments. Beggars were a pitiful throng, for the poor man who was crippled by accident or disease had no alternative but to depend upon alms.

The Markets

On market day, which was usually once a week, the crowds in the street were bigger than usual, and the excitement greater. On this day peasants from the countryside were permitted to bring their produce and other goods into the town and offer them for sale. Usually they set up temporary stalls in the market place, which ordinarily was the main square of the town. Other outsiders were also allowed to set up stalls, on the payment of set fees, and others were permitted to come into the town for the purpose of making purchases. In some towns the market day was so important that the merchants who were residents of the town had to close their shops on that day and, like outsiders, do their selling in market place stalls.

The custom of holding markets within the town once each week, or at other regular periods, grew up with the decline of the fairs, which had flourished in the age before towns were numerous and large. The right to hold a market was an important part of the privileges of a town, stipulated in its charter. Usually the town officials had to pay a tax to the king or lord in return for the privilege. They were not unwilling to do so, because a market brought a regular supply of money and needed goods into the town. In most of the small towns of western Europe the custom of holding a weekly market still survives.

Sixteenth-century Shops. At left, tailors are at work; at right, a man displays tarts and a sugar loaf. In the background, beneath his sign of four basins, a barber is shaving a customer. Paved streets were rare, but half-timbered houses were typical. (Courtesy of the Metropolitan Museum of Art)

THE ECONOMIC AND POLITICAL ORGANIZATION OF THE TOWNS

The men who bought and sought merchandise for a living soon found themselves obliged to band together into organized groups. One reason for this was that the feudal social order made no regular provision for them, since it was based upon the relationships among overlords and vassals and between the lord and the serfs and tenants who resided on his manor. As merchants established permanent settlements of their own in the growing towns, they were compelled to seek some kind of recognition of their status. Within the town, moreover, they had need of both a government and of other institutions for the management of their economic affairs.

At first their economic organizations were quite as important as the government of the town. These organizations, to which were given the name of *guilds,* were of two kinds. One was the *merchant guild,* which included all persons residing in the town who made their living from commerce. The other kind comprised the *craft guilds,* of which there were a considerable number in each town.

Merchant Guilds

The merchant guilds arose first. In some towns the merchant guild lingered on after the emergence of craft guilds, but generally the craft guilds superseded the merchant guild. Because they developed earlier and disappeared sooner, less is known of the merchant guilds than of the craft guilds.

The merchant guild was primarily a trade association including all the merchants of a certain town, who banded together for the purpose of monopolizing and regulating the business of the town. Merchants who were not members of the guild—and who therefore were not residents of the town— were not permitted to enter the town to do business except upon the payment of a heavy fee or by the special permission of the town's merchant guild, often granted only when the outsiders were suppliers of raw materials needed by the merchants of the town for their own businesses.

Merchant guilds attained their greatest importance during the twelfth century. They were often instrumental, especially in France and Italy, in organizing the merchants of the town for the purpose of gaining a town charter. Often this required a bitter, armed struggle against the feudal lords of the region, who were little disposed to give up their right to interfere in the affairs of the towns. (See illustration, p. 447.)

Craft Guilds

Toward the close of the twelfth century, the merchant guilds began to break up. Their place was taken by the craft guilds, which came into prominence at this time and lasted on, in some countries, long after the close of the Feudal Era. The craft guilds differed from the merchant guilds in that they were specialized according to occupation. Consequently, there were many craft guilds in each town, one for every important craft. The transition from a single merchant guild to a number of craft guilds was a reflection of the increasing specialization of business and labor as the towns grew in size.

Among the craft guilds were those of the butchers, bakers, furriers, wheelwrights, carpenters, goldsmiths, brewers, vintners, shoemakers, and innumerable others. Though all were called craft guilds, the name is a little misleading. These guilds were also associations of merchants, engaged in selling a specific kind of product. Some of these merchants were also craftsmen, producing the wares that they sold. Such, for instance, was the master shoemaker, who made the shoes he offered for sale. But the master vintner did not usually produce the wine he sold; he was a dealer, not a craftsman.

The craft guild is not to be confused with a labor union. Though normally all the members of a guild also worked at a craft, only the "masters" had the full rights and privileges of membership in the guild. And the masters were businessmen, who owned their own shops and operated their businesses for their own profit. Much, if not most, of the work in the shop was done by apprentices and journeymen, employed by the master. These were only probationary or prospective members of the guild. They could not enjoy full membership until or unless they became masters and set up shops of their own.

The master craftsmen were the business magnates of the town and usually controlled its government. Ordinarily the right to hold office in the town government was limited to guild masters or to the owners of property, who nearly always were guild masters. This custom still survives in London, where the Lord Mayor is elected by and from the membership of the "liveried companies," which are survivals of the old craft guilds. Nowadays, however, the office of Lord Mayor is merely honorific, and the "liveried companies" are only social organizations of prosperous businessmen.

Even in the Feudal Era the craft guild was a social organization as well as a trade association. Because the guild served as an instrument for suppressing competition among men engaged in the same business, it created an atmosphere of cooperation among its members rather than one of rivalry. Hence the members looked upon the guild as a kind of brotherhood. And since this was an age of strong religious sentiment, the guild took on something of the air of a religious association. Thus the guild took on a number of other functions other than, and in addition to, its strictly business activ-

ities. Some of them established schools for the children of members—one such, the Merchant Tailors' School in London, still survives. Some provided funds for the widows and orphans of deceased members. Usually all the members of the guild attended religious services in a body on feast days, particularly the feast day of the patron saint of the guild. The more prosperous built chapels of their own, and many contributed labor and money to the building of cathedrals. Often a guild would contribute a stained-glass window, perhaps depicting the patron saint of the guild and "signed" by a scene having some association with the work of the members. Famous examples of windows of this kind are to be seen in the cathedral of Chartres, in France. (See also page 470.)

Regulation of Business by the Craft Guild

Each craft guild had a collective monopoly of a specific business, and the guild controlled the business practices of its members. This meant that no one could set up a shop without the permission of the appropriate guild, and, though the owner would operate his business for his own profit, the guild could determine what share of the total business of the guild a particular shop would be allowed to gain.

Furthermore, the guild regulated the recruitment and training of workmen. These regulations provided that no master could have more workers under him than other masters, that the workmen would have the proper skill, and that no more men would be trained in the craft than could be provided with work.

The training of a craftsman began with his apprenticeship. Usually a boy was apprenticed to a master before he reached the age of twelve. The length of his apprenticeship was ordinarily five or six years, though in crafts requiring a great degree of skill it

An Armorer and His Apprentice—from a four-teenth-century German manuscript. The apprentice at left works on a spur; the master holds a hammer while talking to a customer. (Courtesy, Metropolitan Museum of Art)

might be ten years or more. During this period the apprentice lived in the household of the master and worked for him, under the constant supervision and discipline of the master. He was obliged to work hard and for long hours, but in return he was given a thorough training. The apprentice received no wages, and commonly his parents paid the master for taking him in, since it was a great advantage for a lad to be trained in a craft and thus given the chance to work up to the rank of master.

When the apprentice completed his period of training, he was recognized as a journeyman. The name comes from the French word *journée,* meaning *day;* it signifies that the man was now permitted to work for daily wages. He might continue to work for the same master who had trained him as an apprentice, or he might take employment with any other master of the guild. But the journeyman was not yet a fully participating member of the guild. He would have to work many years as a journeyman in order to acquire ripe experience in his craft and save up enough money to open a shop of his own. Then he could apply to the masters of the guild for admittance to their ranks. This would require his passing an oral examination on the lore of the craft, giving proof of his good character, and submitting an article of his workmanship, called his "masterpiece," as evidence that he had command of the skill of his trade. If he passed these tests, he was recognized as a master and given the right to open his own establishment, take in apprentices, and hire journeymen.

Professional Men

Not all the prosperous townsmen were merchants. Some were members of what are now called the learned professions. These included lawyers and physicians, who had guilds of their own, comparable to those of the craftsmen. But not many men with legal training engaged in private practice. More often they were drawn into the royal service as judges and administrative officials. Nor were physicians numerous, for there was no systematic instruction in medicine until universities took up this task. Those physicians who engaged in private practice in the towns were organized into guilds, and they were careful to distinguish themselves from "surgeons" (who were members of the much humbler guild of barbers [p. 487]), and apothecaries or pharmacists, who had their own guilds. As a rule the common people got their medical attention, if any, from surgeon-barbers, apothecaries, and midwives. The physicians usually catered to the needs of the upper classes.

THE TOWNS AND POLITICAL LIFE

Status of the Burgher

The first political efforts of the earliest burghers in the towns were directed toward establishing their personal freedom. Under the customary laws of feudalism and manorialism, a man was attached to some group, and his membership in this group defined his rights as well as his duties. Thus a baron had his specific place in the network of lord and vassal relationships, a monk lived as a member of a religious order, and a serf or free tenant on a manor had certain rights in the small community into which he was born.

But the first burghers had no such customary rights, for they were neither nobles nor churchmen nor free agricultural tenants. Often they were suspected of being runaway serfs—as many of them were—and the townsmen therefore were in constant danger of having their services claimed by some local lord for work on his manor. To meet this threat, the pioneer townsmen banded together, fighting when necessary to preserve their personal freedom.

As time passed, customary law gradually gave recognition to the townsmen as a new social group, and their personal freedom came to be taken for granted. Eventually a legal maxim in most countries held that "town air is free air." That meant that a townsman was not to be regarded as a manorial serf. And even a serf who escaped from his lord's manor would become a free man, provided he lived in a town for a year and a day without being discovered by his former lord and brought back to the manor. This did not mean that, as a townsman, he would have the same rights as all other residents of the town, for usually political rights were limited to only a minority of the population of the town, comprising the well-to-do. But he would be secure against interference with his personal freedom.

Status of the Town

Recognition of their personal freedom from servile manorial obligations was only the first gain of the early townsmen. The next step was to secure some measure of political freedom from the arbitrary rule of the local feudal lord. Nearly every town grew up on land that was within the feudal domain of some baron or on a domain of which the feudal lord was a bishop. Without some formal definition of their rights, the townsmen would be at the mercy of the local lord, who could levy upon their wealth as he pleased.

To gain recognition of their rights, the early townsmen often appealed to the king (or to a great duke or count) to protect them against the local lord. The kings and feudal magnates were not always eager to grant the townsmen this protection, since customary law gave no basis for it, but the great lords, had reasons too, usually for wanting to reduce the power of the lesser lords. Moreover they were always in need of money, and the townsmen were willing to pay either a lump sum or a periodic levy in return for their freedom from local feudal jurisdiction.

The first move, when a town sought to obtain its freedom from feudal interference, was for the citizens—or the most important of them, at least, who were the members of the merchant guild—to form a *commune*, or union for common action. Usually they took a solemn oath to support the commune by acting together in their dealings with the feudal lord. Eventually *commune* came to mean the town itself, as a corporation with a legal personality (in the legal phrase), rather than a mere group of persons.

If the townsmen were successful in their petition to the king, he would grant a charter to the commune. This charter would, first, recognize the right of the commune to act as a corporation, with the power to make agreements under its own corporate seal.

Next, the charter specified the degree of self-government granted to the town. The most favorable terms would wholly free the town from the power of the local feudal lord and place it solely under the authority of the king. Otherwise the local lord would retain a limited jurisdiction, and often he would gain some kind of compensation for the rights that he gave up. He might also have some voice in the selection of the officials of the commune. In any event, the town would have a written statement—a sort of contractual definition—of its corporate rights, and the lord could not make capricious exactions or interfere arbitrarily in the management of town affairs. Ordinarily the town gained the right to establish its own courts for the enforcement of municipal laws, and townsmen were largely exempt from summons to the feudal court of the local lord. But they always remained subject to the laws of the realm, administered in royal courts, and were answerable to church courts for spiritual offenses.

In most instances the town gained its charter simply by a peaceable petition to the king or to a great feudal magnate, usually accompanied by the offer of the payment of money. Sometimes, however, the communes raised troops and fought the king himself to compel him to grant them a charter. In the twelfth century many of the towns of Lombardy, in northern Italy, thus waged war against the Holy Roman emperors, securing the blessing and aid of the pope, who had his own quarrel with the Empire.

The charter of the town, we must note, did not give a town complete political independence. It simply made the town subject directly to the king rather than to a local baron or bishop. In the short run this was a great advantage, for the power of the local lord, if unchecked, was more vexatious to a town than the remote power of the king. In the long run, however, the kings in most countries established absolute power over their realms and, in this process, reduced the liberties of the towns to the vanishing point.

Forms of Town Government

Like the range of communal rights, the forms of town government varied from town to town. Generally the magistrates were elected by a certain number of the residents of the town. As a rule, the right to vote in these elections was limited to owners of property or masters of the guilds. Sometimes the local feudal lord retained the right to approve or disapprove the candidates for office or to appoint certain of the officers. In addition to the executive officers of the town, there was also a deliberative council, usually elective.

The duties of the council and the magistrates included the making of local law, the maintenance of public works, and the raising of taxes both for the support of the municipal government and for the payment of whatever tribute to the king or feudal lord was required by the town charter. The range of matters on which the town council was permitted to legislate varied according to the degree of self-government permitted by the charter. But, usually, the town government undertook a minute regulation of business life within the town. For the most part, this regulation was based on the principles of the "Law Merchant" of the fairs, and the ordinances of the councils were commonly taken over into the regulations of the merchant guilds and, later, of the craft guilds.

One of the important functions of the town government was to provide for the defense of the town in time of war. This might involve repelling an attack by the local feudal lord or keeping the town secure at a time when feudal lords were warring among themselves or even waging war against some other town. Always the town maintained walls for protection against attack, and guards to man the gates. Usually the town maintained a militia, recruited from among its own citizens, or it hired mercenaries as a permanent defense force.

As the town prospered, its council would usually build an elaborate town hall. This hall would normally be built facing a great open square, and the various craft guilds would put up buildings near by to serve as their headquarters. But the town did not normally maintain schools, orphanages, poorhouses, or hospitals, for the nurture of learning and the relief of distress were the functions of the Church.

CHANGING ECONOMIC IDEAS

Though men were slow to realize it, the rise of trade and towns implied the development of a new conception of economic endeavor. Under the manorial regime, men labored each day for the plain and simple purpose of satisfying their own needs for existence. To be sure, the villagers spent part of their time working for their lord, and occasionally they might engage in trade, as when they purchased salt from a peddler or bartered a measure of their grain in exchange for a knife or sickle or some other utensil made of metal. But, as a rule, most of the people in the manorial villages spent their time raising the food that they would eat and providing their own clothes and shelter. And this kind of economic endeavor conformed to the Christian religious teaching that God meant men to earn their bread by the sweat of their brows.

Men who made their living from commerce, however, were guided by other rules. They produced goods that they would not use themselves but that they would sell to other persons; and some of them did not produce goods at all but simply bought wares from one man and sold them to another. At first this seemed a dubious practice, for the merchant appeared to be taking advantage of someone else for his own gain. And this ran counter to the Christian notion that a man should help a neighbor instead of profiting from his wants.

This problem caused a number of theologians to ponder the issues involved in the new kind of economic endeavor. The most famous of those who studied this matter was Thomas Aquinas, who, as we noted earlier (p. 466), was one of the greatest of the theologians of the Feudal Era. The rules for the conduct of business that Aquinas and other theologians proposed were intended to make business practice conform to Christian precepts. But because the theologians of the Feudal Era were more accustomed to the manorial regime than to the new life of the towns, their rules were often at variance with the needs and interests of the townsmen.

As Aquinas and his contemporaries viewed the problem, labor seemed necessary and honorable. And the private ownership of property was also proper, since property arose out of human labor. But trade remained under grave suspicion, because, in the process of buying and selling, a man was always under the temptation of serving his own interest at the expense of someone else, and this would lead him into the sin of greed. To avoid this temptation, the merchant was supposed to charge only the "just price" of the wares that he offered. This meant a price such as would compensate the seller for his labor by permitting him to maintain himself at the standard of living appropriate to his social station. If the price were lower than this "just price," the buyer would be taking advantage of the seller; if it were higher than the "just price," the seller would be taking advantage of the buyer. Under this conception, it is obvious, there would be no profit in our sense of the word, but merely a recompense for labor.

This concept of the "just price" had some practical influence during the Feudal Era. This does not mean that businessmen of that age were more scrupulous than in our own time. We must remember that no businessman in the Feudal Era was free to manage his business quite as he pleased, because he was required to belong to a guild, and the guild imposed strict regulations upon all its members. And though the guild as a whole was not averse to seeing its members grow rich, it was quick to prevent any one member of the guild from outdistancing the other members. If all the members of the guild were making a substantial profit, despite the prohibition upon the taking of profit that was implied by the theologians' concept of the "just price," the guild was not apt to take action. But it would stop a rapacious businessman from reaping an inordinate profit —that is, a profit greater than the average.

A more acute conflict between theological doctrine and business practice arose over the matter of the taking of interest. Generally theologians condemned as usury the taking of interest at even the lowest rate—not simply, as we now define usury, at an extortionate rate. The reason for this was that churchmen regarded money as unproductive. Churchmen could readily understand and condone the charging of rent for the use of land, since land was capable of bringing forth new wealth. The owner who rented his land forewent the chance to raise a crop on it, and the rent was a compensation to him for the loss of this wealth. But a man who lent money to another could not rightfully require the lender to return more than the amount of money borrowed. Hence the lender would have no basis for demanding compensation for the use of his money.

Yet businessmen constantly had need to borrow money, and the prohibition on usury was often circumvented. At first, businessmen had recourse to Jews as moneylenders, because the Jews were not expected to obey the religious regulations imposed upon Christians and were therefore free to ignore the prohibition on the taking of interest. And since the Jews were generally forbidden to own land and were subject to numerous other restrictions, moneylending was one of the few vocations open to them.

Gradually the Christians, too, became moneylenders. The Italians were among the first to make a business of lending, for in Italy business habits conformed to an ancient tradition, dating back to the Roman era, and in antiquity usury was regarded as a normal business practice. Eventually banking developed in other countries, too, and theologians had to give up hope of enforcing their ban upon interest.

Yet we must not think of the businessmen of the Feudal Era as simply self-seeking— eager to make profits for themselves in defiance of all moral considerations. It is true that the businessman thought first and foremost of his own interests, and it is also true that he was usually more concerned with practical economic problems than with the afterlife. Nevertheless, and all unwittingly, he was an agent of social progress.

In the first place, the rise of the *bourgeoisie* represented a challenge to the feudal idea that birth determines a man's station. In the feudal regime a man was born either to labor on the land or to live upon the labor of others as a lord, and he could not choose otherwise. The only way a man born in humble station could improve his lot was by entering the Church; and even in the Church the highest positions were pre-empted by men of noble origin. But in the town a man was given an opportunity to improve his position by his own exertion; he might even make himself as well off financially, if not socially, as a feudal lord. As time went on it became harder for a man to rise to riches in the town, and a large proportion of the town population, like the manorial workers, was condemned to humble toil. But it never became impossible for a man to become rich in a town, whereas on the manor no serf or tenant could ever hope to cross the enormous gap between his class and that of his master.

Even the common people of the villages gained some benefit from the rise of the towns. As towns grew, they had need of ever-larger supplies of food, and thus the market for the produce of the villages became larger. Hence the peasants who brought their surplus produce to the market of the town could gain some share of the expanding wealth created in the towns. Moreover, the growth of towns gave the peasant a protection against his lord, since it now became possible for him to escape from the manor, if his lord mistreated him to the point of desperation, and gain his freedom within the sheltering walls of a town. For this reason, the lord eventually found it to his advantage to give his serfs their freedom and to treat his free tenants with some forbearance in order to keep them from running off. Eventually these facts so undermined the effectiveness of serfdom as to contribute significantly to its abandonment and disappearance in western Europe.

Suggestions for Further Reading

Source Materials

Anthologies and Collected Documents

Columbia College, *Introduction to Contemporary Civilization in the West* (2 vols., New York, 1946), Volume I, pp. 34–101.
An excellent selection of documents illustrative of the economic life and theory of the Feudal Era.

G. G. Coulton, *Life in the Middle Ages* (4 vols., New York, 1931).
An excellent and extensive collection of material, largely sources. Highly interesting, but somewhat uneven in quality.

G. H. Knoles and R. K. Snyder, eds., *Readings in Western Civilization* (rev. ed., New York, 1954), pp. 239–242.
A good, brief selection of documents illustrative of life on the manor.

H. T. Riley, *Memorial of London and London Life* (London, 1868).
An illuminating set of materials illustrative of life in the city of London in the Feudal Era.

J. H. Robinson, ed., *Readings in European History* (2 vols., Boston, 1904), Chapter XVIII.
A fine selection of documents illustrative of the economic life of the Feudal Era.

Contemporary Writings

Thomas Aquinas, *Of Cheating.*

Thomas Aquinas, *Of the Sin of Usury.*
These essays are contained in Thomas' *Summa Theologica,* but they have been published separately. They provide a classic statement of some of the economic thought of the great Scholastics.

Secondary Works

P. Boissonade, *Life and Work in Medieval Europe* (New York, 1927).
An excellent, brief survey of economic life in the Feudal Era.

G. G. Coulton, *The Medieval Village* (New York, 1926).
A graphic description, supported by many sources, of village and manorial life in the Feudal Era.

J. Huizinga, *The Waning of the Middle Ages* (London, 1924).
A near-classic essay on the early phases of the transition to modern times. An excellent, scholarly book.

A. Luchaire, *Social France in the Time of Philip Augustus* (New York, 1912).
An excellent, occasionally racy, description of French society in the time of "the founder of modern France."

C. H. McIlwaine, *The Growth of Political Thought in the West* (New York, 1932).
A standard, dependable survey.

S. Painter, *Medieval Society* (Ithaca, 1951).
A good survey.

H. Pirenne, *Medieval Cities* (Princeton, 1925).
A near-classic. Corrects many old and fallacious impressions relative to the decline and revival of the towns in the Feudal Era.

E. E. Power, *Medieval People* (London, 1925).
A very readable and interesting description of life in the Feudal Era.

J. W. Thompson, *An Economic and Social History of the Middle Ages* (New York, 1928).
A standard general history of the Feudal Era.

20

Western Christianity in the Feudal Era

The Baptism of Christ—Champlevé enamel and copper-gilt mosan, attributed to Godefroid de Claire, second half of the twelfth century. (Courtesy of the Metropolitan Museum of Art)

The history of the Feudal Era in western Europe presents a scene of kings and knights, merchants and peasants, castles and walled towns. But none of these was more characteristic of the age than the lordly bishops and black-robed priests, and the numerous churches, monasteries, and cathedrals.

Throughout the Feudal Era, the Roman Catholic Church held a religious monopoly in western Europe. Membership in the Church was an automatic consequence of birth, and neither law nor custom permitted a man to renounce it. The spiritual dominion of the Church did not extend into Russia or the Balkans, which remained within the realm of the Orthodox Eastern Church, but elsewhere in Europe it reached as far as the borders of civilization itself.

THE BASIC BELIEFS AND PRACTICES OF THE CHURCH

It is impossible to understand the role and influence of the Roman Catholic Church in the Feudal Era without understanding its basic religious doctrines. These stem from the premise that the human race bears an enormous burden of sin. In part, this is thought to lie in the inheritance of mankind from the guilt of Adam; in part, it is considered to be the consequence of the wrongdoing of individual men in their own lives, for, though God has given them the knowledge of right and wrong and the freedom to choose between them, without divine assistance men always succumb to the temptations of evil.

So great is this burden of sin that men, by their own pitiful efforts, can never atone for it. But because God is merciful as well as just, he himself has made it possible for them to be forgiven. This was accomplished through the sacrifice of Jesus Christ, whose death helped atone for the sins of men. However, this Divine Redemption does not assure men of salvation; it merely makes it possible for them to gain salvation. To do so, individual men and women must recognize their sins, repent, and strive to overcome the temptation to sin again. To help them do so, they must submit to the ministrations, performed by priests, that are the sacraments.

The Sacraments

These sacraments were of crucial importance in the history of the Church as an institution, because they were the key to the immense power of the clergy. Without these ministrations, the Christian could not gain salvation. And these rites could be performed only by a specially ordained priesthood.

The number of the sacraments was eventually established as seven. The first of these was (1) baptism, the initiation rite of Christianity, by which the individual's share in the original sin of Adam was washed away, leaving him eligible for salvation. This rite was usually administered to the newborn infant, while sponsors, known as godparents, promised in his name that he would be reared in the Christian religion. (2) Confirmation was administered at the onset of adolescence. It was not regarded as essential to salvation, but it was presumed to give the individual greater moral strength with which to face the moral hazards of adult life. (3) Penance was the rite (usually involving confession to a priest) by which the believer gained forgiveness for serious sins that he himself had committed after baptism had removed the sin he inherited at birth. (4) The Eucharist, or Holy Communion, formed the central part of the greatest public ritual of the Church, which was the celebration of the mass. In this sacrament, consecrated bread and wine would be miraculously transformed into the body and blood of Jesus Christ. This miracle was called *transubstantiation,* and the action of the priest in performing it was regarded as a re-enactment of the "Last Supper" of Jesus and his disciples. After the transubstantiation, the priest consumed a portion of the elements and distributed a portion to those worshipers who wished to partake. The Christian believer was not required to partake of this communion as a necessary prerequisite to his salvation, but this sacrament was believed to give him the strength of soul that he needed in order to gain salvation. He was expected to attend mass frequently.

(5) Extreme Unction was the rite performed for those at the verge of death, to prepare the soul for the afterworld. In the normal course of events all Christians would submit to these five rites at least once in a lifetime.

But not all Christians partook of the two other sacraments. (6) Holy Orders was the rite administered to those who became members of the priesthood, by which they gained the power to administer the other rites to the laity. (7) Matrimony, on the other hand, was a sacrament never partaken of by the priests, monks, and nuns of the Catholic Church, because they were required to remain celibate. Once a couple partook of this sacrament, their marriage was irrevocable.

Ritual and Ceremony

Around the administration of the sacraments and other devotions the Church built an impressive pageant of religious ceremonial. Grand as were the splendid Romanesque and Gothic cathedrals, the buildings of the Church were but the setting for the awe-inspiring rituals performed within them.

The form of the Church ritual was generally the same throughout Europe, and the music conformed to the standard patterns of the Gregorian chant. But the splendor of the scene varied according to the means of the parish, for a humble village church could not provide the costly altarpieces, candlesticks, stained glass, and other ornaments that were used in the great cathedrals, nor did the humble priest wear so gorgeous vestments as the bishop and his attendants.

So great was the dominance of the religious outlook in the minds of the men of the Feudal Era that even the reckoning of time had religious implications. For instance, a man would agree to pay a certain debt on "All Saints Day" rather than setting the date as "the first of November." Even the time of day was kept track of according to the clerical chants of the various psalms and prayers, beginning with matins and ending with vespers.

THE SECULAR PRIESTHOOD

The clergy was divided into two categories —regular and secular. The regular clergy comprised the ordained monks, friars, and others who lived in monastic communities. Their name is derived from the Latin *regula,* which means *rule;* it signifies that they submitted to the special regulations of their monastic communities, which included the three vows of poverty, chastity, and obedience to their superiors. The secular clergy comprised the great number of priests and bishops who lived their daily lives in contact with the world of the laity. Their name is derived from the Latin word *saecula,* which was a figurative term for the world of affairs. All clerics above the rank of subdeacon were bound by the rule of celibacy, but the secular clergy, unlike the regular, was not debarred from owning material possessions.

The Parish Priest

The parish priest (ordinarily a member of the secular clergy) was the representative of the Church who came into daily contact with the mass of the faithful. The whole of Christendom was divided into parishes, and every layman was the member of a specific parish. Ordinarily he was expected to attend the church of his parish for periodic worship and to receive the sacraments of penance and communion, and he was obliged to contribute to the support of the parish priest. In the rural countryside each manor or village constituted a parish, but towns and cities were each divided into a number of parishes. Every parish had its own church, but not every church building was a parish church, for monasteries and friaries usually had their own churches or chapels, in town and country, which laymen were free to attend if they wished.

The normal revenues of a parish came from various sources. Rural parishes, as we have noted earlier, were ordinarily endowed with land, which was tilled by the serfs or free tenants of the manor or village. A town parish might also have an endowment in land, though this might take the form of "income property" within the town. Or the proceeds of some other enterprise, such as a toll bridge, might be the parish endowment. In addition, all members of the parish were expected to contribute a tithe, which was a kind of income tax for the support of the Church. In principle, this was one tenth of an individual's income. Actually, few paid that much, and the well-to-do paid a good deal less, but the tithe still amounted to a considerable burden on the common people. The parishioners were also expected to make an offering to the priest when he officiated at a baptism or marriage or sang a mass for the dead or performed other ceremonies of special interest to the various members of the parish. Such offerings were supposed to be voluntary gifts, for a priest who "sold" his sacramental services was guilty of the sin of simony. But the distinction between a voluntary offering and an obligatory charge was often obscured in the mind of many parish priests and their parishioners.

The Bishop

In the eyes of the Church, the first bishops were the Twelve Apostles of Christ, and these were believed to have passed to other bishops the powers given them by Christ. All bishops thus held their office in an unbroken chain of delegation from the founder of the Church. Their office gave them the power to administer all the sacraments that could be administered by a priest, and they alone could administer the sacraments of confirmation and ordination. By the latter sacrament priests were invested with their spiritual powers.

The bishop was in charge of the administration of the Church within a region known

The Romanesque Cathedral of Pisa—begun in 1063. (Brogi photo)

as a diocese. The whole of Christendom was divided into such dioceses, each comprising a number of parishes and each having a bishop of its own. The "seat" of the bishop— that is, the site of his official residence and the cathedral—was usually in the most important town of the diocese.

The power of the bishop as an officer of the Church was immense. He was accountable to no superior within the Church save the pope, and all the parish priests within his diocese were under his orders. His court tried all cases arising under Church law within his diocese, and he had the right to impose the most severe penalties of the Church. Theoretically, appeals could be taken from his court to that of an archbishop, but often the only effective appeal was to the papal court in Rome, which was both expensive and time-consuming. The judicial authority of the bishop extended to laymen as well as the clergy in disputes affected by matters of religious doctrine. In the Feudal Era these included many cases of a kind that we now think of as wholly secular. For example, a great inheritance might hinge upon the question as to whether a certain marriage was valid under the laws of the Church.

In the Feudal Era, as we have seen on page 448, the bishop also had great importance as a feudal personage. All the land in the diocese belonging to the Church was under his charge, and he was therefore involved in feudal relations as both vassal and overlord. And the holdings of the Church grew larger in each succeeding generation, since gifts were constantly being made to the Church; and once property passed into the possession of the Church it, ordinarily, was never relinquished.

Endowed thus with enormous spiritual and secular power, the bishop was an impressive figure. His attire was in keeping with the splendor of his office—a tall, pointed cap, called a mitre, which was often encrusted with jewels, a great ornamental cloak; and a long, golden staff or crozier, representing a shepherd's crook, which was the symbol of his office.

The cathedral, which was the church attached to the bishop's seat, was usually the architectural pride of the town where he made his residence. The order of services in a cathedral was much more elaborate than in a parish church. The priests appointed to conduct these services in the cathedral were known as canons; as a group, they were called the cathedral chapter. Their number varied between half a dozen and more than a score. Appointments to this body were highly prized, for a canonry was the most important and most dignified office in the diocese below that of the bishop himself. Each canon had the right to a fixed income, called a prebend, which usually was much greater than that of a parish priest.

The Archbishop

The archbishops were the bishops of the greater dioceses. The archbishops had no greater spiritual authority than other bishops, but their prestige was greater, because their dioceses were more important. During the Feudal Era, moreover, the archbishops sought to assume a kind of chairmanship over the bishops of the dioceses neighboring his own. In most respects the bishops succeeded in maintaining their independence of the archbishop, but on ceremonial occasions he took precedence over them.

The Pope

The pope was the Bishop of Rome. As a bishop, he had the same sacramental powers as all other bishops. What originally gave him a much higher rank was not that he held a different kind of office but that the seat of his diocese happened to be Rome, the

Seats of Archbishoprics in the Middle Ages

Sip. : Siponto , Naz. : Nazareth

Some Popes of the Feudal Era

Zacharias	741–752
Stephen III	752–757
Adrian I	772–795
Leo III	795–816
Leo IV	747–855
Nicholas I	858–867
John VII	872–882
John XII	955–964
Sylvester II	999–1003
Leo IX	1049–1054
Alexander II	1061–1073
Gregory VII	1073–1085
Urban II	1088–1099
Paschal II	1099–1118
Innocent II	1130–1143
Eugene III	1145–1153
Adrian IV	1154–1159
Alexander III	1169–1181
Celestine III	1191–1198
Innocent III	1198–1216
Honorius III	1216–1227
Gregory IX	1227–1241
Innocent IV	1243–1254
Alexander IV	1254–1261
Urban IV	1261–1264
Clement IV	1265–1268
Martin IV	1281–1285
Boniface VIII	1294–1303

"capital of the world." This had special significance for two reasons. In the first place, Rome had been, according to tradition, the seat of the Apostle Peter, and Christ had designated Peter as chief among the Twelve Apostles. Hence the Bishop of Rome, as the successor to St. Peter, was presumed to be the chief of all bishops, the others being successors to lesser apostles. This "Petrine theory" was not accepted by the churchmen of the east, but it was acknowledged by those of the west. It became the principal point of difference in the schism dividing the "Orthodox" Catholicism of Byzantium from the "Roman" Catholicism of western Europe (p. 262).

The other significance of Rome came from its prestige as the former capital of the Roman Empire. This did not mean so much in the east as in the west, because such cities as Athens and Alexandria were centers of civilization long before Rome. No city of western Europe, however, could match the renown of the old imperial capital. And inevitably the aura surrounding the name of Rome gave added prestige to the Roman bishop.

During the Feudal Era no one in western Christendom questioned the supremacy of the pope over any other bishop. There was some doubt, however, especially toward the close of the period, as to whether the authority of the pope was greater than that of a universal council of the Church, including all the bishops of Christendom. Apart from this point, the primacy of the pope over the clergy was complete.

Less secure was the supremacy of the pope over secular rulers. The doctrines of the Church on this point were clear: a king or other ruler, being a Christian, was a member of the Church, and, like all others, he was therefore subject to the authority of the clergy, of which the pope was the head. In practice, however, the power of the pope over kings and emperors varied from one time to another. It depended in part upon whether or not a man of great personal vigor occupied the papal throne; and it also depended upon whether the position of the secular ruler within his own realm was strong or weak. The popes of the time of Charles the Great were generally under the domination of that doughty monarch, and a number of later popes were creatures of the early Holy Roman emperors. But toward the middle of the eleventh century a series of energetic "reformist" popes—notably, Gregory VII (1073–1085)—began to assert their authority with increasing vigor and effectiveness. Despite occasional setbacks, the power of the papacy continued to grow thereafter until it reached its zenith early in the thirteenth century, in the pontificate of Innocent III (1198–1216), the mightiest pope in history, who at one time or another laid down the law to nearly every king in Europe.

Excommunication. The weapon that the popes used to bring secular rulers to their knees was the sentence of excommunication. This dire punishment could be imposed by the pope anywhere in the world, or by any bishop within his diocese, upon a sinner who refused to do penance for his sins and submit to ecclesiastical authority. A person thus condemned was cut off from the Christian community. He could not enter a church building or receive the sacraments, and all Christians were forbidden to have dealings with him. He became an outcast, a spiritual leper, whose presence carried contagion. If he died without repenting, his soul would be doomed to suffer the torments of hell until the end of time.

Only at grave risk could a king persist in a quarrel with a pope when the latter resorted to this weapon. The king himself would fear for his soul, if he should be excommunicated. And even if he were willing to ignore the danger to his soul, he could not ignore the threat to his secular power. For once the king was excommunicated, his vassals were freed of their oaths to him, and often this was a sufficient excuse for them to undertake a rebellion. This was what forced the German emperor Henry IV, as we have seen, to make a humiliating submission to Pope Gregory VII (p. 461). As time passed, however, this weapon proved less effective. In the thirteenth century Emperor Frederick II treated the sentence of excommunication as a laughing matter.

The Interdict. Another weapon that the popes sometimes used—as did some bishops —was the interdict. This sentence was imposed upon a whole community—a village or town, a province, even an entire kingdom. It meant that the church buildings would be closed, no religious services would be held and no sacraments administered except those, like extreme unction, deemed essential for the salvation of the soul when death seemed near at hand. Sometimes a bishop would impose this sentence when one of his vassals rebelled against him. On occasion the pope would impose it—or threaten to do so—when a king defied the papal authority. Its effectiveness came from the fact that this punishment affected not only the ruler but all those living within his realm —the populace, terror-stricken at the unaccustomed silence of the church bells and horrified at seeing the churches closed, would exert an enormous pressure upon the ruler to make his submission and thus relieve them of the punishment inflicted upon them for his faults.

The most famous interdict in the Feudal Era was that laid upon the kingdom of England by Pope Innocent III as a consequence of a dispute with King John over appointment to the archbishopric of Canterbury. This interdict remained in force for several years, and it was not removed until John made a humble submission.

Pope Innocent III. The reign of Innocent III, who held office as pope from 1198 to 1216, was the peak of the power of the papacy. His triumph over King John was not the greatest of his victories, for John was a weak-willed ruler. More remarkable was Innocent's victory over Philip II of France, who was a man of tough fiber. Philip had married a Danish princess but, soon tiring of her, had had her shut up in a castle. At his dictate, the subservient French bishops then annulled his marriage, whereupon he took a second wife. But the partisans of the first queen appealed to Pope Innocent, who summarily disallowed the annulment of Philip's first marriage and ordered the king to give up his new wife in favor of the first. Philip blustered until Innocent III imposed

The Palace of the Popes at Avignon. (French Government Tourist Office)

the sentence of excommunication upon him. Then Philip gave in, in order to forestall a rebellion of his vassals. Besides Philip and John, various other kings were also compelled to acknowledge the power of this famous pope.

The Decline of the Papacy. Within a hundred years after the death of the great Innocent, however, the papacy passed into an

---

Popes of the "Babylonian Captivity"

Clement V	1305–1314
John XXII	1316–1334
Benedict XII	1334–1342
Clement VI	1342–1352
Innocent VI	1352–1362
Urban V	1362–1370
Gregory XI	1370–1378

---

abrupt decline. By 1300 another pope, Boniface VIII (1294–1303), became involved in a quarrel with the king of France, as had Innocent III, but this time the pope was the loser. As we have seen (pp. 452–453), when Boniface challenged the right of Philip IV to levy taxes on the French clergy, the king not only persisted in this practice but sent an emissary to intimidate the pope, an affront that hastened the death of Boniface. Soon afterward Philip secured the election of a French instead of an Italian churchman to the papal throne, and this pope—Clement V—removed his seat from Rome to Avignon. For three quarters of a century thereafter—from 1309 to 1378—successive popes reigned at Avignon, virtually as captives of the French monarchy; this period is called the "Babylonian Captivity," after the ancient Jewish captivity (p. 86).

The "Babylonian Captivity," during which the Avignon popes were entirely under the thumb of the French monarch and the College of Cardinals was packed with French prelates, was followed by the Great Schism, 1378–1417. To many, Avignon was no proper seat for the successors of Peter, and at last, in 1378, the College of Cardinals met in Rome and elected an Italian pope, Urban VI. Almost immediately, the French cardinals, insisting that they had been intimidated by the people of Rome, withdrew to a safer spot and elected a French pope, who resumed the seat at Avignon. To the horror of Christendom, the situation of two popes and two Colleges of Cardinals could not be reconciled, and, depending on their friendships and alliances, the nations of Europe sided with one or the other. Under leadership of the University of Paris, the so-called "conciliar movement" began when the majority of cardinals of each pope called the Council of Pisa in 1409. The result was the election of a *third* pope, John XXIII (1410–1415). At last the Council of Constance (1414–1418) was able to end the schism with the disposition of the conflicting claimants and the election, in 1417, of Martin V (1417–1431).

The Papal Court. As the spiritual monarch of the Christian world, the pope presided over a vast and intricate administrative organization. In power and structure, this was comparable to the government of a state—a state embracing the whole of western Christendom.

Highest in dignity at the papal court were those churchmen known as cardinals, who as a group were referred to as the College of Cardinals. One of their functions was to elect a successor upon the death of a pope. Until the eleventh century the election of the pope had been, according to the ancient law and custom of the Church, by "the clergy and people of the diocese." But this had made it possible for the noble families of Rome to influence the choice by stirring up the city mob in favor of a certain candidate, and sometimes the emperor of the Holy Roman Empire had also interfered in this fash-

Popes of the Great Schism

Roman Popes

Urban VI	1378–1389
Boniface IX	1389–1404
Innocent VII	1404–1406
Gregory XII	1406–1415

Avignon Popes

Clement VII	1378–1394
Benedict XIII	1394–1417

ion. To avoid such outside influence, the right to take part in the election had been limited in the eleventh century to the leading churchmen of the diocese of Rome, who came to be known as cardinals. The choice of a new pope was not the only function of the cardinals, however, for the main departments of the papal court were put under the charge of committees of cardinals. Their role was thus comparable to that of ministers of a secular ruler.

Much of the routine work of the papal court consisted of receiving and disbursing the revenues of the pope and hearing suits under Church law, when appeals were made to Rome from the decisions of the local bishop's court. The procedures that were developed in Rome for the handling of this business made the papal court the most efficient government in Europe throughout the Feudal Era.

Church Revenues

We have already discussed the revenues of the parish, the lowest administrative unit of the Church. A portion of the income of all the parishes in a diocese was given over to the bishop. In addition to this income, the bishop also had the income of endowments, usually in the form of land, and revenue in the form of fees charged to persons bringing suit in his court.

The basic revenue of the papacy came from the famous "Peter's Pence." This was a form of poll tax, levied upon all persons throughout Christendom. Though the individual paid only a small sum, the total receipts from this tax were enormous. The pope also had an income from the "first fruits" and "tenths" paid him by certain other bishops—for, in certain dioceses, the man who succeeded to the office of bishop was required to send to Rome a sum equal to the whole income of the bishopric for the first year of his tenure, and one tenth of the income in each succeeding year. Certain abbots and holders of other benefices were required to make similar payments. But this revenue was not paid by all bishops and abbots, and some paid less than the full amount. The pope also gained large income from the fees charged for the settlement of lawsuits heard in his appellate court.

Canon Law and the Church Courts

Since the Church had functions comparable to those of a government, it necessarily developed a body of law and a judicial system, parallel to the courts and laws of secular governments. Ordinarily cases arising under Church law were first tried in the court of the local bishop. Appeal could be taken from the decision of his court to the court of the archbishop and, from there, to the court of Rome. In practice, however, appeals were seldom made to the archbishop's court. If a case were of large importance, appeal would be taken directly to Rome, or the case might be entered at the papal court, without first passing through the lower courts.

The law administered in the courts of the Church was known as canon law. It derived from the legislative enactments, called *canons,* of the general councils of the Church, but it also included the edicts of the pope. The range of topics covered by canon law was great, including a number of matters that are now solely the concern of secular government. On the other hand, secular governments in the Feudal Era regarded as crimes a number of matters that now are presumed to be simply matters of religious belief and practice. Thus the jurisdiction of the two kinds of court overlapped. For example, as we have mentioned, a church court might be involved in a suit concerning inheritance, which now is simply a matter of civil law. Blasphemy, which we think of only as a form of religious disrespect, was not only a sin but a crime, for which a man could be punished in a Church court. And heresy was a crime under civil law, often involving the death penalty, as well as a crime against the law of the Church.

The punishments imposed by Church courts were both spiritual and temporal. The severest of the spiritual penalties was excommunication. Temporal punishments included fines and imprisonment but not the death sentence, since the Church was forbidden to shed blood. However, under civil law, the secular government would put to death persons condemned in a Church court for a grave breach of Church law, such as heresy. And like secular courts at the time, Church courts made use of torture, especially in heresy cases, though not in such form as would involve spilling blood. Much ingenuity was exercised in order to observe that technicality.

THE RELIGIOUS ORDERS

The manifold activities of the Church that have thus far been enumerated were ordinarily under the charge of clerics who were members of the secular clergy. This was not always so, because sometimes monks or other members of religious orders were made bishops or given other duties in connection with Church government. Characteristically, however, the regular clergy pursued a life withdrawn from the world of affairs—even the affairs of Church government.

In the history of the regular clergy, the Feudal Era is notable for the development of the oldest monastic group within the Church, the order of monks following the Benedictine Rule, and for the founding of the new orders of mendicant friars, whose organization was quite unlike that of the Benedictine monks.

The Benedictines

The Benedictine monks were those living in monasteries that observed the regulations first prescribed by St. Benedict. The Benedictines did not form a single religious society, for each abbey was independent of the others so far as its government was concerned. They were alike, however, in their acceptance of the famous "Rule of St. Benedict," which required them to wear a prescribed kind of clothing, called a habit; to pursue a regular daily routine of worship, labor, and rest; and to take the three vows of poverty, chastity, and obedience.

The Benedictine monastery, which usually was located in the countryside, was under the administration of an abbot. He ruled the monastery as an absolute monarch, for the monks were pledged to give him obedience, and the bishop of the local diocese had little or no power over him. Indeed, the abbot of one of the greater monasteries had as much prestige as a bishop, though his power was more limited, since he could not administer the sacrament of ordination or exercise some of the other powers of a bishop.

From the beginnings of monasticism, certain tendencies appeared that were unforeseen by St. Benedict, and in the Feudal Era these produced grave problems. Laymen often made gifts to monasteries, because the monks were believed to have a superior holiness, and gradually the monasteries thus came to possess large and rich holdings of land and other wealth. These furnished an income that released the monks from the need of laboring on the land to support themselves, which St. Benedict had originally insisted upon as a prime condition of the monastic life. The monks who were members of such prosperous monasteries were still bound by the vow of poverty, since the

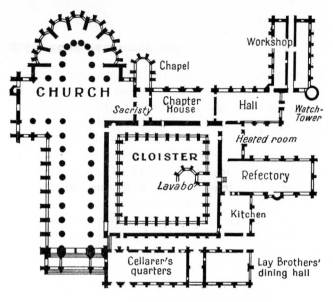

Plan of a Monastery

wealth belonged to the monasteries, not to the monks. But it soon bcame difficult to see what kind of sacrifice was involved in their vow of poverty, when the monks lived in comfort and affluence. To be sure, not every monastery became even moderately wealthy, but some of those that amassed great endowments fell victim to scandalous abuses.

Though the accumulation of endowments sometimes led to a corruption of the monastic ideal, it also had a fortunate consequence. In some monasteries, the monks, being freed from the need to labor in the fields, put their time to good use in intellectual labors. Thus most important monasteries maintained schools, to which were admitted both candidates for ordination to the priesthood and others who had no intention of pursuing a religious vocation. Moreover, most well-run monasteries maintained a *scriptorium,* a kind of workshop in which monks busied themselves with the copying of manuscripts. Before the invention of printing, all books were written by hand, and during the Feudal Era nearly all manuscripts—both sacred and profane works—were produced by monks. Most of the works of Latin literature that have survived from ancient times are known today only from manuscripts

copied by monks of the Feudal Era. These manuscripts are of value not only as works of learning but also as works of art, for the monkish scribes developed beautiful styles of lettering, and the manuscripts were often "illuminated" with lavish artistry (see pp. 452, 472, 473, 513, and 529). Labors of this kind did much to redeem the bad name of those monasteries that became notorious for indolence, immorality, and the general dissipation of their members.

The Cluny Reforms

The abuses of monasticism were considerably abated, moreover, by a reform movement that began in the early years of the tenth century. The initiative in launching this reform came from the Duke of Aquitaine, who was appalled by the sorry state of monasticism at that time. He decided to found a new monastery, where the "Rule of St. Benedict" would be strictly observed. As the site of this establishment, he chose a rural location at Cluny in Burgundy. Within a generation, the abbey of Cluny became celebrated throughout Christendom for the strictness of its discipline and the beauty of its religious observances. Bishops and secular rulers of other places soon besought the abbot of Cluny to establish "daughter houses" in their domains, and within a century, Cluny became the center of a great network of model monasteries. In this expansion, the Cluniac monks established a new pattern of centralized monastic organization, for the new houses set up under the sponsorship of Cluny did not have abbots of their own. Instead they were governed by an officer called a prior, who remained accountable to the one and only abbot of Cluny. Thus, though in other respects Cluny conformed to the pattern of Benedictine institutions, it departed from the Benedictine tradition that each monastery was independent of all others. It created the first religious "order" in the Church.

The wholesome reforms of Cluny spread far beyond the Benedictine world. By the force of its example and by the labor of some of its monks, who were called out of the cloister to become bishops and other high ecclesiastics, it became the center of a reform movement that extended throughout the Church. By the middle of the eleventh century, scarcely more than a hundred years after the founding of the original monastery at Cluny, the papacy itself was showing the beneficial effects of the Cluniac movement, for it was an inspiration to some of the greatest popes of the eleventh century, such as Gregory VII.

The Cistercians

Some of the more ardent spirits of the twelfth century felt that even Cluny fell short of the ideal of monastic devotion. This was not because Cluny or its dependent priories succumbed to the more flagrant forms of corruption, such as the flouting of the vow of chastity, but because the Cluniac monasteries, so it was charged, were filled with well-dressed, well-fed, and well-housed monks, who sang the divine praises in sumptuously decorated churches. Such a way of life, some thought, was far too comfortable, even if the monks avoided sinful irregularities, to measure up to St. Benedict's stern ideal of a life of ascetic self-sacrifice.

So newer groups appeared, to carry on the tradition of reform by which western monasticism constantly renewed itself. Some of these groups, like the Cameldolese monks in Italy and the Carthusians in France, developed new rules that would combine the personal isolation of the old hermits of the early Church with a certain measure of community life within the monastery. Others developed rules that would permit the monk to serve as a priest in a church open to the public in a near-by area, while still adhering to the monastic ideal of personal asceticism. Still other groups combined the life of a knightly warrior with that of the cloistered monk. These were the famous "military orders," such as the Templars, or Knights of the Temple, who took service as consecrated fighters in the Crusades, and the Hospitalers, or Knights of St. John of Jerusalem who devoted themselves to the task of caring for sick and injured pilgrims to the Holy Land.

The most famous of the monastic reform movements of the twelfth century was the one that gave rise to the Cistercian Order, so-called from the site of its first abbey, at

Abbey of Cluny, c.1043. East side of a reconstruction by Kenneth J. Conant, showing the second abbey church and other monastic buildings. (Mediaeval Academy of America)

Miracle of the Spring—one of the frescoes, c.1296–1300, by Giotto (p. 579) in the Upper Church at Assisi that depict scenes from the life of St. Francis. Here the friar kneels in prayer just before saying to the thirsty peasant who has been assisting him: "Hasten to that rock and thou shalt find a living water which in pity Christ hath sent thee from the stone to drink." To pilgrims entering the church, this implied "the living spring of the spirit." (Alinari photo)

Citeaux in France. The founding of Citeaux, about two centuries after the establishment of Cluny, was a sign that Cluny no longer was regarded as a leader in monastic reform, for the harsh Cistercian life implied a criticism of Cluniac comfort. The greatest figure in the Cistercian order, though not its founder, was St. Bernard of Clairvaux. Born of a noble family, as a young man Bernard entered the abbey of Citeaux, and his fervent example inspired most of the male members of his family to follow in his footsteps. After some years he was sent out to establish a new monastery at Clairvaux, which became the first offshoot of the mother house of Citeaux. Thereafter Bernard spent the rest of his life at Clairvaux, which, like Cluny and Citeaux, is located in eastern France. His renown made Clairvaux even more famous than Citeaux, and Bernard himself became a great power in the Church in his time.

Still another reform movement centered in new religious orders, the members of which were known as friars—which comes from their common designation as *brothers,* or *fratres.* The friars devised a new type of religious life, in which the discipline of the monk—epitomized in the vows of poverty, chastity, and obedience—was combined with an active participation in the problems of the world. Hence they did not live in isolated rural monasteries but in the midst of crowded cities and towns, mingling constantly with the laity.

There were several orders of friars. Two of the earliest were the Carmelites, or White Friars, and the Augustinians, or Austin Friars. But the most famous were the Franciscans, or Gray Friars, and the Dominicans, or Black Friars. The founding of these two orders marked a veritable revolution in the history of the Church during the Feudal Era.

The Franciscans

The Franciscans take their name from St. Francis of Assisi (1182–1226), the founder of the order. He himself called the members of his order the "little brothers," and this name is perpetuated in the official name, which is the Order of Friars-Minor. But the official designation has never supplanted the popular name of Franciscans.

No figure in all religious history is more attractive than St. Francis. He was one of a type that appears in every great religion— the believer who gives literal heed to the teachings of his religion and applies them with a deep and consistent seriousness. His fame comes from his uncompromising endeavor to live according to the Gospel precept: "If thou wouldst be perfect, go, sell all that thou hast, give to the poor, and come and follow me." Nor did he fail to note the words: "Take with you neither purse nor scrip nor staff. . . ."

The son of a well-to-do merchant of the Italian town of Assisi, St. Francis spent his youth in normal pursuits, which he later described as singularly sinful but which probably were merely gay. In early manhood he experienced a thoroughgoing religious conversion, whereupon he gave away all his possessions, even his clothes, dressed in a cast-off cloak, and took to a life of cheerful beggary. Of the alms given him each day, he kept only a few crusts, distributing the rest to others in need. Wandering about the countryside, sweeping out churches or washing dishes in a rectory for his daily fare, preaching to the vagrants of the towns he entered, St. Francis impressed everyone he met by his complete unworldliness, his gaiety, and his religious fervor.

The legends are so thick around the figure of St. Francis that it is impossible to separate true from fanciful, but even those that seem incredible serve to illustrate his reputation for unworldly piety and childlike cheerfulness. For example, he is said to have begun preaching to the birds, when their chirping interfered with his preaching to the villagers, and the birds are said to have stopped their noise to listen to him. On another occasion he is said to have met a wolf that had been terrorizing the countryside, and the wolf stopped to chat with him.

Not all the pious were favorably impressed by St. Francis' holy vagabondage, for he was not a priest and therefore had no right to preach. The Church authorities were inclined to look askance at this intrusion upon the priestly monopoly. Moreover, his literal adherence to the words of the Gospel put an unfavorable light upon not only those laymen who succumbed to temptation but also those churchmen whose ways were too much of this world.

St. Francis himself had no wish to question the authority of the clergy, and, in response to the scruple of his own conscience as well as the criticism of others, he appealed to the pope to regularize his position. At length the pope granted his petition, and his band of followers was organized as a religious congregation.

The work that the Franciscans took as their special mission was what we should today call religious evangelism and social service in the cities, especially among "down-and-outers." Francis' own inclination was to serve the humblest of the poor—the unwashed and diseased outcasts of the thick-skinned feudal world. Even the lowliest of men were his brothers, because they were, like him, the children of God.

Yet the order that he founded could not avoid the inevitable. Once the Franciscans were recognized as a religious order, their reputation for piety attracted large numbers of adherents. This meant that the order must develop an organization, administration, government—and, in so doing, it must depart from its founder's example of religious vagabondage, heedless of worldly cares, concerned only for the spirit of Christian love. Nor could the order hold to its founder's example of complete poverty, for inevitably pious persons made gifts to the friars far in excess of their daily need of a crust of bread. Though some of the Franciscans themselves protested at their fate, eventually the order settled into a pattern of monasticism not radically different from that of other orders.

The Dominicans

The founder of the other famous order of friars, the Dominicans, was quite unlike Francis of Assisi. Dominic de Guzmán (c.1170–1221) was a Spanish ecclesiastic. In contrast to Francis, who never became a priest, Dominic was well established in a career in the secular clergy—he was a canon of the cathedral of Osma—before founding his order.

In 1203 St. Dominic set out with his bishop on a trip to Rome, in connection with the business of their Spanish diocese. Their route led them through the south of France, which at that time was a hotbed of the Albigensian heresy (to be explained shortly). At the time of Dominic's visit, the Church authorities had not succeeded in checking this heresy, which was the most serious challenge to the authority of the Church that had arisen up to that time. Dominic became convinced that the reason for the spread of the heresy was that the parish priests were too lazy and too ignorant to combat it. And he resolved to do something toward providing the laity with regular and informed instruction in Catholic doctrine from the mouths of men whose disciplined lives would lend force to the lofty sentiments of the Gospel.

Presently St. Dominic gathered about him a band of fervent and well-educated priests, dedicated to the task he had conceived, and eventually the pope recognized Dominic and his associates as the new Order of Friars Preachers, as they chose to call themselves. The rule of the order included the traditional monastic vows of poverty, chastity, and obedience, but, like the Franciscans, the friars of this new order were destined to serve among the people of the crowded cities and towns and not to live in monasteries.

Their special role was one of study, teaching, and preaching, for the particular purpose of combating heresy. They measured up to their task so well that for centuries the Dominicans were regarded as the Church's academic champions in sacred studies and learned preaching. The most famous philosopher of the Feudal Era, St. Thomas Aquinas (c.1225–c.1274), was a Dominican friar, as was his teacher, the celebrated Albertus Magnus (c.1193–1280). The Franciscans, too, included numerous scholars, but among them learning was a sideline, while it was the first purpose of the Dominicans.

As specialists in the study and teaching of theology, the Dominicans were summoned by the popes of the thirteenth century to be technical experts in the special courts that were set up to check the spread of heresy. These were the courts of the Inquisition. Their association with the Inquisition put a shadow upon the fame of the Black Friars.

The Nuns

Though women were never admitted to the secular clergy, they were not debarred from the monastic vocation. Originally monasticism was a way of life involving a withdrawal from the world and submission to a special discipline of prayer and work, but it was not necessarily coupled with the priestly vocation. In the foundations set up by St. Benedict himself, most of the monks were not priests. Women were therefore not forbidden to take up the monastic way of life, simply because they could not become priests.

The earliest regular nunneries, or monasteries for women, were established by St. Benedict's sister, St. Scholastica. Throughout the Feudal Era nunneries were about as numerous as monasteries for men. The rule governing the routine of a nunnery was generally the same as the Benedictine Rule for monasteries, except that the abbess, whose office was comparable to that of an abbot, was ordinarily under the direction or supervision of an outside ecclesiastical authority. Sometimes this was the abbot of a Benedictine monastery, sometimes it was the bishop of the diocese.

Like men, the women who assumed the monastic vocation took vows of poverty, chastity, and obedience. Commonly they were required to remain within the cloister, and this obligation was more strictly enforced than the similar requirement for men. But not all orders required the nuns to shun the outside world. In some orders the nuns pledged themselves to various forms of service, such as the education of girls or the care of the sick.

Abuses crept into nunneries, as they did into the monasteries for men. But more serious than the corruption arising from the failings of certain individuals was the corruption that sometimes affected the entire institution. As a nunnery became famous for the highmindedness of its members, pious persons would begin to make gifts to it; as the establishment became rich, the nuns would find themselves living in ease and elegance instead of devoting themselves to austere self-sacrifice. Nunneries were especially vulnerable to this kind of corruption, because in the Feudal Era there was no vocation open to women except marriage. Consequently, the nunnery became the normal refuge of women of noble birth who were widowed or who, for one reason or another, failed to marry. Certain nunneries took in only women of this sort, each of whom would be required to make a large gift to the establishment before being admitted as a member. The abbess or prioress of such a foundation was usually a woman of high rank, even a princess.

The Adoration of the Magi—illumination in a fourteenth-century manuscript. (*Bibliothèque Nationale*, Paris)

HERESIES AND THE INQUISITION

An important chapter in the history of the Church in the Feudal Era is concerned with heresy. Under Church law, heresy was the crime of deliberate disbelief in an essential article of the faith preached by the Roman Catholic Church. Evidence of heresy could be either a direct verbal denial of faith or doctrine, or an action or practice that implied such a denial.

In the Feudal Era no heresy arose that repudiated supernatural religion of all forms. However, several heresies developed that either challenged some or all of the tenets of Roman Catholicism or spurned the whole Christian revelation in favor of some other esoteric religion.

Distinct from heresy was another high religious crime that the Church designated as *schism*. A schismatic was a person who accepted all the doctrines of the Church but denied the authority of the hierarchy of the Church. The most formidable schism was the one that involved the Orthodox Church of eastern Europe (p. 262).

Heresy, as we have seen in Chapter 9, was a serious problem of the Church in the time of the Roman Empire. During the earliest centuries of the Feudal Era, this problem virtually disappeared, because the intellectual life of the Dark Ages was too feeble to produce great theological disputes. But in the latter part of the Feudal Era several heresies appeared, some of which became a grave threat to the Church. These were of two kinds: anti-Christian heresies that attacked the basis of the Christian religion, and anticlerical heresies that challenged the traditional role of the clergy but not the basic Christian faith. The most famous of the anti-Christian heresies was that of the Cathari, or Albigensians. The most important of the anticlerical heresies were those of the Waldensians, the Hussites, and the Lollards. These pre-Reformation groups are sometimes called the "first Protestants" in Europe.

The Cathari

The Cathari were so called from a Greek word meaning *purified*. The main tenets of this group were similar to those of heretical groups that arose in the east in the earliest Christian centuries. The cult made its most noticeable appearance in western Europe in the twelfth century, spreading from Italy into southern France, which remained the stronghold of Catharism for several generations. The Cathari were sometimes known as Albigensians, because of their preponderance in the town of Albi in southern France.

The doctrines of Catharism, which are not especially impressive as a body of ideas, seem to have been derived from the old Persian religious conception of a dualism between spirits of good and of evil. This principle, expressed in Zoroastrianism, Mithraism, and numerous other cults, had spread widely in the Roman Empire, and there had become involved with elements of Christianity. According to this conception, two cosmic powers or principles were engaged in a gigantic struggle throughout the universe. One was the principle of good, identified with the realm of the spirit. The other was the principle of evil, identified with the material universe. Their struggle was reproduced in the life of every human being, for the soul of man belonged to the power of good, while the human body was the possession of the power of evil.

This doctrine implied an ethic of the most austere renunciation of the flesh. In rigorous logic, suicide would be the most meritorious of human actions, representing the complete triumph of the spirit over the flesh. Certainly sexual relations, whether within marriage or without, would be evil, since the propagation of the flesh would mean an increase of the realm of the dark power. And any social institution that made a concession to materialism would be tinged with evil. Hence the whole of traditional

Christianity was founded upon an evil premise, because it held that God had been incarnated in the human body of Christ, and this corporeal embodiment of Christ was celebrated daily in the sacrament of the Eucharist.

At the height of the movement, which came at the beginning of the thirteenth century, the Cathari had a full-fledged organization, with priests and bishops. But their clergy apparently did not form a rigidly separate caste above the laity. Generally its members were nonprofessionals, for whom their religious office was an occupation of their hours after work. In some places the movement enrolled more than half the population, including noblemen, merchants, and even some renegade Catholic clerics. For a time the Count of Toulouse, the most powerful feudal lord in the south of France, was a member of the cult. Another stronghold was Carcassonne, page 484.

Since the local clergy was unable to check the spread of this heresy, the papacy took up the task. As the first move, an attempt was made to deal with the problem by means of persuasion, and the best preachers of Europe were dispatched into the affected regions. When the campaign of persuasion failed, the popes, early in the thirteenth century, turned to more forcible measures: more vigorous enforcement of the Church laws against heresy, to which secular rulers were induced to give their assistance.

The Waldensians

Other heresies arose from the protest of poor and humble men against the overweening pride, pomp, and wealth of the ecclesiastical hierarchy. In its origin, Franciscanism expressed such a protest, but this movement ultimately became a support for the Church rather than a challenge to it, because its founder was a man of unquestioning devotion to Church authority. Moreover St. Francis showed great tact in his dealings with the magnates of the Church. But other movements, expressing much the same spirit as that which animated the Franciscans, developed into anticlerical heresies.

One of the most important of these involved those known as the Waldensians or "the poor men of Lyons." Their name comes from that of their founder, Peter Waldo of Lyons in France. Like St. Francis, he was a man of means who experienced a profound religious conversion, leading him to give away his wealth and begin preaching to the common people. Soon he gathered a band of like-minded persons about him.

At the outset the movement did not propound heretical doctrines, for its theological ideas were too simple to give occasion for intellectual discussion. It merely expressed the notion that the clergy was less concerned with religion than with wealth and pride of place. Soon, however, the established clergy declared the movement heretical, on the ground that it permitted laymen to preach, and that it thus implicitly denied the sacramental monopoly of the ordained priesthood. In the course of time, moreover, the Waldensians came to uphold certain practices and ideas that were in clear opposition to the official teachings of the Church. For example, they confessed their sins to one another, and this practice cast an aspersion upon the sacramental doctrine that confession must be made to an ordained priest, as a condition of receiving penance. The Waldensians also supported the idea, common to several heretical sects, that priestly rites were of no effect when the priest himself was sinful. This was an idea that the Church could not admit, since it denied the principle that sacraments are a miracle, accomplished by supernatural power and not by the power of the priest as a man. The Church did not hold that it was proper for priests to be sinful, but it could not accept the idea that only a man free of sin could be a priest, for in a sinful world it would be impossible to recruit priests solely from among the blameless.

The Lollards

The Lollards were the members of an English heretical movement that was inspired by the teachings of a remarkable English priest, John Wyclif (c.1324–1384). Though a priest himself, who had made an English translation of the Bible, Wyclif spent most of his life denouncing clerical corruption, wealth, and arrogance. His earliest prescription for the reform of the Church was to deprive churchmen of all property whatsoever. Naturally this suggestion led to arguments, and in the course of dispute, Wyclif was driven to a still more extreme position. When his adversaries argued that the clergy should have a position of special dignity because they were charged with a special sacramental power, Wyclif questioned the validity of the sacraments, including even the Eucharist. Such sacramental powers as he conceded to the clergy were dependent, he taught, upon the clergyman's purity of life. Despite the boldness of his views, Wyclif himself remained unmolested, for he had powerful lay protection. But his followers, who included priests as well as laymen, were objects of one of the few systematic persecutions of heresy in English history.

The Hussites

The Hussites were members of an heretical movement that flourished in Bohemia, a part of present-day Czechoslovakia. Their teacher was John Hus, a priest of Prague, who was burned at the stake in 1415 as punishment for his having spread heretical doctrines. The ideas of Hus and his followers were so similar to those of Wyclif and his Lollard disciples in England that you may regard them as practically identical. To explain the relationship, it has been suggested that the ideas of Wyclif were brought to Bohemia by some of the attendants in the retinue of an English princess who married a prince of a Bohemian house which at that time held the German imperial throne. The Hussite movement had a political significance, as well as religious, for it became an expression of nascent Bohemian nationalism, directed against German rule in Bohemia. It will be discussed again later.

The Inquisition

Against all these heresies and others, the Church made use of the formidable weapon of the Inquisition. This institution made its first appearance in 1203, when Pope Innocent III sent special papal judges to "inquire into" cases of heresy in certain places where the bishops' courts seemed unable to cope with its rapid spread. These new courts proved much more effective than the regular episcopal courts, and, accordingly, in 1229 they were made a permanent institution for the specific purpose of dealing with heresy.

Though these courts were new in the thirteenth century, the prosecution of heresy was a long-established practice. In the earliest centuries of Christianity, bishops sat in judgment on suspected heretics and imposed on them various spiritual penalties, including excommunication. When Christianity became the official religion of the Roman Empire, heresy was made a crime against the state as well as an offense against the Church. Thus it appears as one of the capital offenses included in the *Corpus Juris Civilis* of the Byzantine emperor Justinian the Great.

The practice begun under the Roman regime carried over into Europe in the early Feudal Era. Persons accused of heresy were tried in the courts of the bishops. If the accused person were found guilty but repented, the bishop usually imposed only a spiritual penance, such as an obligation of prayer and fasting for a specified period, or the requirement that the repentant heretic make a pilgrimage. If the heretic refused to recant and repent, he would be excommunicated and put in prison. In a case of the utmost gravity, the heretic would be "relaxed to the secular arm"—that is, turned over to the secular ruler, who would impose the death penalty. As a churchman, the bishop could not administer a punishment involving the shedding of blood, but such punishments were enforced by secular rulers for religious as well as secular crimes.

This procedure was used throughout the early Feudal Era, and, since heresy was uncommon, it proved a sufficient means of dealing with the problem. In the twelfth and thirteenth centuries, however, when heretical movements flourished with unprecedented vigor, the bishops' courts were swamped, especially those in northern Italy and southern France, where heresy became epidemic.

It was for this reason that the papacy took over from the local bishops the principal responsibility for suppressing heresy. Not only were new courts established, under judges responsible directly to the pope, but secular rulers were induced to take more severe measures in support of the campaign against heresy, and ruthless means, including the use of torture, were used to detect heretics and strike terror into the hearts of those inclined to take up with heretical movements.

In order to be fair, without excusing the excesses of the Inquisition, we must bear in mind how horrible the crime of heresy seemed to the faithful followers of the Church in the Feudal Era. In their view, no crime could be more terrible than that of deliberately renouncing all or part of the religion that God had revealed to men and that was essential to the salvation of the soul. It was the more heinous for the reason that the heretic was apt to corrupt his family, friends, and others, thereby making them liable to the awful risk of hell. Such a crime merited no less a punishment than death, and the best means of inflicting the penalty was by burning at the stake, since the slow agony of the burning would give the victim a last chance to repent his crime. Thus he might save his soul from hell, even if it were too late to save his body.

The Inquisition regularly used torture to force heretics to confess their crimes and also to compel others to give evidence that would incriminate those who were suspected. The Church did not sanction the indiscriminate use of torture—it was not to be used unless other methods of gaining the truth had failed and only when the inquisitors had good reason to believe that torture would bring forth evidence of heresy. Moreover, the inquisitors were not supposed to accept a confession extracted under torture, unless the accused person confirmed the confession after the duress was removed. But these regulations were often disregarded.

Capital punishment was not the usual sentence. Most defendants confessed guilt and professed repentance, even though they

The Pentecost—central figure in the tympanum over the central portal of the Abbey Church of La Madeleine at Vézelay, France, a complex Romanesque sculpture, about 1110. (*Archives Photographiques*)

might remain convinced in their own minds of their innocence, for by bowing to the court, they could get off with the relatively light sentence usually meted out for the first offense. Even those who were adjudged guilty, despite their persistence in professing their innocence, were more often sentenced to life imprisonment than "relaxed to the secular arm" and put to death. But the severest punishment was ordinarily given to the "relapsed heretic"—that is, one who had previously been accused, pleaded guilty, been given a light sentence, and then had again fallen into the hands of the Inquisition on a new charge of heresy.

The peak of the papal Inquisition was reached in the early thirteenth century. The courts in southern France and northern Italy were busiest, but the institution spread over most of the continent, and prosecutions continued throughout the Feudal Era. The Inquisition, however, was never introduced into England. There, cases of heresy continued to be tried in the regular courts of the bishops, not the newer papal courts. But, as elsewhere, the secular government imposed the death penalty for heresy, after conviction in an episcopal court, when the circumstances of the case seemed to warrant the most severe punishment.

CONCLUSION

Until about 1500 the Church succeeded in suppressing at least the public manifestations of all significant heresies. The religion of western Europe, Roman Christianity, was a unity—in doctrine and in practice as well as in its hierarchical organization. In the century that followed the death of John Hus, however, religious differences multiplied and became increasingly difficult to suppress.

With the work of Martin Luther (1483–1546), who challenged the doctrinal and ecclesiastical authority of the Church shortly after the turn of the sixteenth century, that impressive unity was destroyed; western Christianity was broken into many fragments. With this event, the religious history of the Feudal Era came to an end, and the modern era of religious history began.

Suggestions for Further Reading

Source Materials

Anthologies and Collected Documents

F. Le V. Baumer, ed., *Main Currents of Western Thought* (New York, 1952), Part I.
An excellent collection of selections from the writings of the outstanding thinkers of the Feudal Era, including those concerned with religion.

G. H. Knoles and R. K. Snyder, eds., *Readings in Western Civilization* (rev. ed., New York, 1954), pp. 272–279.
Selections from the definition of the sacraments by the Council of Florence (1439) and from Thomas Aquinas' logical proof for the existence of God.

O. J. Thatcher and E. R. McNeal, *A Source Book for Mediaeval History* (New York, 1905).
See the sections on religious thought.

Contemporary Writings

Augustine, Bishop of Hippo, *Confessions*.
There are numerous editions of this classic statement of faith by one of Christianity's greatest saints.

Dante Alighieri, *The Divine Comedy*.
There are many editions, including paperbacks, of this, the greatest poetic work of the Feudal Era.

Francis of Assisi, *The Little Flowers of St. Francis of Assisi*.
A classic of medieval pietism. Available in many editions.

Thomas à Kempis, *The Imitation of Christ*.

A beautiful example of late medieval piety.

Basic Writings of St. Thomas Aquinas, edited by A. C. Pegis (2 vols., New York, 1945).

A fine, well-edited selection from the writings of the greatest Scholastic theologian of the Feudal Era.

William, Archbishop of Tyre, *A History of Deeds Done beyond the Sea;* translated by E. A. Babcock and A. C. Krey (2 vols., New York, 1943).

A classical description of the Levant in the age of the Crusades and of the deeds of the crusaders.

John Wycliffe, *Select English Writings,* edited by H. E. Winn; preface by H. B. Workman (London, 1929).

A good selection from the writings of the great English religious critic.

Secondary Works

S. Baldwin, *The Organization of Medieval Christianity* (New York, 1929).

One of the best brief descriptions of the Roman Christian Church in the Feudal Era.

E. Barker, *The Crusades* (London, 1925).

A standard account.

J. Bryce, *The Holy Roman Empire* (new ed., New York, 1926).

A brilliant classic, now somewhat superseded by later studies.

C. G. Crump and E. F. Jacob, eds., *The Legacy of the Middle Ages* (Oxford, 1926).

The first essay in this book, by F. M. Pourclie, is a brilliant description of the place of religion and the church in the life of feudal Europe.

A. C. Flick, *The Decline of the Medieval Church* (2 vols., New York, 1930).

A scholarly history, especially valuable for its treatment of the relations of the Church with society.

J. Huizinga, *The Waning of the Middle Ages* (New York, 1924).

A near-classic essay on the transition from the Feudal Era to modern times; includes brilliant discussions of religion and the Church and their place in the transition.

K. S. Latourette, *A History of Christianity* (New York, 1953).

A fine general survey.

H. C. Lea, *A History of the Inquisition of the Middle Ages* (3 vols., New York, 1908–1911).

An old book, and somewhat biased, but still a standard work. Highly interesting.

R. A. Newhall, *The Crusades* (New York, 1927).

A fine, brief, and well-balanced history.

S. R. Packard, *Europe and the Church under Innocent III* (New York, 1927).

An excellent brief study of the greatest of the Roman popes and his influence upon his times.

J. H. Randall, Jr., *The Making of the Modern Mind* (rev. ed., Boston, 1940), Chapters I–IV.

This is an excellent survey of the intellectual history of Europe from the beginning of the Feudal Era to the present.

S. Runciman, *A History of the Crusades* (3 vols., Cambridge, England, 1951–1954).

A standard, scholarly account.

P. Sabatier, *The Life of St. Francis of Assisi;* translated by Louise S. Houghton (London, 1894).

A famous biography of the great medieval pietist.

H. O. Taylor, *The Medieval Mind* (rev. ed., Cambridge, Mass., 1949).

A classic history of religion and thought in the Feudal Era.

21

The Cultural Synthesis
of the Feudal Era

A Stained Glass Window—fifteenth-century, German. The illustration on page 470 is a detail of this. (Courtesy, The Metropolitan Museum of Art)

The cultural life of the Feudal Era in the history of western European civilization was a synthesis of Greco-Roman, Christian and Germanic elements, reformulated in terms of the new experiences of men in their struggle to survive and attain the good life in the European wilderness. This cultural life began to show a distinctive pattern about the eleventh century, but it achieved its greatest brilliance in the thirteenth century as we will see later in this chapter.

The prevailing mood of the feudal civilization of western Europe was the mood of Roman Catholic Christianity. Yet we must not think of this civilization as wholly religious in outlook, because it included a vigorous secular and naturalistic culture, which gained expression, for example, in the literature of fantasy, myth, and legend, and in the bawdy songs of the university student. This secular culture, springing from the living experiences of the masses of the people of Europe in the Feudal Era, was no less important a part of the civilization of the time than the religion that Europe inherited from the eastern provinces of the Roman Empire.

The Christian component in the culture of feudal Europe gained its principal expression in the teachings of the Church. Since the Church tolerated no challenge to its doctrines, and these bore upon all aspects of life, it perhaps might seem that religion provided an answer to *all* the questions arising in men's minds, and that thus it became a barrier to intellectual progress. In a sense this is true, and the Church did hinder new intellectual exploration in certain directions. On the other hand, it must be remembered that Catholic dogma was much less rigid in the feudal period than it was to become later, after the Protestant Reformation (see Chapter 24). In the Feudal Era there was wide room for differences of opinion among men who accepted Catholic dogma, and the influence of the Church was therefore less authoritarian than one might suppose. In some fields, moreover, the influence of the Church was remarkably creative and fruitful. This is especially true of painting, sculpture, and architecture, and it also holds true for literature and speculative philosophy. Even in the natural sciences considerable progress was made during the Feudal Era, and some of this progress came through the efforts of churchmen.

Romanesque Mural— from the Hermitage of the "Cruz de Maderuelo" at Segovia, Spain. Segovia, a favored city of the Romans, later conquered and lost several times by the Moors, is noted for its many medieval churches and palaces. Romanesque art there shows a strong Byzantine influence. Compare this mural with the illustration on page 251. (Courtesy of the Prado Museum, Madrid)

Despite the conspicuous role of the Christian heritage in feudal civilization, the inheritance from the pagan world of classical antiquity was also of great importance. From our vantage point, we can see that much learning and literature of the classical world was lost with the breakdown of the Roman Empire, and much of what survived was only dimly understood and appreciated by the monkish scribes who copied and studied the ancient texts. But, in their time, the men of the Feudal Era probably had little sense of a break with the ancient past. Just as some of them persisted in the dream of reviving the Roman Empire, so, probably, some men imagined themselves living in the same civilization as the great pagan writers of Greece and Rome. The illusion is not hard to understand, when we remember that Latin remained the common written language throughout western Europe.

Unlike the classical heritage, the Germanic contribution to the new European civilization was that of a virile, robust people, only recently removed from barbarism. An obvious mark of the German influence was the development of a whole new group of languages, with a literary tradition distinct from that of the Latin countries. In social institutions, Germanic traditions were perpetuated in the development of feudal and customary law. These Germanic contributions were more conspicuous in the lands north of the Danube and east of the Rhine, but traces of Germanic influence were to be found in all lands of western Europe.

If we compare the civilization of Europe in the Feudal Era with that of classical antiquity, we are tempted to look upon it as merely a debasement or distortion of the older civilization. And if we compare it with the civilization of the western world in our own time, we are apt to dismiss it as crude, naïve, primitive. Yet we need not measure it by either of these standards. Instead, we should look upon it as a civilization—or a phase of ours—in its own right, and a truly remarkable one, when we consider the chaotic times out of which it emerged. In some respects it fell short of the achievements of earlier times, and in others it did not measure up to those of later ages. Nevertheless, it produced a number of monumental achievements of its own in thought and art, some of which have survived to enrich the culture of the modern world.

EDUCATION IN THE FEUDAL ERA IN THE WEST

A survey of feudal civilization may conveniently begin with a consideration of its provisions for education. And we may note, as the dominating characteristic in the earlier feudal period, that education was a clerical monopoly. Both students and teachers were clerics, for no one believed that laymen had much need of book learning.

Monastery Schools

In the darkness of the Merovingian Age, the only schools in existence were maintained by the monasteries. They assumed this responsibility in answer to the insistence of St. Benedict that his monks should do a certain amount of reading and studying. The first schools were therefore intended for the instruction of novice monks. Gradually, however, they began to accept as students boys who did not intend to become monks but were destined for the secular clergy. Until the time of Charles the Great, these schools—and the libraries associated with them—were the only places where scholarly activity continued.

Palace Schools

By the command of Charles the Great, a new kind of school was established about the beginning of the ninth century. This was the palace school, maintained in one of the emperor's palaces. As in the monastic schools, the students and teachers were clerics, but not all of them were destined for the service of the Church. Some took posts in the administration of the government, for in the time of Charles, as for centuries thereafter, clergymen filled every office in the government for which a knowledge of reading and writing was required. In the reign of Charles the Great and his immediate successors these schools attracted teachers of

great repute, such as Alcuin of York, who was regarded as the most learned man of his age, and John the Scot, who was the most important philosopher of the Dark Ages. But with the waning of the Carolingian dynasty, these palace schools declined and disappeared, and education became again a monopoly of the monastic schools.

Cathedral Schools

In the eleventh century a new kind of school attained importance. This was the cathedral school, maintained by the bishop for the education of the priests of his diocese. The number of these schools greatly increased when the papacy, under the influence of the Cluniac reform movement, ordered all bishops to make provision for the improved training of the clergy. Despite the intention, the cathedral schools did not bring about a marked improvement in the intellectual level of the parish priests; but they did at least provide a refuge where men of studious tastes could pursue a career of scholarship without having to take monastic vows.

Notable among the cathedral schools was Chartres, where John of Salisbury taught and wrote about ancient Latin literature and political theory, and Paris, which was the scene of Peter Abelard's first academic success.

The "Seven Liberal Arts"

Much the same curriculum was used in the monastic schools and the cathedral schools, and also, later on, in the preparatory "arts" course in the universities. This comprised seven topics, known as the "liberal arts." The elementary subjects were: Latin grammar, dialectic or logic, and rhetoric. These three studies were called the *trivium*. The other four topics, regarded as more ad-

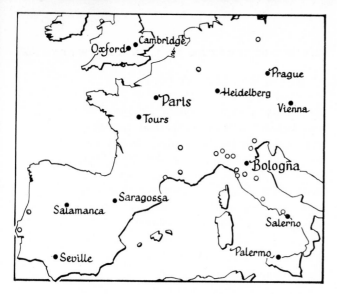

Medieval Universities

vanced, made up the *quadrivium:* geometry, arithmetic, music, and astronomy.

Books were extremely scarce, and those that did exist were, of course, handwritten. Those in the libraries of monasteries and cathedral schools were used largely by masters, less often by students. A student was lucky if he could afford a few sheets of parchment on which to take lecture notes. After committing the notes to memory, he would scrape the writing off the surface of the parchment, so that it could be used again.

The Rise of the Universities

The university as we know it today had its origin in the cathedral towns of the Feudal Era. A number of European universities date their foundation from the thirteenth, fourteenth, or fifteenth centuries. Those of Bologna and Paris go back even earlier, to the late twelfth century.

The first universities developed out of cathedral schools, and it is not easy to say at just what point of time they ceased to be bishop's schools and became universities. But it is possible to establish the marks distinguishing the one kind of institution from the other. In the first place, a university formed a corporation, with a legal identity of its own, and to a large degree it was self-governing. In the second place, a university usually comprised more than one faculty or school. The older monastic and cathedral schools, on the other hand, usually had only a single faculty, that of the liberal arts. Moreover, its members were simply members of the clergy of the cathedral or monastery, wholly under the orders of the bishop or abbot.

The faculties in the universities were commonly those of arts, canon law, civil law, medicine, and theology. In the Feudal Era, however, few universities included all these faculties. Many universities owed their renown to the excellence of only one of their faculties. Thus, for instance, Salerno, in Sicily, which was one of the oldest of all universities, was especially famous for its faculty of medicine. Civil law was the specialty of Bologna, and Paris was foremost in the study of theology.

Nearly every university included a faculty of arts, granting the degree of bachelor of arts. The curriculum leading to this degree was the seven studies of the *trivium* and *quadrivium,* but the level of instruction was higher than in the monastic and cathedral schools. A student receiving the bachelor's degree in the arts might leave the university to take some kind of modest employment in the Church. Or, if he wished eventually to teach in the arts faculty, he would continue until he qualified for the degree of master of arts.

The other faculties ordinarily admitted only students who had already earned the degree of bachelor of arts. The course of study in these faculties, which awarded advanced degrees, might require a total of twelve or fourteen years of university study. Great prestige attached to the doctor's degree in theology awarded by the University of Paris. An advanced degree in civil law, which required mastery of the principles of Roman law embodied in Justinian's *Corpus*

Juris Civilis, would open a career in public administration. Comparatively few universities maintained faculties of medicine. The graduates of these universities served as physicians to important personages; ordinary citizens, as we noted earlier, received their medical care from the more humble surgeon-barber, who learned his art as a guild apprentice. Roman law and medicine were the subjects that eventually attracted laymen to the universities.

The medieval student was generally hard-working, for the course of study was rigorous; and, for want of books, he was obliged to rely heavily upon his memory. Yet students were also given to riotous amusements, which won them a reputation for drinking, brawling, and wenching. Many of them lived as vagabonds, wandering from one university to another, taking courses from famous teachers at each of several institutions in succession. These wandering scholars known as *goliards* were especially notorious. Though most of them were destined for the priesthood, their favorite amusement was composing and singing scandalous parodies of the sacred rituals. This goliardic verse is a picturesque portion of feudal secular literature.

PHILOSOPHY IN THE WESTERN CHRISTIAN SYNTHESIS

The civilization of feudal Europe brought forth an impressive body of philosophical speculation. Since the fundamental assumptions of all men of the Feudal Era in Europe were religious, philosophical thought was derived principally from Christian doctrine. Yet it also was indebted to the pagan Greek and Roman cultures, because the supreme task and brilliant achievement of the philosophers of the west in the feudal epoch was to reconcile classical pagan philosophies with the Christian epic and the body of early Christian philosophy that had arisen around it.

The Influence of Plato

In the early centuries of the Feudal Era the most important and influential of the ancient pagan philosophers was Plato. The writings of Plato himself were not well known to the thinkers of the west, but his influence was transmitted to them through some of the early western Church leaders. The most notable of these was Augustine, Bishop of Hippo (354–430), who had been a Neoplatonist before becoming a Christian. Throughout his writings, he developed one of Plato's basic tenets: that the material world, known to us through our senses, is inferior to another world of immaterial "ideas," which are the perfect prototypes of imperfect actual things. Another source of Platonic influence was in the writings of Boethius (480–524), nearly as widely read as those of Augustine. Boethius was not a cleric, and he therefore did not attempt to expound theology. But in the most famous of his works, *Consolations of Philosophy,* he gave a poetic paraphrase of one of Plato's principal dialogues, the *Timaeus.* In it, he developed the idea that happiness does not depend upon pleasure but upon goodness, and that goodness comes from our perception of the divine pattern behind the mundane world.

John the Scot

After Augustine and Boethius, the history of western philosophy shows a sharp decline until the eleventh century. The one thinker of importance in this period of darkness is John the Scot, or Johannes Scotus Erigena, who lived from about 800 to 877. His was an astonishing achievement, considering that he was a churchman living in the credulous ninth century, for he asserted that "philosophy"—by which he meant human reason—is equal to revelation as a source of truth. Moreover, in contrast to Augustine and despite the condemnation of his views by two church councils, he upheld the principle of the unlimited freedom of the human will.

The Age of Scholasticism

Scholastic philosophy is the name given to the kind of philosophical speculation that prevailed in western Europe after the intellectual decline of the Dark Ages. In a strict sense, it refers to the work of the "school men"—that is, those who were connected with the cathedral and monastic schools. In a more general sense, it signifies the greatest products of philosophy of the period from the twelfth century to the close of the Feudal Era. All the philosophers whom we shall discuss hereafter in this chapter may thus be called Scholastics.

Scholastic philosophy remains the philosophy of Catholic scholarship in our own time. It is characterized by a great reliance upon logic rather than upon the scientific observation of facts, although, of course, modern Scholasticism does not reject the findings of science.

Anselm. One of the first of the Scholastics was Anselm of Bec (1033–1109), whose career gives evidence of the success of the Cluniac reform movement in raising the standards of clerical scholarship. He is most famous for his "ontological" proof of the existence of God. God, Anselm argues, is by definition the greatest being we can possibly think of. God therefore certainly exists as a concept in our minds. But a supreme being that exists outside our minds, as well as inside, would be still greater than one that exists only within our minds. And since we can conceive of such a being, we know that the being that exists within our minds has the attribute of also existing outside our minds.

By this chain of reasoning, Anselm thus made it seem a violation of logic to deny that God exists apart from the human mind. This remains one of the several basic agruments that some theologians cite to prove the existence of God, though it is rejected by many others.

"Realism" *versus* "Nominalism"

The contemporaries of Anselm would have called him a *realist*. Thus they would identify him with one of two factions involved in a bitter philosophical debate that raged all through the twelfth century. The other faction was that of the *nominalists*.

The realists were those who, following the Platonic tradition, held that reality resides in universal "forms" or "ideas" rather than in individual things. For example, mankind is more real than John W. Smith, an individual man, who will soon die and disappear while mankind persists. The nominalists, on the other hand, held that reality lies in the particular things, such as John W. Smith, whereas universal concepts, such as mankind, are only words or names—in Latin, *nomina*. The realists were the more conservative, while the nominalists were innovators. But both sides became involved in difficulties in dealing with such theological concepts as those involved in the doctrine of the Trinity. The realists found it hard to maintain that the three persons of the Trinity were as real as the idea of God, since the persons are more particular concepts. Likewise, the nominalists found it hard to maintain that the idea of God was as real as the three particular manifestations of the divine, since by their view, the particular is more real than the universal.

Abelard. The solution of this dilemma was the achievement of Peter Abelard (1079–1142). His renown as a thinker is overshadowed, however, by his fame as a figure in one of the greatest love stories of history.

As a young man, Abelard was a teacher at the cathedral school of Notre Dame in Paris. His brilliance attracted the attention of an eminent Church dignitary, Canon Fulbert, who engaged Abelard as a tutor for his niece Héloïse. This young lady is said to have been beautiful, and certainly she must have been unusual, for it was uncommon at that time for a woman to be taught to read and write, much less to receive instruction in philosophy. As sometimes happens, the brilliant young tutor fell in love with his pupil, she became pregnant, and they were secretly married. When her plight became known to her uncle, he took a savage revenge, hiring thugs to seize and emasculate Abelard. After bearing a son, Héloïse retired from the world to found a nunnery. Abelard became a monk in the abbey of St. Denis of Paris, later heading a small monastery in Brittany. Finding monastic life irksome, he eventually set himself up as an independent lecturer and made his fame and living as a teacher. He and Héloïse continued to exchange letters, which comprise one of the great classics of romantic literature. The tenderness of these letters gives a more admirable picture of Abelard than other sources, because as a teacher and writer his vanity was as great—and as obvious—as his brilliance.

Abelard's philosophy has been called a breath of fresh air in the dusty Scholastic controversies of his time, for he was a champion of human reason, who boldly insisted upon a rational appraisal of the data of revelation. His most famous book is *Sic et Non* (*Yes and No*), in which he quotes many passages from Scripture and shows contradictory interpretations of them by various official authorities. The only solution to the dilemma, he holds, is the use of reason. And if reason is to stand in judgment over contradictory revelations, then reason, rather than revelation, becomes the supreme guide.

To solve the dispute between the realists and the nominalists, Abelard developed a point of view later called *conceptualism*. This denies the extreme Platonic position taken over by the realists, which holds that universals have the sole claim to reality. However, conceptualism concedes reality to ideas in three "modes": *ante rem* ("before the thing"), *in re* ("in the thing"), and *post rem* ("after the thing"). This means that a universal, such as *cattle,* exists first as an idea in the mind of God before the existence of any particular cow. Then it exists in some particular cow, as the "form" which gives "cow-ness" to the animal. Finally, it exists after the particular cow is dead and gone, as a mental conception in the minds of all those who abstract the idea of "cow" from seeing the particular cow and others like it. This sensible solution of the argument between the realists and nominalists was generally accepted by the leading Scholastic philosophers for the rest of the Feudal Era.

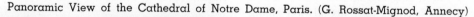

Panoramic View of the Cathedral of Notre Dame, Paris. (G. Rossat-Mignod, Annecy)

The Aristotelian Revolution

Toward the close of the twelfth century there was a great upheaval in western thought. This was caused by the discovery in the west of many more of Aristotle's writings than were known before. Not all the works of Aristotle were recovered, for some had been lost in antiquity, but scholars came into possession of most of the texts that we know today. These were enough to give the outline of a complete system of philosophy.

The texts were not recovered in the original Greek version. They came into western Europe in the form of Latin translations made from earlier Arabic translations. Though the Moslems were not great creative thinkers in philosophy, they were profound students of Aristotle, and some Moslem scholars, notably Averroës (p. 278) and Avicenna, wrote valuable commentaries on his ideas. These commentaries, as well as the texts of Aristotle himself, were introduced into western Europe as a result of the growing cultural interchange between Islam and the west that followed upon the Crusades and the revival of trade across the Mediterranean.

The learned men of the west were electrified by what they now discovered of Aristotle's thought. Unlike Plato, who often merely suggested his leading thoughts, Aristotle had worked out a careful system of metaphysics, and his position was much more congenial to Christian doctrine than was Plato's. Plato, distrusting the world of concrete things because they are always changing or decaying, regarded only "forms" or "ideas" as real. For him, the material world becomes real only insofar as it partakes of "form." And since "form" is of the same essence as God, who is pure form or idea, uncontaminated by matter, the world is real only insofar as it exists in the mind of God. This position approaches pantheism, and is therefore difficult to reconcile with Christianity.

Aristotle, on the other hand, believed that reality requires both matter and form —only God exists as form without matter. This position coincided with the Christian doctrine of two realms: the spiritual and the material, over both of which God rules. Moreover, Aristotle's belief that all things in the universe have a purpose coincided with the Christian conception of a divine design, including God's plan for the salvation of the human soul, which is the supreme end, or purpose, of human existence.

On closer reading, however, Aristotle's thought raised serious difficulties. For example, Aristotle held that both form and matter were eternal, while Christian doctrine held that the material world existed only after a certain occasion, which was the divine creation of the material universe. Likewise, according to the Christian outlook, the human soul, though immortal, does not exist prior to the birth of the particular man with whom it is identified.

The great task of the Scholastic philosophers, therefore, was the reconciliation of Aristotle's ideas with Christian dogma. One of the most prolific of the thinkers who grappled with this problem was Albertus Magnus or Albert the Great, who lived from about 1193 to 1280. A German by birth and one of the earliest scholars of the new Dominican order of friars, Albert spent most of his time teaching in Cologne and Paris. But, though his writings are vast and his personal achievements are considerable, his name is obscured by that of his more famous pupil, Thomas Aquinas.

Thomas Aquinas

The pre-eminence of Thomas Aquinas (1225–1274) among Scholastic philosophers is unquestioned; in our own time his writings form the only system of philosophy that may be taught with official endorsement in Catholic educational institutions. His career exemplifies the cosmopolitanism of the learned world of the Feudal Era, for he was born in Italy, studied there and in Germany, and reached the summit of his career as a professor in the University of Paris.

Thomas's masterpiece is his *Summa Theologica.* As the title suggests, it is a complete compendium of Christian theology. A modern translation of it runs to twenty-four volumes. His *Summa contra Gentiles* is a much shorter work, but it has greater philosophical interest, because it was written to defend Christian dogma against the Moslems and other nonbelievers. It therefore makes less appeal to Scriptural authority, which a non-Christian would not find persuasive, and depends more upon the appeal to reason.

Thomas's philosophizing begins with the problem of the existence of God, and his argumentation on this point is interesting as a sample of Scholastic thought. He is not satisfied with Anselm's ontological proof, which we have noted earlier, because it presumes to deduce God's existence from an idea or mental conception of his essence. That is a good Platonic procedure, but Thomas will have none of it, because no man, he holds, can ever hope to know the essence of God. To replace this argument, Thomas adapts to a Christian context a series of proofs drawn from Aristotle.

His chain of reasoning begins with the observation that there is movement in the universe, and since movement is the result of previous movement, there must be, at the start of the train of movement, an "Unmoved Mover," or God. Similarly, according to Thomas, everthing that happens has a cause, hence there must be an Uncaused Cause, or God. Likewise, since there is such a thing as "necessity"—or order— in the physical world, there must be a source of all necessity, and this also establishes the existence of God. The final argument is that there is an obvious purpose in the universe, and as the existence of a watch implies the existence of a watchmaker, this establishes that there must be an author of

the purpose of the universe. Though theologicans still cite this "teleological proof," as it is called, it has been disputed by the modern philosopher Immanuel Kant.

Thomas Aquinas Conducting a Discussion among Dominican Monks—while a disputatious devil (below) argues a point. This miniature was made by Jean Fouquet (c.1415–c.1480), French illuminator and court painter to Charles VII and Louis IX for a fifteenth-century manuscript. (Courtesy of the Musée Conde, Chantilly, France)

In his theology St. Thomas discussed a vast range of topics, from angels to devils, from sacraments to sin. And in his discussion of moral philosophy he also touched upon some of the basic problems of legal, political, and economic theory—even poetry and art. No other important philosopher has ever attempted to construct on so grand a scale such a consistent moral philosophy to explain rationally every problem in the universe. The degree to which Thomas succeeded or failed in his attempt remains, of course, open to question as between Catholic and non-Catholic philosophers. Some of the latter would question, moreover, whether Thomas was as open-minded as a philosopher should be, since his avowed aim was to use philosophy as a means of proving beliefs, drawn from revealed religion that he was prepared to accept without proof, if necessary, solely on the basis of faith. Yet few philosophers would be unwilling to accord him great praise for the majesty of his attempt and the enormous intellectual labor that went into it.

The Great Franciscans: Roger Bacon and William of Ockham

Thomas Aquinas eventually became the official philosopher of the Church, and, although the prestige of Aristotle was later established through him, the victory of Thomism was not immediate. The Dominicans became the natural champions of Thomistic thought, but other versions of theology and philosophy contested its vogue. Of these, the most important are linked with the names of several distinguished Franciscan friars. One of these Franciscans, Roger Bacon (c.1214–c.1294), was for many years a professor at Oxford University, where he seems to have been an impassioned student of mathematics and science. In philosophy he severely criticized Aristotelian Scholastics. His animus seems not so much against Aristotle as

against poor translations of Aristotle's writings and slavish devotion to Aristotle's every word, real or imaginary. Bacon also blasted the general ignorance of clerics in charge of souls. He was in constant trouble with his Order, which first banished him from Oxford to Paris and later burned his books and imprisoned him for fourteen years.

William of Ockham—or Occam (died c.1349), an Englishman, is often called the greatest scholastic after Thomas Aquinas, but his career was very different. In a great quarrel that divided the Franciscan Order, he was charged with the heresy of denying transubstantiation. The pope excommunicated him, but he escaped to Germany. There he became the protegé and intellectual champion of the Emperor Louis of Bavaria, a bitter enemy of the pope who was also under excommunication. In logic William was a nominalist—of a far more sophisticated type than the old twelfth-century nominalists, drawing a distinction, in surprisingly modern fashion, between true logic of things and the false and misleading logic of words. While Ockham himself did not draw the most radical conclusions from his radical distinction, it was a remarkable anticipation of the later history of philosophy.

In that respect, William of Ockham stands for the weakening of the tremendous religious tradition previously enshrined as the principal concern of Scholastic philosophy. In his thought, as in his antipapal activities, he represents the waning of the Feudal Era. After his time Scholasticism degenerated into more and more fruitless logic-chopping. There would be no new and fresh approaches to the perennial problems of philosophy until after the Renaissance and the Protestant Reformation.

The Christian Mystics

Not all the religious thinkers of the Feudal Era approved the rational speculation of the Scholastics. A certain number of ecclesiastical leaders considered such rational inquiry into matters of faith a sign of impiety. They assumed that a simple acceptance of the creed and tradition of the Church was quite enough for salvation. More important were the contemplatives, or mystics, who, while not hostile to rationalism, did not consider reason the best guide to religious truth. They emphasized, instead, the practice of contemplation, from which would come the experience of a personal union between the believer and God. To some churchmen who did not share their views, their emphasis on contemplation seemed to suggest that the sacraments were superfluous. For this reason, many of the great mystics were suspected of heresy, while other mystics were hailed as saints.

One outstanding orthodox mystic was Bernard of Clairvaux, whom we have already encountered (p. 510) as a Cistercian abbot and leader of the reform movement in the Church. In the next century Bonaventura (1221–1274) became famous for his attacks upon the rationalists and his extravagant praise of the beauties of the mystic experience. Also notable was Thomas à Kempis (1379–1471), whose *Imitation of Christ* is still widely read by Protestants as well as Catholics.

SCIENCE IN THE AGE OF SCHOLASTICISM

By modern standards, the society of western Europe in the Feudal Era was abysmally unscientific. The intellectual leaders of that age greatly preferred the purely mental operations of logical deduction to the physical observation of nature and the performing of experiments. Nevertheless, certain Scholastic thinkers produced a considerable body of scientific lore, which became a stimulus, later on, to further scientific studies. After the twelfth century, moreover, western Europe benefited from the increasing contact with the Moslems, who had made some notable advances in science, and from the recovery of some of the scientific writings of Aristotle.

In astronomy, serious work was done in the observation of the heavenly bodies. This scientific interest was obscured, however, by a magical interest in astrology, by which men sought to foretell the future by study of the stars. Most European astronomers, like the Moslems, continued to hold to the Ptolemaic assumption that the earth was the center of the universe, rather than a planet moving around the sun.

The Alchemist—copper engraving by H. Cook after a drawing by Pieter Brueghel, the Elder (p. 594), shows an early chemist at work. Here the alchemist (*left*) mixes ingredients under the direction of a scholar (*right*), while his hungry children raid the cupboard. (The Bettmann Archive)

A "Bestiary" Elephant with Howdah. Older bestiaries show the elephant without a howdah, fighting the crocodile. The oldest Latin bestiaries, dating back to at least the fifth century, are versions of a Greek book known as *Physiologus*, a generic term. Often a chapter begins with a Biblical text, gives a lesson in natural history, and ends with a moral or spiritual lesson. (From *The Bestiary*, 1928, a reproduction of a manuscript at Cambridge University, by permission of Oxford University Press)

Geography made little progress until the Christians began to learn from the Moslems. The latter developed considerable skill in map-making, because of their historic interest in sea travel across the Mediterranean and through the Red Sea and the Persian Gulf to the Indian Ocean. To what they borrowed from the Moslems, the Christians added the geographical knowledge gained by pilgrims, crusaders, and such venturesome travelers as Marco Polo. Without this gradual improvement in geography and mapmaking during the Feudal Era the Europeans would not have been able to undertake, later on, the great explorations of the age of Christopher Columbus, Vasco da Gama, and Ferdinand Magellan.

Alchemy, the pseudoscience that is the ancestor of the modern science of chemistry, was little developed before the time of the Christian contacts with the Moslem world. The theory of the alchemists was that in addition to the classic "four elements"—earth, air, fire, and water—there was a mysterious and potent fifth "power," called the "elixir" or "philosopher's stone." This wonderful substance, when found, would turn iron or lead into gold. It would also produce a sovereign remedy that would cure all human ills and preserve life in youthful vigor through an indefinite number of centuries. The time spent in search of this "elixir" was not wholly wasted, though the goal of the search was a mirage, because in their experiments the alchemists gained a great deal of experience with metals, minerals, and herbs, which were mixed, heated, decomposed, studied, and analyzed in every way known to the times.

Biology comprised only a host of fantastic stories about animals, which were often gathered into handbooks called "bestiaries." It was believed, for example, that the unicorn is an animal so fierce that he cannot be captured by a man, though a pureminded virgin can walk up to him and lead him away, and that the bird known as the phoenix, supposed to be native to India, lives to an age of about 500 years, then flies to Heliopolis, where he burns himself to death in a fire at the Temple of the Sun—and three days later another full-grown phoenix emerges from the ashes.

Medicine, at the beginning of the Feudal Era, was scarcely more than magic. Later the access to Moslem learning brought to the west the medical knowledge of the ancient Greeks. This included a certain amount of therapeutical common sense but also a great deal of awesome nonsense, to which the physicians of feudal Europe added superstitions of their own. A thirteenth-century prescription for the treatment of eye trouble calls for a mixture of "mountain willow, marjoram, eufragia, celidonia, fennel, ginger, spikenard, pepper, gariofil, thucia, Persian gum, ass's milk, aloes, the gall of an eagle, a hawk, and a mountain goat, balsam, and honey." This stuff was to be stirred daily for forty days, liquefied and pulverized, then dropped into the eyes.

Yet some of the learned men of feudal Europe were not without an appreciation of the worth of scientific experiment. Especially notable is Roger Bacon, whom we have met before (on p. 530), who sharply criticized the reliance of the Scholastics upon the Aristotelian method of pure deductive logic. A professor at the University of Oxford, he became an impassioned student of mathematics and natural science, and he has been praised—perhaps more than he deserves—as a pioneer of the experimental method of modern science.

THE LITERATURE OF THE FEUDAL ERA

The literature of a people gives us the surest insight into their minds and hearts. We may begin the story of the literature of the Feudal Era with samples of two contrasting kinds of poetry.

The first is a Latin hymn:

> Stabat Mater dolorosa
> Juxta crucem lacrimosa
> dum pendebat filius
> o quam tristis et afflicta
> Fuit illa benedicta
> Mater unigeniti, . . .
> Quis est homo qui non fleret,
> Matrem Christi si videret
> In tanto supplicio?
> Quis non posset contristari
> Piam matrem contemplari
> Dolentem cum filio?

> (The sorrowful Mother
> stood in tears beside
> the cross, where hung her
> son. Oh, how
> sad and afflicted was that
> blessed Mother of the
> Only Begotten. Who would not
> weep if he should see
> the Mother of Christ in
> such agony? Who could
> withhold his contrition,
> contemplating the

> loving Mother sorrowing
> with her Son?)

> —from the *"Stabat Mater,"*
> anonymous, thirteenth century.

The second is a student song:

> Praesul discretissime,
>   veniam te precor;
> Morte bona morior,
>   dulce nece necor;
> Meum pectus sauciat
>   puellarum decor,
> Et quas tactu nequeo
>   saltem corde moechor.

> Res est arduissima
>   vincere naturam,
> In aspectu virginis
>   mentem esse puram;
> Juvenes non possumus
>   legem sequi duram,
> Leviumque corporum
>   non habere curam.

> (Most discreet patron,
> I come to confess: I die
> a lovely death, I'm
> sweetly slain—my
> breast is wounded with
> the beauty of girls;
> those I am unable to
> touch, I go to bed with
> in my heart!

It's awfully hard to conquer
nature—to keep a pure mind
at the sight of young girls; we
young fellows can't observe a
law so difficult, and not yearn
for their smooth bodies!)

> —from the *Confessions of Golias*,
> by the "Archpoet," twelfth cen-
> tury.

These two excerpts, the first from one of
the most beautiful religious poems of the
Feudal Era, the second from a famous secular song, reveal the "split personality" of
the early western mind. In the religious
view of life, man was only a sojourner on
this earth, passing onward to his immortal
destiny. His business in this "vale of tears"
was to save his soul by an unceasing struggle against the flesh and the devil. Yet the
human temperament was the same in this
age as in any other. The restraints of religion
were never strong enough to contain the love
of life and its earthly joys. Hence the literature of the Feudal Era includes, along with
sublime religious compositions, some of the
earthiest humor and most fervent tributes
to wine, woman, and song that are to be
found in European literature.

This suggests a natural division of the
literature of the Feudal Era into "religious"
and "secular." But such a division is not
convenient, because the dominance of religion at that time was so great as to influence even the most secular literature. The
most impassioned love lyrics are often punc-
tuated by references to religion, and the clev-
erest comic verses are often parodies of sacred
subjects. The most renowned piece of secular
literature from this era, Chaucer's *Canterbury Tales*, was inspired by the religious occasion of a pilgrimage.

Hence a better division of the literature
of the Feudal Era is the distinction between
compositions in Latin and those in the vernacular languages. We will take up the
Latin literature first, since it was the earlier.

Latin Religious Poetry

Among the earliest and greatest of western
poets was Venantius Fortunatus (d. 609),
an Italian who moved to Gaul and earned
his fame as a poet in the midst of the
Merovingian darkness. The best known of
his writings are two great hymns that still
are used in the Catholic Church. One of
these is *"Vexilla regis prodeunt"* ("The Banners of the King Advance"), and the other is
"Pange, lingua" ("Sing, My Tongue").

Also notable in the early Feudal Era is
Rhabanus Maurus, a German monk of the
ninth century, who was a pupil of Alcuin
at the palace school of Charles the Great.
He is reputed to be the author of *"Veni
Creator Spiritus"* ("Come, Creator Spirit"),
a chant to the Holy Ghost that has been
called one of the seven greatest hymns of
the Catholic Church.

From the thirteenth century dates the
"Dies Irae" ("Day of Wrath"), which has
been called "the greatest of all hymns and
one of the greatest of all poems." It is attributed to Thomas of Celano, (*c.*1200–
*c.*1255), who was a disciple of Francis of
Assisi and his first biographer. The stanzas
below are a portion of it:

> Dies irae, dies illa
> Solvet saeculum in favilla,
> Teste David cum Sibylla

> (Day of wrath, that day when
> the world shall be consumed in
> fire, as David with the Sibyl
> foretold.)

> Quantus tremor est futurus,
> Quando judex est venturus,
> Cuncta stricte discussurus!

> (What trembling there will be
> when the judge will come to
> strike all asunder!)

> Tuba mirum spargens sonum
> Per sepulchra regionum
> Coget omnes ante thronum.

(The trumpet, scattering wondrous sound through the regions of the dead, will call all
before the throne.)

Mors stupebit, et natura
Cum resurget creatura
Judicanti responsura

(Death and nature will be con-
founded when all creatures rise
to submit to the judgment.)

Quid sum miser tunc dicturus
Quem patronum rogaturus
Cum vix justus sit securua?

(What then can I, miserable
one, say? Of what patron can I
beg intercession when even the
just will be scarcely safe?)

Rex tremendae majestatis
Qui salvandos salvas gratis
Salve me, fons pietatis!

(O King of tremendous ma-
jesty, who saves the saved by
grace, save me, O fount of love!)

Latin Secular Poetry

By the twelfth century secular poetry in
Latin had reached a high development. Under the influence of classical models, the
western lyricist imitated not only the language but the spirit of classical antiquity.
The pleasures of life are frankly praised;
pedantry and smugness are satirized; wit and
wisdom are joined in pleasant verses, in
striking contrast to the humorless labors of
the logicians and the theologians who were
writing at the same time in their own pon-
derous idiom.

The best of this poetry is quite fresh in
form and content. It is not merely a sterile

imitation of classical models, though it is
much inferior in poetic technique to the best
of the classics. To be sure, it is sometimes
said that the secular poetry of the Feudal Era
is less original in its themes than the religious
poetry. But this is only because the classical
writers treated much the same themes as the
feudal secular poets—the joys of youth
and spring, the loves of men and maidens,
the general follies of mankind—whereas the
classical poets did not attempt religious
themes; the Christian hymnists were working a fresh new vein of literary inspiration, while the lyricists were carrying on a
tradition.

The most entertaining of the new secular
poetry was that composed by those university students and wandering clerics who were
a unique feature of scholarly life in the
Feudal Era. Well trained in Latin literature, destined to spend long years in the
study of theology or canon law and bored
by this prospect, they gave vent to their
youthful ebullience by writing poetry. Nearly
all of it is amusing; much of it is pleasantly
innocuous; some of it takes the form of
scandalous parodies of the sacred liturgical
hymns and prayers of the Church. Often
hungry, cold, and ragged, these roaming
scholars joke about their poverty with true
Bohemian contempt for bourgeois security
and comforts.

These wandering poets were called goliards, in honor of their patron, a certain
"Bishop Golias," a mythical bishop whom
they invested with their own interesting
traits. He was depicted in their legends as
a good scholar without morals, an amiable
parasite robustly fond of his women and his
liquor.

The best goliardic verse is very distinguished poetry, and even the worst is good
comic doggerel. The finest of it is the Confession of Golias, written by an anonymous
genius known to his contemporaries as "the
Archpoet." An excerpt from it appears at
the beginning of this section, as a contrast
to the "Stabat Mater."

Froissart Presents His Chronicle to King Richard II—late fifteenth-century version of Froissart's *Chronicle*. (British Museum)

Latin Prose

In the later Feudal Era there was a vast output of Latin prose. Much of it consisted of works of theology and philosophy. Most of the rest took the form of either histories and chronicles or devotional works, of which an outstanding example is *De diligendo Dei* (*On the Love of God*) by Bernard of Clairvaux. But the interest of these works comes principally from the subject matter, not the literary style.

Chronicles and Histories. The scholars of the Feudal Era in western Europe had little notion of history as a scientific discipline, but they were fond of writing history for the edification of their contemporaries and descendants. Their historical writings range from systematic "universal" histories to routine local chronicles kept by monasteries or cathedral chapters. These writings are of importance for modern scholars, who must make use of them as a source of information, but they show little sense of historical criticism on the part of their authors or compilers. The men of the Feudal Era were as credulous in their attitude toward history as in their approach toward science. Tales of miracles, divine signs, and wonders were all included in works of history as though they were perfectly normal happenings.

The first western historian of more than ordinary importance is Gregory of Tours (540–594). His *Historia Francorum* (*History of the Franks*) tells us nearly all that we know about certain periods of Merovingian history. Gregory was Bishop of Tours during the rudest and most barbaric phase of the Frankish era. He paints a frightful picture of the manners, quarrels, treacheries, and cruelties of kings, queens, and nobles, and he is no less frank in recounting the gross immoralities of the clergy, which he deplores. Of at least equal importance with the work of Gregory is that of the Venerable Bede (675–735), an English monk, whose *Ecclesiatical History of England* was based largely on original sources and shows flashes of real historical insight.

Among the greatest historical works of the twelfth century were those written by Otto of Freising (c.1114–1158), a German bishop. His most famous work is the *Chronicle of Two Cities,* the title of which suggests the inspiration that the author drew from St. Augustine. Apart from its overtones of philosophical reflection, the book is an excellent systematic narrative of the events of German history within the author's purview. Otto also wrote a biography of the Emperor Frederick Barbarossa, which deserves to be compared with Einhard's *Life of Charles the Great.*

The outstanding historical work of the fifteenth century was written in the vernacular rather than Latin. Jean Froissart (1337–1410), a Frenchman, wrote a voluminous series of chronicles on the history of France, England, Scotland, and Spain. He is the outstanding historian of the Hundred Years' War, in which he took part. His style is a vivid and poetic French, which approaches the superb in his description of great battles.

Early Western Drama

The drama that developed in feudal Europe owed nothing to the models of ancient Greece and Rome, for though the works of the classical dramatists are widely read today, and often produced, they were not known in Europe during feudal times.

The oldest form of drama in the west is the liturgy of the Church, for the mass itself is a stylized re-enactment of the sacrifice of Christ upon the cross, in which gestures, words, and music are artistically coordinated to produce a dramatic effect.

Apart from the mass, the earliest dramatic works developed out of the various antiphons, or verses, chanted by the celebrant with responses by the entire choir, which were added to the liturgy for certain feast days. The development from this liturgical practice to true drama was complete by the twelfth century, when the "miracle plays" were in full vogue. These were re-enactments of miraculous events in the lives of the Virgin and other saints. The actors in them were not clergymen but laymen, and the language was the vernacular.

In the fourteenth and fifteenth centuries, a newer type of drama attained great popularity in the populous and prosperous towns. These were the "morality plays," which were a more sophisticated kind of drama, since the actors portrayed abstract virtues and vices. The central character in the morality was usually named "Everyman,"

and the theme of the play was the progress of his soul through life toward eternal salvation or damnation. The action involved the various temptations that he met, these being personified vices, and the help that he gained from personified virtues. Gradually the themes became less religious and more worldly, until by degrees the modern drama emerged.

Vernacular Literature

The first literary compositions in non-Latin tongues were established by oral tradition long before they were reduced to writing. They were in the form of epic poetry. The epic form is characteristic also of the early literature of many other peoples besides those of western Europe; it is a narrative poetry concerning the deeds of legendary heroes of the past. This kind of theme appeals to the imagination of primitive peoples, and it is usually treated in the form of poetry, because poetry can be more easily memorized and recited than can prose.

The Teutonic Epics. The earliest vernacular literature in western Europe is found among the Germans and Scandinavians, in lands were the competition of Latin was the slightest.

The most primitive Germanic poetry has almost completely disappeared, but knowledge of it can be reconstructed from fragments of the *sagas* of the Norsemen and the *eddas* of the Icelanders. The earliest surviving fragment of the poetry originating in the Germanic mainland is the "Song of Hildebrand," which was probably composed during the Carolingian Age. Familiar to most students as the earliest monument of English literature is the Anglo-Saxon epic *Beowulf,* celebrating the deeds of the Angles, Saxons, and Jutes who conquered England in the fifth century. Originally transmitted by oral tradition, *Beowulf* was reduced to writing in the seventh century or a little later. These early epics are all products of the pre-Christian German culture.

Later versions of Teutonic epics, appearing after the Carolingian Age, are Christianized narratives of semilegendary German history. The greatest of these is the *Nibelungenlied* (*Song of the Nibelungs*), which was written about 1200. Its hero is Siegfried, a character who combines the primitive German virtues with the chivalric traits of Christian feudalism.

Later German literature covered a much broader field than the epic poem. In the thirteenth century appeared the love poetry of the *minnesingers,* or German minstrels, and an increasing number of poems descriptive of everyday life.

French Chansons. The first vernacular literature in France, as in other areas of the Romance languages, was inspired by the epic forms originating in Germany.

Early French epic songs are called *chansons de geste,* or songs of deeds. The most famous is the *Song of Roland,* celebrating the heroic life and death of Roland, Count of Brittany, who was supposed to be the favorite paladin of Charles the Great. The great Frankish emperor himself is the central figure in other *chansons de geste* as well as in the vernacular literature of Germany and Italy. Unlike the true German epics, the *chansons de geste* did not always circulate first by oral tradition; some of them were immediately set down in writing by their authors, though the names of the authors have not survived.

In the south of France a rich literature developed in the Provençal language. (Related to French and to Spanish but distinct from them, Provençal has since become virtually obsolete.) This southern region was the most urbane and civilized part of France. In ancient times, it had been more Romanized than the north, and despite the chaos of the Germanic invasions and the later Moslem incursions, town life had never died out. Hence the south had remained more sophisticated, and its cultural superiority to the north was manifest in its literature.

The characteristic form of Provençal literature was lyric poetry. While the poets of the north were expressing themselves in verses of heroic deeds, the bards of the south were singing of romantic love. The writer of such verses was called a *troubadour.* Usually he did not sing them himself but passed them on to wandering minstrels. The lyrics of the *troubadours* were almost exclusively concerned with the lover's pursuit of his lady's favor. This poetry was governed by conventional rules that prescribed, for example, that the suitor must be knightly and that his lady-love must be a paragon of beauty and gentility. But within these conventions the poets developed an extravagant language of love, virtually unknown in previous literature, which has since become a part of the literature of nearly all countries, especially those of the west. The poet hymns his lady's surpassing beauty, her lovely eyes, her fair hands whiter than snow, her ravishing little waist, and so on, with other beguiling details. The lady, in turn, is always tantalizingly aloof or, as we might say, "hard to get."

The twelfth century was the "golden age" of Provençal poetry. It waned when southern France was devasted in the course of the suppression of the Albigensian heresy but its influence persisted all over Europe. The German *minnesinger,* the Scottish minstrel, and every other bard who sang the praises of knightly love for a noble lady was indebted to the gay and tender songs of the *troubadours* of Provençe.

Meanwhile, there were vigorous literary movements in northern France, in the language destined eventually to prevail throughout the kingdom. Especially notable was the "Arthurian Cycle," comprising a series of poems, based on ancient Celtic legends from Wales and Brittany, which celebrate the adventures of King Arthur, his Knights of the Round Table, and their various ladies. These famous characters, which appear in the prose and poetry of many lands, are familiar to us in the modern verses of Alfred, Lord Tennyson.

In contrast to the poetry celebrating knightly valor and the charms of noble ladies was a literature designed for the amusement of the townsmen. Typical of this was the versified tale of Renard, one of a number of animal stories based on the ancient fables of Aesop. The chief character is a fox, Renard, whose cunning enables him to prosper in a world full of larger and stronger beasts. The allegory is obvious: the magnates of feudalism and the Church were the lords of the earth, while the burgher, like the fox among mightier brutes, had to make his way by his wit and unscrupulous guile.

At the end of the Feudal Era came one of the greatest of French poets—François Villon (1431–1480). He was a student at the University of Paris and therefore a cleric in minor orders. But he was also a thief and a vagabond, as familiar with the lowest dives of Paris as with the lecture halls. His life was one of grinding poverty, relieved only by thievery; he spent time in prison and narrowly escaped the gallows. But the poetry he wrote survives among the classics of early French literature.

Vernacular Literature in England. The earliest vernacular language of England in the Feudal Era was Anglo-Saxon. From the age of *Beowulf* until the Norman Conquest, this Germanic language was used by such distinguished authors as the poet Caedmon and the scholar known as the Venerable Bede.

Despite its promising start, the progress of an Anglo-Saxon literature was retarded by the great political change following the Norman Conquest. Since the invaders, speaking the vernacular French of their homeland in Normandy, became the masters of England, French became the language of court, castle, and high religious circles. French could not permanently displace Anglo-Saxon, because the latter was the language of the vast majority of the population, but its influence was so strong as to bring about the modification of the original Germanic vernacular into the "splendid hybrid" known as English. By the end of the thirteenth century this hybrid tongue that we have inherited was used in popular ballads, such as those recounting the adventures of Robin Hood.

The great masterpiece of English literature in the Feudal Era was written in the late fourteenth century. Geoffrey Chaucer, the author of the *Canterbury Tales*, was born about 1340 and died in 1400. For most of his life he was a civil official of the crown, serving in various capacities, ranging from diplomacy to the collection of customs.

The literary structure of the *Canterbury Tales* is simple. A band of pilgrims is en route to the tomb of Thomas à Becket in Canterbury. To lighten the tedium of their long journey, they tell stories to each other. The characters themselves are as interesting as their tales—the knight (p. 446), the "clerke," the "man of lawe," the shipman, the monk, the nun, the admirable "wife of Bath," and numerous others. For the tales, Chaucer helped himself to the common property of storytellers in his time—the animal stories and *fabliaux* of France, the Italian tales that were later exploited by Boccaccio, old Breton stories, and others as old as Aesop.

Chaucer's Pilgrims—from an edition of *Canterbury Tales* c.1491. See also p. 446. (New York Public Library, Rare Book Room)

Dante Alighieri—the "Naples Bust" attributed to Donatello (p. 583). (Brogi photo)

The tales are vivid, often amusing, sometimes bawdy, and usually bearing a worldly rather than a religious moral. Though the tales are supposedly told by persons on a religious pilgrimage, the attitude of the narrators shows a certain cynicism in matters touching religion that is characteristic of Chaucer's century.

Italian Vernacular Literature. During the early Feudal Era vernacular literature in Italy lagged behind that of France and England. One reason was that Italy lacked a movement toward political centralization. In other countries such movements helped bring about a standardization of the language. But Italy remained a welter of dialects, as of governments.

Ultimately, however, an Italian produced the most powerful work written in a vernacular language anywhere in Europe during the Feudal Era. Dante Alighieri, the author of the *Divine Comedy,* was born in 1265 and died in 1321. A native of Florence and a member of a family prominent in Florentine politics, Dante was a partisan of the "Ghibellines," the Italian faction favorable to the rule of the German emperors in Italy and hostile to the political power of the papacy (p. 462). He is a good example of the man of deep religious feeling who was hostile to the political pretensions of the clergy. In his great poetic work, one may discern both his sincere reverence for the Church and his detestation of the temporal ambitions of the popes. The intrusion of his political thought is a minor note, however, in the tremendous sweep of the *Divine Comedy,* which is a synthesis of all the diverse elements in the intellectual and emotional outlook of the educated man of the Feudal Era.

The *Divine Comedy* comprises three parts: "Inferno," "Purgatorio," and "Paradiso" ("Hell," "Purgatory," and "Heaven"). As the "Inferno" begins, the author relates how he found himself beset with dangers in a dark wood, when he came upon the gentle shade of Vergil, the greatest of Roman poets. With Vergil as his guide, the author traverses the various circles of Hell, passing on to Purgatory, and reaching the verge of Heaven. In describing this journey, Dante not only dramatizes the ideas of the Christian scheme of existence but furnishes a handbook of astronomy, geography, and geology, as these were known to educated men of the Feudal Era.

With Dante, we are at the summit and close to the end of an epoch. In his time, and in his native land of Italy, the intellectual flowering known as the Renaissance was close at hand, and with this new age would come a new emphasis on man and earth—rather than hell, purgatory, and heaven. But never in the modern age would there appear so great a poet of the Christian universe as the Feudal Era produced in Dante.

THE ART OF THE FEUDAL ERA

The men of feudal Europe produced a body of work in the various forms of art that is worthy of their achievements in thought and literature. Especially impressive is the record of their achievement in architecture, because the most lavish effort of the religious civilization of feudal Europe was expended upon religious buildings.

The forms of the architecture of this age fall into two great classifications. The first type of church building was an imitation, in style and method of construction, of the Roman public buildings. Churches of this kind are called Romanesque. The other type, appearing later and a genuinely western creation, is known as Gothic.

Romanesque Architecture

Romanesque architecture is sometimes undervalued because it lacks the lightness and grace of the Gothic, which eventually became more popular. But, at its best, the earlier style need not take second place to the Gothic.

As the name suggests, Romanesque churches were at first mere imitations of classical Roman basilicas and other public buildings. The Roman form was simple but impressive. The building was made of massive stone walls, on a rectangular plan, over which rose a vault, or semicylindrical roof. The more ingenious Roman architects learned how to vary this simple style by the use of a groined vault—that is, one in which a rounded vault intersects another at right angles (see below). But the Romans never succeeded in overcoming a serious limitation on the size of the structure, because the more spacious the vault, the more massive the walls must be in order to support it.

In the Feudal Era the European builders modified the Roman pattern by introducing the use of the ribbed vault and the clustered column. Some architects also succeeded in making the whole building assume the shape of a giant cross, with a dome surmounting the place where the transepts met the nave. (An example of this is Pisa Cathedral, p. 500.) It remained impossible, however, to cut large windows into the walls without weakening them to the point where they could not support the weight of the roof. Hence the interior of the Romanesque building was dimly lighted. This was no great handicap in the southern regions of Europe, where the sunlight is strong during much of the year,

Nave of the Abbey Church of La Madeleine at Vézelay. Although it is considerably smaller than the great second abbey church at Cluny, La Madeleine is the largest Romanesque abbey church still in existence in France. When a fire in 1120 destroyed the wooden portions of the roof, for the first time in France the new principle of cross vaulting or groin vaulting was used. More important than its architecture is Vézelay's tympanum (p. 517) and the sculptured capitals of its columns, which may be seen here. (*Archives Photographiques*)

St. John's Chapel in the Tower of London (p. 457)—built between 1078 and 1097. These Norman Romanesque columns are short and squatty and their capitals have only rudimentary decoration. The side aisle at right, however, shows another early example of cross vaulting. (British Information Services)

and the climate mild. But in northern Europe churches of this kind were dark and cold. Out of their attempts to design a building that would be better lighted, the architects of northern Europe devised the magnificent new "Gothic" style, wholly indigenous to Europe of the Feudal Era.

Gothic Architecture

The name *Gothic* did not come into use until after the close of the Feudal Era, and it originated as a term of derision. Because the new style was unknown to the ancient Greeks and Romans, pedants in a later age of exaggerated classicism thought it necessarily a barbarian style, and *Gothic* was a synonym for *barbarian*. The judgment of the ages, however, has recognized the Gothic style as probably the most beautiful ecclesiastical architecture devised in any age.

As the round arch with massive walls and small windows was characteristic of the Romanesque, so the pointed arch and external buttress are the hallmarks of the Gothic. The virtue of the pointed arch, as compared with the round, is that it has less outward thrust. Hence in buildings which make use of the pointed arch, the walls need not be so mas-

sive as in the Romanesque. This made it possible for the builders of Gothic churches to pierce the walls with large windows. In later Gothic churches the windows became so numerous that they seem to take up the whole of the wall space. This was made possible by the use of "flying buttresses"—that is, a series of stone piers standing outside the building, which served to brace the thin stone arches between the windows in the walls of the church. Because of the use of these buttresses, the Gothic church has been described as a "body with the skeleton outside."

Besides permitting a freer use of windows, the pointed arch and the exterior buttress made it possible to add height to the building. In the best of their buildings, the Gothic architects achieved a soaring effect so magnificent that it is breath-taking. Such buildings are ideal places of religious worship, since the structure carries the mind upward. (See Reims Cathedral, page 8.)

The larger window space that became available in the Gothic church gave rise to another glorious art: that of the stained glass window. Stained glass windows were made of countless small pieces of colored glass, fitted together with strips of lead so as to form a picture. The best stained glass work of the Feudal Era has never been equalled in modern times. In the finest surviving examples, such as those in the cathedral of Chartres and in the Sainte Chapelle in Paris, the windows, when viewed from the interior on a sunny day, seem to glow with the unearthly fire of jewels. (See also page 520.)

The Gothic design was originated by unknown architectural geniuses in the Île de France in the late twelfth century. Its great age was the thirteenth century, and though the style spread far from its place of origin, the finest examples are to be found in France and England. For an effect of soaring lightness, the French Gothic is unexcelled; the best English examples seem heavier, though they have a compensating virtue, for they seem to grow right out of the countryside.

In the Low Countries and northern France there was an impressive development of secular Gothic. Buildings of this kind often served as town halls or guild halls. The finest example of the sort was the famous Cloth Hall at Ypres, which was the headquarters of the drapers' guild, but the building no longer survives; it was destroyed by bombardment in the World War I. Numerous other examples are still to be seen —for instance, the Town Hall of Brussels and the smaller one at Louvain. Interesting as these buildings are, however, they are not characteristic of the Gothic, for the Gothic remained a style primarily for the building of churches.

The work of the unsung architects of the great cathedrals has left us the most impressive religious monuments of any faith at any epoch in history. There is nothing to compare with them, except the pyramids—and that would be like comparing life with death. The pyramids were sepulchres, but the cathedrals were "theaters of religion." They were the setting in which were presented the almost continuous religious ceremonies of the Church, and those ceremonies matched in dignity and beauty the splendid buildings in which they were performed.

Sculpture

The sculpture of the Feudal Era was functional—that is, a statue seldom stood alone on a pedestal. Instead, statues were "worked" as part of the ornamentation of a church or public building. Sculpture is usually classified, like architecture, as Romanesque or Gothic (p. 517).

Though an ingenious sculptor could work human or animal figures into almost any part of the building, most of the best examples of sculpture are found in the portals of churches, as ornamentation on tombs and altars or as the capitals of columns. The portal sculpture developed in answer to the need of the Romanesque architect for some kind of ornamentation to relieve the great

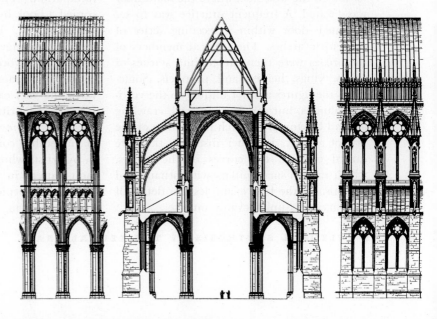

Diagrams of Reims Cathedral—(*left*) longitudinal section of interior along the nave (p. 8); (*center*) transverse section across the nave, showing how exterior buttresses support the vaulting at weak points; (*right*) elevation of portion of exterior along nave. (From *Art Today*, Henry Holt & Co., 3d ed., 1956)

With the coming of the newer Gothic architecture, the sculptor had to work with much higher vertical lines than those common to Romanesque. Hence the figures are more elongated, and consequently less natural, than the rounded figures in Romanesque. For this reason the Gothic carving is often unfavorably compared with the works of classical sculpture. This criticism is too sweeping, because much Gothic sculpture is nearly as faithful to life as the classical.

Animal sculpture was usually competent and often amusing, for the Gothic designers had a taste for the grotesque. The figures of griffons, unicorns, and other legendary monsters were used freely, and the gargoyles that decorate the exterior of the Gothic churches are famous. Taking the form of weird monsters, dragons, birds, and half-human hybrids, they are deliberately fantastic and give a light touch that relieves the solemnity of the religious edifice.

Painting

Both Romanesque and Gothic churches were often ornamented with vast frescoes, but these decorations have almost entirely disappeared. So have most other examples of painting in the Feudal Era. (See p. 522.)

But numerous specimens survive of another kind of pictorial art, in which the Feudal Era excelled. This was manuscript illumination. The scribe who laboriously copied a book by hand took pains to embellish his work. The favorite form of ornament was a huge and elaborate initial letter for the first word at the beginning of each chapter. The most beautiful of all such work was done very early in the feudal period in Ireland and Britain. The *Book of Kells* and the *Lindisfarne Gospels* have initial letters of incredible complexity, with detail filled in by artists who must have been among the most patient in history. These initials glow with gold, purple, and other bright colors—hence the term, "illuminated" manuscripts.

West Portal of Chartres Cathedral. In the tympanum above the doors is Christ in Majesty, surrounded by the apocalyptic beasts—part of the more than 700 carved figures of the west façade that tell the story of Christ from His ancestors to His ascension. Such sculpture was the Bible and art of the poor, and the cathedral was the center of a town's activities. (*Archives Photographiques*)

façade on the west side, where the main door was located. A frequent practice was to set the huge door within a receding series of concentric arches. The vertical members of the arches were then carved into statues of saints, kings, heroes, and prophets. Sometimes the figures are not limited to the vertical columns, but continue upward, crawling around the top of the arch in defiance of the law of gravity. In other instances they are carved only in the curves of the arches, which rest on small pillars with ornamental capitals. In the best examples the detail of the carving is unbelievably minute.

The most exquisite examples of the painting of the Feudal Era, however, were the finely drawn beautifully colored illustrations that were painted (usually in tempera) into the manuscript books of that age (p. 452, p. 513). These paintings varied in subject matter according to the type of book: religious books might have pictures of religious incidents, usually from the Bible; "books of hours" (books giving a sort of calendar of fast days, feast days, and saints' days, along with the hours and instructions for different prayers and devotions) were illustrated with tiny pictures of seasonal activities, such as planting, harvesting (p. 472, p. 473), baking, slaughtering, hunting, courting, etc.; histories and books of chivalry were illustrated with warlike scenes, sieges, and battles. Some of the early copies of Froissart's *Chronicles* were superbly illustrated in this manner (p. 536).

Music

In the course of the Feudal Era the liturgists of the Church accomplished a remarkable achievement in music, adding a third dimension to the plain song they inherited from antiquity. The result of their labors was *polyphony*—the simultaneous sounding of several melodies in an esthetically pleasing manner. In this achievement were also involved the foundation of modern harmony and the development of a system of musical notation capable of indicating exact pitch and time values.

The development of notation, making use of the musical staff, is associated with the name of Guido of Arezzo (d. 1050), who used a four-line staff to fix pitch with precision. As this system of notation was refined, it made possible more complex compositions. About 1200 the composer Petronius, who was attached to the Church of Notre Dame in Paris, took the bold step from two-part to three- and four-part music, but not for another three centuries were all the prob-

lems solved that arose out of experiments of this sort.

The mood of religious music was carried over into the student songs, pilgrim songs, and dance tunes of the era. Hundreds of melodies survive of the music composed by *troubadours* and *trouvères,* who were their counterparts in northern France. The German *minnesingers,* like the *trouvères,* were chivalric; the later German *meistersingers* (mastersingers) were bourgeois. Among the goliards there originated numerous drinking songs and songs of other sorts, often lewd and sophisticated. In the thirteenth century, however, the Church took steps against the scandalous behavior of the goliards, and their music tended to become more respectable.

Town Hall of Louvain. (Courtesy, Belgian Government Information Center)

CONCLUSION

Such was the great cultural synthesis that characterized the Feudal Era in the history of western civilization. In many ways this synthesis was unique in the cultural history of mankind, and it was certainly a high peak in the historical range of intellectual achievements of western Europe. But the Feudal Era, or the Age of Scholasticism, was only the first great creative epoch in the broad historic development of the new civilization of the west, and by the fourteenth century the creative genius of the thirteenth was already giving way before the more secular, more humanistic, and more heterogeneous culture of the succeeding era, the era of the so-called "Renaissance."

Suggestions for Further Reading

Source Materials

Anthologies

F. Le V. Baumer, ed., *Main Currents of Western Thought* (New York, 1952), Part I.
Good selections from the great writers of the Feudal Era, including Thomas Aquinas, Roger Bacon, Dante, and Otto of Freising.

Columbia College, *Introduction to Contemporary Civilization in the West* (2 vols., New York, 1946), Volume I, Chapter 2.
Selections from some of the great writers of the Feudal Era, including Aquinas and Dante.

E. A. Moody and M. Clagett, eds., *The Medieval Science of Weights* (Madison, 1952).
Contemporary treatises on some of the scientific problems of the Feudal Era.

A. P. Newton, ed., *Travel and Travelers of the Middle Ages* (New York, 1926).
Journals of some of the earliest voyages of Europeans outside Europe in the expansion of knowledge which took place with the revival of commerce.

R. Warnock and G. K. Anderson, eds., *The World in Literature* (2 vols., Chicago, 1950–1951), Volume II, pp. 66–263.
An excellent collection of selections from the literature of the Feudal Era; especially good selections from the secular literature, including the *Song of Roland,* the *Song of the Nibelungs, Aucassin and Nicolette.*

Contemporary Writings

P. Abailard, *The Story of My Misfortunes;* translated by H. A. Bellows (St. Paul, 1922).
Peter Abelard's autobiography.

Dante Alighieri, *The Divine Comedy.*
The greatest poetic work of the Feudal Era in European history. There are many editions.

J. Froissart, *The Chronicles of England, France, Spain,* etc. (London, 1911).
Selections from the great contemporary historian of the Hundred Years' War.

Gregory of Tours, *History of the Franks;* translated by Ernest Brehaut (New York, 1916).
One of the famous histories written during the Feudal Era.

Otto of Freising, *Two Cities; a Chronicle of Universal History to the Year 1146* A.D.; translated by C. C. Mierow (New York, 1928).
One of the great classics of historical literature written in the Feudal Era.

Marco Polo, *The Adventures of Marco Polo,* edited by R. J. Walsh (New York, 1948).
One of the great travel books of all time, with valuable descriptions of life in China under the Mongol emperors. Available in many editions.

Secondary Works

H. Adams, *Mont Saint Michel and Chartres* (reissue, Boston, 1936).
A beautiful but highly romanticized description of the religious architecture in two of the greatest Gothic cathedrals of the Feudal Era.

F. B. Artz, *The Mind of the Middle Ages, A.D. 200–1500* (2d ed., New York, 1954).
One of the best surveys of the intellectual life of the Dark Ages and the Feudal Era.

H. E. Barnes, *Intellectual and Cultural History of the Western World* (rev. ed., New York, 1941), Chapters 7–12.
An encyclopedic survey. Good as a reference book.

C. G. Crump and E. F. Jacob, eds., *The Legacy of the Middle Ages* (New York, 1926).
A collection of excellent articles by different authors on various aspects of the culture of the Feudal Era.

S. C. Eaton, *Roger Bacon and His Search for a Universal Science* (New York, 1952).
A good study of the Feudal Era as well as of Roger Bacon himself.

E. Gibson, *The Spirit of Medieval Philosophy* (New York, 1940).
One of the best explanations of what the Scholastic philosophers were trying to do.

C. H. Haskins, *The Rise of Universities* (New York, 1940).
A delightful set of essays on the life and work of the universities during the Age of Scholasticism.

C. H. Haskins, *Studies in Medieval Culture* (New York, 1929).
A brilliant set of essays by one of the old masters.

C. W. Jones, *Medieval Literature in Translation* (New York, 1950).
An extensive and excellent collection of selections from the literature of the Feudal Era, both secular and religious.

C. R. Morey, *Medieval Art* (New York, 1942).
A standard survey.

J. H. Randall, Jr., *The Making of the Modern Mind* (rev. ed., Cambridge, Mass., 1940), Chapters 2–5.
A good survey of the intellectual history of the Feudal Era.

H. Rashdall, *The Universities of Europe in the Middle Ages* (new ed., 3 vols., Oxford, 1936).
The standard work on the universities.

H. O. Taylor, *The Medieval Mind* (4th ed., 2 vols., Cambridge, Mass., 1949).
Somewhat old, but still a standard work.

L. Thorndike, *A History of Magic and Experimental Science* (6 vols., New York, 1934–1943).
A standard work. The second volume deals with the science and magic of the Feudal Era.

H. J. Waddell, *Peter Abelard* (New York, 1947).
Probably the best biography.

H. J. Waddell, *The Wandering Scholars* (7th ed., New York, 1949).
A delightful study.

PART IV

The Commercial Era

The revival and expansion of commerce during the Feudal Era, resulting in the growth of the thriving commercial cities of Italy, France, Germany, the Low Countries, and England, had so profound an effect upon the life of western Europe as to constitute an economic and social revolution. As a part of this revolution—or closely related to it—there took place other profound changes in western European civilization—in political life and institutions, in social institutions and outlook, in religion, and in culture. Even Russia in the east was to be superficially affected.

This so-called "commercial revolution" was extremely slow and gradual. It took about six centuries to accomplish the transition from the typical manorial economy of the twelfth century to the typical commerce-dominated economy of the end of the eighteenth. After 1700 serfdom and the old-style manor had all but disappeared in western Europe, although it continued in Russia. The new measure of wealth, instead of being land, as it had been in the Feudal Era, was now money, for all kinds of property might now be bought and sold outright for money. The great majority of the people still lived on farms and spent their lives in agriculture, but what they raised, where they sold it, and what they received for it was now determined by the people who lived in the towns and made their living, directly or indirectly, from commerce. By the same time, too, European commerce had grown far beyond the confines of Europe itself. It had reached out to all the corners of the hitherto known and unknown world and had established a network of commercial, cultural, and political relationships whose beginning marked the opening of a new era in the history of the world.

Meanwhile, political forms were changing, and on the ruins of feudalism there arose a new political phenomenon, the sovereign state. This political revolution was not due entirely to the rise of commerce, but certainly the Commercial Revolution aided and hastened it. For, as we have seen, the merchants of the cities generally (if with many exceptions) lent the strength of their wealth to support the increasing power and authority of the centralizing kings, especially in France, England, Spain, and Portugal, against the declining power of the feudal barons. The result was the eventual triumph of the kings and the emergence of a new political entity, that of the "state." Presently, however, the merchants would challenge the very kings they had helped to bring to power and would, themselves, take from the kings the attributes of sovereignty in the state, only to have it taken from them, in turn, and centered in "the people" in accordance with a still newer concept, the modern concept of democracy.

Meanwhile, too, the religious unity of western Europe was broken; and in its place stood literally hundreds of divisions, or "sects," of Christianity, especially in northern and western Europe. Even the all-pervasive religious outlook itself, whether the old Catholic or new Protestant, no longer dominated the affairs of men, and men of widely differing faiths had learned to live together, tolerating each other without the dreadful fear and trembling that, in the Feudal Era, had accompanied the name of *heretic*.

Along with the end of authoritarian conformity had come a new intellectual and religious individualism, to accompany the economic individualism of commerce. No longer did men regard life in this world as merely a prelude to life in another, many of them, rather, had begun to think of living in this world so as to enjoy it. Even the sense of human sin that had explained so much of the western Christian synthesis of the thirteenth century was fading. In its place there had appeared a new sense of the individual worth and dignity of individual men, endowed with reason and capable of choosing not only between good and evil but also between alternate courses of behavior in such a way as to bring about an infinite and progressive improvement in their own condition here. Most brilliant achievement of all, the men of

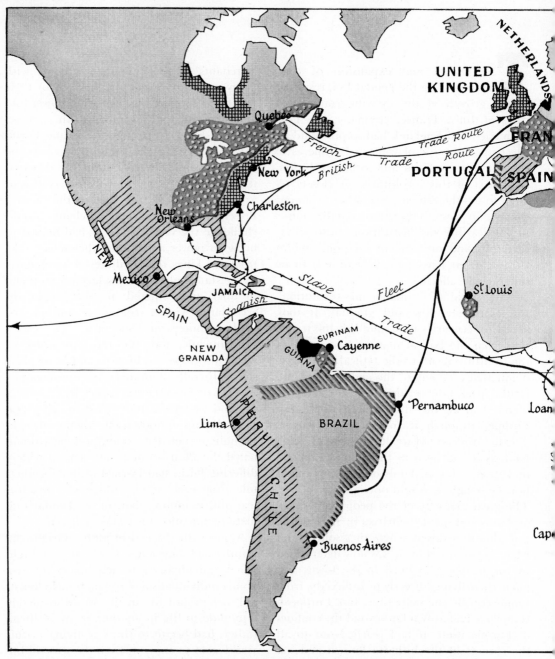

Colonial Empires in the Early Eighteenth Century

the west, having rediscovered the scientific learning of the ancients, had gone on to lay the foundations of modern science. So remarkable were the discoveries of the facts and the laws of nature and so improved was mathematics as an instrument of humanity that man's understanding of the universe and his own place in it was greatly changed.

Even in the eighteenth century the forces set in motion by the Commercial Revolution had already progressed so far that the men of the west had begun to devise new machines to hasten the processes of manufacture, in order to satisfy the growing commercial market of the world. Not only did they invent machines but, in doing so, they also

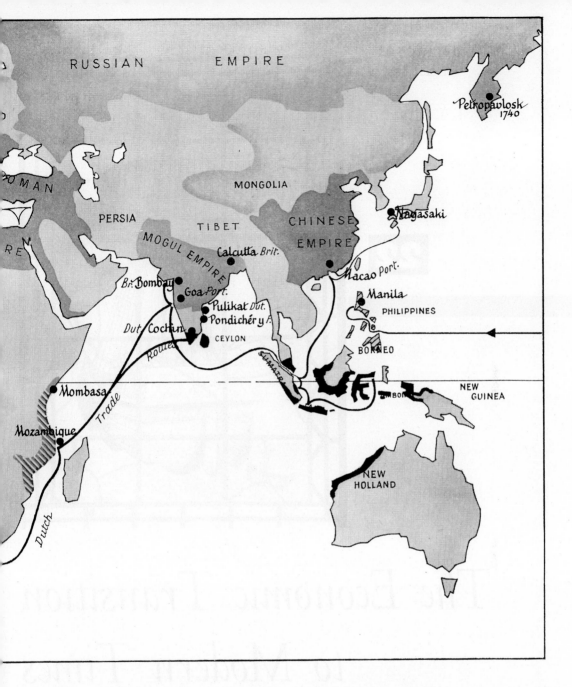

initiated a new revolution—the so-called "Industrial Revolution"—which, aided and abetted by science, would revolutionize the methods of production, distribution, and communication, multiply the hitherto un-dreamed-of mechanical and scientific aids to living, and, at last, draw all states and com-munities into one great world community.

(See Vol. II, Chapter 30.)

The Commercial Revolution began in the heart of the Feudal Era; it was to change many aspects of European civilization and extend it around the Atlantic Basin. The In-dustrial Revolution was an outgrowth of the commercial; it would change the basic eco-nomic aspects of the civilization of the world.

551

22

The Economic Transition
to Modern Times

Fifteenth-century Galley—window in the mansion of Jacques Coeur (p. 554) in Bourges. (*Service Commercial Monuments Historiques*)

By the time when Louis XI, "the Spider King," ascended the throne of France (1461) and Henry VII ascended that of England (1485) the growth of commerce in western Europe, with its attendant accumulation of a commercial type of wealth, had progressed so far as to make commerce almost the dominant factor in European economic life. The majority of the people, about the year 1500, still made their living on the land; but the capital wealth of western Europe was now coming to be measured in terms of commerce and its profits rather than in terms of land and its products. As a part of this shift in the fundamental conditions of economic life, European commerce spread its tentacles around the world, bringing the western world into permanent commercial contact with the older east and opening to commercial exploitation vast areas of the earth's surface hitherto unknown to civilized men. Along with these shifts and reorientations in the fundamental conditions of economic life there went a reorganization of society and the appearance of a new set of economic ideas and ideals.

All these profound changes in the European way of life, taken together, constitute what is called the Commercial Revolution. It was a real economic and social revolution; and it gave a great impetus to the political revolution in the course of which the modern sovereign state replaced feudalism as the dominant European political form. Mentally, too, it broadened men's intellectual horizons, and gave a powerful impetus to the study of science, to literature, to philosophy, and to the secularization of intellectual outlook. It opened a new era in the history of western civilization; and this new commercial era may be said to have been the true *pronaos* (entryway) to modern times.

THE INTERNAL EXPANSION OF EUROPEAN TRADE

When the sixteenth century opened in western Europe the Commercial Revolution was already well under way. The Italian, French, and Spanish Mediterranean cities, whose commerce had been given a great boost by the Crusades (p. 478), dominated the commerce of the Mediterranean area. In northern Europe the Hanseatic League still flourished, although its monopoly was now being weakened by the growing commercial strength of England and the Low Countries. In France, Portugal, England, the Low Countries, and along the western coasts of Spain, the prosperity of commerce through the preceding two centuries had built up the wealth and importance of such western European cities as Cadiz, Lisbon, Bordeaux, Southampton, London, Bruges, Paris, Rouen, Antwerp, Cologne, Augsburg, Amsterdam, and many others. All around the coasts of Europe, and across it in many directions, there was now going on a veritable beehive of commercial exchange, the making of profits, and the exploring of new ways and means of turning an honest—or dishonest—florin.

The Increase of Wealth

It is difficult to come by dependable figures to show the extent and the value of western European commerce about A.D. 1500. It is certain, nevertheless, that the total quantity of exchange between the various parts of Europe and between Europe and the countries around the Mediterranean was very great, and that the merchants of the commercial cities were amassing funds of capital that, relative to the wealth of Europe during the Feudal Era, were enormous. Some measure of this wealth may be seen by an examination of the career of the great commercial leaders who were rising to distinction as key figures in the changing European economy.

The Merchant Princes

One of the most striking and typical phenomena, indeed, of the changing economic life of Europe in the generation of Louis XI and Henry VII was the appearance in Italy, France, Germany, England, and the Low Countries of a number of great individual commercial and financial giants, who were able to accumulate huge fortunes and to exercise, as a result, enormous political power. They also made great contributions to the enrichment of the creative arts and literature by their patronage of artists and writers, thereby providing the economic base for the intellectual and artistic flowering known as the Renaissance.

The Medici family of Florence, for example, from humble beginnings had become substantial merchants in that city by the twelfth century, and their fortune, derived from commerce, continued to grow in the days of Dante and Petrarch. They became spectacularly rich, and the dominant mercantile and political family in this city of merchants in the days of Giovanni di Bicci de' Medici (1360–1429), whose commercial ventures and banking enterprises reached around the Mediterranean and into most of the countries of western Europe. It was Giovanni's sons and grandsons, most famous of whom was Lorenzo "the Magnificent" (1449–1492), who played such important roles among the great patrons of Renaissance art in Florence in the days of Leonardo da Vinci. Similarly, the great French merchant Jacques Coeur (c.1395–1456) amassed an enormous fortune in commerce, and brought the power of his fortune to the support of Charles VII in his struggle to build up the power of France, both against England and against the feudal lords of his own realm. Coeur began by by-passing the Mediterranean trade monopoly of the Italian cities, particularly Venice and Genoa, and then went on to establish branch houses all over France and to acquire mines and other enterprises. He became Charles' Master of the Mint and Steward; and he lent a fortune to the king in support of the king's power. He lost heavily thereby; but his career illustrates clearly both his ruthlessly individualistic ways of doing business and the intimate connection between the bourgeoisie and the monarchy. As a patron of art, he also illustrates the close identity of the economic "renaissance" with the intellectual one.

The Fugger family of Augsburg illustrates much the same general phenomenon. The Fuggers built up an enormous family fortune from the profits of commerce and banking, beginning with the career of Hans Fugger, a weaver, who went to Augsburg about 1380 and got his start by importing cotton from Venice for himself and his fellow weavers and then marketing the finished fustian cloth for them. His son expanded his business, and his grandson Jacob "the Rich" (1459–1525), became one of the outstanding geniuses of early modern capitalism. Jacob was educated and served his apprenticeship in Venice, where he absorbed both Renaissance humanism and economic individualism. When he assumed the leadership of the family business he extended its holdings to mines and industries as well as commerce, and his network of banks and agencies stretched over most of western Europe. He became banker and financier for the popes and for many of the crowned heads of Europe; it was largely with money borrowed from Jacob that Charles V "influenced" the electors of the Holy Roman Empire to elect him Holy Roman Emperor in 1519. When Jacob died the statement of the resources of the House of Fugger included the following:

Mines	270,000	florins
Real estate	150,000	"
Merchandise	380,000	"
Cash	50,000	"
Loans outstanding	1,650,000	"
Private accounts	430,000	"
Miscellaneous assets	70,000	"
Total	3,000,000	"

This total of the capital wealth of one firm probably would be the equivalent of at least $50,000,000 in 1957—perhaps more. The activities of this family firm included mining, real estate, and merchandising; but Jacob Fugger had made its chief and most profitable business that of banking and financing.

Yet the international financial power of the house of Fugger was its own undoing, for, unable to refuse the demands of the Hapsburgs for loans or to withstand the shock of their defaulting, the Fugger fortunes were eventually greatly reduced, especially by the national bankruptcies of Spain and Holland. For two centuries, however, precisely during the period of the Renaissance, the house of Fugger was one of the most important factors in the economic life of western Europe and the most brilliant example of early modern capitalism.

Adoration of the Magi—by Botticelli (p. 587), c.1475. Renaissance artists often commemorated important current events and people in ostensibly religious paintings. Here, kneeling at the feet of the Christ child, is Cosimo de' Medici. The other two kneeling figures have been identified with less certainty as Piero and Giovanni, Lorenzo's sons, the standing figure in black velvet as Giuliano and the man with hands on his sword as Lorenzo (p. 583), Cosimo's grandsons. (Anderson photograph)

The Methods of Early Capitalism

The advent of commercial capitalism as an economic system based upon individual private profit to supplant the agrarian and essentially communal economy of feudal society was an event of major significance in the history of western civilization and, eventually, of the world. And, as this economic revolution progressed, the merchant-capitalists perfected the techniques and the methods that would insure the smooth functioning of the capitalistic economic system and would mark it off from all the economic systems that had preceded it.

One of the most noticeable phenomena accompanying the advent of capitalism was the revival, already related (pp. 482–483), of the use of coined money. This development had been marked, in Florence in 1252, by the appearance of a coin called the florin—so-called because on one side it bore the image of a flower. The gold florin, weighing 54 grains, became one of the standard coins throughout the trading area of western Europe. Other important coins were the Flemish gulden, used by the Fuggers, weighing slightly less than the florin, and the English pound, which originated as a pound of silver pennies (standardized at 240). As these coins accumulated in the coffers of the merchants, capital and wealth came to be measured in terms of money instead of land. But the difficulty and the dangers in transferring large quantities of coin inspired the invention and development of various forms of "paper" to take the place of coin. Thus a merchant from Florence, for example, selling goods in London could get, in payment, a "draught," or "bill of exchange," on a banker in Florence that would relieve him of the necessity of transporting the amount in actual money. He could also get insurance on his goods. Or he could get a loan, covered by the value of his future sales, that would enable him to expand his operations. The extensive use of credit, indeed, and the invention of double-entry bookkeeping and other devices to ma-nipulate and control it, became one of the distinguishing marks of the capitalistic system.

Production: The Putting-out System

The increase in wealth, of course, derived from the steady and continual expansion of commerce. This expansion, in turn, resulted partly from the steady expansion of population in Europe itself, and partly, especially after the middle of the fifteenth century, from the opening of new markets and sources of raw material overseas (see pp. 566–568). It was this increasing demand for manufactured goods that inspired the devising of ways and means of increasing the production of textiles, particularly woolens. Thus a merchant-capitalist facing the expanding demand for cloth would buy the raw materials, such as wool, and, perhaps, the spinning wheels and the looms, and "put out" these materials and tools in the hands of spinners and weavers who, working in their own homes, would produce the cloth and return it to him. He would then sell it; the workers would receive wages or a percentage of the profit.

This system of production, called the "putting-out" system, involved the ownership of materials and machines by the merchant-capitalist on the one hand, and, on the other, labor done by workers who had no share in the ownership of the materials or the machines they used.

Presently, in the eighteenth century, as the world market continued to expand, men of inventive genius began to turn their wits to the invention of new machines to multiply still further the rate of textile (and other) production. With the invention of these new machines, and with the use of power instead of human labor to drive them, the Commercial Era would pass into the Industrial Era in the history of civilization. The important fact to be noted here is that it was the continuous expansion of commerce and the increased world demand for commercial commodities that induced both the application of capitalistic methods of production in the putting-out system and the Industrial Revolution that was to follow (Vol. II, Ch. 30).

Mines

Another important aspect of the capitalistic expansion in the area of production lay in the development of the mining industry. The presence of "Mines" among the assets of the Fuggers calls attention to the fact that there was taking place a great expansion of the kinds and the amounts of metal now being used in European manufactures. Chief among these metals were iron, copper, tin, silver, and brass (an alloy of tin and cop-

per). This increased demand for metals led to a search for new deposits and an expansion of the mining industry, in which the Fuggers shared. The consequent expansion of the supply of metals had a significant effect upon the manufacture of metal objects, the improvement of tools, and the building of machines; coupled with the influx of precious metals from America, it also brought about such an increase in the money supply as to cause a sharp inflation in prices, to be discussed shortly.

Organization of Business Enterprise

Meanwhile the merchants were also learning that, while individual financial geniuses might build up and expand great fortunes

The Amsterdam Exchange—by Job Berckheyde or Bockheyde. The Amsterdam Exchange was the financial center of sixteenth-century Europe, where any respectable businessman could walk in and begin to trade. (Courtesy of Rijksmuseum, Amsterdam)

through several generations, still greater capitalistic power might be achieved, and with less individual risk, by the pooling of resources for common enterprises. Thus, in the sixteenth century there appeared various forms of "companies," which were actually cooperative combinations of capital on the part of the merchant-capitalists. The most significant and successful form of these companies was that of the "joint-stock" company, which was in its essential features an early form of the modern corporation. In such a company a number of investors would contribute capital, receiving in return stock certificates, and the company would operate as a single economic enterprise, directed by a "governor," or "treasurer," and a board of "assistants" or directors. The organization of the company was usually permanent, and each stockholder received periodic (usually annual) dividends in proportion to the amount of stock that he had invested. Such "joint-stock companies," for example, were the great English and Dutch East India companies, organized about 1600, and the Virginia Company, organized in 1606.

The Bourse or Exchange

As the quantities of goods bought and sold in the commercial cities steadily increased, it gradually became the habit of the chief merchants of any given city to meet at some central place where they would offer for sale the goods they had in their warehouses. The exchanges of goods at this place were made by written orders of the merchants upon each other; the place itself came to be called the *exchange*. By the end of the sixteenth century nearly every important commercial city had an exchange or *bourse,* now generally housed in a building erected for the purpose. Presently, as the number of stock companies increased, and as the profits of these companies increased or decreased, it became customary to buy and sell the shares (stock certificates) and the financial obligations (bonds) of these companies for speculative purposes at the exchange. Still later, the exchange for goods and the stock exchange, or bourse, were separated.

The Capitalistic Spirit

But the most profoundly significant difference between this rapidly expanding commercial-capitalistic economy and the manorial economy of the Feudal Era was probably the spirit that animated it. Whereas the spirit of the manorial economy was a "communal" spirit, the new economy was essentially capitalist; that is, it rested upon the concept of capital wealth,—symbolized by, but not necessarily composed of, money—to be used for the increase of wealth by an accrual of profit. The objective was the increase of private wealth in money or property; the "motive" was the individualistic profit motive.

THE SPREAD OF EUROPEAN COMMERCE AROUND THE WORLD

The spirit of capitalism, at its best, was a spirit of adventure, initiative, and resourcefulness. And as capital available for investment accumulated in the coffers of the merchant capitalists, they turned their imaginations to the discovery or the invention of new enterprises for the investment of their surpluses and the making of larger profits. It was some such spirit as this that led the European merchant-capitalists to extend the tentacles of their profit-making commerce around the world.

This reaching-out process had actually begun with those great predatory and commercial enterprises of the Feudal Era, the Crusades. It had continued with the expansion of the commerce of the Italian, French, and Spanish cities around the Mediterranean and, through the Turkish and Arab middlemen of the Middle East, a reaching out of European trade all the way to the rich cities of India and China; the long sojourn of the Venetian Marco Polo in Asia was only the most dramatic of a number of direct contacts which Europeans made with the peoples of the more ancient east.

Westward, the expansion of European commerce into the Atlantic may be said to have begun when, in the year 1317, merchants of Venice tried the experiment of sending a large part of their annual shipments of goods to northern Europe all the way by ship, through the Strait of Gibraltar and along the coast to the Low Countries and to England. The experiment was a success, and for centuries the Venetian fleets sailed annually along this route, bearing Mediterranean and eastern products and returning with hides, tin, lumber, and other products of the north.

The Opening of the Atlantic

Lisbon and Cadiz, standing at the corner of Europe where the Venetian fleet turned northward, became important points of transshipment and exchange. And as their commerce grew and their merchants accumulated capital, their attention began to turn toward the possibility of markets along the coast of northern Africa and, presently, in the "islands of the sea." The Portuguese and Castilian interest in the Canary Islands led to several expeditions to explore and open them to trade, and the Castilian interest led to a request for them to the pope, as the disposer of non-Christian lands. Pope Clement VI, at Avignon, thereupon gave the islands to a grandson of Alfonso X of Castile, Juan de la Cerda. But although both France and Castile claimed them, it was not until 1402 that Jean de Bethancourt, operating

out of Cadiz, conquered the islands and colonized them. This event should probably be taken as the true beginning of European commercial and colonial expansion over the Atlantic.

But the expansion of European commerce outward across the Atlantic really began in earnest with the work of Prince Henry of Portugal (1392–1460), called "the Navigator." For Henry, beginning in 1419, systematically explored the commercial possibilities of the coast of Africa and the groups of islands off the African coast. He gathered a group of mathematicians, geographers, and sea captains about him at Sagres, and year after year he sent expeditions down the coast of Africa to explore the unknown. In 1433 Gil Eannes rounded Cape Bojador, and the next year the first consignment of African slaves arrived in Lisbon—to open the western European slave trade. In 1445 one of Henry's

An Astrolabe. Invented by the Greeks and taken over by the Portuguese from Arab seamen, the astrolabe measured the height of the sun and gave an approximation of the observer's latitude. (*The Arte of Navigation* by Martin Curtis, London, 1561, New York Public Library Rare Book Room)

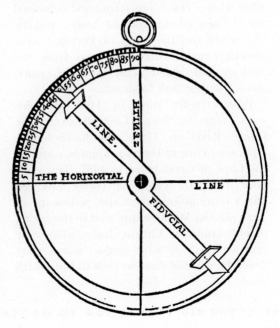

Henry the Navigator—a miniature from the manuscript of Azurara's *Discovery and Conquest of Guinea*, fifteenth century, in the *Bibliothèque Nationale*, Paris. (Courtesy of the Metropolitan Museum of Art)

The Sea Route to the Indies

The dream of Henry was realized. The Atlantic had been opened; scientific geographic knowledge had been vastly expanded; Portugal had established the first overseas European colonial empire; the Italian cities' monopoly of the trade with the Far East was broken; and European civilization had been carried—and planted—in the distant places of the earth.

But that was just the beginning. The wealth and the vision led men on. The year after da Gama's return, Pedro Cabral went back to India, incidentally touching Brazil, a part of the continent just discovered by Christopher Columbus, and at Madagascar. When he arrived in India he established Portugal's first trading stations at Cochin and Calicut. Cabral was followed by a suitable crowd of Portuguese explorers, who discovered St. Helena, Mauritius, and Tristão da Cunha, and conquered numerous areas along the eastern coast of Africa. Within a decade of the expedition of Vasco de Gama, Portugal had extended its already extensive commercial empire around the shores of the Indian Ocean.

But the most dramatic establishment of the Portuguese in the Far East was accomplished by Afonso de Albuquerque. For Albuquerque seized the city of Goa and made it a Portuguese naval base; he conquered Malaysia and sent a successful expedition to the Moluccas, which were added to the Portuguese empire; and he established diplomatic relations with Persia and Thailand. From Goa, the capital of the eastern empire, Portuguese traders went on to Canton, and the Portuguese were given Macao by China as a trading city about 1557. Japan was discovered in 1542, and there, too, the Portuguese established their far-flung commerce and missionaries bearing European religion and culture. Thus by the middle of the sixteenth century the Portuguese commercial and cultural empire, the first European colonial empire, stretched from the homeland

captains rounded Cape Verde and opened the trade along the coast of Guinea, to realize one of Henry's original ambitions. Meanwhile Henry's explorers found and colonized the Madeira Islands and the Azores, and the merchants and the kings of Portugal were growing wealthy on the profits from the African and island trade in gold, ivory, slaves, lumber, and foodstuffs.

Prince Henry died in 1460. But his work went on. Diego Cam discovered the Congo River in 1482, and Bartholomew Diaz, son of one of Henry's captains, rounded the Cape of Good Hope in 1487. Ten years later, in 1497, Vasco da Gama followed Diaz's route around the Cape, picked up an Arab pilot in Mozambique, and in the spring of 1498 landed in Calicut, India, whence he returned in 1499 with cargoes worth sixty times the value of those he took to India with him!

to Brazil, around the coasts of Africa, west and east, to India, Malaysia, China, and Japan.

The Portuguese viceroy in the east, resident at Goa, was a sort of absolute emperor, under the King of Portugal, of one of the most extensive commercial domains the world has ever known. But not only that, the goods, persons, and cultural riches brought back from the empire to Portugal and Europe had, and would have, profound effects upon the civilization of Europe itself.

Westward across the Ocean Sea

Meanwhile the Castilian rivals of the Portuguese, operating out of Cadiz, had also been carrying their commerce and culture outward into the unknown world. Thus the merchants of Cadiz poached upon Prince Henry's commercial domain in Africa, and Castile claimed the Canaries under the old papal grant and first colonization. This claim was recognized by Portugal in the Treaty of Alcaçovas of 1479, on condition that Castile refrain from poaching in Africa. Castile's colonial empire was thus limited to the Canaries. But the huge profits from Portuguese commercial expansion were too obvious and too rich not to arouse envy in the hearts of the Castilians. Consequently, when an Italian adventurer named Christopher Columbus proposed to find for Castile a third commercial route to the east to rival Portugal's and that of the Italian cities, Ferdinand considered it long and carefully. Columbus' scheme, inspired by the Italian humanist, physician, and geographer Paolo Toscanelli, was risky and difficult—much more so than Columbus appeared to realize—so it was rejected. But Queen Isabella, urged by her treasurer to consider how vast, in case of success, would be her profits as compared with her investment, consented. So Columbus was commissioned to try, with the backing of a sort of partnership among the Spanish crown, himself, and the Pinzon brothers, merchants.

The Market at Goa. This scene is a detail from a folding plate made to illustrate the first edition of *Voyage to the East Indies*, by the Dutch traveler Linschoten, published in Amsterdam in 1596. (New York Public Library Rare Book Room)

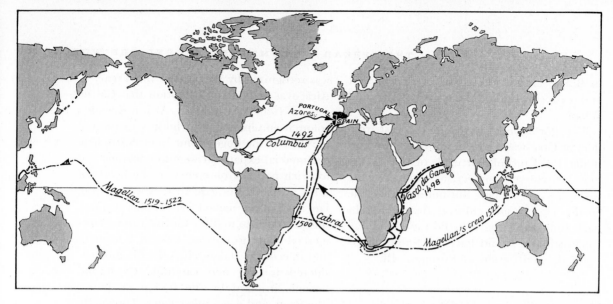

Voyages of Columbus, da Gama, Cabral, and Magellan

The Spanish Colonial Empire

That was early in 1492. Columbus sailed that summer, and discovered land that he thought was Asia. He also established a colony on the island of Española, or Santo Domingo, which became the nucleus for a vast extension of Spain's empire in the western hemisphere. Portugal, suspicious, accused Columbus of trespass upon Portugal's empire, but the pope supported Spain by a series of papal bulls in 1493 that drew a line down the middle of the Atlantic from the north pole to the south and gave Spain all the lands west of the line. Portugal accepted the line; but it was moved farther westward by the Treaty of Tordesillas between Portugal and Spain in 1494.

And now, from Española as a base, a crowd of Spanish adventurers, led by Columbus himself, explored the continent Columbus had discovered. Columbus never doubted that he had found an extension of Asia; but when Vasco Núñez de Balboa discovered the Pacific Ocean in 1513 and when Ferdinand Magellan, a Portuguese captain working for Spain, rounded South America and crossed that ocean eight years later, to add the Philippines in the Far East to Spain's colonial empire, the world knew that "America" was an entirely new continent standing between Europe and Asia. Around the shores of this continent the Spaniards searched for land, gold, adventure, and converts to Christianity. Hernán Cortés conquered Mexico beginning in 1519, and Hernando Pizarro duplicated his exploits, beginning in 1531, in Peru—two conquests that sent a veritable flood of commerce and treasure tumbling toward Spain and imposed Spanish rule, commerce and culture upon the two most highly developed native "Indian" cultures in the western hemisphere.*

English Expeditions

After Portugal and Spain, the other maritime states of western Europe followed suit. Henry VII of England hired an Italian, John Cabot, in 1497 to try to reach and trade with the Indies by a northwesterly route for England. English overseas commercial interest was increased and encouraged under Henry VIII, and about the middle of the century English merchants began to trade with Muscovy (Russia), with the eastern Mediterran-

* For the growth of these colonies, see Chapter 27.

ean, and with Africa, and to search more diligently for a feasible commercial route to China. But English overseas expansion entered a still more spectacular phase under Queen Elizabeth (1558–1603), when such "Elizabethan seadogs" as William Hawkins, Francis Drake, Walter Raleigh, Humphrey Gilbert, and Sir Richard Grenville took their fast-sailing English ships to the four corners of the globe. It reached its climax in the organization of the East India Company in 1600.

Martin Frobisher, searching for the northwest passage to Asia, took possession of "Frobishers' Land" in 1577 to give commercial England its first overseas possession, and a few months later Francis Drake gave England its second "piece of empire" in New Albion (California). In 1583 Humphrey Gilbert planted England's first permanent overseas colony on the island of Newfoundland. The next year Walter Raleigh made his ill-fated attempt to colonize Virginia, and in the next decade several attempts were made to found commercial bases in America—on the St. Lawrence in the north and on the Orinoco in the south. The beginning of success was finally achieved with the permanent establishment of Virginia, beginning with the little colony at Jamestown, in 1607.*

The English commercial empire had thus begun with the work of Frobisher, Drake, Raleigh, and Gilbert in America, and England entered the game of imperialism in the Far East with the foundation of the East India Company in 1600. This company found itself in commercial competition with the Portuguese and the Dutch; but it succeeded in establishing a profitable trade, and, like the Dutch, in turning its "factories" into ports and then in establishing itself as a ruler. Like the Dutch Limited Company, the East India Company was a sort of *imperium in imperio*. It built "factories" at various points along the Indian coast, especially on the Coromandel Coast and in Bengal, Madras, and

* For the growth of the English colonies in America, see Chapter 27.

Bombay, and ruled its ports and possessions as a government. Dutch competition, coupled with the great rebellion in England, weakened the Company, but under a new charter granted it by Oliver Cromwell in 1657 it took a new lease on life and expanded until in the eighteenth century it controlled a major part of India.†

† For the growth of the English colonies in India, see Volume II, Chapters 36 and 37.

"Columbus Landing at Insula Hyspaña." Columbus described his voyage in a letter, *De Insulis Nuper Inventis*, published at Basle in 1493. The artist who made the illustrations for this document portrayed a land of castles, houses, galleons and natives who went naked—a fact that impressed Europeans more than any other. (Courtesy of New York Public Library Rare Book Room)

Seventeenth-century Trade Routes

The Overseas Expansion of the Dutch

The merchants of the Low Countries, already highly successful competitors in the expanding commerce of Europe, had at first gotten their Far Eastern goods from the Portuguese at Lisbon. But after the outbreak of the Dutch war for independence from Spain in 1565, and especially after Spain annexed Portugal and its empire in 1580, the Dutch traders by-passed Lisbon, boldly entered the Indian Ocean directly, and began to share in the rich trade of the Indies, as it were, by trespass.

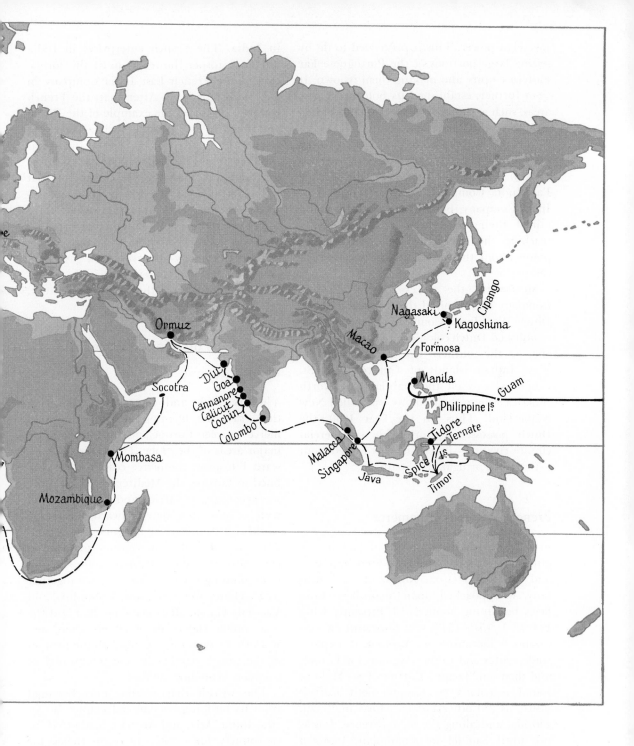

It was not very long, then, before the Dutch established their colonies or "factories" of merchants in the Indian cities. The "factories" soon became ports, and from traders, in many areas, the Dutch became rulers. Dutch trade in India was unified under the Dutch Limited Company, a sort of national joint-stock company formed in 1602. This company was given a monopoly of all Dutch commerce in the area between the Cape of Good Hope and Cape Horn, and was empowered to annex territory, set up governments, make war and peace, and otherwise to conduct itself as a sovereign power. This it proceeded to do by seizing large portions of the Portuguese Far Eastern empire and making them its own. It went further, established its hold upon new areas, such as Surat, Ahmadabad, and Patna, and drove the Portuguese completely out of Ceylon. The expansions of the Dutch brought them into conflict also with the rival English East India Company, the French East India Company, and the Danish East India Company, but they successfully maintained their leadership over their rivals, reaching the apogee of their Far Eastern power about the middle of the seventeenth century.

Meanwhile, the success of the Limited Company had inspired the formation of the Dutch West India Company in 1621, which established Dutch colonies in Brazil and Guiana, on the southern tip of Africa, on the West Indian islands of Curaçoa and St. Eustatius, and on the mainland of North America, where their colony was called New Netherland. Thus, in the year 1650, the Dutch possessed a world-wide commercial empire rivaling—indeed in part carved from —those of Portugal and Spain.

French Overseas Commerce

French overseas expansion had had its beginning in the activities of French pirates and "privateers" from Normandy and Brittany, who poached upon Spanish treasure fleets beginning about 1510. Presently King Francis I (1515–1549) sent Giovanni da Verrazano, a Florentine sea captain, to explore trade routes and to possess lands for France, and then sent Jacques Cartier of St. Malo to found a colony in Canada. But Cartier failed, as did other French efforts in Brazil, Florida, and along the St. Lawrence. It was not until Samuel de Champlain founded Acadia (1604) and Quebec (1608) that "New France" got its start. Thereafter, French colonies were soon established in the West Indies, along the coasts of Africa, and

in India. The French enterprises in India did not prosper, however, until the formation of the French East India Company in 1664 by Louis XIV. After that, the French company followed the example of the Dutch and English and became such a successful rival with the English company in India that the French and English companies fell into a long series of wars for the control of that rich subcontinent. Generally (but not always) merged with European wars, these wars over India finally culminated in an almost complete victory for England in the eighteenth century—an event that gave England an almost complete monopoly of Indian commerce until the twentieth century.

The Effects of World Commerce upon Europe

The sixteenth and seventeenth centuries, then, saw the opening of sea-borne commerce between Europe and most of the other major areas of the globe. From this time onward European commerce ceased to be confined to Europe, the Mediterranean, and the western coasts of Africa and became worldwide. From this date onward, also, the worldwide commercial network grew, from year to year and from century to century, ever more all-embracing, more complex, and more binding upon the areas drawn together by it. Henry the Navigator, Columbus, and Vasco da Gama, all-unknowing, had laid the first commercial cords of an economic network that would one day bind all the peoples of the world together in one community of common economic interest.

The wealth that poured into Portugal from its far-flung commercial empire in Africa, India, Asia, and America made that little country, for a time, one of the richest for its size in the world. The fabulous wealth that poured into Spain from its American empire was in large measure responsible for that country's dominance in international affairs for the century following the exploits of Columbus. The profits from the French commercial and colonial empires were relatively modest, though substantial. The Dutch lost much of their colonial establishment in America to the Portuguese and the English, but their establishments in the Far East paid high dividends. The Dutch, in fact, grew wealthy from overseas commerce less from carrying goods to and from their own colonies than from becoming commercial carriers for all the others, with or without the consent of the governments involved. It was the British Empire, probably, that in the long run was most profitable; and the rest of Europe looked with envy upon the power of England that was thought to derive from its highly profitable colonies.

The opening of a vast, worldwide commerce by the European merchants also had profound effects on the European economy. In the first place, the opening of the new countries around the world introduced an unheard-of quantity and variety of new and old products to Europeans for their consumption—new foods, for example, such as the potato, the tomato, Indian corn (maize), lima beans, yams, tea, coffee, and cocoa. Fruits, such as the banana and the pineapple, were new to Europeans; tobacco was introduced into Europe by Columbus, and its use spread all over western Europe. The supply of other products, some of them already known to Europe, was multiplied. Such were Oriental silks, cotton, furs, perfumes, gems, gold and silver, ostrich plumes, glass, rugs, sugar, and wines; rum, a derivative from sugar cane, was a new—potent—drink from the West Indies.

These exotic products, and a host of others, tended to change the eating and living habits of the Europeans. But if the "new world" of Asia, Africa, and America furnished new commodities for the enrichment and enjoyment of life, it also offered a huge market for such European products as tools, clothing, woolens, firearms, wheat, salt fish, and the gewgaws prized by the primitive peoples with whom the Europeans dealt.

The result was a phenomenal increase in European overseas commerce, which also meant a corresponding phenomenal increase in European wealth. Thus, for example, by about 1700 English imports (including those from continental Europe) amounted to some $27,000,000; exports amounted to some $32,000,000. In the century that followed, English imports mounted to some $157,000,000; exports to $207,000,000. Of these amounts, perhaps one fifth to one fourth derived from England's own colonies; commerce with foreign colonies, such as Portugal's Brazil, may have accounted for an equal proportion. Similarly, French overseas trade rose in value from some $40,000,000 at the time of the Peace of Utrecht (1713) to about $230,000,000 on the eve of the French Revolution (1789). Relatively little of this French commerce was with its colonies; most of it was chiefly with the other countries of Europe and with India.

Ships of the Dutch East India Company—etching by Wenzel Hollar, dated 1647. Beached for cleaning and repairing, the ships bear the arms of the city of Amsterdam. Construction and gun capacity suggest warships, because for long, dangerous voyages the Dutch East Indiamen were armed. (Courtesy of the Metropolitan Museum of Art)

Incidentally, the phenomenal increase in European wealth, including the supply of gold and silver bullion, derived both from the internal capitalistic expansion of Europe itself and from the dramatic blanketing of the earth by the advance agents of European capitalism, brought about a vast inflation. The prices of commodities rose rapidly; within a relatively few years after the beginning of the exploitation of the American silver mines, the prices of certain commodities in Europe were multiplied as much as five times. The result of this price revolution, of course, was a sharp increase in the cost of living and a widening of the economic and social gap between the rich and the poor.

The largest part of European overseas commerce, apart from that among the European states themselves, was around and across the Atlantic Ocean—to Africa, to South America, and to North America. All around the Atlantic Basin, in fact, the Western Europeans now traded pretty much on their own terms and with their own methods, as compared with those people who were employed in the commerce with the more sophisticated peoples of the Far East. In this sense, the trading area around the Atlantic Basin became a "European" trading area, or, to put it more accurately, the European trading area expanded to become the trading area of the Atlantic Basin. This basic fact, alone, is of the utmost significance, because in it lies the key to the transformation of "European civilization" into a "western" or an Atlantic civilization.

SOCIAL ASPECTS OF THE COMMERCIAL REVOLUTION

The growth of commerce and the expansion of wealth that accompanied it brought with them a number of deep social changes. In fact, it can be said that between about 1400 and 1700 there took place in the western world a social revolution that was no less profound than the economic changes that produced it.

The Increase in Population

The population of all western Europe increased steadily during this period. Between 1300 and 1450 the population had increased but little; it is estimated that, if the population of this area was 53,000,000 in 1300, it was still approximately the same in 1450. But it rose to about 100,000,000 in 1650 and amounted to some 140,000,000 in 1750.

The Urban Movement

The majority of these people still lived on the land, but the ratio of city population to rural population was steadily rising: a steadily increasing proportion of the population was now living in towns. In England, particularly, the rising demand for woolen cloth had brought about the so-called "enclosures" movement, which meant that lands were being fenced in for the raising of sheep and the yeomen farmers were being forced off the land into the cities, to swell the available labor force for the textile and other industries or to provide emigrants for the movement of Englishmen to the colonies.

The Class Structure

The class structure that had been characteristic of the Feudal Era continued to be the ideal of the society of western Europe. But whereas the strata in the feudal society were those of landed aristocracy, small knights or squires, and serfs and villeins, by the eighteenth century the commercial and professional classes of the cities were a social force to be reckoned with. Moreover, the steadily increasing number of small shopkeepers and artisans in the towns represented another, and increasingly powerful, social group, as distinguished from the wealthier business and professional *bourgeoisie,* that was already beginning to demand a place in the social and political sun. (See picture, p. 572.)

Society was changing as the economy changed; and as society changed, there was a corresponding change—or demand for change—in politics. But that is another story.

IDEOLOGICAL ASPECTS OF THE COMMERICAL REVOLUTION

One of the most significant changes—or sets of changes—accompanying the Commercial Revolution was the change that took place in the economic thinking of the western world.

Economic Individualism

First of all, it should be noted that the perfection of the practices and the rationale of commercial capitalism by the merchant princes rested upon a new ethos of economic individualism. The merchants, as they became increasingly wealthy, became correspondingly independent of the "communal" ideal expressed by the economic theorists of the Feudal Era. These new merchant-capitalists were economic individualists *par excellence,* and their guiding principle was individual economic gain. They were ruthless and unscrupulous; in their commercial practice, for them, the end justified almost any means.

With the creation of such great mercantile companies as the English Muscovy Company, the Levant Company, and the English, Dutch, and French East India companies, these great corporations received from the governments that created them monopolies of the trade in the areas in which they focused their enterprises. But the creation of these great monopolies, whether of geographic areas or of the marketing of certain commodities, such as tobacco, salt, or woolen cloth, aroused the bitter criticism of the "little men" and the individuals who were excluded. There was a

considerable body of theory thrown off, as a result, by the partisans of the "little men" in the name of economic individualism. Much of this theorizing about economic individualism was, thus, both a rationalization of the original individualism of the rise of capitalism and a sort of defensive ideology against the corporative tendencies of the great monopolies.

Such a theorist of economic individualism, for example, was John Hales, an Englishman who published his *A Discourse of the Common Weal of This Realm of England* in 1581. Hales explained all economic activity upon the basis of individual self-interest; the problem of the times, he said, was to harness this natural human trait to the promotion of the common welfare. His ideas were accepted by many and played an important role in the development of the later ideas of such men as Adam Smith.

Even many of the religious leaders of the new individualistic Protestantism that was sweeping over northern Europe in the sixteenth century (Chapter 24) tied their religious individualism to economic individualism. John Calvin, the "Protestant Pope" of Geneva, for example, said that "the communion of Saints" in the invisible church does not "disturb the order of civil politics, which secures to every individual the exclusive enjoyment of his property, as it is necessary for the preservation of the peace of society that men should have peculiar and distinct possessions." And the Reverend Richard Baxter, one of the great Puritan leaders of England, instructed his followers to use every conceivable means, short of actual sin, to increase their wealth: "Riches for our fleshly ends must not ultimately be intended or sought. But in subordination to higher things they may. . . . But then your *end* must be, that you may be the better provided to do God's service and may do the more good with what you have."

Many of the Protestant leaders were dismayed, to be sure, by the ruthless and scandalous abuses of economic individualism, and they condemned the excesses of "usury." Yet, generally speaking, the idea of economic individualism was accepted by most Protestants and was linked, especially by the Calvinists and Puritans, with the idea of "calling"—that is, that God called every man, individually, to some specific trade or profession, and that it was the duty of the worker by thrift and industry to accumulate all the wealth he could for the furtherance of God's work with men.

Theories of Money and Wealth

Basic to the new capitalist ideology, then, was the assumption, contrary to the "communal" economic ideal of the Feudal Era, of the idea of economic individualism. This individualism rested upon the concept of private (as against communal) property, private economic enterprise, and private individual profits. But the measure of property, or wealth, was now coming to be money as against the feudal measure of wealth, which was land. And some of the earliest theorists of capitalism addressed themselves primarily to this phenomenon.

Bodin. The first European thinker to interest himself significantly in the problem of money and its nature was Jean Bodin (1530–1596), a Frenchman. Bodin was impressed by the price revolution then going on and tried to explain it. The chief cause, he found, was the great abundance of gold and silver; in arriving at this conclusion he gave the ear-

liest expression to the so-called "quantity theory" of money—that is, that prices are largely determined by the quantity of money available: when there is an abundance of money, prices are high; when money is scarce, prices are low. Thomas Gresham, a financial agent of Queen Elizabeth and founder of the Royal Exchange in London (1571), came up, after a life-long study of the various kinds and values of European monies, with the so-called "Gresham's Law" that bad—or "cheap" or "debased"—money tends to drive good—or full-value—money out of the market.

Bullionism. The powerful impression made upon the minds of European economists by the importance of money in the new economy is most clearly to be seen in the theory of national wealth called *bullionism*.

According to this theory, the wealth and international power of a state depend, in the last analysis, upon the amount of "treasure" or gold and silver bullion in the coffers of the state and its citizens. Since the government is bound to promote the interests of the citizens, it should restrict, within reason, the export of bullion outside the national frontiers. Similarly the government, according to this theory, should encourage the import of bullion, as, for example, by requiring exporters of goods to insist upon receiving, as payment for at least a portion of the goods exported, quantities of the precious metals.

This idea of the partnership of the government with the businessmen, or the intervention of the state in international exchange for the sake of building up the stock of bullion within the state, is called bullionism. But it was not long before the theorists and the governments came to realize that wealth is not measured by bullion alone; that, in fact, it is often beneficial to the state to export bullion, if the bullion is used for the purchase of goods that may be re-exported at an additional profit. This consideration, and others like it, led to an increasing sophistication of economic thought, and the appearance of a body of ideas known as *mercantilism.*

Mercantilism. According to the theory of mercantilism, the state may be regarded as being very much like an individual merchant; and, like the merchant, if the state is to increase its wealth and power, it must sell more than it buys. The consequent surplus of profit, whether of bullion or of goods, constitutes a true accrual to the national wealth and eventually benefits every individual citizen in the state.

John Hales had already said: "For we must always take heed that we buy no more of strangers than we sell them; for so we should impoverish ourselves and enrich them." And the European governments had consciously adopted commercial and colonial policies that attempted rigidly to bring this general objective into effect. Thus Edward Misselden (fl. 1608–1654) wrote that the great objective of the national economic policy should be to build up and maintain a favorable "balance of trade." The state should take such measures as it could to encourage exports and discourage imports; if this meant the supervision and regulation of production in order to improve the quality of the national exports and thereby their competitive position on the international market, so much the better.

The best known of the mercantilist thinkers of the seventeenth century was Thomas Mun (1571–1641), an English merchant who was a member of the English East India Company. Mun wrote his classic statement of the mercantilist theory, his *England's Treasure by Forraigne Trade* in 1630 (it was not published until after his death, in 1664). In this book he speaks of the merchant as the most valuable sort of member of society, and he clearly expounds the doctrine that the wealth and power of a country depend upon a favorably balanced foreign trade. But Mun realized, as his predecessors had not, that the measure of this balance need not be bullion but might be goods—"stock" Mun called it.

Incidentally, since this was the period in which European colonies overseas were demonstrating their value to the mother countries, the colonies came in for a good deal of consideration in the thinking of the mercantilists. In general, colonies were looked upon as outlying, controlled sales areas for the products of the mother country and as controlled areas of production for such goods as sugar, tobacco, wine, or precious metals that the mother country could not produce. Naturally, as the colonies were now considered as outlying "factories" that existed largely for maintaining the mother country's favorable balance of trade, it followed that the mother country should enjoy a complete, or nearly complete, monopoly of trade both to and from the colonies—no matter what the interests of the colonies might be. Colonies, however, should not be permitted to produce goods already produced in the mother country and thus enter into competition with it.

Gradually the theory of mercantilism was developed and refined still further. In one direction it developed toward a sort of protectionism for home merchants, industries, and workers against foreign competition. In another it developed in the direction of national economic and military self-sufficiency in time of war. In this way of thinking, colonies began to be looked upon as areas of production for strategic materials the mother country could not produce—such materials as, say, iron or ships' masts or naval stores. All these ideas, along with the basic policy of a national monopoly of colonial trade, strongly influenced, in one way or another, the colonial policies of all the great commercial and colonial states.

Colbert

All of the great commercial states of western Europe based their national economic policies, both internal and external, upon the general tenets of mercantilism. One of the

Nuremberg—German woodcut, 1493. As the power of the feudal nobility waned, traders, artisans, and other townspeople erected the tower at extreme right in defiance of the castle. (Courtesy of the Metropolitan Museum of Art)

most extreme cases of the application of these ideas in national policy was that of France under Louis XIV, whose chief minister, Jean Baptiste Colbert (1619–1683), was one of the most thoroughgoing mercantilist statesmen of all time.

Colbert came to power in 1661 and remained, next to Louis XIV himself, the most powerful man in France. He was convinced of the validity of mercantilist statism, and he put into execution a whole set of codes of law applying mercantilist ideas to the French economy. He was fundamentally a bullionist, but he saw that, to increase the supply of bullion in France, the country must export more than it imported. Commerce was all-important, but one nation's gain was another nation's loss. Commerce, he said is "a perpetual and peaceable war of wit and energy among all nations."

Because of these beliefs, Colbert set up a skillfully devised system of tariffs, encour-aged shipbuilding, and promoted the establishment of French commercial colonies in America and in India. For the promotion of French internal economic life, he created a Council of Commerce and caused it to reduce tolls on roads and bridges, regularize the currency, build canals, and strictly regulate the quality of French manufacturers so they might compete successfully in international trade. It was Colbert, too, who organized the French East India Company (1664) and other great state-sponsored companies, and also built up the French navy to a point where it might successfully compete with the English fleet.

In general Colbert's efforts were only partly successful. Yet they did significantly stimulate French economic life, and they represent the most thoroughgoing conscious effort to use the mechanisms of the state to promote the national economy along mercantilist lines.

The Reaction toward Freedom of Trade

In all this evolution of the economic theories of mercantilism one theme is constant: the political interests of the state were thought to coincide exactly with those of the nation's commerce. The application of this principle in practice brought the power of the state to the support of commerce; but, while in some instances it encouraged the establishment of monopolies, in others it resulted in extensive regulations and restrictions. These restrictions, coupled with duties and taxes upon commerce and industry, severely limited individual enterprise and tended increasingly to subject the interests of the individual to those of the state. As time went on, as strong-minded monarchs tended to override the interests of the merchants, the merchants found it necessary to devise legal limitations or restrictions upon the monarch, and there ensued a contest, particularly clear in England, for the establishment of a basic law or constitution, that even the king must obey (Chapter 25), and some sort of balance, in the control of the state, between the monarch and the various economic and social groups in it.

As commerce continued to expand, the mercantilist regulations and protections, once so highly desired by the merchants, became increasingly irksome, and certain theorists began to suggest that so much regulation, after all, did more harm than good and that commerce would prosper more if left to circulate freely. One of the pioneers of this new line of thought was François Quesnay (1694–1774), a French physician, who, under the influence of the then-popular concept of natural law, made an all-out attack upon the whole mercantilist ideology. The circulation of commerce, he said, is like the circulation of the blood; restrictions and regulations are like tourniquets and have the effect of retarding commerce and causing its stagnation. Therefore, let the state withdraw its interference and allow commerce to flow freely.

Adam Smith

A similar set of ideas was formulated, somewhat more systematically, by Adam Smith (1723–1790), whose *An Inquiry into the Nature and Causes of the Wealth of Nations* (1776) is one of the great classics of economic theory. Accepting John Hales' idea of "enlightened self-interest" as a part of the natural order of things, Smith concluded that wealth is most effectively created by the free and unrestricted exchange of goods. The growth and the flow of wealth follow the dictates of natural economic laws, and regulation is an unhealthful interference with the operation of natural law. Let the state keep its hands off commerce, therefore (with certain exceptions), and let the flow of trade freely follow its own natural channels. This is the beginning of the so-called *laissez-faire* doctrine in economic thought.

With Smith, the rationalization of commercial economy reached its highest expression. European theory as to the nature of economic life dominated by commerce had now come a full cycle: from the naïve and unformulated rugged economic individualism of the sixteenth century, it had moved through bullionism into the thoroughgoing statism of Colbertian mercantilism. But Smith represents an almost equally thoroughgoing reaction against statism in the direction of free trade. Yet Smith was still a philosopher and a rationalizer of the commercial economy; he was the greatest of the theorists of the Commercial Revolution.

Suggestions for Further Reading

Source Materials

Anthologies and Collected Documents

H. S. Burrage, ed., *Early English and French Voyages, Chiefly from Hakluyt, 1534–1608* (New York, 1906).

This is a good and useful selection of explorers' narratives, mostly drawn from the large contemporary collection made by Richard Hakluyt.

Columbia College, *Introduction to Contemporary Civilization in the West* (2 vols., New York, 1946), Volume I, Chapters 4, 8.

A fine selection of documents illustrating the rise and the practices of early capitalism and of excerpts from the chief theorists of the Commercial Revolution.

V. Klarwill, ed., *The Fugger News-Letters* (New York, 1925).

A selection of the news reports of agents of the Fugger enterprises. Very interesting for an understanding of the Fugger network.

G. H. Knoles and R. K. Snyder, eds., *Readings in Western Civilization* (rev. ed., New York, 1954), pp. 439–452, 594–605.

Valuable selections from Thomas Mun, Daniel Defoe, and Adam Smith.

J. H. Robinson, *Readings in European History* (2 vols., Boston, 1909), Volume II, Ch. XXXIII.

Short selections illustrative of the search for new routes and areas for commerce.

Contemporary Writings

R. Hakluyt, ed., *Principal Navigations, Voyages, Traffiques, and Discoveries of the English Nation* (12 vols. Glasgow, 1903).

This is the classic collection of narratives of the great explorers of the Age of Exploration.

Marco Polo, *The Adventures of Marco Polo*, edited by R. J. Walsh (New York, 1948).

An excellent edition of this narrative of adventure.

T. Mun, *England's Treasure by Forraigne Trade* (London, 1664; reprint, New York, 1928).

This is one of the classic expressions of the mercantile theory, by one of the greatest of the mercantilists.

A. Smith, *An Inquiry into the Nature and Causes of the Wealth of Nations* (Modern Library edition, New York, 1937).

This is the classic statement of the doctrine of free trade as contrasted with mercantilism.

Secondary Works

M. Beard, *History of the Business Man* (New York, 1938).

An interesting history of businessmen as a class from ancient times to the present.

E. P. Cheyney, *The Dawn of a New Era: 1250–1453* (New York, 1936).

A valuable summary of the changes taking place in European society in the late Feudal Era.

C. W. Cole and S. B. Clough, *Economic History of Europe* (Boston, 1941).

An excellent survey of European economic development from the Feudal Era to the twentieth century.

N. M. Crouse, *In Quest of the Western Ocean* (New York, 1928).

The story of the search for the westward sea-route to the Indies.

C. Day, *History of Commerce* (New York, 1908).

A standard history of commerce.

J. E. Gillespie, *A History of Geographical Discovery, 1400–1800* (New York, 1933).

A brief history of European explorations between 1400 and 1800.

D. Hannay, *The Great Chartered Companies* (London, 1926).

A standard and highly valuable description of the great companies that developed much of European overseas commerce.

C. J. H. Hayes, *A Political and Cultural History of Modern Europe* (rev. ed., 2 vols., New York, 1932–1936).

A standard, excellent survey of European history from 1500 to the present.

E. F. Hecksher, *Mercantilism* (rev. ed., 2 vols., New York, 1956).

Probably the best analysis and history of mercantilist ideology and practice.

S. E. Morison, *Admiral of the Ocean Sea* (Boston, 1942).

A delightful history of the four voyages of Columbus. Supersedes all others.

W. Notestein, *The English People on the Eve of Colonization: 1607–1630* (New York, 1954).

A delightful description of English life and society in the years when the first English colonies in America were founded.

L. B. Packard, *The Commercial Revolution, 1400–1776* (New York, 1927).

A compact and highly useful history of the Commercial Revolution. Brief, standard.

R. R. Palmer, *A History of the Modern World* (New York, 1950).

An excellent survey of European history from about 1500 to the present.

J. H. Parry, *Europe and a Wider World, 1415–1715* (London, 1949).

An excellent brief history of the expansion of European commerce around the world.

E. L. Roll, *A History of Economic Thought* (New York, 1939).

A standard survey of the development of economic thought in western civilization.

J. Strieder, *Jacob Fugger The Rich* (New York, 1931).

The best biography of the greatest capitalist-entrepreneur of the Commercial Revolution.

W. C. H. Wood, *Elizabethan Sea-Dogs* (New Haven, 1918).

A delightful history of the expansion of the British merchant marine and navy in the sixteenth century.

23

The Cultural Transition
to the Modern Era

Moses. Michelangelo as a sculptor (p. 586) made his *Moses* as the personification of a powerful will and partially as a portrait of Pope Julius II, whose tomb it decorates.

Even in the thirteenth century, when the western Christian civilization of the Feudal Era attained its greatest brilliance, there was a secular aspect to the cultural life of western Europe. Although religion dominated the outlook of the people of that era, at no time were men wholly preoccupied with gaining salvation in the world after death or wholly oblivious of the value of human existence on this earth. By the end of the fifteenth century in Italy and by the end of the sixteenth century elsewhere in Europe, the most striking characteristics of the cultural life of western Europe were its secularism, humanism, and individualism.

This metamorphosis—from the all-pervasive and authoritarian religious mood of the thirteenth century, to the secular, humanistic, and individualistic mood of the sixteenth century—is commonly called the *Renaissance*—that is, *rebirth*. But this traditional name is unfortunate, for secularism and humanism had never been dead. What happened in the interval between the thirteenth and sixteenth centuries was simply that secularism and humanism gained in importance. The so-called "Renaissance" was not a sudden new happening; it deserves to be called a "birth" only when it is remembered that birth is the culmination of a long, slow gestation. It was not a beginning, in the sense of a fresh start, but rather the change by which the culture of the Feudal Era developed into the culture of the modern era. Yet the term *Renaissance* is so well known that we can scarcely avoid using it, even though we must remember that it is inexact and misleading.

THE RENAISSANCE IN ITALY

In tracing the origins of the Renaissance, one must not only consider the men who gave notable expression to secularism and humanism in thought and art, but one must also have some understanding of the economic and political conditions influencing early modern cultural life. These conditions were associated with the growth of towns and cities. Nearly all the intellectual luminaries of the Renaissance were townsmen, who looked upon the world with a point of view unlike that of the feudal lords and churchmen; while the painters and other artists of the Renaissance were inspired by the ideals of master workmanship associated with the guilds, to which nearly all skilled workmen of the towns belonged. Even after the guilds themselves decayed, artisans continued to labor under the moral obligation that the guilds had imposed, to do the best work within their power. And this sense of an obligation to achieve excellence was one influence that urged them on to the artistic triumphs characteristic of the Renaissance.

The culture of the new era required riches, moreover, and it therefore flourished best in cities, where commercial and industrial profits were made and spent. We have already noted that the cities of Italy were the first to gain from the expansion of trade across the Mediterranean, and the largest of these cities—Florence, Venice, and Rome— were to become the greatest in the arts and letters. On the other hand, we will find no important centers of the new culture outside the prosperous cities. The splendid churches, palaces, and villas of the Renaissance could arise only where there were vast funds available to meet the cost of their building.

Not only did these Italian cities command great wealth, but they also provided a favorable political and social environment for the new cultural life. Florence, the queen city of the Italian Renaissance, was a self-governing city-state, and its republican institutions permitted a large degree of freedom—freedom of expression and freedom of social movement from class to class. The Venice of the Renaissance enjoyed a prosperity nearly equal to that of Florence, while Rome grew rich on the revenues of the papacy. Moreover, Venice and Rome were cosmopolitan centers. A wide-reaching commerce gave Venice the advantage of acquaintance with the taste and experience of far-off lands, while the religious leadership of Rome kept its people in touch with the whole of Christendom. The mingling of peoples of differing background, which occurred in both these cities, was always a stimulus to cultural advance. Such conditions did not obtain in rural areas dominated by feudal traditions, nor were they so favorable even in the rising towns of northern Europe.

The Beginnings of the Italian Renaissance

It is all but impossible to establish when the Italian Renaissance began. But, for convenience, we may begin with three great figures of the fourteenth century, each of whom stands at the head of one of the main traditions of the Renaissance. These are: Dante Alighieri (1265–1321, p. 540), the commanding name in early Italian literature; Giotto di Bandone (c.1266–c.1337), the first great painter of the Florentine school; and Francesco Petrarca, or Petrarch (1304–1374), the leader of the humanist movement and also a famous Italian poet.

Dante has already been discussed as the author of the *Divine Comedy,* the greatest literary synthesis of the Christian thought and emotion of the Feudal Era. To the student of the Renaissance, he is also of interest as an Italian urban intellectual, a writer in the vernacular, and one of those who first gave forceful expression to the secular and vernacular interests that were to become characteristic of the modern age. But in his time few others shared these distinctions in similar degree, so we may not speak of Dante's age as beginning the Renaissance.

Like Dante, Giotto looks both backward and forward; he was a man of the Feudal Era, whose work anticipates the modern era. A country boy, raised in the region of Tuscany where St. Francis of Assisi had lived, Giotto seems to have had much the same simple faith as the earlier saint. Some of his paintings depict scenes of the life of St. Francis, and all his work has a Franciscan spirit, giving dramatic expression to Christian sentiment. But as a painter, Giotto stands so far above his contemporaries and predecessors that he seems to belong more to the great age of Italian painting in the Renaissance than to the Feudal Era, in which painting was a minor art, subordinate to architecture and sculpture. Indeed, so remarkable were his genius and his skill that Giotto is sometimes acclaimed as the greatest painter in western history.

Death of St. Francis—Giotto's fresco, c.1320, in the Church of Santa Croce, Florence, an example of the great artist's later work. See also page 510. (Anderson photograph)

Humanism

In the work of Dante and Giotto, along with their religious feeling, there is evidence of a deep and penetrating interest in the earthly, "human" qualities of people. This broad interest in humanity is often called *humanism*. But the term also has a narrower meaning, associated with literature, the arts, history, and philosophy. It was in the age of the Renaissance that men became more conscious than before that the ancients, especially the Greeks, had shared the same love of life and earthly beauty that they felt. Consequently, the term *humanism* came to be associated with the study of the ancient classics. Thus the humanism of the Renaissance implies several things—first, a general interest in humanity, with its virtues, its genius, and its sensitivity; second, a special interest in literature, the arts, and philosophy; and third, a specific interest in the literature, art, and philosophy of the period of classical antiquity.

Petrarch, who provides the best illustration of the dawning humanism, was a Florentine by derivation. However, the vicissitudes of politics caused his father to be exiled, so Petrarch grew up and remained an emigré. For a time he attended the university law schools of Bologna and Montpellier, but the law did not suit his temperament, and he turned from it as from something sordid. He first won recognition as a poet, and in this role he proved a worthy successor to Dante in the development of Italian literature. Yet it was not as a poet but as a humanist scholar that Petrarch won his greatest influence.

From his late twenties Petrarch lived in a manner that would serve as a pattern for the lives of all the Italian humanists. For a time he wandered through northern Europe, gaining a cosmopolitan experience and outlook; in Italy he resided variously in Milan, Venice, Padua, and other cities. In his travels he established numerous intellectual contacts, which he later kept up by means of a vast correspondence in Latin. As his intended contribution to learning, he composed essays, history, and biography in the language of Cicero and Vergil. He had the satisfaction of winning wide recognition at his own valuation of himself; he became the popular and acknowledged master of a whole generation of scholars.

Petrarch's enthusiasm for the literature and history of Rome was unbounded. He composed an epic celebrating the Roman general Scipio Africanus; he wrote on Julius Caesar; he deplored the removal of the papacy from Rome to Avignon; he lauded Cola di Rienzi (*c.*1313–1354), who was attempting to restore republican government to Rome. Though he had respect for Greek literature, he never learned the Greek language, and he remained convinced that Latin letters were superior to Greek. Thus he established the focus of scholarship that defines the "Latin phase" of the humanist movement. In the manliness and austerity of ancient Rome, Petrarch imagined he saw the summation of all the private and public virtues. He and his humanist disciples consequently conceived it to be their task to restore these Roman virtues to the modern world.

Ironically, Florence at once became the center of humanism—although the founder of humanism was himself an exile from Florence. But two of his friends were Florentines. The first was Giovanni Boccaccio (1313–1375). He is best known as the author of the *Decameron,* a collection of 100 comic stories, written in the vernacular. But as a humanist, he also compiled dictionaries of classical lore and made a beginning in the study of Greek. The other prominent disciple of Petrarch was Coluccio Salutati (1331–1406), a less creative mind but an important person because he held the high political office of chancellor of Florence. As a man of position as well as of taste, Salutati helped to make the study of the classics a fashionable cult of society in Florence.

Libraries and Schools

By the fifteenth century humanism was deeply rooted and beginning to branch out. One sign of this was the increasing interest in the collection of books. Until printing came into general use, which was not before the end of the fifteenth century, the texts of classical authors were available only in manuscripts, and scholars who wished to master Cicero and Vergil had to go to considerable trouble to obtain copies of their works. The earliest humanists, like Petrarch, purchased texts out of their own funds; but, as the study of the classics advanced, it became impossible for any but the richest of men to buy the great number of texts needed for a comprehensive knowledge of Latin literature. Of great importance, therefore, was the founding of libraries. In Florence, Cosimo de' Medici (p. 555) established two splendid collections. What he achieved in Florence, his librarian (who later became Pope Nicholas V) surpassed in Rome; for Nicholas became the founder of the magnificent Vatican library, which remains one of the finest in the world. Similarly at Urbino, Venice, and Pavia, Renaissance scholars and Renaissance patrons contributed largely to the establishment of the first modern research libraries.

A related development was the broadening and secularizing of education. Change in this direction was notable in the universities of Florence and Rome, but the Renaissance was not mainly a movement involving universities. Its influence upon education was expressed principally in the new Latin schools, which began to spring up everywhere. These were municipal or court institutions, not ecclesiastical, and were ordinarily under the direction of able humanists. They achieved a remarkably high level of instruction.

The most important educators in this Latin-school movement were Vittorino da Feltre (1378-1446), who taught at Mantua, and Guarino of Verona (1370-1460), who taught principally at Ferrara. These men were attached to the courts of princes, and their task was an essentially aristocratic one: the training of young gentlemen of the ruling order. They conceived of this task broadly, because they insisted on physical training as well as intellectual, and they believed in maintaining a balance between the Christian and classical elements of their teaching.

The social aim of the Renaissance teacher was never so well described as in the widely read dialogue, *The Courtier,* by Baldassare Castiglione (1478-1529), who formulated an almost impossibly high ideal of aristocratic cultivation. The gentleman, in his view, should be refined and accomplished in every respect—an athlete, scholar, connoisseur, a man of integrity and spirit. Yet the education of the humanists was not exclusively reserved to the well born and the rich, for such teachers as Vittorino and Guarino gave instruction to a certain number of poor boys of their choice.

The Greek Phase of Humanism

The recovery of Greek texts presented far greater difficulties than the recovery of Latin. Throughout the Feudal Era Europe had kept at least some acquaintance with the classical literature of Rome, but knowledge of Greek had almost died out. Despite the difficulties, however, Italian humanists of the fifteenth century became avid students of Greek literature as well as of Latin. Many of the texts of Greek works were obtained from Byzantium, with which the Italian cities maintained commercial connections. In the fifteenth century, moreover, Byzantium was under Turkish attack, and the Byzantines were eager to cultivate good relations with the Italians. Their scholars therefore readily cooperated with the Italian Humanists.

The impact of Greek thought is best illustrated in the history of the influential Platonic Academy in Florence. This was not an educational institution in the formal

Florence Cathedral, "Giotto's" Tower, and Baptistry. (Italian State Tourist Office)

sense, like a university, but a meeting place where men of learning gathered for discussion. It was patronized by the two greatest of the Medicis, Cosimo and Lorenzo, and among its leading figures were the able humanists, Marsilio Ficino (1433–1499) and Giovanni Pico della Mirandola (1463–1494). Both these scholars had learned their Greek from an immigrant teacher who was devoted to the religious elements in Plato's thought, and their understanding of Plato accordingly had much in common with the Neoplatonic tradition. Together, Ficino and Pico established a kind of cult of Plato in Florence, which had large influence upon a number of the leading figures of the time, such as the painters Botticelli and Michelangelo. In its brief period of vitality during the later fifteenth century, the Platonic Academy achieved a distinction surpassing that of any of the Italian universities.

The importance of this Greek stage of humanism was not limited to the Renaissance, for it marked the beginning of a study of Greek civilization that was to continue long after the Renaissance. Moreover, the new appreciation of the religious side of Plato's thought, stressing a kind of intuitional religion, was to have important consequences. In the short run, it was to give rise to an impatience with Scholasticism, which placed prime emphasis upon Aristotelian logic, and it was to inspire a more poetic and personal appreciation of Christianity. In the long run, this approach to Christianity, which would eventually undermine the dogmatic and authoritarian elements of Scholasticism, was to contribute to the religious upheaval of the Protestant Reformation.

Critical Humanism

We have taken note of three stages in the development of literary humanism—first, the establishment of a taste for the Latin classics, under the inspiration of Petrarch in the fourteenth century; next, the phase of the accumulation of texts and the education of a greater number of young men in the new interest; and then the widening of humanism to include Greek studies as well as Latin. A fourth and final phase of the movement was the formation of the modern habit of skepticism, or critical-mindedness.

The man who best exemplifies this stage of the Renaissance was Lorenzo Valla (c.1407–1457), who is regarded as one of the fathers of modern critical scholarship in the field of history. Brought up in Rome, Valla was well trained in the classics and became a first-class philologist. This training prepared him for the task that was to win him him greatest fame. By his expert knowledge of texts, he was able to identify as a forgery the document known as the "Donation of Constantine," which purported to be a deed by which the Emperor Constantine gave the pope temporal rule over Rome. So conclusive was his proof that no one since has argued that the document was genuine.

Though the disproof of the "Donation of Constantine" was a blow to the political interests of the pope, it was not an attack upon the Christian religion. In other writings, however, Valla went to one of the extremes toward which the humanists' study of the classics tended: he came to prefer pagan morals to Christian ethics, and Epicurean materialism to Christian idealism. To some, Valla represents the logical conclusion of Renaissance secularism.

Italian Vernacular Literature

The spread of humanism tended to inhibit the development of an Italian vernacular literature, since intellectuals, on the example of Petrarch, long regarded classical Latin as the one language appropriate to the expression of serious thought. After a time, however, writers made the inevitable return to Italian as a literary language.

Notable among the poets writing in Italian during the great age of the Renaissance were Matteo Maria Boiardo (c.1434–1494) and Ludovico Ariosto (1474–1533). Boiardo developed the epic of the Carolingian hero Roland, transforming it into a romantic love story; Ariosto continued the same theme, even more romantically, in his epic *Orlando Furioso*. These men set a new literary style that was to endure and spread outside of Italy. Also noteworthy was Torquato Tasso (1544–1595), a follower of Ariosto, who took the capture of Jerusalem as the theme for a chivalric romance.

Italian was also used in the writing of history and treatises on politics. The foremost of those whose labors were in this field was Niccolò Machiavelli (1469–1527), the author of a *History of Florence* and of the famous little book entitled *The Prince,* which was a rationalized description of the political behavior of the rulers of the city-states of Italy in his time.

Architecture

We must now retrace our steps, returning to the fourteenth century to pursue the progress of the arts after Giotto, as we have ex-

Lorenzo de' Medici—by Verrocchio, c.1480. Lorenzo was not only a statesman and patron of the arts but a true scholar and a great poet. (National Gallery, Washington, D. C.)

Venice in the Fifteenth Century—German woodcut, 1486. At the right is the Palace of the Doge, the city's top official, with the domes of St. Mark's Cathedral rising behind it. In front, men in gondolas unload barrels and bales from merchant ships. (Courtesy of the Metropolitan Museum of Art)

amined humanism after Petrarch. And among the arts we may conveniently begin with architecture, because this provides the setting within which are displayed the works of the other arts.

The enthusiasm of the Renaissance for classical standards naturally had a great influence upon Italian architecture. As scholars studied the literary usages of Cicero, they also pondered the writings of Vitruvius, architect of Augustan Rome; and while collectors searched for manuscripts, they also studied and copied the architectural remains of the "eternal city." It was relatively easy for the Italians to take up Roman building styles. Italy had no firm commitment to the Gothic style that prevailed more generally in northern Europe, and the presence of Roman monuments and ruins all about constantly reminded the Italians that they were them-

selves the descendants of the Romans, and that the Roman style therefore belonged to them.

Foremost of the architects who developed the new style, under Roman influence, were two men of towering genius in the fifteenth century. These were Filippo Brunelleschi (1377–1446) of Florence and Donato Bramante (c. 1444–1514) of Rome. Though their work, like that of others of their age, shows a dubious preference for decorative splendor unrelated to structural needs, we cannot fail to recognize the grandeur of the achievement of these two men. Brunelleschi is famous for the dome of the cathedral of Florence and for the enormous Palazzo Pitti, which he designed for a friend of Cosimo de' Medici. This was typical of numerous palaces built by merchant-princes in all the north and central Italian cities of the fifteenth century. The exterior of these buildings is rugged, resembling the walls of a fortress, but the interior provided spacious accommodation for a life of cultured opulence.

The palaces of Venice are unlike those of the other Italian cities. Because the city is built on an island secure against attack, its buildings do not have the aspect of strongholds. Ground space is too precious to permit the use of large courts and gardens, but balconies and windows are used more freely than in other cities. The close connection of Venice with Byzantium is reflected in the decorative touches of the buildings, in which are to be seen signs of an Oriental influence. The most renowned of the architectural specimens of Renaissance Venice is the great Doge's Palace.

Churches were the principal new buildings of Renaissance Rome, and the greatest of them, St. Peter's, marked the architectural climax of the Renaissance. The idea of building a new basilica was conceived by Pope Julius II about 1505, and, in the competition among architects for the honor of designing it, Bramante was the winner. His original plan was based on a Greek cross, surmounted by a dome. But four decades passed before funds were available for the building; in the interval the original plan was revised several times. The work was taken over by Michelangelo in 1547, and under his direction, the construction was brought nearly to completion.

St. Peter's shows no vestige of the Gothic, but the classical influence is everywhere apparent—from the stupendous dome and the towering Corinthian half-columns of the portico down to the details of decoration. But this is no mere imitation of a classical Roman building. The very size of the church —half again as long as Gothic cathedrals— and the incomparable spaciousness and the brilliance of the colors of the interior express a largeness of feeling that is in keeping with both the spirit of the age and the personal genius of Michelangelo. This great basilica

The New St. Peter's Basilica—that replaced the old building (p. 229).

Mona Lisa—the third wife of Francesco del Giacondo. This portrait is considered the culmination of Leonardo da Vinci's search for an ideal type. (Louvre Museum)

Andrea Pisano (*c*.1270–*c*.1348), Lorenzo Ghiberti (*c*.1378–1455), and Donato Donatello (1386–1466). And in the mausoleum chapel of the Medici family of Florence appears some of the best work of the greatest of all the sculptors of the age, Michelangelo Buonarotti (1475–1564). Unlike many of his contemporaries, Michelangelo was not attracted to portrait sculpture, which is often ill-rewarding, but used his representations of the human body as a means of expressing universal emotions and ideas. In one respect he was closer to the Greek sculptors than were most of his immediate predecessors, for his work was always architectural—that is, it was related to the form and spirit of the building in which it was placed. Yet his work is far more than a slavish imitation of classical models; it is an expression of his own vast genius. (See p. 576.)

Painting

At the beginning of the Renaissance, painting, like sculpture, was subordinate to architecture. In the fifteenth century, however, painting came to be valued for its own sake, not simply as a means of decorating a building. A sign of this change is the increase of easel painting, which came to rival fresco work. Easel painting gave the artist greater freedom of expression. Moreover, it assured him a better livelihood, since he could more easily find a market for the works he painted on an easel than commissions for the painting of frescoes.

The Florentine Tradition. The main stages in the development of painting after Giotto are most plainly to be traced in the Florentine school. In technical advance, there was a progression among the Florentine artists toward greater realism, while in subject matter the movement was away from themes illustrative of Christian piety toward a naturalistic representation of secular life. Among the masters of the Florentine school in the

represents a new synthesis—of Christian and pagan, of classical and modern, of the religious and the humane. It is a symbol of the new cultural era of the Renaissance.

Sculpture

The splendid new palaces and churches of the Renaissance provided the setting for the sculpture of the age, which ordinarily was conceived with thought to the frame within which it was to be viewed.

Florence was the home of the foremost sculptors of the early and middle periods of the Renaissance. Notable among them were

fifteenth century were Fra Angelico (1387–1455), whose pictures recapture something of the poetic Christianity of St. Francis, and Fra Filippo Lippi (c.1406–1469), whose work shows an almost scientific concern for naturalistic representation.

In the judgment of our own day, when abstraction is widely regarded as superior to representation, the esthetic merit of this development has been questioned. But no matter which of these tendencies we favor, we cannot doubt that the Florentine artists of the fifteenth century produced climactic achievements. It is to be noted, moreover, that naturalism never gained a complete triumph in Renaissance Florence. For example, Sandro Botticelli (c.1444–1510), though scientifically accurate in depicting background detail, made frequent use of allegory in his subject matter, and his work is suffused with a lovely atmosphere of fantasy. (See illustration, p. 555.)

The climax of Italian painting came in the sixteenth century, which saw the work both of the trio of the greatest masters of the Florentine tradition—Raphael, Leonardo, and Michelangelo—and of the masterpieces of the Venetian school.

Leonardo. Though they were contemporaries and all had some connection with Florence, it is not possible to treat together such rival geniuses as Leonardo, Raphael, and Michelangelo. If we bear in mind that Leonardo da Vinci (1452–1519) was the greatest master of science in his age (p. 3), we better understand his superb draftsmanship, his unrivaled control of perspective, and the precise knowledge of anatomy that enters into all his known paintings. These qualities are evident in the famous easel portrait, *Mona Lisa,* which indicates the insight of a man who must have sensed the emotional and mental depths of his subject, in order to suggest them so feelingly in paint. His most dramatic achievement was *The Last Supper,* a fresco on the wall of a refectory in Milan. It is a supreme example of the scientific, three-dimensional painting that the Florentine school encouraged. And like the *Mona Lisa* and the madonnas that he painted, it is suffused with a humanity of feeling that assures it rank among the masterpieces of world art.

Raphael. It is easier to characterize Raphael Sanzio (1483–1520), because his merit lies mainly in a wonderful craftsmanship and in his success in utilizing the achievements of the Florentine tradition. He learned the lessons of anatomy, as his Roman murals demonstrate; he knew classical architecture and made use of its forms to frame his paintings; and in his madonnas he showed a singular gift for combining the sensuous and the spiritual. Though lacking the sharp perception of Leonardo and the power of Michelangelo, Raphael was blessed with a gentle charm that has won him enduring popularity.

Madonna and Child—detail of Raphael's *Sistine Madonna.* (Metropolitan Museum of Art)

Sacred and Profane Love—Titian, c.1514. The conflict between earthly, sensual love (the dressed figure) and pure, celestial love (the nude) was a theme that absorbed Renaissance minds. (Anderson photograph)

Michelangelo. Like Raphael and Leonardo, Michelangelo is an ultimate, in the sense that he gave fuller expression to his genius than did anyone else in this amazing age except his two rivals. We have already taken note of his achievements as a sculptor and architect. As a painter he reached the apex of his power in great work of decorating the ceiling of the Sistine Chapel in Rome. Without question, this is the greatest fresco in the world, comprising more than 300 heroic figures, each conceived individually and without repetition, but all bound together in a pictorial and dramatic unity.

Venetian Painting. The artistic tradition of Venice was akin to that of Florence, but there are enough differences between the two schools so that neither need be ranked above or below the other. One reason for the difference was that Venice was especially rich, and the taste of its people encouraged an extreme of opulence in art. Another reason was that Venice was a city without a Roman past and far removed from the centers of the Greco-Roman revival; its art therefore shows a lesser degree of classical influence. The atmosphere of Venice was such as would stimulate the growth of art, but not such as to encourage the austere.

The first of the great masters of the Venetian school was Giorgione (*c*.1478–1510), whose work is noted for lavish coloring and a dreamy sensuousness. His famous *Pastoral Symphony* merits this name, not because of the scene represented, but because it is a concert of color, harmonized and balanced by artistic pull and thrust.

In Titian (1477–1576) we meet the most productive, most creative, and most representative figure in the Venetian school. A man of outgoing temperament, vigorous and dramatic, at home in all circles, Titian rode the wave of Venetian prosperity. He became the most fashionable portrait painter in the city, for his canvases endowed the sitters with the masculine strength that the age admired (see p. 633). In his other works, such as *Bacchus and Ariadne* and *Sacred and Profane Love,* he proved himself a worthy successor of Giorgione, with the same gift for the rhythmical organization of space and color. Though most of his works were worldly and even pagan in spirit, those of his last years, after he reached the age of ninety, deal with religious subjects, which he depicted in a mood of profound tragedy.

The later sixteenth century was a period of slackened artistic impulse in Italy, but Venice nevertheless brought forth one more great master, Tintoretto (1518–1594), and a painter of much skill and charm, Paolo Veronese (1528–1588). Tintoretto's most individual achievement lies in his use of the swirling line and his daring manipulation of light and shadow. His famous *Bacchus and Ariadne* has been acclaimed by a distinguished modern critic as "the most beautiful picture in existence."

A Backward Glance

We may now look back at the achievements of the Italian Renaissance in the three principal lines of its development—humanism, vernacular literature, and the visual arts. And we may ask: What did the movement add to western civilization? With much reason, some would answer that it added nothing new but represented simply an extension of the civilization of the Feudal Era. Unquestionably, many ties connecting the Renaissance with the past can be observed—for example, the mysticism of Christian thought was renewed by the Platonic Academy, the theme of chivalric love was taken up by the vernacular poets, the spaciousness of the Gothic was carried over into the painting of Giotto and his successors.

Yet we must acknowledge much that was original in the culture of the Italian cities. Despite their great debt to earlier ages, the Italians kept an independence of spirit, a mind of their own. And in picking over the heritage of the past, they accepted only such elements as would suit the needs of urban life; and their culture, at many points fresh and individualistic, at some points became greatly creative.

THE RENAISSANCE IN THE NORTH AND IN SPAIN

By the late fifteenth and early sixteenth century, there had appeared numerous manifestations of a Renaissance culture in northern Europe. This culture had many features in common with that of Italy, and the history of the arts and letters shows that there was a great deal of imitation. This was particularly true of the flourishing of the Renaissance in France.

Besides this imitation, however, there were also marked differences between the north and the south, and these contrasts correspond to wider historical differences. To a large degree they are to be explained by the fact that, in ancient times, much of northern Europe lay outside the bounds of the Roman Empire, and the impress of the classical civilization was therefore slighter in this region than in the south. In a considerable measure the Renaissance of northern Europe was an indigenous development rather than a borrowing from either the Italy of the Renaissance or the civilization of classical antiquity.

The Background of the Northern Renaissance

The North European society of the late fifteenth and early sixteenth centuries was at once like and unlike the society of Renaissance Italy. Cities there were, to be sure, but nowhere in the north was urbanism so concentrated or so prosperous as in Italy. The economic area most comparable to Italy was south Germany, where Augsburg and Nuremberg (picture, p. 572) stood athwart the routes of Venetian trade, and great merchant families achieved a prominence like those of Venice and Florence. Flanders, the one region of dense urbanism in northern Europe, passed into a period of change and readjustment in the fifteenth and sixteenth centuries: the grand old towns, such as Bruges and Ghent, were declining as the Hanseatic trade diminished, while Antwerp was rising to new leadership. In Antwerp and in London new concentrations of capital

Erasmus of Rotterdam—by Hans Holbein, the Younger (1497–1593). Holbein was only eighteen when he was commissioned to make the illustrations for Erasmus' *Praise of Folly* (p. 591 and p. 607) in Basel. (Louvre Museum)

buttress Christianity rather than weaken it in favor of secularism and humanism.

Another distinction between north and south was a consequence of the development of printing. This was not a matter of a single invention, but the gradual improvement of several processes: it involved the replacement of the costly parchment by the cheaper paper, the principle of stamping an impression rather than writing upon a page by hand, and the use of movable metal type rather than hand-carved wooden blocks for the making of the impression. The name of Johann Gutenberg is to be remembered for his contributions to the invention of movable type and for the beautiful Bible that he is believed to have printed about 1454; but Gutenberg is not to be regarded as solely or even mainly responsible for the whole complex of innovations that went into the printing of books. It is sufficient to remember that the technique of making printed books was perfected in the latter half of the fifteenth century, and that one of the first great centers of the book-making business was in south Germany.

We need not elaborate upon the general significance of this technological advance, the importance of which is epochal, but we must take note of its immediate influence upon the course of the Renaissance. In Italy the Renaissance began before the development of printing. This meant that it was largely an aristocratic movement, because the collection of manuscripts, which was essential to the study of classical literature, was a costly pursuit. In the north the Renaissance appeared later, as printed books were becoming available, and the new scholarly interests were therefore not so narrowly confined to the wealthiest classes.

were appearing, which were to gain in importance with the development of trade across the Atlantic. In general, however, the city life of northern Europe was not so largely favorable to the characteristic activities of the Renaissance as in Italy. Because the cities were not so close together, the movement of scholars and artists from one town to another was more difficult, and language barriers added to the hindrance. Moreover, the urban centers of the north remained under the influence of a feudal society more conservative and tenacious than was ever known in Italy.

Apart from this difference in social conditions, a contrast in intellectual environment is also to be noted. In the north, universities were more influential than in Italy, and, since these remained ecclesiastical institutions, their influence was of a sort to

Erasmus

The central figure of the northern Renaissance was the humanist, scholar, and publicist Desiderius Erasmus (*c*.1469–1536). A humble son of Rotterdam, Erasmus received his first education in a school of the religious order of the Brethren of the Common Life. He then entered a monastery, but after some years he was sent by his bishop to continue his studies at the University of Paris. Thereafter he spent most of his life as a wandering scholar, locating for periods at various universities, including Cambridge in England, and visiting Italy. At length he settled in Basle, Switzerland, where he spent the last fourteen years of his life in writing.

Erasmus was a thorough humanist, a master of both Latin and Greek, who loved the classics as intensely as ever did Petrarch or Ficino. But, as was true of most northern humanists, his literary and scholarly interests were combined with a religious devotion. In his writings, he set forth a spiritual and moral Christianity, urging the grace that flows from purity of heart and spurning a reliance upon scholastic theology and ritual. In this respect, he upheld the northern tradition of Christianity represented by his earliest teachers, the Brothers of the Common Life, while his anti-scholasticism conformed with the general mood of humanism. Though Erasmus did not approve Martin Luther's break with the Catholic Church (see the next chapter), he was no less quick to point out the worldliness and depravity of his own and Luther's generation, and time was to prove him the most independent of those reformers of his age who remained within the mother church.

The German Humanists

The lesser humanists of the Germanic north gained their importance principally from their association with the Protestant Reformation that Luther inaugurated, and we shall meet some of them in the next chapter. However, the German humanist movement included other interests besides religion, and it has some degree of kinship with the humanism of the south.

Like Erasmus, Rudolphus Agricola (1443–1485) exemplifies the mingling of classical scholarship with religious interests. After studying Greek in Italy, the Dutch Agricola became a professor at Heidelberg, where he lectured on classical literature and opposed the teaching of Scholastic philosophy. Johann Reuchlin (1455–1522) affords an even more striking example, because his study of Latin and Greek led him on to the study of Hebrew, and thus he merged the interests of humanism with those of Biblical scholarship. Ulrich von Hutten (1488–1523), who was to become an ardent supporter of Luther, introduced still another element, for in his writings a new sentiment of German patriotism mingled with the veneration of the classics. While Luther himself is not to be regarded as a humanist, his career (resting as it did upon Biblical scholarship) would have been impossible without the labors of the German humanists who were his predecessors and contemporaries.

As in Germany, humanism in France and England included an interest in religious problems. Thus in England we encounter such men as John Colet (c.1467–1519), who won renown as a Bible scholar, and Sir Thomas More (1478–1535), whose *Utopia*, like Erasmus's *Praise of Folly*, is a Christian satire on the absurdities and injustices of men. In France the leader of the Christian Renaissance was Lefèvre d'Étaples (1455–1536), a teacher at Paris who passed from the study of the texts of Aristotle to those of the Bible. In England and France, however, religion was not the main expression of humanism, nor was classical scholarship. It was to be found instead in the development of the vernacular literature.

French Vernacular Literature

There is no better example of the influence of humanism upon the French vernacular literature than the work of François Rabelais (c.1490–1553). The bawdiness of his masterpieces of satire, *Gargantua* and *Pantagruel,* sometimes makes us forget that the author was a monk, a physician, and a devotee of Greek literature. Beneath the superficial lustiness that gives him his fame was a serious conviction, which becomes apparent in his description of the happy residents of the utopian "abbey of the Thelemites":

> All their life was spent not in laws, statutes, or rules, but according to their own free will and pleasure. . . . In all their rule and strictest tie of their order, there was but one claim to be observed: DO WHAT THOU WILT. Because men that are free, well-bred, and conversant in honest companies, have naturally an instinct and spur that prompteth them unto virtuous actions, and withdraws them from vice, which is called honor.

Here we find a clear expression of the true spirit of the Renaissance—a spirit of respect for individual human integrity and the capacity of human beings to live the good life if nurtured in an atmosphere of intellectual freedom. It was this spirit of faith in the human that was the truly revolutionary element in the Renaissance.

The more refined French literary products of the Renaissance came near the middle of the sixteenth century. In that period appeared a group of poets known as the *Pléiade,* whose leader was Pierre de Ronsard (1525–c.1585). Their argument was that the conscious cultivation of the French language would bring into being a literary medium as great as Latin or Greek, and this would redound to the glory of France as a nation. Unlike Rabelais, they did not make a virtue of spontaneity. On the contrary, their effort was to develop formal rules for delicate literary expression. Often this effort made their writing artificial, even precious, but Ronsard succeeded in giving a sensitive expression to the moods of nature, man, and society.

In the exquisite prose of the great French essayist Michel de Montaigne (1533–1592), we find again the deep convictions of freedom and cosmopolitanism that also flowed from the Renaissance. His breadth of view was derived in part from this study of the Greek and Latin philosophers, but it was reinforced by the reports of diverse continents and peoples recently discovered overseas. In his splendid *Essays,* which are one of the great monuments in intellectual history, one finds no trace of dogmatism or asceticism, only praise of urbanity and the enjoyment of life.

English Literature

After Geoffrey Chaucer the stream of English vernacular literature ran thin until the sixteenth century, when humanist influences from abroad combined with the rising patriotism at home to produce a great flowering of both lyric poetry and poetic drama. Foreign influence is especially evident in the sonnet. Among the masters of this verse form were the great Edmund Spenser (c.1522–1599), Sir Philip Sidney (1554–1586), and William Shakespeare (1564–1616). An Italian model also served for Spenser's romantic epic, *The Faerie Queene,* which imitates Ariosto's epic.

The crowning achievement of England's sixteenth-century literature was the drama. In this medium Shakespeare stands unrivaled. The work of this master would have been impossible, however, had it not been for his predecessors who, before his time, had transformed the mystery and morality plays into secular drama. But if Shakespeare was in debt to those before him, he more than repaid the debt by his own rich contribution. Though not a scholar, he put into his plays great stores of narrative, idea, and color drawn from reports of the new discoveries overseas, from the literature of the classical past, from the traditions of England's feudal age, and from the contemporary scene. Only a man of the Renaissance could have done all this. And in the magnificence of the workmanship that he put into his writing, he exemplified the Renaissance ideal of the supreme value of work superlatively well done.

Spanish and Portuguese Literature

Outstanding in the literature of the Renaissance in Spain and Portugal are the writings of Miguel de Cervantes (1547–1616), whose *Don Quixote* heaped ridicule upon the old knightly ideal, and the epic *The Lusiads* of the Portuguese Luís de Camões (or Camoens) (*c*.1524–1580), patterned after Ariosto's *Orlando Furioso,* which sang the exploits of the Portuguese navigators and heroes who had found their way around Africa to the Indies. Félix Lope de Vega (1562–1635), the greatest and most prolific of Spanish dramatists, embodied the humanistic, secular outlook in hundreds of plays that, for power, versatility, and perception into human emotions, often rivaled those of Shakespeare.

Northern Architecture

When we turn from the literary area of culture, where the play of individual genius is relatively free and change is easy, to the architectural scene, where the force of tradition and the factor of economics are decisive, it becomes plain that the Renaissance was but one element in the civilization of northern and western Europe. There the splendid Gothic continued to prevail throughout the fifteenth and sixteenth centuries, being used both for churches and for secular buildings, such as town halls and guild halls.

Yet in certain areas the architectural forms of the Italian Renaissance began to have an influence during the sixteenth century. One of these areas comprised Paris and the valley of the Loire in northern France. The neoclassical Italian style is evident, for example, in those portions of the Louvre, the royal palace in Paris, that were built during the sixteenth century, and in the chateau of Chambord, one of the finest of the numerous chateaux along the Loire. Likewise, Renaissance influence, merging with the Gothic tradition, is to be seen in certain new buildings of this time in Germany, the Low Countries, and England. Among them are the university buildings at Heidelberg, the town hall of Antwerp, and some of the large country homes of the English nobility. In England this development prepared for the splendid architectural harvest of the seventeenth and eighteenth centuries, in which Inigo Jones and Christopher Wren earned their renown.

In the late fifteenth and sixteenth centuries the rapid rise of Spain to a position of great wealth and world power provided a remarkable stimulus to building. In the architecture of this period, Moorish as well as Gothic traditions are evident and also the influence of Italy, with which Spain was closely associated. Of special interest is the Escorial, an enormous edifice outside Madrid, erected by Philip II, which combined the functions of a palace, church, and education-

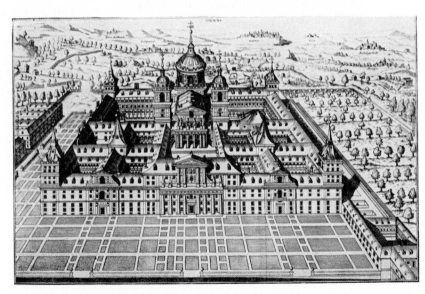

The Escorial—an engraving by Pedro Peret after an elevation by Juan de Herrera. Palace, church, mausoleum, monastery, college, seminary, and national archive, the Escorial was built during 1563–1584 for Philip II of Spain by Herrera, Renaissance architect who had worked on St. Peter's under Michelangelo. It is 675 by 685 feet, with towers 200 feet and a dome 312 feet high.

The Flight into Egypt—Albrecht Dürer. With all the northern love for detail, Dürer, a Lutheran, depicted the Christian faith in symbolic forms evolved by Catholic Italian Renaissance artists. (*Bibliothèque Nationale*)

al institution. Though the conception was academic, the building has an impressive air of noble dignity, combined with severe religious austerity.

Painting in the North

One of the triumphs of the period of the Renaissance is the rise of painting as an independent art in northern Europe. This was, in part, an imitation of Italian art, but it was also, and in larger measure, an indigenous development. To some extent the Italians themselves became indebted to the northern

painters, who were responsible for some important innovations in the craft of painting.

Two brothers, Huybrecht (1370–1426) and Jan (*c*.1390–1441) van Eyck, who worked in Bruges and Ghent during the early part of the fifteenth century, were the founders of the Flemish school and the beginners, as well, of the northern tradition of realistic painting. Not the least of their achievements was their work in perfecting the use of oil paints. They were the first to employ a resin or oil medium, which made possible a more brilliant and lasting color than the Italians had achieved with pigments mixed in albumen or other vehicles. Their paintings show a persistence of the Gothic mood, but also anticipate the later Flemish and Dutch taste for literal detail and secular themes.

The successors of the van Eycks in the Flemish school were of lesser importance until the appearance of Pieter Brueghel (1528–1569), the Elder. His work has a singular appeal, for his homely love of the common folk made him the most socially conscious painter of the age. No matter what its title, whether referring to classical mythology or Christian legend, each of his pictures depicts the land and people of Flanders. As a social observer (see, for example, the illustrations, p. 531, p. 644), Brueghel ranks with the later English Hogarth and the French Daumier; as a landscapist, he belongs with the greatest of those who came after him; and as a lover of life, he is the peer of Peter Paul Rubens (1577–1640), the greatest of all the Flemish painters (Vol. II).

Though Germany never became an important center of painting, the early sixteenth century produced three German artists of note: Albrecht Dürer (1471–1528), Hans Holbein, the Elder (*c*.1460–1524), and Lucas Cranach (1472–1553), the Elder. (See pages 479, 590, and 616 for works by Holbein, the Younger, and page 613 for Cranach). Dürer in particular is noted as the greatest master of woodcutting and copper engraving, although he, like the others, also attained distinction in painting.

Painting in Spain

Spanish painting profited not only from the colonial wealth that came to Spain in the sixteenth century but also from the political association of Spain with both Italy and Flanders, the two leading centers of art at the time. But the greatest of the painters of the Spanish Renaissance was a native of another land. Born in Crete, Domenicos Theotoco-poulis (c.1541–1614) is known as "El Greco" —the Greek. From his homeland, he had made his way to Italy and had absorbed the influence of the great Italian painters of the Renaissance before settling in Spain, where he did the work that was to earn him his greatest fame and was to make him known as the master of the Spanish school. Despite his indebtedness to some of the painters of the Italian Renaissance, El Greco's intense religious emotionalism, introspection, and mysticism made his work less representative of the spirit of the Renaissance than of the so-called "baroque" mood, which was to become characteristic of Europe in a later age. Yet this deviation from the pattern of the Renaissance makes him typically Spanish, for, despite the superficial influence of the Renaissance upon the culture of Spain, the Spanish never quite gave up the old tradition of religious mysticism in favor of the secular and humanistic outlook of the new age. In a sense it may even be said that Spain skipped the Renaissance, passing from the religiosity of the Feudal Era to the introspection of the later baroque age.

Toledo in a Storm—El Greco, the first pure landscape in Spanish art. After El Greco failed to find favor with Philip II, he went to Toledo, religious capital of Spain, to become the greatest pictorial interpreter of the Catholic Reformation (pp. 619–622). But to admirers of the Italian Renaissance art, his religious scenes and portraits seemed highly unconventional. (Courtesy of the Metropolitan Museum of Art)

RENAISSANCE MUSIC

The lilt of popular dances and the possibilities of sheer sensuous charm through combinations of tones enticed the composers of the Renaissance away from the rigidities of the church musical theory of the Feudal Era. A French bishop, Philippe de Vitry (1291–1361), gave the name to the new movement in the title of his treatise *Ars Nova (New Art)*. By 1350 Petrarch, like many other distinguished Europeans, considered Vitry the greatest musician of his age. Characteristic of the new musical style was the use of duple rhythm—that is, a rhythm having two beats to the measure—and the tonal interval of the "third"; tradition prescribed a triple rhythm and intervals of the "fourth" and "fifth."

An early application of the principles of the *ars nova* was in the polyphonic ballads of Guillaume de Machaut (*c.*1305–1377), of which forty survive. As commonly in Renaissance music, one of the parts of these ballads would be sung, while the others were carried by two or three instruments. The leading melody was usually adapted to verses of love poetry and sung by a tenor.

In England, as in France, there was also a freshening of musical composition. The famous Wessex Summer Canon, "Sumer is icumen in," which dates from about 1340, exhibits an extraordinary sophistication of structure, together with the charm of a folksong. Later in the century Chaucer attested the height of musical literacy in England by having a dying child in "The Prioress's Tale" sing the difficult *"Alma Redemptoris";* and in "The Miller's Tale," Absalon improvises on a tune that he plays on the fiddle.

In the course of the late fourteenth and fifteenth centuries the music composed under the inspiration of the *ars nova* attained a degree of complexity that probably has never been equalled, before or since, anywhere in the world. For example, the Flemish composer Jan van Ockeghem (*c.*1425–1495), serving at the French court, wrote a canon having thirty-six voice parts, and this was by no means the most remarkable technical feat of his times.

Ockeghem's pupil Josquin des Prez (*c.* 1445–1521) was the composer who brought western musical art to full maturity. A contemporary of Leonardo, Erasmus, Machiavelli, and Luther, he was regarded in his own time as the greatest living musician, and he is recognized today as the first modern composer. His music has a lovely, deeply reflective expressiveness that still causes the hearer to marvel.

Early in the sixteenth century the printing of musical texts became common. This led both to an internationalization of musical style, since composers in different lands could more easily become familiar with each other's work, and to a wider dissemination of music among the people. Many a home boasted a lute, a recorder, a viol, or a keyboard instrument, such as the small harpsichord or clavichord, and an evening's diversion might include part singing around the kitchen table. Thomas Morley, the celebrated English madrigalist, puts these words into the mouth of one of the characters in his *Plaine and Easy Introduction to Practical Music* (1597):

> . . . supper being ended, and Musicke bookes, according to the custom being brought to the table; the mistresse of the house presented mee with a part, earnestly requesting mee to sing. But when after manie excuses, I protested enfaignedly that I could not: euerie one began to wonder. Yea, some whispered to others, demaunding how I was brought up. . . .

With the increasing secularization of music and the simultaneous development of secular music into a highly sophisticated art form, it became the custom for royal and princely courts to invite distinguished musicians to compose and perform in residence. The most famous and versatile of the sixteenth-century composers who thrived on such patronage was Orlandus Lassus (*c.*

1532–1594), who is also known as Orlando di Lasso and Roland de Lattre. Lassus was a Fleming who gained his first fame as a boy singer in the cathedral at Mons. In 1555 he settled in Antwerp, moving in 1562 to Munich, where he became chapelmaster at the Bavarian court and remained until his death. His compositions, which number more than 2000, include Italian madrigals, French *chansons,* German *lieder,* masses, and magnificats. He and his Italian contemporary, Giovanni Pierluigi da Palestrina (*c.*1525–

1594), were the two giants who brought the music of the Renaissance to its fruition.

This music, taken as a whole, shows the same characteristics of humanism, secularism, and sheer joy of living that distinguished the literature and the art of the age. Like those other arts, music was still put to the service of the Church, but its mood was seldom simply or wholly religious. Like them, its mood was an expression of the prosperous and urbane new civilization that was developing in the European west.

THE SCIENCE OF THE RENAISSANCE

The characteristic interest of the Renaissance in man and his world was not expressed only in art; it also inspired a greater eagerness to observe the natural world in a scientific manner. This new stimulus to the growth of scientific knowledge was later to eventuate in the greatest intellectual and cultural triumph of the modern age.

Like the literature and art, the science of the Renaissance can be traced back to the intellectual stirrings that took place in the time of Thomas Acquinas during the Feudal Era. Thus, in the same generation as Aquinas, Roger Bacon, as we have seen, was beginning to question the deductive method of the scholastics and to urge the method of observation and experiment. He himself dabbled in astronomy, experimental optics, mathematics, and alchemy. Yet the modernity of Bacon's science should not be exaggerated, for it was greatly diluted with primitive magic, and he was content to accept the homocentric and geocentric cosmology of his time. Moreover, he was at one with the scholastic philosophers in assuming that the end of science was to buttress the teachings of Christian theology.

Before Roger Bacon died, men were beginning to show an active interest in one of the more practical sciences: geography. This interest in the features of the earth and the distribution of human cultures was a direct

intellectual product of the expansion of commerce in the late Feudal Era. Traders were vitally concerned with the routes of trade, the resources and markets of distant lands, and the customs of the peoples living in foreign countries and places outside the continent of Europe. Shippers and seamen were equally concerned with shorelines, winds, landmarks, currents, and aids to navigation. Much new geographical knowledge was provided by the travels of Marco Polo, who began his famous journey to the Orient six years before Thomas Aquinas died. In 1291, about three years before Roger Bacon died, the Vivaldi brothers set out from Genoa on an ill-fated expedition to discover whether Africa could be circumnavigated. Petrarch himself records that in his father's day many men set out on expeditions to explore unknown parts of the world, for the sake of the increase of knowledge as well as for greater profits in trade.

The dawn of modern scientific geography may thus be dated from the daring explorations of the Italian merchants. Its progress was materially aided by the introduction of the compass, which Italian navigators were using early in the thirteenth century. At about the same time there appeared the ship captains' *portolani,* or handbooks, containing accurate outline maps of the coasts of the Mediterranean. It was not long before other

The Underground Observatories of Tycho Brahe. The world's first modern observatory was built on an island off Denmark, c.1584. Except for a telescope, invented in 1608, it had every type of astronomical instrument, underground shops, a printing press, and a library. (Culver Service)

aids to navigation—the astrolabe (p. 559)—were invented or rediscovered, and further aid was forthcoming from the development of mathematics, especially trigonometry. The use of mathematics made it possible for Johannes Müller (1436–1476), or "Regiomontanus," to perfect a set of trigonometric tables that aided navigators in determining their latitude by "shooting the sun" with the astrolabe when far out of sight of land. Still further progress in the development of mathematics was marked by the publication of Geronimo Cardan's (1501–1576) *The Great Art* in 1545. This book, devoted to algebra, carried the study of that branch of mathematics further than it had ever gone.

The advancement of practical geography and the navigational sciences thus marched side by side with the expansion of commerce. Not only did traders advance the knowledge

of geography, but mapmakers and geographers also contributed to the expansion of European civilization overseas. The work of the geographers of Barcelona, Florence, Genoa, and other commercial cities was a great assistance to the Portuguese Prince Henry the Navigator, who directed the exploration of the Atlantic coast of Africa. And an Italian geographer, Paolo Toscanelli of Florence (d.1482) gave encouragement to Christopher Columbus when he was conceiving his plan for seeking a westward route to the Orient.

But the greatest advance during the Renaissance in man's understanding of his world far outreached the bounds of geography. This was the bold argument of the Polish astronomer Nikolaj Kopernik (1473–1543), better known as Nicholas Copernicus, that the earth is not the center of the universe but merely a planet revolving about the sun. This theory he set forth in his great book *Of the Revolutions of the Heavenly Bodies,* published in 1543, the year of his death. It was confirmed and elaborated upon by Tycho Brahe (1546–1601) and Johannes Kepler (1571–1630), and, though condemned by theologians, it was soon accepted by all the leading scientists of Europe. No single work of one man's brain ever before or since has done more to change men's thinking, for this marks the first monumental achievement of modern science. Its full impact was not felt until after the period of the Renaissance, however, and accordingly it will be discussed at more length in a later chapter.

Meanwhile, the interest of men in the things about them led many students into the scientific observation of living things, including man himself. There were many studies of plants, insects, and animals. The study of medicine, which, as we have seen, had begun to enjoy a revival at the universities in the late Feudal Era, flourished, and the medical schools at the universities of Padua and Ferrara became famous. The most striking aspect of this new study was its scientific attitude; for the new biologists and anatomists turned away from Scholastic authoritarianism, based upon Aristotle and Galen, and conducted their studies by the method of direct observation of the natural phenomena themselves. In the case of anatomy and physiology, Andreas Vesalius (1514–1564) dissected cadavers before his classes; he scorned and ridiculed the errors of the ancients; and he published his own textbook, called *On the Structure of the Human Body,* illustrated with sketches based upon actual dissection. This book, published in the same year in which Copernicus published his revolutionary study of astronomy (1543), is one of the great mileposts in the history of science.

Vesalius' contemporary, who may have been his pupil, Gabrielo Fallopio (1523–1562), made some of the earliest significant studies of the human foetus; he achieved his greatest fame by his description of the "fallopian" tubes in the female anatomy. Michael Servetus (1511–1553), who would one day be burned at the stake for "heresy" by the Protestants of Geneva, discovered that the blood circulates between the heart and the lungs, thus anticipating the more complete work of William Harvey in the next century. There were also many studies of disease based upon clinical observation. With the work of these men, anatomy and medicine stood upon the threshold of the modern era in the history of these sciences.

"A delineation from the side of the bones of the human body freed from the rest of the parts which they support, and placed in position." Vesalius' explanation of an original woodblock in the 1543 edition of *Icones Anatomicae.* (New York Academy of Medicine)

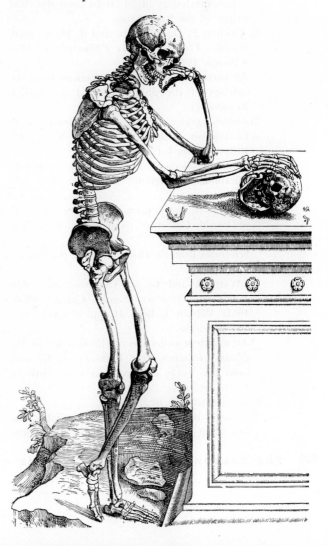

CONCLUSION

As the Renaissance had no obvious and precise beginning, neither did it have an end. To be sure, the points of emphasis in literature, art, and philosophy changed as time went on, but the most precious ingredient of the Renaissance outlook never disappeared. That ingredient was humanism—the sense of the dignity of the individual and of the values of life on earth—that inspired the greatest of the Renaissance thinkers and artists. This humanism was to characterize the western mind from the fifteenth century to our own time, and after the seventeenth century it was to gain still greater strength from the continuing triumphs of modern science.

Suggestions for Further Reading

Source Materials

Anthologies

F. Le V. Baumer, ed., *Main Currents of Western Thought* (New York, 1952), Part I, pp. 103–161.
A good anthology of selections from the chief writers of the Renaissance.

E. Cassirer, P. O. Kristeller, and J. H. Randall, Jr., eds., *The Renaissance Philosophy of Man* (Chicago, 1948).
An excellent collection of selections from the writings of the philosophers of the Italian Renaissance.

Columbia College, *Introduction to Contemporary Civilization in the West* (2 vols., New York, 1946), Volume I, Chapter 5.
Excellent selections from Petrarch, Pico della Mirandola, Castiglione, Erasmus, More, and others.

S. Thompson and J. Gassner, eds., *Our Heritage of World Literature* (New York, 1942), pp. 577–694.
Selections from the chief writers of the Renaissance.

R. Warnock and G. K. Anderson, eds., *The World in Literature* (2 vols., Chicago 1950–1951), Volume I, Book II, pp. 265–414, 425–509, 548–575.
An excellent collection of the writings of the greatest writers of the Renaissance. In most cases the works are given in their entirety.

Contemporary Writings

The following works are widely available and can often be obtained in paper-back form.

F. Bacon, *The New Atlantis.*
Bacon's idea of the ideal society, fashioned along English Renaissance lines, but with an emphasis upon how much science could do for the improvement of the condition of man.

B. Cellini, *Autobiography.*
A racy and exciting autobiography by one of the consummate craftsmen of all time, a typical "man of the Renaissance."

D. Erasmus, *The Praise of Folly.*
A classic of Renaissance satire on the foibles of humanity.

N. Machiavelli, *The Prince and The Discourses,* edited by M. Lerner (Modern Library edition, New York, 1940).
Classic works of the greatest of the Renaissance political philosophers.

M. de Montaigne, *Essays.*
Urbane essays by one of the greatest intellects of the Renaissance in France.

T. More, *Utopia.*
The ideal society, as conceived by one of the greatest humanists of the English Renaissance.

F. Rabelais, *Gargantua and Pantagruel.*
Satirical, humanistic essays by one of the great French writers.

W. Shakespeare, *The Complete Works.*
The greatest figure of the literary Renaissance in England.

G. Vasari, *Lives of Seventy of the Most Eminent Painters, Sculptors, and Architects,* edited by E. H. and E. U. Blashfield and A. A. Hopkins (4 vols., New York, 1901).
A classic set of biographies of the great artists of the Renaissance by a near-contemporary.

Secondary Works

P. S. Allen, *The Age of Erasmus* (Oxford, 1914).
A survey of the intellectual and political world in which Erasmus moved.

H. E. Barnes, *An Intellectual and Cultural History of the Western World* (rev. ed., New York, 1941).
An encyclopedic survey—extremely useful as a reference work. See Chapters XI, XII, XIII and XIV for the history of the Renaissance.

L. Batiffol, *The Century of the Renaissance* (New York, 1916).
A standard history of the era of the Renaissance in Europe. Concerned not so much with the Renaissance as with its historical context.

J. Burckhardt, *The Civlization of the Renaissance in Italy* (New York, 1890).
A classic.

D. Bush, *The Renaissance and English Humanism* (Toronto, 1939).
A good account of the literary Renaissance in England.

H. Butterfield, *The Origins of Modern Science, 1300–1800* (New York, 1951).
An up-to-date, readable, and accurate history.

Cambridge History of English Literature (15 vols., New York, 1933), Volume III.
The standard history of English literature. This volume deals with the literature of the English Renaissance.

S. Cheney, *A World History of Art* (New York, 1937).
This is a general history of art, with a relatively brief treatment of the art of the Renaissance.

T. Craven, *Men of Art* (New York, 1931).
Has a good popular treatment of the chief Renaissance artists.

W. C. D. Dampier, *A History of Science and Its Relations with Philosophy and Religion* (4th ed., New York, 1949).
Has a good treatment of Renaissance science.

W. K. Ferguson, *The Renaissance* (New York, 1940).
Excellent general account of the Renaissance.

W. K. Ferguson, *The Renaissance in Historical Thought; Five Centuries of Interpretation* (Boston, 1948).
A modern examination of the various interpretations of the Renaissance among western historians.

M. P. Gilmore, *The World of Humanism, 1453–1517* (New York, 1952).
An excellent general history of the era.

V. H. H. Green, *Renaissance and Reformation* (London, 1952).
A good, general account of the Renaissance era.

H. C. Haydn, *The Counter-Renaissance* (New York, 1950).
A new interpretation that points out some of the irrational aspects of the thought of the Renaissance.

J. Huizinga, *The Waning of the Middle Ages* (New York, 1926, 1954).
A near-classic of interpretation of the transition from the culture of the Feudal Era to that of the Renaissance.

H. S. Lucas, *The Renaissance and the Reformation* (New York, 1934).
A standard survey.

F. J. Mather, *A History of the Italian Painting* (New York, 1923).
A good modern account.

The Oxford History of Music, Vol. III. (Oxford, 1902).
Probably the best history of music, with thorough treatments of the various phases of the music of the late Middle Ages and the Renaissance. Quite technical and advanced.

J. H. Randall, Jr., *The Making of the Modern Mind* (rev. ed., Boston, 1940).
A general intellectual history of western civilization. See, especially, Chapters VI, IX.

G. Reese, *Music in the Renaissance* (New York, 1954).
The best brief history of Renaissance music.

P. Smith, *Erasmus; A Study of His Life, Ideals, and Place in History* (New York, 1923).
A standard biography of the greatest figure of the Renaissance in northern Europe.

H. O. Taylor, *Thought and Expression in the Sixteenth Century* (2 vols., rev. ed. New York, 1930).
An important survey of Renaissance thought.

J. W. Thompson, et al., *The Civilization of the Renaissance* (Chicago, 1929).
A masterly survey.

L. Thorndike, *Science and Thought in the Fifteenth Century* (New York, 1929).
The stirrings of science prior to Copernicus and Vesalius.

A. Vallentin, *Leonardo da Vinci* (New York, 1938).
A good biography of the most significant figure of the Italian Renaissance.

24

The Religious Transition
to the Modern Era

Door of the Castle Church at Wittenberg
—on which Luther nailed his ninety-five
theses in 1519 (p. 609). Today the theses
are inscribed in bronze on the door.
(Ewing Galloway)

Parallel with the changes in thought and culture that characterized the Renaissance, there took place in the sixteenth century a series of changes that profoundly altered the religious aspect of western society. These changes were of such dimensions as to bring about, first, a breakup of western Christianity into many dissenting, or "Protestant" sects, each subscribing to a sharply modified variant of Christian doctrine, and, second, as a reaction of Catholicism to this rebellion, a new and disciplined restatement of the ancient doctrines of the Roman Church itself. The first set of changes Protestants call the Protestant Reformation and the second they call the Counter-Reformation; Catholics speak of these as the Protestant Revolt and the Catholic Reformation.

PRELIMINARIES OF RELIGIOUS REBELLION

The Priestly and the Prophetic

Religion has been one of the most powerful determinants of human history ever since men first began to seek for the explanation of things. And at all times there have been two kinds of religious movement, which sometimes have coincided but more commonly have competed with each other for the dominant position in the religious life of society. These are sometimes called the "priestly" and the "prophetic."

The priestly type of religion has been described as placing its chief emphasis upon the institutions, philosophy, and practices of religion, rather than upon the individual emotional experience of religion. Historically, this type of religious manifestation has centered in a priesthood, made up of professional religious leaders set apart from the rest of the believers in the religion. Generally the priesthood has been supposed to have a mystical relation with the deity or deities whose worship they carried on and whose will they interpreted to the people, and often the priest has been presumed to hold special powers, by delegation from the god or gods of the cult. As a rule this kind of religion was closely allied to the political power, and the priests were used by the government as a support for the enforcement of its decrees and policies. Examples of the priestly type of religion have already been observed in Egypt, Babylonia, India, and Rome.

Religions of the prophetic type, on the other hand, have generally centered in the personal relationship of the worshiper with his god. Time and again in the history of religion there have been revolts against the sterility, formality, and impersonal coldness of an institutionalized priesthood. Such a mood of protest helped produce the emotional dualism of Manichaeism, and a similar mood was expressed in the revolt of Jesus of Nazareth against the high priests and Pharisees of the Jews, the outcome of which was the spread of Christianity to the poor and oppressed of all the lands about the eastern end of the Mediterranean.

The manifestations of religious experience among the worshipers of these religions were always personal and emotional. Generally they involved the experience of some sort of "salvation" of the individual. For the best examples of the prophetic mood in religion, we have only to recall the Hebrew prophets and their demand for humility, simplicity, and a sincere devotion to the kindly wishes of God. Their outlook is beautifully exemplified in the words of Micah 6:8:

> You have been told, O man, what is good:
> Yet what does the Lord require of you,
> But to do justice, and to love kindness,
> And to walk humbly with your God?

The Protestant Revolt was a forceful expression of the personal or prophetic mood in religion, in protest against the sacerdotalism and authoritarianism that were characteristic of western Christianity in the era of scholasticism. It asserted the need for an emphasis upon the individual and a direct relationship between him and God, an emphasis upon inner experience rather than outward conformity to the sacramental system that played such a large part in the traditional Roman Catholic religious practices.

Early Seeds of Revolt

Christians had never really agreed among themselves as to what they believed. In early times, they had been divided by doctrinal quarrels into hundreds of sects, and it had required almost superhuman effort to arrive at the adoption of the Nicene Creed in A.D. 325 (p. 233). Even then, it had proved impossible to hold the Church together, and Christianity had broken into several great branches. The most important of these were the Armenian, the Abyssinian, the Greek Orthodox, and the Roman Catholic, each having its own refinements of doctrine and separate ecclesiastical institutions, each claiming to be the true expression of God's will on earth.

As we have seen, it was the Roman Church, of which the bishop of Rome was the head, that achieved religious supremacy in western Europe. Its power, both religious and political, had reached its apogee in the thirteenth century, at which time it could correctly claim that practically every individual in western Europe worshiped God according to its doctrine and sacraments.

Already in the thirteenth century, however, the forces were at work that were to bring about the breakup of the Roman Church. The concept of the integrated political state was taking shape as kings, such as Philip Augustus, began to assert their supreme authority throughout their kingdoms. This meant the breakup of Christendom into new political communities, and it likewise meant a challenge to the supreme authority of the pope as the head of Christendom. Moreover, the expansion of commerce during the Feudal Era was producing a class of businessmen who were to demand a new economic ethic, in defiance of the economic doctrines laid down by such philosophers of the Church as Thomas Aquinas. At the same time, too, there was appearing the new mood of humanism, which was soon to eventuate in the Renaissance. This was to affect the traditional Roman religion in two ways:

first, by focusing men's attention upon this world rather than the other world after death, and, second, by encouraging an introspective interest in the individual, which was to run counter to the priestly emphasis upon ritual and sacrament.

These broad new movements—political, economic, and intellectual—were making themselves felt even in the days of Dante and Thomas Aquinas. In the sixteenth century they would develop such force as to shake the whole edifice of Roman Catholicism, requiring the Church to strengthen its doctrinal foundations and buttress its ecclesiastical structure in order to avert a complete collapse.

Early Rebels against Sacerdotalism

During the Feudal Era the voice of prophetic dissent had been heard in many places, both within the Church and without. Thus, for example, Francis of Assisi and Bernard of Clairvaux, in different ways, had both urged an emphasis upon personal communion with God and a pure life rather than mere conformity with a set of prescribed religious practices. These men, we remember, did not break away from the Church, and their ideals were perpetuated by their followers within the Church. Others, however, made an open attack upon the system of worship and salvation prescribed by the Catholic Church. These were branded as heretics, and the Church did its utmost to eradicate the movements that they inspired.

Some of these heretical movements were utterly destroyed. Such was the fate of the most important of them all, the heresy of the Cathari or Albigensians (pp. 514–515). In other instances, however, vestiges of the heresy survived even the most ruthless persecution. Thus many of the leaders of the Waldensians, scattered by the sword of the secular arm and the torture of the Inquisition, fled to Germany, where they spread their simple antisacerdotalism in a new field. Like-

wise, the "Lollards" persisted as a kind of underground movement, even after the Church condemned the teachings of their leader, John Wyclif, and had his bones dug up and burned, as a reminder of the fate he should have had as a heretic. Subsequently, Lollard ideas emerged again in Bohemia, in the movement inspired by John Hus, which lived on after he himself was burned at the stake in 1415 (p. 516).

The survivors of the Hussite movement were especially tenacious. After the death of their leader, those who clung to his teachings banded together in an association known as the Communion of Brothers, or the Moravian Brethren. These people emphasized the importance of moral purity in private life and a direct relationship between the individual and God; they refused to take oaths, denounced war, and demanded the separation of Church and state; most important of all, they preached a return to the simple, pure, and personal religion of Christ and his disciples. In 1467 they completely broke with Roman Catholicism, shortly merging with the remnants of the Waldensians, many of whose doctrines they had already adopted. Their stress, however, was never upon doctrine but upon conduct and spiritual goodness.

The Moravian Brethren were subjected to persecution and were almost wiped out in the course of the religious wars of the Reformation. Yet they held together and their movement endured, exercising a strong influence upon religious developments in both Europe and America.

The survival of these heretics is an indication that the religious mood of Europe was changing. Dissent from the doctrines of the Church of Rome and criticism of its practices were gaining support from the intellectual liberalism of the Renaissance, the developing new bourgeois ethic of economic individualism, and the growing sentiment of nationalism. Provided they could win the help of these other forces, reformers might now successfully defy the Church's power.

Political Challenge to the Church

Not all the challenge to the Church came from spokesmen for the prophetic tradition in religion; some of it arose from the growing political power of kings and princes. In the centuries that brought forth the heresies of the Albigensians, Waldensians, Hussites, and others, the secular rulers of Europe were developing the political institutions that were to eventuate in the integrated sovereign state, usually in the form of a national kingdom. And while the moral authority of the Church was being challenged by the religious dissenters, the political pretensions of the Roman pontiff were being slowly but steadily whittled away in the name of state sovereignty, even in respect to the administrative organization of the Church itself.

In England, for example, the kings had long disputed the pope's power to appoint bishops in England without consulting the king. And as early as 1353 England had prohibited appeals from English courts to the papal court at Rome, on the ground that its sovereignty was "foreign." Thus, as an English state emerged out of feudalism, Englishmen became increasingly stubborn in their refusal to acknowledge their subordination to the outside dominion of Rome. For the time being this did not mean that they were not good Catholics, but it did mean that they were becoming more determined than ever before to manage their own affairs, even in matters pertaining to religion.

Similar trends are to be noted in France. During the "Babylonian Captivity" of the papacy, (p. 504), the subservience of the popes at Avignon meant that, for practical purposes, the Church was subject to the secular sovereignty of the King of France. Then in 1438, in the so-called "Pragmatic Sanction of Bourges," the nationalistic tendencies of the "Gallican" or French branch of the Catholic Church were given explicit statement and acknowledged by the papacy. By this law, the power of making ecclesiastical appointments in France was almost completely taken away from the pope and placed in the hands of the French king, and the pope was also deprived of the right to levy taxes in France for the purposes of the Church.

Much the same tendencies toward the subordination of the Church to the power of the state were to be observed in other countries —Germany, Spain, even Italy, the homeland of the papacy. As a result, any religious reformer or dissenter who could win the protection of his secular ruler could be reasonably sure of escaping ecclesiastical punishment or persecution.

The Renaissance and Religious Criticism

It has already been suggested that the tendencies toward the popularization and individualization of religion were a form of humanism. The placing of the Bible in the hands of the common people by Peter Waldo and John Wyclif were evidence of a faith in the ability of the individual to understand God's word and God's purpose for man without the intermediary services of a priest.

Moreover, the new intellectual mood of the Renaissance brought with it a healthy skepticism toward many old ideas, among which were some of the long-standing tenets of Catholicism. Thus the new humanists not only poked ridicule at the immorality, corruption, and stupidity of the clergy, but they also began to examine with a critical eye some beliefs that came close to the heart of Christian doctrine. For example, Lorenzo Valla not only exposed the "Donation of Constantine" as a forgery but proved that the Latin "Vulgate" text of the Bible differed in important particulars from the original Greek. The humanist Pico della Mirandola was even bolder, for he questioned the Christian belief in man's incapacity to choose between good and evil and glorified man's unique "self-transforming" nature; while Pietro Pomponazzi (1462–1525) went so far as to deny the immortality of the soul. For this, he was persecuted by Church authorities, and his book *De immortalitate* (1516) was publicly burned in Venice.

Other rationalists questioned the doctrine of the Trinity. One of these was Michael Servetus (1511–1553), who antagonized Protestants no less than Catholics and was burned at the stake by the Calvinists of Geneva. Another extremist was Fausto Paolo Sozzini, or Socinus (1539–1604), a member of a famous family of freethinkers of Siena, who, some have thought, denied the "natural" immortality of the soul and attributed only a sort of second-degree divinity to Christ.

But the greatest and most scholarly of the humanistic critics of Catholicism was Desiderius Erasmus. As we saw (p. 590), he denounced the formalism and impious corruption that he discovered in the Church and devoted much of his scholarly effort to bringing the Church back to the piety and sincerity of early Christianity. The *Praise of Folly* was Erasmus's most famous book, but his religious ideas were most clearly developed in his *Familiar Colloquies*, which he published in 1518. Erasmus never left the Church, nor did he directly attack it as an institution; but he brought into sharp relief the absurdities attendant upon the reverence for religious relics, the veneration of the Virgin Mary, and the persecution of fellow Christians in the name of religion.

In the work of all these men and countless others, the intellectual forces of the Renaissance were weakening the intellectual leadership of the Roman Church and its priesthood. Long before the time of Luther,

The Papacy, 1417–1605

Martin V	1417–1431
Eugene IV	1431–1447
Nicholas V	1447–1455
Calixtus III	1455–1458
Pius II	1458–1464
Paul II	1464–1471
Sixtus IV	1471–1484
Innocent VIII	1484–1492
Alexander VI	1492–1503
Pius III	1503
Julius II	1503–1513
Leo X	1513–1521
Adrian VI	1522–1523
Clement VII	1523–1534
Paul III	1534–1549
Julius III	1550–1555
Marcellus II	1555
Paul IV	1555–1559
Pius IV	1559–1565
Pius V	1566–1572
Gregory XIII	1572–1585
Sixtus V	1585–1590
Urban VII	1590
Gregory XIV	1590–1591
Innocent IX	1591
Clement VIII	1592–1605

learning and the critical spirit were linked with the rise of commerce, political evolution, intellectual humanism, and the stirrings of the prophetic mood in religion to prepare the way for the overthrow, in much of western civilization, of the religious hegemony of the Church of Rome.

THE LUTHERAN REVOLT

The spark that set off the religious upheaval known as the Protestant Reformation or Revolt was a disputation between Martin Luther (1483–1546), an obscure Augustinian monk attached to the University of Wittenberg in Saxony and John Tetzel, a papal

agent and salesman. The debate between them hinged on certain questions relative to the Church's custom of selling indulgences.

Born in humble station, the son of a miner, Luther was fortunate enough to receive a university education at Erfurt. He was

Luther Nails His Theses to the Church Door—a contemporary allegorical woodcut. (Culver Service)

a man of keen intelligence, with the gift of winning followers, but he was also a person of deep and explosive emotions and varying moods. At the age of twenty-one he experienced a "conversion," and took the monastic vows in 1506. A visit to Rome revealed to him the corruption of the Church, and his own religious experience led him to believe that the way to salvation lay, not in the sacraments and the "good works" that the Church prescribed, but purely and simply in the grace of God, freely given to any man who would have complete faith in God and his goodness. He found support for this conviction in a statement by St. Augustine that God's grace is not to be earned by good works, which seemed to confirm Luther's own view that salvation was gained solely by faith.

This doctrine that Luther espoused struck at the very heart of the Catholic sacerdotal system. For if faith alone were sufficient for salvation, then men had no need of the ministrations of the priesthood and no need of partaking of the sacraments. Once Luther should make public his views, the Church would have no choice but to brand him a heretic.

The Question of Indulgences

Luther did not at first realize the full import of the doctrinal position to which his thinking led him. But he found occasion to make a public declaration of his beliefs as a protest against the sale of indulgences. This matter came to his attention as the result of the election of Albert of Hohenzollern to the office of Archbishop of Magdeburg and Mainz. On taking office, the new archbishop was obliged, by the custom of the Church, to pay a large sum to the papacy, and, to afford him the means of raising this money, the pope had given him permission to sell indulgences to the faithful. An indulgence was a document that purported to remit a portion of the punishment which a soul must suffer after death for sins committed on earth. According to Church doctrine, the indulgence did not give a man permission to sin without suffering punishment, nor would it have benefit for his soul unless he sincerely repented those sins of which he was guilty. However, these niceties of doctrine were not clearly explained to persons purchasing an indulgence. The new archbishop gave over the selling of them to one John

Tetzel, who proved to be an energetic but none-too-scrupulous salesman. And his eagerness to sell was increased by virtue of an arrangement with the archbishop that permitted him to keep, as his commission, a percentage of whatever money he might raise. Tetzel was reputed to have sold thousands of indulgences on the strength of his assurance that the moment the coin clinked in his box, the soul of him for whom the indulgence was bought was guaranteed release from purgatory.

The Ninety-five Theses

This was too much for Martin Luther. He rushed to denounce the idea that a mere piece of paper could gain men salvation and to assert his own conviction that this could be had only by a genuine repentance for one's sins and a firm faith in God. He set forth these ideas in the form of ninety-five theses, or statements, that he was prepared to defend in a public debate, and on October 31, 1519, he nailed a paper, on which he had written out the theses, to the door of the castle church at Wittenberg. He also had them printed and distributed in other cities.

The response to Luther's theses was surprising, for they seemed to have said the things that many people in Germany were thinking, and Luther was immediately showered with congratulations and encouragement. Tetzel was attacked by a mob and forced to flee the country. Alarmed at this hue and cry, Pope Leo X ordered the Augustinians to discipline Brother Martin, and at the same time he issued an official declaration, explaining the doctrine of indulgences. Haled before a papal legate, Luther refused to recant. However, he escaped punishment for his heresy because he was a friend of the Elector of Saxony, who gave him protection from the ecclesiastical authorities.

But Luther was soon challenged to debate his theses in public with one John Eck. In the course of this debate, which took place at Leipzig in July 1519, Luther was forced to admit that he shared many of the views of John Hus, who had been condemned by the Church as a heretic and put to death at the stake. After that admission, Luther could not retreat—nor did he wish to. Even earlier, in March 1519, he had branded the pope as antichrist. Now he proceeded to attack the Church's doctrine of transubstantiation and to demand that in the communion service both the bread and the wine of the mass be given to the laity.

With the support of many German political leaders as well as humanists, Luther went on to attack still other principles and practices of the Church. Thus he argued, appealing to German national sentiment against the "foreign" power of the pope, that the civil government is superior to the Church

Leo X with Two Cardinals—by Raphael (p. 587), c.1518. Julius II and Leo X were the two great Renaissance popes. Leo X (1513–1521), son of Lorenzo de' Medici, excommunicated Luther. (Alinari photograph)

Luther's Reforms

Once his break with the Catholic Church was complete, Luther began to organize his followers into a new church, which took the place of the old. In its organization he introduced a number of innovations in matters of practice—notably, he permitted the clergy to marry, and he ordered that wine, as well as bread, be offered to the faithful in the communion service. He also revised points of doctrine according to his own convictions. Thus he denied that confirmation, marriage, extreme unction, and ordination are sacraments. The other three of the traditional seven sacraments—baptism, penance, and the Eucharist—he retained. However, he changed the meaning of penance to "repentence," and he substituted a new principle, "consubstantiation," for the traditional "transubstantiation," to explain the miraculous change of bread and wine into the flesh and body of Christ in the rite commemorating the Last Supper.

The Lutheran Revolution

Luther's rebellion against Rome spread like wildfire. Though his doctrines were condemned as heretical and he himself was excommunicated, Luther gained the support of many powerful political figures and a large proportion of the common people. However, the German emperor, Charles V (who was also King of Spain, where he was known as Charles I), remained faithful to the old Church, as did many of the German nobility.

At the order of the emperor, Luther was required to appear before the Diet of the Empire, which was an assembly of the leading princes of Germany and representatives of the more important cities. In an eloquent oration before the Diet, which met at Worms, Luther refused to recant, and many members of the Diet made known their support of him. Thus he and his followers defied the emperor as well as the pope.

Title Page of Luther's Bible—From the original edition of *Das Alte testament deutsch,* published at Wittenberg in 1524. (New York Public Library Rare Book Room)

in political things; that the priesthood is unnecessary and evil, since every Christian is his own priest; and that all Christians should interpret God's word for themselves instead of allowing this interpretation to be a priestly monopoly. Since there was no good German text of the Bible that the people might read, Luther himself set about making a translation. Ultimately this translation became as important for the German-speaking Protestants as the King James version, made half a century later, for the English-speaking world.

The Anabaptists

To some of the poor and downtrodden classes of Central Europe, the news of Luther's defiance of ecclesiastical and imperial authority seemed to herald a great emancipation. Thus Thōmas Münzer (c.1489–1525), the Lutheran pastor of Zwickau, took literally what Luther said of freedom: "A Christian man is the most free lord of all, and subject to none." Accordingly he encouraged the people of his parish to demand certain social and economic reforms of their overlords. These demands brought the congregation into conflict with the local gentry, and Münzer was obliged to leave Zwickau. But the movement spread to other parts of Germany and soon developed into a social war between the peasants and their masters.

In this uprising of the peasants, which broke out into civil war in 1524, the ideal of a simple apostolic religion was merged with a demand for social justice. But Luther and most of his followers, as well as the Catholics, had no sympathy with the social demands made in the name of religion, and the popular rebellion was repressed with surpassing cruelty. Yet the religious ideal of the movement did not perish. Later it was to inspire a group known as the Anabaptists, who advocated a new and more radical pietism. Their influence was to spread throughout Protestant Christendom.

The Schmalkaldic War

Meantime Luther and his supporters were compelled to meet by force of arms the attempt of the emperor to suppress them. The first step of Charles V was to ask the imperial Diet to take action to put down heresy. The Diet refused to go so far, declaring, instead, merely that it would guarantee the freedom of the Catholics to continue their religious observances. The emperor then began to take action on his own, where-

upon the members of the German nobility who were Lutherans banded together for their defense. Their association for defense was called the Schmalkaldic League. Though Germany was thus divided into two hostile camps, Catholic and Lutheran, warfare did not break out at once, for Charles V was occupied with other problems.

But in 1546 fighting at last began. Like many such wars waged in the name of religion, the conflict was as much political as religious, because those German princes who espoused Lutheranism thereby found an excuse to rebel against the emperor, since he was supporting Catholicism. Even had they been less than wholly sincere in their conversion to Lutheranism, they would have welcomed an opportunity to assert their political independence of their imperial overlord.

The war came to its end in 1555. The Peace of Augsburg, which settled the issues that gave rise to it, provided that Lutheran princes might remain Lutheran and impose their religion upon the people under their rule, while Catholic princes could likewise hold to their faith and enforce it within their domains. The settlement was thus a compromise so far as concerned the religious dispute among the princes. But it marked a complete triumph for the princes, Catholic and Protestant alike, so far as it was concerned with political issues, since the emperor was given no authority to impose any religion upon anyone.

Nor was toleration accorded to those who dissented from both Lutheranism and Catholicism. Lutherans living in a region where the prince was Catholic were permitted to migrate to the realm of a Lutheran prince, and Catholics under Lutheran princes were assured of the same right. Such groups as the Anabaptists were given no rights whatever.

Yet the first great breach in the unity of western Christendom had been made; and what one rebellion had achieved another might: already other challengers of the ancient doctrine were arising in other lands.

ZWINGLI AND CALVIN

Martin Luther's break with Roman Catholicism was not an isolated phenomenon but one of several religious rebellions that occurred at about the same time in different places. The success of Lutheranism gave encouragement to the other rebellions, but these might well have taken place without such a stimulus, for criticism of the old Church was in the air throughout Catholic Europe.

One of the most important of these rebellions broke out in Switzerland, under the leadership of Ulrich Zwingli. Even in the Feudal Era, Switzerland had been a breeding-ground of freedom, and as early as 1291 three of the Swiss cantons had banded together and won virtual independence of the Austrian Hapsburgs. Other cantons later entered into the league that the first three had set up, until by 1513 this federation of self-governing provinces included thirteen cantons. And while defending their political freedom, the Swiss had also shown a strong spirit of individualism and independence in matters of religion that often had led them to ignore or resist the authority of Rome. At the beginning of the sixteenth century the wave of religious rebellion that swept over Europe stirred a number of Swiss religious leaders to make a complete break with the papacy. In these men were combined the driving force of the humanism of the Renaissance, the capitalistic interests of the burghers of Zurich, Berne, Basle, and Geneva, and the nationalism of all the cantons that had been forged in their common struggle to maintain their freedom against the machinations of outsiders.

Zwingli

Ulrich Zwingli (1484–1531), a native Swiss, was a child of the Renaissance and a disciple of Erasmus. After taking a master's degree at the University of Basel, he entered the Catholic priesthood, and in 1518 he became the priest of a church in Zurich. But while serving as a priest, he gradually became disgusted with the superstition, corruption, and what he considered the theological errors of the Church. And when Martin Luther began his defiance of the papacy, Zwingli was encouraged to take a similar stand.

On its intellectual side, Zwingli's revolt was a combination of humanistic ideas, which he derived from Erasmus, and the mood of belligerent individualism, which Luther inspired in him. Soon he began to preach against monasticism, and at the same time he attacked the priesthood on the ground that the Bible alone should give guidance as to God's will. Presently he refused to obey the bishop in whose diocese he was preaching, and in this rebellion he gained the support first of his parish, then of the whole town of Zurich (1523). The images in the church were destroyed, and Zwingli stopped celebrating the mass; in its place he substituted a simple communion service. Others of the sacraments were dropped altogether.

Switzerland was split by Zwingli's revolt, but a religious civil war was averted by an agreement among the cantons that each should retain complete autonomy in religious matters.

Zwingli was much more of a rationalist and a humanist than Luther, and for this reason, Luther finally broke with him. The chief point of difference between them was over the doctrine of transubstantiation. After some hesitation, Luther had accepted a modified version of this doctrine, which he chose to call "consubstantiation." Zwingli rejected this as absurd, on the ground that it was contrary to reason. There were other issues between them, but generally, as on this cardinal point, Zwingli placed reason above emotion, while Luther tended to do just the opposite.

Calvin

The greatest leader of Protestantism in Switzerland—perhaps, indeed, the greatest Protestant leader of all time—was John Calvin (1509–1564). He was not Swiss by origin but French, though his name is forever linked with Geneva, where he settled.

Calvin was reared in bourgeois surroundings and given an education at the University of Paris, where he studied Scholastic philosophy, law, and classical literature. About 1533 he was converted to Protestantism, and, in order to escape the persecution of Protestants that was beginning in France, he left his homeland to take refuge in Switzerland. Eventually he settled in Geneva, where he rose to a position of leadership amounting to dictatorship. So great was his power in Geneva that he was sometimes called "the Protestant Pope." Under his influence, an attempt was made to enforce his theological views in morals and politics as well as religion.

The social and political structure that Calvin headed was a marvel of Protestant rigor. The government of the city was given over to the clergy, which formed what was called the *Congregation,* or supreme council. All laws were initiated by the Congregation and submitted for approval to a chamber, called the *Consistory,* comprising twelve laymen in addition to the clergy. Both houses of the government were thus under clerical control, and the government of the city became a theocracy.

The Consistory undertook to supervise the morals of the people as well as to manage their government. The intention was to eradicate sin and create a community made up only of saintly persons. Woe betide any citizen who happened to differ from the ideas of the Consistory as to what was God's plan for men! Adultery, blasphemy, witchcraft, and heresy were all punishable by death. Work on Sunday was a crime, and everyone was required to attend church. The observance of Christmas was prohibited, on the ground that it was a Catholic holiday. The theater was severely condemned, and actresses were viewed with special disfavor. Women, according to one of Calvin's colleagues, should be "shamefaced and shy," but the role of actresses was to "expose their bodies, clothes, and ornaments to excite the impure desires of the spectators."

But Calvin's importance was not limited to Geneva. In his time this Swiss city be-

Luther and His Friends—by Lucas Cranach, the Elder (p. 594), c.1530. Left to right: Luther, John Oecolampadius, John Frederick, elector of Saxony, Zwingli, and Philipp Melancthon. (The Toledo Museum of Art, Toledo, Ohio; gift of Edward Drummond Libbey)

came a refuge for Protestants fleeing persecution in other countries all over western Europe, and the Academy that he established in Geneva became a center for training Protestant missionaries who, in return, would spread the true word of God into other lands. As part of the work of propagating his version of Protestantism, Calvin composed a treatise entitled *The Institutes of the Christian Religion*. In it he gave a more concise and logical definition of Protestant doctrines than any other of the leaders of this religious movement, and his book thus gained a position among Protestants comparable to the *Summa* of Thomas Aquinas among Catholics.

Calvin's basic principle was that the Bible is the one and only guide to an understanding of God's will and plan. The divine purpose of the universe, as Calvin discerned it from his reading of the Bible, was to show forth God's glory. As part of this plan, man was made in the image of God and was therefore endowed, like God, with goodness. However, man had sinned against God, and, as a punishment, God had doomed Adam and all his descendants to suffer forever in hell.

Yet, because God is merciful, he had decreed that certain men would be saved from this punishment. These were known as the *elect*—that is, those chosen by God to attain salvation. Since Calvin believed that the elect were so chosen before their birth, this doctrine is known as *predestination*.

The doctrine of predestination marked a sharp break with Luther's conception of Protestantism. Luther thought of men as having the freedom to gain salvation, if they would have faith in God's goodness. But Calvin had no such principle of freedom. The elect, in his view, did not gain salvation as a result of their free choice; they were simply designated by God as among those to whom his grace was given. Nor was the rest of mankind, to which this grace was forever denied, free to sin, because the elect were supposed to suppress sin on the part of others, as a service to God. And under Calvin's guidance, the righteous few of Geneva did not shirk their task. As we have seen, in their zeal to suppress sin, they undertook a detailed supervision of private as well as public morals, and, as we have also noted, they did not hesitate to put Michael Servetus to death, even though he proclaimed himself a true Protestant, on the ground that he disapproved of infant baptism and denied the doctrine of the Trinity.

Protestantism in France

Protestantism in both the Zwinglian and Lutheran versions made inroads in France before the influence of Calvinism was felt there, but eventually the Calvinists became the most important single group of Protestants in France. By the middle of the sixteenth century the French Protestants, who are known as Huguenots, perfected their national organization and included a number of distinguished personages, such as Gaspard de Coligny, Admiral of France, and the Prince of Condé, brother of the king.

Under the leadership of the dukes of Guise, the French Catholics strove to wipe out their Protestant rivals—for political as well as religious reasons—and France was rent by a series of religious civil wars. The climax of this struggle came with the gruesome massacre that began on St. Bartholomew's Day, August 24, 1572, and lasted until October. In the course of this slaughter, thousands of Protestants were murdered by Catholic officials, supported by the mob. The travail of France was not abated until 1593, when the King of Navarre acceded to the French throne as Henry IV. Though the new king was a Protestant before his accession, he found it expedient to turn Catholic: he is reputed to have said, "Paris is worth a mass." His conversion appeased the Catholics, while the king took steps also to conciliate his former coreligionists. In his reign, peace was restored to France.

Protestantism never disappeared from France, but Protestants have always been a small minority of the population—ranging between perhaps 5 and 15 percent. Its appeal was principally to townsmen and the nobility in certain localities; it never won much of a response among the French peasants.

THE REFORMATION IN ENGLAND

Protestantism swept into England during the 1520's and 1530's. But in England the movement owed less to the influence of outstanding religious reformers, such as Luther or Calvin, than to political figures—in particular, King Henry VIII and Queen Elizabeth I. To be sure, England had had many critics of the Catholic Church, and one of these, John Wyclif, had given voice to ideas that were later to become basic tenets of Protestantism. But the rebellious impulses of religious reformers in England did not gain force until their ideas were linked with the interests of the state and the personal ambition of Henry VIII.

Henry VIII

This lusty young king, the second of the new Tudor dynasty, ascended the throne in 1509. At the beginning of his reign he was a good Catholic, and when he heard of Luther's criticism of the Church, he rushed to its defense, writing a small book which he called *Defense of the Seven Sacraments*. For this service, the pope awarded him the title of *Fidei Defensor*, or "Defender of the Faith," which all succeeding English sovereigns have continued to bear.

Though spurning Luther's religious arguments, Henry was soon driven by the forces of personal ambition, lust, and nationalistic pride to begin an attack upon the institutions of the Church, the outcome of which was the creation of an English Catholic Church and its secession from the ecclesiastic empire of the Roman pontiff. Henry's breach with Rome began when he fell in love with the beautiful Anne Boleyn and sought to divorce his wife, Catherine of Aragon. As grounds for this divorce, he argued that his marriage to Catherine was never valid under Church law, because she was the widow of his brother. The pope refused to grant the divorce, however, on the ground that Henry had asked for and had received a special papal dispensation before marrying Catherine, and their marriage was therefore valid and indissoluble. The pope was mindful, moreover, that Catherine was a relative of the Emperor Charles V, who was also King of Spain, and the granting of the divorce would antagonize this powerful ruler, whose help the pope needed to suppress the Lutheran revolt.

Rebuffed by the pope, Henry promptly declared himself "sole protector and supreme head of the Church and clergy of England." The cowed English clergy accepted this revolutionary action by the king, and Thomas Cranmer, whom Henry appointed as Archbishop of Canterbury, quickly annulled the royal marriage. Thereupon Henry took Anne Boleyn as his second wife, and she soon bore him the daughter who later was to become the great Queen Elizabeth I.

In taking this step, Henry VIII had other thoughts in mind besides his romantic infatuation with the pretty Anne Boleyn. Despite his repudiation of Luther, the king, like many others of his time, had sincere doubts as to some of the practices and beliefs of the Roman Church. Moreover, he was affected by the growing spirit of nationalism, and as a king, like all other monarchs of his age, he was constantly in need of more money. He was therefore moved to bitter resentment by the thought that the Church

Henry VIII—a copy made under the supervision of Hans Holbein of his mural portrait of 1537 that was destroyed by fire in 1698. (Courtesy, Metropolitan Museum of Art)

papal court. In protest at these actions, as well as the divorce of Catherine, the pope excommunicated Henry and declared his offspring by Anne Boleyn to be illegitimate. Thereupon Parliament passed the Act of Succession (1534), which declared the marriage of Henry and Anne to be valid and vested the succession in the children of that marriage. Then, in the Act of Supremacy, Parliament reaffirmed that the king was the "supreme head of the Church of England." Finally Henry dissolved all monasteries and nunneries in England and confiscated their lands. This was a popular move, for these communities were generally regarded as both an economic waste and centers of gross immorality.

Despite these far-reaching moves in matters affecting religious practice, little change was made in points of religious doctrine. In 1536 a new statement of creed, known as the Ten Articles, was promulgated, but the concessions that it made to Lutheranism proved unpopular. In order to appease the protests it aroused, as well as for reasons connected with foreign affairs, the Ten Articles were supplanted in 1539 by a new statement of creed, the Six Articles, which restored a number of Catholic doctrines and doctrinal practices, such as transubstantiation, the offering to the laity of only bread and not wine during the communion service, and the celibacy of the clergy. This Act required conformity, and prescribed the death penalty for those who refused to worship according to the tenets it set forth.

Despite this partial reaction toward Catholicism, Protestantism continued to gain ground. After Henry's death in 1547, when the throne passed to his ten-year-old son Edward VI (1547–53), under a council of regency, the English Church again moved from Catholic doctrines toward those of the reformers. In Edward's reign, moreover, there was a large influx of Protestant leaders into the country, and numerous books and pamphlets were circulated, ridiculing Catholicism and advocating the ideas of Luther,

owned vast properties in England, the revenues of which he could himself use to great advantage for political purposes. And he was likewise covetous of the great sums of money that were sent from England to Rome for the support of a foreign potentate. When this potentate dared to interfere in the internal affairs of the English state and the personal affairs of the king himself, Henry was stirred to explosive anger. His motives were thus a mixture of personal caprice, economic need, and nationalistic ambition.

The breach with Rome was widened when the so-called "Reformation Parliament" began in 1529 to pass a series of laws that removed the English Church from the jurisdiction of the papacy. These laws made the king of England the head of the Catholic Church in England, forbade the paying of annates to the pope, and prohibited the taking of appeals from English courts to the

Calvin, and Zwingli. In the local churches, there were frequent demonstrations against ecclesiasticism and ritualism. Religious images were destroyed, and stained-glass windows broken. Under the direction of Thomas Cranmer, a new *Book of Common Prayer* was published (1549), in which Protestant ideas were popularized, and its use in churches was made official by the Act of Uniformity in 1549.

The Restoration of Catholicism

But England was not yet wholly Protestant, and the old religion was largely restored during the reign of Queen Mary (1553–58), the half sister of Edward VI. The daughter of Catherine of Aragon, whose rejection by Henry VIII had set off the religious upheaval, Mary was an ardent Catholic. She made plain her determination to remain a Catholic and to undo the advances of Protestantism in the previous reigns. Under her leadership, Parliament repealed all the laws enacted since 1529 that separated the English Church from Rome. Though it refused to restore the lands confiscated from the Church, it restored the mass and other rituals of Catholicism and revised the heresy laws so that their force bore upon Protestants instead of Catholics. Consequently many Protestant pastors and leaders fled abroad.

For those who remained, the next few years were a period of bitter persecution. Believing that the execution of the leaders of Protestantism would wipe out the movement, Mary caused the death as heretics of about 300 leading Protestants, among whom was Thomas Cranmer. But this persecution did not accomplish its purpose; instead, it provoked a deep and bitter revulsion against Mary among the English people.

This revulsion was increased by Mary's marriage to Philip II, "His Most Catholic Majesty," the King of Spain. Mary loved Philip—poor woman, for apparently he did not care for her, and he made her desperately unhappy. The English people, however, hated and feared Philip, because they felt that Mary's marriage to him meant the domination of England by a foreign prince and the renewal of the papal dominion over their Church.

Hence the English Parliament, though generally compliant with Mary's wishes, refused to accede to her demand for a restoration of the supremacy of the pope in church matters; instead, it insisted upon maintaining the supremacy of the Crown over the Church of England. Thus the reconciliation with Rome was never completed, and Mary, hated by her people and unloved by her husband, with a record of failure in her effort at reactionary religious reforms, died a lonely and embittered woman.

Burning of the Bones and Books of Martin Bucer and Paulus Phagius—from an early edition of John Foxe's *Ecclesiastical History Containing the Acts and Monuments of Martyrs*, London, 1576. Bucer, who once had been a Dominican friar, became a Protestant reformer, who eventually found a haven in England, where he died in 1551. (*Bibliothèque Nationale*)

The Triumph of Protestantism

The culmination of the Protestant Revolution in England came in the reign of Elizabeth, the daughter of Henry VIII and Anne Boleyn. Though it was said that she was at heart a Catholic, Elizabeth I (1558–1603) was astute enough to win a fair degree of support from all parties and to maintain an effective toleration among them. At the beginning of her reign most of the common people of England were still Catholic in thought and feeling, but the people of the cities, especially London, were Protestant. And the Protestant leaders, who dominated the House of Commons, were the most powerful group in the kingdom. The so-called "Elizabethan settlement," by which these two great parties were held together, was a compromise. It was weighted on the Protestant side, however, and in the long run worked to the advantage of this aggressive minority. By the end of Elizabeth's reign the overwhelming majority of the English people was of the Protestant persuasion.

As soon as Elizabeth came to the throne, Parliament reaffirmed the Act of Supremacy and re-enacted the laws favorable to Protestantism that had been repealed in the previous reign. The *Book of Common Prayer* was restored to official use, though slightly revised in the direction of Catholicism, and in 1563 the Anglican Church adopted the Thirty-Nine Articles, which have ever since been the basic statement of the doctrinal position of the Church of England.

The Thirty-Nine Articles combine ideas drawn from traditional Catholicism with others inspired by Luther and Calvin. They reaffirmed the traditional conception of the Holy Trinity and the redemption of man by Christ, but they departed from Catholicism in placing full and sole authority in the Bible: "Holy Scripture containeth all things necessary for salvation: so that whatsoever is not read therein . . . is not to be required of any man, that it should be believed as an article of faith . . . necessary

to salvation." Moreover, the Articles follow Calvin in the definition of original sin, the doctrine of salvation by grace and not by works, the doctrine of predestination, and the description of the sacraments. Two of these are retained—baptism and communion—but no others.

Though the doctrinal basis of the Church of England thus became largely Protestant, its organization and ritual still resembled that of the Catholic Church. The Archbishop of Canterbury continued to be the administrative head of the Church, though now accountable solely to the king and not the pope, and the hierarchical structure of archbishop, bishop, and parish priest (or curate) remained as before. In spiritual matters the Crown was now supreme, but the ecclesiastical functions of the Crown were in practice delegated to a board of churchmen, called the Court of High Commission. The ritual was governed by the *Book of Common Prayer,* but some of the religious ceremonies retained a Catholic flavor, and, despite the opposition of the more radical Protestants, the queen insisted that the clergy continue to wear the traditional vestments.

After the adoption of the Thirty-Nine Articles, Parliament passed a series of anti-Catholic laws, and Elizabeth refused to send a delegate to the Council of Trent, which the pope convened as a means of rallying the Catholic world against the Protestant menace. She also ruthlessly suppressed a Catholic uprising in the north of England. At last the pope excommunicated her and absolved her subjects of their allegiance to her. But this was to no avail. Elizabeth did not change her position, and England remained Protestant.

Yet the Protestantism established in the Elizabethan settlement was not sufficient to satisfy all Protestants, for, in the view of the more extreme among them, it retained too much of "popery." Accordingly a group of the followers of Robert Browne seceded from the Anglican Church to form Separatist or Congregational churches, which had no hierarchical organization whatever and left each congregation free to manage its religious affairs in its own way. Another group of religious radicals were the Puritans, so called because they wished to purify the Anglican Church of the vestiges of Catholicism. Especially, they wanted to eliminate all ceremonialism from the church services and to prohibit the clergy from wearing vestments. Upon the accession in 1603 of James I, 1000 Puritan leaders in the Anglican Church petitioned the king to inaugurate the reforms they advocated. He refused, however, and there followed an era of the persecution of these "dissenters." To avoid this persecution, many of the Puritans emigrated to America. But in the reigns of James I and his son Charles I, the cause of Puritanism came to

be identified with the cause of Parliament, which was beginning to challenge the power of the king. The outcome of both the religious and the political protest was the Great Rebellion of 1642–1648, in the course of which the parliamentary rebels won a temporary victory over the crown.

But with the ultimate failure of this rebellion in 1660, when Charles II regained the throne, the religious issues were settled by a compromise in much the same terms set down in the time of Elizabeth. This settlement accorded a considerable measure of toleration to Protestant dissenters, though the more extreme groups, such as the Quakers, remained outside the law, as did all Catholics. But the official religion of the land was to remain Anglican Protestantism.

THE CATHOLIC REFORMATION

The Roman Catholic Church had been shaken to its foundations by the revolt started by Luther, Zwingli, and Calvin. This catastrophe, which meant the loss of the larger part of western Europe, induced the leaders of Catholicism to make a threefold effort to restore the Church to its former position of universal authority. One of these efforts took place in the Council of Trent, where the leading churchmen of Catholic Christendom undertook to restate Catholic doctrine. The second was the organization of the militant missionary order known as the Society of Jesus, or the Jesuits. The third was the revival of the church court known as the Inquisition, which was the traditional instrument for the ferreting out and extirpation of heresy.

The Council of Trent

The Council of Trent assembled in 1545, at the summons of Pope Paul III, to consider ways and means of combating Protestantism. It was composed of papal representatives,

archbishops, bishops, and the heads of religious orders. It was charged with three tasks: settling the doctrinal disputes involved in the quarrel between Catholics and Protestants; cleaning up moral and administrative abuses within the old Church itself; and organizing a new crusade against the Moslems, in the hope that this would distract the attention of Christendom from its internal disputes. But the Council suffered from bickering and intrigue among its members, and it accomplished little more than a defensive restatement of the Church's ancient dogmas.

Thus, against the Protestants' claim that the Bible was the sole authority in matters of religion, the Council reaffirmed the authority of the traditions and rulings of the Church and the Church Fathers. As against the Lutheran position that salvation was by faith alone, the Council restated the necessity of both faith and works, including the seven sacraments. Finally, it ordered the preparation of an "Index of Prohibited Books," which Catholics were forbidden to read, issued a new standard edition of the catechism, and laid down a new set of

A Session of the Council of Trent—part of a copper engraving published in Venice in 1565. (The Bettmann Archive)

rules governing the behavior of the priests.

Though the work of the Council of Trent was more negative than positive—it defined the Catholic position but did little to establish a common ground uniting all Christians —it succeeded in giving the Church new moral strength, and this provided some help in checking the spread of Protestantism.

The Jesuits

In 1540, five years before the first meeting of the Council of Trent, a small group of fervent Catholic students at the University of Paris had formed a new religious order, called the Company or Society of Jesus. The leader of this group and first head of the new order was Ignatius Loyola (1491–1556).

Loyola, by birth a Spaniard, was a crippled soldier, who, at the age of thirty, experienced a deep emotional "conversion" while he was recovering from a wound received in battle. Thereupon he had given away his wealth, in the fashion of Francis of Assisi, and had vowed himself to a religious career as a "Soldier of Christ." After

making a pilgrimage to Jerusalem, he had gone to study at the University of Paris, where he gathered about him the band of followers who became the first members of the Company of Jesus. Because of his extreme religious zeal, Loyola had been suspected of heresy, and he had fled from Spain in order to be safe from the Inquisition. Nevertheless, the pope had approved the new order that he formed and had given it a charter.

The stated purpose of the Society of Jesus was to "fight for God under the standard of the Cross." To do so, the order proposed to wage a militant struggle for the Catholic Christian faith by every means possible, but especially by the means of education. It was directly under the orders of the pope, and its members were pledged to serve wherever in the world they might be sent. It thus made an appeal to men of heroic piety, and its numbers increased rapidly. Soon chapters of the order were founded in all quarters of the globe—in North America, Brazil, India, Japan, Africa, and other far-off places. The business of combating heresy came to be recognized as a special field of endeavor for the

Jesuits, and in this work they were remarkably successful. They also gained renown as teachers, and their many schools, to which lay persons were admitted, became famous. It is not an exaggeration to say that the Jesuits were one of the major factors in the reunification of the Catholic Church and the gradual slowing down of the spread of Protestantism.

Jansenism

Not all the battles of the Jesuits were fought against persons who professed themselves to be Protestants, for among their adversaries were a group of Catholics who came to be known as the Jansenists.

Jansenism was the continuation of a movement begun by Michael Bains (1513–1589). Reacting against the Scholasticism of the late Feudal Era, Bains had turned back to Au-

gustine, much as Luther and Calvin had done. From reading Augustine, he came to adopt the idea of predestination, and this brought him into conflict with the official position of the Church. He did not break with Catholicism, but as a professor of theology at the University of Louvain he taught the Augustinian theology as against the official scholastic philosophy of Thomas Aquinas. Later his ideas were taken up by Cornelius Jansen, from whom Jansenism takes its name. Like Bains, Jansen accepted the idea of predestination and emphasized the need for personal piety. In his insistence that the essential element in religion is the individual's relationship to God, he verged upon Protestantism—but he also insisted that this relationship could be achieved only within the Catholic Church.

The Jesuits, sworn to defend orthodoxy, were quick to take note of the deviation of the Jansenists in the direction of Protestant-

The Religious Situation in Europe about 1560

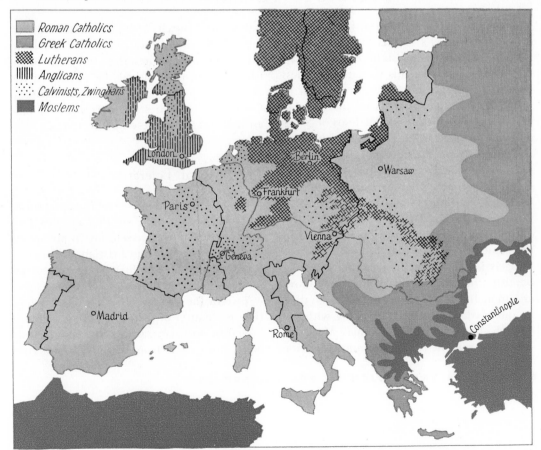

ism, and there ensued a bitter struggle between the two groups that lasted more than a century, ending only when the pope in 1713 condemned the Jansenist position as heretical. Yet, in spite of this outcome, Jansenism represented a genuine reform movement within the Church and a part of the Catholic reaction against Protestantism.

The Inquisition

Meanwhile, the Church revived the Inquisition, or Holy Office, a Church court that had existed for centuries, as we have seen, for the extirpation of heresy. Though it operated in all countries of Europe and America where the Catholic Church was still dominant, it achieved its greatest notoriety in Spain. Its history in that country has been described as a "long record of diabolical cruelty, of protracted confinement in dungeons, of endless delay and browbeating to break the spirit, of ingenious tortures and of racked and crushed limbs and of burning flesh." Many of its victims were burned alive, many were beaten, many were sent to the galleys. The work of the Spanish Inquisition was effective, however, for it checked any slight tendency toward Protestantism—in Spain and in the Spanish colonies. In other countries its record was less lurid.

These various measures by which the Catholic Church mobilized its forces against Protestantism were not sufficient to bring the whole of Europe once more under the dominion of the pope. The campaign, however, did achieve a considerable measure of success in checking the further spread of Protestantism. And though much of Europe remained Protestant, new lands overseas were being won to the Catholic Church. Ultimately, therefore, the area and the number of people under the papal dominion became greater than before the outbreak of the Protestant Revolution.

THE BIRTH OF RELIGIOUS TOLERATION

The century and a half following the publication of Luther's Ninety-five Theses was a period of almost constant religious warfare. In the course of this warfare, countless lives were lost, an immeasurable amount of property was destroyed, and incalculable pain inflicted—in the name of Jesus of Nazareth and for the purpose of human salvation.

The reason for this was plain and simple: religion was identified with power, and religious dissent therefore meant treasonable rebellion against the established power. This was true in Protestant lands as well as Catholic. Thus Luther, though himself a rebel in the name of religious individualism, became savagely intolerant of the peasants and Anabaptists who, starting out as his own followers, took his teachings more literally than he intended. Henry VIII, breaking with the Church, had the kindly Thomas More beheaded because he refused to follow the king out of the Church. Mary, Henry's daughter, lighted the skies of England with the lurid fires of burning Protestants, while the Spanish Inquisition furnished the victims of the disgusting "acts of faith." And professors in Catholic universities were required to take an oath that they were not Protestants!

The Birth of Toleration

It was inevitable that a few of the saner members of society would see that all this warfare, torture, and persecution in the name of Christ was both un-Christian and useless. From them came the first modern pleas for religious and intellectual toleration.

Two of the Protestant sects upheld toleration as a matter of principle. These were the humanist Socinians, who held that religious belief must come from reason and not coercion, and the pietist Anabaptists, who believed that God speaks directly to every individual. But both these sects suffered a persecution, in which Protestants as well as Catholics took part, that all but destroyed them.

Among the individuals who advocated toleration was Sebastian Costellio, a French humanist, who appealed to both Protestants and Catholics to stop torturing and killing one another in the name of religion. One of the most famous of English pleaders for religious toleration was Roger Williams (1604–1683), who showed the tragic inconsistencies inherent in political persecution for conscience's sake and founded the English colony of Rhode Island on the principle that "God does not require" men to worship in any particular way or according to any particular doctrine. John Milton, the great

Puritan poet (1608–1674), also made an eloquent plea for toleration, though he would not extend this so far as to include Catholics and non-Christians.

Meanwhile, the Protestant republic of Holland found it both profitable and intellectually stimulating to welcome religious refugees from persecution, and for a century or more Holland was the greatest sanctuary of religious and intellectual freedom in the western world. Presently this distinction came to be shared by the English colonies in America. Gradually toleration made progress in other countries of Europe. It was established sooner in Protestant lands than Catholic, since the multiplicity of Protestant sects made toleration almost imperative. But eventually religious dissent was also permitted in some Catholic countries, although the Catholic Church never accepted the principle.

THE MUSIC OF THE REFORMATION

The religious movements of the sixteenth century had a marked influence upon the development of music. On the Catholic side, this took the form of an even more sumptuous use of music in the rituals of the Church, with the hope that the heightened beauty of the traditional religious services would combat the appeal of the Protestants. On their side, the most notable new trend among the Protestants was toward the larger use of hymns, sung by the congregation. This was especially important to the Protestants, because their services made much less use of ritual and pageantry than did the Catholic. For the most part these hymns were drawn from a tradition of popular penitential songs, dating back to the fourteenth and fifteenth centuries. In part, however, they drew from the more recent Renaissance tradition of sensuous art-music.

Luther himself was especially fond of music, which he declared was a gift of God, and played a number of instruments. He retained parts of the Catholic ritual and the mass, including its art-music, and gave the-

ological sanction to the growth of a great school of Lutheran organists in the next century. But he also introduced hymns or chorales, drawn from the penitential tradition, to be sung by the congregation. A number of these seem to have been composed by Luther himself, including the defiant *"Ein' feste Burg is unser Gott"* ("A Mighty Fortress Is Our God"), which he sang as he entered Worms in 1521. This is not only the resolute music of protest; it is also the music of the stolid middle class, and of German nationalism.

Calvin disavowed the whole Renaissance tradition of Catholic art-music in church—choirs, organs, even hymns and harmony—but he gave sanction to unaccompanied metrical psalms, sung in unison by the congregation. The best known of the Calvinist psalm-tunes is the "Doxology" ("Old Hundredth"). Also notable is the battle hymn of the Huguenots, "Let God Arise and Scattered Let All His Enemies Be," a setting of the 68th Psalm, which is the Calvinist counterpart to the Lutheran *"Ein' feste Burg."*

CONCLUSION

As an intellectual and religious movement, the Protestant revolt from Roman Catholicism and the Catholic reaction to it, taken together, should probably be considered one of the major events in western history. It split western Christianity from top to bottom. But this religious revolution was also a reaction against religious authoritarianism in the name of an individualism centering about the direct relationship between individual human beings and their God. Despite the corporate authoritarianism that crept into so many of the Protestant sects themselves, this event opened the modern era of religious individualism and toleration in religion that has permeated many other fields of thought. That this religious individualism was closely related to the intellectual individualism of the cultural Renaissance and the economic individualism that marked the expansion of commerce and the rise of capitalism in the same era there can be no doubt. At the same time it could not have succeeded so dramatically or have spread so rapidly had it not been supported by the power of the emerging integral states and the nascent spirit of nationalism. It is to be considered as one of the major aspects of a profound change in the broad mood of western civilization—a change marked by the increasing urbanization of society, the expansion of commerce and capitalism, the first beginnings of modern science, and the increasingly secular outlook on human life and society that was visible in the Renaissance to which it was so intimately linked.

The religious Reformation, like the intellectual Renaissance, had no end, but has continued, from the day when Martin Luther nailed his "Ninety-five Theses" to the door of the church at Wittenberg to our own. Like the Renaissance, too, its most essential and precious ingredients—despite its own ruthless intolerance and the wars, persecutions, and other barbarities committed in its name—were its religious individualism and anti-authoritarianism. Despite all its more sordid aspects and its failures, the successful establishment of the idea that has become one of the most brilliantly characteristic ideas in the Atlantic civilization—that religion is strictly an individual matter between a man and his God, utterly outside the legitimate concern of state or priest—is one of the major triumphs in the history of religion.

As with the moods of the Renaissance, too, the religious individualism and anti-authoritarianism of the Reformation were dramatically confirmed by the later rationalism born of the triumphs of science. Religious and intellectual freedom, introduced into western civilization by the Reformation and the Renaissance together, were written, at last, into the western tradition by this rationalism of the age of science. The story of the religions of rationalism, therefore, and the triumph of religious and intellectual freedom that accompanied them, must await the story of the growth and the triumph of science itself. This triumph was to be achieved in the eighteenth century.

Suggestions for Further Reading

Source Materials

Anthologies and Collected Documents

F. Le V. Baumer, ed., *Main Currents of Western Thought* (New York, 1952), Part I, pp. 165–243.

A fine collection of documents from the great reformers, the "radical" Protestants, and Ignatius Loyola, together with writings illustrating the supposed relationship of Protestantism to capitalism.

H. S. Bettenson, *Documents of the Christian Church* (New York, 1947).

Contains a fine collection of documents illustrating the Reformation.

Columbia College, *Introduction to Contemporary Civilization in the West* (2 vols., New York, 1946), Volume I, Chapter 6.

Documents illustrative of the ideas of Wyclif and Hus, Luther, Calvin, Ignatius Loyola, The Council of Trent, and others.

G. H. Knoles and R. K. Snyder, eds., *Readings in Western Civlization* (rev. ed., New York, 1954), pp. 375–405.

Selections from Luther, Calvin, Anglicanism, and the Roman Catholic Council of Trent.

P. Schaff, *The Creeds of Christendom* (rev. ed., 3 vols., New York, 1931).

A collection of the texts of the historic creeds of Christian churches. For the Reformation, the student is referred particularly to the "Westminster Confession" of the English Calvinists, the "Thirty-nine Articles" of the Anglican Church, etc.

Contemporary Writings

The following books are the basic works of the Protestant Revolt. They are available in many editions and are to be found in nearly all libraries.

J. Calvin, *Institutes of the Christian Religion.*

Catechism of the Council of Trent.

M. Luther, *Address to the Christian Nobility of the German Nation. On Christian Liberty.*

Secondary Works

R. H. Bainton, *Here I Stand: A Life of Martin Luther* (New York, 1950).

A readable and accurate modern biography.

R. H. Bainton, *The Reformation of the Sixteenth Century* (Boston, 1952).

A reliable modern account.

H. J. Grimm, *The Reformation Era 1500–1650* (New York, 1954).

An excellent, up-to-date survey of the rise and spread of Protestantism and of the Catholic reform.

P. Janelle, *The Catholic Reformation* (Milwaukee, 1949).

A fine account of the Catholic Reform.

K. S. Latourette, *A History of Christianity* (New York, 1953).

An up-to-date, accurate history. Contains an excellent account of the religious transition from the Feudal Era to the Commercial Era.

H. S. Lucas, *The Renaissance and the Reformation* (New York, 1934).

A standard, dependable survey.

J. MacKinnon, *Calvin and the Reformation* (London, 1936).

A standard, dependable account of Calvin's life and work.

F. M. Powicke, *The Reformation in England* (London, 1941).

A fine, scholarly account of the English phase of the Reformation.

J. H. Randall, Jr., *The Making of the Modern Mind* (rev. ed., Boston, 1940), Chapter 7.

An excellent, brief survey of religious transition from feudal to modern times.

H. M. Smith, *Henry VIII and the Reformation* (New York, 1948).

A modern history of the reformation of the English Catholic Church under Henry VIII.

P. Smith, *The Age of the Reformation* (New York, 1920).

An old but still valuable history of the Protestant revolt from Catholicism and the Catholic reform that took place, in part, at least, as a reaction to it.

P. Smith, *The Life and Letters of Martin Luther* (New York, 1914).

An old but still useful life of Luther.

E. G. Swiebert, *Luther and His Times* (St. Louis, 1950).

A fine, up-to-date account of Luther's revolt in its historical setting and significance.

R. H. Tawney, *Religion and the Rise of Capitalism* (New York, 1926).

A highly provocative historical essay upon the supposed relationship between the appearance of modern capitalism and the growth of Protestantism in religion.

P. Van Dyke, *Ignatius Loyola, The Founder of the Jesuits* (New York, 1926).

A good biography.

J. P. Whitney, *The History of the Reformation* (new ed., London, 1940).

A solid, standard work by a theologian.

25

The Appearance of the
Sovereign State

Louis XIV, King of France, 1643–1715—portrait of the Grand Monarch made in 1701 by Hyacinthe Rigaud. (Alinari photograph)

What is the State? The very same set of forces that transformed the economy of the Feudal Era into the economy of the Commercial Era also transformed the medieval political form, feudalism, into a new political form, the modern integral and sovereign state. The transformation was slow; but whereas in the year 1300 the feudal network was the almost universal political form in western Europe, by about 1648 the feudal system had broken up and in its place a group of separate, mutually independent "sovereign" states had appeared. In these states, the old, explicit feudal ties between lord and vassal were fast disappearing, and the fundamental political relationship, instead of being a personal relationship between lord and vassal, was now a relationship between the individual and his "state," the corporate body politic into which he had happened to be born. These modern bodies politic have been called *integral* states, because they eventually came to behave as integral political units. And they were—and are—*sovereign* in the sense that, as integers, they had the final power of decision in all matters, both with regard to their citizens, over whom they had an absolute power, even

of life and death, and with regard to their relations with the rest of the world, in which there existed no authority that could challenge their decisions. Government in the sovereign state, to be sure, was now the function of the king and his ministers, and in practice the power of government was well-nigh absolute, so that Louis XIV might actually have said, "I am the State." Yet the new political phenomenon was not merely a form of government: it was a new, corporate, and indivisible form of social and political organism. Increasingly strongly centralized in its direction, it was the antithesis of the loose feudal network of dispersed local authorities that it replaced.

"State" and "Nation." Presently the integral, corporate state would be endowed with a characteristic personality, tradition, and "mission" and, above all, a sort of psychological bond of unity and mutual loyalty among its citizens. This psychological phenomenon, called *nationalism,* was to become one of the great, distinguishing characteristics of the modern integral state; and the body of people bound together by this psychological self-consciousness would eventually come to be

Europe in 1560

called a *nation*. The nation was usually identical with the body politic known as the state, but it was not always so. In France, for example, nation and state were one; in the Holy Roman Empire, on the contrary, the state was in the nature of a federation of many nationalities. The *state* then, was a political unity; the *nation* was a socio-psychological unit. A state that was also a nation came to be called a *national state*.

At the time of the Commerical Revolution, Spain, France, Portugal, Holland, and England were well advanced along the road toward becoming unified, "sovereign" states; and feudalism was clearly on the way out, if it had not disappeared. From about 1500 onward the political history of Europe was largely the history of these several sovereign states and their relationships with each other.

THE AGE OF STATE-MAKING

The Evolution of the English State

The gradual emergence of the English state out of English feudalism had its beginning at least as early as the time of Henry II and John (pp. 458–459). By the accession of Henry VII in 1485 the power of the feudal nobles was rapidly declining and that of the Crown, supported, generally, by the mercantile interests, was correspondingly increasing.

Henry VII was a hard, shrewd, parsimonious king who succeeded in restoring order and prosperity to an England that was badly demoralized by centuries of external and internal warfare. He encouraged the growth of commerce, especially the wool trade with the continent, and he established the power of the monarch so firmly that it was never again seriously challenged by the feudal lords.

Henry VII was succeeded by Henry VIII, who still further consolidated the power of the ruler, most especially by breaking the power of the Roman pontiff in English affairs and confiscating the property of the Roman church in England for the use of the Crown and its supporters (p. 616). This achievement by Henry VIII was of great significance, because, although Henry had no intention of changing the old Roman Catholic religion as such, it took England out of the unity of western feudal Christendom and broke, once and for all, the old ties that had bound England to the continent and made of it a separate and fully sovereign state in the true sense of the word.

Queen Elizabeth I, who ascended the throne in 1558, continued the consolidation of the English state, and while, like her father and grandfather, she maintained the parliamentary forms, she succeeded in finishing the job of almost completely eliminating from English polity the rival power of the feudal nobles. At the same time the establishment of the Anglican Protestant Church strengthened the internal sovereignty of the state by making that Church an arm of the government. While eliminating her chief rival, Mary Stuart, by decapitation, Elizabeth succeeded, probably more than any other modern English ruler, in binding her subjects to herself and to each other in a solid and self-conscious feeling of English nationality. This development was particularly stimulated by Elizabeth's struggle with Philip II of Spain, who attacked England in 1588 with the famous "Great Armada," only to have it strewn as wreckage along the shores of the English Channel by the action of a terrific storm—ably assisted, of course, by the fast-sailing English "seadogs."

The "Elizabethan Era," which was dominated by "Good Queen Bess," saw an almost phenomenal expansion of English overseas commerce all around the Atlantic Basin and eastward around the world as far as India. It was during this era, too, that the first beginnings of an overseas empire were made, in America and in India. It was also in this era that English cultural life flowered in the English "Renaissance" to produce Edmund Spenser, William Shakespeare, Ben Jonson, Francis Bacon, and a host of other literary figures that stand among the greatest of all time.

But the process of integral-state-forming was not completed, even with Elizabeth I. The people were still divided over religious and political questions, and the divisions began to appear in all their depth and breadth when James I (of the Stuart family) ascended the throne in 1603. James believed he was king by "divine right" and felt no strong

Kings and Queens of England, 1485–1694

House of Tudor

Henry VII	1485–1509
Henry VIII	1509–1547
Edward VI	1547–1553
Mary	1553–1558
Elizabeth I	1558–1603

House of Stuart

James I	1603–1625
Charles I	1625–1649

(*The Commonwealth*	1649–1660)

House of Stuart

Charles II	1660–1685
James II	1685–1688

House of Orange

William III ⎫ corulers	1688–1702
Mary ⎭	1688–1694

sense of responsibility to the English people. His son, Charles I, shared his haughty self-esteem, and when Charles flouted both the Puritans and the time-honored English myth of "no taxation without representation," Parliament assumed control of the state, beginning in 1642.

Charles, unwilling to take orders from Parliament, attempted to force his will upon it. But in the Great Civil War that followed, Charles was defeated, captured, and executed for treason against the English state. England then became a republic, under the leadership of Oliver Cromwell; but after Cromwell's death, English leaders invited Charles II, eldest son of Charles I, to return "from his travels" and reassume the throne of his father.

Still the question of the real source of sovereignty in the English state was not yet decided. Charles II got along fairly well, without forcing the issue, but when James II, his brother, succeeded him in 1685, the question was posed once more. James II had apparently learned nothing from the experiences of his grandfather and his father, and set about flouting most of the well-established English prejudices—as, for example, by his excessive favoritism toward Catholics, his highly arbitrary administration of justice, his disregard of the wishes of Parliament, and his friendship for the French king Louis XIV at a moment when Anglo-French commercial and colonial rivalry were becoming acute.

English impatience with this stupid and arbitrary ruler exploded in 1688, when English parliamentary leaders of all parties combined to invite the Dutch *stadtholder*, William of Orange, who had married James' daughter Mary, to come to England and replace James. James discreetly departed for France, and William and Mary assumed the English throne.

The great significance of this almost bloodless revolution of 1688–1689 lies not in the fact that England had a change of rulers but, rather, in the fact that this event settled, once and for all, the question of the nature of the English state and the seat of sovereignty in it. This revolution, in the last analysis, was a triumph of Parliament, which, in theory at least, expressed the will of the body politic in England. And when William and Mary ascended the throne, they did so with a clear and unequivocal acceptance of a set of laws passed by Parliament, such as the Mutiny Act and the so-called "Bill of Rights," that put it almost outside the power of the monarch ever again to interfere with parliamentary supremacy.

At long last the answer to the problem was clear: the "constitution" of England, theoretically derived from the will of the English people as a whole, was recognized as a fundamental law that even the king had to obey. Furthermore, while the government of the English state was through the instrumentality of "king, lords and commons," it was Parliament and, increasingly during the eighteenth and nineteenth centuries, especially the House of Commons, that was the recognized and sovereign voice of the English body politic. With this development, in the century or so that began with the "Glorious Revolution" of 1688, the English state assumed its definite modern form.

The Modern State in France

Meanwhile, across the English Channel in France, the process of integral-state-formation followed lines that were both similar and dissimilar to those in England.

The consolidation of the French state had begun in the thirteenth century, under Philip Augustus, and the earliest expressions of French national consciousness had been inspired during the late phases of the Hundred Years' War by the heroic career of Joan of Arc. The end of that war found France upon the road to national consolidation. Under Louis XI, who died in 1483, the boundaries of France were pushed almost to their present extent, and under Francis I, who ruled from 1515 to 1547, French national consciousness became an important force in French history, and the first beginnings were made toward the foundation of a French overseas empire.

But France, like England, was still divided within itself over questions relative to the succession to the throne, and these divisions were complicated by the religious schisms that appeared with the advent of Protestantism in the Calvinistic faith of the Huguenots. The second half of the sixteenth century was thus marked by a series of civil wars that were both religious and dynastic, that were finally resolved by the accession of Henry IV.

Henry IV, the "Good King Henry" of French history, aided by his able minister, the Duc de Sully, brought order and solidarity to his country, and succeeded in resolving the religious question by the famous Edict of Nantes (1598), by which the Protestants were allowed to control certain cities and to worship freely in them.

Even this, however, did not succeed in finally fusing France into the integral state that it was to become, because the division of the country into "Catholic France" and "Protestant France" made it impossible to administer the country in anything like a unified manner. The feudal nobility were still jealous of their waning power, too. It was the great task of Cardinal Richelieu (1585–1642), therefore, who became Louis XIII's chief minister in 1623, to reduce the power both of the Protestants and of the feudal nobility. The first of these he did by modifying the terms of the Edict of Nantes after a brief civil war in 1627; the second he achieved only partially, and it remained for Cardinal Mazarin (1602–1661), who succeeded Richelieu in power during the boyhood of Louis XIV, to complete this task by the suppression of a series of civil uprisings, called the *Fronde,* sponsored by the nobility in their desire to recover some of their old power. After that, the feudal nobility, while retaining vast estates and a disproportionately large portion of the wealth of France, were almost without significant political power, and were reduced to the position of pompous social parasites swarming about the person of the king.

The reduction of the decentralizing power of the Protestants and the feudal nobility were the clearest indications, in the seventeenth century, that the consolidation of the French state was proceeding apace. This process reached a sort of culmination with the accession of Louis XIV to the full royal power in 1661. Louis' long reign of seventy-two years (he actually ascended the throne as a boy in 1643; he died in 1715) is most significant, probably, in French internal history, for the manner in which he made the power of the monarch well-nigh absolute and made himself the symbol of the French state's unity and its power. Even so, the process of integration was not yet complete, for the local and provincial divisions of France showed an almost infinite, and extremely complex, variety of laws and governmental institutions. Furthermore, there was a vast network of almost-defunct feudal institutions and customs still in force. It was not until the great French Revolution, in the last decade of the eighteenth century, that the hodge-podge of ancient laws, customs, and institutions was finally swept away and France emerged as a state that was truly unified, both administratively and in the self-conscious national feeling of its people.

In the evolution of its political institutions, the French state thus had a history that stood in sharp contrast with that of England. Both countries had emerged from the Feudal Era with parliaments representing the various social classes in the two countries. But, whereas the English Parliament steadily increased its power and eventually became the dominant force in the administration of the English state, the French Estates-General, as it was called, failed to achieve a similar metamorphosis from the old feudal council to a modern constitutional legislature and practically disappeared from French affairs after the reign of Henry IV. It met for the last time in 1614, four years after

ful mercantilist statism of Colbert (p. 571), the French economy made significant progress toward an economic unity and a common national economic purpose that was, if anything, even more solidly that of an integral state than that of England itself. Yet, whereas the English state had fallen under the direction of "the people" (actually, the "middle class"), on the basis of the ideal of a fundamental constitution from which the king derives his power and to which even the king is answerable, the control of the French state had fallen under the rule of an almost-absolute and irresponsible king.

The process of solidifying the state was in both cases the same historic process; it was only the governmental forms and theories that were different.

Henry's death, and it did not meet again until 1789 when Henry's unhappy descendant, Louis XVI, was forced by the bankruptcy of his profligate government to call it together to help him raise some money.

By contrast with England, the sovereignty of the French state was gradually concentrated in the hands of the French king. This aspect of French history reached its culmination under Louis XIV, during whose reign the power of the king became almost unchallengeable. Theoretically, at least, the sovereignty of the French state remained fixed in the person of the king until the French Revolution; and this sort of absolutism was justified by the theory of "the divine right of kings," according to which the state owed its existence, and the king his power, to God (p. 644).

Basically, then, the process of state-formation in France paralleled fairly closely the same process in England. In France, as in England, the power of the feudal lords had practically disappeared. In the place of the feudal network of local governments there now stood the power of the whole country, symbolized and institutionalized in France by the absolute monarchy. Under the power-

State-building in Portugal and Spain

The process of state-formation in the more than two centuries after 1500 was clearest and most advanced in England and France. Yet the process was going on, somewhat less clearly and in relatively varying degrees, in most of the countries of western Europe. Thus the same process is to be observed in Spain and in Portugal, in Holland, in the Scandinavian countries, in Prussia, and in Russia.

One of the earliest countries in western Europe to achieve an integral statehood was Portugal. This small country, on the western tip of the Iberian Peninsula, had been overrun by the Moors in the westward sweep of the Moslem hordes in the eighth century. Then, for several centuries during the wars of the reconquest, it had been a feudal fief of the king of Leon. The rulers of Portugal had thrown off this feudal allegiance, however, and by about 1262 had finally succeeded independently in driving the Moors from Portuguese soil. When the Venetians began the custom of sending their goods to western Europe by sea in 1317, Lisbon became a normal watering-station and port of exchange,

Rulers of Spain, 1474–1788

Isabella (Queen of Castile)	1474–1505
Ferdinand II (King of Aragon)	1479–1516

Hapsburg Dynasty

Charles I	1516–1556
Philip II	1556–1598
Philip III	1598–1621
Philip IV	1621–1665
Charles II	1665–1700
War of the Spanish Succession	1701–1714

Bourbon Dynasty

Philip V	1700–1746
Ferdinand VI	1746–1759
Charles III	1759–1788

with the result that Lisbon—and Portugal with it—became stable and prosperous commercially. In the meantime, the kings of Portugal had succeeded in bringing both the powerful Catholic Church and the feudal barons to a position of subservience to the king. The combination of these three processes came with the reign of John I, father of Prince Henry the Navigator, who ruled Portugal from 1385 to 1433 and who consolidated his commercial and national power by marrying an English noblewoman, the daughter of John of Gaunt.

With the rise of Spain, Portugal fell to a position of relative unimportance. The kingdom, with its colonial empire that now included Brazil as well as parts of Africa and India, was actually annexed to Spain by Philip II in 1580. But Portugal regained independence in 1640, and thereafter it tended to fall under the economic and international dominance of England.

In Spain, the unification of the Spanish state was the culmination of the centuries of struggle by the Catholic Spaniards to overthrow the Moorish domination and to drive the Moors out of Spain entirely. By the middle of the fifteenth century the "reconquest" had proceeded so far as to reduce the

Moorish holdings to the southern kingdom of Granada, while the small kingdoms of Valencia, Catalonia, Aragon, and Spanish Navarre had been united under the leadership of King Ferdinand of Aragon. The kingdoms of Castile and Leon, on the other hand, together with certain other smaller principalities and dukedoms, had been united under Isabella, Queen of Castile. The marriage of Ferdinand and Isabella in 1469

Charles V with His Dog. Charles I of Spain was also Emperor Charles V of the Holy Roman Empire. This portrait, painted in 1530, was the first of several by the celebrated Venetian artist Titian (p. 588). (Anderson)

loosely united—or federated—all these holdings and the long-delayed conquest of Granada in 1492 by the forces of the federated kingdoms at long last drove the Moors forever out of the peninsula.

Under Ferdinand and Isabella the process of consolidation proceeded rapidly, with a partial reduction of the power of the feudal nobility and with a minimum of representation, counsel, and advice from the *Cortes,* a representative body that was comparable to the feudal English Parliament and French Estates-General.

The power of the Spanish state, both internally and externally, reached its apogee in the sixteenth century, under the rule of Charles I (who reigned from 1516 to 1556) and Philip II (who reigned from 1556 to 1598). This power was due in part to the powerful personalities of these two kings; but it was due in even greater part to the wealth derived from the Spanish colonial empire in America that was established by Christopher Columbus under the sponsorship of Queen Isabella just after the Moors were finally driven out of Granada.

After the sixteenth century the international power of Spain declined. The monarchy retained its power internally, however, as the symbol of Spanish unity. Spain would have many internal struggles for the control of the state in the centuries that were to follow, but the Spanish state itself was never again seriously divided after Ferdinand and Isabella unified it in 1492—although Basque, Catalan, and other nationalities within Spain have sought, from time to time, to win a measure of "nationalistic" autonomy.

Germany: The State and the States

One of the most powerful forces upon which Martin Luther had depended for the achievement of success in his religious revolt against Roman Catholicism had been the drive toward independent sovereignty that had motivated a number of the great German lords. Thus his *Address to the German Nobility* had been a frank appeal to the rulers of the German states in the Holy Roman Empire to throw off papal domination, to cease sending money out of their states to Rome, and to become fully masters in their own dominions. A number of the German rulers had supported him and had taken up arms for religious and political autonomy against the Emperor Charles V of the Holy Roman Empire (who was also King Charles I of Spain). Charles, fighting both for imperial control and for the Roman Catholic faith, found it impossible to suppress the Lutheran princes, and at the Peace of Augsburg (in 1555, after Luther's death) he was compelled to recognize the right of the princes to maintain separate Protestant (Lutheran) churches in their own principalities (see p. 611).

Thus the drive toward separate sovereignty among the German states had broken the theoretical political unity of the Holy Roman Empire of the Feudal Era and had brought about a recognition of the quasi-sovereignty of all the member-states of the Empire, although the fiction of the Empire itself was retained. Yet, for many reasons, especially the jealous particularism of their individual rulers, the German states never succeeded in drawing together into the sort of integral body politic, or state, as had by now appeared in England and in France—never, that is, until one strong man, Otto von Bismarck, was able by a ruthless policy of "blood and iron" to force a national union upon the German states in the third quarter of the nineteenth century.

Two strong states did emerge, however, within the heterogeneous galaxy of states that made up the Empire. One of these was Prussia, the other was Austria.

Prussia. The kingdom of Prussia, with the Electorate of Brandenburg as its nucleus, under the leadership of a long line of able but unscrupulous rulers of the Hohenzollern family and with the armed might of the *junkers* of East Prussia, emerged as one of the most powerful of the German states in the course of the fifteenth and sixteenth centuries. When the Lutheran revolt took place, the Hohenzollerns became Lutherans and seized the wealth of the Catholic Church in their territories. Then, under the leadership of Frederick William, the Great Elector, who ruled from 1640 to 1688, the internal power and efficiency of the central government, supported by what was soon to become the most efficient military machine in western Europe, became supreme in Prussia, while one by one a number of the smaller surrounding states were annexed to Brandenburg with its capital at Berlin; Berlin thus became the capital of Brandenburg–Prussia,

Kings of Prussia, 1640–1797

Frederick William (the Great Elector)	1640–1688
Frederick I (actually first king)	1688–1713
Frederick William I	1713–1740
Frederick II (the Great)	1740–1786
Frederick William II (nephew)	1786–1797

which henceforth came to be known generally as the kingdom of Prussia.

The policies of militarism, bureaucratic centralism, and ruthless, unscrupulous autocracy were continued by the Great Elector's successors, to be brought to their great-

The Evolution of Brandenburg-Prussia

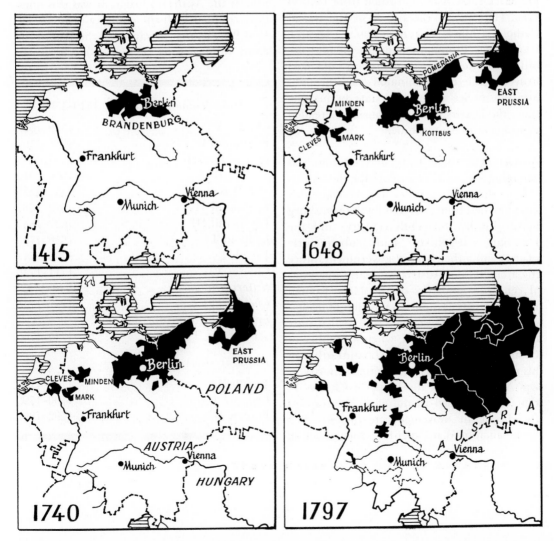

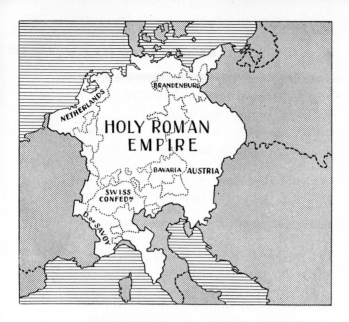

The Holy Roman Empire about 1560

est effectiveness by King Frederick II, called Frederick the Great, who ruled from 1740 to 1786. Here again, the power of the feudal Catholic Church was nonexistent, because Prussia was Protestant. And the feudal nobility, particularly the *junkers* of East Prussia, while not eliminated, were brought into the service of the new state by making them the leaders of the famous and dreaded Prussian military machine.

Austria. The other German state that was emerging as a rival of Prussia for the leadership of the German states was Austria. This kingdom had been acquired by the Hapsburg family in the thirteenth century, and the Hapsburg archdukes had subsequently made Vienna their seat of government. Since the archdukes of Austria were also for several centuries emperors of the Holy Roman Empire, Austria assumed a position of leadership among the German states rivaled only by that of Prussia. Thus, when a number of German princes supported Martin Luther in his revolt from Roman Catholic authority, it was Austria, led by the Emperor Charles V, that took the lead in the effort to suppress the Lutheran movement in the so-called "Schmalkaldic War," (p. 611) which ended in

the Peace of Augsburg (1555). Again, in the Thirty Years' War, which broke out in the Germanies in 1618, it was Austria that assumed the leadership of the Catholic and imperial forces against the Protestants; and when the Thirty Years' War became a battle for power between France (under the leadership of Cardinal Richelieu) and the two branches of the Hapsburg family in Austria and Spain, it was Austria that bore the brunt of the battle in the Germanies. France scored a nominal victory over Austria in the Peace of Westphalia (1648), which also saw a recognition of the power of Prussia; but for a century and more after that peace, Austria continued to be a powerful rival of both France and Prussia.

In 1740, with the death of the Emperor Charles VI of Austria, the question arose whether his daughter, Maria Theresa, could inherit the Austrian throne. It was this question, coupled with the cupidity of Frederick II of Prussia, that precipitated the War of the Austrian Succession (1740–1748). The power

Holy Roman Emperors, 1519–1806	
Charles V	1519–1558
Ferdinand I	1558–1564
Maximilian II	1564–1576
Rudolf II	1576–1612
Matthias	1612–1619
Ferdinand II	1619–1637
Ferdinand III	1637–1657
Leopold I	1658–1705
Joseph I	1705–1711
Charles VI	1711–1740
(*Interregnum*	1740–1742)
Charles VII	1742–1745
Francis I (of Lorraine, husband of Maria Theresa)	1745–1765
Hapsburg-Lorraine Dynasty	
Joseph II	1765–1790
Leopold II	1790–1792
Francis II	1792–1806

of Prussia was increased at the expense of that of Austria in this war. Yet, despite the "unnatural alliance" of Austria and France in the Seven Years' War (1756–1763)—"unnatural" because Austria and France had traditionally been enemies—it was Austria that was to lead the forces of monarchy and reaction against France in the wars of the French Revolution that began in 1792.

Holland and the Scandinavian States

Meanwhile another commercial state, whose international significance was out of all proportion to its size, had arisen in the so-called "Low Countries" that had become part of the holdings of the king of Spain by a series of dynastic marriages and inheritances. These provinces were partly Protestant and partly Catholic. Enraged by the suppressions —economic, political, and, particularly, religious—of King Philip II of Spain, the Low Countries revolted in 1565 (see the painting by Brueghel on page 644) and began a war for independence that was to last almost a century. The Catholic provinces (later Belgium), to be sure, capitulated in 1579. But the Dutch, or Hollanders, of the northern, Protestant provinces, fought on, and eventually had their independence recognized in the Peace of Westphalia of 1648.

A hardy, commercial people, the Dutch federation of provinces became a republic, called

Europe in 1648

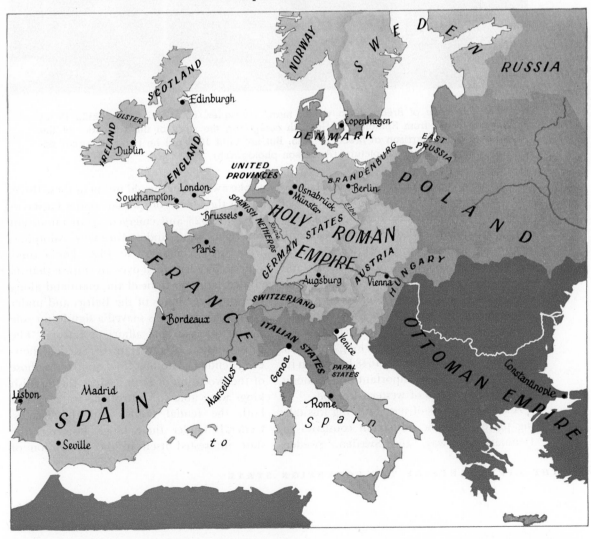

The Surrender of Breda. As a young man, Velásquez, court painter to Philip IV of Spain, heard from Spinola, the Spanish conqueror, the story of the surrender of the heroic Dutch garrison at Breda in 1625. But not until 1647 did he paint his great unimpassioned historical picture. (Anderson photograph)

"the United Provinces of the Netherlands," and proceeded to build up their internal unity by the usually shrewd policies of their joint parliament, called the States-General. Beginning about 1600, the Dutch joined in the European colonization movement, and seized large portions of the Portuguese empire in India and Brazil (later reconquered) and founded new colonies in North America and in the Caribbean. The Dutch state, established in the course of the long, long war for Dutch independence, by 1648 had taken its place—and it was an important one—among the sovereign states of western Europe.

A similar process of state-building was taking place in the Scandinavian countries in Denmark, Norway, and Sweden. Sweden broke away from the old union of these three, called the Union of Calmar, under Gustavus Vasa in 1523 and emerged as an important sovereign state under Gustavus Adolphus, who ruled from 1596 to 1632. For a time, indeed, Sweden ruled over an empire that included large portions of the mainland along the southern shores of the Baltic, and under a series of able kings played a significant role in the international affairs of Europe. The consolidation of the state in Sweden, however, tended to follow lines similar to those of the evolution of France, since the Swedish kings were able to control the state against both the feudal nobles and the Estates-General. Under these kings, however, the state interested itself in the promotion of commerce and industry—even an unsuccessful effort at colonial expansion in America.

Denmark, like Sweden, passed through various vicissitudes of fortune and power. Having adopted the Lutheran brand of Christianity in the sixteenth century, it participated, under King Christian IV, in the Thirty Years' War on the side of the Protestants. But Christian IV, perhaps the ablest of Denmark's rulers, was limited by the power of the feudal nobles; and it was not until their power was broken in 1660, after Christian's death, that the Danish state achieved the degree of unity already achieved by England, France, and Holland. Thereafter the kings achieved a near-absolute power, and the Danish kings of the eighteenth century took their places among the "enlightened despots" by freeing the serfs, encouraging science, and so on.

Norway, since Sweden had broken off from the old Scandinavian Union of Calmar, had been a part of Denmark. Ceded to Sweden in 1815, it was not until 1905 that Norway became a fully independent modern state.

The Rise of Russia

Meanwhile, in the vast plains lying east of Germany and north of the Black Sea, there was taking form another great modern state that would one day play a predominant role in the history of the world, both east and west. This state was Russia.

Peter I, called "Peter the great," who ruled from 1682 to 1725, succeeded in reducing the power of the local rulers and centralizing the power of the state in himself. Furthermore he deliberately set out to modernize (or "Europeanize") Russian customs and outlook —with considerable success—and he made great efforts to establish commercial relationships with western Europe. To this end, he built the great and gloomy city of Petrograd (present-day Leningrad).

But the history of the development of Russian civilization is as closely related to that of Byzantium as it is to western Europe. It is also a sort of connecting link between Europe and the Far East. Indeed, Russian civilization has certain characteristics that mark it off from any other. For these reasons, and because of the importance of the role that Russia has played in modern world history, the story of the rise of Russia will be told in greater detail in the next chapter.

The "Enlightened Despots"

By the second half of the eighteenth century a number of the states of western Europe had come to be governed by kings whose power was very nearly absolute. Yet because many of them had been educated in the philosophies and the humanitarianism of the "Enlightenment" (Volume II), and because they gave patronage to philosophy, literature, and the arts, this entire generation of rulers has been called the "enlightened (or "benevolent") despots." Monarchs such as Frederick II of Prussia, Catherine II of Russia, Joseph II of Austria, and Carlos III of Spain, made a great show of "enlightenment" and were supposed to govern their subjects benevolently, according to humanitarian considerations and under the guidance of "reason." These rulers took their work seriously; they accepted the intellectual progress and moods of their day; they dabbled in literature, philosophy, art, and music. They felt a great concern for the economic development of their countries. Frederick II, for example, encouraged scientific agriculture and the scientific breeding of livestock, built canals, encouraged the immigration of skilled artisans, and took a paternal interest in the welfare of all his subjects, including the peasants.

Still, the power of these rulers was really the power of the state; and the most significant achievement of the benevolent despots may have been the cultivation of a romantic sort of loyalty to themselves that bound their peoples together in an elemental form of nationalism. Actually, by this time, the state in western Europe was more powerful than the king. Practically everywhere the growth of state power had in each state brought into existence a numerous and powerful bureaucracy, a uniform body of national law, and a great and highly influential military establishment. The mechanisms of the integral state had made it a great machine, of which the ruler was only the chief driver. He might manipulate it to his own personal advantage—and often did. But the true "benevolent despot" was a head of the state who directed the machinery of the state for the national benefit, real or imagined, of his people.

It would not be long before this state of affairs would be embodied in basic laws, or constitutions, which even the kings would have to obey. Already in England the state had assumed such supremacy over the king. Already, too, with the ideas of Voltaire and Rousseau and the more pressing influence of increasing national bankruptcies, the time was ripe for a reduction of the power of the kings on the continent. The days of princely irresponsibility were very nearly over; the day of the self-conscious, "organismic" state (that is, a sort of socio-political organism), with or without benefit of monarchy, had very nearly arrived.

THE EUROPEAN STATES SYSTEM

The gradual supplanting of feudalism by the irresponsible sovereign state as the dominant political form in western Europe brought a new set of problems as to the relations among states. In the Feudal Era some superior authority usually had (in theory, at least) the right and power to supervise relations among local potentates, and the pope, in the time of Innocent III, had very nearly succeeded in establishing the idea that the head of the Church, as the vicegerent of God on earth, was the ultimate, universal authority over men and rulers alike. Even as late as the time of Columbus, Spain and Portugal had accepted the ruling of the pope as to how they should share the new world just then being opened to the knowledge of Europeans. But the new states, in their sovereignty, had rejected all outside authority, even the pope's. Now their only authority was their own judgment; the only law they knew, as sovereign states, was the law of their own self-interest.

Relations among States: War and Peace

The three centuries between about 1500 and about 1800 were centuries of almost constant warfare in the Atlantic community of states. And whereas the almost constant warfare of the Feudal Era was most often a matter of personal strife among individual feudal nobles or kings, usually for control of land or feudal power, the almost constant wars of the commercial era were wars among states —for the expansion of the territory of the states, for some state religion, for the commercial supremacy of the state, or for a preponderance of a state or a group of states in the struggle for international power.

We have referred to some of them but it is not our intent to trace the history of these wars, the reasons why each of them took place, the constant rearrangements of the map that resulted from them, the vast destruction they wreaked upon society, or their ultimate futility. Suffice it to say that, in general, there were four major groups of motives that led the protagonists into war, and that, usually, these motives were present, in one degree or another, in nearly every sizeable war that took place.

In the sixteenth century, the century of Spanish preponderance, religion was an important, if not the most important, factor in nearly all international wars. It was one of the major factors in Charles V's long and exhausting wars in the Germanies and in Philip II's wars with England and France. But the other motives were hardly less important. The ambition for territorial aggrandizement was present in nearly every case; so was the desire to acquire and control larger and more profitable areas for commercial and political exploitation.

In the seventeenth century, when the star of Spain declined and the star of France arose to reach its zenith with Louis XIV (p. 626), dynastic and territorial ambitions were more important than religion, though in the Thirty Years' War, which broke out in 1618 and lasted until the Peace of Westphalia in 1648, there were dozens of participants, each with a great variety of motives, dynastic, political, economic, or religious. France played a leading role in this war, under the leadership of Cardinal Richelieu, who was ruthlessly pursuing the logic of his proclaimed ambition to make the king supreme in France and France supreme in Europe.

In the second half of the century Louis XIV's chief ambition seemed to be to push the boundaries of France to the Rhine at the expense of his neighbors, and then, when Charles II of Spain finally died without issue, to join the vast empires of France and Spain under his grandson, Philip of Anjou, who eventually became King Philip IV of Spain.

"The Balance of Power"

But Louis' ambitions were only partially realized. The other states of Europe showed a natural tendency, which sprang from the elementary need for survival, to combine against any state that threatened to become so powerful as to be able to "give the law" to the others. And this habit, or principle, of "the balance of power" they applied very effectively in the case of Louis XIV. The peace of Utrecht of 1713, which brought to an end Louis XIV's long series of fruitless wars, therefore left France pretty much as it had

been when Louis ascended the throne. More important, this peace marked the end of the period of French domination of the power politics of Europe and the beginning of the period of English dominance.

The eighteenth century, then—although there were numerous wars on the continent of Europe in which England did not participate—was characterized in general by the fact that it was in this period (lasting until the Peace of Vienna of 1815) that England emerged as the dominant power. In this century rivalry for commercial and colonial power came to be more important as a cause for war than religion or rivalry for dynastic power. In this century, too, the European colonies overseas began actively to participate in the wars of the mother countries, and "European" wars came increasingly to be fought all round the Atlantic Basin, in Africa, and even in India, and to take on the characteristics of "world wars," with fighting taking place at the same time in Europe, America, Africa, India, and the Far East.

The *leitmotif* in the worldwide conflicts of this century was now the colonial and commercial rivalry between France and England that reached into the four corners of the globe. This rivalry reached a climax in the so-called "Seven Years' War" (1756–1763), in the course of which England, with the aid of Prussia, broke the power of France, which had the support of Austria, and, as a result, acquired by the Treaty of Paris (1763) the greater part of France's colonial empire in North America, Africa, and India.

France was not destroyed, however, and would rise to challenge England again, first in the war of American Independence and later in the wars of the French Revolution and the great Bonaparte. These conflicts, however, belong in Volume II (Chapter 29).

Diplomacy

Out of these centuries of wars and rivalries there arose a set of institutions and procedures in the relations among states that have come to be so customary as to have the effective force of a sort of international common law. As examples we may cite declarations of war, the rules of civilized (!) warfare, and the obligations of treaties. Perhaps the most striking and dramatic of the practices in the relations among states was the habit of attempting to solve the problems growing out of a great war or series of wars by assembling large congresses of diplomats to agree upon over-all settlements. Such, for example, was the Congress of Westphalia (1648) that met in two small towns in the German principality of Westphalia to resolve the problems created by the Thirty Years' War. Another such congress was the Congress of Utrecht (a small town in Holland), which met in 1713 to formulate a set of treaties, known as the Peace of Utrecht. By these treaties the myriad and complicated problems presented by Louis XIV's wars, particularly the War of the Spanish Succession (by which Louis had sought to unite the empires of France and Spain), were settled. Another such congress would be held a century later, in 1815, at the end of the Napoleonic wars, and still another in Paris, in 1918–1919, at the end of the first of the great wars of the twentieth century.

In every one of these great congresses the assembled diplomats hoped to arrive at a general settlement of international problems that would be relatively lasting, if not permanent. There were some, indeed, who even proposed that permanent international organizations be established to maintain peace by resolving international problems as they arose. But these were the dreamers—Emeric Cruce, William Penn, the Abbé de St. Pierre, Immanuel Kant, and others. Their ideas were fine, but all "realistic" diplomats knew that in the face of the selfish, ruthless, and irresponsible national sovereignty insisted upon by every state, no such dreams could ever become reality. Yet the "realists" were never able to propose any better mechanism for the maintenance of peace than the principle of the so-called "balance of power."

The relations among states involved many more problems, in fact, than those related only to war and peace. One of the most important of these was the set of problems arising out of international commerce. How, for example, were the merchants of one country resident in another to be treated? What regulations might properly be imposed by one country upon the commerce of another that must necessarily be conducted within its borders? Could a foreigner own or inherit property? Could a citizen of one state become a citizen of another state? And so on.

It was to provide a mechanism for the resolution of such problems that there were gradually created the institutions and practices of a permanent system of international diplomacy. Such, for example, was the custom, which arose in Italy late in the fifteenth century, of sending an ambassador—"a good man sent to lie abroad for his country"—to reside "near the person" of a foreign king. The ambassador from the king of England to the king of Spain, for example, was his own king's personal representative, and it was his duty to convey messages on high matters of state (including commerce, religion, the enforcement of treaties, the treatment of citizens, etc.) to the monarch to whom he was accredited. But there was also a network of "consuls" who resided in foreign cities, particularly centers of commerce, who were primarily commercial agents. About all these officials and their servants there grew up an intricate set of international rules governing their conduct, their privileges, and their immunities. This system of international agents, and the *protocol* (the body of rules and correct customs) governing them, was a by-product of the emergence of the modern state itself. As time went on it tended to become increasingly complex and increasingly to take on the characteristics of a body of "customary" international law. This body of law, or custom—because it was to their self-interest to do so—the states in the international community observed with a fairly high degree of consistency and dependability.

THEORIES OF THE STATE AND OF INTERNATIONAL RELATIONS

Theories of the State

The emergence of the modern integral state out of feudalism was a phenomenon so obvious and so significant that it could not fail to catch the attention of the most perspicacious and thoughtful political observers, and it consequently called into being a large corpus of political theory, the objective of which was to explain the existence and to justify the behavior of this very new political entity.

Thus, in the course of the three centuries between, say, the accession of Louis XI in France (1461) and the outbreak of the French Revolution (1789), many able men devoted much thought to explaining the origin and the nature of the state. Some explained it as a direct creation of God; others found its origin in the human family; still others explained it as having been formed by men in a state of nature by a process called the "social compact." Whatever its derivation, however, practically all rationalizers of the state accepted the notion that it was "sovereign"—that is, that the state, as a "body politic" composed of its citizens, is responsible to no authority, inside or outside, other than itself, whether it operates as an absolute monarchy (as in France), in which the sovereignty of the state is embodied in the monarch, or whether it operates as a constitutional monarchy (as in England), in which the sovereignty of the state rests always in the people, and in which the monarch is merely the agent of that sovereignty rather than its embodiment.

Machiavelli. It was in the small city-state of Florence that the first outstanding theorist of the state appeared. He was Niccolò Machiavelli (1469–1527), a contemporary of Leonardo da Vinci. Machiavelli, himself both a diplomat and a humanist-scholar, re-jected the old claims of the Church to temporal sovereignty and centered sovereignty entirely in the irresponsible secular state. While he did not attempt to explain the nature of the state as such, in his famous little book, *The Prince,* he spoke of the "prince," or ruler, as the leader of the people of his state. Machiavelli believed that it was the ruler's responsibility to promote the welfare and the self-interest of his people, and that, in doing so, he was subject neither to the wishes of the people nor to any power in the world outside the state, not even to the ordinary rules of ethical behavior. The promotion of the great end—the interest of his state—justified any means whatever that the ruler might see fit to employ: "When the entire safety of our country is at stake," he wrote, "no consideration of what is just or unjust, merciful or cruel, praiseworthy or shameful must intervene. On the other hand, every other consideration being set aside, that course must be taken which preserves the existence of the country and maintains its liberty." Thus the state, for Machiavelli, was completely amoral, and was entirely devoid of responsibility to any higher law. Modern states all too often have followed these precepts; it is for this reason that their behavior has been called *Machiavellian.*

Bodin. Jean Bodin (1530–1596), who was born just three years after Machiavelli died, was a French thinker who was led to study the nature of the state and the power of the ruler by the terrible civil wars that rent France in the second half of the sixteenth century. Bodin believed that the basic origin of the state was to be found in the family; but the family, he thought, was expanded into the state by a uniting of many families under a strong ruler. Like Machiavelli, Bodin reasoned that the state, which he correctly understood to be the "body politic"

Slaughter of the Innocents. This painting by Pieter Brueghel, the Elder, ostensibly shows Herod's soldiers slaying the babies of Bethlehem but reference to Spanish cruelties in Holland is unmistakable. (Museum of History and Art, Vienna)

composed of the citizens, is absolute in its power and is not answerable to any internal law. The ruler, therefore, who is the embodiment of this sovereign and irresponsible power, is himself absolute and irresponsible. Yet Bodin, like some of the rising theorists of international law, accepted the idea that the law of nature in human affairs is the law of God, and that the state is, indeed, subject to that law—although, like the others, he could think of no way of enforcing it.

Filmer. Bodin, in his rationalization of the sovereign state, derived the state from the family, but the authority of the state he derived from the people as a whole. The English writer Sir Robert Filmer (d. 1653) also derived the state from the family; but, as the authority of a father over his children is a divine authority given him by God, just so the authority of the king, who is a sort of father to his people, derives from God

and not from the people. Thus not only is the sovereignty of the state personified in the king; the monarch derives his sovereignty, which is absolute, from a divine source. This theory, shared by such kings as James I in England and Louis XIV of France, came to be known as the theory of the "divine right of kings." It should be remembered, however, that what the theorists were discussing was not so much the rights or powers of the king personally as the sovereignty of the state as personified in the king.

Bossuet. The theory of divine right had another important exponent in Jacques Bossuet (1627–1704), a French bishop, who was the apologist for the absolutism of the French monarchy in the time of Louis XIV. He added little that was new to the theory; he based his convictions upon tradition—upon the argument that, since monarchy always had been the form of government used by human beings, it must therefore have been ordained by God and, therefore, was the best possible form.

Hobbes. The greatest of the rationalizers of the absolute sovereign state was Thomas Hobbes (1588–1679), who was a contemporary of both Filmer and Bossuet. But Hobbes, in his two great books, *De Cive* and *Leviathan,* derived the state neither from the family nor from God but from the voluntary actions of men in the formation, conscious or tacit, of the "social compact."

Now the idea of the social compact was not a new one. It had been suggested as early as Roman times and had found expression in some of the theorists of the Feudal Era, particularly with regard to the reciprocal responsibilities of the feudal system and in the struggle of the emerging integral states against the authority of the Roman Church. But Hobbes reformulated it into a new and brilliant naturalistic explanation of the origins of the state that has deeply influenced political thought from that day to this.

Hobbes started with the idea that men in a "state of nature," or completely without political organization, are savagely and viciously antagonistic to each other. War is a constant condition; life is "solitary, poor, nasty, brutish, and short." Each man is free; each man is the equal of all others; each man is completely sovereign over his own life. But men are intelligent, and in the course of time they gradually discovered certain "natural laws" or "general rules" enjoining upon men peace, order, and good behavior with regard to each other. Then, for the enforcement of these natural laws, and for the maintenance of peace and order, men voluntarily and willingly created a body politic, or commonwealth, by an agreement, or "social compact," in which they conferred upon a monarch, or an assembly, their individual sovereignty and all their natural rights. It is the function of this "leviathan," or body politic—the state—to exercise their

sovereignty for them. But once they have surrendered their natural rights to it they are its subjects and cannot withdraw from it. Its power is absolute, even over religion, and no man or institution may challenge it.

Hobbes, of course, shocked his contemporaries by his ruthless and realistic recognition of the fact that the state had, indeed, assumed an absolute and unchallengeable authority over its citizens, and by his identification of the church with the state. At the same time, he was in a very real sense the "Newton of Political Economy" (he was a contemporary of Newton's), since he applied to the explanation of this most important of modern human institutions the searching logical method of natural science and the then increasingly prevalent concept of natural law. This, too, shocked the religiously minded; for if the state is the product of the operation of natural law in human affairs, what then is God's place in them? Hobbes gave lip service to Christianity; but for him religion, like any other human institution or idea, was a proper subject for scientific investigation.

The significance of Hobbes' thought can hardly be exaggerated. His concept of the social compact, the state, and the role of natural law in human affairs became the point of departure for a veritable host of political philosophers who undertook either to refute his arguments or to enlarge upon them. Even without Hobbes' work, however, there probably would have been much theory expounded on the subject of the state and its sovereignty, since many able thinkers everywhere were now interesting themselves in this phenomenon.

Pufendorf. Samuel Pufendorf (1632–1694), who drew most of his ideas from Hugo Grotius (of whom more later) and Hobbes, added little that was new to the rationalization of the state in terms of the social compact, but he was a great popularizer of the then current naturalistic explanation of political phenomena. Instead, however, of bas-ing the social compact, as Hobbes did, upon the viciousness of men, Pufendorf based it upon a more humane instinct: man's gregariousness or sociability.

Meanwhile the course of political thinking moved forward rapidly. John Milton (1608–1674), who was a contemporary of Hobbes, made some notable contributions, particularly in his advocacy of a limited freedom of thought and publication. Similarly James Harrington (1611–1677), another contemporary of Hobbes, rationalized the British Puritan Commonwealth in his utopia, *The Commonwealth of Oceana,* in which he found the ideal form of government to be a sort of aristocratic republic. Harrington had a considerable influence over William Penn, whose political ideas were tried out in practice in the early years of the British colony of Pennsylvania.

Locke. But the greatest English political philosopher after Hobbes was John Locke (1632–1704), the apologist of the "Glorious Revolution" of 1688–1689. Locke accepted the basic premise that the state rests upon a social compact, but he parted company with Hobbes from that point on. Locke, in contrast to Hobbes' position, believed that, far from surrendering their natural liberties to the state, the men who formed the compact retained a liberty "to be under no legislative power but that established by consent in the commonwealth." Locke, spokesman for the rising mercantile and propertied class, believed that the great ends of the state are the maintenance of peace and the protection of property. Government, he implied, is the servant of the sovereign people and derives its authority from them. He went on to say that there are three aspects of government— the legislative, the executive, and the judicial aspects—and the best government is the one in which these mechanisms function harmoniously. But when the government fails to promote the welfare or obey the wishes of the sovereign people, it may be discharged, or, if necessary, overthrown by force, and a new government set up in its place. It is precisely in this doctrine of "the right of revolution" that Locke departed most radically from the position of Hobbes; and it was this doctrine to which the Americans appealed when they came to take up arms against the government of the British Empire in 1776. Locke became very influential among the British liberals of his time, but his influence has been greater, and more persistent, in the United States than anywhere else in the world.

Meanwhile, a different point of view was developing on the continent of Europe, and particularly in France. Not everyone there accepted the rationalistic doctrine of the social compact; on the contrary, some criticized it on the ground that it was just an imaginary concept, entirely unsupported by any observable or historical evidence. These critics of the so-called "scientific rationalism" and the imagined "natural laws" and "natural rights" of the social-compact school proclaimed that the true scientific method of studying political phenomena was to observe the actual facts and persistently and industriously to amass mountains of data upon which generalizations might be based before trying to proclaim any "natural law."

Montesquieu. The greatest of the political philosophers of this school was Charles Louis de Secondat, Baron of Montesquieu (1689–1755), whose *Of the Spirit of Laws* is one of the great classics of political philosophy. Montesquieu took the whole world as his laboratory and carefully studied the social and political institutions of most of the countries of the civilized world. His sources were not always trustworthy, but his studies were painstaking, thorough, and thoughtful. He finally rose from his study with the conviction —and the thesis—that men are the same everywhere, but that social and political institutions vary from place to place, according to environmental differences; and that the institutions that are suitable for one environment are not necessarily suitable for another. Further, governmental institutions, he says, rest upon social conditions, and they are likely to change when the underlying social conditions change. Montesquieu may have gotten his environmental determinism from Bodin, but, whether he did or not, he was probably one of the most original thinkers of his age. And in the scientific relativism of his political philosophy he was far more "modern" in his thinking than almost any of his contemporaries.

Rousseau. Of very different cast of mind was Jean Jacques Rousseau (1712–1778), last of the great philosophers of the social compact. Emotional, brilliant, erratic, rebel against the privileged and the powerful, Rousseau was an apostle of human freedom. "Man is born free and everywhere he is in chains." How can men be freed from the oppressor and the tyrant? The answer lies in the social compact. The only legitimate basis for the authority of the ruler over the people is the consent of the people. Sovereignty, therefore, resides in all the people; it is expressed by the general will. Rousseau formulated what may well be the clearest definition ever written of the social compact as the foundation of the state:

The social compact, he said, reduced to its essential terms, means simply this, that

Each of us, in common with our fellow-citizens, puts his person and his power under the supreme direction of the general will, and in our corporate capacity we receive each member as an inseparable part of the indivisible whole. . . .

This act of association creates a moral and collective body. . . . This public person which is thus formed by the union of its members, formerly was called by the name of *city,* and is now called a *republic,* or *body-politic,* which is called by its citizens the *state* when it is passive, the *sovereign* when it is active, and a *power* when comparing it with others of its kind. Its members collectively have the name *the people* and are known individually as *citizens,* in the sense that they are sharers of the sovereign authority, and as *subjects* in the sense that they are subject to the laws of the state.

International Law

In all the theorizing about the state that we have noted thus far, the chief concern was with the internal nature of the state itself, its relationships with its component citizens, with its absolute sovereignty, and with the structure, the functions and the nature of its government. While this line of thought was developing, however, a parallel line of thinking was considering the bases and the nature of the relations among states. The European "states system" had become a reality with the emergence of the integral state, and a more or less systematic practice of interstate —or "international"—diplomacy had begun to take shape about the time of Machiavelli.

Francis of Vitoria. Machiavelli, the pioneer of modern political theory, thought of the

Jean Jacques Rousseau. (Ewing Galloway)

Hugo Grotius—by Mierevelt. (Musée Condé)

Indian states of America) that do not offend their neighbors. The other sort of international law is the sort that is embodied in treaties and customs adopted by the community of states. Any state should respect and obey both these sorts of international law. Incidentally, Vitoria was one of the earliest thinkers in this field to discuss an international "community" of states.

Grotius. But the greatest of the founders of the theory of international law and relations was Hugo Grotius (1583–1645), a Dutchman who was a contemporary of Kepler, James I, Galileo, and Roger Williams. His interest in international relations began when, as a young lawyer, he was retained by the Dutch East India Company to defend its right to trade in the Indian Ocean, which was still claimed by Portugal as its exclusive national property under the famous donation of the pope in the bulls of 1493. He distinguished himself in this case by showing, in a brief later published under the title *On the Freedom of the Seas,* by arguments based upon the Bible and upon "natural law," or the law of reason, that the sea, far from being the private or national property of Portugal, belongs to all the people of the world and is, in fact, a highway between the nations, provided by God for their common intercourse and communication.

The great classic of Grotius, however, was his *Concerning the Law of War and of Peace.* In this work, prompted in large measure by his observations of the ruthless and lawless nature of the conflict known as the Thirty Years' War, then going on, he sought systematically to explain the nature of the laws governing the conduct of states, both in peace and in war.

There are, says Grotius, two sorts of law: natural law, based upon reason, and instituted law, as exemplified in treaties and in the practices and immunities of international diplomacy. Both these sorts of law, natural and instituted, have special subdivisions, both with regard to the time of peace and

state as amoral, without responsibility—moral, legal, or other—to anything outside itself. But it was not long before a group of thinkers arose who posed the questions whether the state, after all, was free of moral responsibility, and whether, after all, there was not some sort of law by which even the sovereign state might be bound in its relations with its neighbors. Such a questioner was Francis of Vitoria (1480–1549), a Spanish contemporary of Machiavelli.

Vitoria was shocked by the ruthless conquest of Mexico and Peru by his country, a conquest that was not provoked by any offense of the native Indians against Spain or its people or by any invasion of Spanish territory. Is there not, he asked, some law that will restrain a state from such ruthless and unprovoked invasion and destruction of its neighbors? His answer was in the affirmative. For, says Vitoria, there are really two kinds of law governing the behavior of nations. One is natural law, or the law of God, which provides certain natural rights of freedom and sovereignty to states (such as the

with regard to the practices of war. And his book is a detailed series of demonstrations of how these legal principles should apply in various areas of international relations. It is a masterful statement of principles, many of which have been accepted in the conduct of international relations since Grotius' time. But any law, whether international or municipal, is likely to have very little validity without the backing of some powerful sanction to enforce it; and Grotius ran head on into the fact of irresponsible sovereignty in all the states about him. Grotius could find no sanction more powerful than the moral sense of the leaders of the states themselves and no mechanism for the preservation of peace more effective than arbitration. And in that Machiavellian age (as in the later ages) that sense, as a sanction, and that method of avoiding war proved to be feeble indeed. No modern state, probably, ever came to a decision in its international relations contrary to its own self-interest just because of the pressure of the innate moral righteousness in its leaders to which Grotius appealed! Yet unquestionably Grotius exercised an enormous influence in the formulation of the principles of international law that took place in the centuries that followed him.

Vattel. Emmerich de Vattel (1714–1767), whose book the *Law of Peoples* (1758) was a handbook for diplomats for decades, was somewhat more realistic. For Vattel believed in a positive international law as distinguished from the vague "natural law" of nations. While he did not reject the idea of natural law entirely, as a practical statesman he rejected the idea of a "natural" world community. He did believe in a practical cooperation among states based upon long-range self-interest; he also believed that this long-range self-interest and voluntary cooperation might lead to the elimination of war.

The Idea of International Organization. Other thinkers concerned with the essentially uncivilized and irresponsible nature of war and international rivalry addressed themselves to the possibility of maintaining peace and international order by the formation of international organization.

Emeric Crucé (1590–1648), for example, a French contemporary of Grotius, proposed that there be created a council of ambassadors from all the states of the world to settle all disputes among states, and that rulings of this council should have the force of law upon its members. William Penn (1644–1718), Quaker and pacifist, said men in a state of nature form a social compact by which they surrender a part of their freedom for the sake of order within the state; why should they not make a similar compact for the maintenance of order among states?

But the most thoroughly thought-out plan for international organization was that of the Abbé de St. Pierre (1658–1743), a Frenchman and a thoroughgoing exponent of the "Age of Reason" (Chapter 28). In the first place, said the Abbé, war is irrational; it is, therefore, unreasonable for men to engage in it. And in the second place, if men can solve so many other problems by the use of science and reason, they surely should be able to solve their international problems in the same way. Let them organize, therefore, two great federal unions among the states of the world, one among the Christian states and one among the states of Asia; let them formally repudiate war; and then let these federations turn their collective intelligence and power to the promotion of the arts of peace—commerce, free international movement of persons, standardized weights and measures, monies, calendar, cultural exchange, and so on. The good that such an organization might do for humanity was incalculable. It was a very practical plan, said the cynical Frederick the Great; all that was needed was simply the consent of all the sovereigns in the world, and other trivia!

The great German philosopher, Immanuel Kant (1724–1804) developed the idea of international federation still further. He did not accept the idea of the essential goodness of men, as did the Abbé de St. Pierre, but, rather, he started from the premise of Thomas Hobbes that men are by nature savages and that war between men is a natural phenomenon. But men are intelligent; therefore let the same intelligence that leads to the original social compact among men lead the states, at present in a "state of nature," to form a similar compact among states. But Kant distrusted absolute and irresponsible rulers; such a federation of states should be made up of republican states; for where the making of war is a decision that must be made by the people, there will be no war. And to these practical considerations Kant added the doctrine of a metaphysical human right to peace:

> Right must be held sacred by man, however great the cost and sacrifice to the ruling power. Here is no half-and-half course. We cannot devise a happy medium between right and expediency, a right pragmatically conditioned. But all politics must bend the knee to the principle of right, and may, in that way, hope to reach, though slowly perhaps, a level whence it may shine upon men for all time.

Cosmopolitanism

We should take note, finally, that the eighteenth century was marked by a widespread cosmopolitanism or intellectual internationalism that ran counter to the narrow selfishness of the national state. "Patriotism," cried the English Dr. Samuel Johnson, "is the last refuge of a scoundrel." Johann Gottfried von Herder (1744–1803), German contemporary of Johnson, tried to harmonize nationalism and internationalism, in a slightly romantic fashion, by likening the states to the plants in a garden, each with its own peculiar and individual qualities but all contributing to the beauty and the harmony of the whole. Far from fighting each other, he taught, they should cooperate for the promotion of civilization and the achievement of peace. But the fine cosmopolitanism of the eighteenth century was a voice of reason that found itself in conflict with the unreasonableness of a new and triumphant nationalism. The sovereign states of the western world enjoyed and exploited their irresponsibility; neither the expediency of self-interest nor the force of humanitarian principle was yet strong enough to bring them out of their "state of nature" vis-à-vis each other.

Suggestions for Further Reading

Source Materials

Anthologies and Collected Documents

Columbia College, *Introduction to Contemporary Civilization in the West* (2 vols., New York, 1946), Volume I, Chapters 3, 9, and 11.

Excellent excerpts from the writings of the political philosophers prior to 1800.

F. J. C. Hearnshaw, ed., *The Social and Political Ideas of Some Great French Thinkers of the Age of Reason* (New York, 1950).

Excellent selections from French political philosophers of the age of "the Enlightenment."

G. H. Knoles and R. K. Snyder, eds., *Readings in Western Civilization* (rev. ed., New York, 1954), pp. 329–338, 409–439.

Selections from Machiavelli, Bossuet, Hobbes, Rousseau, and Locke.

J. H. Robinson and C. A. Beard, eds., *Readings in Modern European* History (2 vols., Boston, 1908), Volume I, Chapters 1–4 and 8–15.

A very useful collection of original documents illustrative of the development of the continental European states and international relations in the seventeenth and eighteenth centuries.

Contemporary Writings

H. Grotius, *Commentary on the Law of Prize and Booty* (New York, 1950).

One of the great classics of international law.

J. Locke, *Two Treatises of Government* (New York, 1947).

One of the most fundamental statements of the basic political theory in the Anglo-Saxon political tradition.

C. de Montesquieu, *The Spirit of Laws* (New York, 1949).

A great empirical study of the nature of law and government by one of the outstanding political thinkers of the eighteenth century.

J. J. Rousseau, *The Social Contact and Discourses* (New York, 1950).

Another classic statement of the philosophy of the social compact.

Secondary Works

L. Bertrand, *Louis XIV* (New York, 1928).

A standard history of the great and absolute "true king" of France.

P. W. Buck, *The Politics of Mercantilism* (New York, 1942).

A thoughtful and clear examination of the interconnections between mercantilism and the practice of politics in the age of mercantilism.

W. L. Dorn, *Competition for Empire, 1740–1763* (New York, 1940).

An excellent history of Europe in the second third of the eighteenth century.

L. Gershoy, *From Despotism to Revolution, 1763–1789* (New York, 1944).

An excellent history of the "age of the enlightened despots"—the last generation before the outbreak of the great French Revolution.

A. H. Johnson, *Europe in the Sixteenth Century, 1494–1598* (New York, 1925).

A good general history of Europe in the century of Spanish commerce.

D. Ogg, *Europe in the Seventeenth Century* (London, 1931).

A fine history of the continent of Europe during the century of the ascendancy of France.

L. B. Packard, *The Age of Louis XIV* (New York, 1929).

A fine, brief survey.

P. Roberts, *The Quest for Security, 1715–1740* (New York, 1947).

A broad history of Europe in the first generation after the Peace of Utrecht.

F. M. Russell, *Theories of International Relations* (New York, 1936).

A survey of the history of the theory of international relations. Especially good for the development of the ideas of international law and international organization.

G. M. Trevelyan, *England under the Stuarts* (21st ed., New York, 1949).

A standard, beautifully written history, first published in 1907.

26

The Rise of Russia

Silver Chalice—c.1613–1645. The upper rim is engraved with a Deisis and the traditional inscription in Slavonic: "Drink ye, all of this; for this is My Blood of the New Testament, which is shed for you, and for many, for the remission of sins." (From the collection A La Vieille Russie)

The same centuries that saw the transition from the feudal to the modern era in western Europe also witnessed the appearance of a new and mighty power in eastern Europe, in the vast plain lying between Europe and Asia. That power was Russia. Though its culture was in part derived from western Europe, it was in much larger part a heritage of Byzantium and the product of influences from Asia. Essentially, however, it was an indigenous development, arising out of experiences peculiar to Russia alone.

The people who were to play a major role in building Russian society, the Slavs, had apparently passed through a Neolithic stage of culture among the swamps and forests of the Dnieper River and the Pripet Marshes. In the fourth century A.D. they had begun to move, apparently under pressure of the Huns. As we have seen in Chapter 10, they expanded into what is now Poland and southeastern Russia, and into the Balkan peninsula. A large number of these southern Slavs, or "Yugoslavs," were conquered by the Bulgars and had to join with them in wars against Byzantium. These wars failed to shake the Byzantine Empire, however; and, with the conversion of the Bulgars to Christianity early in the ninth century, the penetration of the cultural influences of Byzantium northward into the Slavic countries, including the invention of the Slavic, or "Cyrillic," alphabet, became more and more powerful and effective.

The original focal point of the emergent Slavic civilization seems to have been the city of Novgorod, near Lake Ilmen, in the forested plateau where three of the chief rivers of Russia (the northwestward-flowing Dvina and the eastward- and southward-flowing Volga and Dnieper) take their rise. According to legend, because of squabbles among themselves, the people of Novgorod in 862 invited Rurik, the great Norse chieftain, to become their ruler, which he did, thus becoming their first prince. Rurik's followers soon moved on to the city of Kiev, on the Dnieper and nearer to Byzantium, and hence it was Kiev that became the true focal center of the emerging Russian culture.

THE KIEVAN PERIOD

The Rise of Kiev

The Dnieper River, along the banks of which this Slavic culture had its rise, had long been a trade route, even in Neolithic and ancient times. During the ninth, tenth, and eleventh centuries this route connected the countries around the Baltic Sea with those around the Black Sea—Georgia and Armenia as well as Byzantine and Moslem-controlled areas. Kiev itself, the urban focal point of this north-south trade, had also been a center of Neolithic culture, and it was already a rich city when Rurik's followers are reported to have seized it about the middle of the ninth century.

Thereafter Kiev continued to grow as a point of exchange for commodities coming from the north and the flotillas of boats that traveled down the river and across the Black Sea to Byzantium. Thus Kiev sent southward Russian furs, wheat, wax, slaves, and other northern goods; in return, Byzantine silks, wine, jewels, works of art, books—and, incidentally, religious and cultural influences—found their way to this frontier culture center. By the beginning of the tenth century, Kiev had become the capital of a new "Russian" state, which probably took its name from a Scandinavian word meaning "rowers"—a reference to its original Viking princes. From Kiev marauding expeditions were sent against Byzantium, but the conversion of Prince Vladimir, "The Saint," in 988 brought about friendlier relations with the Byzantine Empire and made Kiev the first center of Orthodox Eastern Christianity in Russia.

Yaroslav, one of the sons of Vladimir, seized power in Kiev in 1019 and made the city a great center of culture—a culture that was predominantly Byzantine. He built a huge cathedral, established schools, and devoted much energy and money to the collection and translation of Byzantine books. Greek traditions in art and scholarship defi-nitely asserted themselves in Russian intellectual circles, and the Russian people found their customs written down and systematized in a great code of law based upon Greek models. Fortunately, such powerful Greek influence did not stifle the growth of a spontaneous popular literature. Kievan Russia could quite properly boast of its epic songs—or *byliny*—that strongly resembled the heroic legends of western Europe, both in variety of subject matter and in beauty and vigor of expression.

Perhaps the most interesting development in the Kievan state was to be found in its political organization. Despite the many contacts with both Byzantine and Asiatic despotism, the government of Russia remained loose and moderately representative. The town assemblies—known as *veches*—still played an important role, and it was not unusual—particularly in such a great trading center as Novgorod—for the *veche* to control the activities of the local prince. The latter was ordinarily a temporary resident. He belonged to the dynasty founded by Rurik, and he moved from less important to more important towns on a basis of genealogical seniority. The head of the princely family, following this scheme of political advancement, ruled the country from the chief Russian city, Kiev. Yet even such a dynastic and national chief might not be completely free from *veche* influence and control.

Needless to say, the Russian popular assemblies had their shortcomings. They often were unruly in conduct, and at times their meetings might degenerate into bloody rioting. Furthermore, only a limited number of inhabitants of the town and the surrounding countryside could vote—for medieval Russia had its disfranchised freemen as well as a large number of slaves. Nonetheless, the general impression that one receives from studying this early Russian experiment in local self-government is certainly as favorable as that provided by the much better known municipalities of the feudal west. In a sense the Russian record is even better; for the western European nations were just emerging from the economic stagnation of feudalism at the time when Russia's towns became noted for their political and economic achievements.

Yaroslav maintained active relationships with other European kingdoms, and married his sons and daughters to princesses and princes of Poland, Greece, Germany, Norway, Hungry, and France. He and his successors extended their suzerainty over the surrounding territories, and Kiev became the capital of a great empire that stretched from the northern lakes to the southern steppes and from Poland on the west to the Volga on the east. The rule of the Kievan princes was largely a military rule, however, and, so long as the local communities paid the required tribute, they were permitted to keep their old customs and habit of self-direction.

The greatest weakness of the rule of the grand princes of Kiev lay in the principle of genealogical succession and the rotation of the various subdivisions of the Kievan state among Rurik's numerous successors. Conflicting claims to the more important territories became frequent, resulting in bitter feuds and even widespread civil war. By the early twelfth century the authority of Kiev was on the wane, and the city's dominion came to an end in 1169, when Andrei Bogoliubski, a great-great-grandson of Yaroslav, conquered it. Thereafter, other cities, particularly Vladimir, where Andrei established himself as grand prince, and Moscow, where a number of able and crafty princes were building up their influence, began to eclipse the power of Kiev. Kiev itself was crushed in 1240 by the Mongols under Batu, grandson of the great Genghis Khan.

THE MUSCOVITE PERIOD

During the Kievan period of Russian history the culture of this new people was in no way inferior to that of its contemporaries in the feudal kingdoms of western Europe, as the peoples of the west recognized, for the princes of Kiev took part as equals in the politics of Europe, and often their daughters married French and German kings. As might be expected in a civilization of commerce and cities, the spirit of Kievan Russia was one of freedom, and this spirit was expressed in both political and economic institutions.

The Era of Mongol Domination

Russia's destiny, however, was to shape its civilization as Eurasian rather than as purely European, for the broad steppe—a grassland of vast horizons, reaching like a wedge from Central Asia into Europe—proved an inviting highway for invasions. In the twelfth century nomadic peoples coming into Russia across this plain severed the trade routes running from north to south along the rivers, thus hastening the decline of Kiev. And in the thirteenth century the fearful hordes of Mongol—or Tatar—horsemen swept over the plains, to subject the Russians to a dominion that, at its height, reached across all Asia to include even China (see map, p. 367). For two centuries thereafter the Russians had to bear the "Tatar Yoke," as it was called, paying heavy tribute to the Mongol khans in the east.

From their capital at Sarai on the Volga, the khans of the Golden Horde—as these Tatar invaders have been called—ruled directly over parts of Russia. Although they did not occupy the grand duchy of Moscow, merely sending emissaries to extort tribute, their dominion had important consequences for Russia.

In the first place, it slowed down the progress of the Russian civilization. During the fourteenth and fifteenth centuries, while

Russia about 1250

western Europe was experiencing those stirrings of individualism and humanism that marked the beginnings of a new cultural age, the Russians were fighting a rearguard action. By absorbing the Mongol pressure themselves, the Russians prevented the Asiatic invaders from threatening western Europe. But this meant a drain upon the energies of the Russian people, which could not be put to more productive use. In this period the west could use its surplus wealth, for example, in the construction of the great cathedrals of the late Feudal Era; but the surplus wealth of Russia was drawn off as tribute to the Mongols. Moreover, Russia could not defend its own borders against European neighbors. Thus Kiev and other borderlands on the west were seized by the Lithuanians and Poles, while the Swedes and Germans tried to advance on the northwest.

In the second place, the Mongol rule hastened the development of autocracy, supplanting the relative freedom of the Kievan age. This development proceeded with the emergence of Moscow, which had been founded in the twelfth century during the migrations from the unprotected steppe around Kiev to the more sheltered forest land of the north. The Muscovite princes learned well how to exploit a policy of collaboration with the Mongol conquerors. As a reward for their docility, they were permitted to rise from the status of princes of the second rank to one of pre-eminence as grand princes, who became the sole intermediaries between the khan and other Russian princes. And from the Mongols, the Muscovite rulers learned the statecraft of absolutism. While serving as tax-gatherers for the Mongols, they copied the basic principles of authoritarian rule that the Mongols had developed to the utmost. But all the while they nursed the secret hope of building up a military force of their own that would permit them to rid their land of the hated alien yoke.

Ivan III

This was finally accomplished by Ivan III (1462–1505), the founder of the Muscovite state, in whose reign the forces leading Moscow to autocracy and absolutism found full expression. Ivan the Great was the contemporary of the dynastic state-builders in the west, such as the French Louis XI and the early Tudors in England, and his unscrupulous and finely spun policies have often been compared to those of the "Spider King" in France.

Ivan, however, found fewer obstacles to dynastic centralization than did his brother monarchs. In the west the entrenched position of the feudal lords was a barrier to royal power that the kings were obliged to overcome. So, too, was the claim of the popes to a supreme authority over all secular rulers. And even after the political power of the pope was broken, the Protestant Reformation produced religious minorities in many countries that were prepared to resist the power of the state on grounds of conscience.

In Russia there were no such sources of resistance to the ruler. The Russian Orthodox Church took over from Byzantium the tradition that the Church is subordinate to the state, and few churchmen, consequently, ever spoke out for the superiority of the spiritual over the temporal power. Moreover, after the Moslems at last captured Constantinople in 1453, the traditional center of Orthodox Eastern Christianity passed under infidel dominion, and the Russian Orthodox Church therefore became more and more dependent upon the Muscovite prince.

Late in the reign of Ivan III there appeared one of the rare figures of the Russian Orthodox Church who dared to challenge the secular power. This was the ascetic and saintlike Nils Sorski. Nils and his followers, speaking with the voice of spiritual Christianity, denounced the wealth of the Church, opposed the use of force against heretics, and proclaimed that the Church should be free from state interference. But in opposition to this plea, the aggressive abbot Joseph of Volokolamsk became a vigorous advocate of a close alliance between Church and state and the merciless persecution of religious dissenters. The wealth of the monasteries, he argued, was not a corruption of the monastic ideal but was necessary if the kind of men who were required for a strong ecclesiastical hierarchy were to be attracted to the service of the Church.

The government, gave its support to the Josephites, who prevailed against the less worldly faction of Nils Sorski. By the middle of the sixteenth century the Russian Orthodox Church was assured of the protection of the state, and, in return, the Church hierarchy was committed to the support of the autocracy of the ruling prince.

The Russian nobility similarly became dependent upon the prince, although vestiges of its independence persisted until a later reign. When Ivan III entered upon his rule, the northern part of Russia was divided into a number of principalities, of which Muscovy was only one, though the largest and most important. Many nobles held hereditary lands that had been in their family for centuries, and some of these princes traced their lineage back to the ruling dynasty of the Kievan period. But Ivan asserted the Mongol principle that all land belonged to the prince and that lesser noblemen held their land only by grants from him. Such a grant was not hereditary but was to be enjoyed only as long as the nobleman rendered service to the prince. This was comparable to the idea of feudalism in western Europe but unlike it in that the relationship between lord and vassal was even more unequal: the vassal was clearly a dependent of the lord, not the holder of rights that he could assert against the lord.

Though the great noblemen of the old princely families did not accept this new regime without protest, the policy of state service proceeded so far that by 1497 only two classes of persons were legally recognized —the "serving," or nobles, and the "non-serving," or peasants and townsmen.

Serfdom

The absolutism of Ivan III meant more than the subordination of the nobility and the Church to the power of the grand prince: it also led to the establishment of serfdom. This was a late development, because in the Kievan period serfdom was virtually unknown in Russia, though widespread in western Europe. During the Mongol period, however, the uncertainties of life had forced large numbers of peasants into dependence upon the landlords, who provided them with plows and oxen and permitted them to work the land as sharecroppers. With the ending of the Mongol threat and the increase of Ivan's taxation, many peasants sought to migrate to the new territories that were being opened up, where they might get land of their own. But to prevent them from doing so—since their migration would leave the nobles without a supply of labor for the tilling of their land—Ivan took measures to limit the peasants' freedom of movement. Thus his law code of 1497 established that the peasant could leave his landlord only at a certain period each year, during the festival of St. George, and only if the peasant were not in debt to his landlord. Ivan's successors continued to whittle down the peasant's freedom, until by the middle of the seventeenth century he was completely bound to his landlord. Thus the masses of the Russian peoples were legally fastened to the soil at the very moment when in the west of Europe the bands of the peasants were being loosened.

The Reconquest of Novgorod and Pskov

In the commercial towns of Novgorod and Pskov, in the northwest, where the Mongol power had not reached, there still survived some vestige of the freer political institutions of the Kievan period. True to the task taken up by his predecessors as the "gatherers of the Russian land," Ivan set about the acquisition of Novgorod and accomplished it with his customary duplicity. He forced the aristocratic townsmen to acknowledge him as their absolute sovereign, then carted off to Moscow the great bell, the symbol of their self-government, which for centuries had summoned the people for town meetings. When Ivan's son did the same with Pskov, there was left no social force in Russia to stand up against the autocracy. The center of trade also shifted to Moscow, where the merchants were easily controlled and heavily taxed at the ruler's pleasure.

The autocracy that Ivan III thus established in Russia was a new development, not an old tradition. There is little historical evidence for the thesis that the Russians have an affinity for an absolute form of government. Instead, a good case can be made in support of the opposite thesis—that the Russians submitted to despotism only in order to liberate themselves from the Mongol invader and to protect their undefended frontiers. Thus autocracy would represent a grim necessity rather than a spontaneous choice on the part of the Russian people. And there is evidence that even after the establishment of Ivan's despotism, the liberal spirit of the old Kievan Russia did not disappear, for in the reign of Ivan III, the Cossack brotherhoods on the Don and Dnieper rivers continued to grow. These were democratic communities, founded by liberty-loving peasants, refugees from serfdom and Muscovite centralization, who had made their way to the southern frontier country. There they had taken up a freebooting warrior life, combining banditry with religious crusades against the heretic Pole and infidel Turk.

The End of the "Tatar Yoke"

The annexation of Novgorod and its northeastern colonial territories brought Moscow's dominion to the shores of the White Sea. The absorption of other Russian principalities followed, and when Ivan won independence from the Tatars, he was able to style himself the "Autocrat of All Russia." The liberation was in keeping with the spirit of Ivan's other accomplishments. The power of the Tatar khans on the steppe had dissolved, and Ivan was able to play one group against another. After the annexation of Novgorod, he felt himself strong enough to refuse to make any further payment of tribute to the Tatars. A Tatar army advanced to punish him, and Ivan gathered his forces to bar its path. But Ivan was anxious to avoid a test of strength, so he resorted to diplomatic wiles to stir up trouble for the Tatars in their rear. When the two armies met, they camped on opposite sides of a river, and for a long period each watched the other. Then Ivan gave the order to retreat. But in the confusion, the Tatars also retreated, and on their way home, they were

Descent of the Holy Spirit upon the Apostles—Novgorod school, late fifteenth century. The Holy Spirit is represented in the form of twelve rays of light descending from Heaven. The figure in royal garments and wearing a crown embodies the "Cosmos"—the whole world throughout which the Apostles spread the teachings of Christ—holds a wide ribbon on which are twelve scrolls, indicating the preaching of the twelve Apostles in different tongues. The Apostles are shown here in the conventional Byzantine surroundings, with complete disregard for all the laws of European perspective. The more distant figures are the larger, and the towerlike buildings are painted according to the Byzantine reversed-perspective principle. This composition was maintained in Byzantine art until almost modern times, but in Russia, composition began to change in the late sixteenth century. (From the collection A La Vieille Russie)

destroyed by a rival Tatar group. Thus ended the Tatar Yoke—"not with a bang but a whimper"—in 1480.

This event marked the culmination of the rise of Moscow from a small military outpost to its role as the capital of a united and independent state of northern Russia. This development, which came about during the interval between the twelfth and the fifteenth centuries, was largely the result of the policies of Ivan III and his predecessors. But their achievements would hardly have been possible had it not been for the advantage that Moscow gained from its geographical position. Moscow lay in what is called the "Russian Mesopotamia"—the region between the Upper Volga and the Oka rivers. In this region the north-south route from the Baltic to the Black Sea and the Caspian Sea crosses the west-east route from the Baltic to the rivers leading into Siberia. Hence Moscow had easy access to all the great river systems that provide the principal avenues of communication throughout what was to become the Russian Empire. The Muscovite control of vital river lanes had helped make possible Moscow's defeat of Novgorod, and that triumph, in turn, brought Muscovite power to the shores of the White Sea and nearly to the shores of the Baltic. The new lands in the northeast were soon settled by Moscow colonists, following in the path of fur traders from Novgorod and the pioneer monastic establishments.

Expansion to the West and the East

In the reign of Ivan III the new Muscovite Russia also began a career of outward expansion that was to continue for centuries after. In one direction, this movement was to lead the Russians eastward into Siberia, in search of furs, until ultimately they crossed the whole of northern Asia to the shores of the Pacific. This overland expansion was proceeding at the same period, we must bear in mind, as the maritime expansion of western Europe, in the wake of Columbus and the other pioneers who were sailing westward in search of new routes to the wealth of the Indies.

In the other direction, the westward expansion that Ivan III had initiated established the precedent for later Russian diplomacy in relation to the other powers of Europe. One objective of Ivan's policy in the west was to win access to the Baltic Sea, since control of this region would at once make Russia more secure and would permit western artisans to migrate to Moscow, where they could teach the Russians the new technological methods of the west. In the time of Ivan III the Baltic region was under the dominance of Sweden, which held rule over Finland, and of the German Order of Livonian Knights, which had conquered much of the Baltic coastal region south of the Gulf of Finland. Though he waged a war against the Livonian Knights, Ivan III lacked the power to overcome them, and he was not strong enough to challenge Sweden except by entering into an alliance with Sweden's rival, Denmark. But his successors were to take up his interest in this region, and in the early 1700's they were at last to attain his dream of access to the Baltic.

South of Livonia, the lands of the Lithuanians and Poles, stretching from the Baltic to the Black Sea, presented another barrier to Russia's westward growth. The peoples of these lands, which were under the same rule, were Roman Catholic and therefore hostile on religious grounds to the Orthodox Russians. Moreover, they held control of lands that once had been the heart of the Kiev federation. Here lived Ukrainians and White Russians, ethnically and religiously closely related to the Great Russians of Muscovy. Ivan now asserted Muscovy's claim to the legacy of Kiev, and this meant conflict with the Poles and Lithuanians. Ivan won no notable success at the expense of these western rivals, but he initiated a policy that in later centuries was to lead to bitter warfare between the Russians and their Polish kin.

Relations with Rome and Byzantium

Ivan III did not limit his interests to the lands on the western borders of the Muscovite realm. He also entered into diplomatic relations with the pope, who was desirous of reuniting Orthodox and Roman Christendom and forming a Christian coalition against the Turks.

As part of this policy, the pope arranged the marriage of Ivan III to Sophia, a niece of the last Byzantine emperor. This marriage did not, as the pope had hoped, strengthen Ivan's determination to drive the Turks out of Constantinople. On the contrary, Ivan took the revolutionary step of sending an envoy to the Turkish sultan, for the purpose of establishing friendly relations with the infidel ruler.

The marriage did, however, have the effect of strengthening the Byzantine influence at the court of Moscow. Ivan's nobles complained that after the appearance of Sophia, Ivan adopted a more domineering attitude toward them, and this is quite probable, for Ivan welcomed the Byzantine tradition of absolutism. Moreover, the marriage gave Ivan the basis for a claim that he was the successor of the Byzantine emperors, and it was not long before Russian churchmen invented a lineage that purported to show that Ivan was descended from a brother of Augustus Caesar—hence, eventually, the title of *Czar*, derived from the Latin *Caesar*.

The idea of Moscow as the successor to Constantinople found fuller expression in the next reign, when a monk made this public declaration: "Moscow is the successor of the great capitals of the world: of old Rome and of the Second Rome. Moscow is the Third Rome, and a fourth there will never be." The theory was that the First Rome had perished because it subscribed to the Latin heresy, instead of holding to the true faith of the Orthodox Eastern Church; the Second Rome, Constantinople, had likewise suffered God's punishment because, a short time before the Turks took the city, its religious leaders had spurned the true faith and acknowledged the heretical pope, in the desperate hope of thereby gaining western help against the Moslems. Hence Moscow now became the defender of the true faith, and, as such, its mission was to convert the world.

Basil III

The work of Ivan III in founding the Muscovite autocracy was carried on by his son Basil or Vasily III (1505–1533), whose power exceeded even that of Ivan. In his reign a foreign diplomat in Moscow observed that the Russian ruler had a more absolute dominion than any other prince in Christendom. "He has unlimited control over life and property, none dare differ with him. The will of the prince is the will of God." The diplomat went on to speculate whether it was the people who needed such a ruler or whether it was the ruler who had demoralized the people.

Ivan IV

The process of creating the despotic service state—that is, a regime in which all are obliged to serve the state—came closer to its consummation in the reign of Ivan IV (1533–1584), the grandson of Ivan III. He was the first to take the title "Czar of All the Russias," and so ruthless was he in suppressing the hereditary nobility that he earned the sobriquet "Ivan the Terrible." To be sure, this is not an accurate translation of the Russian word that means *commanding respect* or *dread*. Yet Ivan's reign saw such horrible deeds of bloodshed and violence that he deserves the name by which he is known in the west, for his cruelty was exceptional even in the age that saw the massacre of St. Bartholomew's Day in France and the horrors of the Spanish Inquisition.

Ivan the Terrible—from an old woodcut

The excesses that Ivan IV permitted himself in the struggle with the nobles was due, in part, to a mental illness verging on derangement. But they are also to be explained by other factors that led him to treat any sign of opposition with the utmost severity. In the first place, he believed more seriously than any of his predecessors that he ruled by divine appointment, and therefore any disobedience of the czar was disobedience to the will of God. For Ivan was a man of deep religious convictions, and often his bloodletting was followed by periods of brooding repentance and prayers for his victims. Yet this did not mean that Ivan would permit any criticism from the Church. Consequently, when the highest ecclesiastical official sought to restrain the czar, he was dealt with as the rest, suffering the fate of imprisonment and death. Still another circumstance explaining Ivan's despotism was that his reign was a period of almost unbroken warfare against foreign foes, and the czar therefore looked upon those who opposed him at home as traitors serving his enemies abroad.

Involved in this warfare was Ivan's vain effort to reach the Baltic, leading to a struggle with the Poles and Swedes that dragged on for twenty-five years. Russia's enemies, in turn, sought to block Russian trade with the west, in order to prevent war materials and technical knowledge from reaching Moscow. In the south, Ivan was hard pressed to hold back the Tatars of the Crimea, who on one occasion were able to raid Moscow itself. Only in the east was the frontier secure. There Ivan succeeded in suppressing the Tatar kingdoms of Kazan and Astrakan, thus permitting the eastward expansion of the Russians to gain momentum.

The manner in which Ivan IV developed his autocracy followed the pattern set by his grandfather, who had increased the central power by granting land to nobles in return for their service to him. However, Ivan III had not wholly succeeded in subjugating the old princely nobility, which held its lands by inheritance and not on condition of service to the state, with titles running back to the ruling families of the Kievan principalities. During the minority of Ivan IV this group of the highest nobility had sought to increase its influence in the state. But once the new Czar came into the exercise of his rule, he turned his might upon this princely nobility.

To accomplish this purpose, Ivan IV divided the realm into two parts. One of these he ruled in association with the *Boyars' Duma*, which was the traditional council of the nobles. But the other part he ruled alone. In this portion were included the areas that were close to Moscow or were important for reasons of trade or military strategy. Many of the old nobles who held land in these regions were ruthlessly uprooted and transferred to areas on the periphery, where they had no ties of tradition. The lands thus assigned to them, moreover, were held on condition of service. Thus many of the *boyars* were reduced to the level of the other serving nobility. At the same time the lands taken from the *boyars* were given over to reliable servants of the czar, to be held as grants conditional upon their service. To one of these "new men," Ivan wrote: "My father's *boyars* and my own have learned to be traitors, so we have resolved to call upon you, vile varlets, and from you we expect fidelity and truth." To this announcement came the obedient answer: "You are like unto God! You make a little man into a great man." This policy was continued until the political power of the old *boyars* was deemed broken; then the distinction between the two regions was abolished.

Thus the political and social system of Russia was deeply transformed within a period of little more than a century—between the accession of Ivan III in 1462 and the death of Ivan IV in 1584. The old feudal divisions were a thing of the past, and the czar ruled with absolute power over a unified state. Yet the Russian state was not wholly modern, since a vestige of feudalism remained in the relationship of the nobles to the czar and in the institution of serfdom, by which the mass of the peasants was bound to their masters. There was still in the Russian mind no identification between the people and the state. Both the czar and the people looked upon the state as the czar's patrimony: the realm was like a vast manor, of which he was the lord, while the nobles were like the servants of his household.

The Time of Troubles

Because of the persistence of this kind of political thinking, Russian society almost collapsed when the old dynasty came to an end, since its disappearance removed the central, binding element that held the state together. Ivan IV himself helped to bring about the ruin of the dynasty, for in a fit of rage he had murdered his eldest son. His second son, Feodor I, who succeeded to the throne was mentally incompetent, and when, after a short reign, he died childless, Boris

Godunov was elected czar by a popular assembly.

Boris was one of the "new men" of Ivan IV and had married his sister to Feodor I. As a regent for Feodor he had brought about important changes in Russia, including the establishment of the patriarchate of Moscow on an equal footing with other Orthodox churches; as czar he quickly lost his popular support, and the Time of Troubles began. In 1604 the first of a series of four pretenders, claiming to be the youngest son of Ivan IV, appeared on the scene. This first Dmitri, who actually succeeded in being crowned czar, had secured the backing of the king of Poland, whose forces invaded Russia. To meet this threat, the Russians called upon the Swedes for help. But this only made mat-

The Bell Tower in the Kremlin, Moscow. Built by Boris Godunov, it contains thirty-four bells, but the largest—200 tons—was too heavy to hang and stands outside on a platform. (Courtesy of the Metropolitan Museum of Art)

ters worse, for the Swedes took advantage of the situation to make a grab for Novgorod. Briefly a *boyar* reigned as czar, but in 1607 another Dmitri appeared and another Polish invasion followed.

During this period of dynastic crisis and foreign invasion, a social struggle was taking place, releasing all the forces of discontent that had been stored up during the reign of Ivan IV. Thus both the old *boyars,* who wanted to recover their lost power, and the newer serving nobility, who were meeting with economic difficulties, rose up in opposition to the state and to one another. To make matters worse, a severe famine gripped the land, and the peasants, who had been ground down into serfdom and had borne the brunt of Ivan's incessant wars, rose up in a social rebellion. Within a few years these peasant uprisings assumed such proportions that an army of peasants, commanded by a former serf and supported by Cossacks and other discontented groups, was able to storm the gates of Moscow before being forcefully dispersed.

The Romanovs

The disorder reached its ultimate crisis when the Poles seized Moscow. This humiliation induced the Russians at last to put aside their differences. The Church took the lead in calling for a national effort against the invaders, and a "People's Army," led by a butcher and a noble, wrested Moscow from the Poles. In 1613 a national assembly, composed of representatives of all classes, elected Michael Romanov as czar, and thus the "Time of Troubles" came to an end. Michael not only won general recognition as czar, but established a new dynastic succession. This he could do because he owed his position not only to his election but to his connection with the old dynasty, since he was related to Ivan's first wife.

Within a century the Romanov dynasty was to produce a czar, Peter the Great, whose reign was to mark the end of the long Muscovite era in Russian history and inaugurate a new and radically different phase. In the meantime the reign of the first czars of the new line saw a gradual restoration of peace and order and the withdrawal of the Swedes and Poles from Russia. The ending of the foreign threat was purchased only at the price of territorial losses to both invaders, but a compensating gain was made soon after the middle of the seventeenth century, when Russia profited from a revolt of the Cossacks of the Dnieper. The rebellion of these Cossacks, who were under Polish rule, made it possible for Russia to recover the southwestern territory of the Ukraine.

Siberia

Meanwhile Russia was continuing its eastward expansion into Siberia. Late in the reign of Ivan IV the Stroganov family, with government support, began a series of venturesome raids across the Ural Mountains in search of furs. The first of these was undertaken by a Cossack band, under a leader named Yermak. The power of the Tatar khan in this region was soon destroyed, and the government then took up the work that the Stroganovs had begun. Instead of making occasional raids, the government undertook a planned program for the occupation of Siberia, establishing a string of fortified blockhouses, or *ostrogs.* From the farthest of these *ostrogs,* fur traders and Cossack pioneers would proceed into new country, where the fur-bearing animals would be more abundant. In their wake would come government officials and soldiers, who would set up new *ostrogs* and begin collecting tribute from the natives of the region. From this expansion the state reaped a rich harvest, for not only did its officials collect fur from the natives as a form of tribute, but they also levied a 10-percent tax upon the furs of private traders. In the sixteenth and seventeenth centuries furs were Russia's main export.

The Russian movement across northern Asia proceeded at a faster pace than the parallel expansion of the Europeans westward across America. By the beginning of the seventeenth century the power of the Russian government reached as far as the basin of the Ob River in western Siberia. After the accession of Michael Romanov, when Russia's western frontier was about 200 miles from Moscow, the eastern border was already almost 2000 miles away. By the middle of the seventeenth century a government *ostrog* was planted on the Sea of Okhotsk, at the eastern bounds of Siberia. At the same time Russian pioneers reached the Amur River, in what was later called Manchuria, where they encountered the Chinese. The result was a treaty between Russia and China in 1689, which recognized Chinese sovereignty over the valley of the Amur.

Social Consolidation

The internal difficulties of the Time of Troubles were resolved by the victory of the serving nobility. To this group was assimilated what remained of the old *boyar* nobility. The institution of serfdom was officially recognized, and it became more widespread than before, since the peasants were attached to the soil wherever new grants of land were made to the nobility. This was not accomplished without further peasant protest, the most serious of which was expressed in a revolt led by a Cossack, Stenka Razin. For a time, in 1670–1671, this rebellion affected the whole area of the middle and lower Volga. But eventually it was put down by government troops, and Stenka Razin was executed. Though he seems to have been more of an adventurer and brigand than a social revolutionist, his memory has been kept alive in Russian folksong as a popular hero in the struggle for liberty.

With the suppression of such dissidences, Russian society took on the rather rigid form that it maintained into the nineteenth cen-

tury. The government fostered the stratification of classes for the purpose of exacting taxes and state service. Each group in society—nobility, clergy, government clerks, merchants, and soldiers—tended to become an hierarchically organized social caste.

The experience of the "Time of Troubles" served to strengthen the tradition of autocracy. Although the first Romanov czar gained the throne by the election of a national assembly, he received governing power without any conditions being imposed upon him. The early Romanovs continued to convene such assemblies from time to time, and one of them enacted an important new code of laws, but the initiative always lay with the czar, and the national assembly never developed a tradition of parliamentary government.

Russian Rulers, 1462–1796

Ivan III (the Great), Grand Duke of Moscow	1462–1505
Basil (Vasily) III	1505–1533
Ivan IV (the Terrible; first czar)	1533–1584
Feodor I	1584–1598
Boris Godunov (brother-in-law of Feodor I)	1598–1605
Feodor II	1605
(The Time of Troubles	1605–1613)

Romanov Dynasty

Michael	1613–1645
Alexis	1645–1676
Feodor III	1676–1682
Ivan V ⎱ joint rulers	1682–1696
Peter I (the Great) ⎰	1682–1725
Catherine I (joint empress, 1723–1725)	1725–1727
Peter II	1727–1730
Anna (daughter of Ivan V)	1730–1740
Ivan VI	1740–1741
Elizabeth (daughter of Peter I)	1741–1762
Peter III (nephew)	1762
Catherine II (the Great)	1762–1796

A Very Rare Silver Gilt Censer—Moscow, 1681.
(From the collection A La Vieille Russie)

Nikon and the "Old Believers"

The greatest challenge to the authority of the state was phrased in religious terms rather than social or political. This challenge took the form of the great schism precipitated by Nikon, who became patriarch of the Russian Orthodox Church in 1652. Under the influence of westernized Ukrainian churchmen, he immediately set out to correct errors in the Orthodox rituals by the introduction of certain western practices. A large part of the nation, however, refused to accept the new ways, and when the government, supporting Nikon, persecuted those who upheld the old tradition, this persecution only intensified the resistance. Though several of its leaders were burned and others exiled, the opposition continued, and a large-scale secession from the Church took place. Those who thus seceded were known as the "Old Believers." Eventually they won toleration (Nikon was banished and in 1666 deposed) and survived as an important part of Russian society, at one time numbering

perhaps one eighth of the population. But their withdrawal was an unfortunate loss to the official Church, since it removed a large number of persons of sincere and ardent religious devotion. This made it so much the easier for the state to maintain a secular domination over the Church.

This religious crisis provides some important clues for the understanding of Russian civilization. In the first place, the scope of the movement and the fervent passion it aroused are indicative of the great importance that the Russian people attached to religion. Moreover, it suggests the emphasis that they placed on the external symbols of religion, because the controversy aroused by Nikon's reforms was waged about such things as the proper way to pronounce *Jesus* and the proper number of fingers to be used in making the sign of the cross.

This stress upon externals, in turn, indicates how superficial was the impress of Christianity upon the Russian people. Much of the paganism of pre-Christian times survived in the Orthodoxy of the ignorant countryside, and the Church was unable to eliminate these vestiges of paganism, because it lacked the means to provide an educated leadership. Most of the clergy was illiterate, and when in the reign of Ivan III a churchman proposed that no one be ordained who could not read and write, he was told that if this requirement were enforced, there would be no one in Russia qualified to administer the sacraments. Even in the nineteenth century the religion of the Russian peasants was full of ancient superstitions and magic, and the village priest was seldom capable of giving moral guidance. The impression of "Holy Russia" that foreign travelers brought home with them arose from the ubiquitous sound of the church bells, the fasts, and the rich ceremonials—from externals, in short, of the kind to which the "Old Believers" attached supreme importance.

The tenacity with which the "Old Believers" clung to their religious convictions is also interesting as an evidence of the force of the concept of the "Third Rome." Nikon's reforms were intended to restore the Russian Orthodox ritual to the form that it had when it was derived from the Greek Orthodox original. But the "Old Believers" were not impressed by the argument that Russian Orthodoxy should correspond to the Orthodoxy of Constantinople; in their view, Russian Orthodoxy alone had the true faith, and Constantinople had fallen to the Turks because the Greek Orthodox Church had succumbed to heresy.

The schism had social as well as religious significance. Most of the "Old Believers" came from the lower classes, and the movement drew part of its strength from economic discontent. "Old Believers" were to be found in the ranks of the rebels under Stenka Razin, and later they became adversaries of the westernizing reforms inaugurated by Peter the Great. Yet the economic and social discontent that was involved in the movement was obscured by the emphasis upon matters of religion, and once the state accorded them religious toleration, the "Old Believers" ceased their political opposition.

Another social significance of the movement was the widening of the gap between the more educated upper classes, which had little to do with the movement, and the great unlettered multitude, from which the "Old Believers" were generally recruited. This gap was further widened, as we shall see, by the reforms of Peter the Great, and the gulf between the upper and lower classes was to have ominous consequences for the later history of Russia.

PETER THE GREAT AND THE NEW ERA

With the reign of Peter I, who assumed full power in 1696, a new era in Russian history began. It is marked by a much closer connection between Russia and western Europe, and it is symbolized by the transfer of the capital, during Peter's reign, from Moscow to St. Petersburg, a new city on the shore of the Baltic that Peter built and named for his patron saint.

The process of westernizing Russia was not begun by Peter I; it had started two centuries before his reign, when Ivan III threw off the "Tatar Yoke" and called in foreigners to strengthen his army and beautify his capital. But hitherto the process of westernization had been slow, and it had been resisted. Moscow at the end of the seventeenth century included a large foreign colony, composed of merchants, artisans, and soldiers of fortune who had taken service with the czar, but these foreigners were segregated from the Russian people, who wanted nothing to do with "heretics." Even the czars continued the custom of washing their hands after giving audience to "unclean" foreigners.

Peter I, however, became a zealous champion of western influence, giving a tremendous new impetus to the process of westernization that had begun before his time. Peter has been called "a man always in a hurry," and because he wanted to see results at once, he used methods of the utmost cruelty in order to hasten the westernization of the land. As Lenin later put it, "Peter accelerated the adoption of Westernism by barbaric Russia, not shirking to apply barbaric methods to fight barbarism." Thus Peter shed the Byzantine court dress and the religious ceremonial that had surrounded the czars before him, but the instrument that he used to westernize the country was the same autocratic despotism that they had developed and that made Russia seem more Oriental than western. In Peter's time the prisons and torture chambers were fuller than in any reign since that of Ivan IV, and on one occasion the Czar himself served as the headsman at a mass execution, lustily swinging the ax that chopped off the heads of the unfortunate victims.

Thus Peter presents a paradox—but so do his people. The Russians have never been known for their moderation or discipline. Like their boundless and formless plain with its sudden changes of season, their history is full of sweeping violence and extremes. Peter, half-European and half-Asiatic, throbbing with vitality and unbridled emotion, was just such a titan as was Russia itself, sprawling and half-civilized. Though he looked to the west, Peter was not a man of the west; he did not respect the west because he deemed it a source of truth, but because he could draw from it things that he could use for his own purposes. "Europe is necessary to us for a few decades," he is reported to have said. "After that, we will turn our back on it." His purpose was not, as Voltaire and other westerners supposed, to "civilize"; it was to strengthen Russia. Westernization was never more than a means; the goal was conceived in the same terms as before. The basic aims of Peter I were traditional policies, not innovations—the protection of Russia's borders on the west and the south, the reconquest of the portions of the "homeland" that remained under Polish rule, and the attainment of "natural frontiers" on the Baltic and the Black Sea.

The Work of Peter I

Of these aims, the one that Peter pursued with the most success was the winning of access to the Baltic. After a long and bitter struggle with the armies of Sweden, brilliantly led by Charles XII, Russia emerged in 1721 in possession of Estonia, Livonia, and Karelia, and with its new capital, St. Petersburg, established on the Gulf of Finland. In honor of the victory, the czar was hailed as "Peter the Great, Father of the Fatherland, Emperor of All Russia." Poland was no longer a danger, and, though Peter failed to wrest the Black Sea coast from the Turks, he won a measure of security against them and demonstrated that they could be defeated. In the Middle East, where Peter dreamed of expansion to India, he succeeded in reaching the shores of the Caspian Sea after a war with Persia. Even far-off Siberia was not outside his ken. One of Peter's last acts before his death was to sign the instructions for Bering's journey of exploration that eventuated in the mapping of the northeastern edge of Asia and the discovery of the strait between Siberia and North America that bears Bering's name.

These various endeavors meant that Russia was at war almost continuously for all but two of the thirty-six years of Peter's reign. Hence the czar was always on the move from one front to another, as though he were "a guest in his own house." He therefore had little time in which to make careful and elaborate plans for domestic reform, being obliged to improvise instead.

An illustration of his methods is the establishment of St. Petersburg. In 1703, even before the Swedes had been driven from the Baltic, Peter boldly decreed the building of this "window to the west," through which Russia would face Europe after centuries of forced seclusion. It did not matter to him that the site chosen for the new city lay in the middle of marshlands and woods, with a damp, unhealthful climate that caused the death of thousands of the unhappy serfs and prisoners who were forced to labor there. By the will of the czar, the capital of the great empire was to be transferred from its center to its periphery, and Peter's bureaucrats and nobles, no matter how disgruntled at leaving the comforts of Moscow, had to follow him there in 1713 to take up residence, braving the adversities of the inhospitable climate. Moscow with its traditions belonged to the past, and Peter hated it. His new capital was to be the city of the future.

Just as he called St. Petersburg into being by decree, by the same simple manner of command he sought to refashion the whole of Russia. Thus, for example, he dictated that henceforth the peasants must use scythes instead of sickles, pointing out to them:

"You know yourselves that anything that is new, even though it is good and needful, will not be done by our folk without compulsion." And as he created St. Petersburg so that it would give a dramatic symbol of the new orientation toward the west, in other respects, too, he made use of symbols, knowing their appeal to the mind of his people. For instance, on his return from his unprecedented tour of study in western Europe, his first orders to his nobles were to clip their flowing beards, put on western dress, and take up smoking. These superficial imitations of western customs, he realized, would impress upon them and the mass of the people his determination to make Russia over according to western models.

The first thought in Peter's mind, as he undertook his work of domestic reform, was the military needs of the country. He transformed the army from a host of feudal levies into a standing army, recruited by conscription, and he built Russia's first fleet. To support the army, he introduced new measures of taxation, including a sales tax and a poll tax; in order to assure the collection of these taxes, he made the serving nobles responsible for the taxes due from the peasant com-

Evolution of European Russia

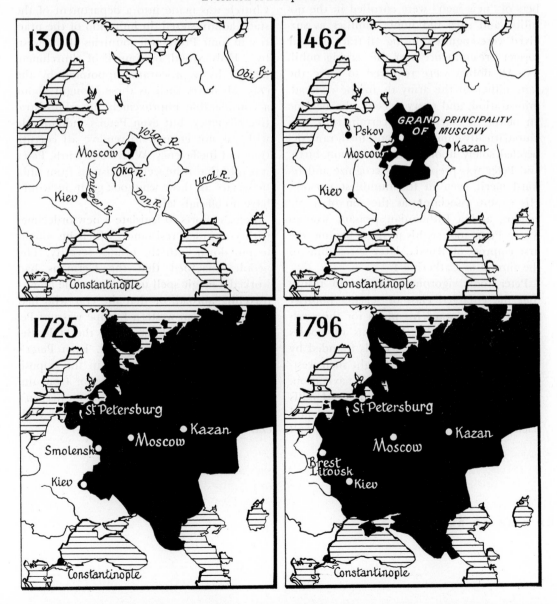

munes belonging to them. As a further support to the army, he encouraged the development of industries that would furnish uniforms and armaments. To hasten this process, the government itself commonly established factories and opened mines, then leased the enterprises to private persons, giving them the right to commandeer the labor of the peasants of the region, who thus became industrial serfs. So far-reaching were Peter's measures of this sort that the Russians could no longer bury their dead in coffins of pine, as had been the custom for generations—the czar needed the pine for building ships!

To make his system work, Peter relied primarily upon the serving nobility. Great numbers of "new men" were enrolled in the nobility, and such old noble families as survived were engulfed, losing all trace of their former pre-eminence over the serving nobility. All nobles were required to serve the state either in the army or in the civil administration, and every person who became an officer or official of a certain rank was automatically ennobled. Henceforth rank depended solely upon merit, not upon birth, and Peter was prepared to recognize and reward merit even in the humblest persons. His closest associate was the son of a pie vendor, and a Lithuanian peasant woman whom Peter took as his mistress became the first empress of Russia, later succeeding to the throne as Catherine I.

Peter took vigorous measures to insure that the enlarged class of serving nobility would help forward his plans for the westernization of Russia. The sons of nobles were required to attend schools founded by Peter, in which they were taught such western sciences as geometry and navigation. Many were sent to learn all manner of skills in western Europe, while technicians and scientists were brought to Russia from all over Europe to staff the new academies and institutes. Etiquette as well as science formed part of the indoctrination in western ideas. Among the new customs that the Russians had to learn was how to treat ladies in society, for Peter's orders brought Russian women out of the seclusion in which they had lived up to this time.

The state ceased to be administered as though it were the czar's household; instead it was administered according to a more logical pattern, comparable to the bureaucratic organization of the absolute monarchies of the west. A high body of nobles consulted with the Czar on legislation, took responsibility for the enforcement of the laws, and served as a supreme court of justice. The Church was made into a department of the state, administered, in imitation of the practice in some Protestant countries of the west, by a Holy Synod, or council of churchmen, headed by a procurator appointed by the czar. Measures such as these brought about a considerable improvement in administrative efficiency, but even Peter's indomitable will was not enough to remove all corruption and inefficiency. With some truth, Peter was told that if he were to dismiss from public service all those who took graft, he would have no officials left.

Peter's efforts to legislate a new order met with continued resistance, which he sought to put down with the utmost severity. The people imagined that the Germans had worked a magic spell upon him while he was traveling abroad, or that the czar who had come back from western Europe was not Peter but the anti-Christ whom the "Old Believers" had long anticipated. Even Peter's son Alexis became involved in the opposition, and to prevent his successor from undoing his work, Peter brought about his son's execution. In the future, he decreed, each czar would designate his successor.

THE EIGHTEENTH CENTURY

This last measure precipitated a period of dynastic confusion that lasted almost half a century, for Peter died in 1725 without having named his successor. Thereupon the throne became the prize of rival forces at the court. The strongest element in the struggles was the Guard, a corps of picked troops of noble birth, which engineered a series of palace revolutions until at last they placed an able German princess on the throne as Catherine II. In the interval between Peter's death in 1725 and Catherine's accession in 1762, Russia's crown was worn by two boys, two dissolute women, who were wholly or partly of foreign origin, and finally by Peter III, a czar who was mentally incompetent. It was this czar's wife, a princess of a petty German state, who became Catherine II after her husband was murdered.

The Emancipation of the Nobility

In this interval, when there was no strong ruler on the throne, the nobility succeeded in throwing off the requirement that they serve the state. Even in Peter's time the nobles had sought to evade the demands of state service, and with the ending of the foreign wars, after the close of his reign, they had settled down on their estates to enjoy the prosperity that came with Russia's agricultural development. Finally, in 1762, they induced Peter III to issue a decree that officially emancipated them from the requirement of service. The reason for this measure, so the decree proclaimed, was that the nobility was now so public-spirited that noblemen need no longer be compelled to render service. But nothing was done to emancipate the peasants from their bondage to the nobility, although the institution of serfdom was originally justified on the ground that the peasants must work for their masters, so that the latter might work for the state.

While the nobles thus gained their freedom, the plight of the serfs was worsened. The nobles now became petty autocrats on their own estates or gave over the administration of them to grasping stewards. There

A Kalmuck, a Finnish Peasant, and a Russian Peasant —as they appear in a vast study of fishing (1769–1777) by Henri Louis Duhamel du Monceau, French botanist and engineer. (*Bibliothèque Nationale*)

Catherine the Great

much of the luster was spurious. For though
the decree that emancipated the nobles from
the obligation of state service lauded their
"public-spirited" character, this praise was
more than they deserved. Though many of
them continued in the service of the czar,
and some furthered economic development
by establishing factories with serf labor,
most gave themselves over to lives of idle-
ness. Nor was their leisure well spent in the
pursuit of culture. Though some of them
dabbled in German culture and later in
French, the veneer of westernization was
very thin and brittle. Evidence of how little
the Russian nobility understood the culture
of western Europe appears in the diary entry
of a nobleman traveling abroad that he observed an interesting statue in Rotterdam,
which represented a certain Erasmus. Apparently he had no notion who Erasmus was.
Even if he had been better informed, he
probably would not have understood the
values that the great humanist expounded,
for the westernization of the upper classes
had led only to confusion. No longer holding to their traditional culture and as yet
not understanding the values of the west,
the upper classes were left without firm principles to guide them, and many of them inevitably sank into immorality.

Meantime the common people of Russia
were still finding their cultural values in the
primitive religious symbolism of the Church,
with its ikons and its liturgical singing, and
in the traditional epics, or *bylini,* handed
down from ancient times. As Peter intended,
St. Petersburg became a symbol—but not a
symbol of the westernization of Russia. Instead it became a symbol of the growing
distance between the czar's court and the
mass of the people.

was no legal limit to the master's power over
the serf. The noble could sell him, order him
mercilessly beaten, or have him exiled to
Siberia. To be sure, he could not have him
put to death, but this was only because the
death penalty was reserved for cases of treason to the state. From a public advertise-
ment we may gain an impression of how
degrading was the status of the serf: "For
sale, a girl of sixteen, good behavior, and a
second-hand slightly used carriage."

This servitude embraced 94 percent of the
Russian population—14,000,000 serfs who
were the property of the state, and another
19,000,000 who were the property of nobles.
Debased as was their status, the demoraliz-
ing effects of servitude were not limited to
those held in bondage, for most of the upper
classes likewise suffered the moral corrosion
that comes when a man has absolute power
over other human beings.

The last part of the eighteenth century,
when serfdom was at its peak, has been
called the "Golden Age of the Nobility," but

Catherine II

Such were the social conditions that continued during the reign of Catherine II
(1762–1796), and though this remarkable

woman gained the name of "Catherine the Great," her reign saw no basic improvement in them. In her time, as we noted in the previous chapter, it was the fashion throughout Europe for sovereigns to make a show of "benevolent" or "enlightened" despotism; thus they professed to labor as rulers to promote the welfare of their people, and they became patrons of the arts and sciences. Catherine saw to it that she kept up with this fashion. Accordingly she corresponded with such intellectual luminaries of western Europe as Voltaire, and at home she made dramatic profession of her determination to rule well. Catherine was actually a person of great ability, and although she found ample time for a procession of favorites and lovers, she also found time for the serious work of statecraft. She left the government more stable than she found it, and it was her triumphs on the diplomatic front that really won her the title of "the Great."

Early in Catherine's reign it appeared that social reforms might be considered. She summoned a Great Commission, charged with the task of drawing up a new law code. This commission was chosen by a popular election, in which all classes took part except those serfs owned by the nobility. Catherine's definition of its task, in the decree known as the Instruction, represented some of the best humanitarian thinking of the time. So advanced were its ideas that it was banned in France as too radical. But though the Commission met for more than a year, discussing the problem of serfdom, among oth-

Europe in 1789 and the Partition of Poland

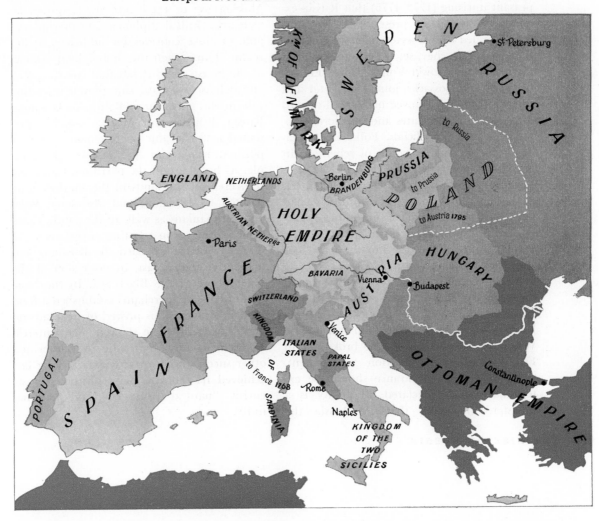

ers, nothing ever came of its deliberations. The nobility was opposed to any kind of change, and it was to this class, after all, that Catherine owed her crown.

Far from relieving the plight of the serfs, Catherine was, in fact, responsible for the further spread of serfdom. In her reign the institution was extended to the Ukraine, and about 1,000,000 serfs owned by the state were given over to private owners, when vast tracts of Crown lands were awarded as grants to her favorites. The only new limitation on serfdom in her reign meant no advantage to the serfs. This was the restriction that decreed only noblemen might own landed estates to which serfs were attached. This did not terminate the ownership of serfs by the state and the Church or their use in industry, but it did prohibit townsmen from becoming serf-owning landlords.

In Catherine's reign occurred the greatest peasant uprising (1773–1775) that Russia experienced before the present century. This rebellion, led by a Cossack named Yemelyan Ivanovich Pugachev, set the whole region of the middle and lower Volga aflame. Embattled serfs and Cossacks, joined by Tatar and Finnish tribesmen, moved northward toward Moscow, burning estates and murdering nobles, priests, and officials. Following a tradition by which the leaders of rebellions in Russia frequently pretended to be the czar, Pugachev proclaimed that he was Peter III, Catherine's husband, whose murder had been the prelude to her assumption of power. But the pretense was to no avail. The revolt was finally put down by the army, and Pugachev was executed in 1775.

The experience of this rebellion caused Catherine to abandon her trifling with liberalism and bound the throne and the nobility more closely together than ever before. When the Revolution of 1789 broke out in France, Catherine's reaction was violent. "The very name of France should be exterminated," she declared. "Equality is a monster." Knowing that in Russia the Church was a bulwark of the autocracy, she recommended that the western powers adopt the Orthodox religion in order "to save themselves from the irreligious, anarchical, abominable, and diabolical plague, enemy of God and of thrones." And in her own dominions she ruthlessly sought to repress any murmur of the ideas she herself had once encouraged.

But in her reign, as often in the history of the czardom, repression at home was accompanied by advance abroad (see map, p. 669). Catherine inherited the army of Peter the Great, which even under poor leadership had been able to raid Berlin in 1760, during the Seven Years' War in which Russia was pitted against the Prussia of Frederick II. She was fortunate, moreover, in having the services of a brilliant general, Aleksandr Suvarov, who proved to be one of the best military commanders in European history. Making use of these military resources, as well as a skillful diplomacy, Catherine was able to make considerable additions to her realm. Thus, when the shortsighted policies of the Polish nobility left that country weak and defenseless, Catherine played a leading role in the partition of Polish lands among Russia, Prussia, and Austria, which represented a remarkable achievement of power politics; even in an age not noted for scruple. As her share in the partition, Catherine recovered all the lands in the southwest inhabited by Russians, and also some Poles and Lithuanians as well. In the south, Catherine's armies won a lasting victory over the Turks, which established the Russians permanently, and at last, in possession of the north shore of the Black Sea. In the same period Russian merchants established a foothold in Alaska. This proved of little advantage, since Catherine showed small interest in the Far East. By virtue of Catherine's other successes, however, Russia at long last achieved its centuries-old aspiration for security, "natural frontiers," and national unity.

Suggestions for Further Reading

Source Materials

J. Cournos, ed., *A Treasury of Russian Life and Humor* (New York, 1943).
A very valuable and amusing collection of documents.

G. P. Fedotov, ed., *A Treasury of Russian Spirituality* (London, 1948).
This is a very valuable collection of documents for an insight into Russian religious history.

B. G. Guerney, ed., *The Portable Russian Reader* (New York, 1947).
A good anthology of selections from Russian literature.

J. S. Martin, ed., *A Picture History of Russia* (New York, 1945).
A useful collection of pictures; it helps the student get an accurate mental image of life in Russia and the Russian scene.

W. Walsh, ed., *Readings in Russian History* (enlarged edition, Syracuse, 1950).
A useful collection of documents and readings.

Secondary Works

N. A. Berdyaev, *The Russian Idea* (New York, 1948).
A survey of Russian thought by a great Russian philosopher.

H. Lamb, *The City and the Tzar* (New York, 1948).
Dependable popular history of the Romanov era through Catherine II.

H. Lamb, *The March of Muscovy* (New York, 1948).
A popularly written, but dependable, survey of early Russian history.

T. G. Masaryk, *The Spirit of Russia* (2 vols., New York, 1919).
The best history of Russian thought in English.

Written by a great Czech philosopher and statesman.

A. G. Mazour, *Russia: Past and Present* (New York, 1951).
A good survey of Russian history.

P. N. Milyukov, *Outlines of Russian Culture*, edited by M. Karpovich (3 vols., Philadelphia, 1942).
This is the standard survey of Russian cultural history.

F. Nowak, *Medieval Slavdom and the Rise of Russia* (New York, 1930).
An excellent survey of early Russian history.

B. Pares, *A History of Russia* (6th rev. ed., New York, 1953).
One of the best textbooks; by an outstanding English scholar.

I. Spector, *An Introduction to Russian History and Culture* (New York, 1949). A good survey, valuable for its discussion of Russian cultural history.

B. H. Sumner, *Peter the Great and the Emergence of Russia* (New York, 1951).
A brilliant study of the great Peter and his reforms.

G. S. Thomson, *Catherine the Great and the Expansion of Russia* (London, 1947).
A penetrating study of the great German-Russian empress and her career.

G. Vernadsky, *A History of Russia* (rev. ed., New Haven, 1954).
An excellent survey by a distinguished Russian emigré historian.

Atlas

G. Goodall, *The Soviet Union in Maps* (London, 1948).
A useful atlas for a study of the historic growth of Russia.

27

The Atlantic Civilization in the New World

An Aztec Calendar Stone. This Aztec sculpture is thought to be a small-scale model of a pyramid or temple surmounted by a calendar stone. (Courtesy, American Museum of Natural History)

In the same three centuries between the beginning of the reign of Ivan III (1462) and the death of Peter the Great (1725), while Russian czardom was spreading steadily eastward across Siberia to link the civilization of Europe with that of China, European civilization was also expanding southward and westward around the ocean, fanlike, to link the newly explored continents of Africa and the Americas with Europe.

This overseas expansion of the European civilization was an event of major importance in the history of civilization in the west, if not in the world. It began, as we already know, chiefly as a capitalistic search for markets and commodities, but it soon grew into a movement of much greater scope, involving the migration of swarms of Europeans and the transplanting into the new lands of languages, religions, arts, and institutions of Europe. It thus represented a great outward growth of the civilization of western Europe, extending this civilization into the vast new lands on the other side of the Atlantic Ocean. It meant, in short, the enlargement of the bounds of the civilization that hitherto had been identified with western Europe into one that ringed the Atlantic Basin.

This does not mean that the civilization that arose in the Americas and South Africa —and that also eventually included New Zealand and Australia after the appearance of the Europeans in those areas—was a replica or a set of replicas of the civilization of the European motherlands. The ideas and institutions that the Europeans brought to this "New World" had to be modified to meet the peculiar geographic, economic, and ethnological conditions found there, and often the modification was so drastic as to change the old ideas and institutions into something new. Often, too, the new conditions confronting the European settlers overseas forced them to create wholly new institutions or to shape their thinking in wholly new ways. In parts of the New World, moreover, a numerous indigenous population of Indians survived after the European migration, and the culture that subsequently arose was in part an outgrowth of the fusion of the Indian culture with the adapted and modified European.

This was not the situation in the portion of North America that passed under English

Painted Buffalo Robe. The pictures represent incidents in the life of the owner, an American Indian of the Neolithic period. Compare with illustration on page 25. (Collection *Musée de l'Homme*, Paris)

dominion, because there the natives were never numerous, and the English drove them back into the wilderness beyond the pale of the European settlements. In other regions, however, where the Spaniards and Portuguese penetrated, the new European culture was merely overlaid like a veneer upon the older, more primitive culture of the natives. But throughout the hemisphere, power—economic, social, and political—was in the hands of the settlers of European stock, and this power assured the dominance of the culture that they had brought with them from overseas or that they had adapted to the needs of their new environment.

THE AMERICAS BEFORE COLUMBUS

When Christopher Columbus first landed on the American continent and with monumental conceit took possession of it in the name of the king of Spain, the land was already populated by peoples—Eskimo and American Indian—at various stages of cultural development.

The Eskimos of the arctic north—"the people who eat meat"—had an extremely primitive culture, with no political or social institutions broader than the family. Depending for their food on the supply of fish and bear or walrus meat, they had no fixed habitation but moved about, following the animals they hunted. Though they invented many ingenious devices to aid them in their struggle for survival, such as the snow hut, or igloo, the fire drill, and an oil-burning lamp, they had no agriculture or commerce.

Scattered over the rest of the two continents, from the timber belt running from west to east across North America to the southernmost tip of South America, were the cultures of Indians. The Indians, most authorities now believe, came to the western hemisphere by way of Bering Strait in a series of migrations. The fact that they all migrated from Asia would explain the similarities of features and traits among the Indians of North and South America. Probably these peoples brought with them a Neolithic culture, because most Indians made fire with a drill, could make baskets, used stone tools, and had domesticated the dog, at least.

The most advanced of the "woods" Indians in North America were the Iroquois and the Hurons, who lived around the Great Lakes. Their culture included the primitive use of metals and pottery, the rudiments of an art, an oral literature made up of the tales and legends of their heroes and gods, social institutions centering in the tribe, and a loose political organization, taking the form of a federation of tribes. Although they were primarily hunters, they also raised crops, and they built walls around their villages, which comprised a number of bark houses in each of which lived several families. During the seventeenth and eighteenth centuries the Iroquois became the dominant group of Indians in the eastern part of North America. By reason of their fur trade and their wars, they exercised a profound influence on the westward-moving settlements of the white men.

In the southwestern section of the continent, about 1500 B.C.—at the time when Minoan culture was at its height—the Basket Makers developed a culture marked by the growth of agriculture. About 1000 years later new tribes of Indians moved into the region, took over the culture of the Basket Makers, and began the manufacture of a painted pottery. These peoples lived in pueblos, large terraced community houses, which they built high up in cliffs or canyons for protection. But this culture came to an end about A.D. 1300, and the numerous pueblo villages found by the Spaniards during their marches of invasion were built after the original pueblo culture had come to an end.

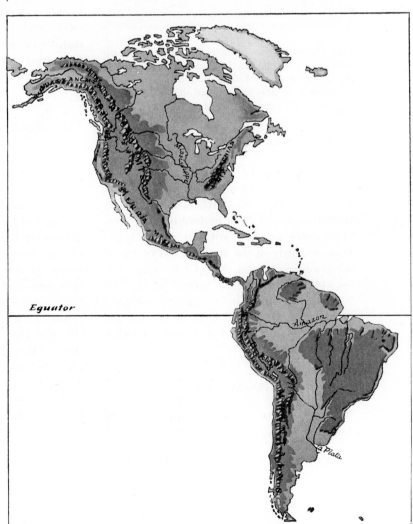

Physical Map of the Western
Hemisphere

Inca Silver Figure—c.1200–1532. The Incas domesticated the llama, a beast of burden ever since, but a silver llama with a rider—in this case a hunchback—is unusual. (Courtesy of the American Museum of Natural History)

These Indians had developed cultures but not civilizations (see p. 5). But in the mountain valleys and plains of Mexico and Guatemala and in the mountain valleys of Peru there had arisen two civilizations that, although somewhat later in development, were comparable to the civilizations that began independently in the river valleys of Egypt, Mesopotamia, India, and China (see map, pp. 40–44). Before the arrival of the Europeans the Aztecs of Mexico and the Incas of Peru had reached a level of culture generally comparable to that of ancient Egypt.

The Aztec Civilization

The Aztecs were a warlike people who took over the culture of the Toltecs, a people whom they had conquered. They were skilled agriculturalists, using systems of irrigation comparable to those of Egypt and Babylonia, and they engaged in trade. They developed the arts of metalworking, in which both gold and silver were used, and of pottery, weaving, sculpture, architecture, and music. Their religion was fierce and brutal, involving human sacrifices. Their deities included a sun god, moon god, and war god, as well as others. The priesthood was a powerful caste. In connection with religion and agriculture, they developed picture writing and gained sufficient knowledge of astronomy to devise an accurate calendar. See page 676.

The center of the Aztec culture after about 1325 was the city of Tenochtitlán on the site of the present Mexico City, where resided their ruler, who was both emperor and high priest. The masses of these people, most of whom lived in villages and cities, were relatively docile. In contrast to their cousins in the northern and eastern forests, they were an easy prey to the European conquerors.

The Civilization of the Incas

The Indians of the lowlands of South America were at a low stage of cultural development at the time of the coming of the Europeans, but the Incas, living on the high plateaus of the Andes, in Peru and Ecuador, developed a civilization as advanced as that of the Aztecs in Mexico. The accomplishments of the Incas in architecture, irrigation, and road building were such as to rival the engineering achievements of the Europeans. Agriculture was well developed, and the government was centralized under a ruler called the Inca, who was both a god and the emperor. Society was stratified in castes, but the economy was run on a communistic basis, so that the lower classes were preserved from poverty. Religion centered in the worship of the sun god, from whom the rulers were thought to have descended. There was no written language, but the Incas developed a system of counting and a kind of calendar, and their religion encouraged both the arts and the science of astronomy. Like the Aztecs, the Incas worked silver, gold, and copper and engaged in commerce. Also, like the Aztecs, they proved too docile to withstand the Spanish conquerors, and their land became one of the most profitable of the realms in America that the Spaniards took over.

The Mayan Civilization

Another highly developed indigenous civilization was that of the Mayas, which arose in the Yucatan Peninsula and in what is now Guatemala. This civilization, which probably had its beginnings in the second millennium B.C., seems to have been older than that of either the Aztecs or the Incas.

The Mayan civilization had a high degree of political organization, based on a federation of city-states. From its ruins, the principal city, Chichén-Itzá, seems to have been nearly as splendid as the ancient Egyptian cities of the Empire, for the Mayans created a magnificent architecture (see the Mayan temple illustrated on page 7) featuring terraced pyramids on which were built their temples and palaces. The ruins of the palaces show that the Mayans were masters of the column and the corbeled arch. The walls of their buildings were made of rubble, set in concrete and faced with stucco. Their sculpture, used chiefly for architectural decoration, showed a high degree of sophistication and symbolic beauty. They were skilled also in the making of pottery and the weaving of textiles, and they made use of metals, though only in jewelry.

Mayan society was divided into classes, with warriors and priests at the top, farmers and traders in the middle, and slaves at the bottom. Religion was vastly important, dominating every aspect of the life of the people. The chief place in the hierarchy of gods was given to the sun god, but the serpent seems also to have been important. The priests were the most powerful group in society, for they monopolized the secrets of writing and of science as well as religious functions. Like the priests of the Aztecs, they practiced human sacrifice.

Sometime after the end of the first millennium of the Christian era, the brilliance of the Mayan civilization dimmed. The reason for its decline is not known, but its greatest time was past before the Spaniards began their conquest.

"NEW SPAIN"

The Spaniards were the first of the Europeans to transplant their civilization to America. Their empire was founded by Columbus on his first voyage of discovery in 1492, and three centuries later it included all the mainland of the continent south of the Rio Grande del Norte with the exception of Brazil, which belonged to Portugal. In addition, the Spaniards held three islands of considerable importance—Cuba, Puerto Rico, and Hispaniola or Española.

The whole of this domain was under the rule of the king of Spain. For convenience of administration, it was divided into four viceroyalties, each of which was a separate kingdom under a viceroy, representing the king. The oldest of these viceroyalties was New Spain, established in 1535, which centered in what is now Mexico. The second, Peru, which was established in 1542, included most of the western coast of South America. New Granada, established in 1718, took in the northern ports of the South American continent, while Buenos Aires, established in 1776, comprised the lands in the region of the La Plata River.

Colonial Administration

The viceroys who governed these kingdoms were not supposed to rule at their own discretion but to administer the policies decreed by the king of Spain. In the formulation of these policies, the king consulted bodies of experts, charged with the supervision of imperial relations with "the Indies," which were attached to his court in Spain.

The most important of these bodies of experts was the Council of the Indies, which corresponded to the commission known as the Council of Castile that assisted the king in the government of his Castilian kingdom. The Council of the Indies, founded in 1511, was composed of leaders of Spanish affairs and men who had had experience in the colonies. Its members were appointed by the king, and it became, in effect, the central government for the entire overseas empire. It nominated viceroys, captains-general, bishops, and other officials whom the king appointed to the leading offices in the colonies. It set the boundaries of the administrative, judicial, and ecclesiastical divisions of the colonies, and it exercised a general supervision over all aspects of colonial life. It gave special attention to the problem of the Indians, entrusting their welfare principally to the care of the Church.

The Council was particularly concerned with the financial and commercial policies to be followed in the exploitation and government of the colonies, and it drafted the many mercantilistic laws that sought to control the profits of the colonies for the benefit of the mother country. Moreover, it served as the highest court of appeals for cases dealing with colonial affairs, whether these cases originated in the colonies or the homeland. Its functions were therefore legislative, executive, and judicial, and—in the last analysis—it determined both the formation and the execution of Spain's imperial policy. This policy—as was to be expected in an age of mercantilistic statism—was arbitrary, absolute, and extremely paternalistic.

In 1714, after the Bourbon Philip V had become king of Spain, the Council of the Indies was shorn of its legislative and executive functions, which were given instead to ministers responsible to the king. It continued to exercise its judicial functions, but its decisive importance was gone, and thereafter its power steadily declined.

Commerce and communications between the colonies and the homeland were under the management of another board, the *Casa de Contratacion,* or House of Trade, established in 1503. Because of its responsibility for commerce with the colonies, the *Casa* concerned itself with the conditions of navigation, maintaining a school for navigators and seamen and a center of scientific and geographical information regarding America and the ocean trade routes. From its headquarters in Seville, the *Casa* issued licenses for trade or travel in America, supervised the collection of import and export duties, regulated the quantity of goods imported from other European countries for export to the colonies, and performed countless other functions in the conduct of colonial commerce. It even had some judicial power in cases involving disputes between sea captains, foreign merchants, and others. Thus the *Casa* was both a great trading house and a ministry and court, with virtually complete power over all matters arising out of commerce with Spanish America. In the eighteenth century, however, its power was somewhat reduced. For example, the English gained the right to engage in the slave trade, bringing slaves from Africa to the Spanish colonies without having to submit to the supervision of the *Casa*. Licenses were also given to foreign merchants to trade directly from Cadiz, to which place the *Casa* was transferred in 1717.

The decisive power over the colonies was thus exercised by the king of Spain, the two great agencies in Spain to which was delegated the task of managing colonial administration, and the four viceroys overseas, who put into effect the policies determined in Spain. For purposes of local administration, the four viceroyalties were subdivided into smaller areas. These were of two kinds: the *audiencias,* which comprised the more settled and civilized areas, and the *capitanías,* which included the more remote regions, where a military form of government was needed. The *audiencias* and *capitanías* were, in turn, subdivided into local units. But all the officials were appointed by the viceroy, who was responsible to the king. Thus, with the exception of the *cabildos,* or town councils, which for a time were elected by the townsmen, there was nothing in the imperial government that even resembled representative institutions. But this is not surprising, when we remember that absolutism was the accepted rule in European political institutions during the age when Spain ruled her empire in America. And even if Spain had been willing to give the colonies a measure of self-government, this would not have been feasible, because the masses of the people in Spanish America were ignorant savages, without the slightest conception of the functions and institutions of government among civilized men.

The People of New Spain

The vast bulk of the population of the colonies was Indian. The number of Spaniards who came to America was never large, and although they and their descendants, the *creoles,* multiplied by the natural process of reproduction, they never constituted more than a powerful minority of the population. Despite the encouragements offered emigrants in the form of free passage and grants of land, livestock, and equipment, the policies of the Spanish government were not such as to favor emigration. Prospective emigrants had to prove that neither they nor their ancestors had ever been tainted by heresy; unmarried women were not permitted to go to the colonies unless they were

members of the families of emigrants; and foreigners were rigorously excluded.

Yet some foreigners managed to get into the Spanish colonies. The number of Portuguese and Jews was considerable. Moreover, many Negroes were brought in as slaves, and these Negroes soon mixed with the Indians to form a large class of mixed breeds. The Europeans also mixed with the Indians to produce another mixed-breed class called *mestizos.*

The proportion of pure-bred Europeans to the native and mixed peoples may be seen by the following estimate of the population in 1810 at the end of the colonial period:

Region	European stock	Total
New Spain	1,100,000	5,760,000
Guatemala	150,000	1,200,000
Cuba	275,000	600,000
New Granada	250,000	1,555,000
Argentina	300,000	1,150,000
Venezuela	160,000	800,000

Economic Life of the Colonies

The economic life of the colonies was closely regulated in the interests, first, of the king and the homeland, and, second, of the Spanish and creole settlers in the colonies; scarcely any heed was given to the interest of the mass of the people in the colonies.

In accordance with the ideas of mercantilism, all the commerce of the colonies with Europe was monopolized by the homeland, and in order to make it easier to enforce the regulations to this end, ships were required to sail from and to only one port in Spain—Cadiz. The articles passing to the colonies consisted mainly of manufactured goods, such as textiles, hardware, tools, flour, and wine. The imports from America were hides, sugar, dyewoods, cacao, and the supremely important gold and silver bullion.

The European goods were sent out to the colonies in two great fleets, each making

The Port of Acapulco. Acapulco, on the Pacific coast of Mexico, was the only port in New Spain permitted to trade directly with the east. One ship a year, beginning in 1565, sailed from the Spanish trading center in Manila to this port. To the annual fair at Acapulco, merchants from Mexico City traveled over what was known as the "China Road." (From De Bry's *Voyages*, New World Series, Part XL, first German edition, Frankfort on the Main, 1619, New York Public Library Rare Book Room)

one voyage a year. One of these, known as the *galleons,* was dispatched to the fairs at Cartagena or Porto Bello; the other, known as the *flota,* was destined to serve the fairs at Vera Cruz and Mexico City. At these great trading centers were accumulated the stores of colonial goods that were to be sent back to Spain. The ships picking them up would meet at Havana and would return to Spain together, usually under the escort of warships.

Despite its intention of monopolizing the profit of trade with the colonies, Spain was unable to keep the whole advantage. Since the homeland produced few manufactured goods that could be shipped to the colonies, Spain had to obtain these goods from French, English, Flemish, Dutch, and other northern European merchants. Thus much of the profit of the trade was drained out of Spain to these northern countries. To lessen this drain, the Spanish government levied a tax upon the goods purchased abroad for shipment to the colonies. Yet it could not wholly prevent a leakage, because Spain lacked ships of its own and therefore was obliged to hire foreign ships to carry the colonial commerce. And this gave foreign

shipmasters an excellent opportunity to engage in smuggling.

The Negro slave trade was also placed by contract, or *asiento,* in the hands of foreigners, since Spain had no slave-producing territory of its own. In 1715 this *asiento* was granted to the English South Sea Company, which was also given the privilege of sending one ship each year bearing merchandise for the fair at Porto Bello. The *asiento* was never very profitable to the English, but it gave them a cover for a considerable amount of smuggling.

By the eighteenth century so much of the colonial commerce was in the hands of foreigners that Charles III (1759–1788) instituted a new economic policy. Giving up the attempt to keep the trade wholly in Spanish hands, he chose to give still wider freedom to foreigners to trade with the colonies and to take measures to increase the volume of commerce. He hoped thus to make the colonies more prosperous, expecting that their prosperity would redound to the benefit of the homeland as well as the empire. Accordingly, foreigners were more readily given permission to enter the colonies and to make investments in them; roads were built so as to make it easier to bring products to the seaports; cattle-breeding was encouraged; and the burden of taxes on the colonies was considerably lightened. At the same time the administration of commerce in the colonies was put under the supervision of *intendants,* who improved the efficiency with which it was carried on. These reforms had a salutary effect upon commerce, although, as we shall see, the infiltration of foreign influence was to have social, intellectual, and political consequences that the Spanish government did not foresee (p. 687; also Chapter 29, Volume II).

The profits that Spain first took from its colonies were in the form of gold and silver. After taking from the natives whatever stores of these precious metals they had accumulated, the Spanish put the Indians to work opening up new mines as well as exploiting the old. Especially important were the great silver mines of Potosí, in what is now Bolivia, and Zacatecas, Guanajuato, and Taxco in what is now Mexico. During the sixteenth, seventeenth, and eighteenth centuries these mines produced silver to the value of billions of dollars, which enriched both the homeland and such English pirates as Sir Francis Drake and Sir Henry Morgan. Even in the eighteenth century mining remained an extremely important part of the colonial economy, but its relative importance declined as the Spaniards developed other economic resources.

The economic pursuit that occupied the masses of the population was agriculture. Farming was encouraged by the Crown, which granted a remission of taxes to those who undertook the cultivation of the land and the raising of cattle, and the Crown made grants of tools, seeds, and livestock to those emigrants willing to settle on the land. The native Indian corn was cultivated almost everywhere, as were also potatoes, yams, tobacco, and cassava. To these were added such plants of European origin as wheat, vines, sugar, and olives. Of those raised primarily for export, the most important were sugar and tobacco. But the exports also included cacao, indigo, ginger, and certain medicinal plants.

More important than crops in the export trade were the products of ranching, in which more persons were occupied than any other single industry. Vast expanses of the land in Spanish America are more suitable for grazing than farming, and the huge herds of cattle, horses, mules, goats, and swine that ranged over the open country multiplied rapidly. The export of hides became one of the most profitable items in the Spanish colonial trade.

Silver Mining in Peru—an artist's conception of the "Silver Mountain" at Potosi, discovered in 1545, the richest silver mine known in the sixteenth century. The Spaniards worked the mine with a day and a night shift of natives. Six men were always on the long ladders, three carrying the ore upward while three descended. At left, llamas carry the silver down the mountain. (From De Bry's *Voyages,* New World Series, Part IX, first German edition, Frankfort on the Main, 1601, New York Public Library Rare Book Room)

Social Organization

With scarcely any exception, the social and economic life of the Spanish colonies was controlled by the Spanish and creoles. In theory, all the land belonged originally to the Crown, and individuals gained possession of it only by grant or purchase from the government. To provide for the control of the natives and their conversion to Christianity, the *encomienda* system developed. Under this institution, which first appeared about 1503, the natives were grouped in villages near the Spanish settlements, and each village was placed under the charge of a Spanish overlord, who was responsible for civilizing and converting the natives. In return, the overlord was permitted to require the natives in his charge to work for him or to pay him tribute. Though invented for a laudable purpose, this system led to scandalous abuses in Hispaniola and Cuba, where it was first instituted, and resulted in the rapid annihilation of the native population in those islands. But despite widespread criticism both in Spain and in America, the system was eventually established on the mainland and became the basic institution determining the structure of Spanish American economic and social life.

From time to time, efforts were made to ameliorate the inhumane conditions prevailing under the *encomienda* system, and it was legally abolished in 1720. Thereafter government officials were in charge of the natives. In spite of this reform, however, the natives remained in economic subjection.

Another form of the exploitation of the natives developed under the system of *repartimientos,* instituted in 1609. This was a system by which the Crown authorized private persons to draft the Indians for work in agriculture, herding, mining, or public works. Theoretically, the natives were to be taught how to do the work required of them and were to be paid wages. But, in practice, the *repartimiento* became simply a device for exacting forced labor.

As the abuses of the systems of *encomienda* and *repartimiento* led to a decline in the native population, Negro slaves were imported to provide an additional source of labor. Their use was never universal, but in some colonies the institution of slavery attained considerable economic importance. By the end of the eighteenth century, the number of Negro slaves in the Spanish colonies was about 700,000.

Thus the social structure of the colonies comprised an aristocracy of officials and Spanish landowners, many of whom held *encomiendas;* a middle class, comprising merchants and artisans of the towns, often mestizos; and a working population of Indians, Negro slaves, mulattoes (half white and half Negro), and *zambos* or persons of mixed Indian and Negro stock.

Religion

Of all the Spanish institutions in the colonies, the most widely influential was the Roman Catholic Church, for it touched all classes, including the lowest, and affected all aspects of their lives. Its organization in Spanish America was under the supervision of the Council of the Indies and of archbishops in Hispaniola, Mexico, Peru, and New Granada. Under their direction, churches were built in the towns, and missions were established among the Indians in the countryside. In the more remote and primitive areas, such as California in the late eighteenth century, these missions became the principal center for the dissemination of Hispanic culture among the natives.

The Church was the only agency for education in the colonies. Its schools admitted the children of townsmen and Indians as well as those of the Spanish emigrants. In various places, such as Mexico City and Lima, the Church founded universities, which afforded secular instruction as well as advanced training for the clergy.

The Church was an important economic institution, as well as the guardian of religion. In many places the Church held large *encomiendas,* and in some areas, notably present-day Paraguay, its missions assumed complete governmental control over the natives, regulating their economic life as well as providing for their moral and intellectual formation.

A Culture Synthesis

In cultural life, as well as economic and political affairs, Spain sought to maintain an exclusive dominance over the colonies, and in great measure it succeeded in extending its culture to America and imposing it upon the natives. Thus the religion of Spanish America was Spanish Catholicism, its art was Spanish Baroque and rococo, its music was Spanish music, and its literature was part of the "Golden Age" of Spanish literature.

In those aspects of cultural life that did not intimately touch the lives of the Indian and mestizo masses—in art and literature, for instance—there was little modification of the original Spanish forms. But in religion, social customs, and such arts as pottery and weaving, the native Indian traditions persisted with but little change. The religion of the masses was a mixture of primitive Indian beliefs and practices with other ideas and forms taken from Europe. Likewise, social customs became an amalgam of primitive Indian mores and the imposed European moral code. For the masses, art similarly retained much of its original character as an expression of the native esthetic instincts of the primitive Indian peoples.

As part of its endeavor to impose the culture and the religion of the homeland on the colonies, the Spanish government introduced the Inquisition. First established in America in 1569, this powerful Church court kept a vigilant watch for foreign heretics, Jews, Protestants, witches, and bigamists. It also took heed of the printing presses, and no one was permitted to publish or read books that were listed in the Church's *Index* as inimical to the purity of faith and morals. Generally, however, the Church was lenient toward the religious practices of the Indians, and the persecution of others was never so severe as in the homeland.

Despite all the efforts of Church and government, the new ideas of the Enlightenment (see Volume II, Ch. 28) began to seep into Spanish America about the middle of the eighteenth century. Even in the universities the works of Descartes and Newton began to receive attention, and an occasional bold voice was raised in criticism of the old Scholasticism. And though the political ideas of such thinkers as Rousseau were excluded and the American Declaration of Independence was placed on the *Index,* colonists traveling or studying abroad brought back word of the new spirit of freedom that was stirring throughout Europe in the Age of the Enlightenment.

More important for the history of civilization in America, however, was the birth, by the end of the eighteenth century, of a self-conscious colonial culture. Though Spanish in its superficial aspects, this outlook on life was to be distinguished in many ways from its European source. The Church was gradually losing its hold upon the mind of the colonists, and a resentment against the motherland was developing as a result of the exclusion of the creoles from important governmental posts. Hence Spanish American art and literature began to take on a more "American" cast, in both subject matter and style. This was true not only of the culture of the natives, which never had been deeply influenced by Spain, but also of the culture of the creoles, who formerly had kept closely in touch with the culture of Spain. Out of the synthesis of European civilization with the native cultures of America, there thus began to emerge a new civilization—that is, a new, American variant of the civilization of the European peoples living in the lands bordering upon the Atlantic.

"NEW PORTUGAL"

During the sixteenth century, while Spain was laying the foundations of its great empire south of the Rio Grande del Norte, the Portuguese were beginning to bring their own brand of European civilization to Brazil.

For about thirty years after Pedro Alvares Cabral discovered Brazil in 1500 while on his way to India, the Portuguese did little or nothing to plant colonies in this part of their empire. The savage wilderness of the new land promised little profit, and the Portuguese were deeply preoccupied with the rich domain they were bringing under their sway in the Far East. Only a few private persons visited the coast in search of brazilwood, from which dyes were made and from which the country got its name. Some of these individuals settled along the shore and developed a trade with the Indians. But many of these first settlers were not Portuguese, and other countries, especially France, soon began to show an interest in the region. Therefore, in order to make sure that Brazil would not be lost to foreigners, the king of Portugal in 1530 appointed a governor for the Portuguese coast of South America. The first governor was Admiral Martim Afonso de Sousa.

Administration

As a device for stimulating settlement in the colony, the Brazilian coast was divided into twelve *capitanías*. Each of these was assigned to a *capitão*, or lord, who was given the land on condition that he settle it with colonists and bring it under exploitation. The Crown reserved the right to collect customs and receive one fifth of all gold and silver mined in the region. But apart from these reservations, complete authority was given to the captains, who were to govern both the natives and the Europeans living on their lands. Though the plan did not

work well and was eventually abandoned, a few of the capitanías prospered and grew. Among these was Sousa's own grant, São Vicente, and the capitanía including Pernambuco.

Presently it was discovered that sugar could be raised with profit, and Brazil soon became one of the world's principal sugar producers. But the raising of sugar cane required a plentiful supply of cheap labor. Since the Europeans would not stoop to menial work and the Indians were averse to work of any kind, the proprietors of the sugar plantations began to import Negro slaves from the Portuguese colonies in Africa. These unwilling immigrants contributed another element to the mixture of races, as well as to the labor that brought riches to the land.

Brazil was annexed by Spain when Spain and Portugal were temporarily united by Philip II in 1580. During this interval portions of Brazil were occupied by the Dutch, who were at war with the Spanish. But in 1640 Portugal regained its independence of Spain, and eventually the Dutch were dislodged.

Immigration from the homeland increased during the latter part of the seventeenth century, and by the beginning of the eighteenth there were many towns and plantations along the coast. In the temperate southern parts of the colony, the frontier began to move inland toward the plateau in the interior. Rich deposits of gold were discovered in the interior between 1698 and 1725, and diamond fields in 1729. These discoveries stimulated a new rush of immigration, which quickly increased the population. By the middle of the eighteenth century Brazil was a populous and valuable part of the Portuguese Empire, with a civilization, in and about the towns along the coast, that, while predominantly Portuguese in style and culture, was already showing traits that were peculiarly its own. European influence never reached inland except in the region of the mines or where Catholic missionaries ventured among the Indians.

The development of Brazil, as thus appears, owed little to the government, because the administration was never so effective as that in the Spanish viceroyalties. The Portuguese king retained, theoretically, an absolute rule over Brazil, but no body developed in the homeland comparable to the Spanish Council of the Indies or the House of Commerce, which would take over the burden of devising and enforcing policies for the government of the colonies. The king's authority was represented in Brazil by a governor, who after 1714 resided at Bahia. But the governor never established effective control over the captains or the local governors who later replaced them. Moreover, governors were frequently defied by the clergy and the owners of large plantations or mines.

Economic Development

The economic life of the colony centered in ranching, mining, and the production of sugar, tobacco, and brazilwood. The raising of vines was prohibited—on the ground that it would produce competition for the wine industry of the mother country—and certain other economic pursuits were likewise forbidden out of mercantilistic considerations.

But because Portugal could not furnish enough ships to handle the commerce of Brazil, foreigners were permitted to trade with the colony, except during the interval of Spanish dominance from 1580 to 1640. Before this period, the Dutch had built up strong commercial connections with Brazil, but after the end of the Spanish regime their place was taken by the English, who received special privileges under the Anglo-Portuguese treaty of 1654 and the Methuen treaty of 1703.

Brazilian Sugar Works. Beginning in the center foreground with (2) cutting and selecting (1) the sugar cane, the artist depicted, counterclockwise, ten scenes in the production of sugar, (10) the refining being at the lower right. (From Pierre van der Aa, La Galeries Agreable du Monde, Vol. III, Leyden, 1733, Bibliothèque Nationale, Paris)

By the end of the eighteenth century Brazil was both prosperous and populous. Rio de Janeiro, the chief city, ranked next to Mexico City in importance among the cities of the New World. But the wealth of the land was in the hands of a small ruling class, made up of Portuguese landlords and officials. Of the population of 3,500,000, two fifths were slaves. The great mass of Indians, Negroes, and half-breeds shared in the economic life of the colony only as laborers and were wholly excluded from its political life.

Cultural Development

As in the Spanish colonies, the original cultural pattern of Brazil was that of the European homeland. But under the influence of geographical and ethnological conditions, it quickly began to take on an American aspect.

The religion of the colony was the Catholicism of Portugal, but the Portuguese were never so zealous in spreading their religion among the natives as were the Spanish. Heretics and foreigners were permitted to enter the colony, and the Inquisition was never introduced. The Jesuits, however, did undertake vigorous missionary endeavors in some regions, sometimes forcibly converting the natives to the Christian faith.

The intellectual life of Brazil was far less developed than that of the Spanish colonies. There were no printing presses, and almost no books were imported except those of a religious character. Such schools as existed were both scattered and poor. Those persons who could afford an education went to Europe to the universities either of Portugal or of France and England.

Despite this backwardness of Brazilian intellectual life, the new radiance of the Enlightenment began to relieve the gloom of the eighteenth century, and gradually signs appeared of a new cultural activity distinct from that of the mother country. As in all the other colonial areas of the New World, the conditions of the frontier brought about an adaptation of inherited institutions as well as a general lowering of the level of culture. From the amalgam of Portuguese, native, and foreign peoples, a new synthesis emerged, and this creative intermixture was apparent in culture as well as in the new stock produced in the Brazilian melting pot of peoples.

"NEW FRANCE"

France, England, Holland, Denmark, and Sweden were a century behind Spain and Portugal in extending their national brands of European civilization to the western hemisphere. To be sure, France and England began to share in the speculative exploration of the world about the beginning of the sixteenth century, while the Protestant Revolution was taking place. In 1497 the parsimonious Henry VII of England had engaged John Cabot, an Italian, to sail westward to the land of the Great Khan, and Cabot reached a land that was probably Newfoundland. And in 1523 the quixotic Francis I of France had engaged Giovanni da Verrazano, another Italian, to stake out France's claim in the New World. About a decade later Verrazano was followed by Jacques Cartier, a French mariner of St. Malo, who explored the gulf of the St. Lawrence and sailed some distance up the river. But nothing substantial came of the work of these explorers in French and English service. It was not until the beginning of the seventeenth century that the commercial interests of these and the other Northwest European countries were prepared to invest their capital in colonizing enterprises overseas. Then all began to do so at about the same time.

This wave of colonization by the seaboard nations of northwestern Europe presents a sharp contrast to that of Spain and Portugal. In the first place, the colonizing ventures of these countries were carried out by private companies, organized for the purpose of exploiting the New World for private profit, whereas the Spanish and Portuguese ventures had been begun largely under royal auspices. In the colonies of the northwestern nations, therefore, private initiative was of more importance than the action of the national government, which ordinarily limited its interest in the colonies to the mercantilistic regulation of their commerce. In the second place, the colonies founded by the northwestern nations developed by the mass migration of European settlers, who drove the natives before them in an irresistible movement that eventually was to drive most of the Indians out of the continent. This was quite unlike the Spanish and Portuguese pattern of a relatively small-scale European migration, producing a settlement in which a European minority ruled over a larger population of mixed-breeds and natives.

The first of the northwestern European nations to establish an offshoot in America was France. After several unsuccessful ventures at colonization—in Canada, Brazil, and Florida—the French made a plantation at Port Royal in Acadia, or Nova Scotia. This settlement, established in 1605, preceded by two years the first successful English colony, which was established at Jamestown in Vir-

The Western Hemisphere about 1750

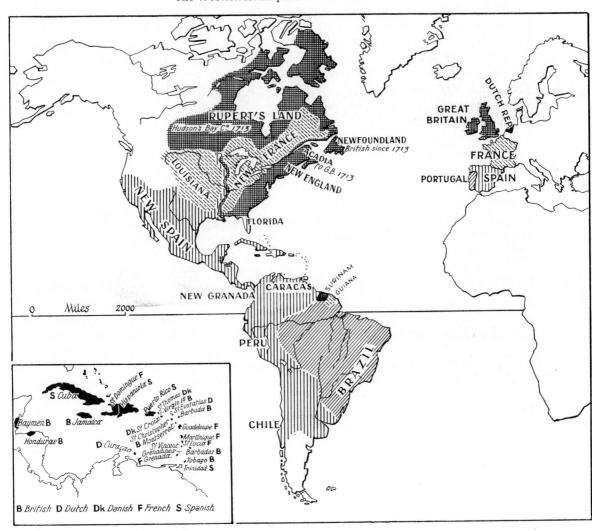

ginia in 1607. A second French settlement in Canada was begun at Quebec in 1608. Both these new communities drew their economic sustenance from the fur trade.

A few years later, in 1625, another French colony was founded in the West Indies, on the island of St. Christopher's, and a few French found a precarious foothold on the continent of South America in what is now French Guiana. Both these Caribbean colonies thrived on the cultivation of sugar, and, as time went on, the French extended their settlements into Martinique and Guadeloupe and other islands in the Caribbean. Later, too, Frenchmen settled along the Mississippi, founding Louisiana.

But the real cultural center of New France was Quebec, founded in 1608 by Samuel de Champlain, for a company of French merchants. The growth of the colony was extremely slow until 1627, when Cardinal Richelieu organized the great Company of New France that undertook to settle the country in exchange for a monopoly of the fur trade. The colony was not profitable, and its growth remained slow until 1665, when Louis XIV made it a royal enterprise. For a few decades thereafter, under the paternalistic patronage of the "Grand Monarch," its development was rapid. By the work of such men as Louis de Buade, the count of Frontenac, Jean Baptiste Talon, and Robert Cavelier, sieur de La Salle, the economic and social life of the colony was firmly established, and the greater interior region, comprising the Great Lakes Basin and the Mississippi Valley, was brought to the knowledge of Europeans and opened to European exploitation.

Canadian Economy and Society

The pattern of economic, social, and cultural life in New France was determined in the era of the Company of New France. The intention of the Company was to establish agricultural settlements along the banks of the St. Lawrence, under a kind of feudal and manorial system. Large grants of land were made to proprietors who were styled *seigneurs,* and these were subdivided into smaller holdings, assigned to peasants, or *habitants.* Though not attached to the land like serfs, the habitants in a seigneury were supposed to render dues and services to the *seigneur,* and he was likewise supposed to owe a kind of feudal allegiance to the Company.

As the Company hoped, substantial settlements were made along the St. Lawrence and its tributaries, but the feudal regime never worked quite as planned. The main reason for this was the vastness of America that made it unnecessary for the *habitant* to remain on the holding that the *seigneur* allotted him, if the *seigneur* proved too demanding or if the *habitant* took it into his head to strike out for himself. Consequently, the *seigneurs* were obliged to reduce to a minimum the dues and services that they required of the *habitants.* And instead of living in feudal splendor, the *seigneur* often found it necessary to labor in the fields alongside his people.

In these settlements the Roman Catholic Church gained a position of moral and intellectual dominance. It was from the first the only church permitted in New France, and it had complete control of education. Its strong position among the settlers in this early era gave a Catholic religious cast to French Canadian society that has persisted to our own time. From the settlements along the St. Lawrence, the Jesuits and other missionaries spread French religion and French culture into the villages of the savage Indians, deep in the heart of the continent.

But there was also another side to Canadian society, more "American" than the semifeudal and clerical society along the St. Lawrence. This was represented by a new class, the *coureurs de bois,* or bush-rangers, that arose out of the trade in furs with the Indians of the interior. The center of this trade was at great fairs, the most important of which was held at Montreal, to which the Indians brought their packs of skins, to barter for guns, lead, gunpowder, scalping knives, and various European trinkets. But the bush-rangers, eager to make an extra profit, went into the interior, sometimes hundreds of miles from the settlements, to trade with the Indians in their own villages. In the course of their travels, these woodsmen lived among the Indians, consorting with Indian women and begetting a race of half-breeds who, in turn, became traders and an important link between the French and the natives. Loving the wild, roving life, the *coureurs de bois* were a semisavage group, culturally not far from the Indians among whom they lived. Many efforts were made by the Church and the government to limit their activities and prevent their increase, but to no avail. The social dynamics of the frontier could not be contained.

Government

The government of New France was autocratic, paternal, and mercantilistic. The king had his representative in the colony in the person of the governor, who was the military commander. The king also appointed the bishop, who administered the religious life of the colony, and the *intendant,* who was responsible for the routine of civil administration. These men and their subordinates acted upon direct orders from the king; there was nothing in Canada even remotely resembling representative institutions, except the government of the towns, which usually included some of the town merchants.

Economic life was closely regulated in the interest of the homeland according to the principles of mercantilism. Immigration was limited to French Catholics, and the trade of the colony, both import and export, was restricted to the mother country. Naturally, therefore, the colony of New France could never show the vigor and self-sufficiency of the English colonies along the sea-board, with which New France was almost constantly at war.

Rivalry with the English

The struggle between these rivals was primarily for control of the interior of the continent, to which the French laid first claim. By virtue of the explorations of Champlain, the Jesuit priest Jacques Marquette and his companion Louis Jolliet, La Salle, the sieur Du Lhut, the sieur de La Vérendrye, and a host of others, by 1682 France asserted its possession of the whole of the basin of the Great Lakes and the valley of the Mississippi. Numerous outposts were soon established in this region. Among them were

Death of the Jesuit Fathers—Jean de Brébeuf and Gabriel Lallement being burned at the stake by Iroquois near Lake Huron, March 16–17, 1649. (Detail from illustration in François du Creux, *Historiae Canadensi,* Book 10, 1664, New York Public Library Rare Book Room)

Fort Frontenac (1673), Detroit (1701), New Orleans (1718), and Mobile (1710). This spread of French power into the interior meant the creation of a barrier, shutting the English colonies into the Atlantic Coastal Plain east of the Alleghenies. In view of the expansive vitality of the English colonies, conflict was inevitable. The outcome, after a series of wars, was the conquest of the whole of New France by the English, which was accomplished by 1763.

After the English triumph, nearly every trace of French influence disappeared from the interior except in the region around New Orleans. The settlements along the St. Lawrence, however, remained an offshoot of France, for the language of the people remained French, as did their religion and culture. Yet this French plantation in America was never a replica of the motherland.

Under the influence of the new land, with flora and fauna of its own, a climate unlike that of the homeland, and a native population, the frontier culture became something quite different from the culture of the mother country. But because the people had become conscious that they were distinct from France—as well as resentful of the flagrant neglect of the colony by the mother country during the eighteenth century—the settlers of New France were not deeply troubled by their separation from France in 1763. Once the English made plain they would not disturb the language, religion, and customs of the French colonists, the latter were willing to accept English rule without protest. Their culture, flourishing today on the banks of the St. Lawrence, remains one of the distinct and significant variants of western civilization in America.

"NEW NETHERLAND"

The story of Dutch overseas settlement begins with the Dutch War of Independence, which started about 1565. During that war the Dutch gained their independence of the king of Spain, who formerly held rule over their land. But while this war was going on, the Spanish annexed Portugal and thus gained control of the Portuguese Empire in Asia and America. Hitherto, the Dutch had been accustomed to voyaging to Lisbon, where they bought the products that the Portuguese brought back from the Far East and Brazil. And as wholesale distributors of these often exotic commodities, the Dutch had become deeply interested in the overseas trade. Now that they were at war with Spain, and Lisbon was under Spanish rule, the Dutch found themselves shut off from their customary supply of goods. Consequently, they determined to voyage directly to the Far East to obtain for themselves the goods that formerly they had bought from the Portuguese.

The Dutch East India Company

As the means of prosecuting this venture, the Dutch merchants formed, in 1602, the Dutch East India Company. Immediately the Company became involved in conflict with the Portuguese in Far Eastern waters, and eventually the Dutch drove their rivals out of many of their bases in this region, leaving Portugal only the merest fragment of her once great and profitable empire in the Orient.

In the Far East the Dutch East India Company established a number of trading stations, or "factories" (pp. 563, 565), but the Dutch made no attempt to plant large settlements of their own people in the region east of the Indian Ocean. At the southern tip of Africa, however, a small Dutch colony developed, eventually becoming another outpost of the Atlantic civilization.

This area had been discovered by the Portuguese, who had christened it the Cape of

Good Hope. But, although their ships usually put in at Table Bay to take on fresh water and give the seamen a respite, the Portuguese had not established a permanent colony.

On the shore of this bay in 1648 a group of shipwrecked Dutch sailors built a shelter and began to raise crops while awaiting rescue. So promising was this impromptu settlement that the Dutch East India Company decided to develop a colony at the Cape to provide a way station for ships making the long voyage to India. This colony grew slowly, until by the end of the eighteenth century it numbered about 16,000 persons of European descent and 17,000 Negro and Asiatic slaves. Thus the "Cape Colony," as it was called, became a counterpart of the European colonies in the western hemisphere.

New Netherland

Meanwhile the Dutch also had planted outposts in America. Their interest in the western hemisphere dates from the explorations of Henry Hudson, an Englishman in Dutch service, who in 1609 sailed along the northeastern coasts of America and entered the river that bears his name. A little later, in 1621, the Dutch West India Company was chartered, on the model of the more famous Dutch East India Company, for the purpose of harassing the Spanish and the Portuguese colonies in the Americas and establishing Dutch bases in this region.

A beginning was made in 1623 with the settlement of New Amsterdam (New York) and Fort Orange (Albany), and a few years later other settlements were made on Curaçao (taken from the Spanish in 1634) and St. Eustatius and in what is now British Guiana (1616). (Surinam or Dutch Guiana was settled later, but its history is too complicated to relate here.) Except for Curaçao, none of these proved very profitable, but Curaçao and the colony at New Amsterdam did become significant as outposts of Dutch culture in the New World. Here the Dutch language was spoken; agriculture and commerce followed Dutch patterns; and the official religion was the Dutch brand of Calvinist Protestantism. True to the tradition of the mother country, however, the colonies maintained a relatively large measure of religious toleration.

The main economic pursuit of the colonists of New Amsterdam was trading with the Indians for furs. Unlike the French in Canada, the Dutch did not mingle with the Indians or seek to Christianize them. But they began the slow process by which the natives were deprived of their hunting grounds and thereby forced to withdraw, step by step, into the interior.

The First Known Picture of New York. It is possible that the original drawing was made by Cryn Frederickzs, sent in 1625 to lay out New Amsterdam for the Dutch West India Company. The engraving, first published in Joost Hartgers *Beschrijvinghe van Virginia, Nieuw Nederlandt, Nieuw Engelandt,* etc., Amsterdam, 1651, inverted the drawing. To be viewed correctly, with Governor's Island at left and the mill on the west shore, it must be looked at in a mirror. The five-bastioned fort was never completed. (New York Public Library, Stokes Collection)

t' Fort nieuw Amsterdam op de Manhatans

The colony of New Netherland remained in the possession of the Dutch only until 1664, when it was seized by the English. But even in that short time, its life, like that of other European colonies in America, became differentiated from that of the mother country. One reason for this was the influence of the frontier and the fur trade. Another was the near-by presence of the English colonies on the seaboard, for many of the English moved into the Dutch colony, thereby giving it a cosmopolitan character. Because of this cosmopolitanism, and also because of its religious toleration, its importation of Dutch art, and its achievement of opening up the Hudson River gateway to Canada and the Great Lakes, the influence of this short-lived Dutch colony on the subsequent history of civilization in North America was much more profound and more enduring than might have been expected.

"NEW ENGLAND"

The colonies that the English planted on the continent of North America and the islands of the Caribbean were the most advanced, vigorous, and self-sufficient of all the colonial offshoots of the European civilization in the western hemisphere. These colonies differed from those of the Spanish and Portuguese in that they were purely European, including no Indian or mixed-breed population. But, unlike the other colonies, their white population was not drawn wholly from the mother country, because the English permitted foreigners of all kinds to settle in their colonies.

The English began their American colonization ventures in the latter part of the sixteenth century, notably under the initiative of Sir Walter Raleigh, but none of their settlements endured until the establishment of a colony at Jamestown in Virginia in 1607. Thereafter their interest in the New World quickened, and in the third and fourth decades of the seventeenth century there was a large-scale migration of English colonists to the western hemisphere.

Several factors combined to bring about this great westward movement. One was the interest of the English merchants, who had accumulated sufficient capital to take the risks involved in investment in colonial enterprises—with the hope of reaping great profits from fishing, tobacco-raising, mining, or trade with the natives and the colonists.

Another factor was the desire of large numbers of the English people to gain land of their own in the New World. Still another was the wish of some, who were "Dissenters" from the established Anglican form of Protestantism, to escape religious persecution or harassment in the homeland, while others were anxious to escape the political upheaval produced in England by the struggle between Parliament and King Charles I. Most of these emigrants—about 37,000 of them—went to the West Indies. But about 18,000 went to New England, and another 12,000 to Virginia, Maryland, and Bermuda.

During these decades, colonies were founded at Plymouth (1620), on the islands of St. Kitts or St. Christopher (1625) and Barbados (1627), on Massachusetts Bay (1623–1630), in Maryland (1634), in Rhode Island (1636), in Connecticut (1635), and in what later became New Hampshire and Maine. Thus by 1650 England had more than a dozen colonies along the coast of the American continents, from the Orinoco to the St. Lawrence. Some of these were under the private control of individuals, as in Nova Scotia, Maryland, and the West Indies; some were operated by commercial companies, as in Massachusetts and Rhode Island; and one, Virginia, was under the direct control of the Crown after 1624.

In the second half of the seventeenth century several more colonies were added.

These included Jamaica, taken from Spain in 1655, New Netherland, or New York, taken from the Dutch in 1664, Carolina, settled in 1670, and Pennsylvania, settled in 1682. Meantime New Jersey was split off from New York, and Delaware from Pennsylvania. In 1670 the great Hudson's Bay Company was chartered—its first expedition had gone out two years before—to exploit the rich fur trade of the lands lying around the northern sea.

English Colonial Policy

In sharp contrast to the Spanish, French, and Portuguese colonies, where even the most minute details of daily life were regulated by orders from the mother country, the English colonies were almost wholly free from parental interference. Nearly all of them were founded by private enterprise, and not until nearly half a century after their founding did the English government take official cognizance of them. Then England began to make an effort to control American shipping and commerce for the benefit of Englishmen.

Beginning in 1651, the English Parliament passed a series of laws seeking to exclude foreigners from maritime intercourse with the English colonies and to control the movement of certain American exports, such as sugar and tobacco, and certain American imports, such as manufactured goods, in such a way as to insure that English

businessmen would gather profits from this trade. These mercantilistic regulations reached their climax in the Great Navigation Act of 1696.

But despite the strenuous efforts of England to control the economic life of the colonies, it was not until the eve of the American Revolution that the mother country effectively interfered in other aspects of their affairs. For a century or more, therefore, these colonies grew up separately, with a strong feeling of independence, and in the course of time they became differentiated from each other as well as from the mother country.

Economic Divergence

The most striking differentiation was to be observed in colonial economic life, which by the eighteenth century took on a clearly regional aspect.

The Englishmen who went to Virginia and Maryland found the economic basis for their survival in the profitable cultivation of tobacco. This crop, which is native to America, was already known in Europe before the English settled Virginia, but preference was given in the English market to tobacco raised in this colony, and eventually a strong demand for Virginia tobacco also developed on the continent. Even though the English Navigation Acts put hindrances in the way of marketing the crop, the area planted to tobacco steadily increased, and

The Restored Governor's Palace at Williamsburg—typical of English domestic architecture. Williamsburg, with a population of about 3000, was the capital of the colony of Virginia from 1699 to 1779. (F. S. Lincoln, photographer)

throughout the eighteenth century this remained the staple product and principal export of both Virginia and Maryland.

The concentration upon tobacco production had several significant effects upon the social and political life of these communities. For various reasons, the business passed into the hands of large planters, and these great landlords gained a dominant position in both politics and society. Moreover, it was discovered that Negro slaves were a cheaper supply of labor than free whites, and large numbers of Negroes were therefore brought into the colonies from Africa. This created a deep and impassable social gap between the white settlers and the Negro slaves, and the whites were led to adopt an aristocratic outlook, regarding manual labor as a badge of social inferiority.

The colonies of South Carolina (1670) and Georgia (1733) present a history of adaptation comparable to that of Virginia and Maryland, except that the economic basis of their developing culture was the cultivation of rice and indigo and trade in deerskins with the Indians of the southern Alleghenies. In these colonies, too, there developed a plantation economy built upon slave labor, supplemented by the commerce of Charleston and Savannah, and a society marked by an aristocratic attitude on the part of the whites.

All the southern colonies were closely attached to the mother country. Since the navigation laws required that their principal exports be shipped to England, the southern planters were dependent upon the merchants in the mother country, known as *factors,* who purchased their crops. Commonly, moreover, the colonists were in debt to these factors. And because their income was earned in England, through the sale of their products by the factors, the southern colonists bought most of their imports from English suppliers.

Along with goods of English make came English ideas regarding social institutions and customs, English fashions in art, architecture, furniture, and dress, and English views as to education and religion. Hence the plantation society consciously copied the culture of England. Nevertheless, the ideas imported from England underwent important modifications in America. Though superficially English, the culture of the plantation colonies remained basically American, rooted in the American experience and differing in many ways from that of the England from which it sprang.

The development of civilization in the English West Indies had its economic base in the cultivation of sugar. This led to the development of large plantations, using great numbers of slaves, who eventually outnumbered the whites by four or five to one. The plantation owners of the West Indies were even more closely attached to the homeland than those of the southern colonies of the mainland. If possible, they resided in England, regarding their plantations as overseas investments rather than homes. Those whites who resided in the islands were aristocratic in outlook, living like conquerors among the masses of their slaves. But despite the conscious effort of the settlers to remain English, the society and civilization of these island colonies were profoundly different from those of their motherland. The necessary adaptation of European civilization to a new environment produced a culture that, if not entirely new, was no longer English, but West Indian.

The development of civilization in the northernmost of the English colonies was in sharp contrast to that of the southern colonies. Because of its discouraging soil and climate, New England never produced any important agricultural surplus for export. But the sea provided an abundance of fish, which could be dried and salted and sold in all the countries of Europe bordering on the Atlantic and the Mediterranean, and the forests provided the timber for building ships. Hence the New England "Yankees" specialized in shipbuilding, fishing, and maritime commerce.

Ideas, however, rather than economic factors, probably played a more important role in the cultural development of New England than in any other part of the British Empire. The leaders who directed the establishment of Massachusetts, Rhode Island, and Connecticut were highly educated men, imbued with strong convictions as to the sort of society they wished to build. Nearly all of them were men of Protestant mold, determined to build in America societies that would better conform than did England with what they thought was the will of God. And the people who followed these leaders generally sympathized with their high purposes. Hence New England led the American colonies in its efforts to direct its own religious and cultural evolution by all the devices of education, preaching, politics, and the press. The result was that there was a higher level of literacy in New England than anywhere else in America.

The so-called "Middle Colonies" deserve their name for more reason than their location between New England and the southern colonies. In New York, which the English took over from the Dutch, and Pennsylvania, which was founded by William Penn and the Quakers, commerce and agriculture combined to make an economy that was both prosperous and well balanced. Moreover, this region was the most cosmopolitan and tolerant of the areas of English settlement, because numerous European peoples besides the English settled in these colonies. Among them were the Dutch, Danes, Swedes, great numbers of Germans, some French, some Jews, and many Scotch-Irish emigrants from Ulster in northern Ireland.

An American Culture

We have pointed out that the economic and social institutions of the four sections of the English colonies in America differed according to the geographic and economic conditions in the diverse regions. We must also note, however, that the culture of all the colonies had much in common. All of them shared, for example, the English tradition of representative government. This set them all apart from the French, Spanish, and Portuguese colonies, where there was little trace of representative institutions.

Yet, from the outset, the American political institutions differed from those of the homeland. In England, political life continued to rest, even in the eighteenth century, upon the representation of social classes. But because social classes were not well defined in the colonies, Anglo-Americans had to devise another basis for representa-

The Old Boston State House—built in 1748, when the city's population was about 10,000, is probably the oldest public building in the United States. (The Bettmann Archive)

tion, resting upon territorial area and the size of the population. Moreover, because the settlers were engaged in the gigantic task of building a new society where none existed before, they were more conscious than their cousins at home of the role of the government as the agent of the people as a whole, in the management of their common affairs. In England, on the other hand, the tradition persisted that government was a prerogative of the ruler and of a ruling class. This different sense of what government meant was one of the factors that eventually led to the protest and eventual rebellion of the American colonists against the rule of the mother country.

In other ways, too, the colonies had much in common. Commerce among the colonies made for the exchange of ideas among them. Preachers, artists, scientists, and travelers moved up and down the seaboard in increasing numbers. Newspapers circulated widely, and readers in all the colonies were familiar with the scientific and literary works of such persons as Benjamin Franklin, Jonathan Edwards, Cadwallader Colden, William Byrd II, John Bartram, Lewis Evans, and others.

Rivalry with the French. Still another factor drawing the colonies on the mainland together was the struggle between the French and the English for dominance in the interior of North America. This struggle was linked with issues of European politics and with rivalries in the Far East as well. It was thus part of a worldwide conflict, in which England challenged the pre-eminence of France and, later, of Spain, which was linked with France after the accession in 1700 of a Bourbon ruler to the Spanish throne.

Even apart from these other points of friction, however, it was inevitable that trouble should develop between the two powers in the forests of North America, for the spread of the French dominion into the heart of the continent meant, as we have seen, that the English were being hemmed in on the narrow seaboard plain. And given the compactness and vigorous expansiveness of the English colonies, it was hardly to be expected that the thin line of French outposts might stand against the English tide. The decisive stage of the struggle came in the period between 1756 and 1763 as the French and Indian War, the American counterpart of the Seven Years' War in Europe. In the outcome, the French empire in America was completely destroyed, and the English colonies were left free to expand into the valleys of the St. Lawrence and the Mississippi.

CONCLUSION

Between the fifteenth and the eighteenth centuries, then, the swarming of the Europeans overseas, that had begun with the work of Henry the Navigator (see p. 559) and had centered upon America after the discoveries of Columbus and his contemporaries, had produced many "little Europes" around most of the shores of the Atlantic Basin. The original European settlements in the new world differed from each other, of course, in language, religion, culture, and political institutions, according to the differences between the European nations that founded them. In the course of their growth, however, these new colonial societies had become differentiated from their mother countries; they had also become differentiated within themselves. Thus there were sharp differences between Mexico and Argentina, between northern and southern Brazil, between French Canada and the French West Indies, between New England and Virginia.

By about the middle of the eighteenth century this process of differentiation had gone so far, and such a strong sense of colonial or regional interests had developed, that the colonists were beginning to question, and even resist, the dominance of their mother countries in their affairs. They had become, in significant ways, "American," and this fact would lead, in time, to their independence. But they were still "western"; many of the basic elements in their cultures were derived from European origins; they could never completely divest themselves of their cultural lineage. From being a "European" civilization, the civilization of the western world had now become an "Atlantic" civilization; and the new societies were local or regional variants of that civilization, just as France, England, Spain and the other European countries were.

Suggestions for Further Reading

Source Materials

Anthologies and Collected Documents

J. F. Jameson, ed., *Original Narratives of Early American History* (New York, 1909).

An extensive and valuable collection of accounts and descriptions by early settlers and travelers in the British colonies, chiefly in the seventeenth century.

M. Jensen, ed., *American Colonial Documents to 1776* (London, 1955).

An excellent collection of documents illustrative of the founding and the growth to independence of the British colonies in North America.

B. Keen, *Readings in Latin-American Civilization, 1492 to the Present* (Boston, 1955).

An excellent collection, which includes records of Mayan, Aztec, and Inca civilization as well as of the Spanish and Portuguese colonial empires.

P. Miller and T. H. Johnson, eds., *The Puritans* (New York, 1938).

An excellent collection of the writings of the Puritan leaders, preachers, and writers of colonial New England.

H. R. Warfel, R. H. Gabriel, and S. T. Williams, eds., *The American Mind* (New York, 1937).

A fine collection of selections from American writers—See Part I for the colonial period.

Contemporary Writings

R. Beverley, *History and present state of Virginia* (London, 1705; Chapel Hill, 1947).

A description of one of the most important English American colonies by a contemporary Virginian.

A. Burnaby, *Burnaby's Travels through North America,* edited by R. R. Wilson (New York, 1904).

A description of life in the middle and British colonies by an Anglican clergyman who visited them.

B. Franklin, *Autobiography.*

Available in many editions. Provides a delightful personal insight into the mind and culture of the greatest British-American of the eighteenth century.

A. von Humboldt, *Political Essay on the Kingdom of New Spain* (4 vols., London, 1811–1822).

An almost-classic account of life in New Spain at the end of the eighteenth century.

G. J. and A. de Ulloa, *Voyage to South America;* translated by J. Adams (London, 1807).

Travelers' descriptions of the society in the Spanish colonies, particularly Cartagena, the chief city of "the Spanish Main."

P. Kalm, *The America of 1750: Peter Kalm's Travels in North America,* edited by A. B. Benson (2 vols., New York, 1937).

An entertaining and highly informative description of life in the British-American colonies in the mid-eighteenth century by one of the most celebrated travelers of the time.

H. Koster, *Travels in Brazil* (London, 1816).

A contemporary description of the administration of Brazil by a traveler who visited it in the early years of the nineteenth century.

P. de Magalhaes de Gandaso, *The Histories of Brazil;* translated by J. B. Stetson, Jr. (New York, 1922).

A famous contemporary history by a Portuguese historian of the sixteenth century.

C. R. Markham, trans., *Narratives of the Rites and Laws of the Yncas* (London, 1873).

Contemporary description of aspects of the Inca civilization conquered by Pizarro.

J. Mawe, *Travels in the Interior of Brazil* (London, 1812).

A description of certain aspects of life in the Portuguese colony of Brazil by a traveler who visited it in the first years of the nineteenth century.

A. Vázquez de Espinosa, *Compendium and Description of the West Indies;* translated by C. U. Clark (Washington, 1942).

An eyewitness account of life in the Spanish colonies in the seventeenth century—especially good for a description of religious, educational, and cultural life.

Secondary Works

On the Expansion of Europe

J. B. Brebner, *The Explorers of North America* (New York, 1933).

A standard history of the principal explorations on the continent of North America.

E. P. Cheyney, *The Dawn of a New Era 1250–1453* (New York, 1936).

A brilliant survey of the European background of the colonization of the American hemisphere.

W. L. Dorn, *Competition for Empire, 1740–1763* (New York, 1940).

A fine survey of the European states and their societies in the era of the great Anglo-French imperial rivalry of the eighteenth century.

J. E. Gillespie, *A History of Geographical Discovery 1400–1800* (New York, 1933).

A standard brief survey of the history of the great explorations.

E. F. Heckscher, *Mercantilism* (2 vols., New York, 1935).

The standard analysis of the politico-economic ideology governing the colonial policies of the colonizing nations.

S. E. Morison, *Admiral of the Ocean Sea* (2 vols., Boston, 1944).

Also available in a one-volume edition. The best and most interesting study of Columbus and his "enterprise."

W. Notestein, *The English People on the Eve of Colonization, 1603–1630* (New York, 1954).

A very interesting survey of the society of England from which sprang the British colonization movement of the early seventeenth century.

E. Prestage, *The Portuguese Pioneers* (London, 1933).

An excellent history of early Portuguese explorations.

W. P. Webb, *The Great Frontier* (Boston, 1952).

A new and important interpretation of the long-range significance of the expansion of Europe.

On the Spanish Provinces in America

E. G. Bourne, *Spain in America, 1450–1580* (New York, 1904).

An old, but excellent survey of the early history of the Spanish colonies.

C. H. Haring, *Commerce and Navigation between Spain and the Indies in the Age of the Hapsburgs* (New York, 1947).

The standard history of the commerce between Spain and its colonies in the seventeenth and sixteenth centuries.

H. C. Herring, *A History of Latin America from the beginnings to the present* (New York, 1955).

A new and up-to-date textbook.

F. A. Kirkpatrick, *The Spanish Conquistadores* (London, 1934).

A fine, dramatic account of the great Spanish conquests in the American hemisphere.

R. B. Merriam, *The Rise of the Spanish Empire in the Old World and the New* (4 vols., New York, 1918–1934).

A very large, standard work.

B. Moses, *The Spanish Colonies* (New York, 1940).

Especially good for cultural history.

D. G. Munro, *The Latin American Republics* (New York, 1942).

A dependable textbook.

W. H. Prescott, *The Conquest of Mexico* (reissue, New York, 1943).

A classic old history of the Spanish conquest of Mexico—still useful and highly exciting reading.

W. H. Prescott, *History of the Conquest of Peru* (New York, 1890).

A classic. Old, but still useful; provides highly interesting reading.

W. Roscher, *The Spanish Colonial System* (reprint, New York, 1944).

A good study of Spanish colonial administration.

L. B. Simpson, *The Encomienda in New Spain* (rev. ed., Berkeley, 1950).

A scholarly and penetrating study of the economic and social organization of Mexico in the first century of Spanish occupation.

A. C. Wilgus, ed., *Colonial Hispanic America* (Washington, 1936)

An excellent collection of historical essays, by many authors, on the life, institutions, culture, and historical development of the Spanish and Portuguese colonies in America.

On the Portuguese Empire in Brazil

J. P. Cologeras, *A History of Brazil;* translated by P. A. Martin (Chapel Hill, 1939).

A standard work by a Brazilian historian.

H. C. Herring, *A History of Latin America from the beginnings to the present* (New York, 1955).

Contains good chapters on Brazil.

L. F. Hill, ed., *Brazil* (Berkeley, 1947).

A series of excellent essays on aspects of Brazilian history by various authors.

D. G. Munro, *The Latin American Republics* (New York, 1942).

See the chapters on Brazil—a good textbook account.

A. C. Wilgus, *The Development of Hispanic America* (New York, 1941).

Contains a good survey of Brazilian history.

On New France

N. M. Crouse, *French Pioneers in the West Indies, 1624–1664* (New York, 1940).

An interesting history of the earliest French colonies in the West Indies.

M. H. Long, *A History of the Canadian People* (Toronto, 1942), Volume I.

An excellent survey account of the founding and development of French Canada.

S. L. Mims, *Colbert's West Indian Policy* (New Haven, 1912).

A standard study of the formation of French policy with regard to the French colonies in the West Indies.

A. P. Newton, *The European Nations in the West Indies, 1493–1688* (London, 1933).

A good survey of the foundation of European colonies in the islands of the Caribbean.

F. Parkman, *Count Frontenac and New France under Louis XIV* (Boston, 1885).

A classic by the greatest of American historians.

F. Parkman, *Montcalm and Wolfe* (2 vols., Boston, 1884).

A classic history of the most dramatic part of the Seven Years' War in America.

G. M. Wrong, *The Rise and Fall of New France* (2 vols., New York, 1928).

A standard survey of the history of French Canada.

On the Dutch Colonial Empire

A. C. Flick, ed., *The History of the State of New York* (10 vols., New York, 1933–1937), Volume I.

A standard, collaborative history. Volume I gives the history of the Dutch period.

A. P. Newton, *The European Nations in the West Indies, 1493–1688* (London, 1933).

Contains a good brief account of the Dutch colonies in the Caribbean area.

J. H. Nunes, *New Amsterdam and Its People* (New York, 1902).

An old, but still useful, description of life in New Amsterdam.

W. R. Shepherd, *The Story of New Amsterdam* (New York, 1926).

A pleasant, brief history of the Dutch period in the history of New York.

On British Colonial America

J. T. Adams, *Provincial Society* (New York, 1928).

A standard, interestingly written description of life in Britain's North American colonies in the eighteenth century.

L. H. Gipson, *The British Empire in the Era of The American Revolution* (9 vols. to date, New York, 1936– – – –).

This is the standard description of life and society in the British-American colonies in the third quarter of the eighteenth century.

M. Kraus, *The Atlantic Civilization: Eighteenth-century Origins* (Ithaca, 1949).

A survey, chiefly of the intellectual changes between the British colonies and Europe in the eighteenth century. Very useful.

L. W. Labaree, *Royal Government in America* (New Haven, 1930).

The standard work on the dominant form of government in the British colonies in America.

F. W. Pitman, *The Development of the British West Indies, 1700–1763* (New Haven, 1917).

A standard, interestingly written account.

M. Savelle, *Seeds of Liberty* (New York, 1948).

A description of the intellectual life of the British-American colonies in the eighteenth century.

INDEX

705